Books by Jay Robert Nash

Fiction

On All Fronts

Nonfiction

Dillinger: Dead or Alive?
Citizen Hoover, A Critical Study of the Life and Times
    of J. Edgar Hoover and His F.B.I.
Bloodletters and Badmen, A Narrative Encyclopedia of American
    Criminals from the Pilgrims to the Present
Hustlers and Con Men, An Anecdotal History of the
    Confidence Man and His Games
Darkest Hours, A Narrative Encyclopedia of Worldwide Disasters
    from Ancient Times to the Present
Among the Missing, An Anecdotal History of Missing Persons
    from 1800 to the Present

Poetry

Lost Natives & Expatriates

Theater

The Way Back
Outside the Gates
1947 (Last Rites for the Boys)

Murder, America

Homicide in the United States from the Revolution to the Present

by Jay Robert Nash

Simon and Schuster
New York

Published by Simon and Schuster
A Division of Gulf & Western Corporation
Simon & Schuster Building
Rockefeller Center
1230 Avenue of the Americas
New York, New York 10020
SIMON AND SCHUSTER and colophon
are trademarks of Simon & Schuster

Designed by Irving Perkins
Manufactured in the United States of America
Printed and bound by Fairfield Graphics, Inc.
1 2 3 4 5 6 7 8 9 10

Library of Congress Cataloging in Publication Data

Nash, Jay Robert.
   Murder, America.

   Bibliography: p.
   Includes index.
   1. Murder—United States—Case studies.   I. Title.
HV6529.N37   364.1'523   80-10371

ISBN 0-671-24270-9

All photographs not otherwise credited come from the author's collection.

ACKNOWLEDGMENTS

My deep gratitude goes to my friend and associate researcher, James Patrick Agnew, whose many months of search handsomely yielded vital information for this book.

My tireless typist, Mrs. Sandy Horeis, also deserves a sincere thank you for her herculean efforts on this book's behalf.

Those who aided my efforts in the search for graphics include William Kelly of the Associated Press (Wide World) and the late Lou Tempke of United Press International (Compix), and Al Wolff, Arthur Levine, Bernard Van Marm and Thomas Buckley.

For special collections of private letters, trial records and miscellaneous memorabilia, and printed matter of all kinds, from rare books to broadsheets and pamphlets, I am indebted to Edgar Krebs, Phil Krapp, Neil H. Nash, and Jack Jules Klein, Jr. Rewarding "leads" were helpfully supplied by Leonard Des Jardins, Jack Conroy, Hank Oettinger, Art Kluge, Elmer Gertz, Patrick Agnew, Bruce Spivey, Jim and Edie McCormick, Neal and Joan Amidei, Curt Johnson, Marc Davis, Bob Abel, Bill Granger, and Mike LaVelle.

Of the newspaper community, I would like to thank for their help Clarence Page, Nancy Adams, Anne Keegan, Phillip Watley and Dick Griffin of the Chicago *Tribune;* Mike Royko, Tom Fitzpatrick, Art Petacque, Roger Ebert, Paul Galloway and Lynn Sweet of the Chicago *Sun-Times;* Tom Ray and George Lakehomer of the Chicago *Sun-Times* Public Service Bureau.

Many law enforcement officers were extremely helpful in the research for this book, and I would especially like to thank Sergeant Tony Consieldi of the Chicago Police Department's Training Academy.

Libraries, archives, museums throughout the country responded to requests for help with considerable aid; these include the New York Public Library, Joseph C. Lutz of the Chicago Public Library (downtown branch), the staff of the Newberry Library of Chicago, the staff of the Joseph Regenstein Library of the University of Chicago, the staff of Northwestern University Library, the staff of the John Crerar Library of IIT, the Chicago Historical Society, the New-York Historical Society, Agatha Fullam of the Waterville (Me.) Historical Society, the San Francisco Historical Society.

This book is for John Agnew, Sr.,
and all his sons,
both of blood and spirit.

Contents

Murder,
America

Preface

The crime of murder is more far-reaching, diversified, and complicated than any other. The motives that propel killers to the completion of their dark acts have astounding variety which all the more dumbfounds police and historian. Unlike the forger, the bank robber, the political terrorist—whose crimes have but a single purpose, following an exact course of action, and whose modus operandi is therefore somewhat predictable—the murderer is a much more elusive creature; and his or her offense, whether it be coldly premeditated or a *crime passionnel,* is the supreme attack upon any society coveting law and order. As such, police confront a wholly different and distinctive kind of ego, one that demands from them an all-out commitment to combat with the deadliest and most sinister of criminals.

In this class of murder the reader will not readily discover the everyday gangster killer who is in the business of murder as an indifferent professional, although America has produced some notable exceptions in this category, if only for the style employed in the manner of execution. Nor will the murder devotee find informative the sluggish acts of lurking street cretins who artlessly strangle and knife their random victims for no other reason than that the local pool hall has been closed down for repairs. No, those who relish a good murder are more demanding, requiring of their subject material some intelligent assemblage to the crime, even intellectual propensity as was the case of the inventive Dr. Buckanan, found in these pages, or the intricate deviousness in the scheme of Arthur Perry.

In his perceptive 1827 essay, "On Murder Considered as One of the Fine Arts," Thomas DeQuincey aptly pointed out that "something more goes into the composition of a fine murder than two blockheads to kill and be killed, a knife, a purse, and a dark lane. Design, gentlemen, grouping, light and shade, piety, sentiment, are now deemed indispensable to attempts of this nature."

The selections made for *Murder, America,* it is felt, are of this genre. The entries are cross-sectioned, representative of their respective eras, lifestyles, and community positions, from the most socially respectable such as Bathsheba Spooner, the Reverend Carawan, Martha Place, to the highly esteemed professional types such as doctors Coolidge, MacGregor and de Kaplany, the dentist Waite, attorneys Patrick and Payne, the businessman Keller.

The reader will also find enterprising blue-collar killers displaying as much creativity as their white-collar counterparts, for murder in the U.S. is as democratic as our political process —the farmer Watkins, the handyman Probst, streetcar driver Walsh, seaman Bram, sexton Piper, housekeeper Peete, policeman Erler, porter Jackson, and furniture mover Cowan. To be sure, there are the dedicated killers slaying on a mass level— Samuel Green, the deadly poisoners Lydia Sherman, Thomas Neill Cream, Johann Otto Hoch, Tillie Gbrurek, Nannie Doss, lonely-hearts murderers Fernandez and Beck, thrill killers Kelbach and Lance, the kidnappers Hightower, and Hall and Heady, and the outright bizarre bloodletters such as the intellectual Rulloffson, the love-embittered Barberi and Stopa, the ambitious Kenneth Neu, the possessive Mildred Bolton, the marrying Robert James.

In many ways, these citizens of our imperfect republic, born and nurtured in violence, reflect the mores and mentality of successive generations. They are of the commonplace and the exalted, their historical footnotes, either infamous or obscure, as well fixed in the annals of murder as the recorded permanence of our muster roll of presidents.

Those profiled in this book represent all points of America's compass, and, in traveling that geography of murder, the author has discovered that certain types of murders are indigenous to particular areas of the country, relating, as it were, to topographical deadly trends. In New England, for instance, always a hardscrabble land of caution and reserve, homicide has been enacted with traditional adroit secrecy. Along the Eastern Seaboard murder has been historically a matter of business, like the efficiency of its great cities; in the South acts of murder are customarily committed by those driven by a passion smoldering like their own long, hot days and unrelieved cotton fields. Always the seat of America's strongest moralities, the midwest has characteristically spawned murders planned with fearful care, then acted out, for the most part, in savagery—like the unpredictable weather sweeping across the flatlands. In the West, particularly in the Southwest, the utter barrenness of the land, the hopeless horizons, have apparently affected the lives of that area's most notorious killers, calling forth in style wild rampages equal to the frontier past and an untamed land hostile to civilized notions about the sacrosanct state of life. These consistent curiosities of topographical murder do much to detail the psychological pressures of locale upon the minds of murderers. But wherever their homes, their motives are always divergent.

Many killers are motivated by greed, others by love, revenge, jealousy. Some have killed out of boredom, others out of sexual aberration and excitement, religious fanaticism, even berserk patriotism. Their methods ranged from the prosaic to the positively ingenious. Guns and gunpowder were never considered, as a whole, to be anything other than the tools of war in our early-day society, to be employed in open conflict justified by all nations. Murder was confined from the Revolution to the gaslight era, for the most part, to the insidious device of poison, a subtle agent of death. As science twisted convention and progress with dizzying speed, the murderer modernized with knife, gun, and bomb. And, as the hundreds of examples in this book's chronology should show, the murderer entered the so-called modern era with lethal sophistication, keeping pace with indifferent science, to shatter the concept of life-held-dear through wholesale killing.

In the deeper past the mass killer was the exception, almost a medieval rarity, but with the coming of the social revolutions, specious or not, of the mid-1960s, the lunatic fringe of murder appeared to become the ghastly norm. Murder was no longer a singular and personal affair but a nameless, ongoing slaughter that was only of incidental interest to the drug-cultured, sex-deviated perpetrator. He committed his acts over long periods of time as would a farmer obliterating pesky starlings each season.

The Wayne Henleys, Juan Coronas killed and continue to kill not with unconscionable reason but without reason at all. Religious leaders have pointed to the decline of organized religion and the disintegration of the family unit as potent factors contributing to this murderous perspective. Sociologists murmur about fluid environments, psychologists about alienation of identities, law-enforcement authorities about the shabby conduct of the courts. All of these are handy explanations and full of their own truths, yet the plain fact is that it is *easier* to murder now than ever before, because these explanations serve as lines of reason for the killer's defense should he be caught and tried. It is the attitude of the murderer that has so radically changed. For the most part, he considers *himself* to be a victim. His defense counsel, he knows, will provide any number of qualifying reasons for his deed later in court. For today's murderer, there is little between the angry past and the permissive present to frustrate his acts or fret his future.

JAY ROBERT NASH
Chicago, 1979

1778 WORCESTER, MASSACHUSETTS

A Lady's Patriotic Gore

Lust and politics ruled equally in the heart of the beauteous Bathsheba Spooner, a constant emotional condition that inevitably led her to hate her doddering, ancient husband and embrace murder as a fervent lover. Her marriage was a bad bargain from the beginning, most knew, arranged by Bathsheba's illustrious, stern-minded father, General Timothy Ruggles, whose devotion to the English king branded him a staunch Tory long before the birth of the American Revolution.

Ruggles was a strategist, especially with the lives of his offspring, promoting in 1766 the marriage of his favorite daughter, eighteen-year-old Bathsheba, to wealthy Joshua Spooner, a man old enough to be her grandfather. Yet there were compensations. Spooner's vast land holdings outside of Worcester, Massachusetts, included a large, comfortable home peopled with several servants to do young Bathsheba's bidding.

But the headstrong woman was unhappy from the start. Her own parents had served as disastrous examples of wedded bliss. Ruggles and his wife had argued constantly throughout Bathsheba's early youth, and, on one occasion, the impressionistic girl was present when her mother served her father his favorite dog for dinner, roasted.

General Ruggles doted on Bathsheba, implanting his own stringent thinking in her mind, particularly his Tory sentiments. She grew to be a stunning woman, but young men were

17

wary of her. Historian Peleg W. Chandler described Bathsheba in his noted *Criminal Trials* as "extremely prepossessing in her personal appearance, and she was noted for great strength of character; but her temper was haughty and imperious, and the circumstances of her birth and early education were not favorable to that delicacy and refinement, which constitute the greatest charm of the sex."

Indelicate situations became numerous in the Spooner household, Bathsheba's enfeebled and dominated husband suspecting but unable or unwilling to combat his wife's flagrant flirtations with other men. Joshua Spooner was a born cuckold. Beautiful Bathsheba began to bat her eyes at almost any young male passing the Spooner mansion in the early 1770s; it was well known through Mrs. Spooner's own loud complaints that her husband had long ago been incapable of meeting any sexual requirements.

By the time the Revolution broke out, Mrs. Spooner was sending her servants into the road to ask soldiers, both Continental and British, to partake of her ample table and, later, with full stomachs, her warm bed. One such passerby was Ezra Ross, who had served in the American Army with his three brothers from the outset of the war, fighting at Bunker Hill and in other battles. He was but sixteen when Bathsheba spotted Ezra straggling down the Worcester Road past her home. She sent a servant to fetch him inside. Ezra happily gorged himself on the sumptuous meal Bathsheba had served. Suddenly he fainted. So emaciated and ill was the young revolutionary that Bathsheba ordered her servants to put him to bed. For several weeks Mrs. Spooner doted on the boy, nursing him day and night. When his strength returned, Bathsheba, though twice his age, made romantic advances to him. Ezra responded with enthusiasm.

The youthful soldier rejoined General Washington to serve with him in several campaigns for a year. He then returned to the waiting arms of Bathsheba in 1778. The elderly Joshua Spooner looked upon the amiable youth as a family friend, liking him, never for a moment suspecting that Ross was trysting with his wife.

It was during this passionate period that Bathsheba decided to rid herself of her wealthy husband. Her reasons were twofold: Joshua Spooner was useless to her as a sex partner, and he was an ardent supporter of the American Revolution. Bathsheba, like her father, was intensely loyal to the British crown, so her husband's demise became in her troubled mind an extension of her own patriotism. (General Ruggles had planned his exit from the colonies with precision. His vast estates, purchased in 1755, were in Hardwick in Worcester County. He kept thirty horses and a twenty-acre park for deer, plus several houses. Ruggles put his properties into Bathsheba's name before fleeing to Nova Scotia to live out his life, dying in 1795 at age eighty-four. Ruggles shrewdly figured that Bathsheba, being married to Spooner, a staunch supporter of the Revolution, would thereby be able to hold onto his estates.)

Spooner, who traveled widely on business, planned a trip to Princetown. He asked young Ross to accompany him. Ross agreed, playing his role of family friend to the hilt. Before they left, Bathsheba took her teenage paramour aside and handed him a half bottle of aquafortis, telling the boy to put a few drops into Spooner's ale on the trip. But Ross appeared squeamish about poisoning his benefactor.

"Do it," ordered the headstrong Bathsheba. "It will make a man out of you."

Once before Mrs. Spooner had tried to convince Ross to murder her husband. At the time the boy had agreed to slit Spooner's throat when he was asleep, but he cowered at the old man's bedroom door and could not go through with the killing. It would be the same with the poison, Bathsheba reasoned. She was right; Ross grew fainthearted on the trip and failed to poison his sponsor.

Mrs. Spooner continued to search desperately for a way to rid herself of her shriveled spouse. Then her deliverance appeared on February 8, 1778, in the form of two ragged men, British soldiers who had been taken prisoner with Burgoyne at Saratoga and had escaped the prison camp at Rutland, Massachusetts, attempting to make for Canada.

Spotting the bedraggled pair shuffling down the snow-swept roadway before her house, Bathsheba ordered her servant, Alexander Cummings, to ask them into her house. James Buchanan, a thirty-year-old sergeant, and William Brooks, a twenty-seven-year-old private, accepted with alacrity. Once they were inside, Bathsheba prepared a large meal for the soldiers, joined them in the sitting room, and confided that she was a loyal supporter of the British Army, that her father and one of her brothers had served in it.

"My husband is away on business," the attractive Mrs. Spooner told the escaped prisoners. "You are welcome to stay until he returns." The men were put up in spare rooms, grateful to be out of the snow and cold.

After two days, Bathsheba grew bold enough to tell Buchanan that her husband might not return at all; that her young lover, Ross, would, hopefully, poison Mr. Spooner. Then again, the beauty sighed, Ezra might weaken. According to Buchanan's later confession, "She said at the same time we should stay till we saw whether Mr. Spooner returned or not."

Bathsheba's intimate hints to Buchanan were clear. If Ross could not murder her husband, the troopers of the cause she endorsed should do it for her. Buchanan and Brooks, she knew by then, were not upstanding men, both having admitted to her that they had been professional thieves. She would be willing to pay handsomely for the deed, at least a thousand dollars.

When Spooner returned alive and well from his business trip, a sheepish Ezra Ross in tow, Bathsheba clucked knowingly and nodded to her British friends. Joshua Spooner, in contrast to his reaction to the likeable Ezra, became suspicious of the two new guests, asking who they were.

"Mr. Buchanan here," explained the quick-witted Bathsheba, "is the cousin of Alexander Cummings." Spooner eyed the two men and then went to a nearby inn to chat with neighbors. Upon his return, he found Buchanan and Brooks sitting by the fire, drinking ale with Mrs. Spooner. He ordered them out of his house. The troopers pointed to the window, beyond which a snowstorm raged. They begged to remain overnight. Spooner reluctantly agreed and moved into a sitting room, where he fretted alone. Bathsheba went to bed, Ross leaving his own room to join her—no doubt to be scolded for botching his murder assignment.

As the troopers paced before the fire, contemplating the destruction of old man Spooner, a neighbor, Reuben Olds, appeared. Joshua was more than glad to see him, taking his friend into the sitting room and telling him of his fears. Olds suddenly walked into the kitchen where Buchanan and Brooks idled.

"The old man fears you think to rob him," he said to the troopers. "You must leave."

Replied Buchanan: "What is the old fellow about? He will not come to say much to me." Then anger spilled from the trooper's mouth. "It won't be healthy for him, for I would put him in the well for two coppers!"

Olds left them with a warning to conduct themselves properly, distinctly recalling Buchanan's remark some weeks later in court. The idea of tossing someone down a well was not original with Buchanan. Mrs. Spooner, it was later revealed, had thought much in recent weeks of the well just outside the large house. Bathsheba had read of a sensational murder in England, that of Daniel Chater in February, 1748. Chater had been seized by seven brigands in Lady Holt Park, England, and thrown down a well; his killers were all apprehended and hanged in Chichester the following January. The chilling case undoubtedly inspired Bathsheba.

The following morning, Brooks and Buchanan left the house, Spooner shaking his walking cane at them and telling them never to return. Alexander Cummings accompanied the two men. He took the troopers to Cooley's tavern and bought them drinks, the money provided by Bathsheba. When Joshua Spooner retired that night, the men crept back to the estate, staying in the barn.

For more than two weeks the hiding game went on, the troopers staying in the barn, their food and drink sent to them from the mansion by Bathsheba. Often she delivered the meal trays herself. At such times she promised the men a great deal of money if they would kill Joshua. One night, Brooks got drunk and agreed to shoot the old man. He changed his mind at the last moment. Bathsheba went to work on his military superior, Buchanan, knowing he was the real authority of the pair. That she slept with Buchanan there is little doubt. He finally consented to the murder, but insisted that Ross and Brooks help him kill the old man.

On the night of March 1, 1778, the three conspirators, all amply endowed with ale supplied by Bathsheba, watched for Spooner to return from Cooley's Tavern. In Buchanan's words: "Mr. Spooner was at length seen coming, and then was the time for the Devil to show his power over them who had forsaken God. William Brooks went out and stood within the small gate leading to the kitchen, and as Mr. Spooner came past hime, he knocked him down with his hand. He strove to speak when down. Brooks took him by the throat and partly strangled him. Ross and Buchanan came out; Ross took Mr. Spooner's watch and gave it to Buchanan. Brooks and Ross took him up and put him into the well head first. Before they carried him away, I, Buchanan, pulled off his shoes: I was instantly struck with horror of conscience, as well I might. . . . Had we all been immediately struck dead, after the perpetration of so horrid a murder, and sent to hell, God would have been justified and we justly condemned."

When the three killers entered the Spooner home, Bathsheba stared wild-eyed at them for some time. She then flitted about the house in great confusion, looking for her husband's money box to pay the promised price, her speech next to babbling. She finally found the money box in Spooner's bedroom and raced downstairs, giving Brooks $243, stating that she would give the killers more in a few days. The trio set off for Worcester wearing Spooner's clothing. Bathsheba went to her room and collapsed.

Early the next morning Bathsheba Spooner awoke a free woman. To cover the deeds of her accomplices, she dressed hurriedly and ran downstairs, pretending to search frantically for the missing Spooner. She raced outside through snow drifts, Alexander Cummings at her side. Standing next to the well, Bathsheba cryptically remarked to Cummings: "I hope he is in heaven." Then she said to the servant, "Get a horse, ride to the tavern, and inquire as to the whereabouts of my husband!"

Cummings rode to the tavern, announcing that Joshua Spooner had utterly vanished. Ephraim Cooley, the proprietor and a close friend of Spooner's, rode to the house and began looking over the grounds. In a mound of snow he found a hat and took it inside.

"This is Mr. Spooner's hat," he told Bathsheba, holding it out to her. He added suspiciously: "What do you think now?"

Mrs. Spooner lowered her head. "It is his hat," she replied quietly.

The bloodhound in Cooley prompted him to continue his search. He reached the well and noticed blood spots on the curb. Peering down, he could see the mangled body of his friend at the bottom. Ephraim Cooley mounted his horse and rode madly to town to inform authorities.

Buchanan, Brooks and Ross were quickly rounded up at Brown's Tavern in Worcester, their presence raising eyebrows hours before the discovery of Spooner's body. They were not only wearing the dead man's clothes but had brazenly worn his silver shoe buckles, which bore his initials, and had passed around Spooner's magnificent watch for all to see. They readily confessed to the killing.

At about the same time, constables and a physician arrived at the Spooner home to inspect the body. Bathsheba refused to look at it. The physician, Dr. Jonathan King, one story relates, insisted that Mrs. Spooner touch the body, to try out the old idea that should the flesh of the deceased turn red beneath the touch of the suspect, guilt of murder would be proven. Nothing of the sort occurred. Bathsheba bravely stood up, walked to the corpse stretched out upon the table and placed her lovely long hand upon the dead man's forehead. Calmly, she sighed: "Poor little man."

Some time later Mrs. Spooner was taken to Worcester, where she confronted her fellow killers. She broke into great sobs and then admitted that she had put the trio up to the killing. It was a different story at the trial, which began on April 1, 1778. All four prisoners loudly entered pleas of "Not Guilty." The prosecuting attorney, the illustrious Robert Treat Paine, who had signed the Declaration of Independence, charged all four prisoners with first-degree murder, stating that Bathsheba was "an accessory before the fact and that she invited, moved, abetted, counselled and procured" the murder to be committed.

Thus began the first capital case of American jurisprudence in Massachusetts—a nonstop trial that took sixteen traumatic hours. Levi Lincoln, one of the most eloquent lawyers of the day, represented the accused. Lincoln, who had graduated Harvard in 1772, was to prove himself distinguished in the early history of American law. He would rise to become the Attorney General of the United States under Jefferson and later the lieutenant governor of Massachusetts. (He would also, in 1811, be appointed an associate justice of the Supreme Court but decline to serve.)

Lincoln knew there was no hope for the British soldiers. He abandoned their cause. He did attempt to save Ross, claiming he had been a hero of the Revolution, a mere boy confused by events and made senseless by drink. He had merely been present at the time of the murder and that did not, the defense counsel thundered, prove guilt. Lincoln went further in the case of Bathsheba Spooner, claiming for the first time in an American murder trial that she had been insane at the time of the slaying. Cautioning the jurors to banish political feelings against the Tory-bent Bathsheba, Lincoln theatrically reenacted the crime, depicting all of Mrs. Spooner's erratic behavior, stating that for all her high-ranking birth, her lofty education and social accomplishments, she had acted like a person who "was not in a sound mind."

He went on to point out how "after the murder, she gives the murderers his [Spooner's] watch, buckles, waistcoat, breeches and shirts, and even puts them on, to be worn in the eye of the world, where they were well known to be Spooner's clothes, and from their goodness and fashion might be known not to belong to the persons wearing them, being low and vulgar. Was this the conduct of a person in the exercise of reason? Would it have been less rational to have written on their foreheads, in capitals, 'THE MURDERERS OF MR. SPOONER!' "

Lincoln's masterful arguments were wasted on the jury, who quickly returned a verdict of "Guilty" against all four defendants. Massachusetts Chief Justice William Cushing, who had heard the case along with four associate justices, pronounced the death sentence. The four were to be hanged on June 4, 1778.

In their jail cells, the three men broke down, becoming "mighty in the scriptures." Buchanan penned his long confession and he and Ross signed it. Brooks, who could not write, affixed his mark to the document.

There was still a fight for life. Jabez and Joanna Ross of Ipswich petitioned the court, begging for the life of their young son, Ezra. Their plea pointed out that the boy had been mesmerized by the beautiful vixen Bathsheba. "At the evacuation of Ticonderoga," the Jabez document read in part, "in his march to reinforce the northern army, gratitude for past favors led him [Ross] to call on his old benefactress, who then added to the number of her kindnesses, and engaged a visit on his return. With a mind thus prepared and thus irresistibly prepossessed, by her addresses, kindnesses on his tender years, he for the first time heard the horrid proposals; tempted by promises flattering to his situation, and seduced both from virtue and prudence, a child as he was, by a lewd, artful woman, but he too readily acceded to her measures, black as they were."

It mattered not; Ross and the others were to die. The date of the execution, however, was altered by a drastic new turn of events. From her death cell, Bathsheba, who had shown little emotion during and after the trial, sent word to the court that she was pregnant and asked to be examined by midwives.

Bathsheba and her convicted accomplices received a reprieve while state authorities ordered two male midwives and "twelve discreet lawful matrons" to examine Mrs. Spooner. Midwives Elijah Dix and Joshua Wilder, along with twelve matrons, headed by Elizabeth Rice, inspected the condemned woman and reported that she "is not quick with child." Bathsheba protested, begging for another examination. Four more midwives were dispatched to Mrs. Spooner's cell, where she was meticulously inspected. These midwives informed authorities in Boston in a letter dated June 27, 1778, that "she is now quick with child." On the same day, Elizabeth Rice, a powerful influence in Worcester and one of the midwives who had first examined Bathsheba, sent the authorities another letter in which she emphasized that her finding, not that of the second group of midwives, was correct. Elizabeth Rice had enlisted the aid of another midwife, Molly Tatman, to support her statements. That matron Rice was a political sachem in Worcester at the time was evidenced by the reaction of Boston authorities. They took the word of the Rice woman, a staunch Revolutionary who hated all pro-British Americans, and set a new date for Bathsheba's execution. She and the others would hang on Thursday, July 2, 1778.

Bathsheba took the news in solemn silence. She insisted that her claim of being pregnant was naked truth and asked that she be examined after death. In her cell on the morning of the execution date, Mrs. Spooner appeared calm but weak. A few moments before leaving her cell she was baptized by Rev. Thaddeus Maccarty, who also delivered a loud sermon to the condemned prisoners, which ended with: "Thine eyes shall not pity him, but thou shalt put away the guilt of innocent blood from Israel, that it may go well with thee." His paraphrase from Deuteronomy was apt.

Immense crowds filled the narrow streets of Worcester on execution day—more than five thousand, some estimated. The town selectmen had urged in the *Worcester Spy* on June 24, 1778: ". . . taking into consideration the large concourse of people who will probably attend the execution of the unhappy persons under sentence of death here . . . caution and request all . . . persons having lately had the smallpox, not to appear in the assembly of spectators, unless sufficiently cleansed. Otherwise their attendance may prove fatal to many, and render the execution, which is intended for the warning and benefit of all, a public detriment."

About 2:30 P.M., Bathsheba and the others were brought out of the Worcester jail. The three men walked ahead on foot. Mrs. Spooner, "through great bodily infirmity," was carried on a chaise. As they neared the execution spot, the skies split wide and the darkened heavens burst forth with one of the most terrifying thunderstorms in the state's history.

A local scribe witnessing the event wrote a few days later: "There followed an awful half hour. The loud shouts of the officers, amidst a crowd of five thousand people, to 'make way! make way!' the horses pressing upon those in front; the shrieks of women in the tumult and confusion; the malefactors slowly advancing to the fatal tree, preceded by their dismal coffins; the fierce coruscations of lightning athwart the darkened horizon, quickly followed by loud peals of thunder, conspired together and produced a dreadful scene of horror. It seemed as if the Author of nature had added such terrors to the punishment of the criminals as might soften the stoutest hearts of the most obdurate and abandoned."

Ross, Buchanan and Brooks ascended the ladder to the makeshift stage (located at what is now Washington Square). While Ross said a prayer aloud and the others mumbled their offerings to God, Mrs. Spooner remained on the chaise, staring out at the crowd, nodding silently to spectators she recognized. The hangman looked down at her and slowly beckoned with a long arm. Bathsheba gave a thin smile and then crawled up the ladder on her hands and knees, her beautiful face now sunken and pale. Hoods were placed over the heads of the soldiers.

The hangman approached Bathsheba. She grabbed the sheriff's hand and spoke in a loud, clear voice: "My dear sir! I am ready! In a little time I expect to be in bliss; and but a few years must elapse when I hope I shall see you and my other friends again."

Without another word, the four were hanged, the execution being the last of such public spectacles in Massachusetts. Inside of five minutes the murderers were pronounced dead. The three men were nailed into their coffins and removed for burial. In accordance with her last request, Bathsheba Spooner was for the last time examined by surgeons. A fetus of five months was taken from her body.

1797 HEIDELBURG, PENNSYLVANIA

The Determined Inheritor

John Hauer was a frustrated man. He had planned his life carefully, his future fortunes plotted the way an expert fisherman baits a hook. Yet his prize catch slipped away from him time and again. Hauer had, after a long and expensive courtship, wooed and won the hand of Elizabeth Shitz, whose father, Peter, was the wealthiest man in Dauphin County, Pennsylvania, his estates centered about the peaceful town of Heidelburg.

When Peter Shitz died in 1795, Hauer expected to inherit through his wife much of the vast Shitz fortune. But in keeping with the male-oriented customs of the day, the family patriarch bequeathed the bulk of his estates to his two sons, Francis and Peter, leaving Elizabeth only a thousand dollars. Most of this money was a paper inheritance since Elizabeth had drawn upon her share before her marriage to Hauer.

Almost from the moment of the old man's death, Hauer embarked upon a fanatical crusade to capture the Shitz fortune. At first he tried the courts, entering a claim against his father-in-law's estates. His petition was denied. Next, Hauer attempted clumsy persuasion, going to both Francis and Peter Shitz and telling them they must divide their inheritance with their sister on an equal basis.

"And why would we do that?" inquired Francis, the older son.

"Your father has willed it," answered Hauer, his eyes rolling heavenward. "Not in the courts of the land but from beyond the grave."

"Is that so?" smirked Francis. "How does such knowledge come to you, Hauer?"

"Your father appeared in a vision to me last night and ordered justice done in the matter."

The Shitz brothers laughed in Hauer's face.

To emphasize his contact with the spirit world, Hauer then warned the youths that their father would haunt the family mansion until they agreed to set matters right with the estate. John Hauer then proceeded to provide these ghostly apparitions himself, or rather the *sounds* of old man Shitz's troubled spirit. In the dead of night Hauer crept into the large Shitz house and

27

made his way to the attic where he clomped about in heavy boots, rattling chains and moaning loud in his best impersonation of his dead father-in-law's bellowing voice. Before he could make his escape, the Shitz boys found him. Hauer's explanation for his presence in the attic was that the ghost of old man Shitz had summoned him there. He was thrown out of the house.

Hauer decided that the brothers must destroy themselves. He went to work on Peter, then only seventeen years old. The gullible Shitz boy visited Hauer at his farm, where his brother-in-law inveigled him into a drinking bout. Drunk, Peter allowed Hauer and his halfwit brother, Solomon, to tie him up. In his incoherent state the youth allowed a rope to be put about his neck. At Hauer's order, and with the promise of five gold pieces should he take the dare, the boy jumped from a loft, the rope about his neck tied firmly to a high beam above. (Peter Shitz's later testimony concerning this ridiculous incident was fuzzy, but it seems that Hauer's challenge was that Shitz could not survive a hanging.) Fortunately for the youth, the rope about his neck broke, though it tore the skin away and left a permanent scar.

For two years, John Hauer stayed awake nights, devising schemes to obtain the fortune he felt he had been unjustly denied. With sighing resignation he accepted the only course left open: he would simply murder the two Shitz boys and be done with the play-acting.

Drawing funds from his meager accounts, Hauer strolled into Heidelburg and entered Geiger's Inn, looking for some recently arrived Irish immigrants. Here he met Charles M'Manus, Patrick Donagan, Peter M'Donoghy and Francis Cox. He bought the men several rounds of drinks. Then, in whispered tones, he explained his problem. Should they help him kill the entire Shitz family, he would reward them handsomely from his subsequent inheritance. The bone-poor Irishmen shrugged and accepted the chore.

On the night of December 28, 1797, a maid in the Shitz home heard noises coming from a bedroom. Investigating, she saw men holding pistols, their faces covered by handkerchiefs, crawling through a window. Before the maid could warn Francis Shitz, who was sleeping on a nearby bed, one of the intruders rushed forward and fired a shot. As the woman and other servants fled screaming into the night, the man who had fired

the weapon raced into the kitchen, picked up an axe,
turned to the fallen Shitz, striking him four times on the
The intruders then forced their way into Peter Shitz's
where the boy was attacked. Peter fought for his life with
desperation that, even though he received several blows fr
the axe, he managed to knock down two of the men and escap
into the fields.

The next morning John and Elizabeth Hauer were summoned to the Shitz house. Elizabeth fell upon her slain
brother's body, weeping. A constable pointed out the gashes in
the head from blows made by the axe, but none were death
wounds. Hauer, sitting passively in a chair nearby, grunted:
"Perhaps he has been shot in the mouth." Francis, it was found
some minutes later, had been shot in the ear; the bullet had
lodged in his brain.

No one stood to benefit from the killing, authorities quickly
concluded, more than John Hauer. The Irishmen who had hired
themselves out for the murder were quickly rounded up after
the pistol used to kill Shitz was identified as belonging to
M'Manus. All were indicted but only Hauer and M'Manus were
found guilty. Throughout the trial, Hauer sat mute and staring
at his accusers. He had no comment after he and M'Manus were
sentenced to death.

Yet, once in his cell awaiting execution, Hauer appeared to
go berserk. He refused to eat. He stripped himself naked and
remained so. He would not bathe, "remaining in the most indelicate and filthy situation," according to one report. Then he
began to bite anyone who came near him; he injured one jailor
so badly that the man was hospitalized. Such conduct was obviously designed to convince authorities that John Hauer had
gone insane.

All pretense, however, was abandoned when he and
M'Manus stood upon the gallows on July 14, 1798. Hauer was
calm and a knowing smile played about his lips as the noose
went around his neck. Unlike the one in the game he had
played with Peter Shitz, this rope did not break. In minutes,
the man who had tried to scare his relatives to death for the
sake of fortune was dead. Two days later the bank where Hauer
kept his deposits declared the deceased insolvent.

1801 DEDHAM, MASSACHUSETTS

A Rejected Suitor's Revenge

For Jason Fairbanks, luck wore only a sneer. From his birth in Dedham, Massachusetts, in 1780, Fairbanks suffered a weak constitution. He was always short of breath, tired easily, and was afflicted with an obscure bone disease. A quack administered an inoculation to Jason in his tenth year, intended to cure the child. The shot caused the boy to lose the use of his right arm, which became stiff and failed to grow from the elbow to the hand. Because of his being an invalid, Fairbanks' education was limited.

Relationships with attractive Dedham females seemed out of the question. Especially vexing for Fairbanks was his tenuous affair with one of the town's most alluring young women, Elizabeth Fales.

Fairbanks and the Fales girl had known each other since early adolescence. Elizabeth was friendly with the crippled youth but never his lover. She was enamoured with an older man from New York named Sprague. When Sprague returned to New York City, Elizabeth, feeling sorry for the mooning Fairbanks, dated him on occasion. Fairbanks fell in love, but, as some witnesses later claimed, the Fales refused to have the deformed youth in their home, actually closing the door in his face one evening when he came to visit their daughter.

One Abner Whiting, Dedham's town gossip (who many claimed was of unsound mind), later recalled standing with Fairbanks in a shop in 1799. Mrs. Fales, who allegedly had scorned the lovestruck Jason, walked by, and Fairbanks cursed in a low voice, saying: "I will have my revenge upon her!" Whiting also stated that Fairbanks on different occasions had uttered both love and hate for the fair Elizabeth. When he was twenty-one and Elizabeth nineteen, Fairbanks told Whiting: "Betsy is a nice girl, but damn it, for all that, I don't know what to do. I don't know but I must be the death of her."

In the early spring of 1801, Whiting later claimed, he was standing in the doorway of a shop when he saw the Fales girl and Fairbanks approach each other in the street. Said Jason to Elizabeth, clutching her with his good arm: "Damn you, I must have you in the bushes!" Some days later, Whiting said, he overheard Fairbanks shout at the now frightened girl: "Damn you, I will be the death of you!"

There was no doubt that Fairbanks intended to marry Elizabeth Fales despite the fact that she had refused his proposals many times. He had obtained an official certificate intended for the publication of marriage banns. Jokingly, Fairbanks induced a friend, Susannah Davis, to fill it in, and sign it as would the town clerk, inserting his own name and that of Elizabeth Fales.

Some days later, on the morning of May 18, 1801, Fairbanks met his friend Ephraim Handy. In the course of their brief conversation, Jason casually asked if he could borrow Handy's ten-cent penknife. That afternoon, a prearranged meeting between Elizabeth and Jason took place in Mason's pasture, which was adjacent to the Fales' property. The pasture was enclosed by shrubs almost six feet high. No one saw the couple walking in the bright day, but one passerby on the road nearby later testified that she heard Elizabeth Fales suddenly shriek, "Oh, dear! Oh, dear!"

A few minutes before three o'clock, Jason Fairbanks emerged from the pasture. He walked unsteadily, eyes open and glazed, toward Mrs. Sarah Fales, Elizabeth's mother, who stood in the doorway of her house, transfixed by his strange appearance. Fairbanks moved past Mrs. Fales and, as he did so, he almost absentmindedly dropped the ten-cent knife into her hand. It was coated with blood.

"Jason," cried the frightened mother. "What horrid thing have you done?"

The youth moved off a bit in silence until Samuel Fales, Elizabeth's uncle, grabbed him and held him on the spot. The uncle thought Fairbanks had gone insane. Froth bubbled from a deep wound in his throat, which had been slit wide. There were apparent wounds in the youth's abdomen; his shirt was dripping blood. While one of the Fales sons held on to the incoherent Fairbanks, Samuel Fales raced into the pasture, joined shortly by Elizabeth's father, Nehemiah Fales.

A moan from a pile of rocks caught their attention; the men ran to the spot to find Elizabeth. She was dying, slashed to pieces. Her shoes were off and her loose calico gown and green shirt were covered with blood.

All Nehemiah Fales could do was pick up a greatcoat lying nearby (it belonged to Fairbanks) and, bundling it up, place it under the head of his dying daughter. Her uncle brought her water but she could not drink, as her throat was slashed deeply. Mrs. Fales arrived in time to see her daughter die in the open field a half hour later while the sun poured down upon the grisly scene.

Dr. Nathaniel Ames arrived to itemize Elizabeth's many wounds. She had received a two-inch-deep slash in the throat; a four-inch-deep wound in the back; four wounds in the left side, all three inches deep; six wounds in the left arm and two in the right. Elizabeth's left thumb was almost completely severed. Dr. Ames was later to testify strangely that Elizabeth might have inflicted these wounds herself, but could not explain how the girl could have driven a knife into her own back.

Found strewn about the body were several bits of paper. These were meticulously pieced together and proved to be the fake banns certificate Jason had asked Miss Davis to write. Also found were Fairbanks' purse and other belongings known to be his.

It was apparent that Fairbanks had attempted suicide after murdering his reluctant sweetheart. His efforts had been awkward. Though he claimed to be dying while doctors patched up his wounds, Fairbanks was a healthy specimen when he was brought to trial on August 6, 1801, before the Supreme Judicial Court of Massachusetts, then sitting in Dedham.

The prisoner stood mute. After a ten-hour trial, Fairbanks was found guilty on largely circumstantial evidence. When he was sentenced to death, many in Dedham felt he had been wronged, that he was innocent. Five of these staunch supporters resolved to set him free. Fairbanks, on the night of August 17, broke through his cell bars with tools smuggled to him and climbed down the jail wall; then quickly mounted a horse awaiting him, no mean feat for a person as sickly as he claimed to be.

Riding off into the night with a friend named Dukeham, Fairbanks headed for Canada. Sheriff Cutler of Dedham offered five hundred dollars for his capture. Subscriptions instigated by the fury of press reports detailing the escape brought the reward up to a thousand dollars. Printed on the morning of Fairbanks' escape, the Dedham paper was full of wrath, its editor exclaiming: "The stain of blood is upon the land. Jason Fairbanks, the murderer, has escaped; we cannot tell where to look for him; we must look everywhere. Therefore, we agree to submit to three things: —That our houses and premises shall be searched: —That we will give an account of ourselves and our intimates during the night of the past and this day: —That we will exert ourselves in every way to apprehend the culprit and his accomplices. No honest man's eyes must sleep in Dedham this night."

One man's eyes were wide, those of M. P. Holt, as he rode pell-mell along the trail Fairbanks had left, spurring his horse through Worcester, Hadley, Cheshire, and into Vermont, through the sleepy villages of Bennington, Arlington, Greenville and finally Whitehall, on the southern tip of Lake Champlain. It was August 23 when the weary Holt reined in his near-dead horse at an inn next to the lake. He spotted two strangers having breakfast and quickly realized that they were Fairbanks and Dukeham.

Holt chatted pleasantly with the pair, who told him they were about to sail a small boat they had rented for fifteen dollars to St. Jean, Canada. The pursuer, knowing he could not apprehend both men, stalled for time; there were more men behind on the trail, Holt knew, and he must await their arrival.

"What good fortune," Holt told Fairbanks and Dukeham. "I, too, am journeying to St. Jean."

Dukeham, a friendly sort, told Holt that he was welcome to sail with them.

"My luggage is arriving in one hour," Holt said. "It is coming by wagon. Will you wait?"

Fairbanks seemed edgy but Dukeham agreed, no doubt eager to dismiss any suspicion that might arise if they protested the delay. Inside the hour, Holt, realizing that other pursuers might not arrive in time, approached a cluster of men in the inn, explained his desperate gamble, and asked them to help hold the pair until his friends arrived. They agreed, but were so fearful of Fairbanks, the much-publicized murderer, that they told Holt he must capture the killer himself.

As the men jumped Dukeham and held him to the ground, Holt slipped behind Fairbanks and held him in a fierce armlock. Though Holt called out to the other men to assist him, none came to his aid. Here the once puny, crippled Fairbanks had been transformed in the frightened minds of others into an all-powerful creature of superhuman strength. Holt held on to the squirming Fairbanks for more than ten minutes until, to his relief, his fellow pursuers, Captain H. Tisdale and M. S. Wheelock, rode up on lathered horses.

Fairbanks was returned to Dedham and, on September 10, before a large crowd, he mounted the scaffold. The youth seemed resigned to his fate. Although he never made a formal confession, he had earlier admitted that he had brought about Elizabeth Fales' death and praised the jury and court that had sentenced him to the gallows.

As the rope was placed about his neck, Fairbanks asked that the final act be his own. He then produced a white handkerchief and held it aloft in the gentle breeze for some seconds. Then he released it. Before it fluttered to earth, Jason Fairbanks had been sent through the trap.

1817–22 NEW ENGLAND
The Family-Made Monster

"He was not the type of person a traveller would want to meet in a lonely spot," wrote one early-day crime historian of Samuel Green, the terror of New England, and one of America's first archmurderers. Heavyset, muscular, the five-foot-eight-inch Green showed the world a savage-looking face and burning dark eyes, but the strange fires raging inside him were more fierce and threatening than his physical appearance.

Green was a product of the whip, that cherished item of a young United States. To say that this inhuman killer was created by the stern-minded adults who ruled his childhood is an understatement in the annals of murder.

Born in the hamlet of Meredith, New Hampshire, Green's poor, hard-working parents thought the child possessed at an early age when he played the truant from school. As was the case with most simple folk of that era, they resorted to thrashing their child with switches. As a teenage apprentice to a blacksmith, Green was caught stealing. He was horsewhipped. He was sent home, where he was whipped again. He angrily sought revenge by destroying a bed of onions. He was whipped for this offense but refused to admit to the deed. Instead he grabbed the family dog and threw it in the well. The drowned dog caused the water to turn bad and the well had to be cleaned at great expense to the Greens. For this transgression Green was, naturally, whipped.

In childish rage, Green stabbed the family pig. He was beaten severely. His parents finally threw up their hands to Heaven and sent their son off to Newhampton to live with a man named Dunne. For a short time Samuel settled down and attended school without incident. He then grew bored with classes and began to play hookey. Apprehended, he was beaten. The boy stole a jew's harp from a local store and was flogged. Green fled back to his parents, who, upon hearing of his theft, beat him into unconsciousness, sending him back to Dunne, who, in turn, flayed Green's back until a layer of flesh was peeled back.

For this last beating, Samuel decided to kill Dunne. The boy cleverly arranged a large axe to fall upon his master when he entered his workshop. In case this failed, Green fixed a pitchfork, points aimed downward, at the top of the barn door. Dunne proved lucky. When he entered his workshop, the axe fell but only sliced away a part of his coatsleeve. As he raced into the barn in search of Green, the pitchfork shot downward, giving Dunne only a minor wound in the foot. For these clumsy attempts at homicide, Green was tied to the barn door and whipped until his back was a welted, bloody mass of flesh.

Again Green retaliated, destroying a hogshead of cider and stealing some bushels of Dunne's corn. He was whipped when caught. Green tried to burn down Dunne's barn. His master quickly put out the blaze. Green was beaten senseless with whips and fists.

This seesaw battle between guardian and boy continued for months until Dunne gave up the fight. By then the youth was old enough and strong enough so that no man could hold him. He then embarked on a career of passing counterfeit notes, along with another embittered youth named Ash, both of them supplied by a crafty old Fagin whose name they never uttered. They operated about Newhampton at the time. When both young men came under suspicion as having too much money for their station and age in life, they moved to other towns. As they passed a schoolhouse where children were playing, Green decided to wreak more vengeance upon those who represented his misspent youth. He threw a large timber beneath a speeding sleigh loaded with children, almost killing them.

The schoolmaster, a large man, collared both Green and Ash

35

and beat them severely. That night the bruised youths waited for the man, waylaid him in a remote spot, and knocked him unconscious with rocks. They stripped him naked, tied him up, and left him to freeze to death. (The schoolmaster was found hours later and narrowly recovered.)

Green and Ash then moved through the town of Guilford, and then over to Burlington, Vermont, where Green enlisted with the army, being paid a bounty for his services. He immediately deserted but was caught and thrown into a guardhouse where, of course, he was flogged. He broke loose and fled back to his family in New Hampshire. Green was rich by then, having passed hundreds of dollars worth of counterfeit notes. With more than a thousand dollars to his name, the young man purchased a cow for his mother, the only sign of love he ever manifested in his life. The remainder of his loot he lavished upon himself in the purchase of fine clothes, jewelry, a fine horse and sumptuous meals.

When the money ran out, Green and Ash went back to passing counterfeit bills. Their elderly mentor and supplier taught the dedicated felon Green some backup trades in the lucrative fields of crime, showing him how to become an expert card cheat and how to pick locks and duplicate keys to enhance his methods of burglary.

Green went to Boston, where he hired out as a servant to wealthy men. Once inside their houses he played the dutiful servant, but late at night he robbed them of their valuables and fled.

Next, Green again teamed up with Ash and, outside of Bath, New Hampshire, they encountered a jewelry salesman in a tavern. The peddler imprudently allowed the two cutthroats to inspect his fine gems. Later that day, Green and Ash waited in ambush for the peddler. When he leisurely rode past them, they sprang forth from bushes, knocked him off his mule with cudgels and took his money. Ash thought they should kill the man. Green hesitated. "A dead cock never crows," advised the wily Ash. Green winked at the reason and then brought his club down upon the unconscious man, bashing in his head and killing him on the spot.

Green's wild exploits became less secretive as he ranged through New England, robbing and murdering at will. He was jailed several times on suspicion but evidence was lacking to indict him. On several occasions, Green did not wait for judgment. His friend Ash always managed to help him escape his cell. Once, when looting a jewelry store in Montreal, Green fought his way through an entire posse, shooting several men. He was apprehended and thrown into jail. He was soon tried, convicted and sentenced to be hanged. Green, as his jailors half-expected, broke jail with his friend Ash's help and returned to the lonely mountains of New Hampshire. After hiding out for some months, Green again went on a crime spree, burglarizing stores in Albany, New York, and in New York City. He then went up to Middlebury, Vermont, where he robbed and shot to death a wealthy French traveler. Nothing was beyond the ambitions of Samuel Green. He left a trail of rape, horse-stealing, burglary, counterfeiting and murder from Montpelier, Vermont, to Schenectady, New York; from Saco, Maine, to Barre, Vermont. He became America's first Public Enemy Number One. In scenes reminiscent of the terrified villages with flickering torches and howling dogs searching for the Frankenstein monster, Green had aroused all of New England. Half the country was looking for him; the bounties to be paid for his capture were enormous.

The great fugitive's end began when he was arrested in Danvers, Massachusetts, for stealing thirty dollars' worth of goods from a store while blind drunk. He was convicted of this burglary. Green was sent to the State Prison at Boston to serve a four-year term. He attempted to escape many times, for which he was fitted for special shackles with weighted clogs to slow his movements; several more years were also added to his term.

Green learned that a Negro prisoner named Billy Williams had informed on him moments before his last escape attempt. Once released from solitary confinement, Green vowed revenge. He put poison into Williams' food but the wary convict did not eat it. Green finally cornered Williams alone in a shop on the morning of November 8, 1821. Wielding an iron bar, he pounced upon the informer. He brought the weapon down on Williams' head, giving him a fractured skull. While the man lay unconscious at his feet, Green kept hammering at him with the bar, breaking all of Williams' ribs and his arms and legs. Williams died a week later of these injuries.

It was the finish for Samuel Green, juvenile delinquent, whose final punishment, following a long trial, occurred on April 25, 1822. A rope was put about his neck instead of being applied to his back. Before Green was dropped to death, he told

An old print of New England brigand and killer Samuel Green, circa 1821.

Father Taylor, who prayed at his side, that he had no words for those gathered to see him hang. "They shall not know my fate," he said cryptically. "I have written out my confession in full."

"Are you penitent, my son?" asked the priest.

"If you wish it," droned Samuel Green.

1826 EN ROUTE TO NOVA SCOTIA

Piracy over an Insult

Captain Edward Selfridge, skipper of the American schooner *Fairy*, was shy two crew members. By the middle of August 1826, with his ship still docked in Boston Harbor, Selfridge was beginning to get a little desperate about signing on the needed able-bodied seamen. He didn't like the looks of Charles Marchant and Sylvester Colson as they stepped forward to volunteer for duty, but he was late sailing and his cargo, bound for Gottenburg, Germany, was highly perishable. He signed on Marchant and Colson, who joined the mate, Thomas Paine Jenkins, and crew members John Murray and John Hughes.

The *Fairy* sailed from Boston on August 20, 1826, its holds filled to the brim with sugar, rice, coffee, fustic and tobacco. The twenty-three-year-old Selfridge, as he was to learn with the spilling of his own blood, had every reason to mistrust his two new crew members. Marchant's real name was John Duncan White. He had been, among many things, a British seaman, a thief, and a pirate who had sailed with Lafitte a decade earlier. "Colson" was an alias for Winslow Curtis, American-born, with a criminal record as long and deadly as his friend Marchant's.

There was trouble from the start. Jenkins, on the day of sailing, spotted Marchant shirking near dockside. The mate pointed to a pile of wood that had to be taken aboard ship, shouting at Marchant: "Bear a hand!"

The burly, scar-faced Marchant glared at Jenkins, saying: "Do you think you're speaking to a slave?"

"Get on with it," ordered Jenkins, ending the squabble.

Colson was equally lax in his duties. When he fell asleep on watch a few nights out of port, Selfridge shocked him awake by tossing a bucket of cold water on him. Marchant and Colson, both good seamen, were kept at the helm during the captain's and mate's watches for extensive periods. They complained bitterly about such treatment.

After only a few days at sea, the grumbling Marchant and Colson met in the crew's quarters. Colson urged the murder of Captain Selfridge and Mate Jenkins. He then suggested that the crew members, Murray and Hughes, should also be killed to prevent them from talking. Marchant, according to his later statements, at first refused to take part in such cold-blooded retaliation for the harsh treatment he had endured. Yet in the early evening of August 24, with the *Fairy* riding easy in calm seas, Marchant stole one of the two axes stored in the Captain's cabin and secreted it near the helm. Crewman Hughes thought it odd some minutes later when he spotted Colson slipping a heaver, a large staff employed to fix the halyards, into a lifeboat.

At nine o'clock that night, Captain Selfridge left the helm and went below. Hughes and Colson remained on deck. At midnight Hughes awoke Marchant and the mate, and he and Colson were relieved.

Hughes slept soundly until he heard someone calling the next watch. He moved to an adjoining berth but Colson was not there. Rubbing the sleep from his eyes, Hughes clambered up to the deck. He saw Marchant idly sitting on the weather rail and Colson at the helm.

"Where's Mate Jenkins?" Hughes said, a bit dumbfounded.

Marchant's answer chilled him to the bone. "We killed the captain and the mate! We threw them overboard!"

Colson gave him a maniacal smile. "We have killed the damned rascals, that's right. By this time they are in hell with the devil!"

Then Marchant added in his most sinister voice: "You may thank God that we did not kill you as we did them!"

"I may thank God," replied the terrified and shivering Hughes, "but I don't know but that you will kill me anyway later as you did them."

Marchant gave him an assuring look. "No, no, we will not kill you, if you behave yourself."

Hughes began to weep. Through his sobs he found the courage to inquire: "Who killed them?"

"I killed one," Marchant said in a matter-of-fact voice. "He the other."

"Why did you kill those men?"

"No cause at all," answered Marchant. He hung his head a bit. "I'm sorry now that I did it."

Colson flared up, almost spinning the helm in anger. "What! Sorry! For killing them two fellows? I would kill them two rascals as I would a dog." He looked disapprovingly at Marchant. "If they had been good men, it would be worthwhile to be sorry."

According to a report published the following year by Dutton and Wentworth, the mutineers then told Hughes they intended to sail the *Fairy* to Newfoundland. They would scuttle the ship there and sign aboard other vessels sailing for European ports. Both Murray, the cook, and Hughes were told that they would not be harmed when they reached land as long as they kept their mouths shut. They would all tell the same lie, Marchant and Colson said, that they were the only survivors of the ship *Fame* out of Philadelphia, which had sprung a leak and sank. (The *Fame* was a product of Marchant's imagination.) Hughes and Murray fearfully agreed.

The *Fairy* never made it to Newfoundland. Sighting the shores of Nova Scotia, the mutineers decided to land there. They used an auger to bore holes into the ship below the waterline, then quickly plugged the holes. Next they filched all the valuables on board, filling three large chests with their loot—which made them official pirates. On August 29, when close to the flickering lights of Louisburg on the island of Cape Breton, both pirates raced about the ship pulling the plugs. They then swung the lifeboat over the side, lowered it, and rowed quickly away from the sinking *Fairy*. The four men and three chests touched land an hour later.

Once ashore, Murray managed to free himself from the pirates, using the excuse that he would arrange passage to Halifax on board the *Sally*, a schooner anchored in the harbor. Murray immediately told the skipper of the *Sally*, Captain Hook, that Colson and Marchant had murdered his captain and mate. The pirates and Hughes were then rounded up. From the outset of their capture, Marchant and Colson turned on each other. Marchant, apprehended first, was being tied up on a Louisburg dock when he blurted to Captain Hook that it was Colson who had murdered Selfridge and Jenkins, claiming that Colson had bashed in the mate's brains in the hencoop while he, Marchant, was manning the helm, helpless. Then, he said, Colson, who had "haunted" Marchant for three days, went below to the captain's cabin. Wielding the bloody axe, Colson ignored Selfridge's screams and chopped him to pieces. Asked how he came to have blood on his pants, Marchant quickly explained that, since the deeds were done and he would, no doubt, be incriminated anyway, he had helped Colson drag the captain's blood-soaked body on deck, where it was tossed overboard.

Canadian police captured Colson after he led them on a wild chase. He was brought to a magistrate's room where Marchant was held. Both men glared at each other. Then Colson spat out at Marchant: "Charles, if you had only listened to my advice, we should not have come to this." (His meaning was quite clear: they should have killed Murray and Hughes.)

Before the magistrate could further grill Colson, the tough seaman put across his own story of gore. "I know that I must die and will tell the truth," Colson said quietly to the magistrate. "I was forward when I heard Marchant strike the blow that killed the mate, and I then heard the mate fall off the hencoop onto the deck. I went aft and found Marchant throwing Jenkins' body overboard. When he was discovered, Marchant took up the weapon, and swore that if I did not instantly go below and kill the captain, I would share the fate of Jenkins. Fearing for my life, I went into the cabin with an axe. But as I approached the berth where the captain was sleeping, my heart failed me and I ran back to the steps of the companion ladder. Marchant came to me and again told me that if I did not kill the captain, I would be killed. I returned to the berth and struck the captain with the axe. The captain screamed and cried 'Murder!' At this Marchant sprang into the cabin, seized the captain and pulled him from his berth. I then killed him on the cabin floor. I helped Marchant to haul the body up the companion ladder and thrust it through a porthole into the sea."

During his recitation, Colson never once took his eyes from Marchant, whose response was a stony silence. The two men were removed to Boston and, on November 29, 1826, were charged with murder and piracy. Marchant testified that Jenkins, on the night of the double murder, had found him asleep at the helm and had slapped him in the face twice. He struck back at the mate with such force that Jenkins was hurled into the sea and disappeared. When Colson heard this news he gleefully, according to Marchant, ran down to the cabin and killed Captain Selfridge with an axe as a retaliation for the captain's throwing water on him days earlier. Marchant obviously attempted to convince the jury that he was guilty of manslaughter, not murder.

Colson tried to share the blame for both murders, but his pleas for mercy, along with Marchant's, went unheard. Both men were found guilty and, on December 23, were sentenced to death.

"I am innocent," yelled Marchant, "innocent, innocent!" He burst into tears.

Colson's face seemed to cloud over, a crazy grin formed. "That's the best news I've heard in six months," he told the judge.

Marchant regained his composure. "I wish I could die tomorrow. I would do so and be happy, for Jenkins got what he deserved. I took two blows from a Yankee. There is too much English blood in me for me not to return one!"

Colson began to rave incoherently, his sentences running down in spittled madness to shrieking curses, foul words. "Damn you, damn all of you!"

Both men were physically removed from the court, which took some time for they struggled violently with the guards. Marchant and Colson were placed in separate cells to await the hangman, the date of their execution fixed for February 1, 1827. Marchant remained surly during his last hours; one prisoner overheard him whisper to Colson, who was in an adjoining cell, that "they will never take me to the gallows." Early on the morning of January 31, 1827, Marchant tore a strip of cloth from his blanket, tied this to his bandanna in a perfect sailor's knot and affixed it to a grating on his cell window. He tied the loose end around his neck and, using the cell's tub as a platform, jumped, hanging himself.

Colson was executed on time. Before being swung off, he turned to a small crowd and said, "God forgive me, we did it." He then expressed hope that there would be a safe place for him in the hereafter.

But there was no safe place for the bodies of Colson and Marchant. Both corpses were delivered for anatomical observation to the Harvard Medical School. The bodies were received by an odd-looking character, Dr. John White Webster, who would perform one of the most gruesome murders in American history two decades later (see Chronology, 1849). Webster, at the time, was conducting bizarre experiments with bodies, employing a galvanic battery to view the reactions of nerves and muscles to battery charges. Webster inserted dozens of pins with wires into Colson's body. The wires led back to the enormous battery, which had a switch control. (Webster's odd-looking device was somewhat similar to a crude electroencephalogram machine.)

This experiment, reported in detail by the *Columbian Centinel* on February 3, 1827, created an image not unlike that conjured by Mary Shelley or the brothers Warner when depicting a mad scientist manipulating his life-support machines in the making of human monsters. The account read in part:

> The first experiment was made by introducing a negative wire into the mouth [of Colson], and a positive wire into the utera, and convulsive motions ensued. Applied to the eye the organ opened, and rolled wildly and the face distorted.
>
> One wire placed over the carotid artery, the other in the mouth, and at every contact the mouth opened and shut. . . . One wire being placed to the top of the shoulder and the other to the wrist, the arms were convulsed and raised. . . . One wire placed near the carotid artery and the other to a wire pushed to the imbileas, the chest rose and fell, and the mechanical action of breathing was induced. . . . At the same time a flexible tube was passed into the windpipe and oxygen gas thrown into the lungs, the belly swelled out, and there was, as before, appearance of breathing.
>
> The wire applied to each wrist, the arms extended and the hands became clenched forcibly, and on another trial the convict's forefinger extended and pointed at the bystanders. . . . The hand being turned down and the wires applied to the arm and wrist, the hand was violently thrown out, and one wire applied to the upper part of the thigh, and one in the heel, the knee previously bent, the leg was much agitated at every contact, and more than once thrown forward with force and the toes moved briskly.

A short, squat man who peered myopically through thick-lensed glasses, Professor Webster squirreled about the corpse like a man possessed while performing his strange chores. After an hour he turned and bowed to his gaping-mouthed, popeyed audience. "The experiment, gentlemen," he said with a slow smile, "is a great success."

But Webster, fiendish murderer-to-be, did not explain what it all meant, ever.

1829 STERLING, CONNECTICUT

The Woman Who Could Predict Murder

During the presidency of Andrew Jackson, the sleepy hamlet of Sterling, Connecticut, was torn asunder by a spectacular female named Waity Burgess, a lady who had murder on her mind.

When Waity married Welcome Burgess, it was known that she had carried on with many lovers. And much to Welcome's consternation, she continued to frolic with her former associates even after the wedding. After fathering five children, Welcome died and Waity and her brood moved to Chestnut Hill, Connecticut. At age thirty-eight, Waity was considered an attractive widow and a notorious Jezebel. Her sexual antics caused the local inhabitants to storm her house and bombard it with rocks. Waity quickly packed and descended upon hapless Sterling, where she picked out her next victim—Oliver Watkins, a farmer.

Watkins was married and had two children. He was a tall, strong man and was known for his quick anger and cruelty to animals. On one occasion, Watkins became so vexed at his oxen that he wore out his whip on them and was stopped only by his neighbors' intervention.

Waity moved in with her father, a resident of Sterling, who agreed to house her on the condition that she refrain from decimating the local male population. The widow, however, was soon seen with Watkins, and the couple took excursions to neighboring towns, visiting fairs and markets. Roxana Watkins was a patient woman (and feared her husband's temper), and said nothing.

Waity began working on Oliver Watkins, telling him that his wife was a "lazy and indolent person who lets her clothes lay outdoors until they rot." Waity, however, kept her house "neat and tidy. . . . I used to spin my own wool and flax, make my own cloth and had some to sell at the same time."

Roxana Watkins finally approached her husband one day and told him that his behavior with Waity was something more than shocking. "What business is it of yours where I go?" Oliver roared. "Shut up your mouth, wretch. I'll go where I please and when I please, and were it not for my family, I would never hear any more of your jaw!"

Such bombast was sufficient to silence Roxana, but Waity Burgess would not settle for an affair. She subtly began to suggest that Watkins send his wife off. To where, she did not say, but in the days that followed her meaning became clear: Oliver was to murder the oppressed lady.

Waity then appeared in several of Sterling's stores, ordering broadcloth and startling all by stating that she would soon be marrying a widower. Her father, disgusted with her affair with Watkins, threw her out, and Waity took up lodging in a rooming house. This move, the widow explained, had traumatized her into being psychic. Waity insisted she could tell the future. One night she was found racing about town in her nightgown, crystal ball in hand. When stopped by puzzled citizens, Waity said: "There will be a sudden death in the neighborhood, for there was a winding sheet on my candle when I looked at it this morning, and I never knew it to fail but that a sudden death followed."

On the night of March 21, 1829, Oliver Watkins pretended to be asleep, waiting for his wife to drop off. He then rose, crept from the bedroom, got a horsewhip and returned to the sleeping chamber. Oliver slipped the whip about Roxana's neck and, using his gigantic strength, quickly crossed the ends over her throat. So great was the pressure that a string of beads Roxana was wearing burst and scattered. She was dead within minutes. Oliver then returned the whip to its post and slipped back to bed.

Some hours later he rose with a bellow, shouting for his mother-in-law, who was asleep in an adjoining room. "She has choked herself with her beads," he told old Mrs. Adams, and held to that story when the authorities arrived.

A coroner's jury found Roxana's death accidental, but the state's attorney nurtured dark suspicions and caused Oliver's arrest for murder. Throughout the trial, Waity kept her distance, telling everyone, "I hardly know the suspect." The trial resulted in Oliver's conviction and he was scheduled to hang. The murderer refused to admit his guilt, however.

Oliver Watkins was hanged Aug. 2, 1831, in the last public execution in Connecticut. It was a memorable affair. One report said: "A company of the old state militia was present and the hillside was black with people."

Waity Burgess didn't attend. Some days later she placed her children in an orphanage, then moved to Foster, Rhode Island,

This early engraving depicts the much-bedeviled Oliver Watkins strangling his sleeping wife, Roxana.

where she convinced a widower to take her in. Within a week, though, local residents assembled at her new residence, battered down the door, and dragged Waity into the night. She was sent down the road to wander into an aimless future.

The last report of the woman who could predict murder had her living in seclusion in the aptly named town of Killingly, Rhode Island.

1844–71 UPPER NEW YORK STATE

An Intellectual Killer

From the age of four until he was hanged in 1871, Edward Howard Rulloffson was a fanatical reader, a strange scholar, and an intellectual of the rarest breed. Born in 1819 in Hammond River, New Brunswick, Canada, Rulloffson stemmed from Dutch ancestry, his parents being hardworking farm folk who could not spare him from chores for a formal education.

A bookish mother, however, filled young Edward's head with smatterings of knowledge, Greek and Latin, the classics. He became an avaricious reader, consuming any and all books he could find, having no preference for any particular field of study. At age twelve, Rulloffson entered school, but he only received a few years of formal study. He worked for a while for a grocer in St. John, then as a clerk for a local lawyer.

It was while clerking for the lawyer that Rulloffson first got into trouble. A number of burglaries occurred in the St. John area; one of the ransacked homes was Rulloffson's employer's. A few days later, the lawyer entered his office and blinked in amazement at his young, studious clerk. Rulloffson was attired in a suit owned by the lawyer, one that had been pilfered during the recent robbery. Confronted with the theft, the apprentice merely shrugged. He would neither affirm or deny his guilt in the robberies. Rulloffson's indifference was enough to earn him a two-year sentence in New Brunswick Prison. Discharged at age twenty-two, after serving the full term, Edward Howard Rulloffson completely vanished.

In the deep summer of 1842, Rulloffson, calling himself Edward Rulloff, appeared in Dryden, New York, obtaining a job as a canal laborer. He was a broad-backed, thickly bearded young man many a Dryden maid thought handsome, yet there was an outstanding peculiarity to his physical make-up; his head was enormous—larger, many commented, than Daniel Webster's—a massive head covered with shaggy hair and further ornamented with extremely wide-set, penetrating dark eyes.

Rulloff may have worked with pick and shovel, but the townsfolk soon learned from his lips that he knew several languages and was an expert on the law, medicine and botany. When questioned as to what university he had attended, Rulloff only gave a wry smile and kept his silence.

When he learned that the small school in Dryden was in need of a teacher, Rulloff applied for and was given the position. As the town's teacher, he amazed his students with stupefying rhetoric and startling knowledge of the roots of words in many languages. Professor Rulloff, as he took to calling himself, displayed methods of teaching that were no less than spectacular as he filled the blackboard with simple drawings to explain the origins of words, bringing in to play involved Chinese dialects and ancient cavemen's symbols.

One fascinated student, sixteen-year-old Harriet Schutt,

found it impossible to resist falling in love with the colorful Rulloff. The following year, despite objections from Harriet's parents and brothers (who were put off by Rulloff's unknown background), the professor married his most ardent student. On the day of the wedding, December 31, 1843, Rulloff quit teaching, suddenly assuming the role of "Doctor" Rulloff, telling all in Dryden that he was a whiz at healing all manner of ills through his incredible knowledge of herbs, a claim that was not altogether untrue. As a botanical physician, Rulloff found his practice blossoming; the naive natives of Dryden flocked to his grubby offices for natural healings. But with success, Rulloff's temperament seemed to sour; he fell into black moods and his anger flared at any annoyance. Once, while his wife was preparing a meal for him, Doctor Rulloff inexplicably grabbed a pestle and struck Harriet on the head, heaping curses upon the fallen woman. Such conduct brought a warning from Harriet's brothers, William and Edward Schutt. The haughty Rulloff bristled and moved, tight-lipped, with his wife to Lansing, New York, settling in a remote cabin near the shores of Lake Cayuga.

Rulloff's fame as an herb healer had spread to neighboring communities by 1844. His ability to cure myriad maladies was known as far as the large city of Ithaca, and more than once he was called to aid the stricken of that city. One of these was William Schutt, his brother-in-law, whose wife and child had been suffering from an unknown disease. Doctor Rulloff treated both woman and child but they died shortly thereafter. "They were beyond all help," Rulloff told his wife.

When Harriet gave birth the following year, the famous doctor ignored his baby daughter, Dorothy, as well as his wife. He was too busy with his practice to be interested in the mundane events of his own homelife. Part of that business was done in secret in late June 1845, when Rulloff went off in the direction of Lake Cayuga. He returned to tell his neighbor, Mr. Robertson, that his wife and daughter had journeyed to see relatives in Ohio. Rulloff asked if he could use Robertson's horse and wagon to transport a large box containing his wife's and the baby's belongings for shipment to Ohio; they would be visiting for an indefinite period of time.

Robertson not only loaned Rulloff his horse and wagon but helped the good doctor load the large, weighty crate. Rulloff waved a thank-you and drove off whistling a happy tune. On June 25, Robertson saw Rulloff return and was amazed to see how easily the doctor lifted the same heavy box from the wagon and took it into his home. When the doctor returned the horse and wagon to his neighbor, Robertson's suspicions grew. He noticed that the horse was not lathered. (Rulloff had claimed his journey was to be a long one.)

Further perplexing Robertson was Rulloff's announcement some hours later that he was off to be with his wife. The large man's spirits were no less than ebullient as he joked and laughed with neighbor Robertson, setting off with a smile and saying over his shoulder: "Don't let anyone carry away our house while we are gone."

Rulloff was next seen in Ithaca, where he dropped in to see the Schutts, telling them that Harriet and Dorothy were staying with a friend, one N. Dupuy, of Madison, Ohio. His remarks were met with nerve-pricking questions. Why would she go off like that without telling them? the Schutts asked pointedly. Flustered, Rulloff immediately sat down and, as if to prove his statements were true, wrote a letter to his wife that gushed endearment. Later, in the presence of the Schutt brothers, he mailed it off to Ohio. This seemed to allay the family's fears but when Edward Schutt heard that Rulloff was going to Auburn some days later, he followed the doctor, finding him on a train headed for Buffalo.

Without any trace of apprehension, Rulloff told Schutt that he was on his way to visit Harriet and his child. "Why don't you come along?" To his surprise, Schutt did, but once in Buffalo, Rulloff lost him, jumping from the train bound for Madison, Ohio, at the last minute. Schutt went on to Madison to discover that there was no one named N. Dupuy living there, and that his sister and niece had never been seen in the area. Hurriedly, the brother went to Cleveland and reported the facts to the police. An alarm went out for Edward Rulloff who, with his unusual appearance, was not hard to find. He was arrested in a Cleveland hotel. Schutt, as was often the custom of the day, was deputized; he returned to New York with his shifty brother-in-law handcuffed to him.

Authorities in Tompkins County, where Rulloff was held prisoner, realized that without any corpses, the eccentric doctor could not be indicted for murder. (Lake Cayuga had been repeatedly dragged in an effort to recover the bodies of Harriet Rulloff and her child without success.) However, Rulloff was charged with abduction and was convicted, receiving ten years

49

in Auburn Prison. The self-appointed doctor-professor became a model prisoner, broadening his education by reading thousands of books on various subjects, particularly those dealing with ancient and modern languages. He taught his fellow prisoners in a school he organized, and, when he was released in 1856, it was thought that Rulloff had been victimized, such was his sterling reputation in prison.

Yet officials of Tompkins County had other ideas. They had learned during Rulloff's imprisonment that a large man who gave no name had sold the bodies of a woman and child to the Geneva Medical College for study shortly after the disappearance of Harriet and Dorothy Rulloff. The bodies bore no marks of violent death but the woman did fit the description of Mrs. Rulloff. Unfortunately, the bodies had long ago been dissected. Still, police figured they had gathered enough circumstantial evidence to convict Rulloff and he was once again arrested and charged with his wife's murder.

With a smug appearance and much sneering at the court and jury, Rulloff acted as his own attorney during the trial, an event he had apparently anticipated as he had immersed himself in the studies of intricate law during his long prison term.

In court, the accused killer's blue eyes blazed; his heavyset five-foot-eight-inch frame moved in jerky motions as he defended himself with great self-confidence. At one point, he boomed at the prosecuting attorney: "You cannot try me again for the unfortunate disappearance of my wife. Even a backwoods shyster ought to know that much!"

He was right. The state dropped that charge but brought another murder indictment against Rulloff, that of killing his child. Though convicted of the charge and sentenced to death, the doctor-professor remained unruffled. While being held without bail, he filed a brilliant appeal to the higher courts and told his friendly jailor, Deputy Sheriff Jacob Jarvis, that the decision would be reversed and he would soon be free.

Jarvis not only believed the cunning Rulloff but asked that the brilliant prisoner tutor his son, eighteen-year-old Albert. Rulloff accepted the chore with delight, teaching the boy French and Latin. The youth grew to admire Rulloff so much he arranged for the prisoner's escape on the storm-shrouded night of May 5, 1857. The professor-doctor wasted no time in deserting Albert Jarvis. Rulloff fled to Meadville, Pennsylvania, which housed Allegheny College. He became the darling of the intellectual community, proving that he had no equal in the study of languages; he also displayed some genius as a mineralogist, a conchologist, and an expert on insects, birds and machines. He worked in Meadville for a scientist, A. B. Richmond, perfecting a new invention, but the pay was meager and Rulloff, who had been calling himself Professor James Nelson, was off to Warren County where he robbed a jewelry store.

Exhausted and frostbitten after hiding in cold barns and beneath bridges, Rulloff next appeared in Jamestown, New York, entering a drugstore and so thoroughly convincing the owner of his expert knowledge in pharmacology that he was allowed to compound his own frostbite prescription.

"It's no good," Rulloff grumbled to the druggist after applying the medicine and staring at a sorry-looking big toe. "It's got to come off." He borrowed some surgical instruments from a local doctor and amputated his own toe. Hobbling away, Rulloff traveled to Ohio, where he began teaching in a small Columbus school. All seemed calm in his life, but dogged lawmen were not far behind. Dozens of sheriffs had been searching for him since his escape from the Ithaca jail. One determined lawman, Sheriff John Dennin, clutching one of the many thousands of wanted posters that had been printed of the fugitive, tracked Rulloff to Columbus and arrested him, extraditing him to New York with the Ohio governor's blessing.

Fortune was with Rulloff. After being held for several months on fragile charges, the long-awaited decision of Rulloff's appeal arrived. Since no body had ever been found, the high court pronounced him innocent of killing his daughter.

The citizens of Ithaca, enraged at the decision, threatened to storm the local jail. Rulloff narrowly escaped with his neck intact as deputies spirited him to Auburn Prison for safekeeping. Police attempted to try Rulloff on another murder charge, that of killing William Schutt's wife and child while treating them in 1844. Authorities went so far as to exhume both bodies, turning them over to a Professor Ogden Doremus, who flatly insisted that the remains, although they were fourteen years old, contained definite traces of copper poison. His views, however, were not supported by other testifying physicians, and these charges too were dropped. The illustrious doctor-professor Rulloff was once again set free.

The slippery Rulloff wandered throughout New England for the next six years, being implicated in a New Hampshire bank robbery and a theft in a Connecticut store, among many other crimes, but Rulloff always managed to ease out of the jittery hands of the law. His luck ran out in November 1861, when he was caught flagrantly looting another store in New York and was sent to Sing Sing for two years for burglary. Again, the ever-studious Rulloff begged and borrowed every book he could obtain, reading them until he wore out the pages. He took out enough time during his sentence to befriend a professional burglar named William T. Dexter.

When Dexter and Rulloff were released about the same time in 1864, they teamed up with none other than Albert Jarvis, the jailer's son gone wrong, and put together the most formidable burglary team ever seen in New York City with Rulloff as the mastermind.

The remarkable rogue Rulloff had not lost his original touch, displaying the type of ingenuity that would make a Poe salivate at his writing desk. Much like the archcriminal portrayed some seventy-odd years later by Rudolph Klein-Rogge in the German-made films about the sinister Dr. Mabuse, Professor Rulloff became a man with many lives, all of them acted out superbly.

Inside Dexter's ancestral Brooklyn home on Graham Street, Rulloff was known as Professor E. C. Howard, master of almost all known languages, and self-appointed patriarch to the large Dexter family, directing the lives and fortunes (not to mention the rents from the family's considerable real estate holdings) of its members. In this role, Rulloff-Howard also maintained offices in Hoboken, New Jersey, where, two days out of each week without fail, he taught immigrants the simple wonders of the English language, as well as improved their own native tongues.

Three days out of every week, Rulloff took on the identity of a distinguished philologist, Professor Edward Leurio, proficient in three dozen languages and dialects, working out a new tongue for the world's babbling nations, which he called Leurio's Universal Method. For this important study, Professor Leurio rented offices at 170 Third Avenue in Manhattan, where he also maintained living quarters should they be needed.

The need might arise from Rulloff's third and most provocative life-role, that of a master planner of super burglaries. Since he possessed rare knowledge of the value of Chinese silk, taffeta and other fabrics, Rulloff directed his charges, Dexter and

Jarvis, to loot several silk-manufacturing warehouses and retail shops in and about Manhattan, after the scholarly professor had properly "cased" the objective buildings. Thousands of dollars' worth of these rare goods were fenced by Rulloff and his partners, enough to keep them in high style.

Luxury, however, no longer appealed to bibliophile Rulloff. He lived more simply as time passed. Except for a black top hat, his wardrobe remained inexpensive. He spurned jewelry. Meager, bland food he wolfed down while squeezing time from his studies, which more and more preoccupied his waking hours. He was developing his Universal Method of Language through an enormous manuscript, which he claimed would make it possible for anyone to travel from one point of the globe to another with no difficulty in communicating with a host of peoples accustomed to polyglot tongues. The project grew into an obsession until even his rather cretinous co-burglars realized they were supplying Rulloff-Howard-Leurio with funds to complete his monstrous academic dream.

So fanatical did Rulloff become in his literary efforts that he addressed, as Professor Edward Leurio, the August American Philological Association in Poughkeepsie, New York, in July 1869. With his black top hat perched on his great head, Leurio-Rulloff swept back the tails of his black frock coat, gripped a podium, and thunderingly announced that he had invented a new language that would undoubtedly cause all wars to cease and turn all nations into instant brotherhoods. He submitted his study, hundreds of pages of handwritten script, for acceptance. The Association examined the manuscript and then turned it down.

Rulloff cursed these would-be savants and proclaimed to his burglar pals that he would publish the work himself, no matter the cost. To acquire funds, the dedicated intellectual selected Halbert Brothers' Silk Shop in Binghamton, New York, for his next burglary. The goods from this emporium alone would enable Rulloff to publish his masterwork. Dutifully, Dexter and Jarvis broke into the store on the night of August 21, 1870, but were surprised as they were gathering rolls of silk by two of the store's clerks, Gilbert Burrows and Fred Mirrick (or Mirick), who happened to be sleeping on the premises. As the four men struggled, a huge man wearing a top hat, which wobbled upon an enormous head, stepped into the store, firing a pistol. At first Mirrick and Burrows thought the man was a detective, but this hope quickly burst when the large man, his eyes blazing beneath heavy eyebrows, calmly walked up to Mirrick and sent a bullet into his head. He then turned the pistol on Burrows and shot him. The burglars ran from the store without taking one piece of silk with them.

Mirrick was killed instantly but Burrows lived. He staggered from the store to give the alarm. Half of Binghamton responded; posses were quickly formed, fanning out over hilly terrain. A short time later, possemen discovered two bodies floating in the nearby Chenango River. They had been beaten to death before being thrown into the water. Burrows quickly identified the men as the two burglars he and Mirrick had surprised. In the pockets of the dead men, proving their killer had hurriedly disposed of them, were found identification cards listing them as William T. Dexter and Albert Jarvis.

Possemen searching the railroad tracks outside of Binghamton came upon a towering man with a large head and piercing blue eyes. The man, who told officers that his name was Charles Augustus, explained that he had been forcibly thrown from a passenger train after he had lost his ticket and that it was urgent he get to Ithaca where he was expected to lecture before a collection of the most learned men in New York. As the queer-looking man mesmerized the lawmen, a freight train passed between them and, when it had gone, Charles Augustus, lecturer, had disappeared. He was found hours later hiding in a barn a half mile from the tracks. Augustus was hauled off to jail under suspicion of being the gunman in the attempted store burglary. While awaiting a formal charge, Augustus yelled from his jail cell: "You will all regret the day you falsely arrested me! What a case of false arrest my lawyers will make when I sue!"

So cowed were the anxious police that they unlocked the cell holding Augustus and were leading him into the foyer of the police station to release him when an Ithaca magistrate, Judge Bolcom, glanced at the man with the giant head and shouted frantically: "Grab that man! That's Rulloff!"

Rulloff was promptly stopped at the front door of the police station and dragged back to a cell. He was identified as the killer of Mirrick by the wounded clerk, Burrows. Through Dexter's family, the many roles Rulloff had played in New York City were exposed. A jury found the evasive intellectual killer guilty of Mirrick's murder in January 1871.

Even though Rulloff was championed by literary lions and newspaper pundits—such as Horace Greeley—as a great mind (his murderous pursuits notwithstanding), there would be no further reprieve for the marvelous linguist. Knowing his fate finally sealed, Edward Howard Rulloff confessed all, stating that he had killed his wife and child in 1845 and that, among many other deaths, he was responsible for poisoning William Schutt's wife and child a year earlier. "I wanted him to suffer for his opposition to my marriage to his sister," Rulloff stated.

"The Educated Murderer," as the press had dubbed Rulloff, was marched to the front of the Binghamton jail on the morning of May 17, 1871, and, before a large crowd, openly spurned any spiritual aid from clergymen expectantly standing nearby. As he had on the last night of his life, Rulloff bragged of his intellectual accomplishments while bellowing "revolting blasphemies and obscenities," according to one on-the-spot reporter. His was a sorry end for a much-vaunted man of language, his last words being "vulgar and profane mouthings, horrible to hear." The rope cut off his curses.

Still the scholarly Rulloff ironically ended by finding a home of sorts inside a great seat of learning. After his hanging, Rulloff's corpse, like those of his wife and child, was turned over to physicians for study. A Dr. George Burr removed the arch-villain's head, weighing and studying Rulloff's massive brain, which was found to be larger than that of Thackeray's or of Daniel Webster. Burr, after writing of his findings in the *Journal of Psychological Medicine*, turned over Rulloff's impressive brain to Cornell University, where it was displayed for years—enduring far beyond Edward Howard Rulloff's severed body, which vanished after body snatchers dug it up and made off with his unsavory remains.

1847 WATERVILLE, MAINE

"I Thumped Him on the Head"

The most successful physician in Waterville, Maine, was Dr. Valorus P. Coolidge. He was also one of the town's most extravagant residents, living the high life in expensive quarters, dining on the best meals, moving about in an elegant carriage with liveried servants to do his bidding. Even the largest practice in Waterville could not sustain such tastes, so it was inevitable that Coolidge sought more funds in the form of loans.

Privately, Coolidge approached one wealthy townsman, asking for a loan of two thousand dollars over a four- or five-month period, desperately offering five hundred dollars in interest. He was refused. The doctor went to another well-endowed citizen and begged a loan of a thousand dollars for a six-month period. He would return an interest of five hundred dollars. Again, Coolidge was rebuffed. His next attempt proved more rewarding. Well-to-do Edward Matthews nodded yes to a Coolidge proposal of loaning the doctor fifteen hundred dollars for a ten-day period, at the end of which the entire sum would be repaid, along with four hundred dollars' interest. It seemed like a good business deal to Matthews; to Coolidge it was a contract for murder.

Matthews, a drover, told the anxious doctor that he intended to sell a herd of cattle in Brighton at the end of the month— September 1847—and with the proceeds would make his loan to Coolidge. No sooner had the cattleman departed Waterville than Coolidge dashed off a note to Hallowell's, the local apothecary, for one ounce of prussic (hydrocyanic) acid, "as strong as it can be made." It was delivered the next day. Two days later, on September 19, the physician wrote to a Boston drug firm, ordering the same potion, also specifying that it should be "as strong as it can be made." This order, too, was promptly delivered to Coolidge.

Dr. Valorus P. Coolidge, who resorted to poison and a club to settle his debts.

The cash-frantic doctor then made inquiries as to how much money Matthews' herd of cattle might bring. He scurried to the inn where the stage stopped to tip the bartender there, asking him to report to him the minute Matthews returned to Waterville. Matthews himself had made arrangements with his bank in town to withdraw fifteen hundred dollars on his return, the amount of the agreed-upon loan, a fact the meticulous Dr. Coolidge took pains to ascertain.

On September 30, Matthews returned to Waterville and was immediately handed a note as he alighted from the stage. It was from Coolidge, asking that they complete their transaction at eight o'clock that night in the doctor's offices. At six that night, Thomas Flint, Coolidge's student-helper, entered the doctor's offices. Coolidge arrived in a nervous state.

"I have arranged through Charles Stackpole," Coolidge told his assistant, "to have a body delivered here for dissection tonight. It will arrive at eight P.M. Before it does, I want you to leave." Flint nodded.

At eight P.M. there came a loud knock at Coolidge's office door. Flint obediently went out a side exit and walked to his boardinghouse where he played backgammon with the proprietor's daughter, Miss Williams, who was also his sweetheart. An hour later, drowsy from the game, Flint took a lamp and began to make his way to his room. In the middle of the dark hall, the lamplight flickering on his open-mouthed, wide-eyed face, stood Dr. Valorus P. Coolidge. His clothes were disheveled and his hands twitched as he spoke.

"Flint," he said in a whisper. "I want you to go to my office with me." He blew out the lamp. "Right now."

Flint placed the lamp on the floor and followed Coolidge in the darkness to his office. Once there, with only a dim lamp to illuminate the twisted features of his face, Dr. Coolidge turned to his apprentice and, in a moment of silence, studied him with darting eyes.

"I am going to reveal to you a secret which involves my life," Coolidge finally said to Flint in a low voice. "That cursed little Ed Matthews came in here, and went to take a glass of brandy, and fell down dead. He now lies in the other room. I thumped him on the head to make people believe he was murdered."

This startling bit of news, especially Coolidge's last puzzling explanation, caused Flint to sink ashen-faced into a rocking chair. He rocked slowly, staring at his employer, speechless.

"What do you think we should do with him?" Coolidge said.

"I don't know," replied the shocked Flint.

"We should get him out of the office," mused the doctor. "I wish he was in the river."

Flint, innocently accepting Coolidge's version of events, and wishing to protect his mentor, suddenly said: "I don't think we can get him in the river. There's a full moon. It's much too bright outside."

"Perhaps we should put him in back of the building?"

"We might be seen," volunteered Flint. "I tell you what. We can carry the body safely to the cellar. That's as far as I will go, the cellar."

"But that's crazy," objected Coolidge. "The body will be found in no time."

"Yes," said the ever-precise Flint, "at seven o'clock tomorrow morning by the janitor, but the cellar is as far as I go."

Doctor Coolidge picked up the lamp and walked in circles about his office, thinking. He finally shrugged and motioned for Flint to follow him into the back room. Flint saw Matthews' body behind a counter, his head bashed in, and blood in small pools nearby.

For all of his once-cool reserve, the doctor seemed in a quandary about the smallest details. "Do you think we ought to wrap his head in something?" he inquired of Flint.

"I think that would be a good idea," answered the apprentice.

Coolidge retrieved Matthews' hat and jammed it down on his head so that it almost covered his open dead eyes. The doctor then dragged the body around the counter and oddly suggested that "we take off our boots." Both did.

Flint went to grab the dead man's ankles but Coolidge stopped him, saying: "Take him by the shoulders. You can carry him better than I." The student took the shoulders and both men struggled awkwardly as they carried the corpse, which slipped several times from their grasp, downstairs. They finally managed to deposit their gory load on a woodpile next to the door of the cellar of a neighboring shop that was part of the same building.

Once again in Coolidge's office, the doctor spent some time wiping up the blood on the floor of his back room. When all was tidy, he turned to Flint and said through a grimace: "They can't suspect me, can they?" Suddenly he laughed in near hysteria. "Oh, no, no, no! My popularity is too great!"

Dr. Coolidge swore Flint to secrecy, telling him he intended to go to the town of Skowhegan the following morning, but at dawn, just as the apprentice had predicted, the janitor found the body of Edward Matthews and sent for the police. A coroner's jury was convened that day and, to Flint's amazement, Dr. Valorus P. Coolidge performed the autopsy on the dead man. Hours later, Coolidge crept back into the operating room when no one was about and tried to dispose of the dead man's stomach, but he was interrupted by an attendant. He quickly left for Skowhegan after giving Flint a thousand dollars to hold for him.

During his absence a Dr. Thayer reexamined the stomach of the dissected Edward Matthews and discovered the presence of prussic acid. When Dr. Coolidge returned from Skowhegan some days later, he asked Flint for his money, as he was planning a long trip. But he was too late. Police had discovered the bottles containing prussic acid on the shelves of Dr. Coolidge's office. He was charged with murder; his trial took place in Augusta, Maine, in March 1848.

Flint was no help on the witness stand, relating exactly what had happened on the night Matthews died. The prosecution carefully pieced the killing together, stating that Coolidge had committed premeditated murder. He had inveigled Matthews to his office, given him a shot of brandy liberally laced with prussic acid—a drink that certainly killed his usurious financier—and then, apparently losing his senses, struck him several times on the head with a hatchet. He then rifled Matthews' pockets and took the fifteen hundred dollars.

Coolidge admitted the killing as it was reconstructed in court. He was sentenced to hang the following year, but, as he languished in the Augusta jail, the inventive doctor somehow procured more prussic acid and committed suicide. To this day, Dr. Valorus P. Coolidge shares with only one other doctor-poisoner, Dr. William Palmer of Rugeley, England, the dubious distinction of having performed an autopsy on his own victim.

1852 GOOSE CREEK, NORTH CAROLINA

Murder from the Pulpit

One of the most powerful representatives of God, a marvelous and bellowing orator, was the Reverend George Washington Carawan. In his hortatory capacity as pastor for Pungo Church in Goose Creek, North Carolina, he was known as a true "Bible belter," one who could turn the devil's legions back to Hades with his rhetorical fire. And he was, in the secret, dark side of his own character, a most self-righteous murderer.

Baptized in 1827 at age twenty-eight, Carawan feverishly waded into religion, a flaming-eyed zealot not unlike Sinclair Lewis' public-dedicated Elmer Gantry, who knew by holy instinct that evil did, indeed, lurk in the land, and, also, by the heart's own reason, where to locate and stamp it out.

From the pulpit Carawan called out the most likely looking

sinners of this thriving congregation, and, with heavy-handed chastisement, did cleanse, purify and forgive. He was immensely successful, both as a minister and, in flourishing corporeal terms, as a wealthy land squire with two sprawling plantations in his dominion. He owned scores of slaves, none of whom benefited from the Christian charity he so ardently lavished on the neatly dressed white folks who humbly lined the pews of his church.

In fact, Carawan's slaves were terrified of him. He would tolerate no shirking of duties on their part and frequently employed the whip. A more politic man would have been mindful of such abuses, for one of his slaves, Seth by name, would be the cause of his fall from public grace. The Reverend Carawan's slaves had noticed peculiarities in the pastor's lifestyle for some time. His first wife died quite suddenly, and it was more than ironic that her death immediately followed Carawan's purchase of a large dose of arsenic. (Portions of the poison were later found hidden in the reverend's trunk.)

Remarrying almost at the graveside, Carawan then took umbrage with a youth named Hudson, who, he claimed, made improper advances toward his second beauteous spouse. Hudson also exited with the help of arsenic. Evidence of this second murder found its way secretly to Reverend Albin R. Swindell, who practiced in Carawan's county.

Swindell made public his discoveries, and in scarlet speech accused pastor Carawan not only of murder but of fathering an illegitimate child by a naive, God-struck parishioner of sixteen. The latter charge in 1852 was apparently deemed the more serious and for a brief spell Carawan was dismissed from his religious duties.

Seething with fitful vengeance, Carawan went in search of his nemesis, Swindell, and found him on a lonely road near one of his plantations. Carawan, a shotgun filled with buckshot held breast high, jumped from his own buckboard and raced with loud oaths bleating to the covered buggy in which the terrified Swindell sat. Fortunately for Swindell, he was traveling with another man and when Carawan noticed the companion he drew back and stammered: "Oh, I'm having some trouble with runaway slaves . . . you haven't seen any about, have you?"

Swindell and his friend shook their heads and traded glinty stares with the good pastor, who was apparently reluctant to commit a double murder then and there, perhaps thinking the two loads of buckshot, even at point-blank, might fail to kill both men.

Clamor from pockets of discontented parishioners ebbed and Reverend Carawan was soon reinstated as the head of his church. Unshakable proof of his bloodletting was wanting. It was not lacking in Carawan's third murder.

For weeks a young corpulent teacher of "singing geography," one Clement Lassiter, was a constant visitor in the Carawan household. At times, the withdrawn, chubby young man stayed overnight at the parsonage.

Pastor Carawan later stated that Lassiter had made lecherous advances toward his wife and that the situation became unbearable one day when the reverend was conducting a "housemoving." Lassiter, the parson claimed, stood about smirking all day and inanely whittling while he and his wife sweated laboriously with massive furniture. The reverend called him an ingrate and Lassiter, according to the pastor's claim, swiped at him with his knife "twice across the bowels." Carawan seized an old rifle from above the mantle and drove the rake from his home. Lassiter, said Carawan, stood swearing in the road at the pastor for some time and then sauntered off.

The youth, incensed with Carawan's public accusations, sued and was quickly awarded eight thousand dollars in court for the slander. Only a few days after the settlement, Lassiter was seen entering a densely wooded area on Carawan's plantation. He was followed by Reverend Carawan and his wife who, several slaves noticed, carried the pastor's shotgun beneath an apron. Minutes later Carawan's wife emerged from the woods *sans* shotgun. The pastor appeared hours later. Lassiter was not seen.

One of Carawan's slaves, the aforementioned Seth, then went to local authorities, stating that the pastor had "blown a load" through the dallying schoolteacher and that he had helped the reverend to bury the body in the woods. Seth was not believed and Carawan was left to his dark pursuits. Another man, however, soon appeared, telling essentially the same story: that he had seen Carawan and his wife overtake Lassiter in the woods and kill him. The fact that this witness was also the pastor's nephew convinced the local sheriff and, later, a perturbed jury of Carawan's guilt. (Mrs. Carawan was never arrested.)

Pastor Carawan was a step ahead of the arresting officers and fled to Tennessee, after telling a group of his slaves: "Boys, they have found Lassiter's body and I must leave or stay and be hanged."

A short time later he returned, imperious, to Goose Creek to sell some of his land, but this was a mistake. Carawan was promptly arrested and thrown into jail. His trial commenced almost at once. It was one of the strangest trials in American court history. Carawan denied everything, insisting that his accusers were jealous of his communion with God. The nephew's story remained intact and the good reverend was convicted.

At his sentencing a day later, Carawan looked furtively about the courtroom for his errant nephew and, not spotting him, settled for venting his wrath on a prosecuting attorney named Warren. Leaning down between his own two lawyers, Carawan tore open his shirt and withdrew a one-shot pistol. He jumped up and aimed it at Warren, sending a ball at his heart.

Carawan's face registered shock even beyond that of those in the court when the bullet bounced harmlessly from Warren's chest after striking a metal chain he was wearing. (Warren fainted.) It was obviously not the custom to frisk parsons on trial for murder in that genteel era; Reverend Carawan, realizing, as we would now say, "the jig was up," produced yet another pistol. With "everything being in the wildest confusion" he, like Richard Cory, sent a bullet into his own brain.

Spectacular? God's will, said some. Amen, said most.

1859 ST. PAUL, MINNESOTA

". . . A Sacrifice to the Law"

Mary Ann Evards Wright was a lady first by all standards and one who set an unforgettable precedent in the darker annals of Minnesota lore. Tall, gray-eyed and blond, Mrs. Wright, a widow of thirty-eight, first appeared in St. Paul in the summer of 1858, summoned from her ancestral home in Fayetteville, North Carolina, to attend to her sick nephew, the handsome, curly-haired John Walker. (At least he said he was her nephew, which was later to raise the eyebrows of those who make it their business to record the more flamboyant displays of incest.)

Walker, a young carpenter, introduced Ann to his friend,

Stanislaus Bilansky, a one-time saloon-keeper and wealthy landowner whose shrewd real estate deals in the 1840s, when St. Paul was an infant city on the heavily trafficked Mississippi, had assured him of a large bank account and early retirement. Bilansky, who had migrated from Poland to Minnesota, was as hardheaded in his love life as he had been in business; he went through four wives and produced several children before reaching middle age and meeting the tempestuous Mrs. Wright.

Though it seemed improbable to those who knew the couple, Ann and Stanislaus vowed their love for each other in September 1858 and were soon married. Rosa Scharf, Bilansky's house girl, was only one of those who thought it more than peculiar when John Walker moved into the Bilansky home almost immediately following the wedding ceremonies. Within a few weeks, Ann's affections for her new spouse changed drastically. She remarked to housemaid Rosa that she "did not want to sleep with" Bilansky, and that she "hated him and could not treat him well." Further, Rosa more than once saw "Mrs. Bilansky undress right before Walker."

Even though stories about the ravishing Ann's slipping into Walker's room late at night and returning to her own room just before dawn reached Bilansky's ears, the truculent husband only grunted and did nothing. He had his own worries, chiefly an illness that befell him in the early part of 1859, one that eyeballing neighbors attributed to Bilansky's usual pastime—furiously guzzling whiskey—which caused violent retching, incessant headaches, and an overall physical condition that made him a wobbling wreck. He was bedridden most of the time but Ann, who treated Bilansky "in a rough manner," was concerned enough to nurse him through his vexing delirium tremens. The suffering wife began to make cryptic remarks to intimates, especially Mrs. Lucinda Kilpatrick, a neighbor and close friend. Once, when complaining of her husband's constant ailment, Ann remarked that she "wouldn't mind giving him a pill if the doctor was attending him." What kind of pill, Ann Bilansky did not specify.

Meanwhile young Walker was seen often in the company of his "aunt," which also caused much gossip. The devoted attention the two showed for each other was unnatural, most said, not to mention immoral. The odd Bilansky *ménage à trois* ended in March 1859 when the sick man died in convulsions.

An inquest was held and Ann Bilansky was portrayed by several witnesses as a firm but loving wife who had patiently nursed her impossible spouse through his illness. Rosa Scharf stated that her employer had suffered instant nausea after eating and complained of a burning sensation in his stomach that never let up. His diet consisted of soup, toast and arrowroot (the latter supplied by John Walker), all of which he vomited. Physicians who attended the sick man were at a loss to explain his death and marked it up to Bilansky's staggering consumption of alcohol. The inquest closed without charges' being hurled at anyone. Mrs. Bilansky and Walker settled down to a cozy time in Bilansky's home, going over Ann's sizable inheritance.

The very night Bilansky's body was sealed into a coffin, Mrs. Lucinda Kilpatrick tossed and turned in bed, waking up in a sweat. She answered her husband's alarm with a startling confession. She had been with Mrs. Bilansky on February 28, two days before Bilansky fell ill. Ann had purchased a packet of arsenic at Day and Jenks' drugstore, after Mrs. Kilpatrick had refused Ann's urgent request to buy it for her. Mrs. Bilansky told the druggist that the arsenic was to kill the army of rats infesting her basement. Further, Mrs. Kilpatrick revealed to her husband, Ann had nervously said after purchasing the poison: "If arsenic was found in the stomach they would have to prove who gave it." To make matters worse, the troubled Lucinda admitted that while she gave her testimony at the inquest, held in the Bilansky home, Ann had hidden behind a curtain to make sure that Mrs. Kilpatrick colored her as a loving wife in her remarks to investigators.

The shocked Mr. Kilpatrick threw on his clothes and raced to Police Chief Crosby with the awful news. Early in the morning of March 12, Crosby, accompanied by Ramsey County Coroner John V. Wren, three doctors, a coroner's jury, and many witnesses, barged into the Bilansky home to hold another inquest. Bilansky's corpse was removed from its coffin and examined. Arsenic was found in the stomach.

Dr. J. D. Goodrich, who had visited Bilansky during his illness, then revealed that his patient had exhibited all the signs of one being slowly murdered by arsenic poisoning—the burning sensation in the stomach, inability to retain food or liquid, and a cracked tongue of brownish color. Why Goodrich had not informed authorities of his findings while his patient still lived was never explained.

Ann Bilansky and John Walker were immediately arrested.

Walker was released on March 15, but Ann was held on a charge
of first-degree murder. Her trial opened on May 23, 1859. She
was found guilty on June 3 but Ann's only response was described as "emotionless indifference." Perhaps Mrs. Bilansky
felt that Minnesota would never hang a woman; she may have
been positive that her appeals would result in a commutation
of her sentence to life imprisonment. Yet all her appeals were
denied; her death sentence was upheld, and, on Friday, March
23, 1860, Ann Bilansky was marched to the gallows, a company
of smartly uniformed Pioneer Guards solemnly in step with her.

Several thousand St. Paul residents had turned out for the
spectacle. Ann mounted the scaffold stairs without faltering.
She glanced at the black coffin awaiting her at the front of the
gallows, then knelt upon the trapdoor, displaying in prayers the
fervor of the religion she had found while awaiting execution.

There was grumbling in the throng; the hanging was going to
be routine, many carped. However, Ann Bilansky seemed to
make it worth the while for those who had traveled great dis-
tances to witness her finish. She leaped up and, arms akimbo,
yelled at the crowd: "I die without having had any mercy
shown me, or justice. I die for the good of my soul, and not for
murder! May you all profit by my death. Your courts of justice
are not courts of justice, but I will get justice in Heaven. I am a
guilty woman, I know, but not of this murder, which was committed by another! I hope you all may be judged better than I
have been, and by a more righteous judge! I die prepared to
meet my God—"

A deputy walked up behind Ann Bilansky and slipped the
noose over her head, whispering: "That's quite enough, don't
you think?"

Ann turned an angry face to him, spitting indignantly: "How
can you stain your hands by putting that rope around my neck
—the instrument of my death?"

"I assure you," replied the deputy in a polite tone, "that it is
only my duty which compels me to do so." With that, he covered her head with a black cap.

From beneath the cap, the woman murmured: "Be sure that
my face is well covered." This last vanity uttered, Ann Bilansky, poisoner, gave out her final words: "Lord Jesus Christ receive my soul."

The trapdoor snapped open at her last word and she dropped
four feet, her body convulsing only once before being stilled by

death. Ann Bilansky's last-second reprieve, which she had so confidently expected, never arrived. The state of Minnesota had dared to hang a woman—its first executed, and its last. The crowd must have sensed the historic moment, for hundreds broke through the cordon of troops and, ever-mindful of souvenirs, tore the hangman's rope to pieces.

1860 NEW YORK CITY

Revenge for an Injured Party

New York in the early eighteen-sixties, before the bloody upheaval of the Civil War caused its low-life citizens to burst loose in the frenzy and killings of the Draft Riots, was far from a pastoral, peaceful place. Broadway, the Great White Way, was going full blast. The city was already established as the American capital of nightlife, represented by Barnum's mighty museum, Niblo's saloon where George Christy's Minstrels strummed and stepped, and hundreds of other naughty spas and emporiums shedding their warm gaslight upon the happy street throngs rippling by.

It was also a city of dark creatures who thought no more of slitting a neighbor's throat than of belting down a shot of rye. Several of these already awaited the hangman by June 1860. One man named Harden had poisoned his pretty wife as she sat on his knee eating a red apple. Another was the inhuman river pirate Albert Hicks, who had slaughtered an entire crew on the oyster sloop *A. E. Johnson* while it was docked in New York Harbor one fog-bound night.

But these atrocious humans were far from the thoughts of middle-aged John M. Walton, who had migrated from England twenty-five years earlier to set up a retail liquor store on Mulberry Street, then moved to Warren Street to establish a wholesale liquor business that did so well he was able to buy his own distillery. As he sat on a large barrel in his distillery laughing and joking with several friends on the night of June 30, 1860, he was in the prime of life; and, nestling in his secure bank account, was more than a hundred thousand dollars. True, he had marital problems; in fact, he was in the process of divorcing his wife. And his stepson, Charles Jefferds, had often threatened him with bodily harm, but the boy was merely being overly protective of his mother. No, John Walton felt he had nothing really to fear as he spun his tales for his chums, Terrance Dolan, John W. Matthews, and his sometimes bodyguard, Richard Pascal. Their laughter spilled out an open doorway with the flickering lights of the distillery to a quiet Eighteenth Street.

Watching this group from the shadows of the street, a tall man wearing a light coat and a Panama hat leaned casually against a tree. He was a young man with a sallow complexion, a lamp jaw, and a whispy sand-colored mustache. In his pocket was a six-shot American Adams pistol, fully loaded.

The group in the distillery broke up at about 11:15 P.M. Walton, Pascal and Matthews began to walk down Eighteenth Street. Matthews went briefly into a drugstore at the corner of Third Avenue. At the corner, the man "leaning against a tree in the shadow of the moon," as one officer later described him, stepped calmly up to Walton, placed the pistol next to his ear, and fired a single bullet. The liquor magnate fell dead into the arms of the shocked Pascal, who stood petrified, holding the body of his employer and staring at the killer retreating into the shadows.

At that moment Matthews stepped from the drugstore, and, witnessing the astounding scene, raced in pursuit after the murderer, yelling: "Watch [police]! Watch! A killer afoot!" A good runner, Matthews began to close on the fleetfooted gunman, but, just as the running men approached Sixteenth Street, the killer turned, stood stone still, and took careful aim at the approaching Matthews. He fired only one shot but his aim was true; the bullet struck Matthews square in the heart. As he fell, Matthews screamed: "I am killed! Oh, I am a dead man!" He was quite dead before he struck the cobblestones. The gunman wheeled about and ran on. Now *he* began to yell: "Stop, thief! Murder! Help, police, police!"

As officers of the watch began to respond to the various alarms, the killer spotted a high stoop in front of 37 East Sixteenth Street. Reaching this house, he vaulted over a low iron fence, dashed into the areaway and crouched beneath the stoop. In moments, his police pursuers clattered by down the street. The murderer remained silent in his hiding position for several minutes. Then, thinking no one had seen him, he calmly got up and walked away through the moonlight shredded by the thick trees above.

But one person had seen him; in fact, several had gotten fleeting glances at his face, a face set with determination and gritting hatred. Mary Ann Davis, a black cook, peering out the window from 34 East Sixteenth Street, had seen the killer lurking under the stoop and caught a glimpse of his face in the moonlight. Richard Pascal, who had been standing next to Walton when he was executed, plainly saw the murderer. And there was even a butcher named Hessel who saw the gunman shoot down Matthews; so close to Matthews was Hessel that he touched the slain man a moment after he fell. (Coroner Jackman was quick to upbraid Hessel at the inquest, fairly screaming at the butcher: "You should have leaped upon the villain then and there! You could have taken him red-handed!" The beefy Hessel responded with vein-popping incredulity, yelling back, "What! And have been shotted myself?")

All of these witnesses uniformly voiced one name as that of the killer: Charles Jefferds, stepson of the slain Walton. An arrest warrant was immediately issued for Jefferds. The wanted man, however, had been persuaded by a friend, William Betts, to turn himself in. Jefferds and Betts left the Union House in Brooklyn where Jefferds was staying, and took the ferry to New York. They walked to the Tombs prison late at night, but the guards told them: "It's after hours. If you want to give yourself up, find a judge who will sign the order." Impossible as it seems, the two men spent the next four hours tracking down New York judges. They were finally shown into the study of a Judge Osborne who complained with sleep-clogged eyes that they were "damn fools" to wake him up and ordered them to "go back to the Tombs in the morning."

Jefferds was finally admitted to the Tombs after dawn. In the afternoon a bearded attorney with snake eyes, employed by Jefferds' mother, eased into the accused killer's cell. He assured his client in no uncertain terms that he would be free in a few days, adding that District Attorney Nelson J. Waterbury had no case at all. "And if Waterbury is crazy enough to indict you," the lawyer grinned, "we'll make him wish he'd never heard of this case or my name isn't A. Oakey Hall."

The indictment and subsequent trial, however, were what the politically bent Hall was hoping for. He would turn the courtroom exercises into a hollering circus, gleaning enough publicity for himself to run for and win Waterbury's own office, which is exactly what Hall did do in the fall of the year following Jefferd's sensational trial, becoming one of the pinwheels in the incredibly corrupt political ring headed by Boss Marcy Tweed.

Waterbury produced two indictments against Jefferds, one for first-degree murder in the shooting of his stepfather, John Walton, and another for second-degree murder in the killing of Matthews; but Jefferds' case did not come to trial, the accused languishing inside his Tombs cell all through the winter and into the spring. Though such procrastination on the D.A.'s part puzzled and worried Jefferds, his shrewd lawyer only smiled, patted his client on the back, and told him to relax; he would never be found guilty.

Oakey Hall's confidence stemmed not from any miraculous bag of legal tricks but from his knowledge of a grand *faux pas* committed by the state legislature only ten weeks before Walton and Matthews had been shot. This group of politicians, most of them well-intentioned reformers, had, on April 14, 1860, totally changed the New York laws dealing with capital punishment, restricting such execution to those convicted of murder in the first degree and treason. The legislators, however, in their zealous and sweeping reform of the old law, had committed a monstrous oversight by nullifying Section 25 of the old law, which allowed that "the punishment of death shall in all cases be inflicted by hanging the convict by the neck until he be dead." In short, the means of any kind of execution had been eliminated by mistake, an error Waterbury was all too aware of, and, to prevent himself from becoming a laughingstock should he win his case against Jefferds and not have the legal apparatus to send him to death, the D.A. stalled until the legislature corrected its blunder. But the Assembly, though it did nominally reinstate the death penalty by July 1861, failed to specify the means of execution.

It was then that Oakey Hall demanded and got his trial for Charles Jefferds. Waterbury nervously presented his case, trotting out his witnesses, who, by then, displayed skimpy memory of the killer. Hall told the court he would not waste its time with any defense witnesses and then, in a show of bravado, waved for his untried junior partner to address the jury on his client's behalf, as if to state that the entire proceedings were nothing more than the sweaty maneuverings of a district attorney without a case. The jury swallowed the ploy and acquitted Jefferds of the murder of his stepfather.

The bored Hall yawned to the court and moved that, the case of Matthews "being founded on the same style of facts as that in the case of Walton, the charge be withdrawn and the prisoner discharged." A beaten Waterbury agreed. Jefferds was set free within an hour.

So humiliating a defeat was the Jefferds acquittal that Waterbury vowed to somehow once again place the youth on trial for murder. To accomplish this end, the vengeance-seeking D.A. employed a Broadway walkabout and gambling tout named William Moore to play an undercover role, one in which he would trap Jefferds into admitting his guilt in the shooting. Moore's funding was simple. If the Jefferds acquittal were to stand, the brother of the murdered man, William Walton, had much to lose—his brother's fortune and half his business, which the now-divorced Mrs. Walton was legally moving to acquire. William Walton gave Moore several hundred dollars and for some weeks the undercover man not only befriended Jefferds but became so chummy with him that the youth let down his guard, drinking so heavily with his newfound friend that he slurred out his innermost secrets to Moore.

Moore's job involved a race against time, to inveigle Jefferds through camaraderie and booze into an admission of murder before the November elections swept Waterbury from office and replaced him with Jefferds' own attorney, A. Oakey Hall, whose election to the D.A. post was a certainty.

The naive Jefferds was overheard by Moore incriminating himself several times in the murder of his stepfather. In a brief argument with his mother, Jefferds blurted, "I did it for you!" The final self-condemnation came on the night of November 14, 1861, when Jefferds became sloppy drunk with Moore and —after a tour of the Tombs, where they visited Jefferds' old cell —a binge through the Bowery bars ensued. One of these saloons, at 32 East Bowery, was owned by none other than William Walton.

When Moore and Jefferds went into Walton's saloon, the youth stared at the man behind the bar. He staggered forward, ordered a drink and tossed a coin on the bar. Walton picked up the gold piece and disdainfully threw the coin to the floor, saying: "I will take nothing from you."

"Do you know who I am?" menaced the youth, drawing himself to his full height and glaring at Walton. Then he shouted: "I am Charles Jefferds who shot your brother, and I will shoot you as quick, for you are the man who kept me in prison a whole year!"

Before he could speak further, the man sent to trap Jefferds into just such a public statement ironically ushered the young man from Walton's saloon. The next morning found both men still together and, as they emerged from a Bleecker Street cafe, Officer George H. Webb of the Fourth Precinct barred their path. He served Jefferds with a warrant and promptly arrested him for the murder of John W. Matthews.

As he was once again being led away to the Tombs for lockup, Jefferds shouted: "I defeated Waterbury! That's why he won't let me alone!" To Moore, Jefferds begged: "Go see Oakey Hall. He'll know what to do."

Oakey Hall's response was typical of his double-dealing nature. He quit the Jefferds case immediately, instructing his aides never to mention the accused killer's name to him again. Since the courts had absolved Jefferds in the Walton slaying, he could not be tried again for that offense; but the youth had not expressly been acquitted of the Matthews killing, for which he was now tried on a charge of first-degree murder.

The same judge who had presided over Jefferds' first trial, John T. Hoffman, was the man on the bench in the Matthews case. Though it had lampooned this jurist, along with Waterbury, in the Walton trial, the *New York Times* did a turnabout in covering Jefferd's second trial, its chief editorialist musing: "The present trial will doubtless clear up the mystery which has hung about the case, or else consign it forever to the long catalogue of horrible murders, whose undiscovered and unpunished perpetrators are a living contradiction of the popular notion that 'Murder will out!' "

Mary Ann Davis, the butcher Hessel, Pascal and others were once more brought forward to testify against Jefferds as the murderer of both Walton and Matthews. A surprise witness, one Robert Shultery, a clerk at Alfred Woodham's Gun and Pistol Store at 424 Broadway, testified that he had sold Jefferds the American Adams pistol used by the killer, which had been found by police the next day on Sixteenth Street where the fleeing slayer had dropped it.

Walton, Moore, and a captain of police who had been in Walton's saloon wearing civilian clothes (at the request of Waterbury, some later claimed), all testified to Jefferds' rash admission to Walton during his drinking spree. It was William Walton who proved the most damning in his courtroom accounts.

From the witness stand, Walton detailed in a clear voice: "I told him since he'd been acquitted and stood in no jeopardy he could tell us how he'd done it [shot Walton]. 'Tell us, Charley,' I said to him. 'I've always wondered.' So after we talked for a while, he told us how he'd watched John Walton sitting on a barrel and laughing there in his distillery on Eighteenth Street, and then he'd gone ahead and laid in wait for him under the tree. Then he says to me, 'Bill, why are you so down on me? I know I murdered your brother, but it wasn't because I hated him. I had to do it, Bill. Bill,' he says, 'if you'll come down with the dimes, I'll give you information that'll be worth ten thousand dollars to you.' " (The last remark referred to helping Walton in his suit against Jefferds' own mother over the disposition of John Walton's estate.)

It was all but over for Charles Jefferds. The jury took no more than an hour to discuss the case and render a verdict of guilty. As the word greeted him, Jefferds, standing and gripping the edge of a table, cried out: "Gentlemen, gentlemen, you have convicted an innocent man!"

Though he was sentenced to die on February 20, 1863, the court made no provision for the method of death to be imposed since the state legislature had still failed to specify the type of execution for condemned prisoners; Charles Jefferds grew old in prison, filing petition after petition from Sing Sing, where he was killed some years later in a fight with another inmate.

The shrewd A. Oakey Hall, Jefferds' one-time legal champion, took no notice of his former client's plight in Sing Sing. He was, at the time, too busy combating the law himself, having been placed on trial for embezzling city funds.

1864-71   NEW YORK—CONNECTICUT

"We're Alive with Rats!"

Lydia Sherman was one of those rare humans who, despite an extraordinary ability to display emotion and concern, had not, by her own admission, the slightest compassion for the life and welfare of her fellow creatures. She was also devoid of remorse, regret, and conscience as she poisoned her way through town after town, America's first infamous mass-murderess, whose toll in human life has been put as high as forty-two by some journalists but whose victims at least numbered more than a dozen.

Lydia's first well-documented movements centered in New York, where, as the wife of policeman Edward Struck, she maintained an image of domestic simplicity and hardworking motherhood, having had six children with Struck—Lydia, Ann Eliza, William, George, Edward and Mary Ann.

Born about 1830, Lydia's background then, as it is today, was hazy. Though she had been married to Struck for seventeen years when murder interrupted her housewifely role in 1864, there is much to suggest that Lydia had often dabbled in the not-so-fine art of poisoning earlier in life. She was to become known to the newspaper readers of America as "Queen Poisoner," her personality invested with all the insidious traits of her trade. This sobriquet conjured an image, as the image does with all poisoners, of a killer with the mind of a master criminal. It was a generally held belief that poisoners were the most clever of murderers, carefully planning in detail each guarded step of their premeditated killings; intellectual murderers, as it were, who seldom if ever failed to obscure any trace that would lead to suspicion, let alone capture and conviction.

Nothing could be further from the actual truth. The poisoner on all social levels has proved to be anything but a precise and cautious character, one who will practically advertise his or her intentions, and, after accomplishing the desired death of another, leave a trail of clues and perform such incriminating antics that even the most doltish of detectives could not eventually fail to identify the killer. Lydia Sherman was no exception to this dark rule, but she did possess an amazing ability to act the part of the bereaved widow and grief-stricken mother, which disarmed those suspicious of her. She also lived

73

in an era when naivete and ambiguous knowledge of diseases on the part of physicians confused the minds of would-be accusers—which abetted her in her sloppy run of adventures with murder.

Toxicology was a little-known science in the days of Lydia Sherman and, in fairness to the medical men who inspected her victims, those dying of arsenic poisoning displayed symptoms analogous to those of many illnesses, chiefly gastritis and dysentery, and doctors could easily be deceived. Arsenic, the favorite of early-day poisoners, was later discarded as a safe murder method when it was learned that the poison remains in the human tissue after death, although detection of arsenic was an elaborate process. (British forensic scientist James Marsh created the first apparatus to detect arsenic in 1836 but the device was not perfected until many years later, and only a few medical men were expert in the field of such detection.)

Lydia and her family resided in a rented New York flat on Lawrence Street near old Broadway in 1864. Her apparently tranquil world was splintered forever, she was later to carp, one spring day when her husband, Edward, a member of the Metropolitan Police Force, heard of a crazy man creating an uproar in Stratton's Hotel on Bloomingdale Road, which was part of his beat. To the man bringing him the news, Struck hesitated and asked: "Does the man have a gun?" When the citizen replied he thought the disturber might, Struck beat a hasty retreat, seeking assistance. A passing private detective did Struck's work for him, entering the hotel and shooting the madman dead as he ran toward the detective armed with a large knife. Struck next appeared but, for all his showy authority, it was obvious to one and all he had blatantly shirked his duty. He was dismissed from the force for cowardice.

When Lydia heard of this shameful conduct, she condemned her husband outright, which caused him to turn to drink. She goaded her embarrassed husband into wild fits of rage so that she could appear justified in her remarks about him. "He is insane," she told one friend. "Captain Hart [Struck's one-time superior] has advised me to have him sent to an asylum," she lied.

Since Struck found no employment other than visiting his favorite bars, Lydia sought work to support her large family. Dr. L. A. Rodenstein of Harlem hired Lydia as a practical nurse. After working only two weeks for Rodenstein, she went to the doctor and asked, as if it were merely in the nature of her work: "What will kill a person without leaving any visible signs?"

The doctor thought her question academic and replied: "If not given in too large a dosage, arsenic would work as well as anything."

Arsenic it would be. But still Lydia paused and sought out one more opinion, or rather a directive for her nightmarish ambitions. After taunting Struck into another drunken rage in which he threw the furniture about and bellowed curses and threats, Lydia raced downstairs to the apartment below and asked a policeman living there to accompany her back to her flat. The man did, sorrowfully witnessing Struck's impossible behavior.

"This can't go on," Lydia wept to the officer. "One day he will kill me, I guess."

Nodding in the affirmative, the officer muttered that she was no doubt living with a madman and that Lydia ought to "put him away, as he would never be any good to her or himself again."

Queen Poisoner pounced on this line and unswervingly interpreted the officer's suggestion that Struck be institutionalized to mean that he should be murdered, as grim and unreasonable a rationale as any killer might put forth, but pure logic to Lydia Sherman. (Years later Lydia was to recall with her convenient memory that the police officer suggested she purchase a "certain quantity of arsenic, and give him some of it," a quote invented in her own boiling mind.)

On May 24, 1864, Lydia visited a Harlem drugstore and bought ten cents' worth of white arsenic. When the druggist asked if she had rats in her abode, Lydia replied: "Rats, my goodness, yes, we're alive with rats, the entire building is crawling with rats!" That night Edward Struck was treated to Lydia's special concoction of oatmeal gruel, liberally laced with arsenic, of course. He immediately took to his bed, too ill even to take a drink of his favorite whiskey.

To prevent her children from becoming suspicious, Lydia had them scurry about bringing towels and making hot water as she went through the motions of being the very concerned housewife, spooning patent medicines into Struck, who promptly disgorged them. Throughout the night Struck suffered body-wracking cramps and convulsions. His writhing and moaning caused the children to beg their mother to send for a doctor. Lydia waited until dawn before sending for Dr. N. Hustead, who lived nearby, even though she could have had Dr. Rodenstein's services for free. When Dr. Hustead arrived, he found Struck dead.

Lydia by then was apparently an emotional wreck, her bosomy body heaving with uncontrollable grief; she flitted about the flat, sobbing, hand-wringing, head-flopping, tears running down like wild rivers over her reddened cheeks. When the doctor asked what Lydia thought might have killed her husband she blubbered: "I am a nurse. . . . Poor Edward must have taken the wrong medicine when I was out of the room."

Dr. Hustead inspected the medicines on the bedside table. "But these are all harmless," he stated.

Lydia was quick to jump to another track. "Then it was the consumption that did him in."

Hustead shrugged and perfunctorily signed a death certificate stating that Edward Struck had died of consumption. To his credit, the good doctor, however, was somewhat suspicious about Struck's symptoms and intended to go to the authorities after Lydia's "grief" subsided. A few days later Hustead discovered to his chagrin that Struck had already been buried (Lydia was never one to tarry in her grim adventures) and he could not convince city officials to authorize exhumation of the body for further study. As with many noteworthy poisoners, Lydia had made careful plans for the disposition of her victim long in advance, having purchased a burial plot in Trinity Churchyard months earlier; on the day Struck died the enterprising Mrs. Struck had the late Mr. Struck quickly carted off to the cemetery and planted while she calmly stood at the foot of the grave, instructing cemetery workers to "dig a nice deep hole."

That Lydia had pumped poison into others before murdering Struck is a widely held belief. Her blasé commitment to such an act after seventeen years of marriage certainly suggests that she was no stranger to the use of poison, which served as an expedient to settling any gritty problems. In the words of crime archivist Thomas M. McDade: "She simply found a family an inconvenience, and poison such an easy solution." Lydia's own words, written while she paced her cell years later, were succinct, to say the least. "I gave him [Struck] the arsenic because I was discouraged," she wrote. "I know that that is not much of an excuse, but I felt so much trouble that I did not think about it."

Murder for Lydia became easier with each new death. Only weeks after she had dispatched Struck, the widow, properly sporting her black mourning attire and dabbing her eyes at the slightest mention of her departed mate, decided that her children "hindered her," and resolved to get rid of them. "On July 1st," she later scribbled, "I made up my mind that my two little children, Mary Ann, six years old, and Edward, two years younger, would be better off if they were out of the way. So I made the same kind of gruel their father had eaten. . . . They only survived a short time."

Even the mass-poisoners Locusta, the Empress Agrippina, and Madame Brinvilliers would have blinked at Lydia's industry. Not only did the determined woman kill off Edward and Mary Ann, but added enough arsenic to the milk of her nine-month-old baby, William, to have him join his sister and brother in death on the same day, July 5, 1864. Their ends were attributed to remittent fever and bronchitis. Dr. G. Jackson and Dr. B. Gross, unwitting new doctors, signed their death certificates before the children joined their father in Trinity Churchyard. (Lydia was shrewd enough always to call a different doctor to attend those afflicted by her self-inspired epidemics.)

George Struck, fourteen years old, was next. He was given the entire contents of a ten-cent packet of white arsenic, which Lydia purchased in a Harlem drugstore in August. The motherly Lydia fretted and wept as a Dr. Oviatt stated that George's death was due to "Painter's Colic."

Ann Eliza—uncommonly for the Struck household—genuinely became ill the following March. Dr. Rodenstein said that she was suffering from typhoid fever. A child in agony was too much for Lydia to endure. This sympathetic murderess went to Ann Eliza's rescue with a cup of medicine laced with arsenic. "Ann was continually sick during this time," Lydia recounted. "It made me downhearted and discouraged. . . . I had some arsenic in the house . . . and I put it in the medicine I bought for her to cure the chills. I gave it to her twice, then she was taken sick as the others were, and died about noon, four days afterward. She was the happiest child I ever saw."

Only young Lydia was left of the Struck children, and she quickly followed Ann to the grave two months later, in May 1866. Her passing, unlike those of the other children, did not go unnoticed by the suspicious. The pastor of the Harlem Presbyterian Church, Reverend Payson, attended to Lydia's spiri-

77

tual needs in her final hours. He was alarmed at the convulsions that seized the child; he had witnessed the work of poisons on humans before. Unfortunately, the pastor reserved action until some days later, when he mentioned the way Lydia had died to her half-brother, Cornelius Struck, a New York streetcar conductor. Struck went to District Attorney Garvin, demanding that not only Lydia's body be exhumed for examination, but also those of his father and other half-brothers and -sisters. "All of them down there in Trinity Churchyard," said Cornelius in an ominous-sounding voice, "is victims of poison, you can be sure. It's that woman, full of black evil who done it, sure."

The district attorney, a typical bureaucrat with about as much enthusiasm for his job as a chimneysweep, yawned and had the medical records pulled on each death. All had been certified by reputable doctors, he explained, and each had succumbed to "acceptable" diseases that had plagued the country for decades. No, there was no legitimate reason to order the exhumations. The Struck family members stayed buried and their murderess went free to seek a new life, as well as new victims.

Many adventures befell the active widow. She worked briefly for the Maxom family in Sailorsville, Pennsylvania, as a "kind-hearted" nanny. Then she moved back to New York, where she worked as a housekeeper for a man named Cochran who owned a small sewing-machine shop. One of Cochran's friends, James Curtiss of Stratford, Connecticut, was overheard by Lydia to remark that his elderly mother, who was quite well-to-do, needed a practical nurse and efficient housekeeper. Lydia promptly presented herself to Curtiss as just such a rarely available person. Curtiss hired her for eight dollars a month, but, upon her arrival in the Curtiss homestead in Stratford, Lydia discovered that Mrs. Curtiss was a sharp-minded person—one who was not only far from being senile, but was wary of her new nurse from the beginning. Queen Poisoner looked about for more susceptible prey.

While working in the Curtiss home, Lydia learned that Dennis Hurlbut, a seventy-five-year-old farmer, was in "bad need of a housekeeper." She investigated Hurlbut's background, discovering that he was extremely wealthy but naive when it came to women. Borrowing the Curtiss horse and buggy, Lydia drove out to Hurlbut's country estate in Corum and alighted at the old man's front door, hailing him with sweet smiles, rustling her crinoline dress, which she had fashioned in such a way as to accent her curvacious form. Old Hurlbut hesitated not for a second, hiring Lydia on the spot. Two days later, Hurlbut begged the pulchritudinous Lydia to become his wife. They were wed on November 22, 1868.

With Hurlbut, Lydia took a new turn in her demeanor. The women of the area thought correctly that Lydia was nothing more than a fortune-hunter, as she knew they would. Therefore, her game was a slow and tedious one, where she never failed to appear as the loving and considerate wife, meeting the old man each day when he returned from his fishing and bestowing upon his cheek a wifely kiss. She took advantage of every opportunity to dote publicly on Hurlbut, making him tasty lunches for his walks and knitting him sweaters, which he proudly displayed to the neighbors.

More than fourteen months of such ostentatious bliss went by before Old Hurlbut began to be "subject to fits of dizziness," as Lydia later put it. Prior to these alleged fits, Hurlbut had returned Lydia's kindness and consideration by making out a new will in which she was the sole heir to ten thousand dollars in cash and as much in his real estate holdings.

As usual, the rats came next. They seemed to follow Lydia throughout the land, her garbage, no doubt, more appealing than that of any other citizen of the Republic; or, at least, one would think so to hear her complain of the diehard rodents. She was soon visiting the local drugstore, announcing that "we're overrun with rats" in explanation of her purchases of arsenic.

Hurlbut fell ill some days later. A Dr. Church was called but he was perplexed by the ailment, recording only that his patient had "acute pains in the head and stomach, accompanied by an intense burning as if the patient had a violent fever." He lasted only a few days. Lydia had him buried an hour following death. Though Dr. Church called two specialists into the case for consultation, the old man was underground before they could examine him.

Queen Poisoner's explanation of the affair was tidy, her lethal additives to Hurlbut's diet only incidental in her notes: "One day he was unwell and he ate clams and drank cider with saleratus in it.... Finally, Mr. Hurlbut became worse, and about five o'clock one morning the old man died. I wish to say that I never gave Mr. Hurlbut anything that would cause sickness—though there may have been some arsenic mixed with the saleratus which he put into the cider." This off-and-on admission by Lydia of killing Hurlbut was undoubtedly put forth to convince the world her avarice was not at the root of the old man's death; that she would *never* murder for anything as vile as money.

Inheriting what was then considered a wealthy estate made Lydia an attractive widow. Many a swain thought to woo her, but Nelson Sherman, a widower himself, won the lady's attentions in April 1870. Lydia later claimed that Sherman had proposed at their first meeting, but told him that they "ought to be better acquainted." The scheming widow thought it prudent, unlike her unstinting pursuit of old Hurlbut, to put off Sherman to maintain ladylike decorum. The couple were not wed until the following September and only after Lydia had practically bribed her way into marriage with Sherman by loaning him six hundred dollars. She went to live with Sherman in Derby, Connecticut, where he was a foreman at the Shelton tack factory, with a fifty-dollar-a-week salary.

The accommodations in the Sherman house at the edge of the scenic Housatonic River were spacious but the occupants worried Lydia. There were four Sherman children by a former marriage to contend with, besides Sherman's mother-in-law, Mary Jones, who was critical and leery of Lydia from the onset. The baby, nine-month-old Frank Sherman, was of particular annoy-

"Queen Poisoner" Lydia Sherman encouraging her second husband, the elderly Dennis Hurlbut, to partake of her specially prepared wine.

ance to Lydia. Despite the fact that she had hired a housemaid to take care of the child (who was also fiercely attended to by Mary Jones), just hearing the infant's occasional cries caused her to be "full of trouble again."

Lydia managed to unburden herself by slipping baby Frank some arsenic Mary Jones had kept on hand. The town health officer, Dr. Beardsley, was summoned at Lydia's request by Addie Sherman, Nelson's fourteen-year-old daughter. The child had vomited up most of the poison by the time the elderly physician arrived. Dr. Beardsley pronounced him better as he was leaving, but Lydia corrected the improvement by sneaking more arsenic into the infant's food. He died at 11 P.M. that night.

The loss of his youngest child caused the distraught Sherman to seek consolation inside a bottle. He became a hopeless drunk. Addie Sherman was the next to vex the darkly troubled Lydia. She was just too popular, being the most attractive belle in Derby. During a slight illness in December 1870, Queen Poisoner administered two cups "of very strong tea" to the girl, naturally peppered with poison. Lydia's reason for murdering the girl, she was to later state, was because her father had to borrow ten dollars from her to pay Dr. Dutton for his house call. When Addie died in paroxysms of pain, Nelson Sherman became a hopeless drunk. He was not so far gone, however, that he did not become suspicious of his solicitous wife, telling her in one of his sober moments, "I know too much of you."

Bright and early the next day Lydia Sherman was inside Peck's drugstore, decrying the pest population at the Sherman house. "We are overrun with rats," came her favorite refrain. She was soon scurrying home with a packet of arsenic, which she promptly used to dose her husband's chocolate. Sherman proved to have a stomach of iron, perhaps fortified by the massive amounts of alcohol he had been consuming in recent months. It took dozens of cups of chocolate over a three-day period to finish him off. His death on May 12, 1871, caused Dr. Beardsley to seek out officers of the law. As the doctor in attendance, he had noticed similarities between the types of illnesses that had befallen Sherman, his son Frank, and his daughter Addie. He brought two other physicians into the case. The medicos concluded that all three had been poisoned with arsenic and that Lydia Sherman was the most likely killer.

With Nelson Sherman already buried, Beardsley decided to boldly confront Queen Poisoner. He went to the Sherman home

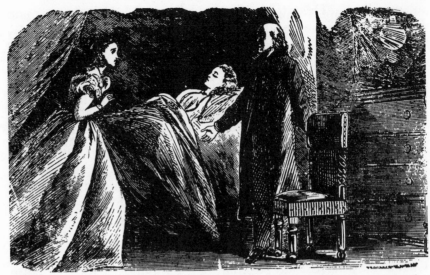

Lydia attending the death of her stepdaughter, Addie, whom she poisoned over a ten-dollar bill.

and discovered Lydia strolling through the garden. He came quickly to the point. "Did you ever give your husband poison?" nerved the doctor.

"Certainly not," replied Lydia without a twitch of muscle.

"Will you then permit a post-mortem examination of the corpse?"

"I don't see why not."

Sherman's body, as well as those of his children, was exhumed. Following an autopsy, Sherman's stomach and liver were sent to Professor Barker of Yale University, an expert on poisons. (Such were the inadequate scientific processes of the day that only a few medical men were accepted as true specialists in diagnosing poisons in the human body.) Without waiting for Barker's findings, S. B. Platt, at Beardsley's urgings, issued a warrant for Lydia's arrest on a charge of murder, handing the summons to Deputy Sheriff Blakeman. This officer realized that without official word from Yale, he risked being charged with false arrest, so he merely kept Lydia under surveillance.

Blakeman chose an unorthodox but, no doubt, to him an inventive method with which to keep tabs on the mass poisoner. He posed as a junk dealer and went to the Sherman house, asking if Lydia had a piano for sale, according to rumors he had heard in Derby. Without a word, she closed the door in his face, but Blakeman did manage to see Lydia's front hall, a sight that caused him alarm. There were several large trunks piled in the hallway. Off to the train station dashed Blakeman where he learned that Mrs. Sherman had bought two tickets to New Brunswick, New Jersey.

Blakeman frantically contacted Dr. Beardsley. He was told that the poison expert in New Haven had not yet responded. Worse, the samples of Frank and Addie Sherman's bodies had not been sent to Yale. The deputy sheriff did the next best thing to arresting the fleeing Lydia; he wired the chief of police in New Brunswick to have Lydia followed wherever she went. The New Jersey lawman replied that he would be all too happy to have his detectives trail the suspected killer.

Professor Barker finally, on June 1, 1871, sent the results of his meticulous examinations to the Derby, Connecticut, doctors. His chemical analysis proved that Nelson Sherman's body had enough arsenic in it to do away with a half dozen men; the vital organs of the children were also permeated with the same poison.

Deputy Blakeman then began a hit-and-miss legal odyssey. He obtained extradition papers from the Connecticut governor and departed with his best detective, Officer Mitchell, for New Brunswick. Lydia, he learned, had already left for Philadelphia

Dr. Beardsley confronting Lydia with her murderous ways.

on a shopping tour. Blakeman missed her in New Brunswick upon her return. He missed her again when she left for a pleasure visit to New York with a male friend, a man who later turned out to be a gigolo Lydia had rented for the excursion. When they once again returned to New Brunswick, Blakeman and other officers arrested Lydia on the platform of the train depot.

The deputy and his captive left for Connecticut the following day, but the long train ride offered nothing in evidence as to Lydia's horrible deeds. As usual, Lydia Sherman proved to be a great actress, for "she manifested surprise either real or very well assumed, gave no appearance of grief, and beyond the simple surprise and the assertion of her innocence did not seem to be at all affected."

Blakeman pointedly asked her if she had purchased any amounts of arsenic recently. Yes, of course she had, Lydia said without a quiver. It was to dispose of "large swarms of rats" about the Sherman house. (As if to prove some truth to this claim, the defense at her trial later produced the lone carcass of

While being hunted, Lydia fled to New York and the high life; here two detectives are shown "shadowing" her through her revels.

a dead rat that, after much hunting, had been located near the outdoor well on the Sherman property.)

Defense Counsel George H. Waterous could do little to undo the murderous image his client projected, especially when Lydia's past was revealed, along with the astounding number of deaths surrounding her activities. Her trial in New Haven, beginning on April 16, 1872, was covered by the most important newspapers in the country. The *New York Times* reporter on the scene took pains to write that the accused poisoner walked calmly into court wearing "neat, black alpaca, trimmed with black velvet, a mixed black and white woolen shawl, white straw hat trimmed with black velvet and brown plume, from which dropped over her face a thin veil, through which her features were plainly marked." Lydia would face murder charges in the height of fashion.

The circumstantial evidence against Lydia Sherman was overwhelming. Not only did Horatio Sherman, Nelson Sherman's teenage son, testify against his stepmother, recalling how she dosed his father, but Dr. Beardsley presented the damning evidence developed by Barker, the New Haven specialist in poisons. Further, George Peck, the druggist, stated that Mrs. Sherman had purchased large quantities of arsenic before the deaths of Addie and Nelson Sherman. Following a ten-day trial, on April 26, 1872, the jury found Lydia Sherman guilty of murder in the second degree after a fifty-minute deliberation. (Judge Park had directed the jury to consider only second-degree murder should Lydia be found guilty, since the main body of evidence was circumstantial.)

Queen Poisoner was cool on hearing the verdict and was led wordlessly to her jail cell, where she fainted. Upon being revived, Lydia presented her keepers with one of the great crying jags on record. She remained in her cell for a year while her lawyers attempted to get her a new trial. They failed. Judge Sandford sentenced her to life imprisonment on January 11, 1873. Lydia was taken to Weathersfield Prison where she died on May 16, 1878. During the last five years of her life, the mass killer occupied her time with long, passionate displays of weeping worthy of Joan of Arc in her torment and writing her lengthy horror-filled memoirs of mass murder. None of her words showed repentance, let alone recognition of her acts as ghastly, unconscionable deeds. She felt matter-of-factly justified in her role as slayer, particularly when she eliminated Nelson Sher-

Lydia Sherman reflecting on her mass murders in Wethersfield Prison.

man, who, she wrote (thus perplexing a plethora of crime historians to come) was supposed to benefit from her arsenic. Queen Poisoner had slipped him the poison "not to kill him, but to cure him of liquor."

1866 PHILADELPHIA

Massacre by a Considerate Handyman

Much has been said and written in recent years of the increasing brutality among American criminals, particularly killers whose compassionless bloodletting shocks and bewilders police, public and the press. But the notion that there ever was a gentler quality to murder is pure fiction; Anton Probst proved that as early as 1866 when, for a few dollars, he brought about a massacre that sent Philadelphia and the nation into paralyzing shock.

Probst, born in 1842 in Germany, immigrated to the United States when the Civil War was at its bloody zenith in 1863. Almost immediately upon his arrival in New York, the German youth volunteered for service with the Union Army, which, for lack of patriotic support, was at the time paying recruits three hundred dollars. Probst knew a good racket when he saw one; he volunteered several times, becoming a professional "bounty jumper." He would collect the bounty for his enlistment, serve a few weeks at training camp, then desert, moving on to a different northern city where he would again enlist for the three-hundred-dollar bounty. He never saw action but he did manage to make a comfortable living while many able-bodied men were bleeding to death at Gettysburg, Cold Harbor, and the Wilderness.

The lucrative racket came to an end with Lee's surrender and, by the fall of 1865, Probst found himself in Philadelphia, penniless. Wandering aimlessly about, Probst learned that Christopher Dearing, who owned a small farm on Jones' Lane, in Philadelphia's first ward, needed a handyman. The twenty-three-year-old Probst applied for his first honest work in the New World.

The Dearing Farm was only a few acres in size, with a small house, a barn in which were kept one horse and a pig, and some grazing area for cattle; the buying and selling of cattle provided Dearing, his wife, Julia, and their five children with a meager existence.

Probst's lackadaisical attitude and his lewd remarks toward Julia caused Mrs. Dearing to ask her husband to fire the strange young man after only three weeks. Claiming that he was in bad health, Probst was taken in by a Philadelphia charity hospital, the Almshouse, where he lingered from December 1865 to the following February. Here, while lying awake nights on his cot, Probst schemed to rob the Dearings. He returned to the small farm on March 2, 1866, begging Christopher Dearing to employ him again. Dearing, a kindhearted soul, agreed.

Working hard for a little more than a month, Probst ingratiated himself with the family. Then, on April 7, a Saturday, he put his plan into action. While Christopher Dearing traveled by buggy to the docks of Philadelphia to meet a visiting family friend, Miss Elizabeth Dolan of Burlington, New Jersey, Probst and Cornelius Carey, a boy employed to help about the farm, were working in a field. At about nine in the morning, Probst decided that he would slaughter the entire family to more easily steal the family's wealth.

It began to rain. Probst and Carey took shelter beneath a tree. When Carey looked away for a moment, Probst struck the boy with the blunt end of an axe. He then turned the instrument around and decapitated him. He quickly hid the body in a haystack.

Then, with methodical precision, the killer enticed the family

87

members, one by one, into the barn. There he struck them with a hammer, then chopped them several times in the neck until Mrs. Dearing and four of her children, including an infant, were slain. When Dearing arrived with Miss Dolan, Probst was ready for him. He told him there was a sick steer near the barn. He followed his employer there and again used a hammer and axe to murder. Miss Dolan, who had gone into the house, was also lured into the barn, where she was slain.

A tidy sort, Probst lined the bodies of his victims neatly in a row inside the barn and covered them with hay. Then he returned to the small house, which he ransacked, looking for money. He found ten dollars in Dearing's wallet, of which four dollars were later discovered to be counterfeit. Probst added to this miserable loot three dollars which he took from Miss Dolan's purse. Nothing else of value could he find.

The killer was unconcerned about the slaughter. He used Dearing's razor to shave off his beard and, discarding his own clothes, which were soaked with blood, put on Dearing's clothes and boots. Then he ate some bread and butter before going to his loft room for a nap. When he awoke, the phlegmatic

Handyman Anton Probst preparing himself for the slaughter of the Dearing family.

Probst thought it best to feed the dogs and chickens. He also fed the pig and the horse in the barn as his shadow crossed the prone bodies of his victims. He then leisurely strolled away from the farm, staying in lowlife dens for several days.

Neighbors, finding no one about on the Dearing farm, discovered the bodies and sent up the alarm. Police had little difficulty in tracking down Probst. He had sold Dearing's revolver to a saloonkeeper and his employer's watch to a jeweler. On April 12, five days after the killings, Philadelphia's first mass-murderer was arrested by a lone policeman as he sat swilling ale in a groggery at Twenty-third and Market Streets. He surrendered meekly.

At first Probst pleaded innocent, but circumstantial evidence against him was so overwhelming that, at the conclusion of his trial on May 1, 1866, the jury took only twenty minutes to convict him. Before his execution on June 8, Probst made a lengthy confession.

Only two survived the Dearing Massacre. Willie Dearing, the oldest son, had been sent to visit relatives a few days before the mass murders. Probst himself survived in a peculiar fashion. Following his execution, the killer's body was delivered to the Jefferson School of Medicine, where it was dissected. Probst's mounted skeleton then went on display in the museum of the college, an artifact of murder not too enthusiastically advertised by the City of Brotherly Love.

1869 CHICAGO

Attentions from a Stranger

Revenge and love are cranky bedfellows; seldom do these passions cohabit without the eruption of violence. Often, as was the case of Civil War veteran Daniel Walsh, the reaction between the two emotional forces ended in murder.

Walsh seemed to be the ordinary American youth of ambition and innocence when he arrived in Chicago from Buffalo, N.Y., in 1861. He briefly migrated to St. Louis where, his heart full of patriotic zeal, he enlisted in the Union cause and marched south to do mortal combat with boys in butternut gray. He fought with valor in the battle of Wilson's Creek and was at the side of General Nathaniel Lyon when Lyon was shot.

Mustered out, Walsh returned to Chicago, where his pursuits were mundane and his days peaceful. He drove a hack and later became a streetcar driver. One day, the most beautiful girl Walsh had ever beheld climbed aboard his horse-drawn trolley. She was Rose Weldon, who worked in a millinery shop on Lake Street. Such was Walsh's ardor for the attractive young woman that he stopped his trolley in the middle of the street after Rose alighted and chased her down, begging a date.

The romance flourished, even though the Weldons did not approve of Walsh, a man without a checkable background. Family opposition, however, all the more readily disposed the lovebirds to obstinate plans for marriage. Overcoming all odds in the name of love, in typical American fashion, the couple wed in Chicago's Church of the Holy Family on February 6, 1869. Following the ceremony, the lovebirds adjourned to the bride's ancestral home on the West Side, but, wonder of wonders, Daniel Walsh, after a few hours with his wife's family, utterly disappeared.

The smitten swain had given no excuse for his frenetic departure and, try as she might, Rose found it impossible to locate her errant new husband. She returned to her job but persistently attempted to dig up background information on her trolleycar lover. Buffalo police finally informed her that Walsh had abandoned a wife and child in that city. Rose lost no time in filing for divorce based on desertion. When the decree was granted, Walsh's employers learned of the matter and promptly fired him.

Walsh, who had been working another trolleycar line at his request, and hiding out in a Twenty-Second Street boardinghouse, took the news of his discharge poorly. He purchased a revolver and was overheard to grunt: "Nobody can ruin the life of Daniel Walsh without paying up in blood!"

The next day the vengeance-seeker lolled about outside the shop where Rose worked. When she emerged, Walsh stepped from a doorway. The jilted woman glanced at him in fear and rage. Then she began to run. Walsh ran after her, mouthing peace and consideration: "Listen, sweet Rose. It's a reconciliation I'm after!"

Rose had deaf ears to such blandishments and raced on until

she reached the door of her father's house. Walsh gave up the playacting, reached for his revolver, and shot his estranged beloved in the side. As the love-lost Rose fell to the pavement, her brother Dick rushed from the house and knocked Walsh down, leaping upon him, his hands about the attacker's throat.

For a moment, Walsh freed himself and blurted, just as the brother came to use the weapon on him: "Don't shoot me, Dick! Give me the gun and I'll shoot myself!"

Dick Weldon glanced at his bleeding sister and the cringing wretch she had married. He helped Walsh to his feet and handed him the revolver. "Here. Do it!"

Daniel Walsh was not a man to be trusted. True to his crafty nature, he dashed off down the street, laughing hysterically. A policeman, however, who had seen the shooting from a block away, collared Walsh and led him to the nearest precinct station, despite a hurriedly collected crowd clamoring for the killer's neck.

Rose lingered for ten days before dying of her wound. Her grief-stricken father, who would take no food as he sat by her bedside, died an hour after his daughter. Nor could Rose's mother bear the grief; she died five days before Walsh entered the penitentiary.

Walsh was promptly tried and convicted; he was sentenced to hang on December 10, 1869. Several prominent Chicago citizens reacted to the sentence with compassion. They felt Walsh was a victim of Rose's revenge. They petitioned the Governor to spare his life, the head of the committee traveling to Springfield to plead personally with the Governor, who refused to grant the reprieve. The petitioner then sent an unsigned wire to Chicago, reading: "All right; I will return by next train." This was somehow construed, on the day of the execution, as meaning Walsh had been reprieved. Newspaper extras quickly announced that the killer had been spared.

On hearing the news, Daniel Walsh did clog dances in his cell. The compromised Governor signed a four-week stay of execution. Walsh's attorneys put the borrowed time to good use and, mounting a barrage of petitions from thousands of do-gooders, overwhelmed the Governor who, at the last moment, changed Walsh's sentence to life imprisonment.

Walsh lived another twenty-five years in Joliet, dying inside his cell white-haired and embittered. He felt cheated by the

State; he had righted a wrong, he felt, to his final hours—when he turned his face from the bars and moaned to a cellmate: "Hell, I thought they were gonna let me out!"

1873 BOSTON

The Monster in the Belfry

In the twentieth century, the popular cliche in murder mysteries is "The butler did it." Given the exploits of Thomas W. Piper in the nineteenth century, however, it is little wonder that police of that era instinctively singled out another trade in which to search for bizarre killers.

It was Piper's job as sexton of the Boston, Massachusetts, Warren Avenue Baptist Church to ring the bell every Sunday as the members arrived. He would stand in the belfry looking down at churchgoers with a wide smile that curved upward into a long, black mustache.

The twenty-six-year-old Piper had been an acceptable fixture at the church until the winter of 1873–74, when he began to act strangely. Piper took to sitting at the back of the church and reading risque novels during sermons. Worse, the sexton approached several teenage girls and whispered comments that made their faces go scarlet. It was also known that Piper kept a bottle of whiskey and laudanum in a dark corner behind the last pew.

Yet Piper's outward services to the church were beyond criticism, and he continued to smile and wink at the pretty girls from the belfry.

On the night of December 5, 1873, however, an event took place that overshadowed Piper's rakish antics. A resident of Dorchester (which was incorporated into Boston the following year) was tramping home when he was startled by noises from a thicket at Upham's Corner. He plodded into the wooded area only to see a dark figure leap and race away. On the spot, naked, was the body of Bridget Landregan, a local servant girl whose head had been bashed in. A club nearby was covered with gore.

Enraged, the citizen gave pursuit, but the dark figure escaped by climbing over a railroad embankment.

Soon after that, a girl named Sullivan was also sexually molested and battered senseless. She died in a hospital without regaining consciousness.

Next, Mary Tynam, a "girl of the town," was attacked as she slept. Although horribly mutilated, the girl managed to survive a year in an asylum before succumbing to her injuries. She never regained her senses enough to identify her attacker.

The killer grew bolder until, on May 23, 1875, he took little pains to disguise his whereabouts. On that morning, churchgoers arriving at the Warren Avenue Baptist Church noticed Piper standing at the front door next to what appeared to be a cricket bat leaning against a wall.

After church, the sexton invited five-year-old Mabel H. Young to visit the belfry to see his pet pigeons. Excitedly, the youngster followed him.

Sexton Thomas Piper of Boston waylaying five-year-old Mabel Young.

Once in the belfry, Piper attacked the girl, striking her with massive blows to the head. At that moment, however, Mabel's aunt, Augusta Hobbs, led a search party into the church.

Piper panicked, threw the bleeding child into the belfry recesses and tried to descend the stairs. Hearing footsteps coming upward, he threw open a window and dropped to the ground outside. The sexton then casually walked back into the church.

Piper was thunderstruck as he heard screams from the tower. Mabel was still alive. Several men raced to the belfry, broke down the door and carried the child away. Although the girl died some hours later without identifying her murderer, Piper's bat was found covered with Mabel's blood, and he was arrested.

For weeks, Piper shouted out his innocence from his cell. At his trial, the sexton admitted he was drunk the day Mabel died, but insisted he had nothing to do with the death. His escape from the belfry had been seen, however, and the cricket bat was introduced as belonging to Piper. The jury found the sexton guilty, and he was scheduled to hang in May of 1876.

A few days before his execution, Piper called his attorneys and confessed to killing not only Mabel but also Bridget Landregan, the Sullivan girl, and Mary Tynam. The sexton left nothing out, and ended his gruesome monolog by saying, "I am a very bad man."

Piper's image didn't fade for decades after his execution.

Piper leaping from the tower window to escape pursuers.

Each new murder, especially those involving women and children, led police to round up every sexton in Boston. Said one sexton after being yanked from his belfry for an intense grilling, "It's not safe up there anymore, thanks to that monster!"

1881–92 CHICAGO

"I Am Jack the . . ."

He thought of himself as a master criminal; his ego knew no bounds. In the pursuit of his dark deeds he grew enchanted with evil until he loved it, became its embodiment, a sinister killer gliding paradoxically through Victoria's innocent era. Ubiquitous, half-mad, the calculating and insidious Dr. Thomas Neill Cream revolutionized the concept of murder in the last quarter of the nineteenth century. His murky motives would later give broad play to the twisting theories of psychologists, and in his day he schemed at the finish to mock the police and baffle the criminal historian for generations to come. His specialty in murder was women.

This new breed of slayer was born in Glasgow, Scotland, on May 27, 1850, and immigrated to Canada with his parents four years later. Though little is known of Cream's early life, it was certain that his father and mother were hardworking, decent parents and little Thomas (along with younger brother and sister, Daniel and Jessie) lacked nothing of comfort and education. Yet a fatal flaw somehow developed in his character, perhaps in early youth, that caused a gnawing hatred for all women. British crime writer Colin Wilson thought this one-time Sunday School teacher to be "one of the oddest figures of the Nineteenth Century, a kind of criminal Leopold Bloom; like Joyce's hero, he was an introvert with feelings of sexual inadequacy, given to writing strange letters to women, and sometimes to men." (Bloom's missives to upper-class housewifes were blunt and crude, replete with obscene suggestions that such prim and proper ladies must "soil his letter unspeakably"; in sharp contrast Cream was ever the gentleman in his mad letter-writing, as in his attire, couching his words in the formal style of the period.)

Piper is ordered to touch the body of Mabel Young; it was then superstitiously thought that if the corpse bled at the touch of a suspect, that person was guilty of murder.

It had always been Cream's ambition to become a doctor, and, after attending McGill University in Montreal for four years, he qualified as a physician. Judging from his later actions, Cream must have fallen asleep during the dean's address to his 1876 graduating class, a speech entitled "The Evils of Malpractice in the Medical Profession." (The university would later remove Cream's name from its graduate rolls.)

During his senior year at college, Cream met and seduced a beautiful young woman named Flora Eliza Brooks of Waterloo, Canada. Discovering her pregnant, Cream performed a crude abortion, which left Miss Brooks permanently ill. Her father compelled the errant student at shotgun point to marry his daughter, but shortly after the nuptials, Cream fled, borrowing money from his father, William Cream, by then a well-to-do businessman.

In that year, 1876, Cream sailed for England, enrolling in a postgraduate course at St. Thomas' Hospital, which was situated in the Lambeth–Waterloo Road section of London, a seedy, sleazy area teeming with diseased prostitutes. It was here that Cream first became a night-prowler and obsessed with having sex only with whores. And it was in the human cesspool that was the Lambeth district, which he was to revisit with a vengeance some fourteen years later to carve out his lasting infamy, that Thomas Neill Cream first contracted syphilis, which would turn his mind to jelly and, many later claimed, his constant thoughts to murder.

Early in 1877, Cream learned that his Canadian wife had died (the cause was given as consumption, but Cream's butchering abortion upon the woman undoubtedly contributed to her youthful demise). He didn't bother to send his regrets. Cream had other problems. His wenching had consumed so much time that he had failed his examinations at St. Thomas'. He packed his bags and journeyed to Edinburgh, Scotland, where, painfully parted from his London doxies, he used his considerable intellectual abilities to earn the double certificate of the Royal Colleges of Physicians and Surgeons. He was now *Dr.* Thomas Neill Cream, and, pocketing his illustrious degree, he sailed back to Canada and set up practice in London, Ontario.

Once again, Cream's dark passions boiled over into a plethora of crime. In the words of Edmund Pearson, writing in *Murder at Smutty Nose*, "frauds on insurance companies, medical and other malpractices with women as their victims, charges of blackmail and of other malodorous deeds, were the principal events of his professional career." Add to these enterprises bigamy, firesetting, and eventual murder, the first known occurring right in Cream's backyard.

It gave Cream special sexual delight to perform illegal operations, particularly on women, and specifically abortions. As he had done with his first wife, Cream seduced and made pregnant a young hotel chambermaid named Kate Gardener in London, Ontario, in 1878, and then performed a savage abortion on her. It failed. Miss Gardener was found dead on the back porch of Cream's office-apartment with a bottle of chloroform beside her, such was the doctor's indifference as to the girl's fate and his own crime. He was arrested without a murmur and stood trial, claiming that the young woman had merely committed suicide; how could he be held responsible for such irresponsible behavior? The jury was apparently convinced that Dr. Cream's claim was correct and freed him, pointing to a lack of evidence put forth by the prosecution. Kate Gardener's death was ruled a suicide. (Had anyone bothered to check at McGill University, they would have discovered Cream's lengthy paper on the uses of chloroform, written while he was a student.)

This was the first in a series of miraculous escapes Cream would experience; these narrow squeaks with the law and his evading subsequent punishment undoubtedly fortified his self-image to the point where he felt immune to the law itself, his conceited exploits growing bolder with each murderous step. The Gardener death, however, focused too much attention upon him, Cream knew, so he decided to quit Canada and move to a large metropolitan center where he could appease his roaring sexual appetite and practice his quackery unmolested. Chicago, still untamed, its red light districts in full scarlet bloom, was his selection.

Abortion was no longer Cream's lucrative sideline; he made of it a full-time occupation. There were plenty of patients—thousands of sickly strumpets from the wide-open Levee district to service—and plenty of victims. Cream enjoyed inflicting pain upon these hapless prostitutes, but was especially interested in operating upon proper young ladies who had been compromised. One such was Julia Faulkner, who died on his operating table late in 1880. He was charged with murder but Chicago authorities lacked proof and Cream was released, even though he was suspected of having given Miss Faulkner strychnine in the guise of a painkiller.

The poison by then was a Cream favorite. He knew full well as a practicing physician that strychnine, unlike arsenic, was all but impossible to trace unless a medical examination and autopsy were made shortly after death.

In 1881, two months after Miss Faulkner's death, a Miss Stack, who had also received the Cream abortion treatment, died after taking medicine Cream had prescribed, a dosage that contained strychnine. *Before* authorities even suspected Cream of murdering Miss Stack, the thirty-one-year-old doctor brought attention to himself by writing a blackmailing letter to a chemist, accusing him of putting too much strychnine (used minimally in some medicines of the day) into Miss Stack's prescription. Cream demanded money to keep his mouth shut about the chemist's lethal error, although he himself had dosed the medicine with the poison with the full intent of murder. Instead of paying off, the chemist turned the letter over to the police, who promptly arrested Cream. Again he was tried and again he was released for lack of proof.

Thomas Neill Cream came to believe that he could all but advertise his guilt and yet remain sacrosanct from the law. This letter-writing provided Cream with another dimension to his many perversions; he actually received a sexual thrill from involving himself in his own murders by being the first to publicize such infamous acts, and then defeating authorities who strove to convict him. He himself threw down the dare, picked up the challenge, and decided the outcome in his favor long before stepping into court. The impossible letters Cream was to so carefully write would become his hallmark.

Even given the deaths of Julia Faulkner and Miss Stack, and the police keeping an unblinking eye on his activities, Cream did not openly reform, or even attempt to maintain a pose of respectability. His sexual drive was astounding; in Chicago, when not seducing or conducting abortions on women in his thriving clinic, Cream roamed the red light districts, bedding as many as a half dozen women before sunrise. He was as insatiable with his patients, seducing one and all. "It was a bisected existence that was due, at some time or other, to end in disaster," wrote Leonard Gribble in *They Had a Way with Women*. "Neill Cream was not the kind of man who can stave off disaster when it threatens. That was an art he never acquired. He was always too hopeful about the outcome of his own plotting, and accordingly was often confident about his own quality of acumen at times when such confidence was very far from being justified."

Beautiful Julia Stott was to burst that bubble of confidence. The youthful and well-endowed Mrs. Stott appeared in Dr. Cream's office, telling the abortionist that she had read his advertisements, in which he claimed to have a remedy for epilepsy. Her husband, Daniel Stott, a station agent on the Northeastern Railway, Julia explained, was an epileptic. Cream took one look at the curvaceous Mrs. Stott and led her into his examination room, where he promptly seduced her. She was most receptive, complaining that her husband's disease, as well as his advanced age, had ruined her sex life.

What Mrs. Stott saw in Thomas Neill Cream was unfathomable. He was a scrawny man, his stoop-shouldered, five-foot-nine-inch frame all bone and points. His brown hair was thinning. He squinted over gray eyes already failing at thirty-one. However, to Mrs. Stott's sublime edification, Cream was sexually insatiable, *ravishing* her—she used the word—several times at their first meeting.

To explain her long absences from her Garden Prairie, Illinois, home, Julia Stott used as an excuse the necessity of fetching her husband's medicine from the mild-mannered Dr. Cream. Daniel Stott nevertheless grew suspicious, more than once accusing her of having an affair with his own physician. Instead of changing doctors, or getting rid of his unfaithful spouse, Stott contacted Cream, telling him he was going "to make life difficult" for him and his wife. Cream's response was typically decisive; he liberally laced Stott's medicine with strychnine on June 11, 1881.

Mass poisoner of American and British prostitutes, Thomas Neill Cream.

Cream's action was not spur-of-the-moment. He had long envisioned a profit from Stott's death, having taken out a large amount of life insurance on the doddering epileptic. Mrs. Stott was not unaware of her doctor-lover's intent. She watched him "put some white powder" into the prescription when it was delivered from the drugstore. Julia scurried home with the medicine, which her husband promptly gulped down. He was dead twenty minutes later.

The death of Daniel Stott was diagnosed as resulting from an epileptic seizure. He was buried without a whisper of suspicion. Then, befitting Cream's mad egotism and paranoia, the murdering doctor, while attempting to collect the insurance monies, wrote two letters, one to the Coroner, another to the District Attorney, insisting in both missives that Daniel Stott's body be exhumed. Daniel Stott, the enigmatic Cream claimed, had been murdered; the authorities should find poison in the body!

After posting his own guilt, Cream fled with the widow Stott. They were tracked down and arrested. Cream yelled at his trial that a chemist had blundered and put too much strychnine in Stott's medicine. Not only the finger of the law pointed at the doctor. Mrs. Stott proved her undying love by quickly turning State's evidence. Cream was convicted, but again his amazing luck held. A jury found him guilty of *second-degree* murder, a verdict that still puzzles crime historians. Remarked crime writer Edgar Lustgarten: "It is an odd, but a true, reflection that this sentence sealed the fate of several girls who at the time when it was passed, were playing tag or hopscotch 3000 miles away."

Sentenced to life imprisonment, Cream was sent to Joliet, having given Boone County as his place of residence. This was specious information since Cream had never set foot in that northern Illinois county, but it was all part of his strange plan, no doubt, to confuse the police of his day. He also stated that he had been born and raised in Scotland, never mentioning his parents or his Canadian background. He mixed truth and fiction as was his shifty style. The Joliet prison ledger reads today: "No relations, no religion; Habits of life: Moderate; Education: Good."

Cream was admitted to Joliet in 1881, a model prisoner who spoke little to other inmates and always did what he was told by guards. Over the years the only complaints received about him were that cellmates would be awakened in the middle of the night at the sound of his low, hissing laughter. At such times, Cream was seen to be sitting on his bunk, knees drawn to his chest, his face turned toward the dim moonlight slanting through the barred window. He would address phantom women with murmuring curses and obscenities, promising painful death to an imaginary race of females. His thoughts at such times no doubt centered about Mrs. Stott's betrayal.

Like many a mass murderer after him, Cream's solitary thoughts in prison created wild, horrific visions of the revenge he would wreak if he should ever be released. Such fantasies heightened his sexual appetite and implanted within him a lust for the murder of women, chiefly whores, which is what he thought all females to be.

Though he resigned himself to a life in prison, kind fate once again took a hand in the case of Thomas Neill Cream. His father died in 1887, leaving his errant oldest son sixteen thousand dollars, a sizable fortune for those days. William Cream's account-bookkeeper, Thomas Davidson of John Ross Co. in Quebec, wrote to Illinois authorities at the time, asking for complete transcripts of Cream's trial. After studying the case, Davidson was convinced that young Cream was innocent. He began petitioning Illinois authorities for Cream's release. Family members and friends in Canada joined in the fight, sending petitions in droves to Illinois each year. Finally, Illinois Governor Joseph W. Fifer relented, commuting Cream's sentence. With ten years already served, he was set free on July 31, 1891.

Cream went immediately to Quebec where he picked up his inheritance from solicitor Davidson. "In my first interview with him," Davidson later wrote, "I concluded he was unmistakably insane, and stated my conviction to his brother, Daniel Cream, in whose house he was stopping."

In attitude and attire, Thomas Neill Cream was certainly arresting to the casual eye. He had lost all his hair in prison and he wore small gold-rimmed glasses, through which he constantly squinted. He affected an upper-crust costume of long black frockcoat, vest, wing-collar shirt and cravat. He wore a silk top hat and flowing about his shoulders was a black cape with purple velvet lining. His bushy mustache was heavily waxed and turned up at the ends.

With ample money to fund any caprice, Cream sailed for England on the *Teutonic*, arriving in Liverpool on October 1, 1891. He headed straight for London and the fleshpots he had so often dreamed about while in prison, renting rooms in a boardinghouse run by a Miss Sleaper at 103 Lambeth Palace Road on October 6, 1891. He was back at the hub of his youthful debauchery, nightcrawling among the whores in London's seamy East End.

Known as Dr. Neill to Miss Sleaper, Cream told his landlady that he was at work in postgraduate studies at nearby St. Thomas' hospital. When he failed to keep regular hours or see patients in his rooms, Cream explained his odd schedule by telling Miss Sleaper that he had been ill, that he was recovering from a strange disease. He made a point of letting her know that he had consulted an oculist, James Aitchinson, of 47 Fleet Street, who had diagnosed Cream's eye trouble as hypermyopia (extreme shortsightedness), which undoubtedly brought about his raging headaches and caused him insomnia. Aitchinson made up two sets of new glasses for Cream, but that did not alter his nocturnal meanderings. Mrs. Sleaper heard her odd-looking boarder pacing the floor overhead throughout the night, except when he was out, which was always after dark. She knew also that Dr. Neill, to lessen the agony of his headaches, took great quantities of morphine and cocaine. But drug-taking for medicinal purposes at the time was not condemned. Poor man, Mrs. Sleaper thought. She hoped his health would improve.

Some time in the second week of October 1891, a man wearing a black silk high hat and talking in a decidedly American accent entered Priest's pharmacy at 22 Parliament Street. Squinting through his glasses, he introduced himself as "Thomas Neill, M.D.," also stating that he was attending a series of lectures at St. Thomas' Hospital. He then wrote out an order reading: "Nux vomica, one ounce, ten to twenty drops, diluted in water."

The request did not raise any eyebrows. Nux vomica was then properly used by physicians as a tonic, being a liquid taken from "the nut that causes vomiting." But only doctors could obtain the prescription; it contained two alkaloid poisons, brucine and the lethal strychnine. Dr. Neill was given his order promptly and without question. He departed with a cheery wave.

On the morning of October 13, Dr. Neill was back at Priest's. He ordered some gelatin capsules, which had recently been put on the market. Designed as two parts, one half sliding over the other, the capsules were to be used with distasteful medicines. Dr. Neill took a case of five-grain capsules with him. Somewhere in his recent travels Dr. Neill also purchased large quantities of ink and paper, for he busied himself with letter-writing of a most peculiar nature.

On the same morning Cream bought the gelatin capsules, a nineteen-year-old prostitute he had recently patronized received two perplexing letters from him. They were addressed to Miss Ellen Donworth of 8 Duke Street, Lambeth. The first read:

Miss Ellen Linnell [the surname of her pimp, Ernest Linnell]

I wrote and warned you once before that Frederick Smith, of W H Smith and Son, was going to poison you, and I am writing now to say that if you take any of the medicine he gave you, you will die. I saw Frederick Smith prepare the medicine he gave you, and I saw him put enough strychnine in it to kill a horse. If you take any of it, you will die.

HMB

A second letter had arrived in the same mail. "HMB" asked Ellen Donworth to meet him at the York Hotel in Waterloo Road that evening and to bring the letters with her. Ellen did not understand any of it. She told her friend Annie Clements, a cleaning lady who lived in the same building, about the letters and said she had decided to meet her patron. "He's a queer duck—bald, cross-eyed, but he's easy with the money." That night Ellen Donworth kept her appointment.

Some hours later Ellen Donworth was seen to stagger down New Cut Street, off Waterloo Road. She suddenly fell smack on her face; her large hat, bearing an atrocious green bird, flew off. Fruit vendor James Styles and a man named Adam raced up to the fallen woman. Turning her over they saw by flickering gaslight that the young woman's face was the color of chalk.

"Where do you live, dear?" quizzed Styles.

"Eight Duke Street," Ellen replied through heavy breathing.

"What's wrong?" Adams asked.

Her eyes rolled; she trembled and shivered. "Pain—pain—all over me," she gasped out.

An Inspector Harvey of the Lambeth District approached and asked if he could help. The vendors told him they would carry Ellen home. Harvey summoned a doctor from the South London Medical Institute, and then continued his beat. At first glance, he thought the young woman was probably drunk.

An hour later Harvey looked in at 8 Duke Street to find the seedy rooming house in an uproar. In a second-floor bedroom, Ellen Donworth was dying in convulsions. Her face was twisted in pain; her body arched and sagged as the seizures mounted. Inspector Harvey knelt by her bed and softly questioned her. Weak, but conscious, Ellen answered in a soft voice.

"A tall gentlemen with cross eyes, a silk hat and bushy whiskers gave me a drink twice out of a bottle with white stuff in it," she told Harvey. "I drank it in the street."

"Did you know this man? Had you seen him before?"

"Yes, I knew him . . . before. He sent me two letters."

"Where are these letters?"

"I gave them . . . back . . . to him."

With a jolt, Ellen Donworth's body convulsed in quivering pain. A medical man named Johnson from the South London Medical Institute arrived in answer to Harvey's summons. He took one look at the sweating, convulsive girl and instantly diagnosed her condition. "She's dying," he whispered to Harvey. "It looks like strychnine poisoning."

Inspector Harvey and others bundled up the girl and raced to the street, climbing into a cab, which tore clattering toward St. Thomas' Hospital. As the cab swung before the hospital entrance, Inspector Harvey leaped down and opened the cab door. Ellen Donworth fell like a marble statue into his arms, quite dead. She had perished in excruciating agony.

Two days later Coroner George Percival Wyatt, who was handling the inquest into the Donworth murder, received a strange letter which read:

> I am writing to say that if you and your satellites fail to bring the murderer of Ellen Donworth, alias Linnell, late of 8 Duke Street, Westminster Bridge Road, to justice, I am willing to give you such assistance as will bring the murderer to justice, provided your Government is willing to pay me £300,000 for my services. No pay if not successful.
>
> G. O'Brien, Detective

Wyatt dismissed the letter as the work of a crackpot. The letter-writer, of course, was Cream. He did not stop with this missive. Such was his perversion that the letter-writing had become an unbreakable habit, a sort of ghoulish masturbation over the grave of his victim where he toyed with those attempting to identify him. The game went on. Cream's play turned to blackmail. As he had done in his letters to Ellen Donworth, he implicated Frederick Smith in the Donworth murder, writing —as "H. M. Bayne"—directly to W. F. D. Smith, an M. P. and head of the W. H. Smith bookselling firm in the Strand, stating:

> Ellen Donworth of 8 Duke Street, Westminster Bridge Road, was poisoned by strychnine. Two letters were found among her effects, incriminating you, which, if published,

will surely convict you of the crime. If you employ me at
once to act for you in this matter, I will save you from all
exposure and shame, but if you wait till arrested before re-
taining me, I cannot act for you, as no lawyer can save you
after the authorities get hold of these two letters. [Cream
boldly enclosed a copy of one of the letters he had sent to
Ellen Donworth.] If you wish to retain me, just write a few
lines on paper saying, 'Mr. Fred Smith wishes to see Mr.
Bayne, the barrister, at once!' Paste this on one of your shop
windows at 186 Strand next Tuesday morning, and when I
see it I will drop in and have a private interview with you. I
can save you if you retain me in time, not otherwise.

Smith's reaction was precise; he called in Scotland Yard. He
showed the letters to inspectors who advised him to place the
notice in the window, which he did. Smith and the Yard detectives waited and watched the rippling throngs along the Strand.
No one seemed to read the notice in Smith's window, although
one well-dressed gentleman in a silk top hat passed the shop
several times in a two-day period, pausing and smiling but
swiftly moving on.

To landlady Sleaper, Dr. Neill seemed avidly interested in
the Donworth case. He pored over the papers reporting the
murder and openly discussed the killing with Miss Sleaper and
his fellow boarders at breakfast. The time he spent in his room
was occupied by reading and writing. He was absent from the
house most of the day, seldom taking dinner, and returning very
late at night, his footsteps falling heavy above Miss Sleaper's
back bedroom beneath the stairs, which creaked her awake in
the still hours.

On October 19, 1891, a twenty-seven-year-old unmarried
mother with a two-year-old child, Matilda Clover, who had
turned to prostitution to survive, received a letter from a client
in which he arranged to meet her the following evening. The
letter was received at Matilda Clover's home, a brothel on Lambeth Road run by a toothless harridan named Mother Phillips.
Matilda's client seemed to be a decent sort. He had taken her
to Lilley's Boot and Shoe Emporium on Westminster Bridge
Road the day before and bought her expensive new boots. He
had also been upset with her, saying in his letter to her that he
would only meet Matilda the next night "if you can come clean
and sober." He complained in his careful handwriting that she

had been too drunk to carry on a proper conversation when he bought her the boots. He told her to bring his letter with her.

Matilda met her client on time at seven thirty at the Canterbury Theatre. She returned home a little after ten. Lucy Rose, the bordello maid, opened the door for her. With Matilda was a thin man squinting through small spectacles. He wore evening clothes and a black silk top hat. He twisted a heavily waxed bushy mustache with the ends of delicate fingers as he followed Matilda upstairs to her rooms. Matilda had previously explained to her visitor that her boyfriend Fred had made her pregnant and deserted her when her child was born. She had named the boy Fred. That was curious, the visitor in the top hat had remarked. His name was Fred, too.

A few minutes later Matilda left the brothel and fetched some beer for her guest. The elegantly attired gentlemen departed a half hour later. Lucy, the maid, heard Matilda say to him at the front door: "Goodnight, dear."

It was three o'clock in the morning when the entire house was aroused by Matilda Clover's screams. Rushing into her room, Mother Phillips and Lucy found Matilda bathed in sweat, her body wracked with spasms. She shuddered and quaked uncontrollably.

"What's happened to you, dearie?" asked Lucy Rose.

"That wretch Fred gave me some long pills," replied Matilda. "It was to cure my drinking." Through labored breathing, she said to Mrs. Phillips: "Something on my chest . . . in my throat. I'd be better if I could get it up."

A Mr. Coppin, assistant to Dr. McCarthy, was summoned. He gave Matilda some milk, which she vomited. Matilda's agony was prolonged; for hours the seizures twisted and turned her slight body. Between spells, she gasped: "I think I'm dying. I should like to see my baby." Her son, Fred, was brought from his bed. She kissed him. Coppin gave her some medicine. Her face turned black; her eyes rolled wildly in her head. By eight o'clock, Matilda Clover was dead. A Dr. Graham, who had been treating Matilda for alcoholism, arrived and wrote out a death certificate, stating the cause of death as "Delirium tremens followed by respiratory arrest."

Early that morning, Dr. Neill came downstairs from his room, having bathed and shaved. He smelled of heavy cologne. While munching his toast and sipping his breakfast milk, the lodger devoured the morning newspapers, hunting for any word of

Matilda Clover's demise. So curious was he of the effect of his "long pills" that he walked to Miss Sleaper's back room where he found the door open and the landlady at her desk, sorting bills.

"Would you do me a favor, ma'am," Cream said in a serious voice, brushing some dust specks from his coat lapel, firmly clutching his top hat. "You know the house, Twenty-seven Lambeth Road?"

"I don't actually know it," replied the landlady. "I know whereabouts it must be."

"Then would you be so kind as to deliver a letter there, when I have written it?"

"Who is the letter for?"

"I know a girl there, and I think she has been poisoned. I want to know if she is dead or not."

"Heavens above! I really think you had better take it."

"Well, perhaps so." He started to go, then turned. There was a thin smile on his lips. "I think . . . I think I know the person who poisoned her."

"God!" Miss Sleaper's hand twitched and her bills fluttered to the floor. "Who do you think it was?"

"Lord Russell!" he said as he quickly stepped from the room.

He went out and returned that afternoon, carrying with him a half dozen papers. These he took to his room and spread over a table. He found the incomplete stories about Matilda and read them over and over again, occasionally looking up to stare out the window of his room, which gave him an expansive view of the glistening Thames and the Houses of Parliament beyond. Then it was back to the newspapers, avariciously gnawing on and consuming, as would a hyena jawing carrion, each morsel of newsprint that dealt with the murder, *his* murder.

What vexed him most was the report that "a person unknown" was responsible for the killing. The taking of Matilda Clover's life *belonged* to him, and beyond the immediate lust-fulfilling sensation he felt at knowing he had brought about her end, coupled with the sexual-sensual feeling he derived in fantasizing her prolonged agony and miserable death throes, he felt robbed of the recognition. Thomas Neill Cream was no "person unknown." He was a genius murderer, a master criminal, an untouchable killer of whores, exemplifying deft, cunning techniques that put him above the fumbling of any ordinary killer.

Matilda Clover that day joined Ellen Donworth in a pauper's grave in Tooting. Matilda's sponsor, Mother Phillips, promptly pawned the boots her lover-killer had bought for her. None of this troubled the spinning mind of Dr. Cream. He turned his attentions to Lord Russell, the man he had blamed for the murder he himself had committed. Young Lord Russell had been much in the news, as Cream knew, since May 1891, when Lady Russell petitioned for a separation between her son and his bride of three months, Lady Scott's daughter; charges and countercharges of homosexuality had scandalized the Russell family, perversions aplenty flung about by the press.

Cream penned a letter addressed to Lady Russell. This was sent to her at the swank Savoy Hotel where she was staying. In it, Cream identified himself with another alias, "M. Malone," telling the distressed countess that her cherished, scandal-smothered son was the poisoner of poor Matilda Clover. Lady Russell called Scotland Yard and turned over the letters. Yard inspectors were putting together quite a collection of these letters, noting that though they bore different signatures, the handwriting, especially the decidedly constant Greek *e*'s, was the same in all.

Next, Yard inspectors were called to the home of a much-disturbed Dr. W. H. Broadbent, who lived in upperclass Portman Square at 34 Seymour Street. Broadbent, one of the most distinguished physicians in London (he would later receive a baronetcy), had received a letter from a madman on November 30, 1891. The good doctor had choked on his breakfast of bacon and mushrooms as he read a letter from an "M. Malone" with his morning mail.

A Yard Inspector soothed the doctor and then held out the letter, reading it aloud:

London, 28th November, 1891. Dr. W. H. Broadbent. Sir, Miss Clover, who, until a short time ago, lived at 27 Lambeth Road, S.E., died at the above address on the 20th October (last month) through being poisoned with strychnine. [Cream erred; Matilda Clover actually died in the early morning of the 21st.] After her death a search of her effects was made, and evidence was found which showed that you not only gave her the medicine which caused her death, but that you had been hired for the purpose of poisoning her. You can have the evidence for £2500, and in that way save yourself from ruin. If the matter is disposed of to the police it will, of course, be made public by being placed in the papers, and ruin you forever.

Now, sir, if you want the evidence for £2500, just put a personal in the *Daily Chronicle*, saying that you will pay Malone for his services, and I will send a party to settle the matter. If you do not want the evidence, of course, it will be turned over to the police at once and published, and your ruin will surely follow. It is just this—£2500 sterling on the one hand, and ruin, shame and disgrace on the other. Answer by personal on the first page of the *Daily Chronicle* any time next week. I am not humbugging you. I have evidence strong enough to ruin you for ever. M. Malone.

At the urging of the police, Dr. Broadbent did place the personal ad and his house was carefully watched for weeks after, but no one responded.

Scotland Yard investigators concluded that the letter-writer was the same in all recent instances, and was quite possibly the killer of the Lambeth prostitutes, but his identity was another thing. They could only wait for him to strike again. There was no way in which the Yard could station men to watch the thousands of whores and their clients in the Lambeth district. Unfortunately, another "fallen angel" would have to be poisoned first, before the Yard could get a break.

The next victim had been selected by Cream at random, almost by accident. Her name was Louisa Harris; she called herself Lou Harvey, after her pimp, Charles Harvey. This young trollop was a cut above the Lambeth district ladies. She lived at a good address in St. John's Wood and she worked the theaters; she was well-dressed and belonged to that upper class of whoredom then known as "flash women."

Lou Harvey first met Cream outside the elegant Alhambra Theatre just as he was about to buy his ticket. She smiled at him and he immediately asked her to dinner. They left the Alhambra without seeing the show, going to the St. James' Restaurant in Piccadilly. From there they adjourned to a Berwick Street Hotel, spending the night together.

Between his many sexually varied assaults on Lou Harvey, Dr. Cream, as he had introduced himself, sat on the edge of the bed, showing the young woman dozens of obscene photos he carried about with him. He then put these aside and drew forth a tintype of his mother, sentimentally weeping over the photo. Being an accommodating courtesan, Lou Harvey wept, too.

In the morning, Cream held Lou Harvey's face in his hand and scrutinized her. "Those blemishes on your forehead," he said in a paternal voice. "I'll give you something to clear them up." He made arrangements to see Lou Harvey that night at seven-thirty on the Embankment by the Charing Cross underground station.

That evening Cream was waiting for Lou Harvey on the Embankment as the river fog swirled about him, the pale yellow light from a gaslight silhouetting his tall top hat, his lean figure all in black, his cape fluttering in a light breeze.

Louisa Harvey was prompt, meeting Cream in the shadows of the Embankment promptly at 7:30 P.M.

"It's chilly," he told her. "You need some wine to warm you." With that, he firmly grasped her arm and led her to the Northumberland Public House nearby where they each drank a glass of red wine, Cream studying the prostitute with a bemused expression on his long face.

Minutes later, at Cream's urging, they walked back to the Embankment. Once there, Cream reached out, took Lou Harvey's hand, spread the palm and pressed two capsules into it.

In a low, kind voice he told her: "These will clear up your blemishes, my dear. Swallow them. Now."

Lou glanced down at the capsules. Something about them, or perhaps the way Cream had forced them on her, made her suspicious. Quickly, she turned her head to look up the Embankment.

"Is there someone watching us, Dr. Cream?" she asked him.

As Cream momentarily peered up the Embankment, the wily Lou tossed the pills over the Embankment into the darkness, then put her hand to her mouth just as he turned back to her. She returned his stare as she made swallowing noises. Even when Lou dropped her hand, Cream continued to scrutinize her, squinting hard behind his gold-rimmed glasses.

Leery, the poisoner squinted in the shadows. "Let me see your right hand," he ordered quietly. Lou showed an empty palm. "Now your left." That, too, was empty.

Cream was content; she had taken the pills, he was sure. He quickly told her that he could not attend the show at the Oxford Music Hall as previously planned. He had an urgent appointment at St. Thomas' Hospital. He gave her enough money for a cab and her ticket to the hall, telling her to meet him outside the theater at eleven that night. Lou Harvey waited for a half hour after the show that night but her doctor-lover never appeared. She shrugged and headed home, carefully scanning the faces of male passersby should there be time for a late night trick.

Comfortable in his rooms that night, Cream had delicious visions of Lou Harvey screaming in the sweaty throes of strychnine poisoning right in the theater. Such perverse fantasies were the mainstays of his abnormal sexual diet, these mental feasts far more appeasing to his raging appetite for sex than the three or four whores he consumed each night in the Lambeth bordellos. Just the thought of reading the newspaper reports of Lou Harvey's terrible and agonizing death the following morning sent Cream into paroxysms of pleasure. Yet there were no reports the next day, or the next.

While Cream tried to puzzle out what had gone wrong he occupied himself by window-shopping during the day and whore-hunting at night. One day in December as he was leaving Euston Station, Cream accidentally bumped into a petite, dark-haired woman, knocking a package from her grasp. He gallantly picked it up and asked her to take tea with him in a nearby restaurant. The woman blushed but agreed; he looked like a real gentleman, and she felt there was no harm in it. Besides, she had a considerable wait before her train left for Berkhampstead, Hertfordshire, where she lived with her mother.

Over tea, Cream learned that she was Laura Sabbatini, a dressmaker; she was thirty and had never had a beau. He gave the name "Dr. Neill," saying he was studying in London. Cream learned that Laura traveled to London regularly to make purchases for her shop. He asked if she would attend a concert with him two days later at St. James' Hall in Piccadilly. The quiet, attractive Laura agreed.

They met often after that, Cream's attitude toward her being one of consideration; to him she was lofty, like his mother, a woman in complete contrast to the whores he had been busily killing. His conduct with her was always proper. So drawn to Laura Sabbatini was Cream that he actually proposed. He bought her a ring and they were officially engaged over lunch in the Euston Station Tea Room where they had met.

What plans Cream had for Laura were never discovered. On the way to meet her one afternoon he stopped to stare into a glove shop on Regent Street. He looked up to see a young woman, her face heavily made up, smiling at him. She was a good-looking prostitute, he thought, and he immediately took her to a public house where they drank wine. Just as Cream was about to ask her to bed down with him, the woman laughed. He stared myopically at her.

"Don't you know me?" the woman said.

"No," he answered weakly, squinting at her. "Who are you?"

"You promised to meet me outside the Oxford Music Hall."

"I don't remember. Who are you?"

"Lou Harvey."

"What!" He shot up out of his chair. Without a word, Cream walked away, out the door, quickly disappearing down the street.

The dangerous fact that Lou Harvey, his intended victim, was still alive no doubt prompted Cream to make arrangements to visit Canada once again. He told his fiancée, Laura, that he had to settle up his father's inheritance with solicitors in Quebec. He would leave shortly after New Year's Day. They enjoyed the Christmas holidays together and Cream seemed in excellent spirits. On Christmas Day he sat with the other boarders of Miss Sleaper's rooming house, singing hymns in a fine tenor voice and playing the zither. Cream sailed on the *Sarnia* on January 7, 1982, arriving in Quebec on January 20, where he registered at Blanchard's Hotel, one of the city's most fashionable resorts.

While settling business matters, Cream occupied his time by frightening other hotel guests half to death. He befriended a salesman, John Wilson McCulloch of Ottawa, who was also staying at Blanchard's. Inviting the salesman to his room for a drink, Cream boldly produced a small bottle, one-third full of white crystals. He grinned maniacally as he held it up. "That's poison," he told McCulloch.

"God help us," replied the salesman, his eyes popping. "What do you do with that?"

"I give it to women to get them out of the family way."

"How do you do that?"

Cream produced a small, flat box and displayed some gelatin capsules. "I give it to them in these." Enjoying the shock he was producing in the salesman, Cream then capriciously slipped on a set of false whiskers, telling McCulloch that when conducting an abortion, he always wore this disguise "to prevent identification." He went on to explain to the salesman that he took strychnine himself, along with large amounts of cocaine and opium. "I need it to keep my head quiet," Cream said.

On one occasion during his long stay at Blanchard's, Cream spotted a wealthy American registering at the desk. The man flashed a wad of bills Cream immediately estimated to be about two thousand dollars. The guest departed the following day and Cream told McCulloch about him, adding with a sinister tone: "I ought to have had that man's money."

"How could that be?" asked McCulloch.

His eyes squinting, Cream said in a deliberate way: "I could have given him a pill and put him to sleep and his money would have been mine."

"My, God," said McCulloch. "You wouldn't kill a man for two thousand dollars, would you?"

"I ought to have done it," said Cream, almost as if speaking in a trance.

Aside from convincing all he met in Quebec that he was a man to be feared, Cream spent his time writing long letters to Laura Sabbatini. They would be married upon his return to London, he promised. Before sailing for England, Cream purchased a large tin box and equipped it with many bottles of his favorite companion, strychnine. He then went to a Quebec printer, thinking in his warped mind to correct a terrible slight he had received in London's Metropole Hotel. Cream had stopped in its lounge one night and ordered a drink. The waiter never returned and he sat alone for an hour, ignored by all, purposely shunned, he thought, by the opulent guests as well. He would have his revenge by spreading panic.

Cream had the Quebec printer make up five hundred circulars that read:

Cream's terror proclamation to residents of the Metropole Hotel in 1892.

> To the guests of the Metropole Hotel
> Ladies and Gentlemen,
> I hereby notify you that the person who poisoned Ellen Donworth on the 13th last October is today in the employ of the Metropole Hotel and that your lives are in danger as long as you remain in this Hotel.
>
> Yours respectfully,
> W. H. Murray

Cream ordered the circular dated London, April 1892. The circulars were later sent to him in London but he never had them distributed. When arriving in London, Cream took up residence once more in Miss Sleaper's Lambeth Road rooming house. He wanted to be close to his prey and he immediately sank into fleshpot pleasures. Cream took time out to visit Laura Sabbatini and her elderly mother in their Berkhampstead bungalow, making final arrangements for his marriage. Yet the old lusts drew him back to the sinkholes of London's East End. He decided, as had Jack the Ripper before him in 1888, that he would have two girls in one night; two girls, and two deaths.

On the night of April 11, Cream met two young women who had left their Sussex country homes to seek fortune in London, deciding on prostitution as the most convenient way to earn money. Cream gave them money after spending the evening with them, indulging both eighteen-year-old Alice Marsh and twenty-one-year-old Emma Shrivell for several hours in their rooms at 118 Stamford Street, off Waterloo Road. Constable George Comley was passing the address at 1:45 A.M., April 12, when the door opened and he saw a thin man in a top hat and dark overcoat being let out the front entrance by a young woman.

Almost an hour later, Comley was again passing the Stamford address when he saw a cab standing outside. Suddenly another constable, named Eversfield, was rushing to the cab with the girl Comley had earlier seen ushering her guest to the street. The girl was Emma Shrivell and her body convulsed and quivered in pain as the constable moved toward the waiting cab. Seeing Comley, Eversfield shouted: "Another one inside, first floor. Quick!"

Comley raced inside the house and scooped up Alice Marsh, whom he found writhing in pain on the floor. He took her to the cab and placed her next to her friend on the floor. The cab dashed off to St. Thomas' Hospital.

En route Eversfield gently asked Emma Shrivell: "What have you had to eat?"

"Some tinned salmon and some beer," came her weak response. Then she added: "And a gentleman gave us three pills each."

"Was that the gentleman with glasses on," remembered Comley, "that you let out of the house at quarter to two?"

"Yes," she gasped, "long thin pills."

Though Emma Shrivell fought the body-wracking spasms all
the way to the hospital, Alice Marsh was quiet. When they
reached St. Thomas' Hospital she was discovered to be dead.
Emma Shrivell's condition was quickly diagnosed by a Dr.
Wyman to be strychnine poisoning. He gave her emetic and
some chloroform, but he knew this was only a delaying action.
The girl would die. Emma Shrivell went through almost six
hours of hellish torment before the end. But this time, the police, thanks to the memory of Constable Comley, now had an
accurate description of the infamous poisoner.

The news of the double murder delighted Cream. He could
speak of nothing else for days, startling Miss Sleaper with the
news that he knew the identity of the killer. He told her it was
none other than a roomer in her own house! His name, Cream
said through a smirk, was Walter J. Harper, a medical student
attending St. Thomas' Hospital school.

When Miss Sleaper demanded proof of such an outlandish
charge, Cream replied: "The police have proof of it. I have a
friend who is a detective." Miss Sleaper thought it all unreal
and that Dr. Neill seemed to be coming unhinged with his
suspicions. She said nothing, closed her door, and retreated to
her magazine reading.

Cream did not let up on pinning these most recent murders
on Harper. He wrote Harper's father, Dr. Joseph Harper of
Barnstable. Using the name W. H. Murray, Cream wrote the
elder Harper that he had proof that his son had murdered the
two prostitutes but that he would turn over this "evidence" for
a sum of fifteen hundred pounds. He asked Harper to contact
him by placing a personal ad in the London *Daily Chronicle*.

Dr. Harper held on to the letter but did nothing. Cream, getting no response in the *Chronicle*, next wrote Coroner Wyatt,
informing him that W. J. Harper was the killer of Shrivell and
Marsh. He said that Wyatt was to contact George Clarke, a private detective, who would supply the proof. Next he wrote
Clarke, telling him he would be contacted by the Coroner and
that he should charge well for his services, and that the proof
the Coroner sought would be sent to Clarke shortly. He signed
both letters as W. H. Murray. This time, perhaps out of strange
caution, Cream dictated the last two letters to his fiancée, Laura
Sabbatini, who scribbled the notes. He explained to the perplexed girl that Scotland Yard had asked for his help, that he
was writing the letters for a detective friend named Murray.

The naive girl believed him, as she had believed all the other lies he told her.

Cream could not stop. He next told John Haynes, a photographer who lived in his building, that Harper was the much-sought-after poisoner of Shrivell and Marsh. Apparently, Cream's memory was shattered, for he also told Haynes that Harper had killed another prostitute, named Lou Harvey. Haynes' suspicions of Dr. Neill as being the killer himself caused him to go to Scotland Yard.

After a few days of cat-and-mouse interviews, Thomas Neill Cream was arrested by Yard detectives and charged with sending blackmailing letters, even though they suspected him of the mass poisonings. He was later charged with killing Matilda Clover on June 3, 1892. Next he was charged with murdering Ellen Donworth, Emma Shrivell, and Alice Marsh.

Piece by piece, letter by letter, the prosecution built up an insurmountable case against Cream in his five-day trial, which opened on October 17, 1892. All the while he proclaimed his innocence, telling the court that he was a learned doctor being victimized. His story captured and held the nation's headlines. Lou Harvey read of the "long pills" given the other girls and came forward to testify against Cream. McCulloch, the Canadian salesman, even traveled to London and told of his bizarre experiences with Cream. Only a sobbing Laura Sabbatini spoke up for the squinty-eyed killer, a pathetic love plea for his life. Cream's tin box containing dozens of vials of poison was placed on exhibit in the court. (It was later put on display in Scotland Yard's "Black Exhibits" room.) Pharmacists from Priest's drugstore testified against Cream. Constable Comley identified Cream as the man he saw leaving the home of Shrivell and Marsh before they were poisoned.

Jarring the proceedings was a letter the court received, one that brought back the nightmare of 1888. Coroner Braxton Hicks read it aloud in court:

Dear Sir, The man that you have in your power, Dr. Neill, is as innocent as you are. Knowing him by sight, I disguised myself like him, and made the acquaintance of the girls that have been poisoned. I gave them the pills to cure them of all their earthly miseries, and they died. Miss L. Harris has got more sense than I thought she had, but I shall have her yet . . . If I were you, I would release Dr. T. Neill, or you might get into trouble. His innocence will be declared sooner or later, and when he is free he might sue you for damages. Beware all. I warn but once.

> Yours respectfully,
> Juan Pollen, alias Jack the Ripper

The mere utterance of the name of this gruesome specter caused the entire court to gasp, except for one loan lean figure standing in the dock. Thomas Neill Cream smiled wide. The letter was later dismissed as the work of a crank. (Cream himself had no way of sending such a missive, being securely locked in Holloway Jail.) The grisly apparition of bloody Jack, however, stayed long in Cream's troubled mind.

It took the jury only ten minutes to find the diabolical Cream guilty. Judge Sir Henry Hawkins was known as "the hanging judge." He lived up fully to his reputation by ordering Cream to be executed on the gallows on November 15, 1892.

When asked if he had anything to say, Cream only sneered. As he walked from the court he was heard to say "They'll *never* hang me!"

While awaiting execution, Cream babbled incessantly to his keepers, his nonstop talk a mass of contradictions. He was consistent about only one thing: He was a great man and the world had failed to realize it. His greatness stemmed from his courage to poison these hapless whores—he claimed to have done-in scores more than those he was found guilty of murdering—as a way of ending their misery and aiding society.

On the night before his execution, Cream could be heard moaning in his cell, crying out his innocence. At dawn on November 15 he went calmly to the scaffold. He was bound hand and foot and placed upon the trap by Billington, the hangman. The hood was slipped over his head. He saved his bravura show, undoubtedly sparked by the Ripper letter read at his trial, for the last. (Cream had often spoken of his admiration for the Whitechapel madman.)

Craning his head to hear the grinding lever that would release the trap, Cream was distinctly heard to say from beneath his deathcap: "I am Jack the . . ." The rope cut him off, according to his evil plan, in that split second of eternity as he fell through space. It was the last grinding defiance of Thomas Neill Cream, whose immortality in crime was his own self-created enigma.

Cream's last words have inspired many sleuths and writers to seriously think of him as the eternally sought Jack the Ripper. Sir Edward Marshall Hall, who had once defended Cream on a charge of bigamy, later wrote that he believed Cream had a double, an exact *doppelganger* who used his name, and that both men "used each other's terms of imprisonment as alibis for each other," according to Hall's biographer, Edward Marjoribanks. Cream had earlier told Hall that he refused to plead guilty to bigamy charges because he was in prison in Sydney, Australia, at the time of the offenses. A check with Australian officials brought word that a man of Cream's description had been in prison at the time of the acts of bigamy, a report that won Cream's release.

"This has led to the suggestion," wrote Jack the Ripper authority Donald Rumbelow, "that while Cream was serving his life sentence in America, his double was committing the Whitechapel murders. As the double had given Cream an alibi for the bigamy charges, Cream subsequently tried to repay the debt by shouting those last words from the scaffold." (One could also add to this thin theory that the preposterous letter read aloud at Cream's trial was, indeed, from Cream's double, the real Jack the Ripper, attempting to save the life of his underworld twin.)

An even more preposterous claim that Cream was absolutely the Ripper was offered in 1974 by Donald Bell, who insisted that Cream bribed his way out of Joliet Prison in the mid-1880s, such being the typical state of corruption in Illinois at the time, and then traveled to London, committing the Ripper murders in 1888. Bell's notion is patently ridiculous. The author has personally checked with officials at Joliet. The prison's general ledger of that era is still intact (although Cream's personal "jacket" and glass-plate photo were long ago destroyed by fire). The ledger stipulates that Thomas Neill Cream, inmate No. 4374, was imprisoned in Joliet on November 1, 1881, and not released until July 31, 1891. Coupled to this are records of the Governor of Illinois, commuting Cream's sentence in June 1891; press announcements confirming his release date; plus the affidavit of Thomas Davidson, who handled Cream's inheritance, who fought for the freedom of his client's son and swore that he "succeeded in getting him [Cream] released in the early part of the summer of 1891."

No, those still questing for the identity of Jack the Ripper must look beyond the mocking murderer Cream. It is certain that the Ripper and the transcontinental poisoner Cream did have chilling similarities in style. They both killed whores and wrote letters to the authorities about it (although the Ripper selected aging prostitutes, where Cream picked only youthful trollops). They were both megalomaniacs who drooled over their images as archfiends. And, thankfully, they are both quite dead.

1885 CHICAGO
The Killing of a Boyhood Friendship

One of the most publicized slayings in the nineteenth century, a murder that attracted worldwide attention, pointed out to proper Victorians in gruesome detail how boyhood friendships could not only turn sour but fail to protect one against the greed of thieves. On May 2, 1885, Francesco Caruso barged into the main offices of the Chicago Police Department, excitedly explaining to officers that his brother Filippo, a wealthy fruit peddler, had utterly vanished.

Francesco had searched all of his brother's known haunts in the city without a trace of Filippo. Ironically, Chicago police had received a message from authorities in Pittsburgh a day earlier, informing them that a body in a trunk shipped from Chicago on April 30 had been discovered in the baggage room of the Union Depot. The victim had been trussed hand and foot and had been strangled.

Chicago police suggested to Francesco that he travel to Pittsburgh to see if he could identify the body. He left on the next train and, to his horror, discovered that the murder victim was the missing fruit peddler. Detectives immediately interviewed the baggageman at Chicago's Union Station. Yes, he remembered the trunk that was shipped to Pittsburgh, he told police, and the jittery dark man who had checked it. In one of those rare instances, officers discovered a man with total recall; the baggageman described the man shipping the trunk to a mole on his chin. Nationwide bulletins were sent out with the full description. Another man with total recall, the remarkable Inspec-

tor Thomas Byrnes of the New York Police Department, was to
break the Caruso case with a memory that proved astounding to
his peers and devastating to criminals at large.

Byrnes read the description of the man who had shipped the
death trunk to Pittsburgh and concluded that the suspect was
none other than a thief who worked both Chicago and New
York, one Agostino Gelardi. The fugitive was arrested a few
days later in a roominghouse on Wooster Street, the pinch made
personally by Byrnes. Gelardi was returned to Chicago, where
positive identification of him as the sender of the trunk containing Caruso's body was made by the baggageman at the Union
Depot. Further, a boy living in an apartment building on Tilden
Avenue in Chicago, where Gelardi and two friends also resided, identified Gelardi as a man dragging a trunk down the
stairs of the building—the murder trunk, which the boy later
identified. When he had inquired what Gelardi was doing, the
swarthy young man had pulled out a long knife and told him he
would slit his throat unless he went away.

Gelardi's roommates, Aguazio Silvestri and Giovanni Azari,
were arrested in Chicago. Terrified, the three men quickly
began to implicate one another in the murder of Filippo Caruso,
each suspect desperately attempting to exonerate himself.

Though all three were later found guilty of murder, what
most shocked police and public alike was the revelation that
the three men had coldly killed their boyhood friend Filippo
Caruso. The fruit peddler had grown rich in America and,
knowing the impoverished plight of his three dear friends in
Italy, had furnished the money for their immigration to the
United States. Upon their arrival in Chicago, Caruso had vigor-
ously tried to obtain jobs for them, paid for their room and
board, and loaned them money.

Knowing that their friend Caruso carried large sums of cash
on his person, the three young men decided to kill him, following a rather ingenious plan. When Caruso arrived in their apartment on the morning of April 30, the foursome decided to shave
each other in a makeshift barber chair Gelardi had rigged together, ostensibly to earn a living. When it came Caruso's turn
in the chair, he was carefully, almost lovingly shaved by one of
his Old World friends. Hot towels were then placed about his
face to soothe him. One of the three—it was never determined
which—then quickly threw a rope around Caruso's neck and
strangled him to death.

119

The leg of Caruso's trousers was then torn apart and, from a secret pocket the thieves knew to exist, his cash—a total of three hundred dollars—was taken. The money was divided and Gelardi fled to New York where he had often visited to commit robberies, while Azari and Silvestri went into hiding in Chicago.

"The Case of the Three Italians," as the murder case came to be known in the press, ended on July 1, 1885, when all three men were found guilty of murder. They were hanged together some weeks later, all refusing, not unexpectedly, to shave before walking to the gallows.

1885 ST. LOUIS

When Opportunity Knocked and Murder Answered

Murderers are not always dedicated to the task of taking life. Often enough the concept of killing is an afterthought, a slowly formed idea brought about by expediency in the pursuit of something else. In the case of W. H. Lennox Maxwell, money was mostly on his mind, not murder.

On April 1, 1885, Maxwell, the scion of a wealthy British family, who was traveling in the United States for pleasure, registered at the Southern Hotel in St. Louis. A few minutes later, another young man, C. Arthur Preller, registered at the swank inn. The two men were given rooms next to each other. Preller ran into Maxwell as both men were going to lunch hours later. Striking up a pleasant conversation, the young men became friends, taking in the sights of St. Louis together.

So much did they enjoy each other's company, hotel employees learned, that they intended to continue their travels together; at least that is what Maxwell often remarked in the two weeks the men were guests at the hotel. They would be going on to Auckland, New Zealand, the Englishman was heard to state loudly.

On April 15, the dapper Maxwell checked out of the Southern Hotel. Preller was nowhere to be seen. His whereabouts remained unknown for several days but the hotel manager was not alarmed; many young men disappeared from their hotel rooms for days, only to return after brief escapades. Besides, Preller's clothing and personal effects were still in his room.

That room became the object of concern some days later when hotel employees and guests complained of a sickening odor coming from it. Investigating police found a large zinc trunk in the room and opened it. Inside, barely recognizable due to decomposition, was the naked body of C. Arthur Preller. Stuck in the mouth of the corpse was a note reading "So perish all traitors to the great cause," which perplexed detectives.

Maxwell was the immediate suspect. Officers, told that the youthful Englishman intended to go to Auckland, concluded he would leave by way of San Francisco and traveled to that port city. There they learned that Maxwell, who had posed as a Frenchman (although he could speak no French) and had registered at a hotel under an assumed name, had already left for Auckland. New Zealand officials were contacted and Maxwell, wearing a disguise, was arrested when he arrived in Auckland. He was returned to the United States and brought to trial for murder in St. Louis in May 1886.

Circumstantial evidence was heavily against him. Maxwell had been found with some of Preller's clothing, which bore the initials C.A.P. A St. Louis druggist testified that Maxwell purchased four ounces of chloroform from him on the day of the murder and, hours later that same day, returned and excitedly asked for two more ounces, which was sold to him.

It was then determined that Maxwell's name was an alias; his real name was Hugh M. Brooks. This was discovered when the suspect's father, who was, indeed, a wealthy English merchant, arrived in St. Louis to hire the best lawyers available for his accused son.

Pinned by the prosecution, Maxwell-Brooks took the stand and admitted that, yes, he had been responsible for Preller's death, but that the killing had been entirely accidental. He then told a preposterous story that even he had a hard time relating without a smile. Preller, stated Maxwell-Brooks, "had long been afflicted by a disease of a private nature and requested that he be treated by me in a professional way." The disease, the witness inferred, was venereal. That Maxwell-Brooks knew nothing of medicine meant little. He was Preller's friend and that would do. The witness claimed to have consulted with medical authorities and then conducted his "examination,"

121

using chloroform to deaden whatever pain Preller might have during the process. He had accidentally overturned the chloroform bottle, Maxwell-Brooks said, which was why he had gone back for more. He then realized that he had administered too much chloroform and Preller died. Fearing a lynch mob because he was a foreigner, the witness went on, he stripped his friend, wrote the cryptic note to make the death appear to be that of a conspiratorial group, and left St. Louis.

The prosecution was able to prove that the suspect's story was pure bunk. Maxwell-Brooks had arrived in St. Louis with less than fifty dollars to his name. Preller, Maxwell-Brooks learned, was well-fixed. When Preller refused to loan Maxwell-Brooks money, the suspect resorted to murder, chloroforming Preller in his sleep and stealing six hundred dollars, along with most of the victim's wardrobe.

Though Maxwell-Brooks was convicted of murder and sentenced to death by hanging, he never admitted his guilt. Yet wry words escaped his lips as he stood during the last moments of his life upon the scaffold: "America was certainly not the land of opportunity for me."

1885 NEW YORK CITY
One for the Sob Sisters

Scorning a woman for any reason has often provoked murderous passions; in the case of the hot-blooded Maria Barberi, the mere thought that she was an unacceptable bride produced in her lethal rage and revenge, far greater than any dispute steaming out of the annals of the Mafia. Her 1885 trial in New York City was one of the zaniest and most bizarre in American jurisprudence.

This case set a number of startling precedents—that a woman could get away with murder under the jiggling banner of "equal rights," that lunacy of love excused all bloodletting, and that the mighty grip of that era's sob sisters of the press could bend the law and break the spine of any jury.

In April 1885, Maria Barberi, thirty, from southern Italy, met Domenico Cataldo in New York's Little Italy. Cataldo inveigled the naive Maria to move into his lodgings on Thirteenth Street by promising eventual marriage. However, the callous cad had nothing of the sort in mind. After Maria repeatedly begged her lover to go to the altar, Cataldo finally spat out: "Only pigs marry!"

Obviously, this was the wrong reply. A few days later, Maria crept up behind Cataldo, who was sitting in a bar, and slit his throat with a razor. Having a sense of drama about him, the lover jumped up, raced from the bar, and, at the corner of Avenue A and Fourteenth Street, commented to fairly disinterested passersby: "I die." He then did.

Maria's first trial was speedy and to the point—she was found guilty and sentenced to death.

A disturbing gnat began to sting members of the press, though, biting mainly the bevies of "sob-sisters," so-called because their editorial chores centered on stirring the passions of female readers to sobbing bathos with maudlin stories.

In that Victorian era, it was unthinkable that such a charming creature as Maria would be the first woman executed in the electric chair. The sob sisters' prose inspired countless wailing social groups, from the "Italo-Americans of Texas" to palsied summer guests of the Griswold Hotel at New London, Connecticut, to bleat "reprieve" and petition New York's jittery Governor Levi Parsons Morton.

The sob sisters kept pounding away, chattering about Maria's being "a mere child of 15," thus reducing the killer's age by half. They extolled the virtues of a kind soul who pampered her pet canary, Cicillo, in her "dank, dark cell" in the Tombs. A man in Fort Scott, Kansas, even wrote Morton that he would be willing to be strapped into Sing Sing's electric chair instead of Maria, if the governor paid his travel expenses to New York.

Publicity about the cruel injustice soon to be administered to Maria brought a new trial, if any sane person could label it that.

The "Tombs Angel" who "prayed in the light of a solitary sunbeam falling on the cold stones of her cell" was the essence of propriety in court. On the opening day she handed her lawyer gifts—a silk purse and a chatelaine bag, which she had crocheted in her cell.

Her defense had already been established by the sob sisters. The press had been running sketches of Maria's ears and asking "Is she a degenerate?" This tactic was based on the concept advanced by some "alienists" and phrenologists that a person's mental condition could be determined by the shape of the head and contours of the body.

Defense attorneys shrieked that Maria was a victim of "psychical epilepsy." She had been ruined mentally, they argued, when some unnamed villain years earlier put unknown drugs into her soda water and beer! They also produced charts of Maria's family that insisted her ancestors were loaded with epilepsy and insanity.

The highlight of this presentation involved an uncle of Maria's who was an exhibitionist, to say the least. It was the habit of this uncle to gather his friends about him in a favorite bar, buying all drinks. After paying his bill—which may have served as the catalyst for subsequent acts—he would tear off his clothes and scamper stone naked down the streets, shouting incoherently.

Maria's neighbor, Angelo Piscopo, testified that the girl had fits. He reenacted one of Maria's alleged epileptic seizures with such fervor that several sisters at the press table became hysterical and some of the women jurors fainted.

The prosecution went lame. It battled only once, against a Dr. Hrdlicka, who said his studies of Maria's skull proved her a lunatic. The prosecution showed the phrenologist several unlabeled charts of human craniums, which the learned physician promptly termed "abnormal." These were charts of the heads of President Grover Cleveland, George Vanderbilt, and Henry Alger Gildersleeve, the presiding judge of Maria's trial.

In the end, the prosecution crumbled. The chief prosecutor kissed Maria's hand and told her: "My dear, I never doubted for an instant that you were a good, honest girl." Maria Barberi returned to the Tombs, but only to retrieve her canary. When she emerged from that forbidding prison, thousands stood in her path, cheering.

But the impossible triumph belonged to the sob sisters of the press, who were at the zenith of their tearful hour.

1887–1906 THE MIDWEST

The Lady Killer

Inspector George Shippy of the Chicago police knew he had a mass-murderer on his hands, a man he knew had slain perhaps a dozen women, and yet Shippy was compelled to set him free. The detective's tedious investigation into the murky career of Johann Hoch—one of the scores of aliases used by this unique killer—had produced a sinister portrait of an American Bluebeard that, at least in the sense of longevity, was unequaled in the annals of homicide.

Johann Otto Hoch, who married and murdered for nineteen years until his own lethal bigamy overcame him, was born John Schmidt in 1862 in Horweiler, Germany. He married Christine Ramb, and deserted her and three children in 1887. While investigating a charge of bigamy and another charge of swindling a used-furniture dealer, Inspector Shippy first came in contact with Johann Hoch in 1898, when he was using the alias "Martin Dotz."

Shippy had no way of knowing that Hoch-Dotz had murdered a dozen women from coast to coast but his suspicions were aroused when he received a letter from a Rev. Hermann C. A. Haas of Wheeling, West Virginia. Rev. Haas, who had good reason to look for Hoch, had recognized the bigamist's picture in a Chicago newspaper. He sent along another picture of Hoch, stating it was this man who was suspected of killing a Mrs. Caroline Hoch in the summer of 1895.

Hoch, a middle-aged, balding, burly man of medium height with piercing, light blue eyes and a thick handlebar mustache, stood behind the bars of his cell and looked at the picture Shippy held in his hand.

"Is this you, Dotz?"

"It is me," Hoch replied.

"That's curious," Shippy mused. "According to my information, the man in this picture committed suicide in the Ohio River three years ago."

Hoch glared at the detective for a moment and then turned to his cot, remaining silent. Shippy managed to collect enough evidence to convict Hoch-Dotz of swindling. While Hoch was serving a year in the Cook County Jail, Shippy, acting on a tip, began to search for a dozen missing wives. The detective began with Hoch's murderous exploit in Wheeling, West Virginia.

Hoch first appeared in Wheeling in February 1895, using the name Jacob Huff. He opened a saloon in a German neighborhood. He played the zither and led boisterous customers in drinking songs. Upon arrival, Hoch also began to seek out marriageable widows or divorced women with money. He found Mrs. Caroline Hoch, a middle-aged widow.

The couple married in April. Three months later, Rev. Haas, who had performed the wedding ceremony even though he suspected Hoch of foul play, found his once healthy parishioner, Mrs. Caroline Hoch-Huff, dying in agony. The parson saw Huff administer a white powder to his wife and concluded it was poison. He did not act, however, and the woman died some days later in great pain. Huff insisted she be buried immediately. After withdrawing all of the nine hundred dollars from his wife's bank account, selling her house, and collecting twenty-five hundred dollars on her life insurance, Jacob Huff disappeared.

Rev. Haas, in a series of letters sent three years later to Inspector Shippy, described what he thought happened. Huff walked to the nearby Ohio River on the night of his disappearance. He stripped naked and waded into the waters. Hoch placed his good watch, with his picture inside the locket, and a suicide note on his pile of clothes and then, holding a heavy sack aloft, walked up the river in neck-high water for a hundred yards until he reached a rowboat. He climbed into the boat, which he had earlier anchored, and then quickly dressed in another set of clothes. Next he calmly rowed up river, pausing only once in deep water to drop the large weighted sack he had so carefully carried. He continued on until he reached the Ohio side of the river, where he set the boat adrift and continued on his strange journey. But he was no longer Jacob Huff; now he was Johann Otto Hoch. It was peculiar to Hoch that he often took the last name of the woman he had either deserted or murdered. "A warped keepsake stored in that evil mind," Inspector Shippy concluded years later.

For almost a year Shippy tried to follow Hoch's strange, fading trail. He found a score of dead and deserted women, from San Francisco to New York, most of the victims being in the Midwest.

He would unearth more years later, as many as fifty and per-

haps more than that—women in St. Louis, Minneapolis, Philadelphia. Incredibly, Inspector Shippy could not produce
enough evidence to convict Hoch. Desperately, he wrote to the
authorities in Wheeling, West Virginia, and begged them to
exhume the body of Mrs. Carolina Hoch, telling them to look
for arsenic poisoning.

In Wheeling, the body of Mrs. Hoch was dug up, and officials
gasped as the coffin lid was opened. There was no middle to
the body; all of the widow's vital organs had been surgically
removed. (That, authorities later decided, was what Hoch had
carried in the weighted sack and dropped into the middle of
the Ohio River when feigning his suicide.) There was no case
against Johann Otto Hoch. At the end of his term for swindling,
he was let loose, "to murder again," moaned Shippy, "God
knows how many women, God knows where."

From 1900 to 1905, Hoch, under various aliases, married at
least another fifteen women, murdering most of them. His
modus operandi was to marry and then slowly poison his wives
to death, calling in doctors he knew would innocently diagnose
the wife's disease as nephritis, a disease of the kidneys, for
which there was then no treatment. Hoch, at the beginning,
took his time, spending patient months to murder his wives
systematically.

Hoch's careful method, however, fell to pieces after his release in Chicago. He knew he was a suspected killer and prolonged stays in any city would invite further suspicion. He
began killing in record time—marrying rich widows he met
within hours and heavily dosing them with arsenic within days,
his gruesome job sometimes completed within a week. Such
lethal frenzy ended his career. He married his last victim, Mrs.
Marie Walcker, in Chicago on December 5, 1904, and quickly
poisoned her.

On the night of Marie Walcker's death, the victim's estranged
sister, Amelia, appeared. Hoch embraced the sister and kissed
her. "Upstairs my poor wife is dying," he said. "I cannot be
alone in this world. Marry me when she goes."

Amelia Walcker was stunned. "What? How can you say such
a thing?"

Hoch drew back into the shadows, his massive chest heaving.
"The dead are for the dead," he intoned. "The living are for the
living."

Marie Walcker-Hoch was buried the next day without being

embalmed. Amelia Walcker married Hoch within six days. The killer had received $500 from Marie's insurance policy and Amelia gave him another $750. Then he disappeared and Amelia went to the Chicago police. Inspector Shippy immediately had Marie Walcker's body exhumed and Hoch's poison was found. Shippy sent photos of Hoch to every major newspaper in the country.

In New York, a landlady and widow, Mrs. Katherine Kimmerle, spotted Hoch's picture and realized that it was a photograph of her new boarder, Henry Bartels, a strange lodger indeed since Bartels had proposed marriage to the widow only twenty minutes after he took a room. Mrs. Kimmerle rushed to the police. Hoch-Bartels was soon in custody.

"I'm Hoch, all right!" he admitted to the police. "But I am a very much abused and misrepresented man." Found in Hoch's room were $625, several wedding rings with the inscriptions filed off, a dozen suits with labels ripped out, a loaded revolver and a fountain pen that contained fifty-eight grams of arsenic. ("The poison is for me," Hoch insisted. "I was planning suicide.") While being extradited to Chicago to stand trial for the murder of Marie Walcker-Hoch, the killer told his train guards: "There are lots of Hochs but I'm not the one they want."

"You're the one," Inspector Shippy shouted when he picked up the killer at Union Station.

During his long trial, the mass-murderer hummed, whistled

Johann Otto Hoch (left, front), a methodical Bluebeard who may have slain as many as fifty females, awaits trial in Chicago, 1905. (CHICAGO HISTORICAL SOCIETY)

A boxed set of rules by which mass-murderer Hoch won the hearts of his victims as it appeared in the Chicago Sun, *1906.*

and twirled his thumbs in court. He was innocent, he insisted to the end. When convicted of murdering Marie Walcker-Hoch and sentenced to be hanged, Hoch only whispered: "It's all over with Johann." Then he murmured as he was led away, "It serves me right!"

Yet Hoch clung to hope to the hour of his death. He remained awake all night before the day of his execution, eating huge meals and demanding more and more food. Every now and then he would smile at his astonished guards and say: "Now look at me, boys. Look at poor old Johann. I don't look like a monster now, do I?" No one replied.

On the scaffold on February 23, 1906, Hoch piously proclaimed his innocence, and then nodded for the sheriff to place the rope around his neck. "I am done with this world," he growled. "I have done with everybody." He shot through the trap moments later and died of a broken neck.

A reporter standing next to the gallows spoke to the still-swinging corpse: "Yes, Mr. Hoch . . . but the question remains . . . *what* have you done with everybody?"

1889 LITTLE FALLS, NEW YORK
Death Along the Mohawk

In the latter part of 1889, peaceful Herkimer County, New York, was jolted by a slaying that equaled the terror the once-fierce Indian tribes had spread along the Mohawk in Revolutionary

129

days. Outside the city of Little Falls, New York, dwelled a farmer named John Druse; his wife, Roxana; his twenty-year-old daughter, Mary; and his twelve-year-old son, John, Jr. All appeared well and sane upon the small tract of land and inside the Druse cottage but murder was definitely afoot.

Though John Druse, a man weakened by his seventy-odd years, was much liked and respected in the small community, his wife, Roxana, was known as a mean-mouthed and tyrannical shrew who insulted neighbors and strangers alike, and ruled the household with an iron hand. She made no secret of the fact that for many years she had detested both her low, backbreaking lot in life and the man who had brought her to farming servitude, her husband.

In early November, nearby residents became apprehensive when they noticed that none of the Druse family members were seen to work the farm, and that the cottage, unlike its former appearance, was kept tightly closed. Moreover, neighbors were alarmed to see dense black clouds of smoke belching from the chimney of the Druse cottage. The smoke continued for two days. Druse's friends, not seeing him about the farm, approached his wife and questioned her.

Roxana Druse answered their questions with firm replies. Her husband had gone out-of-state to visit relatives, she stated. No, she did not know when he would return; in fact, she added, he might never return. John Druse had mentioned these relatives and his friends lost no time in writing to them, inquiring as to the well-being of the missing farmer. The relatives surprised few of Druse's friends by replying that they had not seen him. Instead of going to the authorities, farmers around Little Falls spotted John Druse, Jr., in the town, took him aside, and grilled him as to the whereabouts of his father. The boy, in an obvious emotional state, immediately blurted out the story of a heinous murder; his mother and sister had brutally slain his father and disposed of his body in methods that harkened back to the Dark Ages.

Both Roxana and her feeble-minded daughter, Mary, were arrested. Mrs. Druse did not parry with investigators but confessed the slaying on the spot. She was a simple farming woman without guile who had decided in her practical way that her doddering husband would soon be of no use around the farm and become wholly dependent upon her slaving self. There was nothing else to do but murder him, and this she promptly did, she admitted, as he walked into a small pantry in their home. She came up behind him, striking him on the head with an axe, killing him instantly. The daughter Mary was present at the slaying, approving of her mother's act, but the son was in another room when his father was slain. Dispassionately, Roxana Druse severed her husband's head with the axe for arcane reasons. (Testified John Jr., at her trial: "I saw my father's head resting upon a plate in the pantry.")

Following the murder, Roxana turned to her daughter and commanded her to "put on the wash boiler and fill it with water." This done, both women diligently dismembered the body of old John Druse, placing the remains in the huge pot hanging inside the large stone fireplace. The remains were boiled for hours. This completed, the body was then burned piece by piece in the kitchen stove—hence the billowing black clouds emanating from the chimney. Roxana Druse reasoned that the boiling process would reduce the odor of burning flesh and bones. Contrary to her plans, the entire neighborhood was aroused by the tell-tale smoke and sickening stench.

The murder axe was found at the bottom of a pond after Mary Druse told police where her mother had thrown it. The head of John Druse was never recovered. "I didn't burn it," Roxana stipulated in a calm voice, "for fear that the burning hair would bring the authorities." She refused to disclose its hiding place and it remains missing to this day.

Mrs. Druse and her daughter were convicted in a speedy trial. Mary Druse was sent to prison for life; her mother received a death sentence; and the innocent son was sent with his horrid memories to live with relatives.

Roxana Druse spoke little of her fiendish crime while awaiting the gallows. She did say that when she had heard years earlier that boiled flesh gave off no odor, the false idea had taken root in her mind, preying upon her thoughts and becoming an irresistible attraction.

Oddly, this woman who had no criminal past, and who lived a worthy life aside from her incredible act, mounted the scaffold without remorse or acknowledgement of her human insensibility. As the noose was placed about Roxana's neck, she droned: "I have nothing more to say. Be done with it." And it was done.

1892 NEW YORK CITY

A Dose Too Clever

Dr. Robert Buckanan reeked of self-confidence and reveled in his intellectual prowess, a man whose ego and vanity insisted that he was above the minds of most men and beyond their laws. Buckanan, like the prolific killer Dr. Cream, studied medicine in Edinburgh, Scotland. At the age of twenty-four, he married an attractive woman, moving from Nova Scotia in 1886 to New York where he established his practice at 267 West Eleventh Street, in what is now Greenwich Village.

His practice soon bloomed and with his new riches, Dr. Buckanan maintained himself and his wife in style; he also, like the lust-tripped Dr. Cream, sought out fleshpot pleasures almost every night in New York's flashiest Tenderloin bordellos.

In his travels, Buckanan befriended saloonkeeper Richard Macomber and one of his wealthy patrons, William Doria, a retired British Army captain. The trio became regulars in the posh whorehouses, favoring the brothel owned and operated by Anna Sutherland on Halsey Street in Newark, New Jersey. The trip to Madam Sutherland's was tedious in 1890, the dedicated rakes having to travel by train and ferry, but Madam Sutherland and her four girls made life merry for the good doctor and his roisterous companions.

Despite the repelling fact that Anna Sutherland was obese, sported a wart on the end of her large nose, had dyed orange hair and was twice his age, Dr. Buckanan seemed enamored of her. Doria and Macomber saw him several times retreat with the whorehouse proprietor to her room. He later told his companions that he was merely treating Mrs. Sutherland for a kidney ailment, but, in truth, he was wooing the woman, after learning that she had accumulated a fortune from her years of prostitution. Some months later Buckanan informed his friends that he intended to divorce his wife, which he did on November 12, 1890; the decree was granted on grounds of *her* adultery. Two weeks later Macomber and Doria accompanied Buckanan to Newark where they witnessed Anna Sutherland's new will, which specified that her best friend, Dr. Buckanan, was to receive all her worldly possessions in the event of her death, unless she subsequently married; in that case, her future husband would inherit her fortune. Buckanan took no chances. He and Anna were wed on November 29, despite the grumblings of Anna's long-time janitor and part-time paramour, James Smith, who had thought all along that he, not the interloping doctor, would marry the thrice-divorced Mrs. Sutherland. "I would never bind myself to a man who lives off girls," the suddenly reformed madam told her one-time associate Smith.

With that she moved to Buckanan's New York home and served as his office receptionist. Nothing went smoothly for the calculating doctor after that. He was soon complaining to his drinking cronies that his new wife had a nasty way of treating his patients, that her flippant tongue wagged such greetings as "Hello dearie, which shall it be, a blonde or a brunette?" At parties, the flamboyantly attired Mrs. Buckanan shocked all by prattling racy stories and luridly commenting on the sexual attractiveness of the doctor's male guests. Such conduct was increasingly glaring when Buckanan was appointed a police surgeon and then a Lunacy Commissioner for the city.

The solution to Dr. Buckanan's alarming social situation was hinted at in a conversation he had with his chums at Macomber's bar in early 1891. The murder trial of a young medical student, Carlyle Harris, was brought up. It was pointed out that Harris (see Chronology), who had provided a lethal pill dosed with morphine to his secret wife, Helen Potts, had grossly erred in his method. The morphine poisoning, the first in New York court history, was easily diagnosed, Doria told Buckanan, since the pupils of the victim's eyes were contracted.

"Harris was a stupid fool," snorted Buckanan. "Only a bungling amateur would make such a mistake!" He then went on to sneer that Harris had no idea how to disguise the symptoms of morphine poisoning.

"Do you know a way?" quizzed Macomber.

"Yes, a way has just occurred to me. Every acid has its neutralizing base and every chemical agent its reagent. If one is expert in the field"—he nodded, as if to acknowledge his own profound presence—"the preparation of an undetectable poison could be easily accomplished."

The thought of committing the perfect murder undoubtedly took root in Buckanan's mind some months later when his life with Anna Sutherland became unbearable. He announced to one and all that he was returning to Edinburgh to study, planning to sail April 25, 1892. Before his departure, Anna informed her thirty-year-old spouse that if he left the country without her, she would disinherit him.

Four days before his scheduled departure, Buckanan scurried from Macomber's bar after telling his friends that he had to get home in a hurry; his wife had become ill, so ill that he had canceled his European trip. Anna was attended by Dr. B. C. McIntyre, who had been called in by Buckanan. The visiting physician noted Anna's hysteria and her complaints of throat contractions. When she lapsed into a coma, McIntyre ordered a nurse, Mrs. Crouch, to watch the patient while he fetched another doctor, H. P. Watson. Twenty-six hours later, on April 23, Anna Sutherland Buckanan was dead, her death, both McIntyre and Watson concurring, attributed to cerebral hemorrhage, stemming from epilepsy.

Buckanan showed no remorse at Anna's death. Dutifully he collected the fifty thousand dollars she had left to him in her will and blithely he sailed for Nova Scotia, but not before hiring a private detective to watch his wife's grave, with instructions to report to him if it was disturbed.

While Buckanan was abroad, the rejected suitor, James Smith, read of the death of his former benefactor and went to see one of New York's coroners, a Dr. Schultze, telling him that Buckanan had only married Anna to obtain her money and that he most likely had murdered her to get it. Dr. Schultze shook his head, telling Smith that the doctors who had signed Mrs. Buckanan's death certificate were highly respected, their word beyond doubt. Smith left in a rage but his visit accidentally stirred a spectacular inquiry.

Isaac White, a reporter for the *New York World*, had overheard Smith's accusations, and, following him into the street, obtained more information from the enraged man that led him to interview Dr. McIntyre. The physician told him that Mrs. Buckanan's death was most probably due to epilepsy, answering White that morphine poisoning would cause similar symptoms but such poisoning, in his opinion, was not in evidence; he pointed out to the reporter that the pupils of the dead woman's eyes showed no contraction. Dr. Watson shared Dr. McIntyre's belief, adding that both physicians had been careful to check Mrs. Buckanan's eyes at the time of death since Dr. Buckanan had made a point of telling them that he had been treating his wife with morphine for her kidney ailment.

White was persistent, smelling a classic murder story, one

probably more sensational than the Carlyle Harris killing a year before. He learned from Buckanan's friends, Macomber and Doria, that the doctor had canceled his trip to Scotland because of his wife's threats. Buckanan's boasts of being able to conceal the symptoms of morphine were also related to the reporter. White next called at the steamship line and discovered that the doctor had canceled his original plans on April 11, 1892, ten days before his wife became ill.

The reporter's wire to Halifax authorities also proved beneficial. He was informed that Buckanan had remarried his first wife only three weeks after Anna's death. She had traveled to Nova Scotia ahead of him and was waiting for him when he docked.

Armed with such unsettling information, White convinced authorities to open Mrs. Buckanan's grave and examine the corpse. Careful anatomical analysis revealed no lesions of the brain, ruling out death by cerebral hemorrhage. Then a Professor Witthaus, one of the leading toxicologists in the country, discovered one-tenth of a grain of morphine—the remains, he estimated, of five or six grains undoubtedly administered to the woman: a fatal dose . . . murder.

Yet Witthaus was perplexed. When he lifted the dead woman's eyelids, there was still no characteristic symptom of morphine poisoning; the pupils were not contracted. There was no doubt now that Buckanan had killed his wife, said Witthaus and others, yet there was no evidence, thanks to the lack of contraction of the pupils. "Amazing," murmured the professor, "but apparently Buckanan *has* found a way to conceal those symptoms."

Undaunted, White asked that the body be kept from its grave for another twenty-four hours; Dr. Buckanan had returned from Nova Scotia and White tracked him down in Macomber's saloon. The short, mild-mannered, bespectacled doctor flew into a rage when White asked him why he had remarried his first wife, denying that he had done so. In an attempt to learn how Buckanan had disguised the morphine poisoning, the reporter tried to get the doctor drunk, but Buckanan revealed nothing— nothing with his tongue, that is; his eyes betrayed the secret. While White was staring at the doctor, he noticed how Buckanan's eyes were enlarged by the thick lenses of his glasses. White thought back to his days in school, remembering that a classmate had once received an eye examination, and, to enlarge the pupils, the doctor had administered a few drops of belladonna.

Leaving Buckanan in a silent stupor, White rushed to the coroner and persuaded his experts to check Mrs. Buckanan's body for belladonna. They did, finding quantities in both eyes. The nurse, Mrs. Crouch, then stated that she recalled Dr. Buckanan's inexplicably giving his ailing wife eyedrops shortly before her death.

By this time, Buckanan had been warned by the detective who had been watching his wife's grave that the body had been removed. The doctor packed his clothes and prepared to flee but he was arrested as he stepped from his front door.

Charged with murder, Buckanan went to trial on March 20, 1893, telling reporters that it was all a hoax, a stunt dreamed up by Isaac White to sell newspapers. He was innocent, he was wronged, and his lawyers, Charles W. Brooke and William J. O'Sullivan, a young doctor-turned-lawyer, would prove it.

The prosecutors, District Attorney Delancey Nicoll, Francis L. Wellman and James Osborne, now famous names in American criminology, knew their case was mostly circumstantial but they attacked with vigor, parading the discarded suitor, James Smith, to the witness stand. Macomber and Doria also testified for the state, telling of how Buckanan had boasted of his ability to disguise the symptoms of morphine poisoning, of witnessing Mrs. Buckanan's strange will and her subsequent marriage to the doctor.

Jurors were treated to a gruesome state exhibit: a cat was killed with a dose of morphine and then belladonna was dropped into its eyes, which disguised the symptoms of the poison. O'Sullivan, however, brought forth his own experts, who thoroughly confused such dramatic presentations with elaborate toxicology tests. There was every indication that Buckanan would be freed, yet he condemned himself by insisting, against his counsel's wishes, on taking the stand.

Buckanan had thought long about the Carlyle Harris case, and the bungled methods that had actually inspired him to use morphine to poison his unwanted second wife. Harris, Buckanan knew all too well, was condemned when he refused to take the witness stand on his own behalf. Dr. Buckanan would not make that fatal mistake, pompously mounting the stand to give his own evidence. A ruthless cross-examination destroyed him.

Why had he boasted that he could disguise the symptoms of morphine poisoning? Why had he hired a detective to watch his wife's grave? Buckanan blubbered and fumed but could not answer. The jury found him guilty of first-degree murder after twenty-six hours of deliberation.

Valiantly, Buckanan's lawyers fought for his life, but all his appeals were denied, including requests for clemency. He went to the electric chair on July 2, 1893, a man whose perfect crime would stand today as a sinister, singular achievement in the history of murder had it not been for his strutting cleverness.

1896   HIGH SEAS, EN ROUTE TO THE ARGENTINE

Slaughter Below Decks

The fact that the barkentine *Herbert Fuller* sailed out of Boston Harbor, bound for Rosario, on the Parana River, Argentine Republic, on a Friday, July 3, 1896, endorsed an evil omen of long standing among seamen. Ships departing on Fridays had always encountered trouble; many were doomed to destruction, mutiny, and even murder, the legends muttered. The Argentine voyage of the *Herbert Fuller* proved the soothsayers of the sea correct in awful detail, for its decks were to run with blood shed by an unknown maniac whose dark purposes were never fully brought to light.

Eleven men and one woman set sail that day: Captain Charles I. Nash; his wife, Laura; Lester Hawthorne Monks, a passenger; and nine crew members. The Captain, at age forty-two, had had twenty years of sea experience and was a native of Harrington, Maine, the spot where the three-masted vessel had been built in 1890. His wife, two years younger, was an attractive, well-endowed woman; Laura Nash had several times previously sailed with her husband. They were a childless couple who enjoyed each other's company. There had never been any trouble with crew members dealing with the lone woman—none until the Argentine voyage.

The lone passenger aboard the *Herbert Fuller*, Monks, was a sickly twenty-year-old Harvard student whose bronchial ail-

The Herbert Fuller, *at dock in Boston Harbor, after returning from its bloodstained voyage in 1896.*

ments, he felt, would improve with a long sea voyage. Monks had thought about the trip only a week before sailing, talking to the ship's new first mate, Thomas Mead Chambers Bram. The mate ominously told Monks not to take the voyage, but his reasons for rendering such advice were not forthcoming.

In addition to Bram, the crew was an odd lot who shipped aboard the *Fuller* only days before she sailed; among them were a few spectacular, if not suspicious, characters. The second mate was a Russian Finn named August W. Blomberg, a burly silent type who was as big and rough-and-tumble as Captain Nash himself. Jonathan Spencer, the steward and the only member of the crew who had sailed with the Captain before— on a voyage to Martinique—was, perhaps, the most intelligent person on board, a twenty-four-year-old mulatto whose lone good sense would prevail during the coming hours of chaos.

The other seamen included two Swedes, Folke Wassen and Oscar Anderson; Henry J. Slice, born in Hamburg, Germany, but a naturalized American citizen; Francis Loheac, a deserter from the French Navy; Hendrik Perdock, a youth from Holland; and another Swede known as Charley Brown, but whose real name was Julius Leopold Westerburg.

Her holds full of lumber, the good ship *Herbert Fuller* sailed toward its destination without incident until the night of July 13–14. All aboard were in their cabins, presumably sleeping, except for Mate Bram, who had the midnight-to-four watch; Charley Brown, who was at the wheel; and Loheac and Perdock, who were the forward lookouts.

The early evening had been calm as the ship sailed the mid-Atlantic, almost exactly halfway between Portugal and the eastern United States. Everyone had eaten supper early and retired just after eight that night. Henry Slice, who was to be relieved at the wheel by Brown, could see the Captain lying down in the chartroom (also known as the afterhouse), where he usually slept, directly in front of the wheel; Slice's view was through an eleven-by-sixteen-inch window and he could see Nash's legs as far as the knees as the Captain reclined—an all-important view, as events later proved.

In his small cabin, Monks, the passenger, had gone to sleep a little after eight. The rattling of his door caused him to lock it, an insignificant gesture at the moment, but one that probably saved his life. The sea was calm until about midnight when a fresh breeze filled all the available canvas, causing the *Herbert Fuller* to skate forward at six knots. With the increased movement, the barkentine's timbers groaned and creaked, and the wind sang in the halyards. Mingled with these natural noises was the unnatural piercing scream of a woman. Monks woke drowsily from his bunk, sat up and listened. It was a dream, surely, the Harvard student concluded. As he slowly settled back against the pillows, he heard it again, a sharp, quick scream of a woman.

Monks leaped from his bunk, pulling open a drawer beneath it and withdrawing a box of cartridges. Hurriedly, he slipped his revolver from beneath the pillow and loaded it. He put on his slippers and then, pajama-clad, Monks unlocked and threw open his door, stepping hesitantly into the chartroom. He strained to see through the murk, his only dim light coming from the lamp swaying in the forward cabin. He made out the Captain's cot, which had been toppled to its side.

At first Monks could see little else. Then he heard a gurgling sound. "Captain Nash!" he yelled. Walking forward, he almost stumbled in the dark over the Captain's body. Nash was sprawled on the deck, strange noises rattling through his throat. He did not respond to Monks' calls. The passenger felt the Captain's shoulder; it was wet and sticky with blood.

Recoiling in fear, Monks raced to Mrs. Nash's stateroom to ask her to help her husband, thinking there had been some kind of freak accident. It was almost two in the morning, Monks later estimated, when he threw open Mrs. Nash's cabin door, recalling for authorities later: "I suddenly realized that the scream I heard meant something." Laura Nash was lying on her bunk, her nightgown pushed high on her legs. She had literally been chopped to pieces, the skull smashed in front and back, the jaws broken. There were deep gashes in her arms and hands, as if she had received these terrible blows while attempting to ward off the lunatic attacking her.

Dazed, Monks staggered from the cabin and lurched up the forward companionway. Looking up through the hatchway, the passenger saw Mate Bram walking the deck. Without realizing that he was pointing his revolver at the mate, Monks called to him: "Mr. Bram!" The mate took one nervous look down at the passenger with the gun in his hand and quickly picked up a plank and threw it at him, but it fell harmlessly across the hatchway.

Monks lowered his revolver, pleading: "Come below. The Captain has been murdered! Come below, for God's sake!"

"No, no, no," Bram said rapidly, as if to deny Monks' claim.

"Come below and see for yourself."

Reluctantly, Bram descended and the two men entered the afterhouse. Monks held up a lamp to reveal Captain Nash gurgling his life away. Bram stood like a rock, saying nothing, making no attempt to help his skipper. Both men then returned to the deck and sat nervously near a rail. "What about Mr. Blomberg, the second mate? We should awaken him," Monks finally volunteered.

Bram's face clouded with fear. "There is mutiny," he whispered. "The second mate is forward with the crew."

"What time is it?" Monks asked him.

"I don't know . . . but I do know that someone has tampered with the cabin clock . . . they set it back." Suddenly Bram began to cry, his body heaving with great sobs. He slipped to the deck and, to Monks' amazement, the burly man desperately hugged

Monks' legs. "Protect me, please," he begged in a whimper. "I've been hard on the crew . . . I know they're going to rush aft to kill me!"

"I'll do what I can," Monks replied.

"I'm sick, Mr. Monks. The second mate was on deck at twelve o'clock. He gave me a drink of whiskey. He said he had gotten it from you—"

"I never gave the second mate any whiskey for you."

"It was in a tin cup. I drank some. Blomberg threw the cup overboard. I suspected it was drugged. I heaved it." Bram pointed to a patch of vomit on the deck.

"You better get up and walk about. I'll help you." Monks pulled the heavyset man to his feet. They walked the deck for about five minutes, Bram staggering about in an exaggerated manner. "I think we should wake the steward. He may be able to help you," Monks soothed.

Fear again gripped the mate. "If you do, somebody may rush at us around the forecastle house."

Both men sat down, Monks facing forward with his revolver, Bram pointing his pistol aft toward the wheel manned by Loheac, who had relieved Charley Brown at 2:00 A.M. They sat that way, tense, expectant, waiting for daybreak, as the ship silently skimmed the sea.

At dawn, urged by Monks, the two men went to the galley, knocking loudly on the door. Spencer, the steward, opened it, wearing only his pants.

"The Captain has been murdered," announced Monks.

The steward thought he was joking. "I guess not," he sniggered.

"Well, you can go and look for yourself," Monks told him.

Spencer said he would and started for the afterhouse.

"Do you have a revolver?" Bram asked.

"No," said Spencer.

"Well, here, you take this one." Bram gave him his revolver.

"I'll try it," Spencer said and fired a shot over the side. Bram jumped at the explosion.

Spencer then cautiously went to the afterhouse, looking through the skylight first, to see the Captain sprawled dead below. He descended, and checked the body; the Captain's head had been gashed by seven or eight blows, several penetrating the brain. Seeing that Second Mate Blomberg's cabin door was open, Spencer stepped inside. The second mate was in his bunk, feet crossed. He was covered with blood. His head was gashed in several places, like that of Captain Nash. It was odd, the steward noted, that one of Blomberg's fingers had been sliced off. Spencer had had enough. He ran screaming to the deck: "The second mate has bled to death. Jesus Christ! What does this mean?"

Monks turned with suspicion toward Bram. "I thought you said the second mate went forward?"

"Well," replied Bram indignantly, "he was forward!"

Loheac was asked if he had seen anything from his wheel position. He tersely told the three men no, he had seen nothing. Spencer, Monks and Bram then walked forward, pausing to confer when they reached the main rigging on the starboard side.

Mate Bram suddenly squinted at the far side of the deck and then shouted: "There is an axe! This is the axe that did it!"

"I don't see anything," Monks said.

"Neither do I," added Spencer.

They followed Bram across the deck. Bram kicked aside a lashing plank used to bind the deck-load. Before them was a

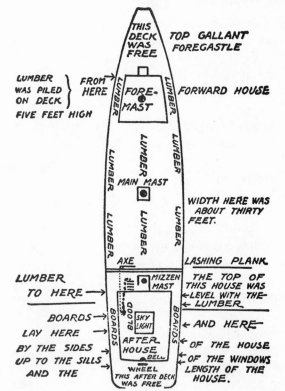

An 1896 sketch showing the deck areas, including the fatal "afterhouse," of the Herbert Fuller.

new axe, its head and handle fairly dripping blood. It had hung in the storeroom.

Spencer picked it up, and with amazement in his voice, said: "This is the axe that done it, this is the axe that killed the Captain."

Bram took the axe from him. "This done it all right." A strange light came into his eyes. He grinned at the axe. Tears rolled down his cheeks as he crazily repeated: "This is the axe that done it, this is the axe that done it." Abruptly he turned to Monks. "Shall I throw it overboard?"

Monks paused a moment, looking about, his mind still on mutiny. "Yes, for fear the crew may use it against us."

Spencer stepped forward, holding up his hand. "No—"

He was too late. Bram, giving a shriek, hurled the bloody murder weapon into the sea.

"You shouldn't have done that," Spencer told Bram.

The first mate gave him a weak smile and a near-wink of instant wisdom. "But we don't find no axe."

Spencer was angered. "What do you take me for—a Goddamn fool?" He hooked a thumb in the direction of the helmsman, Loheac. "Don't you know a man has seen you with the axe?"

Bram's attitude reversed itself, from assurance to terror. He suddenly grabbed Spencer, weeping, sobbing. "You will look out for me, take care of me, Steward?" He babbled out his theory of being drugged by Blomberg, showing the steward the vomit on deck.

By then Spencer was all business. "We will put some of that into a bottle and have it examined when we reach port."

Bram readily agreed, walking toward the waste matter and then appearing to stumble so that he stepped in it and wiped it away, more evidence destroyed.

The other crew members were then called on deck and informed of the mass slaying. No one had an explanation as the seamen eyed each other. They toured the grim cabins, noting the bodies. They stood again on deck. Bram burst into tears again, shouting: "My Captain—I'd die for him! We were both Freemasons, you know," he informed the bewildered crew. "Oh, my poor, poor mother!"

Monks slapped him rudely in the back. "Brace up, will you?"

Bram, as the first mate, was now in command of the *Herbert Fuller,* but he exercised no authority. He seemed confused and stunned by it all. He looked around at the little circle of men

143

staring at him. "You will stand by me, boys, won't you?" To their response of silence he next said with a weird smile: "Let's all shake hands." He stepped nervously forward, grabbing a few limp hands. "Well, now, that's settled," he said in a firmer manner. "We will now take those bodies out of there and throw them overboard, and wash up the blood in the cabin."

Henry Slice shook his head firmly. "We don't throw no bodies overboard. We take them in as evidence. And we don't clean the cabins out either. We leave them as they are." Everyone nodded agreement at this logic, including Bram. At Slice's suggestion, the bodies were put in the jolly boat amidships and the boat and bodies covered with canvas.

Bram continued to act in an eccentric fashion, wailing and praying to God for the soul of his Captain, his hands clutched high above his head as he paced the decks.

Several crew members sought to console him. Monks brought a box of cigars from his cabin and passed them around. The men smoked and sat in a circle on the deck, each suspecting the other. There were some questions about the blood. The clothes of all aboard were clean of blood, yet the killer, who had chopped three humans to pieces, certainly must have been coated with gore. He had obviously changed his clothes and thrown the incriminating garments into the ocean. As they sat about pondering the killer's identity, Bram suddenly said: "We all here is one." They were a happy family, he added, comrades, friends, united against the sea and the terrible events of that morning. But none of the men were friends; all were strangers, all suspects, and they knew it. Bram had become the congenial mediator of the tragedy on the *Fuller,* telling one and all that "We must not blame the living for the dead. The dead can't speak for themselves."

As early-day crime historian Charles E. Grinnell put it in *The Green Bag,* Bram's conduct was "as if it were not an uncommon thing anywhere to have three murders before breakfast on a week day." Crime writer Edmund Pearson was to later call Bram a "blithe optimist," whose simple plan for solving the dilemma was to "throw the dead overboard, blame everything upon them, and go forward light-heartedly into the future."

Bram later told Monks his theory of the murders. It was all quite prosaic. Blomberg, the brute, tried to rape Mrs. Nash, and was interrupted by her husband. He then slew the Captain and the wife, but in turn was slain, managing somehow to make it back to his cabin bunk to perish. (When Charley Brown later repeated this story in court, it took the judge several minutes to quiet the roaring laughter from the gallery.)

After the bodies were placed in the small boat and covered with canvas, Monks said it would be proper that prayers be read over their grisly cargo. Bram was so excited by the idea that he suggested having music at the prayers; he had the brainstorm of bringing the organ up from the cabin.

"No, that's foolishness," Monks solemnly pronounced. With that he produced the Book of Common Prayer and read in a grave voice the Order at the Burial of the Dead at Sea. Following these services, Monks sat down and wrote a complete account of the murder events, including the absurd theory advanced by Bram. Everyone on board attested to its accuracy by signing it, although the steward hesitated when reading the account, remarking before affixing his signature: "That ain't so. Them people didn't kill themselves—nothing of the kind."

Though the ship was estimated to be only four hundred miles from Bermuda, when asked what course they should take, Mate Bram thought they ought to sail for Cayenne in French Guiana, fully fifteen hundred miles distant. The crew finally agreed to go with the best winds, heading for Halifax, Nova Scotia or St. John's, Newfoundland.

For six days, the *Herbert Fuller* groped for a port, its crew and lone passenger in constant fear of all, thinking that danger was everywhere, for all knew that the berserk killer was aboard the ship, talking among them, eating and drinking with them. He had moved through the ship's quarters with them as they discovered the gruesome murders, and he pretended to be shocked and dismayed by such bestiality. No one slept. Every act was suspicious. When Charley Brown threw overboard a pair of pants he had worn that were smeared with blood, he was manacled in irons and locked in a cabin. He protested, pointing out that he had stained the pants when preparing the bodies in the jolly boat. On that day, the steward, Spencer, remarked to Monks: "The mate killed them people," meaning Bram. He refused to add more. (Later, at the trial, Spencer told the court that he signed the paper with the bogus theory of the murders "because I didn't want them to know that I knew as much as I did; didn't want to be too smart; signed it more for peace than anything else.")

It was Bram who convinced the others that Brown was acting

suspicious. After Brown had been locked up, the first mate said to the passenger: "Now that we have got the murderer, we will tear up the paper that you wrote."

"We don't know that we've got the murderer," Monks replied, "and we won't tear it up. We will keep it."

Each night those on board stayed on deck, afraid to go below where they might also be killed. Shivering in the cold and damp, their sleepless eyes glanced in all directions. As they moved northward, the days were still hot, so much so that the odor from the bodies in the jolly-boat was overwhelming. They lowered the boat and towed it.

Bram took one of the seamen, Wassen, aside, and whispered to him: "If we don't get Brown guilty we will get two years each."

Monks and other seamen were then called by the manacled Brown, who told them he had some startling information. While at the helm on the night of the murders, he had seen the first mate step into the charthouse and chop the Captain to pieces; he had seen it all through the eleven-by-sixteen-inch window directly before the wheel. Brown then stated that he had heard Mrs. Nash scream. Some minutes later he saw Bram come on deck carrying something, probably the bloody axe; he could not be sure because of the gloom of night. Monks and the crew members wasted no time. They found Bram sitting on deck and seized him, chaining him to the mast.

"What is this for?" Bram boomed, his face turning scarlet with rage.

"For killing the Captain," Spencer told him.

"I am innocent, Steward."

The *Herbert Fuller* lumbered into Halifax on July 21, its jolly boat with its pathetic cargo trailing behind. Police and newsmen swarmed over the exhausted crew and Monks, most of whom collapsed into deep sleep only an hour after reaching port. All were eventually removed to Boston where a Grand Jury refused to indict Charley Brown, but did indict the first mate, Thomas Mead Chambers Bram. His trial commenced on December 14, 1896.

One of the first witnesses for the prosecution was a detective from Halifax, Nicholas Power, who had questioned Bram just after everyone had left the ship. "Bram, we are trying to unravel this horrible mystery," he had told the first mate at the time. "Your position is rather an awkward one. I have had Brown in this office and he made a statement that he saw you do the murder."

"He could not have seen me—where was he?" Bram had responded.

"He was at the wheel."

Such answers were almost an admission of guilt. To make sure of Brown's point of observation, the court adjourned to the *Herbert Fuller,* which had been sailed to Boston, and inspected the area, jurors standing behind the wheel and peering toward the small window of the afterhouse at night. With the glow of a single lantern, such as had been used during the night of the murder, it was clear that one could easily see the bunk where the Captain was lying and anyone trying to kill him in that position.

Added to that were the salient points of Bram's suspicious behavior. He had tried to put the murders on a nonexistent mutiny. He had discovered the murder weapon and had gotten rid of it. He had destroyed evidence of his claim of being drugged. He had tried to pin the blame on the murdered second mate. He had then tried to blame Charley Brown. He had tried to destroy the written account Monks had penned and he had signed. He had acted suspicious from the start, hysterical.

More was to be revealed. Spencer took the stand and related how Bram had ranted against the Captain and the second mate to him on the first days of the voyage, even once insinuating that Nash might be killed and that he had told more than one crew member that Laura Nash ought "to be taken care of by a real man."

It was not by whim, the prosecution pointed out, that Mate Bram thought to take the *Herbert Fuller* the long distance to Cayenne. He undoubtedly thought to murder those remaining on board one by one; the lengthy voyage would allow him time enough to perform the killings. There, he would sell the cargo as a pirate, and the ship, too.

Bram's past was disclosed piecemeal. He began work as a youth waiting tables in the Dennett restaurant chain in New York City, cheap eateries that provided an evangelistic atmosphere, murals depicting the fires of hell, waiters scolding with Biblical quotes, religious zealots hectoring the crowds from special platforms. Bram was proved to be emotionally unstable, railing against customers when he was promoted to the night managership of a Dennett restaurant in Boston. When the res-

An unflinching Thomas Mead Chambers Bram, first mate of the Herbert Fuller, *on trial for his life.*

taurant closed, Bram went to sea, where he rose through the ranks to the status of mate, sometimes Captain, on board several ships. A sailor named Nicklas testified that while he was first mate of the ship *White Wings*, Bram, the second mate, approached him and suggested they kill the captain, take the vessel, and sell it and its cargo. Nicklas thought he was kidding, but recalled that Bram offered an alternate plan, saying to him: "If you don't want to kill this particular Captain, let us go on board a Norwegian vessel where they have fewer men before the mast, where they don't talk our language, and where they are laden with coffee. . . . We can give the crew knockout drops . . . and then kill the Captain, and the crew of the vessel will obey our orders."

Bram had gone on to tell Nicklas that when he was the skipper of a ship called *Twilight*, he collected the cargo money and then scuttled the ship, telling the owners that the money sank with the vessel. He also claimed that as captain of another ship, the *China*, he had sold its cargo of coconuts in Belize, pocketing the profits, and then told the owners that the freight had been destroyed by seawater.

Prosecutors then produced a certificate from the American Vice-Consul in Rio stating that Bram had been fired as second mate on the *White Wings*, "on complaint of the Master, R. E. M. Davisson, that he had well-founded suspicions of said Bram having intentions to steal the vessel." The affidavit was dated February 1, 1896, only a few months before Bram signed on as the *Herbert Fuller*'s first mate.

Piratical, untrustworthy, a man who had often before schemed at murder on the high seas, Bram was unconvincing when taking the witness box, his answers all too brief, his face grimly set. Coupled with all the statements of the witnesses regarding his actions, plus the unshakable identification of him as the killer by Brown, Bram was convicted of mass murder on January 2, 1897, after fifty ballots and a twenty-six-hour recess. On the following March 9, Bram was sentenced to be hanged.

Bram's lawyers energetically filed appeals, going to the U.S. Supreme Court, where, because of certain technical errors in the first trial, the verdict was set aside and a new trial ordered. Bram's second trial began on March 16, 1898, and ended the following April 20. Between the two trials, new federal legislation permitted jury members to convict someone of murder but allowing them to qualify their verdict with the words "without capital punishment." This is exactly what the jury recommended in Bram's second conviction. He was sentenced to life imprisonment on July 12, 1898, and removed to the U.S. Atlanta Penitentiary in Atlanta.

There Thomas Mead Chambers Bram would no doubt have died had it not been for the desperation of a hack mystery writer scrounging for material. Mary Roberts Rinehart, hearing of the *Fuller* killings, did some cursory investigation and then produced a fanciful mystery tale entitled *The After House,* in which she put the blame for the murders squarely on hapless Charley Brown, whom she called "Charley Jones," labeling him a homicidal maniac who had murdered the Nash couple and second mate in a moment of unreasoning madness. She stated that her tale, published in 1914, was written in protest against the conviction of Mate Bram. One of her avid readers was ex-President Theodore Roosevelt, who was convinced of her theories. He wrote to authorities, asking that Bram be released. Another ardent reader, President Woodrow Wilson, apparently believed the Rinehart fiction, and, on April 22, 1919, signed a presidential pardon that released the murderous Bram from prison.

By the time he stepped from prison a free man, the ship on which he had once created havoc had perished, a victim of World War I. The *Herbert Fuller,* renamed the *Margaret B. Rouss,* had been torpedoed on May 29, 1917, by a German submarine, sinking forty miles off Monaco.

Bram apparently liked the Atlanta climate so much he decided to settle in the area. He lived out his life as a prosperous broker of a wholesale peanut business. He was always eager to talk about the murders of which he had been convicted and for which he had served over fifteen years in prison (a little more than five years for each victim). He enjoyed his terrible fame, as evidenced by the letter he sent to his counsel upon his release:

> My dear and honorable lawyer:
>
> It gives me indescribable pleasure to inform you that President has this day granted a full and unconditional pardon to your innocent client.
>
> This is the closing chapter of a wonderful case. I am gratefully and respectfully your humble servant.
>
> Thomas M. C. Bram

1898 NEW YORK CITY

The Busy Housekeeper

Not unlike that of many a twentieth-century counterpart, house-work was at the core of Martha Place's seething discontent. Since childhood, Martha had undertaken household chores that mounted into drudgery as her mother plied her with more and more work, changing her from "mother's helper" to "mother's slave." Yet Martha cheerfully labored, even seeking out more work to complete for the edification of her mother.

During the 1880s, Martha worked not only as maid for her mother but took on the full-time position of a seamstress in a local sweatshop. She turned forty without any other major interest in life than work. Then in 1894 she spotted a newspaper ad for a housekeeper and replied, finding insurance executive William Place, a widower with a twelve-year-old daughter.

The girl, having lived long alone with her father, objected to the hiring of Martha, telling her father: "We don't need a house-keeper and besides, it's costly." The eventual cost of hiring Martha was higher than Ida Place and her father could ever have imagined.

William Place prevailed. Martha soon had the Place home in tidy order, serving meals that Place thought a great improvement over his daughter's imaginative cuisine of banana souffles. Released of her own chores, Ida Place began to enjoy the freedom and fun of girls her age. Martha, too, though she labored long in the Place home, felt there was a secure future. This hope became a reality three months later when William Place proposed to her. She accepted without a murmur of hesitation.

It was obvious from the start that William Place had no romantic notions but sought to make Martha's position as a house-keeper more secure through marriage. At first, all went well. Gradually, as Ida grew into young womanhood, a cautious resentment, then simmering dislike, grew between stepdaughter and stepmother. William Place, a taciturn, silent man, did alleviate Martha's workload by hiring another housekeeper, Hilda Palm, who found Martha an exacting taskmaster.

Realizing that connubial bliss was a myth in her life, that she was no more than a figurehead wife, Martha Place became sullen, her anger mounting. She insisted upon absolute silence during mealtimes. Moreover, she resented the freedom enjoyed by Ida and insisted that the girl help Hilda with the heavier chores, snapping at the girl: "She's as good as you are."

Martha's thoughts turned to money. As wife she received no salary and only cursory recognition of her marital status. She vied with daughter Ida over the smallest amounts of allowance William Place bestowed upon his daughter. Such was Martha's rage over her impossible situation that violent headaches sent her reeling to bed, where she munched on Munyon's Headache Pills.

Tradesmen calling at the Place home found Martha a veritable tigress at bargaining. She complained about the price of carrots and meat, shrieking at costermongers that they were crooks, their scales were rigged, their prices exorbitant. They dealt with her in slinking terror.

Cajoling, wheedling, threatening, Martha finally managed to obtain from husband William a meager twenty-dollar-a-week allowance for household expenses. She secretly saved as much from this sum as possible, hoping to purchase someday a small cottage by the seaside where she could stroll with the only love of her life, her dogs. As she drew more and more into herself, her expressions and conduct toward Ida and William stiffened into calculating spite. Her behavior began to embarrass Place and stimulate the nonstop tongues of neighborhood gossips.

On one Sunday afternoon, a sweaty August day, a couple known to Place before his marriage called to have refreshments. Martha, as glorified housekeeper, was expected to serve them. She entered the parlor dressed in a heavy coat and shawl, her feather-bedecked bonnet firmly fixed upon high-piled hair. With a grab, Martha snatched a piece of cake and jammed it into her mouth. As the startled guests stared, she swilled down a huge glass of lemonade, slopping much of it down the front of her dress.

William Place shook his head in disgust and, as a way of apologizing for his wife's odd behavior, told his guests: "This is not Ida's mother, you know."

The outburst of the frustrated woman was thus labeled the tolerated aberrations of an outsider, a social cruelty not beyond the hardheaded Mr. Place. Martha further compounded the embarrassing scene by then filling up her glass several times and walking to the open window, where she poured the lemonade onto the front lawn bushes. "I didn't care about appearances any more," she was later to state.

Martha not only discarded her own efforts at appearances but began to systematically destroy her stepdaughter's wardrobe. Ida found her expensive new bonnet "of almond straw, wide-brimmed, with a wreath of blue cornflowers" shredded next to her bed. Next to the remains of the bonnet, Ida discovered a neat pile of her hosiery and undergarments, which had been missing for some weeks. Here then was a sign, a telltale signal that Martha Place had begun to demonstrate her rage in a physical manner, but in that pre-Freudian era of stoic notions and lamentably stern indifference to matters of the heart and mind, the incident passed with William Place's turgid comment: "She must have another one of her headaches."

In desperation, Martha attempted to salvage her sanity by feverishly trying to inspire her husband to romance, to show some kind of affection, showering him with passionate endearments. His response was to ignore and rebuff her. Martha resigned herself to a loveless life, spitting to her husband: "I'm leaving you. But I want three hundred dollars or I won't go."

"That's too high," the ever-business-minded Place responded. "I'll make it one hundred and fifty dollars."

"That's too low," Martha whimpered, refusing to be bought off for such a paltry amount. The price was also too low to ward off disaster.

A few mornings later, William Place argued with Martha over breakfast, telling her not to persecute his daughter. As he walked to the office, this normally unthinking man stopped in his tracks; he felt some strange apprehension and returned home. There he found Ida in a panic, being chased around heavy tables by a red-faced Martha full of curses and venomous threats. Turning to her husband, Martha screamed: "You'd better keep her out of my sight! I've warned her!"

"Idle threats," muttered William Place. He took his daughter to live with relatives, where she stayed for six weeks. A hateful hiatus set in, with Martha throwing herself at a disgusted spouse who spent most of his time telling her how deeply he missed his daughter. Ida returned and Martha made herself scarce, running off to the theater almost every night, a costly pleasure that began to eat up her small savings.

On February 7, 1898, a Monday morning, Martha and Ida stood by the front door as William Place prepared to leave for his office. "Goodbye," he said tersely to Martha and then leaned forward to kiss Ida.

Martha squinted at her husband; for two days he had adamantly refused to advance her the twenty-dollar household allowance. She had had enough. "I want my money," she said quietly to him. "I'm going downtown. I need it."

"I shall not give you that money," Place said gruffly. "I've said plainly what I mean, and I intend to stand by it this time."

"If you don't give it to me I will make it cost you ten times more" came her hissing retort.

Place ignored her, kissed his daughter, and strolled away. He could not understand the low muttering tumbling from Martha's mouth.

The minute Place was out of sight, Martha turned to Ida: "Did he give you any money?"

The seventeen-year-old snapped: "None of your business!"

"When he gives you money, he won't give me any." Martha advanced on Ida. The girl was certainly a physical match for Martha, not much shorter than Mrs. Place at five-foot-two, and weighing 125 pounds. Yet she retreated under the menacing glare of her stepmother, throwing a cigarette box at Martha and then running up the stairs to her room, shouting: "I'm leaving now, and this time, believe me, I'm never coming back."

What happened next was later related by the maid, Hilda Palm who heard, at 8:15 that morning, the sounds of doors being banged shut and locked, followed by a piercing scream from the top floor, then silence.

A short time later Martha called Hilda to her room on the second floor, handing the maid some bills. "You'll have to leave," Martha told her in a quiet voice, "but here's five dollars above salary for notice."

Hilda noticed that Martha quickly began to pack. She raced downstairs and called a truckman to carry her luggage to the ferry. When the man arrived, Martha changed her mind, sending him away and saying almost to herself that she would take a later ferry.

"Should I do the washing?" Hilda asked her mistress. "Everything is dirty."

"No, leave it alone," Martha replied lamely, then hastened to add: "If anyone rings the bell asking for Ida, say she has gone on downtown. No matter who comes, don't let them in." Seeing the look of concern on the maid's face, Martha confided: "I am leaving my husband, Hilda. He's really hurt me this time, and I can't stand it any more."

A Mrs. McArran, one of Martha's few friends, received a note that day from Mrs. Place through Hilda. The note stated that Martha was departing. "I will make you a present of my rubber plant and bicycle," Mrs. Place had written her. Mrs. McArran's surprise at the hasty departure caused her to immediately visit her friend.

Later that afternoon, she went to the Place home and found Martha lounging in the parlor, seemingly unruffled by her decision to leave her husband. Said Martha in a matter-of-fact voice: "I'm going to live in New Brunswick, Mrs. McArran, dear. I won't need my bike because I'm leaving him at last, I'm glad to say."

"What about Ida?"

"He's boarding her out. She hasn't even been here today."

Mrs. McArran left with thanks for the gifts Martha had bestowed upon her. Other callers rang the Place doorbell that afternoon but none were allowed inside.

When William Place returned home at 6:30 P.M., he was greeted with the pleasant kitchen smell of roast beef. He was moving down the hall toward the kitchen when out of a hall closet burst his Martha with an axe in her hand. With a vicious swipe, she just barely missed Place, whose instincts caused him to duck. The axe was wielded with such force that it lodged in the woodwork. As Martha tugged wildly to free it, William Place ran for the front door. She was faster, freeing the axe and running behind him, swinging, finally striking him in the arm and causing a wicked gash that made Mr. Place's blood spurt onto the carpet. Screaming, the dazed, injured man, leaving a trail of blood behind him, staggered into the street, calling for help.

Police came on the run. William Place was taken to the hospital for mending. Officers barged into the house, looking, at Place's desperate instructions, for his daughter, Ida. They found her in her bedroom, horribly mutilated and quite dead, murdered, it seemed, by one who knew the business of murder.

Ida had been blinded by acid; her eyes had been covered with a towel. She had then been asphyxiated with a pillow. Authorities found the skin about her mouth discolored. Her head, angling toward the foot of the bed, rested on a pillow. She wore only bloomers. The killer had been careful to spread a

Martha Place, a New York housewife who thought to end her marital problems with an axe, circa 1898. (UPI)

sheet that hid only the upper portion of the girl's body. The body was cold and stiff, rigor mortis already in possession. Only a small chair, broken on the floor between two beds, showed signs of a struggle. Ida's clothes were neatly arranged in a pile on one of the beds, Martha's handiwork.

One of the investigating officers sniffed gas. He pointed to an adjacent room. Rushing inside, police found two gas jets turned on. In the middle of the floor, as if hiding like a child, they found Martha Place, bedclothes piled high over her head. She was carried to the parlor below, where officers administered artificial respiration. A police surgeon arrived and helped revive the unconscious woman. She moaned: "I want to die, I want to die."

Martha's first response to police questions was to claim that Ida, "that poor child," had committed suicide over a few harsh words that she, Martha, had leveled at her. So full of regret was she, sobbed Martha, that she decided to join her dear stepdaughter in death and turned on the gas. The police were having none of it, one officer cracking: "And you thought you'd chop up your husband to calm your grief, ma'am?" They took her to the Kings County Jail on Raymond Street and booked her for murder.

Martha swept into her cell with an indignant air. It was all a mistake because of that unstable child. Mrs. Place was entitled to a lawyer, she was told, but if she cared to make a statement first, the police would be most grateful. A statement? Of course, she had nothing to hide.

Martha seated herself on a wooden chair in the detective office and told of seeing her husband off early that morning.

> I told him I was going downtown and would like to have some money. So when he said he would not give me any more I sat down on the front stoop and waited there till he came out. . . . I had a headache and I went upstairs and took off my hat, and read in the parlor. . . . I . . . had been picking up the papers around, and she [Ida] said, "You and Pappa have been having more quarrels." I said, "Yes." She said "I am getting sick and tired of it." I said, "I am sick and tired of it too." She said, "I'm not going to stay here." I said, "Did he give you any money this morning?" She said, "None of your business." I said, "When he gives you money, he won't give me any." She said, "That is nothing to you." And she picked

up a cigarette box out of the basket and threw it at me, and I
went for her, and she jumped up and said, "I am going away.
I won't stay here any longer." And she went upstairs and I
went in the back parlor, and got the water bottle and watered
the rubber plant. After that I went up to my room . . . to make
preparations to go, and while I was doing that I heard Ida
going downstairs. . . .

Ida came upstairs, and went to her room. And I went into
Mr. Place's desk and got a little bottle of salts, about that
large [holding up her fingers to indicate size], not very much
of it. It wasn't half full. I took and put it in a glass, in a goblet
I had in my room. I dumped it out in that, and went to the
bathroom to put water in it, and while there, Ida came upstairs and she went to her room, and after I had fixed the salts
and was just going to take it . . . and I stopped at her door,
and I threw the salts at her, and the door knocked the glass
out of my hand. . . . I went to my room, and I was there a little
while, and I thought I heard her going downstairs, and I
thought she would be going out for the day. . . . Then I . . .
went out in the kitchen, and fed the little dogs we had, and
lit the gas, and put the supper on the table for Mr. Place, and
then went in the cellar, and fixed the furnace fire, and then I
came upstairs, and went to my room, laid down for a few
minutes, as I was tired, busying around so all afternoon.

Yes, the police concluded, it had been a tiring day for Martha,
one so tedious they found it hard to believe that she had enough
strength remaining to try to axe her husband to death when he
arrived home for dinner.

Undaunted by the charges against her, Martha was much
more concerned with what people would think and how she
would appear in court, writing from her cell to her best friend,
Mrs. McArran, asking that she retrieve her wardrobe for her:

The horrible news is circulating. I should prefer death to it.
Through Will's threatening I was driven to desperation, but
enough, I say no more about him. . . . I want a pink wrapper,
and another, black and white, same closet; some waists and
skirts also; in closet of my room, whatever you think best,
bring. I want my winter cloak, colarette, is like the fur on my
cloak. Also little fur cape in same closet, and several things

out there I may need. I want my brown derby or purple one out of closet. Shoes, good pair, black ones, I have nothing but slippers to go out in. Also stockings, underwear, my flannels are downstairs, kitchen closet; skirts, drawers, and other things necessary, etc. . . . Little black cape with fringe on it, satchel in my closet, or grip in garret stairway. Please go at once. . . . I have a right to all that I want. Handkerchiefs, combs, etc. Bring the grip or satchel *full*, all that you can send. . . .

Mattie Place

P.S. I can write and receive letters here.

The appearance of Mrs. Place at her trial was not disappointing. She wore a completely new ensemble for each day as the prosecution firmly established her as a willful, plotting murder-

Mrs. Place (third from left) is led to her execution as the first woman to sit in the electric chair. (UPI)

ess who knew perfectly well that the substance she threw into her stepdaughter's eyes was not salts but acid, which she found in her husband's desk, acid she knew he used in his hobby of photography. She also knew, the prosecutor droned on, that the acid would blind the girl and make her an easier victim to be smothered, that the girl had fainted in pain and was helpless on the floor when Martha kneeled on her and suffocated her with a pillow.

The jury had no other choice than to find Mrs. Place guilty. Her sentence was another matter; in a more enlightened time, she would undoubtedly have been sent to an insane asylum. The judge sentenced her to death in the electric chair, the first woman so condemned in the state of New York. None of her appeals were effective. Reviewing the case, Theodore Roosevelt, then Governor of the state, threw her file down upon his desk in disgust, refusing to commute her sentence to life imprisonment. She would die on schedule, and did, murmuring about money and love as she was led to the chair at 11:05 A.M. on March 20, 1899. For her the distinction of being the first woman to be electrocuted was only more "horrible news" to a busy housekeeper.

1900 NEW YORK CITY
"The Most Wonderful Man in the World"

In keeping with the lamentable concepts of some of this century's prominent lawyers, Albert T. Patrick longed to become a counselor only for the riches the position would let him reap— a desperate lust and a lethal one, as the spectacular events of his life would prove.

Born in the Lone Star State in 1865, Patrick graduated from the University of Texas and then went on to study law, being admitted to the Texas bar in 1890. In his first Texas cases Patrick displayed an unorthodox, if not highly suspect, technique; he wielded his legal talents as a double-edged sword, hacking at the purse-strings of both sides. One of the first cases of his infant practice involved a man named Volk whose wife's affections had been snatched by a railroad official. Patrick handled the alienation suit and won a settlement of $5,000, promptly taking half of the amount as his fee. He then went to Volk's wife, and, at his insidious encouragement, the injured lady sued her frustrated husband. Patrick won a divorce for her in record time.

Shortly afterward, the enterprising Patrick brought charges of barratry against a congressman named Hutcheson and worked for his disbarment. The suit was halted by a judge of the U.S. District Court, who instructed the District Attorney to start disbarment proceedings against Patrick. Packing up his wife and two small daughters while the case was pending, Patrick fled to New York and was quickly admitted to that state's bar in 1892.

Patrick was all front. He and his family appeared to live well. As a stern teetotaler, Patrick gave lectures against Demon Rum before an edified congregation of the fashionable Fifth Avenue Baptist Church. An ardent parishioner of this institution, Patrick was fond of prattling to any casual acquaintance: "I attend John D. Rockefeller's church." He became active in the Y.M.C.A., playing handball and basketball with dexterity at least three nights a week at the West Side Branch. Upstanding citizen though he appeared to be, Patrick's legal conduct was as shoddy as it had been in Houston, Texas.

One of his escapades involved millionaire William H. Moore, president of the Knickerbocker Phosphate Company, against which Moore held notes of $5,500. Moore assigned these notes to Patrick, who collected the money. The millionaire then complained that the lawyer had had no right to obtain this money as the notes had been assigned only on a technicality. Moore sued Patrick to recover the funds. Only days after the elderly Moore began the litigation, he was visited in his suite at the Occidental Hotel by a man unknown to the hotel staff. The millionaire died hours after the visitor left. A physician stated that Moore's death was the result of "debility" and that no suspicion was attached to Moore's demise.

Some claimed that Patrick had brought about the old man's death, but the barrister was not indicted. Patrick's wife suddenly died in 1896, and, after sending his daughters to live with relatives in Austin, Patrick moved into a boardinghouse at 316 West Fifty-eighth Street. While he fielded about for a legal bonanza, fortune flashed a grin in Patrick's direction; another lawyer from Texas, O. T. Holt, knowing of Patrick's unsavory

159

reputation, had an equally unsavory chore for him, one he found too repugnant to handle himself.

Visiting Patrick in his boardinghouse rooms in 1896, Holt unraveled a tale that made Patrick's natural greed whirl in his brain: the story of Texas multimillionaire William Marsh Rice. This stubborn, selfmade man, Holt related, had been born in Springfield, Massachusetts, in 1816, venturing into the frontier of Texas in the 1830s to glean his fortune. Everything Rice touched turned to gold. He became a merchant prince, retailing, exporting and importing merchandise. He bought hotels by the score and these prospered. He dug for oil and it gushed forth. With his millions he bought land, until he possessed city blocks in a half dozen boomtowns, then whole townships, not only in Texas but in Oklahoma, Georgia, and Louisiana. And this vast real estate empire yielded more millions.

Rice had married twice but remained childless. He lived in Dunellen, New Jersey, with his second wife, Elizabeth, dwelling in a pretentious mansion peopled with liveried servants, an image befitting his wealth, or so thought his Wisconsin-born wife. But upon her death in July 1896, the normally retiring Rice moved to New York, taking a spartan suite of rooms in the Berkshire Apartments at 500 Madison Avenue. By then he had given up the manners of the rich, dispensing with catered meals and groveling servants, his only companion being a personable youth named Charles F. Jones.

Rice had met Jones on a visit to the Capitol Hotel in Houston, an inn he owned. The twenty-three-year-old Jones, then employed at the Capitol as a storekeeper, ingratiated himself with Rice who hired him as his personal secretary, for he possessed some skill at penmanship and at the typewriter. Jones also served as valet, pressing Rice's suits and polishing his shoes. When the multimillionaire departed for New York in May 1897, he took Jones with him.

Rice gave the youth a spacious room in his Berkshire suite and made of him his sole confidant. Rice and Jones seldom went out, dining in the drab decor of the suite on meals of bouillon and bread sent over from the Woman's Exchange, located down the street. The diet, whether or not it was to Jones' liking, was of Rice's design; the old man explained that he suffered from dyspepsia and the bread and soup (sometimes supplemented with fresh eggs, which Rice ordered from a

A portrait of William Marsh Rice, which currently hangs in the Rice Institute's administration building.

farmer from his former town of Dunellen) were all he could stomach.

Jones always accompanied the old man in his infrequent jaunts about the city, strolls that left the young man apologizing to and pacifying indignant fruit peddlers who became the objects of Rice's parsimonious behavior. It was the old man's custom to approach a fruit stand, select an apple and bite into it before paying. If the taste was not to his liking, he adamantly refused to fork over the expected two pennies.

In addition to faithful companion, Jones served as unofficial business manager to the elderly millionaire, wholly in charge of the Rices' bankbooks, checking accounts and considerable paper holdings. In fact, as the *New York World* was later to report, Rice had "so many stocks and bonds that he had to get someone to help him cut the coupons," which was also one of Jones' tasks. Dutifully, Jones made collections for the old man and placed bank deposits. He wrote out all checks for Rice's signature. The only other visitor to the Rice apartment was a cleaning lady, who appeared three or four times a week.

One night, as the two men sat sipping their bouillon, Rice started blurting out invective over the actions of his late second wife, telling Jones how Elizabeth, before her death, had betrayed him. The second Mrs. Rice had left a will that dispensed many of Rice's millions to her own relatives under the "community law" of Texas, a law that states that husband and wife are equal partners and owners of all property, even though it be only in the name of the husband. This was unthinkable to Rice, who stubbornly maintained he was a resident of New York, not Texas, and therefore not liable for any such whimsical settlements bestowed by the late Elizabeth Rice. To that end, Rice had instituted a federal suit in Galveston against O. T. Holt, executor of Mrs. Rice's will, seeking to have Elizabeth's will declared void.

Such meddlesome gestures from the grave interfered with the millionaire's own dream, the establishment of "The Rice Institute," a not-for-profit educational corporation for the advancement of literature, art and science, to be located on Rice-owned property in Houston. The old man had, shortly before his wife's death, made up his own will, which left fifteen-sixteenths of his estate for such an institution, and the remainder to his own relatives.

This was the fight lawyer Holt faced in 1899 when he sought out the aid of Patrick. He preferred that Patrick "do the dirty work," offering the shady lawyer a small week-to-week retainer to dig up evidence that would prove Rice to be a resident of Texas, which would uphold Mrs. Rice's extraordinary will. Patrick instantly saw himself brushing once more against millions. He accepted Holt's offer with alacrity and went about the "dirty business" with a vengeance.

Patrick settled down to a long legal hassle, busying himself with taking depositions from all who knew old man Rice in his attempt to prove the millionaire's Texas residency. In the process he learned much about the magnate's sources of wealth. In November 1899, making sure Rice would not notice his presence, Patrick called briefly at the Berkshire apartment, telling Jones that his name was Smith and that he was a cotton buyer and a friend of the millionaire. He left abruptly but returned inside of a week, asking to see Mr. Rice.

"Ah, Mr. Smith," Jones said, remembering him and showing him into the living room. "I'm sorry, but Mr. Rice is not available; he is preparing to go to bed." Patrick heard a dull bumping sound from the old man's bedroom. Jones explained that his master had a peculiar habit before retiring. For exactly two-and-a-half hours Mr. Rice, as a form of self-conceived exercise, would wrap his scrawny, naked body in a single blanket and roll furiously about his bedroom floor. Then, sweating mightily, he would hurl himself into the bed and await slumber.

While old man Rice was going through his nightly contortions, Patrick eyed the gullible Jones and decided to risk all. He told the valet-companion that he had nothing to do with cotton, that he represented the Holt forces in Mrs. Rice's much-debated will, and that his real name was Albert T. Patrick, a man Rice had never seen but one he had heard of and hated, knowing that Patrick had been gathering evidence to disprove his New York citizenship.

Patrick came to the point. If Jones would write a letter on Rice's stationery in which Rice admitted his Texas residency, Patrick would somehow manage to have it signed by the old man. (The lawyer had already obtained copies of Rice's signatures and had spent months forging his name.) For such a service, Patrick offered Jones $250. The secretary went to a typewriter and tapped out the letter, but Patrick hedged at giving him the money. Apparently, Jones was not that much of a fool. "No money," he said, slipping the typescript into a drawer, "no letter."

Patrick rubbed the short-cropped, thinning red hair on his massive head and scratched his stubby beard. He studied the valet-secretary with deep-set, piercing eyes for a moment. "What does old man Rice pay you, Jones?"

"Fifty-five dollars a month," the youth replied, "and all expenses."

"You ought to have double that amount."

"I agree," Jones replied without hesitation.

"See here, if you go into a little deal of mine you'll have it, and much, much more."

Jones was eager to hear of the deal. Patrick then produced a draft of a will of William Marsh Rice, one he unabashedly admitted was of his own making. In the will, Rice left half of all his holdings to Albert T. Patrick, who was named its executor; the balance was to be left to relatives, and only a small portion to the proposed Rice Institute.

"I want you to type this on Mr. Rice's typewriter and using his stationery," ordered Patrick. "I'll make sure it's witnessed and signed."

They talked price; Jones was to receive a fortune for this, as well as "going on the witness stand" to prove the bogus will legitimate if it came to a court action following Rice's death; it was mutually assumed that the old man had not long to live, whether his demise be in the natural course or resulting "from an accident."

The murder plot was thus hatched, but the plotting pair had much work to do before they helped Rice into eternity. For months Patrick appeared each Thursday night at the Rice apartment, conferring with Jones and taking away with him great volumes of correspondence, files and canceled checks bearing Rice's signature. The lawyer diligently labored at perfecting his forgeries. The old man, who had never met Patrick, once stepped into the living room as the two men sat conspiring against him, apologizing for the interruption before he withdrew. He later asked Jones who his "handsome bald-headed" visitor was, to which the valet replied with a shrug, "just an old friend of mine." No doubt, had the old man known that Patrick, his avowed enemy, was lounging about under his roof, he might have hastened his own end through an apoplectic stroke.

To add to their "foolproof" plan, a physician, designated to

The gullible co-killer of William Rice, Charles F. Jones.

163

attend to the old man, was introduced by Patrick. In March 1900, Jones was taken ill and the lawyer sent Dr. Walter Curry to him. Dr. Curry prescribed for Jones and, at the secretary's urging, was later presented to Rice, who liked him so much he made Curry his own doctor. Thus, Dr. Curry believed Patrick to be in Rice's confidence.

A new will was drawn up on June 30, 1900, by Patrick. At the bottom of this will he listed Morris Meyers and David L. Short as witnesses. These gentlemen both worked in Patrick's office in minor capacities, but when Jones introduced them to Rice, he passed Short off as a commissioner of deeds for the State of Texas and Meyers as his friend; both impersonators insisted that they were sympathetic to the old man's battle with Holt. They were merely more "plants" who could be seen in Rice's company and later be known as Patrick's employees, thereby cementing the idea of Patrick's close ties to the multimillion-aire.

As August began to make Manhattan swelter, Patrick visited Jones once more on a Thursday night, sitting in the living room of the Berkshire apartment, sipping tepid tea. He slowly nodded in the direction of the old man's bedroom, and then asked: "How is Mr. Rice's health?"

"Oh, he is better than he was."

"Don't you think Rice is living too long for our interest?"

"It does seem that way," Jones said in a calm voice.

Then, in a hushed tone, Patrick leaned forward and said: "You let me in some night and I will put him out of the way."

Jones reacted to that remark as if contemplating a grocery list. "If anything like that is to be done, Dr. Curry should do it, I would think."

"Dr. Curry!" Patrick was on his feet, glaring down angrily at his junior partner in murder. "He wouldn't do a thing of that kind!" The lawyer composed himself and sat down. "Let's discuss this problem. There must be some simple measure we can take."

Anxious to contribute, Jones volunteered an idea: "I read an article in a magazine recently, about chloroform and how it acts."

"Do you know of a place to obtain chloroform?" inquired Patrick.

"I think from the nurses at the Presbyterian Hospital." (Jones had recently been a patient there.)

"A good idea. Get the chloroform."

"Maybe," suggested Jones, "it would be better if you got it."

"No, no. That's a poor idea."

"Why?"

"It would excite suspicion. You get it."

The youth agreed to obtain the chloroform, but he undoubtedly realized that such a move would bring *him* under suspicion. Without informing Patrick, the valet sent five dollars to his brother in Texas, and some days later received a four-ounce bottle of chloroform sent express in a wooden box.

To make sure of the drug's use, Jones boldly asked Dr. Curry on one of his routine visits to Rice what effects chloroform might have on humans—especially whether its effects could be detected following death. Dr. Curry, thinking the question academic, told Jones that such detection would be difficult. The valet lost no time in informing Patrick about Dr. Curry's reassuring remark.

Moreover, the pair decided to also use laudanum. Jones again wrote to his brother and shortly received a one-ounce bottle of laudanum and another two-ounce bottle of chloroform. Patrick was taking no chances, telling his disciple to obtain some mercury "to break the old man down." When ill, Jones had taken some mercury tablets ordered for him by Dr. Curry. He had this prescription refilled and began giving two tablets each day to Rice as a dietary supplement. This caused the old man extreme diarrhea.

One of Rice's friends, a Mrs. Van Alstyne, visited him on September 14. Hearing of the old man's problem, she recommended he eat bananas. Rice sent Jones out for a dozen and a half. The old man later baked five bananas and wolfed them down. He ate four more raw and then became so sick he was bedridden. Jones gave him four mercury tablets "to clear him," and these provided some relief.

When Patrick heard of this he became enraged, shouting at Jones: "It was silly to have given him the mercury pills! Idiot! If he had been left alone he might have died of eating the bananas!"

Rice's condition was by no means stable. He seemed unsure of foot and went into crying jags when old friends called on him. Jones was surprised one afternoon to find the old man "pulling the furniture around. . . . He didn't seem to know what he was doing."

An event in Texas suddenly interrupted the pair's slow killing process. One Sunday, September 16, 1900, the Merchants and Planters Oil Company of Houston, 75 percent of which was owned by Rice, was utterly devastated by a raging inferno. Lacking rebuilding funds, company officials notified Rice of their need for a quarter of a million dollars. The old man agreed to send the money. When Jones heard of this he immediately called Patrick, who had had a new phone, then quite a novelty, installed in his boardinghouse room for just such emergencies. "If the old man sends those funds, he will deplete his New York bank accounts. The amount of two hundred fifty thousand dollars is all he has on hand here."

"But he's got millions," said Patrick.

"And I have the bankbooks in my hand. That's all he has here. Most of it is in Texas."

"We've got to move fast," said Patrick through gritted teeth. The anxious lawyer knew that if the funds were paid to the Texas firm, he and Jones would be left without the necessary operating capital to complete their swindle-and-murder plot. It was decided to give the old man oxalic acid mixed with alum to finish him off. On Sunday afternoon, September 23, Jones prepared this vile brew and gave it to his employer, telling him: "This should pep you up."

The bedridden man took one swallow and spat it out. "That's awful!" roared Rice as he waved the nervous Jones from his room.

Early that evening Jones met with Patrick at Seventh Avenue and Fifty-sixth Street. He was shaking with fear. Patrick soothed him. "Now, Jones. Everything is going along fine so far. You'll simply have to put the old man out of the way tonight."

"But you said you would—"

"I am a man of family and I can't afford to do this that I have said I would do. You will have to administer the chloroform."

"You went back on your word. I won't do it."

"Of course you will, Jones. There's no choice. Those drafts from Texas will be paid tomorrow if you don't and all the money the old man has in the bank will be lost to us."

"I don't think I can do it alone."

"Nothing to it, my boy. Now listen to me. I will tell you what to do in detail . . ."

Some minutes later Jones was back at the Berkshire apartment. Rice was sleeping soundly. The valet took a sponge and soaked it thoroughly with chloroform. He next made a cone from a towel, placing the sponge at the small end of the cone. He tested Patrick's homemade device by placing it for a few seconds over his own face and "got a very strong effect from it." Regaining his senses, Jones poured more chloroform on the sponge and then tiptoed once more into Rice's room. He paused only a few seconds to view the sleeping multimillionaire. Then, with a firm hand, he placed the makeshift cone over Rice's nose and mouth. Remembering Patrick's warning to stay out of the old man's room for at least thirty minutes, Jones ran from the room. He sat in the living room staring at the mantle clock, watching the seconds tick off. The doorbell began to ring and Jones jumped in alarm. He crept up to the front door of the apartment and squinted through a small viewing hole to see two old ladies, dowager friends of Rice's, standing impatiently in the hall. (These untimely visitors later proved to be Mrs. Martha E. Thompson and a Mrs. Moody, old friends of Rice's from Galveston, Texas.) Jones backed away from the door in terror. The women kept ringing the doorbell. The sound drove the valet near mad. He trembled, his eyes darting from the clock to Rice's bedroom door. After twenty terrible minutes, the ringing ceased. Jones collapsed in an exhausted sweat on the couch.

At the end of thirty minutes Jones walked slowly into Rice's bedroom and removed the cone. He saw instantly that the old man was dead. Following Patrick's instructions, Jones carried the towel with the sponge still in it to the kitchen, where he removed a lid on the range. He crammed the murder weapon into it, ignited it with a match and watched it burn to ashes. He then went to the phone and called Patrick, telling him in their prearranged code, "Mr. Rice is very ill," meaning that he was dead.

"Call Dr. Curry. Tell him you think the old man has passed on."

Jones called the doctor, who arrived twenty minutes later. Patrick was with him, entering with a wink to Jones. Both men proceeded into Rice's bedroom where Dr. Curry officially pronounced him dead, making out the death certificate and listing the causes as "old age, weak heart and collacratal diarrhea with mental worry." Dr. Curry had been carefully hoodwinked into believing that, since Patrick had recommended him to Jones, the enterprising lawyer was, indeed, Rice's faithful legal servant and confidant. Patrick had told Curry for months that he was in charge of all of Rice's legal affairs; Jones had confirmed such status with each visit of Dr. Curry to the Rice household. He had no reason to doubt the facts cleverly woven by Patrick, who, for the first time in his life, was really meeting Rice face to face as he took charge next to his victim's deathbed. He was ready for the next stage of his plan.

Patrick immediately called Charles Plowright, an undertaker he had cultivated for this moment. Patrick had often told Plowright in the past that he was Rice's attorney, and that upon the old man's death, Plowright would have the honor of burying the millionaire, as well as a handsome fee. Plowright appeared at the Rice apartment a little after nine in the evening on September 23.

"Plowright," intoned Patrick in his most authoritative voice, "I want you to take charge of the remains of Mr. Rice. He is to be cremated and not embalmed. I would like to have the body cremated as soon as possible."

"But it will take at least twenty-four hours to prepare the crematory. Mr. Rice wanted this done?"

With an assuring flourish, Patrick withdrew a letter from his pocket—a forgery, replete with Rice's known grammatical errors, he had prepared long in advance for just this purpose. It read:

New York, Aug. 3, 1900

Albert T. Patrick, Esq.
No. 277 Broadway, City.

Dear Sir: —

Concerning the matter of cremation. I sent down to the United States Crematory Office for information and got two circulars which are very interesting. I will show them to you when you come up. Ever since Col. Robert Ingasoll and Col. Waring were cremated, I have thought that I should like to be cremated also.

Col. Ingasoll was a very smart man, and a man of great judgement about all things which is possible for a man to know, but about religion a man cannot know. Ingersoll may be right or he may be wrong that is all guess work.

Col. Waring was a great sanitary man, and it seems to me

that the law should not allow dead bodies to be buried all over the Country, after dying of all kinds of deseases. I would much rather have my body burned than eat by worms or stolen by some medical student and carved to pieces. If I should die I want you to see that I am not embalmed as they fill you with chemicals when they embalm you, but I want you to have my body cremated at once and my ashes put in an urn and interred with my late wife Elizabeth B. Rice. As to funerals I do not think my relatives would care to come to mine and I see no use having one until my ashes are interred with my wife.

I write these things because I happen to think of them although told me to give you written directions some time ago. But I expect to live twenty years, as I came of a long lived family and am in pretty good health for a man of my age.

Yours truly,
W. M. Rice

After studying the letter, Plowright repeated the reasons for the delay in the cremation.

Patrick told him to hold onto Rice's letter and show it to the officials at the crematory the next day. He then asked: "What do you suggest we do with the body?"

"It should be embalmed before it is cremated," Plowright said.

"Go ahead," ordered Patrick, ignoring the directives of his own forgery.

Plowright removed Rice's body to his mortuary, where John S. Potter, his embalmer, prepared the old man for burial. Dr. Curry left. Patrick and Jones immediately adjourned to the old man's office where Patrick took several hours to examine everything on hand—files and valuables. He stuffed a valise with documents and then pocketed $450 in currency, $9 in silver, and two watches belonging to Rice.

"It's been a long and tiring day, my boy," Patrick told Jones, paternally placing his hand on the valet's shoulder. "Get some rest. I shall return early in the morning."

Jones obediently went to bed after Patrick left. He slept soundly.

It was eight o'clock when Patrick returned the next morning. He went immediately into Rice's study with Jones, sat down at the desk, and brought forth six checks signed "W. M. Rice." He handed these forgeries to Jones. "Check these."

Jones scrutinized the signatures. "Two of these aren't very good."

Patrick then dictated to Jones what should be filled in on the four remaining checks. Two were drawn on the banking firm of S. M. Swenson & Sons on Wall Street, one for $25,000, another for $65,000; two more were drawn on the Fifth Avenue Trust Company, one for $25,000, the other for $135,000. These amounts, as Patrick and Jones had carefully calculated from Rice's bank records, represented all the cash the multimillionaire had on hand in New York banks. Jones made all four checks payable to Patrick. The lawyer stood over him as he wrote them out in a nervous manner. Pocketing the checks, Patrick departed, saying that he would be in touch as soon as the checks cleared.

It was eleven o'clock on the morning of September 24 when David L. Short, Patrick's associate, appeared at Swenson & Sons, presenting a check for $25,000 drawn on Rice's account to teller John H. Wallace. The teller examined the check, noting that it was made out to one *Abert* T. Patrick and endorsed by *Albert* T. Patrick. Instead of certifying the check, Wallace took the check to another clerk, Walter O. Weatherbee, who also carefully examined it. Weatherbee, along with another of the bank's clerks, William F. Harmon, had long dealt with the Rice account, both having signed the old man's 1896 will as witnesses. He, too, noticed the discrepancy of the missing *l* in the name of the payee. Wallace returned the check to Short, telling him in his crisp banker's voice: "We require another endorsement in accordance with the name on the face of the check. Thank you."

Short walked away without a word. He was back inside of twenty minutes. The check now bore a second endorsement, *Abert* T. Patrick. The check was this time taken to Eric Swenson, a member of the firm. Not only did Swenson think the name of the payee and different endorsements on the check peculiar, but, after comparing Rice's signature with those in his own records, Swenson had serious doubts about the signature on the check. He called Rice's home.

Jones answered. His response to Swenson was to blurt: "That check is all right." He then hung up. Swenson had the check certified, but before he returned the check to the waiting Short, he shook his head slowly, suspiciously. No, he would not guarantee the authenticity of this check. He drew two lines through the certification stamp.

While the banker was reaching his plodding decision, Jones called Patrick, explaining that in his nervous state, he must have omitted the *l* in his name when making out the checks earlier that morning. "What'll I do if they call again?"

Patrick thought for a moment. "The checks are dated September 22, the day before *you* took care of the old man. It's all right. Just tell them he has passed on."

Minutes later Swenson was again on the line, demanding to speak to Rice.

"He can't come to the phone."

"Why not?" Swenson wanted to know.

"Because he's dead. He died last night."

Swenson returned the check to Short, telling the emissary that his bank could not honor the check. Short left without a word of protest.

A little after noon, Albert T. Patrick, all smiles and full of bright cheer, strode into the bank and asked for Swenson. He was shown to the banker's office where he offered his legal credentials and once again presented the check for $25,000, apologizing for the fact that he had been unable to endorse the check in person.

Swenson, wary of the man before him, could not be budged. "I'm a bit amazed," he said, "that you as an attorney should expect us to certify Mr. Rice's check after his death."

"Ah, but the check was made out before Mr. Rice passed on," Patrick said matter-of-factly. He then presented another check for $65,000 drawn on the same bank.

"These amounts represent every dime Mr. Rice had with us." Swenson decided to be as cagey as Patrick. "It is my decision to hold the property of the late Mr. Rice until hearing from the administrator of his estate."

Patrick's broad smile never weakened. "There will be no administration of property in New York. Mr. Rice has assigned it all to me."

"To you?"

"Yes. And, of course, I very much respect Swenson & Sons, a trustworthy, old-line firm, and would be much disposed to keeping my account here."

"Nice of you."

"Perhaps you would care to attend Mr. Rice's funeral, Mr. Swenson," Patrick said in a solicitous manner. "He is to be cremated immediately."

"Cremated?"

"Yes. You know the old man was a crank on the subject of cremation."

"No, I didn't know anything of the kind."

"Well, he was."

Swenson studied the handsome bald-headed man before him and then said: "What did he die of?"

"Bananas."

"What!"

"Yes," said Patrick without a glimmer of the humor he certainly must have felt in his own statement. "Baked bananas. You know Mrs. Van Alstyne, don't you?"

"I do."

"Well, old Mr. Rice had indigestion, and Mrs. Van Alstyne advised him to eat baked bananas. She said they agreed with her perfectly. He got nine of them and ate them, and I believe that is what killed him."

Again Patrick pushed to have Swenson certify both checks in his possession, but the banker was disinclined to do so. Patrick diplomatically backed away from his demands, telling the banker they could handle it all later, following the burial of Rice. He had many pressing matters to attend to, said Patrick. He was gone, scurrying from the bank with friendly waves and broad smiles.

The lawyer rang up Jones. "Get those telegrams off exactly as I have worded them for you," he barked.

Jones sent out telegrams to Rice's only brother, two sisters, and nephews and nieces, along with one to Captain Baker, Rice's Texas lawyer. They were as follows:

MR. RICE DIED EIGHT O'CLOCK LAST NIGHT UNDER CARE OF
PHYSICIANS. DEATH CERTIFICATE: OLD AGE, WEAK HEART,
DELIRIUM. LEFT INSTRUCTIONS TO BE INTERRED IN
MILWAUKEE WITH HIS WIFE. FUNERAL 10 A.M. TOMORROW
AT 500 MADISON AVENUE.

Then came the first real opposition to the spidery plot of Patrick and Jones. Baker, a shrewd attorney, wasted no time, replying by wire within an hour:

PLEASE MAKE NO DISPOSITION OF RICE'S REMAINS UNTIL WE ARRIVE. WE LEAVE TONIGHT, ARRIVE NEW YORK THURSDAY MORNING.

"The Most Wonderful Man in the World"

Suspicions aroused Eric Swenson to action, too. Minutes after the strange-talking Patrick left his office, he called his lawyers, Bowers & Sands, asking them to look into the Rice matter. They, in turn, asked their best counsel, James W. Gerard, to take charge. (Gerard was later to become celebrated as Ambassador to Germany just before the outbreak of World War I.) Gerard contacted the New York Detective Bureau and investigators soon began to move in on the conspirators.

Patrick's careful plan was beginning to come apart. He had to postpone the old man's funeral after receiving the unexpected response from Baker in Texas. The banks were balking at his forged checks (the Fifth Avenue Trust Company had certified, but not cashed, the two checks drawn on its Rice account). Jones had called him to tell him that city detectives were snooping around the apartment. Then, late that Monday night, a man named Gerard and a detective introduced by Gerard as a fellow lawyer appeared at Patrick's boardinghouse. Gerard was investigating Rice's extraordinary death on behalf of Swenson's, he said.

Patrick invited his visitors to sit down. He then affably launched into a speech: "I may as well tell you, in the first place, that I have a will in my possession in which I am executor, and I also have an assignment of all of Mr. Rice's property of every kind. I expect to have the settlement of the estate in my hands. I intend to leave that with Swenson & Sons, and I hope we will have very pleasant relations. I hope there will not be any friction whatever between us. As far as these checks go, why, I have arranged to get the money from another source, and I shall leave everything at present at Swenson's. Nothing will be disturbed there."

"What is the use of having an assignment and a will, too?" asked the detective.

"That," Patrick replied through a confidential smile, "is a secret."

What tremulous moments Patrick spent after the two men left can only be imagined. The steely plotter, however, was beginning to make mistakes. He went to his office the next day and tore up a great many documents and letters belonging to Rice.

173

He attempted to dispose of these by flushing them down his office toilet. His efforts proved useless: the pipes became clogged, and he had to call in the janitor—who looked over some of the soggy documents. Witnesses were sprouting.

Next, thanks to Captain Baker's wire, Patrick felt compelled to call Plowright, the undertaker, and cancel the cremation, ordering a regular service on Thursday.

Before the services commenced, Captain Baker arrived from Texas, meeting Patrick in Rice's Berkshire apartment. Patrick still acted as if he were in complete control of the situation, greeting the Texas lawyer with: "Well, Captain Baker, I suppose you are surprised to find me in charge."

Said Baker: "I certainly am!"

Patrick then explained that he had known Rice for some time; that he had met Rice while working for Holt, and Rice had taken a liking to him; that Rice had "lost confidence" in Baker. "To be frank with you," Patrick said, ending his self-aggrandizing refrain, "the old man became, as it were, stuck on me. He thought I was the most wonderful man in the world."

Accompanying Patrick to his home, Baker was shown the forged copy of Rice's 1900 will. Patrick's audacity and nerve still hadn't quite fled. He was banking on the acceptance of this will by Rice's relatives, who would stand to inherit much more than the magnate had decreed in his 1896 testament, Patrick's theory being that "every man has his price." (He had once told Jones that "I can buy any man in Houston, Texas, for five thousand dollars.") The greed of Rice's relatives, Patrick was positive, would make them insist to one and all that the fake 1900 will was genuine.

Baker, upon reading the will, exploded: "In view of your antagonistic and hostile relation to Mr. Rice, if you expect this will and this assignment to hold in any court in Christendom, why did you not have some friend of Mr. Rice—the Swensons, for instance, who had known him for thirty years—or some other good people in New York who knew you and Mr. Rice, go with you to Mr. Rice's apartment and in their presence offer this will and this assignment, and tell those witnesses in the presence of Mr. Rice that this was his act? Why didn't you do that?"

Patrick's response to this record-long question was anemic. "I expect I ought to have done that. But Mr. Rice, as you know, was peculiar, and he insisted always that our relations should be secret. As far as I know, not anyone, no living man, ever saw me in the presence of Mr. Rice—unless it was C. F. Jones. And I don't know if he ever saw me with him."

When asked why he had attempted to cash checks that would entirely deplete Rice's New York bank accounts, Patrick was ready. "To pay off his poor dead wife's relatives, of course."

That afternoon Patrick played his trump cards, all against the greed of Rice's relatives. He moved about the funeral home, greeting those in attendance, calling them by name and uttering in happy confidence his intention, as sole executor of the 1900 will, to bestow fortunes upon them, wealth they would not have inherited under Rice's 1896 will. "How are you," he would say to one, "Mr. Rice has bequeathed you forty thousand dollars . . . and another ten thousand for your infant sons . . . each." In his spread-the-wealth display, Patrick even included Rice's cleaning lady and the elevator operator of the Berkshire, promising them thousands.

By that time, Patrick had turned over his bogus checks to Baker and, after authorities studied them, both Patrick and Jones were arrested for forgery.

"I'm shocked, gentlemen," a confused Patrick said to officers taking him and Jones away to the Tombs. "If these checks are forgeries, I cannot conceive that they are so."

Once inside a Tombs prison cell, Patrick turned to his young accomplice, the willing Jones. "It's over, boy," he said sadly.

"What can we do?"

"I suggest that *you* commit suicide," Patrick advised. The lawyer handed the youth a small vial of oxalic acid and a penknife, which had been secreted on his person. By then thorough autopsies had been performed upon Rice's remains. Several doctors performed the operation, including the renowned Dr. Rudolph Witthaus, the man who had discovered the intricate poisons in such famous cases as Carlyle Harris, Doctor Buckanan, and Roland Molineaux. The congestion of Rice's lungs indicated the use of an irritant gas or vapor, most probably chloroform, said Witthaus. It was then a murder charge Patrick and Jones faced.

Jones refused to face it. After giving contradictory statements to the Assistant District Attorney, he used Patrick's penknife in an awkward attempt to cut his throat. He was dragged by guards from his cell and patched up. He then confessed the entire plot in detail. Patrick denied all.

Albert T. Patrick (right, in custody), the scheming lawyer who planned the meticulous murder of multimillionaire William Marsh Rice. (UPI)

175

The state offered to drop its charge against Jones if he supplied evidence, which he agreed to do. He was in for a long wait. Lawyer Patrick, directing his own defense and pleading "Not Guilty" in a loud, commanding voice when indicted, managed to stall the beginning of his trial for murder until January 22, 1902, sixteen months after Rice had been killed at his orders.

All was not lost for the conniving Patrick. He was not the only member of his family who "had a fad for millions," as the *New York World* described him. Both his sisters had married wealthy men. One of these brothers-in-law, millionaire John T. Milliken, a St. Louis chemist and mine-owner, completely believed in Patrick's innocence and threw his fortune behind his defense.

Said crime reporter Arthur Train, writing in *The American Magazine* during the case's heyday: "Technically, the case against Patrick was not a strong one. Dramatically, it was overwhelming."

The trial staggered forward for nine weeks, swelling court files by three thousand pages. Jones' testimony was the prosecutor's greatest strength. He admitted that he had killed the old man, but at Patrick's command; the lawyer had planned everything and he had been totally under his sway. Without much debate, the jury, on March 26, 1902, found Patrick guilty of murder. The great New York jurist John William Goff (later a State Supreme Court Justice) sentenced the crafty lawyer to death in the electric chair the following April 7.

Jones was set free and returned to Texas where he disappeared. His convicted partner, Patrick, had no intention of giving up. With his brother-in-law's millions backing him, he made one appeal after another through 1905, all being turned down. Again Patrick was sentenced to die, the new date being January 22, 1906. Milliken's money went to work. Many believed the millionaire bought the state legislature, which voted to grant Patrick a new trial—a move vetoed by the governor. Following a denial of Patrick's last appeal before the U.S. Supreme Court, Governor Higgins commuted the killer's sentence to life imprisonment, stating that there had been technical errors in Patrick's trial.

"I am either innocent or I am guilty," boomed Patrick from his cell in Sing Sing. "I refuse to accept Governor Higgins' commutation of my sentence. I believe that to a certain extent its acceptance by me would be an admission of my guilt. I propose to continue my fight for freedom."

The commutation, said the *New York Tribune,* was a scandal. Crime writer Edmund Pearson remarked: "Now that Patrick's life had been saved, there would be demands for his release. If he got out, he would be invaluable as a counselor to tell murderers how to escape."

Patrick went on battling for his complete exoneration; Milliken prepared to spend his entire fortune to free him. The lawyer's next move was a spectacular one that caused his name to be emblazoned in headlines again in December 1909. It was Patrick's loud claim that the New York Court of Appeals had on one hand affirmed his conviction and on the other ordered a stay of execution. The stay, therefore, was void, insisted Patrick, and it was a logical presumption, by virtue of this order, that he was "legally dead." His continued confinement as a nonexistent person, Patrick argued, was illegal.

So taken aback with this stance were officials that Patrick was allowed to leave prison for Brooklyn and argue his own case in the Appellate Division of the Supreme Court, which promptly denied his claim.

The celebrated prisoner went back to the limbo of Sing Sing, but in 1912 he again made headlines with the mighty help of Governor John A. Dix, who astonished almost everyone in the state of New York by granting Patrick an unconditional pardon on November 28, 1912, as a last gesture before leaving office. To startled newsmen Dix lamely explained that "there has always been an air of mystery about the case." When badgered by the press, Dix stated that "in 1910 the Medico-Legal Society of New York had published a brochure of their 'researches' and had concluded that the condition of Rice's lungs as found on post-morten could not have been caused by chloroform."

Author Francis X. Busch later wrote that "there was a storm of protest and more than vague hints of corruption which had reached into high places" over Patrick's release. The hints were explicit. The *New York Sun* exposed the Medico-Legal Society as being backed "by the never-ceasing efforts of John T. Milliken of St. Louis, who married Patrick's sister." Further, Milliken had met with Dix at a banker's convention two years before Patrick's pardon, making the following offer to the Governor: "I will deposit one hundred thousand dollars in any financial institution in New York City which may be chosen, and I will forfeit that sum to charity, if within a year after his release Albert T. Patrick does not absolutely prove his innocence."

Newspapers, criminal lawyers, professionals in the field of law enforcement condemned Dix's outrageous actions. Frederick B. Crossley, writing in the *Journal of Criminal Law*, summed up the universal attitude regarding the pardon, calling it "one of the most striking abuses of executive clemency in recent times, and an example to the entire country of the failure of the law to work justice."

Patrick, smug and haughty as ever, walked from Sing Sing a free man, first going to St. Louis and then disappearing into the Southwest where he practiced law briefly before dying. He never proved his innocence, and Milliken obviously "forfeited" his money, although it is doubtful it was ever paid.

It undoubtedly pressed upon Patrick's mind to the end of his days that the very core of his planned escape never materialized; the heirs of William Marsh Rice did not rush to his defense to uphold his phony 1900 will by which they stood to more handsomely profit than by the will of 1896, which gave them a pittance. They knew full well of the old man's dream for the Rice Institute, approved of it, even admired him for dreaming it, even though the establishment of such an academy meant they would do without.

It stands today in Houston, a marvelous campus of stunning Romanesque buildings through which hundreds of tuition-free students move to classes in philosophy, architecture, literature and engineering. The figure of the white-bearded old man towers as a bronze statue in the center of the Academic Court of the Rice Institute. The dust of his murderer mingles with the anonymous moving sands of New Mexico.

1904 WESTON, MASSACHUSETTS
A Stroll to Kill

Charles Louis Tucker was out of a job. The twenty-four-year-old widower—his wife had been dead for less than a year—had worked in many capacities about the Boston area, renting canoes on the Charles River, handling baggage in the South Station, running an elevator, clerking in a stationery store. But unemployment didn't worry Tucker; something would turn up. As he strolled out of his Auburndale home, nothing occupied Tucker's mind other than the fine spring day of March 31, 1904, a bright, breezy, almost balmy day.

He had worked on his parents' lawn until noon. After changing his clothes and nibbling a quick lunch, Tucker strolled down to the Weston bridge with a friend named Bourne and there Tucker spotted another acquaintance, Arthur Woodward, who was driving a fishwagon. Next to Woodward on the wagon seat was perched a young lovely Tucker later named as one Mabel Walker from Damariscotta, Maine.

Mabel actually caught Tucker's attention by waving a handkerchief at him, inviting him and Bourne to ride along on the wagon. Bourne hopped in back with the fish; Tucker climbed to the seat. A short time later, Tucker and Mabel left the odorous wagon, Woodward and Bourne, and walked to a trapshooting area where they gaped at marksmen banging away at clay pigeons. An hour or so later, according to statements Tucker was to subsequently make to authorities, he parted company with Mabel and returned home.

Another acquaintance of Tucker's, Harold Page, did not see Tucker that day; he was busy at his job in the South Station where he worked as a clerk for the Boston and Albany Railroad. His father, seventy-eight-year-old Edward Page, a retired businessman, had also taken advantage of the inviting weather and had been strolling, returning to his Weston home a little after two that afternoon. Edward Page thought it peculiar to find the front door unlocked, which was not the family habit. He called for Amy Roberts, the housekeeper, and got no answer. She was apparently shopping. His spinster daughter, forty-one-year-old Mabel Page, who was usually home this time of day, oddly did not answer the old man's call.

After a drink of cider and a lunch of buttered bread, Edward Page roamed through the house, looking for his daughter. He found her in her room, dressed in walking boots, hat and underskirt, lying face up on the floor, her eyes staring into oblivion. He felt her hand, which was cold, and listened for her heartbeat, which had ceased. She was quite dead, a jagged wound gaping in her neck. As the old man ran downstairs to call for help, he found on a table a note from his daughter. It read:

Have just heard that Harold is hurt and at the Massachusetts Hospital. Have gone in 12 o'clock. Will leave key in front side door with barn key. Will telephone Mrs. Bennett.

Authorities responding to the old man's cry for help soon discovered two more wounds in Mabel Page's body, one in the chest, the other in the back, made by a blade five inches in length. Found near the body was another note, which read "J. L. MORTON, CHARLESTOWN, MASS." The note had been written in pencil, its letters slanting first one way, then the other. Nothing had been taken except about fourteen dollars from a purse owned by Amy Roberts, which was found ransacked downstairs.

Police began a thorough investigation, sifting through all known suspects; relatives, even those with the most meager acquaintance with the dead woman were called in and interviewed by officers. One of these was Charles Louis Tucker. Harold Page recalled Tucker's coming to his rural Weston home a few times, once in 1902 to buy a dog. At that time Tucker had talked with Mabel Page.

Tucker was questioned by police but he appeared innocent enough and his alibi of being with friends seemed acceptable. One of those friends, however, Arthur Woodward, the driver of the fishwagon on the day of the murder, gave Tucker a good deal of thought as he pondered the brutal slaying of Mabel Page. The *Boston Post* had routinely published Tucker's picture, along with many others questioned by the police, and Woodward had seen it. He had also read that the victim had been killed by a knife with a five-inch blade. This fact troubled Arthur Woodward much, since he had found on the seat of his wagon after Tucker's departure a sheath for a knife, one that would accommodate a five-inch blade. He also recalled Tucker's wearing the knife under his belt. The sheath was turned over to the Weston police, who noted that it bore teeth marks in a corner.

The police took Tucker into custody and grilled him. He denied ever owning a sheath and a knife. The local cops, however, were far from naive. One detective had picked up several of Tucker's coats when he was taken from his home. The detective held one of these coats, showing it to Tucker, and then drew from one of the pockets the sheath. Tucker recoiled in shock, telling the police that the sheath was his, that he had lied out of fear. He had, he said, three days after the murder, taken the sheath out of a bureau drawer and hid it in the coat pocket. This, too, was a lie, officers told him. The sheath had been in the possession of his friend Arthur Woodward.

"Well I never even owned a hunting knife!"

"No?"

"Well, except the one I sold a year ago."

"When?"

"A year ago, and I had one two years ago but I lost that in the river."

"We want a dentist to take a cast of your teeth, Charles," he was told. The suspect shrugged. It was all right with him. The plaster cast was taken; it matched perfectly the teeth marks on the sheath.

While he was being grilled, police searched his room and found in a coat pocket three pieces of a knife blade. The handle was missing.

Tucker went to trial for murder on January 2, 1905, in East Cambridge. Though no one had witnessed Tucker entering or leaving the Page house, Amy Roberts did identify a pin found in Tucker's room as having been owned by her mistress, Mabel Page. The odd note with the name Morton on it was identified as having been written by Tucker; the strange penciled hand-writing matched his. The broken knife still had Mabel Page's blood on it, the prosecution demonstrated. Tucker's motive, the prosecution insisted, was the rape of Mabel Page. He had ar-rived at the Page house, telling Mabel that her brother had been injured—thus the note Mabel hurriedly wrote to her fa-ther. Apparently, Mabel resisted Tucker and he stabbed her to death, plunging the knife five inches straight into her heart.

Tucker was found guilty on January 24, 1905. His appeals came to nothing. On June 12, 1906, Charles Louis Tucker was baptised. A few hours later he read a religious statement from the gallows in which he neither admitted his guilt nor claimed innocence in the slaying of Mabel Page. He was then hanged.

1906 SEATTLE, WASHINGTON

Finish for a Mad Prophet

The hypnotic ability to inspire once-normal humans into acts of frenetic lunacy was not the exclusive province of Charles Manson. Many decades before devilish Charlie put his dreams of madness into the minds of killer dupes, a wild-eyed prophet named Joshua the Second became the sexual scourge of Oregon. He began as a rather lame evangelist whose real name was Franz Edmund Creffield.

The thirty-five-year-old Creffield first appeared in Corvallis, Oregon, in 1902 as a humble tambourine shaker for the Salvation Army. There was a noticeable trace of his native Germany in his accent but what most captivated people who met him were his large brown eyes, which, when blazing with the word of the Lord, held all transfixed.

Within months, Creffield dropped from the ranks of the Army and vanished into the tall timbers surrounding bustling Corvallis. He reappeared in early 1903 wearing a flowing gown and a luxuriant beard that spread across his small chest. He then introduced himself to one and all as the prophet Joshua the Second, head of the Church of the Bride of Christ. The prophet immediately set about Corvallis in search of converts, announcing in a booming voice that the ways of the world would have to be changed or doom would be the reward of the sinful.

Joshua's changes consisted of holding orgiastic rites in the homes of some of Corvallis' most prominent citizens, duped into believing he was sincerely searching for a holy vessel, a chaste female who would become the Mother of a Second Christ. To that end, scores of females—spinsters, married women and their daughters, young and old—attended Joshua's meetings, where all clothes would be shorn and holy rolling commenced with the prophet doing most of the rolling.

The scores of women following the mad prophet were hypnotized, it was later claimed, by his trancelike gaze and thunderous voice. They would sway and chant and cry out in strange tongues as the prophet instructed them in his special ways of "cleansing the soul"—mainly, mass fornication. The group's religious activities created such scandal in Corvallis that a mob of irate fathers and brothers finally drove Joshua from the city; he moved to deserted nearby Kiger Island, and dozens of

women followed him, living in makeshift tents and crude wig-
wams.

To drive the devils from the bodies of these misguided souls,
Joshua took to whipping the females until his arms ached.
Other oddball rituals, such as cremating cats and dogs, were
put into practice. The welted group received financial aid from
a few husbands, especially O. P. Hunt, one of Corvallis' richest
(and most naive) citizens. Hunt's wife and daughter were
staunch residents of the Kiger Island community.

An enterprising citizen slipped unseen onto the island one
day and captured with his Brownie camera the rites practiced
at the high tide of Joshua's exhortations. The clear photo
showed the prophet quite naked, surrounded by a bevy of ador-
ing females, also in the stark altogether, in a frenzy of sexual
frolic. This photo—so many hundreds of prints were made and
sold that the negative was worn out—provoked the male population of Corvallis into violent action. Joshua's religious love
nest on Kiger Island was raided, the women dragged home, and
the prophet driven off after he had been properly tarred and
feathered.

But Joshua II was a stubborn prophet, one who returned to
live in a dank hole in the ground beneath the Hunt house. He
was finally discovered and sent off by the Corvallis menfolk,
told he would suffer death if he ever returned. The prophet
returned; he was arrested, tried, and convicted for something
akin to mass adultery, and given two years in the state prison.
Creffield served fifteen months, and upon his release he again
set up his sect near Waldport, just south of Corvallis. To one
astonished male, Joshua announced that "I have called down
the wrath of an angry God on these modern Sodoms of Seattle,
of Portland, of San Francisco, of Corvallis. . . . Have no fear . . .
my faithful will return to the fold—all of them. They will leave
all behind them—the scoffing fathers, their brothers, their husbands—and come to our Eden. A curse, oh God, on San Francisco, on Portland, on Corvallis, on Seattle!"

Only a few days later, on April 17, 1906, San Francisco was
destroyed by fire and quake. Naturally, Joshua II took the
credit, booming: "I knew that God would respond. . . . We must
rouse the faithful before it is too late." Scores of women left
their homes to be with the prophet, some of them walking more
than a hundred miles to his campsite, without money and carrying babies. But Joshua II was not present. He had run off to

Seattle to marry one of his most ardent followers, young Esther Mitchell. Her brother, George, tracked the pair, and found them sauntering down a Seattle street on May 7, 1906. George Mitchell calmly walked up to Joshua II as he peered into the window of Quick's Drugstore, put a revolver to the prophet's left ear, and pulled the trigger. Joshua II sank to the pavement quite dead.

Mitchell was hailed as a hero and was acquitted of murder. As he later stood amidst admirers in the Seattle train depot before returning to Corvallis, his sister, Esther, walked up to him and drew a small pearl-handled revolver, which she placed against his left ear and fired. George Mitchell fell dead at her feet. The seventeen-year-old Esther was sent to the Washington State Asylum for the insane.

Thus ended Joshua's crusade to find the Bride of Christ. His career, like that of the addlebrained Charles Manson, ended in violence born out of babbling gobbledygook. His body lies in Seattle's Lakeview Cemetery. San Francisco was rebuilt without the knowledge that Joshua II had brought about its ruination, a dubious fact of which most residents are happily ignorant to this day.

1909–11 BAD AXE, MICHIGAN

"All Ain't Well There!"

Most thought the Sparling clan to be upstanding farm folks who tilled the hardscrabble land of Huron County, Michigan. Their spread, a neat and modern farm, was situated only six miles from Bad Axe. Head of the family, John Wesley Sparling, age forty-six, was one of the most respected farmers in the county; he paid his bills on time and he slaved through his fields from dawn to dusk, aided by his four strapping sons, Peter, Albert, Scyrel (an alternate spelling of Cyril), and Ray. His attractive wife, Carrie, and his daughter, May, worked no less hard keeping the house.

To this typical family of rural America in the halcyon days of President William Howard Taft, with honest labor in its heart and a zesty future on its horizon, came a weird and stalking death. The Sparling menfolk began to die.

John Wesley Sparling, who had never had a sick day in his life, suddenly in the early afternoon of a sweet June day in 1909 turned away from his haying chores, telling his sons that he felt ill. "I'm going up to the house and lie down for a few minutes."

Sparling was bedridden for a week, vomiting and in agony, before he died. At his bedside throughout the ordeal was the family physician, Dr. John MacGregor. Mrs. Sparling was so moved by the doctor's kindness and solicitude that she promptly appointed MacGregor the family adviser. In their extensive conferences, the two decided to insure the lives of Mrs. Sparling's robust young sons. All four boys were insured for a thousand dollars each with the Sun Life Assurance Company of Canada, the policies written by MacGregor's father, who owned an insurance firm in Ontario, Canada. More policies with the Gleaners Insurance Company, also written by MacGregor's father, were taken out on the Sparling boys. On both sets of policies, Dr. MacGregor acted as the examining physician, writing to the insurance firms that the Sparlings were in wonderful physical health.

But they kept dying. The eldest son, Peter, age twenty-six, went the way of his father, taking sick in the middle of a June day in 1910, returning to the house from the haying chores, and perishing five days later after much vomiting and great pain. Albert was next, almost collapsing in church in May 1911; within five days, showing the exact symptoms of his father and brother, he was dead.

It was a mystery, this strange malady that was continually striking down what the people of Bad Axe came to label pathetically "the dying Sparlings." In all three cases, the good doctor MacGregor was in attendance. No one thought the deaths suspicious except an uncle, John Sparling, who was overheard to carp about the lethal homestead of his kinsfolk: "By Jesus! I don't like the way things are going. I figure all ain't well there!" But his was the only voice to question what all others deemed the will of God.

MacGregor was equally baffled. The handsome thirty-six-year-old doctor was married to an attractive woman, yet he seemed to be spending more time with Carrie Sparling than with his own spouse. Ever since the death of her husband, Mrs.

Sparling had felt it necessary to have MacGregor call on her almost once a day to treat a pesky eye infection, one that lingered for years. Following the deaths of Peter and Albert Sparling, MacGregor was constantly at the Sparling farm. He was forever in conference with the beauteous Mrs. Sparling. He became the actual director of the farm, telling Carrie Sparling when to plow and when to sell her livestock.

Apparently, Dr. MacGregor was well paid for his eye examinations and advice. Mrs. Sparling, with the proceeds of the insurance on Peter's life, purchased a comfortable cottage in the nearby village of Ulby, but she never lived inside the house. Dr. MacGregor and his wife moved into the home and, as far as any records ever revealed, never paid one penny in rent. Further, Dr. MacGregor became the proud possessor of a new automobile, one of the few in Bad Axe in that horse-and-buggy era, just after the death of Albert Sparling. There was some strange talk about town concerning MacGregor's purchase of the motorcar. He had paid for it with the insurance check sent to cover the death of Albert Sparling, a check made out to Carrie Sparling, who had endorsed it in MacGregor's name.

Before gossip inflated this strange transaction, the residents of Bad Axe were shocked to learn that husky Scyrel Sparling had taken ill on August 4, 1911, and was bedridden. He, too, was vomiting uncontrollably. Dr. MacGregor, perhaps reacting to public concern, thought this time to call in outside medical opinions to help him determine Scyrel's puzzling condition.

With MacGregor standing by, two doctors, Harrington and Conboy, examined Scyrel Sparling. Dr. Conboy was then approached by MacGregor, who asked him: "Do you suspect arsenic?"

"I do," replied Conboy.

"So do I," said MacGregor.

Dr. Conboy wasted no time in visiting the prosecuting attorney for Huron County, one Xenophon A. Boomhower. The physician told the attorney: "I think somebody is feeding arsenic to young Sparling. I've been there twice, called in by MacGregor, and I'm as certain as I can be of anything that the Sparling boy is suffering from arsenic poisoning. You ought to look into it."

Boomhower immediately sought counsel with Dr. MacGregor, an old friend. "There's a mystery around here, Mac," he confided to the Sparling family physician. "As you already know, Dr. Conboy thinks the lad is being poisoned."

"I'm mystified about it myself. I told Conboy the thing is completely baffling. Who would want to kill him?"

At Boomhower's suggestion, MacGregor arranged to have a nurse named Gibbs stay with the Sparling boy night and day. No one, including Mrs. Sparling, was allowed to give the youth anything—except the nurse, who slept on a cot in the boy's room. Another doctor named Holdship was called into the case when Scyrel did not improve. He was as mystified by the youth's worsening condition as the others. Scyrel Sparling, continuing to vomit, finally died on August 14. Holdship and MacGregor performed an autopsy, stating the following day that the youth had died of cancer of the liver.

Boomhower remained suspicious. Though Carrie Sparling objected, as did MacGregor, the attorney had Scyrel's organs sent to the University of Michigan, where pathologists determined that arsenic was, indeed, present. The prosecuting attorney, thus armed, ordered Albert Sparling's body exhumed and examined by the same experts, who reported identical findings: death by arsenic poisoning.

It was not surprising that, friend or not, Boomhower ordered MacGregor's arrest on a charge for murder, the warrant also naming Carrie Sparling and Nurse Gibbs as accomplices in the death of Scyrel Sparling. All three pleaded "Not Guilty"; MacGregor was put on trial in April, 1912. It was the most sensational event that ever occurred in Bad Axe.

Boomhower's prosecution was deft. He stuck to the facts: Posing as the family physician, MacGregor systematically poisoned four of the Sparlings, collecting, ostensibly as his fees for medical services, the insurance on three sons, a huge amount. The doctor's scheme was abetted by Carrie Sparling with whom, the attorney blatantly inferred, MacGregor was having a prolonged affair. There could be no other possible explanation for the amounts of money bestowed upon the doctor. Further, MacGregor had been the doctor who had examined the sons and pronounced them fit for the insurance firms; yet, as later testimony revealed, he had, at the same time, confided to Sheriff Donald McAuley, that the Sparling sons were "suffering from an unfortunate disease," a comment that undoubtedly supported premeditated murder.

The incredible fees paid MacGregor by Carrie Sparling were

mocked by Boomhower, who had estimated that, according to the regular medical rates of the day, MacGregor would have had to make four calls daily, every day for four years, on Carrie Sparling for her eye ailment to justify his payments from her.

On the stand, MacGregor could offer little rebuttal, except to say that the Sparlings were addicted to patent medicines that contained arsenic, a habit he had unsuccessfully tried to get them to quit. It was quickly proved by the prosecution that such medicines contained a negligible amount of arsenic, certainly not enough to cause death.

The jury found MacGregor guilty of murder, and he was sentenced to life imprisonment by Judge Watson Beach. (The case against Mrs. Sparling and the nurse was dropped.) The doctor's lawyers appealed to the state supreme court, which upheld the lower court. John MacGregor began to serve out a lifetime behind the bars of the state penitentiary in Jackson.

In one of the strangest moves in state history, Governor Woodbridge Nathan Ferris granted Dr. MacGregor a full pardon in November of 1916, declaring that he had information that convinced him that MacGregor was innocent. (Ferris never revealed that information, and to this day it has not been made available.) Moreover, this extraordinary pardon was followed by the Governor's appointment of MacGregor as the official doctor to the Jackson penitentiary where he had once been an inmate.

Ferris died in 1928. In that same year, still the prison doctor, MacGregor joined his benefactor in death. Pardon or not, many of the unsettled citizens of Bad Axe felt Ferris had acted in a most inexplicable, if not suspicious, manner, and that the mass murderer of the Sparling family was not only guilty as charged but had been rewarded by the State of Michigan for dark, unknown services.

1914–21 CHICAGO
A Female Bluebeard's Deadly Stew

There have been legions of men over the centuries who have married and murdered their spouses for profit, from the original Bluebeard, Henri Landru of France, to the notorious H. H.

Holmes (real name Herman Webster Mudgett), who may have killed as many as two hundred females, making him America's, if not the world's, all-time mass-murderer (*See* chronology). Such gory occupations, however, on the part of females are relatively rare. A roaring exception to this historic rule was Tillie Gbrurek, a native of Chicago's Little Poland.

Tillie, born in 1865 to immigrant parents, went early into a North Side sweatshop, a tragedy shared by many lowborn American females in the nineteenth century. At twenty, Tillie still slaved from dawn to dusk in the shop with little hope of marrying her way out of such miserable servitude. She was utterly homely, a beefy, red-faced woman with piano legs who smothered her broad, muscular body with mannish clothes. Yet there was a glimmer of salvation.

Taking the fifty dollars she had saved over a three-year period, Tillie risked all with a marriage broker. Her investment yielded a dull young man, one John Mitkiewitz, who promptly proposed, knowing Tillie to be one of the best cooks in the Polish community. The marriage did not save Tillie from the sweatshop, for Mitkiewitz proved to be a shiftless type who would rather eat and drink than support his young wife. For twenty-six years, Tillie labored silently in support of Mitkiewitz, who lazed about the apartment guzzling beer and warming his friends' hearts with cackling stories.

Then, in 1911, the long-suffering, meek-mannered Tillie underwent a traumatic experience that altered her wearisome life. She looked up from her worktable one day that year to grit her teeth in anguish and rage when her bullying sweatshop boss ruthlessly upbraided a sick child. Tillie stomped up to him and let go with a roundhouse right to the nose that knocked the owner flat unconscious. Her fellow sweatshop slaves leaped up with a deafening cheer.

Taking heart from the event, Tillie's ego ballooned to the point where she marched home that evening and thrashed her worthless husband into a sickbed. She compelled Mitkiewitz to go to work. Tillie's prestige was even more enhanced when she suddenly announced that she could predict the future. Gazing from her window one sultry night, she pointed to a dog rummaging in the garbage and told her neighbors as they sat in their windows: "That dog will be dead in a week."

"How do you know?" she was quizzed.

"The ancient powers tell me so."

Within a week, the mongrel was found dead, and the community at large, holding superstitious beliefs nurtured from the Dark Ages, instantly accepted Tillie as a soothsayer. In the summer of 1914, Tillie made a similar prediction, but this concerned her errant husband.

"I don't think that John is long for this world," Tillie mused to her neighbors as she languished on a fire escape. "The powers tell me that I'll be a widow within three weeks."

Tillie's powers never lied after that. Within three weeks, almost to the hour, John Mitkiewitz no longer resided with the living. Tillie announced his death quite casually to the local butcher and to neighbors while buying meat for her famous stew: "He just got numb all over. Where's a good place to buy a coffin—cheap?"

Collecting a thousand dollars in life insurance on Mitkiewitz, Tillie again went to her trusty marriage broker. She was soon the bride of railroad employee John Ruskowski, a man absolutely delighted with Tillie's cooking, especially her beef stew. "I don't know what she puts in them stews," Ruskowski told a friend, "but I never tasted anything like them."

Three months later, Ruskowski was still gulping down Tillie's culinary delights, but one night he complained that the stew tasted different. "What did you put in it?" he asked the most industrious cook in Little Poland.

"A new spice," Tillie smiled back. "Was it bitter?"

"A little bit," belched Ruskowski, "but I liked it."

Some days later, Tillie, while finishing a bottle of wine, told her neighbors that she feared for her husband's health. Ruskowski was gone in two weeks. "He just got numb and died," shrugged Tillie.

Undaunted, Tillie went on making her stews and marrying unhealthy men, collecting considerable insurance along the way. In 1914 she married Joseph "Blunt Joe" Guszkowski. Her third husband also loved her stews and soon "ate himself numb," according to Tillie. In 1916, the widow, her bank account fattening, wedded Frank Kupczyk, who lasted until 1920. During the heady stew-brewing years of Tillie's fourth marriage, a neighbor, Rose Chudzinski, suggested to the fabulous cook and seeress that it was unnatural for her previous husbands to have died in the prime of life. For these uttered suspicions, Tillie predicted Rose's death, shaking her head with "the powers have willed it that way!" Rose died on schedule.

Then Tillie the soothsayer visited a store and purchased some black cloth, telling the clerk it was for a funeral.

"Whose?" inquired the clerk.

"My husband's," droned Tillie.

"When did he die?"

"Ten days from now," Tillie announced. She then bought a coffin for Kupczyk, who filled it exactly ten days later.

Tillie married Anton Klimek in 1921 and shortly predicted his end. By this time, Chicago Police had heard of Tillie's incredible string of bad luck with perishing husbands, and decided to check on Klimek, who was sick in bed when officers called on October 27, 1921. He had just had a double portion of Tillie's marvelous stew; his wife insisted that he eat to "keep his strength up," almost force-feeding the hapless male. Of course, the stew was loaded with arsenic, the method Tillie employed to make all her dire predictions come true. Klimek proved to be the rare exception in Tillie's murderous career, surviving a massive poisoning after his stomach was pumped.

His portly wife fought police tooth and nail, sending several officers to the hospital before she was tossed into a cell. Her trial for killing three earlier husbands quickly commenced. Inside the courtroom, Tillie strutted and posed, lapping up the limelight. Found guilty of murder, the self-styled seeress snarled a last prediction: "I'll never stand on the gallows!" She didn't. Tillie was given a life sentence, but it was expressly ordered that she never cook for her fellow inmates.

1915 PHILADELPHIA

The Tell-tale Body in the Trunk

Of all the cases that have plagued the homicide division of the Philadelphia Police Department, none proved more baffling than the one beginning on December 13, 1915. Two workmen shoveling in a cellar were preparing to set down a new floor in a building once used by the Red Star Laundry Company. One of them struck a piece of wood. The men unearthed a large packing case, and, breaking this open, found an old leather trunk covered with mildew and powdered lime. The leather straps wrapped about the trunk were so rotted away that the workmen had little difficulty breaking inside.

The men peered into the trunk, one reaching forth. He pulled back with a yell. Crumbling under the lime inside the trunk was a half-decomposed corpse, a fleshless head with a jawbone sagging down so that gleaming teeth were parted in a ghoulish grin. The workmen ran screaming for the police.

Lieutenant William J. Belshaw of the Philadelphia Homicide Department answered the call. From the medical examiner who later inspected the remains, Belshaw learned that a flat-nose .32-caliber bullet had been sent into the dead man's head at the base of the skull, which meant murder.

Belshaw scooped up some small change, a nailcutter and a bunch of keys found in the trunk with the body. Inside the coat of the murder victim he found a tailor's tab, which gave an address on Walnut Street. The detective knew the corpse would not remain nameless for long. In addition to the artifacts found with the corpse, the medical examiner supplied the officer with the information that the murder victim had been dead for approximately twenty months. Belshaw immediately went to the police files of missing men. There it was: Daniel J. McNichol, a partner in a leather goods firm, had been missing since March 14, 1914, a period of twenty-one months.

Interviewing Mrs. McNichol, Belshaw was told that the missing man had given no reason for his departure but that his partner, Edward Keller, had reported seeing McNichol in New York. Keller had informed Mrs. McNichol that her husband needed clothes and money. Perplexed at her husband's odd behavior, but desperate to help, she sent the clothes and money along to her errant spouse through Keller.

Belshaw went to Keller, who had owned the Red Star Laundry after his leather goods partner, McNichol, vanished. At first glance, the detective suspected Keller of murdering his partner to steal the business. In his purple report, Belshaw described Keller thusly: "The cruelty and ferocity of his nature were perfectly mirrored in the right side of his face, which was marked by a malicious gleam in the eye and a cynical, upturned lip. But the mild and almost pious expression on the left side of his face negated one's suspicions. It was one of the most marked cases of dual physiognomy I have ever seen."

Though he was grilled constantly, Keller stuck to the same story. He had dissolved his leather business partnership with

McNichol in April 1914 and had begun the Red Star Laundry, which later went broke. Keller claimed that he had some months later met McNichol by chance in New York—the time McNichol asked his former partner to contact his wife in order to obtain money and clothes before disappearing into tramp-dom once again. He had delivered the requested items and tried to talk McNichol into seeing his wife, but the young man, who had been married for only a few months (his wife gave birth some months after McNichol's disappearance), inexplica-bly refused to return home.

Belshaw believed none of Keller's story and departed to track down, for several months, his meager clues. He established the corpse's identity as that of McNichol when the tailor on Walnut Street identified the dead man's blue worsted suit, one cut es-pecially for Daniel McNichol. After learning that McNichol had been wearing an expensive gold watch and carrying more than fifteen hundred dollars, Belshaw and his men combed the pawnshops. After several weeks, a pawnbroker was found on Kensington Avenue who possessed the missing watch. It had been pawned by one "J. McNamee of 826 Wensley Street."

Edward Keller, Belshaw knew, had lived on Wensley Street at the time of McNichol's disappearance, but at a different ad-dress, number 1818. Going to that address, Belshaw got incred-ibly lucky; the landlady told him that Keller had moved all his belongings to a new address on the day of McNichol's dis-appearance. She remembered his having a very large trunk with special leather straps. Hours later this woman identified the trunk in which McNichol's body had been jammed.

Edward Keller was arrested. Belshaw's careful check of his background proved him to be Edward Keilblock, who had served fourteen years in Sing Sing for embezzlement, burglary, and grand larceny. Keller was tried for McNichol's murder, but the circumstantial evidence against him brought in only a ver-dict of "voluntary manslaughter." The celebrated trunk mur-derer slipped out of the hangman's noose and into a ten-to-twelve-year sentence in Eastern State Penitentiary in 1916. He was released in 1924.

Upon his release, Keller somehow got the position of night watchman at the Corn Exchange National Bank, which he looted of twenty thousand dollars on December 20, 1925. He dashed into a street, jumped into a taxi, and ordered the driver to take him to New York. The cab had not gone more than a few blocks when the driver heard a loud thump on the back floor. He turned to see his passenger sprawled dead of a heart attack, large bills spilling from a sack across his chest. The cabbie spotted a squad car and stopped it. A plainclothesman walked to the cab and peered inside the window. He stared down at the gaping-mouthed dead thief. The detective smiled wryly at the astounding irony: He was none other than Lieutenant William Belshaw.

1916 NEW YORK CITY

The Determined Dentist

Current murderers seem tame and phlegmatic for the most part when it comes to *modus operandi,* preferring either to bludgeon their victims to death or blow them away with an unimaginative elephant gun, lacking that certain *élan* that marked the clever killers of a half century ago. Warren Waite was no impatient slayer by any standard, but a man of infinite care and overwhelming kindness.

Waite, born and bred in Grand Rapids, Michigan, of struggling farm folks, looked early upon the richest family in town as his exclusive prey, yet he took his time in his lethal walk to wealth. He dated Clara Louis Peck through high school while attending the University of Michigan, where he studied dental surgery before going to Europe to study and practice. Clara's father was the lumber king John E. Peck, worth millions.

The local papers regularly reported Waite's social and professional progress, giving him the laudatory comments reserved in that era for international scholars of renown. It was reported that he had graduated from the University of Glasgow with honors and had gone on to practice his artful dentistry on the mouths of the mighty, finally being appointed the chief dentist to the most powerful mining corporation in South Africa. Clara, who had been pursuing Waite for years, and had written him long, love-gushing letters in Europe, swooned with delight when news arrived that her hero was returning home.

The beamish dentist returned to Grand Rapids on Christmas Day, 1914, when the lovelost Clara met him and proposed. Despite the objections of seventy-six-year-old father Peck, who thought Waite too ambitious for a son-in-law, the couple were wed on September 9, 1915. Peck gave the newlyweds a lavishly furnished rent-free apartment on Manhattan's Riverside Drive, and an allowance of three hundred dollars a month. Ostensibly, Waite set up his practice, but he spent most of his hours playing tennis. He had little time for Clara. His wife was more than understanding about his long absences. "But he has his profession and his tennis," she explained in letters to her parents. "He's Metropolitan Amateur Champion. Isn't that wonderful?"

The enterprising Warren Waite, however, was not playing tennis, but carrying on a torrid affair with Margaret Weaver Horton, the wife of Henry Mack Horton, a distinguished aeronautical engineer. To keep the beauteous, raven-haired Mrs. Horton in style (their trysting was elitist, confined to the Plaza Hotel), Waite needed money, much more than his in-laws had given him. On his wedding night, Waite had exploded, telling Clara that the apartment and allowance were but a pittance. "I expected fifty thousand dollars outright!" he had roared.

There were other ways, the dentist reasoned, to obtain necessary funds. He invited Mrs. Peck to visit New York. She arrived on January 10, 1916. Ten days later she was dead. Her unexpected illness shocked all, but the family fondly remembered how kind Warren had been to his suddenly sick mother-in-law, bringing her flowers and footwarmers, and playing her favorite records as he crooned at her bedside. It was also Waite, explaining that a drawn-out funeral would vex the family, who suggested that Mrs. Peck be cremated. She was, John Peck telling his associates how thoughtful his son-in-law was. The old man then went to New York to stay with Warren and Clara. In less than a month, on March 12, 1916, he, too, was dead. Waite again urged cremation but Clara and her brother, Percy, refused; the lumber king would be sent back to Grand Rapids where he would be given a funeral a man of his achievement deserved. The Waites accompanied the body. Warren, however, was a busy man and returned to New York.

In his absence Percy Peck received a telegram from a mysterious "K. Adams," which read: "Suspicions aroused. Demand autopsy. Examine body." Peck, who had always thought his brother-in-law to be less than honorable, had his father's body examined. There were great quantities of arsenic in the intestines and chloroform in the brain. Try as he might, Percy could not convince his sister that her husband was a killer and fortune-hunter, coveting their one million-dollar inheritance.

"Clara," he yelled in exasperation, "don't you honestly think Warren killed Mama and Papa?"

"Nonsense," replied the dutiful Clara. "He wouldn't have poisoned them. He loved them too much."

Even Clara's maiden aunt, Mrs. Catherine Peck, rushed to Warren's defense, stating that her wonderful nephew-in-law "neither drinks or swears. I like him so well I gave him a three-thousand-dollar wedding present." She also gave Waite thirty thousand dollars to invest for her on the Stock Exchange.

New York police turned up an atomizer Warren had filled with "medicine" for the Pecks. It was loaded with typhoid and antrax germs. Police then talked to Elizabeth Hardwicke, a distant Peck relative, who had spotted Mrs. Horton with Waite, put two and two together and had sent the mysterious telegram to Percy Peck. The motive was clear. Warren Waite was poisoning off the Pecks for money to support his affair. He was arrested but laughed at police. "Why, the thing is too absurdly amusing even to discuss it," he chortled. It was then police discovered that Waite had intended to kill off the entire family. He had tried to use the germ-filled atomizer on Clara once when she had a slight cold, after getting her to revise her will to leave her inheritance of a half million dollars "to my beloved Warren."

Further, police grilled Oliver Eugene Kane, the embalmer who had prepared John Peck's body. He broke down immediately, blurting: "Waite told me the D.A. was going to ask me for a specimen of my embalming fluid. He asked if I could put some arsenic in it. I said I couldn't because it's against the law to have arsenic in embalming fluid." Waite thrust nine thousand dollars upon the timid little embalmer, quivered Kane to police. "I-I—kept the money. I was so scared I buried it out in the sand at Orient Point on the tip of Long Island. But I didn't put any arsenic in the fluid."

Confronted with the evidence, Waite broke down, tried to commit suicide by taking sleeping pills, was revived, and then pretended insanity. "A bad man from Egypt dwells in my body," he screamed. "He makes me do bad things! He struggles for possession of my soul!"

Then came the confession. Warren Waite admitted a lifelong sham. He had graduated from the University of Michigan by

Mrs. John E. Peck, a victim of the murderous dentist, and her doting daughter, the ever-trusting Mrs. Warren Waite. (UPI)

Dr. Warren Waite, beamish at the murder of his in-laws, surrounded by
New York City police officers in 1916. (UPI)

using another student's work. He had forged his postgraduate
certificate at Glasgow and had secretly written and mailed all
those newspaper accounts of his sterling career in Europe. He
had been after the Peck fortune since impoverished boyhood,
planning to kill the entire family.

Briefly working at New York's Flower Hospital, Waite stole
drugs and collected deadly bacterial slides. "In November
1915," he droned to police, "to test my knowledge and to test
the effect of germs, I inoculated myself with cultures of anthrax,
typhoid, and pneumonia. By the time Mrs. Peck arrived in January 1916, I was ready for her." He admitted spraying Mrs.
Peck's food with anthrax and typhus germs and spraying her
throat with typhoid, influenza, anthrax, diphtheria, and tuberculosis, plus giving her powdered sleeping tablets each night.
"It took just ten days," he gloated. The same routine was practiced on John Peck, but he proved too tough. Waite put damp
sheets on the old man's bed and let him lie in drafts. He burned
flypaper and left open containers of chlorine gas in Peck's room.
"Finally I resorted to arsenic. Even that didn't kill the old fellow. On the last night I tied a rag of chloroform over my father-
in-law's face and I held it in place with a pillow until he was
dead."

Waite added as an afterthought: "Oh, yes, Aunt Catherine. I
tried to kill her, too." He grinned at his police interrogator. "I
kept her car windows open when I took her riding. I put ground

The wealthy John E. Peck
proved almost too tough
to kill. (UPI)

*Dr. Waite claimed he
"did it all" for this
woman, the ravishing
Margaret Weaver
Horton.* (UPI)

glass in her marmalade but she thought it was sand and returned it to the grocer."

"Are you crazy?" asked the interrogator.

"I think not, unless it is crazy to want money."

Upon his conviction and sentence to death, Waite sighed and said in court: "What a relief!"

Warren Waite, poor boy gone wrong from the start, sauntered to the electric chair on May 1, 1917. He sat down calmly in the death seat. As the electrodes were fixed to the shaved areas of his body, he looked about and with his last words commented: "Is this all there is to it?"

1919 AKRON, OHIO
Ending the Force

In the spring of 1919, police Lieutenant Michael Fiaschetti, head of New York City's Italian Squad, answered a call from Harry Welch, chief of detectives of the Akron, Ohio, police force. Fiaschetti listened amazed as Welch told a tale of murder without reason, slaughter without pattern. Members of the Akron police force were being killed systematically, it seemed, and at an alarming rate. Patrolman Robert Norris had been shot in the back and killed as he made his rounds on a residential street on December 26, 1918. Some days later officers Joe Hunt and Edward Costigan, also on night patrol, were shot dead. A week later Patrolman Gethin Richards was murdered in a similar fashion.

The murders were inexplicable. No crimes, other than the killings of these officers, could be detected. A reward of twenty thousand dollars had been posted for information leading to the arrest and conviction of the killer but no one stepped forward. Welch and his detectives had turned up nothing, except one thin cryptic clue, which Welch delivered to Fiaschetti, telling him that a suspect in the killings was somewhere in New York City. He had no name and the description, supplied by an Akron informant, would have tingled the spine of Sherlock Holmes. "All we have is this," sighed Welch. "Look for the man with a hole in his hand. He is Italian. Period."

Fiaschetti had come up through the ranks under the fearless Lieutenant Joe Petrosino when the celebrated Italian squad had been formed to combat the Black Hand, the Camorra, and the Mafia shortly after the turn of the century. He was conditioned to the bizarre. His squad members went to work activating the elaborate informant system, a host of "stool pigeons" Fiaschetti and others had cultivated for a decade. Three weeks after the hunt began, Fiaschetti received a call from a poolroom operator, one of the lieutenant's regular informants.

"He was in my place last night," the informant stated. "Says he's coming again tonight. Looks like he had been shot through the hand."

Fiaschetti went to a Brooklyn hall that night and waited until two men entered and began to play pool. One of the men rested his hand on the green of the table, and, under the glare of the overhanging lamp, the police detective saw the livid scar in the middle of the right hand. Fiaschetti arrested Tony Manfredi and Pasquale Biondo and two days later escorted them by train to Akron. Both men had been in New York for only a few weeks, traveling from Akron. The detective studied his captives on that trip and tried several times to get them to explain the Akron police murders. They merely snarled defiance, especially Biondo, whom Fiaschetti described as being "right out of the book, type and figure of the Italian gangster—fierce, wary, grim, and silent."

Manfredi, however, was a different matter. His features were delicate, his manner somewhat gentle. His speech was that of a man with an education; he was also a braggart, impressionable and egotistical. Fiaschetti locked Biondo in a stateroom, chaining him to a bar. He then took Manfredi to the lounge where he ordered drinks and allowed the handsome gangster to gnaw on his own vanity.

Detective and gangster chatted for some time until Fiaschetti casually inquired: "How did you get that scar on your hand?"

Manfredi brightened. "You wouldn't believe anybody could be so dirty," the gangster spat out, eager to talk about himself. "Four of us were out visiting a friend in the country. And they were my buddies, my pals—at least, I thought they were. It was night, and we sang as we walked along, songs of my province. I was out in front singing loudest. I got some sweet voice." Manfredi burst into a Neapolitan song as a sample.

199

"What happened?" Fiaschetti asked, nodding approval of the gangster's irritating tenor voice.

"Well, I was out in front singing, when bang, bang—would you believe me? They were shooting at me. One bullet got me in the hand. But I was too smart for them. I can move fast when I have to. I ducked and ran, and beat it away from them and got into the brush and hid. I could hear them stamping around and hunting but they couldn't find me." Manfredi smiled at the thought of his clever escape.

"Why did they do it?"

"I don't know—some grudge."

"Was Biondo with them?"

"Biondo?" Manfredi's eyebrows arched. "Not on your life. He's what I call a friend. If he'd been there he wouldn't have let 'em do it. He came to me later and said how dirty they were." Manfredi went to explain that Biondo had suggested they both leave Akron for a while, go to New York.

A talker, Fiaschetti knew well, has a short life with a mob. The detective then played a colossal bluff. "Listen, Manfredi. I know all about those policemen killed in Akron. You were in on it and so was Biondo. The gang that tried to knock you off had planned to take you for a ride because you knew too much and they were afraid you would talk. When they made a mess of the job, what else could they do? Biondo wasn't in on the shooting." The wily detective went on to explain that Biondo was assigned to kill Manfredi in New York, to "get the job done right this time." Manfredi stared bug-eyed at the detective. "That's the tip that's come from Akron," Fiaschetti lied. "When the word came it was up to me to keep Biondo from sending you to the morgue. I jumped in just in time to save your life."

Pale and silent for some moments, Manfredi digested the underworld logic put before him. Fiaschetti sipped his drink and puffed his cigar nonchalantly, pretending indifference while anxiety jangled his nerves. Then the detective threw his bone: "Come through, Manfredi . . . and you won't burn. Do the right thing and you'll get away with a prison sentence, instead of the electric chair."

Suddenly, Manfredi let loose a torrent of curses, screaming: "And I thought he was my friend!" As the train plunged through the night toward Akron, Tony Manfredi gushed out the incredible story of the Akron police murders. "It all began with Rosario Borgio," he growled, describing a swarthy, savage re-

The Akron, Ohio, mobsters who intended to wipe out the entire police force (from top to bottom): Pasquale Biondo, a coast-to-coast killer; Rosario Borgio, who gave the order and paid off; Paul Chiavaro.

Borgio's murderous boys (top to bottom): Johnnie Mazzano, Lorenzo Biondo, and the talkative Tony Manfredi.

sortkeeper in Akron. Borgio was a fantastically vindictive enemy of the police, who had incensed him by repeatedly raiding his resort and arresting him for myriad violations.

Borgio had sworn vendetta and his grudge became so much a personal craze that he called in every Black Hander, every thug and hooligan he knew in the vicinity. He was a *padrone* and his word was law in Akron's underworld. As more than twenty men stood in the shadows of a back room of his saloon in the fall of 1918, Borgio boomed: "Two hundred and fifty dollars a head for policemen!"

In American police annals, Borgio's offer ranks as the most astounding proposition ever; he intended to kill the entire Akron, Ohio, police force, every last officer, the money for each dead cop to be paid spot cash on delivery. The gang thought it a sound offer and enthusiastically embarked on exterminating the entire force. The patrolmen died and Borgio paid off. The methodical eradication would have gone on undetected had it not been for the boasting Manfredi, who subsequently testified against the gang and received twenty years in prison (as did Biondo). Borgio, Paul Chiavaro, Lorenzo Biondo (Pasquale's brother), and Vito Mezzano went to the electric chair.

The indomitable Michael Fiaschetti received a gold medal from the Governor of Ohio and returned to New York to chase down more criminals, content with the knowledge that he had halted a murder campaign with savvy and soft-soap.

1919 CLEVELAND, OHIO
The Curse of Big Emma

Killers have resorted to a horrible host of methods in dispatching their victims, but one of the most bizarre murder procedures was that followed by the slayer of Daniel D. Kaber, a wealthy Cleveland publisher. Kaber had suffered a paralytic stroke and lay bedridden in his mansion on the night of July 18, 1919. In another room, Kaber's step-daughter, eighteen-year-old Marian McArdle, a student at Smith College, told funny stories to a friend, Anna Baehr. Mrs. Mary Brickel, Kaber's mother-in-law, moved slowly in a rocker on the colonnaded front porch. The publisher's wife, Mrs. Eva Catherine Kaber, was out of town, visiting her sister at Cedar Point, Ohio.

Sharply at 10:20 P.M., Kaber's terrified voice could be heard in piercing screams. F. W. Utterbach, a male nurse attending Kaber who had been taking a nap in an upstairs room, leaped from his bed and raced to Kaber's room to find the millionaire on the floor. He was slashed to pieces and gushing blood. Utterbach called for an ambulance, then the police. He searched the room and found a bloody razor, a nail file that had been used as a stiletto, and a blood-soaked glove. When police arrived, they found nothing beyond these gruesome clues.

Kaber was rushed to Lakewood Hospital but doctors could do little to save his life. The publisher died a few hours later, gasping at the last: "The man in the cap did it—the man in the cap. That woman had me killed."

Moses Kaber, the victim's seventy-five-year-old father and business partner, was positive who "that woman" was—Eva Kaber. Prosecutor Samuel Doerfler agreed with Moses Kaber and at the coroner's inquest interrupted Eva's weeping jag to shout at her: "You had him killed and you know you did it—didn't you?"

Eva Kaber bolted upright in her chair. "Absolutely not! Are you crazy?"

Beyond Doerfler's bursting accusation, Eva Kaber was judged guiltless; her alibi of being out-of-town at the time of the murder was unshakable. The coroner's jury found that Daniel Kaber had been killed by "a person or persons unknown." Eva promptly collected insurance money and sold the Lakewood house, telling one and all that Cleveland only held painful memories. She moved to New York, where she opened a millinery shop and her daughter joined a chorus line.

The victim, wealthy Daniel Kaber. (UPI)

Moses Kaber, however, refused to give up pinning his son's murder on Eva. He hired the Pinkertons to follow her and posted a two-thousand-dollar reward. Answering the reward were two enterprising Cleveland matrons, Mrs. Ethel Berman and Mrs. M. A. Deering. Mrs. Berman followed Eva to New York, where she befriended the attractive widow. Months later, she became a secretary in Mrs. Kaber's millinery shop. Mrs. Deering remained in Cleveland, ingratiating herself with Eva's mother, and often visiting the Brickel house.

Mrs. Berman learned that Eva's climb had been hard and embittered. Two marriages before Kaber's had ended in di-

*Mrs. Eva Catherine
Kaber, who sought black
magic to end her
marriage, then settled
for murder.* (UPI)

vorce. When she wedded the publisher in 1911 her only
thought was to obtain wealth. After her husband suffered his
stroke, Eva complained long and loud about hospital expenses.
Mrs. Deering learned from Eva's mother that Eva had consulted with many fortunetellers to find out how long she would
have to put up with her husband's illness. A year elapsed before
the two apprentice detectives were able to piece together the
murder plot of Daniel Kaber.

Mrs. Berman learned that Eva had overheard her husband
telling Moses Kaber that he intended to change his will, leaving
nothing to his unfeeling wife. Eva promptly contacted one
Frank Di Carpo, a chauffeur. "I'll give you a two-hundred-
dollar down payment against five thousand dollars if you'll run
over my husband," the woman told Di Carpo. The chauffeur
refused. Next, Mrs. Kaber went to a medium, Mrs. Mary Wade,
asking that she conjure up spirits to frighten her husband to
death. "My power is for good, not evil," rebuked the medium.

Eva scurried to another mystic, Mrs. Maria Matthews, throwing down a wad of money on the medium's table, and insisting
that she stick pins in a wax doll, the likeness of her husband, to
bring about Kaber's death. Mrs. Matthews threw her out.

*One of "Big Emma's" killers-for-
hire, Salvatore Cala (center).* (UPI)

Then Eva heard of a woman named Mrs. Erminia "Big Emma" Colavito in Sandusky, Ohio, a most accommodating woman, even in the realms of murder. Mrs. Kaber asked Big Emma for some special "medicine" to speed her husband's demise. The poison Big Emma gave Mrs. Kaber, however, proved ineffective. A more direct means had to be found. Big Emma called in two thugs, Vittorio Pisselli and Salvatore Cala. These two professional killers were the visitors to the Kaber house on the night of the publisher's death.

Police rounded up Mrs. Kaber, Big Emma, and Cala (Pisselli was arrested and sent to prison in Italy, where he had fled after the killing). All were given life sentences, Mrs. Kaber dying in 1931 inside the Prison for Women at Marysville, Ohio. Eva, who was called "the meanest prisoner in Ohio," attempted many escapes and made life unbearable for her fellow prisoners all through her incarceration. Big Emma, on the other hand, proved to be a model prisoner. She applied for parole several times but was always refused. "I pray to God I may not spend all my life in this place," Big Emma told reporters at the age of seventy in 1953. She did.

Erminia "Big Emma" Colavito; she had the death answer in her crystal ball. (UPI)

A self-styled sleuth, Mrs. Ethel Berman uncovered evidence that led to Mrs. Kaber's guilt. (UPI)

1921 SAN FRANCISCO

The Best-Laid Murderous Plans

A business scheme propelled every action William A. Hightower ever made. He was a born Babbitt, a man oozing with enterprise; ideas gushed from his fertile though disorganized mind, all seemingly sure winners. But Hightower's much-expected profits never materialized. Success, always just a few steps away, eluded him with a taunt and a jibe. Approaching middle age and haunted by the nagging thought of failure, Hightower lay awake nights in a seedy San Francisco Hotel in the late summer of 1921, finalizing the details of his most spectacular scheme, an act of total madness he thought to be perfectly sane, properly businesslike.

Hightower was born in Texas in 1877. He left his impoverished home before he was a teenager, working at myriad servile jobs, from picking cotton to sweeping streets. In his travels through the western states, Hightower worked in dozens of restaurants and picked up an amazing knowledge of the culinary arts. His specialty was baking, particularly inventive pastries. In 1910 he met a girl in Fresno and married her, but their relationship was skittish from the start, she being a member of a Fundamentalist religious sect, he being a devout hedonist. Hightower left both his wife and the Fresno religious group after one shocked parishioner discovered the baker taking "liberties" with his daughter.

For a while, this restless wanderer settled in Bakersfield, California, where he owned and operated a bakery. During this period, while World War I was raging, Hightower claimed to have invented, among many marvelous inventions, a "darn good machine-gun," but, typical of his inevitable penchant for failure, his revolutionary invention was stolen. According to his later claim, "I was going to have it patented and give it to the government when the models got into the hands of German sympathizers."

With the crush of the Depression following the war, Hightower's bakery failed and he once more took to the roads, trying to sell a candied fruit substitute, another of his creations. No one was interested. By the beginning of 1921, William A. Hightower had been reduced to cooking for a section gang working on the Southern Pacific railroad outside of Salt Lake City, Utah.

The sledge-slingers did not appreciate his high cuisine and Hightower quit in disgust, motoring to San Francisco with his last few dollars. Here he schemed for a way to create the one majestic success that would line his pockets and lift his sagging ego. He bought a paper and read that fifteen thousand delegates to the Thirty-ninth International Supreme Convention of the Knights of Columbus would momentarily be descending upon San Francisco. Suddenly, he laughed aloud—more a shriek of joy—when he realized what the convention would really mean to him, the long-sought elusive bonanza, riches, perverse, delightful fame.

On the fog-bound night of August 2, 1921, a weird-looking man stood before the priest's residence of the Holy Angels Church in Colma, just outside the limits of San Francisco. When housekeeper Marie Wendel opened the door she was greeted by a man wearing a long overcoat, the collar shielding his face from view. Further hiding his identity were the kind of driver's goggles worn by motorists a decade earlier. "I would like to see the Father," the odd-looking stranger asked, seeming to speak in a foreign accent. "He is very needed. My friend is dying. We want the Father at once."

Father Patrick E. Heslin hurriedly threw on his overcoat to protect against the night chill, common in San Francisco even in mid-summer. Although he was sixty years old, Father Heslin was a burly sort, standing six feet tall and weighing about two hundred pounds. He was especially energetic when anyone needed his religious aid. Quickly, after hearing the man's story about a driver, his friend, mortally injured in an accident, the priest raced to the Church, retrieved his bag containing his last rites paraphernalia, and then joined the goggle-clad visitor who had his car idling at curbside. Housekeeper Wendel watched the car drive off and disappear into the fog.

Father Heslin did not return that night, much to Miss Wendel's mounting fears, nor the following day. It was not unusual for Father Heslin to stay away while comforting the dying but it was strange that he did not call, informing the housekeeper about any extended absence—as was his custom, and the usual protocol with any priests in the Catholic Church.

Upset, housekeeper Wendel called the residence of San Francisco's Archbishop Edward J. Hanna. The archbishop decided it prudent to wait a few hours before notifying police. He waited several hours. Still no word of Father Heslin arrived. A moment before the archbishop reached for the phone, an aide walked into his study with a special delivery letter. It was a carefully worded kidnapper's note declaring that Father Heslin, who had not been heard from in fourteen hours, was being held for a ransom of $6,500. Police were contacted immediately; someone on the force tipped the press.

San Francisco's newspapers roared into action. Enormous headlines of the kidnapping (the papers were not given the contents of the ransom note) incited to near pandemonium the thousands of Catholic delegates to the Knights of Columbus convention. A team of handwriting experts were assigned to study the ransom note. Little was forthcoming from Carl Eisenshimel and Chauncy McGovern, the much-vaunted experts in graphanalysis, other than that the writer was "a deranged person . . . a demented person."

Miss Wendel could give but a scanty description of the man. The housekeeper described the abductor as "a small dark man, sort of foreign-looking."

San Francisco police, aided by sheriff's deputies, state police and local officers from adjoining communities, organized massive posses, mostly augmented by volunteers from the Knights of Columbus. Hordes of shotgun-carrying men doggedly searched the streets of San Francisco, scrambled up and down the brown hills around the city, slogged through the sandy surfside of its beaches. After eight days, nothing new had been uncovered. The newspapers had run out of headlines, invective and speculation. Interest began to die. Then, a second ransom note was delivered to Archbishop Hanna in which the kidnapper repeated his demand of $6,500 (a sum both police and newsmen found curious, not like the usual even-numbered $50,000 or $100,000 typical of kidnappers). The kidnapper, however, failed to specify where or when such a payment should be made. "Fate has made me do this," whimpered the words of the second ransom note. "Sickness and misery has compelled my action. I must have money. Please forgive this act, if you can. The father is not dead YET."

Again the handwriting experts went to work. Their summation of the writer: "He is a goof!" (Eisenschimel) "The handwriting shows the writer to be a jellyfish!" (McGovern) With these ringing words of indictment, the handwriting experts walked out of the case. The police were as stymied as ever.

Late in the afternoon of August 10, a pleasant-faced, medium-sized man, wearing a Palm Beach suit and carrying a Panama straw hat in a pink hand, slipped into Archbishop Hanna's study just as a reporter from the *San Francisco Examiner* entered for an appointed interview with the clergyman.

"I don't know this man," apologized the reporter to the archbishop." "He just walked in with me . . . I'm not responsible for him."

"I came to see the archbishop, too," piped the smiling man in the tropical clothes. The archbishop gave the stranger a puzzled look. The intruder then dropped his bombshell: "I think I know where the missing priest is."

"You do?" quizzed the startled reporter.

"Yes," the man said in a calm voice, "a man who fries flapjacks all the time is watching over him."

At first the reporter thought the man was insane, but then remembered the famous Albers Milling Company billboard displaying a rugged miner tossing flapjacks over an open campfire. "You mean near that sign on Salada Beach?"

"The very one." The reporter dove for the archbishop's phone, blathering his news to the police. He listened for a moment and then turned to the mild-mannered stranger. "Police Chief O'Brien wants to know your name."

"Ah, it's William A. Hightower, sir."

It was night before Hightower, reporters from the *Examiner*, and chief O'Brien and other law enforcement personnel climbed into a large touring car and headed for the wave-crashing gloom of Salada Beach, its headlights hardly piercing the dense fog along the San Pedro Road running from San Francisco. By then, Hightower had carefully explained that an attractive female of his acquaintance, one Dolly Mason, had told him about a cache of illegal imported booze, Scotch to be specific, that was buried near the billboard. This amazing information was supported by another young lady, named by Hightower as one Doris Shirley; both "dear things" earned their daily bread as "ladies of the evening."

Hightower grumpily admitted to Chief O'Brien as they drove that he had visited the spot the previous evening in hopes of digging up the buried booze and selling it—well, it was a way to make a living, illegal or not, and these were hard times. As he had dug for the illicit liquid treasure, oblivious to the Fundamentalist law of Prohibition, Hightower patiently explained, he unearthed a black scarf. He had at once realized that it must be that belonging to the missing priest so much in the news of late. "I left the scarf as a marker on the beach," Hightower proudly told the occupants of the car. "Father Heslin, poor soul, is probably at the other end of it."

They would soon find out; Chief O'Brien and the others had taken the precaution of bringing along several shovels. En route, Hightower talked nonstop, regaling the riders with tall Texas tales, such as the time when he inexplicably shot the hat off the head of an enraged Texas Ranger during his cowboy days. "I sneaked over the county line and kept on going that night, boys," laughed Hightower. "Strange way for a man to lose his job, don't you think?"

Hightower's tongue wagged incessantly as Chief O'Brien at the wheel encouraged his garrulousness. During the long drive the would-be inventor and unemployed baker rattled off a dozen stories, interjecting bits of the saga of his nomadic life. Just before reaching the designated spot, he chirped: "Say, is there any kind of reward for finding poor Father Heslin?"

"Could be," grunted Chief O'Brien. He looked hard into the rearview mirror to see Hightower beam with pleasure.

"I kind of figured that might be the case. Mind you, I only told you boys about the find because of my civic duty and all that."

"And all that," nodded O'Brien.

Reaching the billboard, the group stumbled around on the sand dunes; holding lanterns high, bumping into each other in the swirling fog.

"This is useless," complained one of the newsmen.

"Press on, boys, press on," encouraged Hightower. He darted into the fog ahead of them. Suddenly his voice pierced the gloom. "Over here, boys, just this way!"

The group made its way to Hightower, who was on his knees, digging in the sand with his hands at the side of a hill. In one hand, held high for them to see, appeared a black scarf. "Here's my marker."

Everyone began to dig with the shovels, including the triumphant Hightower, who positively tore away at the sand with deep, aggressive strokes. Constable Silvio Landini looked up at Hightower and said: "If the body is in there, you ought to be a little easy with that shovel. You might strike the face and mar it, and we don't want any of that."

Father Patrick E. Heslin's body being removed from its shallow beach grave. (UPI)

Without pausing, Hightower loudly replied: "Don't worry, I'm digging at the feet."

Chief O'Brien edged his way over to the shoveling Hightower. "Didn't you say you didn't know if there was a body down there or not?"

"That's what I said, Chief," Hightower emphasized in a calm voice. He did not pause, but kept digging.

A shovelful of sand turned by a reporter revealed an arm. It was Father Heslin's body. When it was removed from its shallow grave, the silent group stared at the place where the feet had been. William A. Hightower stood at that exact spot, smiling his good citizen's smile.

The body was removed and Hightower was taken to police headquarters for further questioning. He repeated several times the story of the two girls who, he insisted, had told him of their booze cache, dumped by rumrunners to be retrieved at a later date.

211

*William A. Hightower, as he
appeared in the San
Francisco police station in
1922 only hours before
leading officers to the body
of the slain priest, Father
Heslin.* (UPI)

The coroner had already released his gruesome report that Father Heslin had been knocked unconscious and "the entire back of the skull has been crushed and the brain mashed. A blunt instrument, used with very powerful force, caused these injuries. Two shots had been fired into the body."

The killing of a priest on an errand of mercy not only shocked San Francisco but made howling headlines across the country. Nothing, save the murder of a child, all agreed, could be more horrible. Added Archbishop Hanna: "That a poor priest, going to assist a man in the throes of death, could meet foul play seems so incredible that the archbishop hopes that in the clearing up of the death of Father Heslin some excuse may be found that will save the name of San Francisco."

That excuse was not long in coming. The police charged Hightower with the murder. Inside his hotel room, officials found the typewriter on which the ransom note had been neatly typed. Also discovered on the premises was a homemade machinegun of rather inventive origin, which, as one of the notes had said, would destroy any who attempted to apprehend the kidnapper when the ransom was paid.

A search for the two girls proved disappointing to Hightower's story. The first, Dolly Mason, never existed. The second, Doris Shirley, was, by the time she was located, found to be engaged. Yes, she had known Hightower, she admitted, but only for one night in his hotel room, that was all. She knew nothing of rumrunners, secreted booze, or, least of all horrors, the kidnapping and killing of a priest.

On August 13, a pawnbroker informed police that Hightower had pawned a .45-caliber automatic, the same weapon, authorities were to determine, used to kill Father Heslin.

The game was up with William A. Hightower. To a barrage of questions from reporters, Hightower could only answer: "Ish ka bible!" In a brief trial he was found guilty of murder. Why the convicted man was not sentenced to be executed is unclear; the jury concluded he was a bit daffy, too zany to be executed. Though the *San Francisco Examiner* lobbied for Hightower's death, he received life imprisonment and was sent to San Quentin, where he became inmate number 35458, entering the prison with a copy of the *San Mateo Times* that said he had perpetrated "the most heinous and revolting crime that has ever been committed in the annals of the state."

Hightower was as reclusive in prison as he had been in the

outside world. This was mostly the decision of other inmates who made him a pariah; other than killers of children and women, no offender was thought by the prisoners to be more despicable than the slayer of a priest. Convict Hightower didn't seem to mind. He busied himself in the kitchen, where he displayed his true talents as a master cook and superb dietician (his food preparations were to become standard practice at San Quentin). Naturally, he excelled in pastries and delicacies. Warden Duffy was to remember how "he made a candy out of fruit which was so delicious that Gladys [Duffy] asked him for the recipe. Neither she nor anyone else could duplicate it even after he wrote it out for her."

Most of Hightower's time was spent printing his own newsletter, which he called "Observations from A. Hightower," a weekly one-page affair on which he sketched himself, a bald-headed little man peeping out of a turret in the clouds, and words ballooning from him that read "Clouds of popular conception."

The newsletter was slightly above gibberish and lavished with rotten puns, stale epigrams and verse that would not pass for kitsch. Well or sick, Hightower continued to produce his newsletter, coming to believe that he was another H. L. Mencken. (One of his fellow prisoners, Gordon Northcott, a sex deviate who had slain more than a dozen women, died in San Quentin and, among others, inexplicably bequeathed part of his secreted fortune—never unearthed—to H. L. Mencken.)

Such was Hightower's opinion of his own literary talents that he demanded that the *San Francisco Examiner* publish a regular column written by him. It was only fair, he argued, since the *Examiner*, with its snoopy reporters, had "railroaded" him into prison. William Randolph Hearst was disinclined to make him a prison pundit in his newspaper. Yet Hightower's ego not only remained intact but blossomed to megalomania. In 1960, this mentor to miscreants sent a letter to Warden Duffy: "Hightower that WAS SUPPOSED TO BE VERY IGNORANT when sent to prison—is NOW—such a *'wizard of words'* that he has SURPASSED ALL OTHER MEN in writing 'punch lines.' " This note, plainly enough, displayed the same writing style, such as combining all-caps and lowercase words, Hightower had employed when penning his ransom notes for Father Heslin, a man he never mentioned in prison to his dying days. Near the end, Hightower yearned for his last moments, writing that

"Death is a brief wait between the acts." He considered, however, the writing he had done before his imprisonment to be
the highwater mark of his "genius," proudly pointing to a poem
found in his rooms by news-hungry reporters in 1921:

Somewhere someone is waiting
Someone with a heart that is true
Somewhere someone is longing
Waiting and watching for you.

1922 LOS ANGELES

The Scratch of a "Tiger Woman"

Former showgirl Clara Phillips thought herself a happily married woman. Her husband, Armour Phillips, was a well-to-do
oil stock salesman with unlimited prospects, what with newly
discovered black gold gushing from the ground in southern California in the early 1920s. The Phillips home in Los Angeles
was definitely upper-class, replete with maids and three sets of
silverware.

At twenty-three, the attractive, brown-haired Mrs. Phillips
found her life with Armour suddenly less than amorous. He was
beginning to spend a great deal of time elsewhere—unknown
time and in unknown places, particularly in the evenings.

Clara spent several weeks checking on her husband, following him in cabs, listening in on the upstairs phone extension
when Armour Phillips received calls at strange hours. The results of her sleuthing she confided to her best friend, Peggy
Caffee, another former showgirl who had once trouped the
backwater vaudeville circuits with Clara.

"He stays out late," complained Clara to Peggy; and, what
hurt most of all, "he doesn't care to come near me.... He's
running around with some girl." And Clara had discovered the
identity of the other woman, the beautiful Alberta Meadows, a
twenty-one-year-old widow. Clara and Alberta had briefly met
a few days before, an icy, stare-down encounter.

The girls decided to drown Clara's sorrows in some Prohibition gin. Peggy and Clara took a cab to Long Beach to a swanky

speakeasy where Clara was known, and for several hours they swilled the stinging Jazz-Age hooch. By late that afternoon, July 6, 1922, Clara and Peggy, at Clara's insistence, found themselves standing in a parking lot behind a Los Angeles bank. Somehow, Clara knew that her love adversary would arrive momentarily. Alberta Meadows appeared within minutes, coming from the bank and going to her car.

She was startled to see Clara and Peggy standing before her, a bit wobbly-legged and thick of tongue as a result of their speakeasy revels. Clara was all charm, smiling toothily and calmly saying: "Hi! We need a ride. How about a lift to my sister Etta's place?"

Alberta first hesitated, then shrugged, no doubt concluding that it was time she had it out with Clara; she would not deny seeing Armour Phillips. They were in love and Clara, if reasoned with, would surely agree to abdicate her matrimonial throne. Alberta agreed to drive the girls.

Clara chatted good-naturedly to Alberta as the widow drove, her mood almost gay. Then, reaching a sparsely populated district on Montecito Drive, at the top of a hill, Clara's attitude abruptly changed. "Stop the car here!" she ordered.

"What for?" Alberta said.

"Some things need talking over."

Alberta nodded and pulled the car to the curb. She turned off the ignition and gave Clara back her defiant look. "Well?"

With a quick move, Clara got out of the auto. Alberta slipped from behind the driver's wheel. Both women stood in the road glaring at each other. Peggy Caffee got out of the car and stood nearby.

"He's awfully nice, isn't he?" Clara spat at Alberta with a sneer. "How many things has he bought you lately?" She looked down and pointed to an expensive-looking wristwatch on Alberta's arm. "He gave you the watch, didn't he?"

"No, he didn't," Alberta said defensively. "I bought it myself."

With that Clara's eyes blazed; her clenched fist came forward with a terrific smash to Alberta's face that sent the youthful widow reeling backward, knocking her hat to the ground. One look at Clara's face contorted with rage and Alberta began to run down the hill, one of her high heels breaking off, and Clara, panting curse words, in pursuit. Peggy ran after them, wedging between the two women.

With one motion, Clara produced a hammer she had secreted
in her handbag and shoved Peggy aside, roaring: "Get out of
the way." She lifted the hammer and brought it down full force
into Alberta's face. Again and again, to Peggy Caffee's astonish-
ment, Clara Phillips struck the widow, raining blows upon her
head and face until she sagged to the pavement, her skull a
pulpy piece of gore. Peggy, by then hysterical and vomiting,
also collapsed; she managed to scream "Help! Help!" She
watched in horror as her friend Clara bent over Alberta's
crushed form and twice more raised the blood-dripping hammer to strike the woman.

Peggy fainted. She revived minutes later when she heard the
sound of a car horn. Clara was at the wheel of Alberta's car and
beckoned to her, opening the door for her and giving her a
crazy smile with the soothing words of "It's all right now, dear,
get inside. Time to go home."

Dazed and horror-struck into silence, Peggy climbed into the
car. She watched Clara hold up Alberta's handbag, open it and
then, with hands coated with blood, take off her wedding rings
and drop them into the bag. A strange smile clung to Clara's
lips. Clara drove Peggy home and then returned to her own
house, parking the widow's car in her driveway. Her husband,
Armour, met her in the living room, disturbed at the strange
way his wife acted. Clara poured herself a drink and then told
him: "I guess it's murder."

"What's murder?"

"I killed your lover, Alberta."

Whether by self-defensive instincts or a mad act of compassion, it was never known which, Armour Phillips responded to
this lightning-bolt news by immediately offering to help his
murderous wife. "You've got to escape, get out."

Within minutes Clara was driving the widow's car to Pomona,
her husband following her in their own car. They parked the
murdered woman's car in a secluded spot and returned to Los
Angeles. Clara packed her bags and took the next available train
from the city, heading for Mexico—the plan man and wife
thought best.

While Clara rode southward, Armour Phillips reconsidered
the insanity of it all and then called his lawyers who, in turn,
notified the police. Officials went aboard Clara's train in Tucson
and arrested her in her drawing room.

Her trial was a newspaperman's delight, headlines depicting

Clara as "The Tiger Woman" who had stalked her prey, Alberta Meadows, for days, until pouncing for the kill. Clara claimed innocence; someone else had done the foul deed. Her lawyers could offer only a feeble defense. They referred to a large rock that had been found on the dead woman's chest, but the jury was unimpressed, realizing that Clara had placed the rock there as false evidence. The blood-caked handle of the hammer was placed in evidence (the head had broken off during the repeated blows; it had been embedded in Alberta's skull, and then was somehow lost by pathologists examining the body).

Peggy Caffee's testimony doomed the defiant Clara who, incredibly, then charged that her friend Peggy had bought the hammer and had killed poor Alberta. When pressed, Clara could give no motive for such lethal wrath on Peggy's behalf. The jury quickly decided that "Alberta Meadows came to her death of a fracture of the skull inflicted with hammer blows by Mrs. Clara Phillips." The Tiger Woman was given ten years to life on November 16, 1922. But before she was sent to San Quentin, Clara again made sensational headlines.

While her lawyers filed appeals, Clara, residing in the Los Angeles County Jail, was aided by a gallant old lover, Jesse Carson. The two plotted an unbelievable escape. During a violent storm on the night of December 5, 1922, Clara Phillips obtained a hacksaw, apparently smuggled to her from the outside by Carson, and sliced through the bars of her cell window, squeezing through an opening thirteen by ten inches. While the heavy rain beat upon her, the intrepid Clara, groping in the dark, made her way along a slippery third-story ledge, down a drainpipe to another lower roof and then, somehow, managed to slip over a fifty-foot wall to an alley and a waiting car.

Clara fled to Honduras with Jesse Carson, and her sister, Etta Mae Jackson. Her freedom was short-lived. Police arrested Clara on April 20, 1923, in downtown Tegucigalpa while she was shopping. She was extradited to Los Angeles. After extensive psychiatric examinations, Clara Phillips was pronounced sane. She had hoped for another trial based on temporary insanity at the time of the murder.

Clara was sent to San Quentin where she maintained her innocence through the wearisome years behind bars. Despairing of ever being released, the Tiger Woman tried to commit suicide, but her wrist-slashing attempt was feeble and she recovered. In 1933, Clara, along with all other female prisoners

Clara Phillips, the "Tiger Woman" of Los Angeles, upon her release from Tehachapi in 1935.

in San Quentin, was removed to the new woman's prison at Tehachapi. She was paroled, much against the vociferous arguments of Alberta Meadows' relatives and friends, on June 21, 1935. Standing before the wire fences of Tehachapi, Clara smiled for cameras. Newsmen yelled out to her: "Look this way, Tiger Woman! Hey, Tiger Woman, look fierce for the camera!"

There was nothing of the jungle left inside Clara Phillips, who pooh-poohed the newshounds with: "Oh, stop that . . . it was all nonsense, so long ago."

Nothing more was heard from Mrs. Phillips until August 30, 1961, when the California Parole Board was petitioned by Clara, then living in La Mesa with her seventy-seven-year-old mother. She asked permission to relocate in Texas where she wanted to practice dentistry. Even at that late date, she complained, there was no peace for her in California. With unthinking neighborhood children, whispering gossips, even the milkman, it was always the same refrain: "Tiger Woman, Tiger Woman."

1924 CHICAGO

The Sting of a Bohemian Butterfly

The lure of the artistic life was overwhelming to Wanda Stopa. Since a childhood that had scrabbled through the toil-sweated streets of Chicago's Little Poland on the near-northwest side of the city, Wanda had dreamed of becoming a writer of great prose and moving through the gossamer circles of successful artists as a recognized talent. Hers was the ambition for sophisticated fame and the whirlwind lifestyle of those romantic Bohemians respected and feared by the pedestrian public—particularly the ethnic horde of Polish that Wanda reluctantly called her own people. Her fate, toward which she hurled herself with feverish vigor, was to be that of Edna St. Vincent Millay's candle that burned at both ends. Wanda was the wax; her lover and unwitting catalyst to her crime, the fire.

As a child Wanda proved herself to be an excellent student, encouraged by her mother to make more of herself than those children predestined to poverty and a sweatshop future. She clutched inspiration in the hand of a father who had been an artist. Everywhere in the Stopa home on Augusta Street were her father's etchings of cathedrals and miniature statuary made in the old country before the family immigrated to Chicago. Prior to entering college, Wanda became intrigued with the rituals and drama enacted in the municipal courts, visiting them daily. She decided to make a profession in the legal world and, by working at night and using the meager allowance her parents gave her, she managed to save enough money to finish college and law school, becoming the pride of Little Poland and, according to one of her professors, "one of the most brilliant women ever to be admitted to the local bar." Within months she was sworn in as an assistant district attorney in Chicago.

Wanda's legal career began with the birth of Prohibition and smoke-filled twenty-four-hour jazz joints, of fast flivvers and even faster flappers. Chicago's toot was equal to that of New York and spiced with more of everything—more gin, more vice, more violence and glamorized gangsters. Wanda, growing restless with the routine of court, soon bobbed her hair and bought some tight-fitting, knee-length dresses, slipping into the wicked swirl of Bohemia centered in the early 1920s on the Near North Side of Chicago.

At one of the endless parties roaring through the city nights of 1922, Wanda was introduced to a tall, stately émigré from Russia, an impoverished count named Vladimir Glaskoff (later anglicized to Glaskow). His regal airs and manners, his handsome profile, his talk of art and *belle lettres* soon captivated her. The two had a brief affair before motoring to Crown Point, Indiana, just across the state line, to wed.

Marital bliss with the count was short-lived. Glaskoff, for all his imperial style and sartorial splendor, was a deadbeat, moving from one party to another, borrowing money and apartments in which he and Wanda could sleep off the long hangovers. In her traveling revels, Wanda met and became enamored of Yeremya Kenley Smith, a wealthy advertising executive who gently prattled of Nietzsche and Schopenhauer. He became the center of Wanda's world; she sat at his feet while Smith played intellectual mentor.

The count flitted away with other paramours while Wanda spent most of her time in the company of Smith and his music-loving wife, Vieva Dawley Smith, actually moving into their

A Jazz Age flapper, Wanda Stopa was both beautiful and lethal. (UPI)

studio at 190 East Ohio Street in the heart of Chicago's synthetic artistic community on the Near North Side, called Towertown in those days. In her distorted view of phony artists and fake writers, Wanda came to believe the gobbledygook Smith spewed forth as words of genius; she fell in love with him, believing he no longer cared for his wife.

To her mother the bronze-haired beauty confided that she would obtain a divorce from her philandering count and, once Smith did the same with wife, Vieva, they would marry. Her mother, Inez, shook her head sadly and then burst forth with: "Only a bum would make love to my little girl when he is already married. No good can come of it."

Smith had made no such arrangements. In fact, he was amused by Wanda, loved her spirit for life and art, but, as he adamantly proclaimed afterward, he had no carnal ideas about the attractive assistant district attorney. Rebuffed, Wanda became despondent. She spent long nights sobbing hysterically. The Stopa family doctor visited her at her mother's and then duly reported that Wanda "is on the dope." Indeed, by that time, Wanda Stopa had become a heavy morphine addict.

Worried about her menacing outbursts, Smith decided to send Wanda away to an even bigger and brighter Bohemia, Greenwich Village in New York. There she would meet professional writers who could encourage her desire to pen a great novel. She fought with him, but when Smith insisted that he would never divorce his wife, she relented, and, with money he had given her (Smith promised to keep sending her money until she established herself in New York), Wanda entrained for the glittering artistic world of Bodenheim and F. Scott Fitzgerald.

It was the same in the Village, Wanda swimming through endless parties. She was a hit. Her money assured her of street fame in an area of penniless, fawning would-be artists and writers. She rented a comfortable flat in the Village and gave, by most standards, sumptuous parties. To any who asked, and there were scores, Wanda loaned out her money. When not high on morphine or hungover from rotgut booze, Wanda struggled to complete a story that had begun to take place in her mind, slowly, agonizingly, as she brooded darkly about her lost love, Smith. It was a murder story, one she managed to sell to a popular magazine for several hundred dollars.

Using Smith's final check, Wanda threw a lavish party. Her

swan song to Greenwich Village was awash with social misfits, literary leeches and artistic poseurs who gladly got drunk on her Prohibition gin. As the party increased in tempo, Wanda, dressed all in black, studied her phony friends. Unnoticed, she stepped to the center of the living room of her flat and then shouted: "I have an announcement to make!"

The startled guests were rocked to silence. Said the beautiful Jazz Age butterfly: "You and your theories and platitudes, listen to one who has heard them all time and again . . . they don't work out. Life—can't you see it crumbles like a handful of ashes? And I won't have ashes of life. . . . So now I'm going to try death. . . . Tomorrow I'm leaving here for Chicago and when I arrive I'm going to kill a woman—perhaps a man. But anyhow a woman. I'm going to kill her, do you hear? Shoot her because she refused to give up the man I love, one of the people who taught me theories that didn't work . . . I'll probably kill myself afterwards."

With that, Wanda tore away the costume jewelry she was wearing—bracelets, rings, a necklace—and threw them into the stunned crowd. The awesome silence was broken when a drunk lumbered up to Wanda and, placing a heavy arm about her shoulders in mock camaraderie, sloshed forth: "Atta girl. . . . But, listen, kid, when you shoot, aim straight, 'cause dead ones don't tell tales!"

The laughter was uproarious; it was a joke, all thought. While the party went on, Wanda went into her bedroom, grabbed two bags she had packed earlier and left, catching the train for Chicago. Reaching Union Station on the morning of April 24, 1924, Wanda picked out a cab that had no license plates, driven by Ernest T. Wood, an elderly man whose sight and hearing, she learned in a few seconds, were failing. She jumped into his taxi and told him to drive to Eighty-ninth and One hundred twenty-third streets in Palos Park. This was the country estate of Y. Kenley Smith. On the way, Wanda withdrew a .38-caliber revolver. She made sure it was loaded.

Her bronze hair glittering beneath a bright sun, the twenty-five-year-old writer and lawyer ordered Wood to stop his cab a block from the Smith residence. She walked calmly up the block and into the house, looking about. Pistol in hand, Wanda stepped into a bedroom off the living room to see Vieva Smith in bed, sick with influenza. The woman's eyes fluttered in the direction of Wanda Stopa.

"Where is Kenley?" screeched Wanda.

Mrs. Smith was so weak she could not lift her head from the pillow.

"Where is he?" the beautiful Polish girl demanded. "Aren't you going to divorce him? I tell you he loves me! You don't really love him, but you won't give him up!"

"Of course I'm not going to give him up, Wanda," Vieva finally replied. "Don't be silly. I have no reason to divorce him. Kenley doesn't want a divorce. And you're making yourself ridiculous. Kenley's tired of it and so am I."

Henry Manning, the sixty-eight-year-old caretaker of the Smith estate, had seen Wanda enter the house. He stood close to the bedroom window, listening to the confrontation. He jumped when he heard the intruder shout, "I'm going to kill you!"

Wanda produced her revolver, aimed and fired. The bullet slammed into the wall only six inches from Mrs. Smith's head. The sick woman, adrenaline now pumping, suddenly leaped from her bed, and, with a bounding stride, dove through the window, taking the screen with her as she bounced on the lawn. Wanda fired two more shots at her but they went wide, smacking into the bedroom wall.

Mrs. Smith got up and, with a wild yelp, dashed across the lawn, her grass-stained nightgown flowing behind her as she headed for the safety of a neighbor's house. Wanda calmly approached the window for a final and fatal shot. Manning suddenly blocked her path, stretching out his arms in front of the window to protect his mistress. Wanda fired. The old man fell backward without a word, a bullet through his head.

Seeing her prey escape, Wanda put away the revolver and walked slowly from the house and down the street, where she slipped back into the cab, ordering Wood to take her to the Illinois Central Depot.

When police arrived at the Smith home, they found caretaker Manning quite dead. A desperate womanhunt then ensued. Wanda's picture adorned the front pages of newspapers across the nation inside of twenty-four hours. "A flapper gone wrong," said one newspaper in New York. "Another Chicago girl went gunning today," said a hometown sheet.

Police frantically searched the city, especially the Near North Side and Little Poland, keeping an around-the-clock watch on her mother's home. Wanda was nowhere to be found. Her pic-

Chicago advertising mogul Y. K. Smith, for whose love Wanda Stopa murdered. (UPI)

ture stayed on the front pages, long enough for Eugene Chloupak of Indianapolis to recognize her as he passed her in the mezzanine of Detroit's Hotel Statler two days later. Wanda, Chloupak noted, was writing a letter at the time.

Chloupak notified authorities. Police were checking the Statler's register at 1:30 P.M. that afternoon. They found no "Stopa" registered. One officer, knowing Wanda's background, suggested they check the name Glaskoff, her married name. They found the room number. Detectives raced upstairs but when they came to Wanda's room, the house physician was standing before them. He had been called there minutes before by a woman who could only mutter weakly, "I am very ill."

Wanda was dead, fully clothed, on the hotel bed. Next to her lay an empty bottle; she had taken poison. There was no farewell note. On the floor was a small overnight case, expensive lingerie and toilet articles inside. On the bureau was her diary, which carefully told the story that had financed the killing of hapless Henry Manning.

The body was removed to Little Poland in Chicago, where a great throng assembled at the time of the funeral two days later. As her coffin was being removed from her home en route to burial, more than two thousand persons, all Polish, came to bid farewell to "the brainiest woman ever to come out of Little Poland," as one newsman wrote. To these uneducated, unsophisticated masses of hard-working people, Wanda was a bright star in their otherwise gray lives, one of their own who had managed, despite the violence and sorrow of her plight, to escape the drudgery of their economic caste. Such was the hysteria as her casket was carried through the crowds that many ripped away the flowers adorning it.

People leaned far out their windows on Augusta Street to catch sight of the departing hearse. Women held up their babies so that they could see the last of all their ambitions drive slowly down the street, see the "one of them who made good" vanish at the corner and disappear.

1927 BROOKLYN, N.Y.

Homicide Bit by Bit

A short, thick-set man, his collar buttoned tight about a bull neck, his black hair glistening, was seen Sunday morning, July 10, 1927, leaving a boardinghouse in Brooklyn, carrying a bundle. He returned within an hour and left again with another bundle. He lugged bundles from the three-story building at 28 Prospect Place all morning long.

At two o'clock the following morning, a beat cop patrolling Battery Park poked his nightstick at a heavy bundle wrapped in brown paper nestling at the corner of a subway air vent. He opened the bundle. Inside were some old clothes and two laundry bags. Untying the laundry bags, the cop gasped. In each was a human leg, neatly severed.

The following day added more mystery to this disgusting find when an officer was called to a Brooklyn Church where a small boy had found a bundle on the lawn. This, too, was wrapped in brown paper. Inside, officers found the hips and back section of a woman's body. Some ten blocks from the church, a theater manager, inspecting his building before the afternoon matinee, found another bundle, also wrapped in brown paper, at the base of his theater's fire escape. It contained the arm and left shoulder of a woman's body; its ring finger had been cut away but the remaining fingers were clenched around strands of black hair.

The bundles kept turning up all over Brooklyn and parts of Manhattan. Police realized that they were now in possession of not one, but two bodies, both females, as they put the pieces together; but they lacked positive identification. The heads were still missing. One of the bodies was that of an elderly woman, the other middle-aged. There was only one clue, a thin one. On the wrapping paper bundled around one of the grisly finds was a series of numbers, such as one might make when tallying a grocery purchase, detectives concluded. The paper itself was distinctive and police soon learned that it was a brand used only by two grocery chains, Bohack's and A&P.

The impossible task of tracing down the paper through hundreds of stores in New York was begun, detectives seeking out the clerk who had undoubtedly penciled the numbers on the one sheet of wrapping paper. Before officers visited a half dozen stores, the search was called off. Luck, the greatest aid police ever have, next to informers, in solving their cases, intervened in the form of a missing persons report.

Alfred Bennett of 16 Lincoln Place, Brooklyn, reported his wife missing. Investigating officers learned from one of Mrs. Bennett's four children, nineteen-year-old John Bennett, that he had last seen her cross a backyard courtyard from their home, entering 28 Prospect Place, a boardinghouse she had recently sold to a seventy-six-year-old spinster, Sarah Elizabeth Brownell. Miss Brownell had been late with her monthly payments and Mrs. Bennett had gone to collect. She had not returned home.

Arthur A. Carey, Deputy Inspector for the Homicide Bureau of the NYPD, went to 28 Prospect Place that night. He was greeted by a dark-featured thirty-eight-year-old man who identified himself as Ludwig Lee, a Norwegian who did odd jobs and was down on his luck. He explained to Inspector Carey that he had been living for several years in the boardinghouse. No, he had no idea where they could find the landlady, Miss Brownell.

Carey and other detectives edged past the man, stepping into the dark entrance hall. "Are you sure you don't know where Miss Brownell is?" asked Carey in the dark.

The man hesitated, then said: "Oh, yes, I remember now. I think she went to visit relatives in Gloversville, New York. That was on July Fourth . . . to celebrate the holiday."

"What about Mrs. Bennett? Have you seen her?"

"Yes, she, also. Some days ago. She come over here to complain to Miss Brownell about the water pipes in the building. They are leaking. They have flooded Mrs. Bennett's yard, I think. I went to the basement with her. I left her standing next to the furnace. That is the last time I see her."

As the detectives stood in the gloom they sniffed a familiar odor, damp and sickeningly sweet.

"I think you're coming with us," Carey told Lee.

"What for?"

"To see what else you can remember."

Minutes after Lee was escorted to the Brooklyn Police headquarters, detectives left at the boardinghouse stopped a man from entering. He gave his name as Christian Jensen; he was a clerk in a Brooklyn A&P store. Jensen was coming to visit his friend Lee; he had roomed in the house for years.

At that moment, Ludwig Lee stood mute in an interrogation room at headquarters. He stared sullenly at the officers about him. "That smell at the boardinghouse," one detective said to another in front of Lee.

"Yeah?"

"Take a whiff of this character. He's reeking of it."

"What smell is that?" asked Lee innocently.

"Death," snapped the detective. "The smell of dead human flesh."

Detectives at the boardinghouse were by now conducting a thorough search of the building. In the basement they found part of a female torso and other parts of bodies in an ashcan. Leaning against the furnace was a large axe, which had been washed and polished recently.

Jensen, interviewed by detectives in the boardinghouse parlor, was shown the wrapping paper from one of the bundles with the numbers written on it. He identified the writing as his own. He next told police that he had given Ludwig Lee quite a bit of wrapping paper some days before; the Norwegian boarder wanted to bundle up some "gifts," he had told Jensen, which he intended to mail to relatives in Norway.

Lee had acted strangely as of late, Jensen recalled. He had wanted to chat with him on Saturday night and had looked all about the boardinghouse for Lee. He tried the door to the basement and found it locked. Thinking Lee might be in the basement, he had rattled the door repeatedly. Finally, Lee's angry voice shouted through the door: "Don't do that!" Jensen had gone away.

Medical examiners were sent to the Brownell house, taking with them the gruesome pieces police had discovered. There, with the parts of bodies found in the basement, including Mrs. Bennett's head, they pieced the bodies back together on the kitchen table. All of this gory work was done by plan, a shock treatment, as it were, for the close-mouthed Ludwig Lee, who was then taken back to the boardinghouse and shown the corpses in the kitchen.

"Who killed them?" Inspector Carey asked him, pointing to the bodies.

"I don't know!" screamed Lee, his manner fierce. "How should I know?" He sneered at what he thought to be the remains of Miss Brownell. "The old woman begged me to marry her and I first refused, then consented."

Detectives coming from Lee's room had found Miss Brownell's savings book listing an account of more than four thousand dollars. Lee weakened and told police that he had, with the old woman's blessings, cashed several checks against her account on different occasions.

Jensen was brought in to face his friend. Lee's face drained of blood when the clerk told how Lee had borrowed the wrapping paper. The odd-job man lost his nerve altogether, confessing the double murder on the spot. He had not meant to kill Mrs. Bennett. She had stepped into the basement on Thursday night, July 7, 1927, looking for Miss Brownell. She had found her, lying in pieces, Lee standing over the ghastly remains with a raised axe. He had killed Mrs. Bennett, too, to cover up his murder of the old woman, a landlady killed for her bank account.

"There was nothing to do but chop them into little pieces and drop them out of sight," Lee sighed. "It was a lot of work doing all that running around."

Ludwig Lee, a man of grim opportunity, was convicted in a quick trial and electrocuted in early 1928.

Brooklyn handyman Ludwig Lee (right, under arrest) dropped pieces of his victims all around New York. (UPI)

1930 AMARILLO, TEXAS

A Newsman Smells Murder

A. D. Payne was a contented man, successful as one of the most sought-after attorneys in Amarillo, Texas. He had wealth, a handsome home and a cherished family; he was devoted, as the town knew, to his wife and three children. All the more shocked were citizens when they learned of violent death striking into the heart of the Payne family on June 27, 1930.

On that day Payne broke a longstanding habit and told his wife that he would be walking to his office. She and the children could use the family car, a coupe, for their errands.

As Payne was leaving the house, Bobbie Jean, his small daughter, caught his hand at the door. "Daddy, can I walk with you to your office?" Payne bent down and kissed the little girl's forehead. "Of course you can, sweetheart," he replied, and went off with her.

A few hours later, Mrs. Payne and her son, A. D., Jr., climbed into the coupe and set off for the grocery store. After going no more than a half mile, the front of the car began to gush smoke.

The boy sniffed and remembered: "Mother, that smells exactly like the smoke of that powder fuse I found in the backyard and burned."

"Daddy told me to drive faster if the car smoked," said Mrs. Payne, ignoring her son's remark and stepping hard on the accelerator.

A terrific explosion tore the auto to pieces a few seconds later. Mrs. Payne was blown through the roof of the car, her body hurtling forty feet in front of the car. A. D., Jr., was also sent through the top of the car. Running, gasping neighbors lifted the bleeding, horribly disfigured boy and found him still alive. He was rushed to a hospital where he survived. There was nothing anyone could do for Mrs. Payne except call the morgue and notify her husband.

Townspeople were enraged; the police, who examined every detail of the explosion, were baffled; and Gene Howe, the dogged editor of the *Amarillo News* and *Globe,* vowed he would unearth the true cause of the explosion.

It was Howe's unswerving opinion that Mrs. Payne had been murdered. He said so in his newspaper, stating that he might have himself deputized so that he could personally investigate the case, a statement made more from bravado than intention.

To this bombast responded A. D. Payne, who walked quietly into Howe's office and thanked him for the interest in his wife's death. Not only did he encourage Howe to delve into the case but offered a reward of five thousand dollars through Howe's newspapers to anyone who could solve the mystery.

Understaffed, Howe contacted the *Kansas City Star,* asking that it send one of its many experienced reporters to help him on the Payne matter. The paper dispatched a dogged snooper named A. B. MacDonald.

The big-city reporter had long talks with Howe. Did he suspect anyone? The editor paused, then said: "I don't know. Sometimes I think Payne killed her and again I think that he did not. I am completely baffled. So are all the authorities. Ninety percent of the people here suspect Payne killed her, but there isn't a shred of proof."

What pointed to the lawyer's guilt was Payne's provocative background. The mild-mannered Payne had become a school-

Texas attorney A. D. Payne resorted to a bomb to rid himself of his family.

teacher upon graduation from college. He was named a high school principal within a short time. During this period, Payne put himself through law school, concentrating on criminology courses. His practice was strictly devoted to criminals, whom he defended with great legal acumen and whose fees made him a rich man. All who knew him were aware that Payne spent most of his off-hours studying criminals and their crimes, particularly murder.

Those who had been following his career were not wholly shocked at the awful death of his wife. They remembered the previous March when his wife had opened a closet door in her home and had received a discharge of birdshot through her hand from a shotgun. Most thought the calculating lawyer had planted the gun and rigged it in such a way as to kill Mrs. Payne. The lawyer innocently claimed that it had been a clumsy accident, that the shotgun, standing on top of a sewing machine, had been jarred when Mrs. Payne pulled the closet door open too abruptly, setting it off.

MacDonald discovered in his investigative interviews about Amarillo that Payne had heavily insured his wife and children

*The shattered remains of the
Payne auto.*

with himself as the beneficiary. But by the same token, he had also taken out massive insurance on himself with his wife and children to receive the benefits. The *Star* reporter decided to confront Payne directly.

The lawyer welcomed the reporter into his home, chatting affably with him and offering him any kind of information asked. MacDonald, a streetwise reporter of a thousand criminal cases, didn't like the lawyer's demeanor and instinctively thought him guilty. "There was something about him that made me suspect him," he later wrote. "He was nervous. His long fingers kept fidgeting and pulling at his cheeks and chin. Behind his thin-lipped mouth I felt there was a cruel, heartless nature. I never once thought he was innocent after I first saw him and heard his even-toned voice; it seemed unnatural."

During the interview Payne's fourteen-year-old daughter, now the family cook, nervously wrung her hands as she moved in and out of the rooms of the house. Tears seemed to swell up in her eyes. Little Bobbie Jean was asked to relate how she narrowly missed being killed. She told her story wrong, according to Payne, who coached: "No, honey, it wasn't that way. Don't you remember—" Bobbie Jean burst forth in tears and wracking sobs. Reporter MacDonald felt both children had been told by their father what stories to recite when asked about their mother's death, and the fear of their father was real.

The motive for Payne's killing of his wife remained unclear. He certainly didn't need the money he collected from his wife's insurance—his bank accounts proved that. Not until checking into Payne's business affairs did MacDonald think he had pinpointed the cause.

Payne had had four different secretaries in less than one year. Vera Holcomb had been with Payne only a short time in 1929. Also in that year, from August to December, Verona Thompson had gone to work for Payne, who had let her go. Mabel Bush had also worked for the lawyer, and been replaced by Ocie Humphries. All of the girls were young.

Returning to Payne, MacDonald asked him what he thought of the secretaries.

"How do you mean?"

"Were men attracted to any of them?"

Payne couldn't say. Then he studied the reporter and stated that Vera Holcomb was all right. Of Verona Thompson, Payne said "she is twenty-four or twenty-five years old, just an ordinary-looking woman. No man would get sweet on her." He described Mabel Bush as a hot number. "She's young and very attractive, a redhead full of pep and wide awake. She is only nineteen or twenty." Ocie Humphries was a good-looker, said Payne with a shrug.

The lawyer, MacDonald instantly felt, had given him the key to the mystery. He went directly to Verona Thompson, whom Payne had insisted would draw no man's attention. Greeting him at her apartment was a voluptuous young woman with a wide smile of even, bright teeth. "She was that type of working girl who knows," wrote MacDonald, "how to dress attractively and be agreeable to men."

Playing all his cards at once, MacDonald, who was to win the Pulitzer Prize for his audacious investigative reporting, stared into the eyes of the young woman and said: "Verona, how many times has Payne taken you out for lunch?"

"Many times," came her instant response. "But there was always another girl with us."

The reporter suspected that Payne would never have taken Verona to any of the local hotels, but could have easily slipped away with this sexy brunette to any of the oil boomtowns nearby, especially Borger, Texas, where no questions were ever asked. "Have you been to Borger with him?"

Verona hesitated and then blurted, "Yes, to Borger."

"Do you think he killed her?"

"Yes, I think so," the secretary said matter-of-factly. "My! It was an awful thing, wasn't it?"

Verona Thompson admitted to authorities that Payne had been her tempestuous lover for months prior to Mrs. Payne's death, that he had promised to get rid of his wife and marry her. Confronted with this, Payne lost all composure and sobbed out a confession of murder by dynamite. His guilt was not for his dead spouse but for his now scandal-ridden lover.

"I am the meanest man that ever lived," Payne blabbered. "I love that girl, Verona Thompson. She is as pure as the driven snow!"

In a speedy trial, criminologist Payne was convicted and sentenced to die in the electric chair. He proved too clever for that. Two days before his execution was to take place, A. D. Payne once more displayed to the world his inventive knowledge of explosives by discharging a small explosive contraption he had secretly strapped to his chest. It blew out his heart.

Mrs. Payne, who took one shopping trip too many.

1933 NEW YORK CITY—NEW ORLEANS

"Look at Those Nerves!"

Affable, twenty-five-year-old Kenneth Neu was a heart's delight to women young and old, sporting wavy brown hair, piercing blue eyes, and chalk-white teeth. He had a talent of sorts for singing and dancing; his ambition was to be a nightclub entertainer, but though he warbled his way through many a honky-tonk, Mr. Neu's real talent was in murder.

Little is known of Kenneth Neu's early life, except that he drifted young into vagrancy and then upper-class trampdom during the early 1930s. Without any special training, Neu wholeheartedly believed himself blessed with a marvelous voice and dancing feet. (The voice was adequate; the feet could patter somewhat-less-than-dazzling, uneducated steps.)

Neu badgered almost all the nightclub owners in Manhattan to allow him to sing with their bands. The pay he politely requested was no more than a handout, a not-unusual ploy; the country was swamped with young men on the bum during the Depression and any job for any price meant survival. Neu's skimpy talent assured him limited engagements. By September 2, 1933, Neu found himself wandering through Times Square, broke and tired, too weak even to sing a song for quarters.

A middle-aged man named Lawrence Shead spotted him and invited him to his hotel room for a drink, telling Neu that he owned a string of theaters in Paterson, New Jersey, and that he might be able to advance his career. Neu spent the next twenty-four hours drinking with Shead, asking about the promised job. Shead put him off, plying Neu with imported liquor, and eventually making homosexual advances. Kenneth Neu finally had enough and told Shead he was through with the game.

"I want you to feel good," Shead told the would-be crooner, putting his arms about him. "We're going to have some real fun."

Neu exploded. He lashed out at his scabrous benefactor, landing a blow to Shead's head that sent him to the floor. Shead got up, belching revenge. The two men fought wildly about the room. As Shead fell off balance, Neu grabbed an iron from a shelf and crashed it onto the older man's head. He then jumped upon Shead and strangled him, but he was choking a corpse.

He then went to the bathroom and took a shower. He put on one of Shead's best suits, stuffed the businessman's wallet into a pocket and left.

A week later Kenneth Neu was strolling the streets of New Orleans, singing in what nightclubs could endure his act. He met a waitress named Eunice Hotte and told her he would take her to New York: "We'll have a big time in the big town."

"Are you sure you'll have the money, Kenneth?"

"I'll have it," beamed the enterprising Neu. He found it at the Yung Hotel some hours later, in the pockets of Sheffield Clark, Sr., head of a Nashville, Tennessee, hardware firm. After striking up a conversation with the elderly Clark in the lobby, Neu pawned his watch, bought a blackjack, and returned to the hotel. He went to Clark's room and demanded money. Clark refused and Neu blackjacked him to death. He took three hundred dollars of Clark's money and the parking stub for the merchant's car, and was soon driving northward with a deliriously happy Eunice Hotte at his side.

To avoid Clark's license plate's being detected, Neu replaced it with a crudely scrawled sign reading "New Car in Transit." This guaranteed a speedy arrest. New Jersey police pulled Neu over and he was soon in a station giving a dozen different stories for the sign. Detectives learned that a young man answering Neu's description was wanted for killing a prominent Patterson, New Jersey, businessman.

"Did you ever know a man named Lawrence Shead?" they asked Neu.

The boyish dancer grinned. "Sure, I killed him. This is his suit I'm wearing now!"

Neu just as happily admitted killing Clark. He was extradited to Louisiana and placed on trial for the Clark murder. Though lengthy arguments ensued over Neu's sanity, he was convicted and judged mentally fit to be executed. Upon hearing the jury's verdict, Kenneth Neu bowed to the judge, turned to the jury and cried out: "Gentlemen, you have my best wishes." With that he went into a wild dance and sang "Sweet Rosie O'Grady" at the top of his lungs before being led away.

Neu's conduct while awaiting execution in Parish Prison in New Orleans was a virtuoso performance. He sang and danced all the time in his cell, giving out interviews to startled reporters as he flipped a coin and shouted: "Look at those nerves, boys! Look at those nerves!"

Kenneth Neu, singing the song he composed for the hangman in New Orleans and wearing the suit of one of his murder victims. (UPI)

233

On the morning of his execution, February 1, 1935, Neu treated guards to a song he had composed entitled "I'm Fit as a Fiddle and Ready to Hang." He gingerly tapped his way up the gallows stairs and did a clog dance upon the steel trap. As the hood was being lowered over his head, Kenneth Neu finished his last performance by crooning "Love in Bloom." The trap sprung open and Neu shot downward, his neck breaking almost instantly. From the guards and visitors present there was no applause, only silence for a bad actor.

1935 LOS ANGELES
"The Damned Snakes Didn't Work"

A successful barber in Los Angeles, Robert James seemed to have nothing more than a good meal on his mind when he drove up to his LaCanada home at six o'clock on the night of August 5, 1935, tooting the horn of his car to signal his wife, Mary, that he had brought company for dinner.

"That's funny," James remarked to his two friends as they strolled into the richly furnished bungalow, "Mary's usually got the feedbag on by now. Wait till you meet her. What a cook!"

But Mrs. James, the former Mary Bush, age twenty-five, James' one-time red-hot blond manicurist, would be cooking no more dinners. The trio found her in the garden, sprawled face down in a shallow lily pond.

Responding to James' alarm, the Los Angeles County Sheriff's office sent two officers and a doctor. The physician pronounced Mary James dead, drowned in six inches of water. He noticed that her left leg was horribly swollen to twice its normal size.

"Some strange insect must have bitten the poor woman," the doctor commented. Authorities quickly concluded that Mary James, who was pregnant, had gotten dizzy while watering her flowers, and collapsed into the lily pond. James was not under suspicion. He easily proved he had been in his luxurious five-chair barber shop in downtown Los Angeles at Olive and Eighth Streets at eight that morning—the time Mary's unfortunate death was fixed. "Accidental death" was written on the police report and the case forgotten. The grief-stricken Bob James went back to cutting hair. Three months passed before the barber was awarded thirty-five hundred dollars by an insurance company for the accidental death of Mary James.

A few days later, while James was shaving a customer, he spotted a ravishing redhead walking past the window of his shop. The auburn-haired, beefy six-footer suddenly put down his razor, took off his barber's white jacket and threw on his suitcoat.

"What about my shave?" carped the customer in the chair.

"To hell with that," James said and raced from the shop, chasing the skimpily clad redhead across the street. He grabbed her by a milky arm. "How about it, beautiful?" he smiled. "You and me—right now—I'll make it worth your time."

"Police!"

A beat cop came running and arrested Robert James for mashing; he was let off with a small fine and told to mind his manners. One cop, however, was not prepared to forget the incident. Jack Southard, Captain of Detectives in the Los Angeles District Attorney's Office, heard of the incident. He decided that such conduct in a recently widowed man was not only unbecoming but highly suspect. He began to look into James' background.

"The Damned Snakes Didn't Work"

Mrs. Mary James, the victim of one of the most bizarre murders in American history.

Detectives inspect the lily pond in which Mary James was found; Charles Hope, handyman for murder, stands at left; his inventive employer, Robert James, is in the center of the group. (UPI)

The insurance firm, he learned, had contested James' claim on his wife, awarding him considerably less than the payment called for on Mary James' life. The barber, Southard was told by an insurance investigator, had not been legally married to the former Mary Bush when the policy had been taken out.

There had been a marriage of sorts. James had been having an affair with his manicurist, Mary. When she discovered herself pregnant, the blond yelled for matrimony. James responded in typical fashion. Encountering a stew-bum in a bar, one Joseph Riegel, the barber offered him fifty dollars to impersonate a minister.

"For that kind of money you could get somebody murdered."

"Just a marriage," James told him.

The mock ceremony took place the following evening in James' barber shop. Mary Bush gullibly accepted Riegel as a legitimate reverend; he had rented a smock and collar for the ceremony, lifted a Gideon Bible from a nearby hotel. Following the inauspicious wedding, the happy couple rented the spacious bungalow in LaCanada, a suburb northeast of Los Angeles. James took out a ten-thousand-dollar insurance policy on Mary's life and anxiously waited for some weeks before legally marrying her; he had neglected to tell Mary that he was already married. When his divorce decree was finalized, James once more marched the naive Mary to a clergyman, a real one.

Insurance agents looking into Mary's death unearthed the parsimonious Joe Riegel, who promptly disclosed his role as a bogus reverend, earning himself another fifty dollars from a grateful claims adjuster.

The story goaded Southard to delve further into the oddball activities of barber James. Visiting with Alfred Dinsley, a retired major of the British Army and James' next-door neighbor in LaCanada, the detective got both ears stuffed with more than gossip.

Just after the Jameses moved to LaCanada, Dinsley and his wife were awakened late at night by frightful screams wafting over the hedge separating their house from that of their new neighbors. This went on for several nights until Dinsley's curiosity compelled him to slip through the hedge and peek through a window of the James house.

"The lady had a horsewhip," Dinsley told Southard. "She chased him around the bedroom, lashing the bloody hell out of him and him screaming all the while. Both were stark naked. Disgusting!"

Yes, agreed Jack Southard, downright repulsive conduct. He also learned from Dinsley that a green Buick sedan had been parked outside the James home several nights before the sad demise of the whip-wielding Mary. A few days later, Southard discovered that James was receiving countless phone calls from a man named Charles Hope—one of James' disgruntled under-paid barbers.

Hope, the State Motor Vehicle Department informed Southard, owned a green Buick sedan. While Hope, a rather slow-witted type who worked as a bread cutter in a restaurant, was away, detectives entered his apartment and conducted a methodical search. Their pains were rewarded when one of them found in an old pair of Hope's trousers a receipt for two rattle-snakes, signed by a Long Beach resident named Snake Joe Houtenbrink.

Details concerning Mary's swollen leg had always bothered detective Southard; now he had what appeared to be an explanation. He visited Snake Joe Houtenbrink, who gladly told him that Charles Hope had gotten two Crotalus Atrox rattlers from him in late July 1935, a short time before Mary James' death. The reptile collector had sold the Colorado vipers, named Lethal and Lightnin', at seventy-nine cents a pound.

"Funny thing," Snake Joe mused to the detective. "Hope came back here about two weeks later with them rattlers. Said they didn't work—whatever that meant." Houtenbrink had bought the snakes back from Charles Hope for half price.

Armed with this information, Southard, with the D.A.'s blessing, arrested Hope (who was by then using the alias of Jack Conti) on suspicion of murder. The dim-brained bread cutter went to pieces under the first interrogation in May 1936. "It's murder, all right," moaned Hope, "but I didn't do the thing."

Hope related how he had entered James' barber shop in June 1935, telling the barber that he was broke and asking for a haircut on credit.

"Sure thing," James had said. When Hope sat down in the chair, the barber asked: "If you know anything about rattle-snakes, I think you can earn a hundred bucks."

Hope knew nothing of snakes but he was certainly aware of what a hundred dollars could provide in those Depression-torn

days. "There isn't a man alive who knows more about rattlers,"
Hope assured the barber. "What do you want to know?"

James bluntly told his customer that "I have a friend whose
wife is bothering him and he wants a couple of snakes used to
bite her."

That sounded reasonable enough to Charles Hope, so he
busied himself in the following weeks with obtaining snakes
for "the friend," who proved to be none other than barber
James. He located two snakes in a carnival sideshow but their
rental proved disappointing. When James placed them in a box
with a chicken, the reptiles cowered. Hope came up with another rattler and James put it into a cage with a rabbit. The
following morning he found the rabbit frisky as ever, but the
snake was dead. Still pursuing the hundred-dollar finder's fee,
Hope finally unearthed Snake Joe Houtenbrink, who guaranteed his venomous pets. That night Hope and James retired to
the LaCanada bungalow where Mary made them a meatloaf
dinner. James told his pregnant wife that Charlie Hope was a
respected physician, a role for which he had prepared the bread
cutter through long hours of coaching.

Over the dinner table, Mary James looked up to see Hope
staring at her. "Why are you looking that way at me?" she asked
him.

From beneath a frown, Hope intoned: "You don't look so
good. I don't think you should have that baby. It could kill
you."

*Witnesses for the prosecution: two lethal
rattlesnakes Robert James thought would do
the job.*

Mary panicked, begging the "doctor" for his advice. Hope suggested an abortion. It was providential, he explained, that he had brought along his instrument case. "Why, I can do it right here, now. You won't have to leave the house and the neighbors will never know."

"Do I have to take ether? I get sick on the stuff."

Following James' script and knowing Mary's love for alcohol, Hope responded in crude bedside manner: "All you have to do is get good and drunk. Then you won't feel a thing."

Mary went to the liquor cabinet, took out a bottle and proceeded to drink herself into a stupor. Murmuring the expected "there, there" blandishments, James and "doctor" Hope undressed Mary. They strapped the naked woman to the kitchen table. When she passed out, James went to his garage and retrieved Lethal and Lightnin'. He placed his wife's foot into the snake box and then retreated with Hope to the garage, where they gulped great quantities of liquor.

"I don't like this, Bob," Hope said when in a boozy state.

"You bought those snakes, so you're in this as much as me," snorted the barber. "Look, you don't have to worry about a thing. I'm gonna collect ten thousand from the insurance people on her and I'll give you two grand."

The hours passed. James made several trips throughout the night into the bungalow to check on his wife. The snakes had repeatedly bitten her. But Mary didn't die. Her leg began to swell up horribly. Once more in the garage, James became disgusted with his carefully plotted scheme. "Hell," he said to Hope, "the damned snakes didn't work." He went on to explain that he now remembered that whiskey was an antidote for snakebite. The barber threw up his hands in resignation. "I'm going to drown her."

Mary James came to just as the barber entered the kitchen and began to untie her.

"Is it over?" she asked her understanding spouse.

"You bet, honey."

"But it don't hurt where it should. It's my leg that hurts."

"Something must have bit you." James had, by that time, removed the snakes to the garage where Hope waited. The accomplice noticed some black widow spiders crawling about in a box and later learned that his niggardly employer had tried to get these also to bite his wife in her sleep, but that attempt had proved unsuccessful.

One of Robert James' back-up murder weapons, a deadly black widow spider found in the murderer's garage. (UPI)

239

Hours passed and in the house Mary James hobbled about on a leg ballooned to twice its normal size. "It feels awful," she complained to her husband, who sat sipping coffee at the kitchen table.

"Go on and walk on it. That will make it feel better," he soothed.

Mary James stomped about. A little after six in the morning she walked out to the patio to water the flowers. Robert James went to the bathroom and filled the tub. He then suggested she take a bath to alleviate the pain in her leg. As she stepped into the tub, James pushed her down, yanking her legs high so that she was helpless to lift her head from beneath the water. She drowned in seconds. He removed her body, dried her off and dressed her.

The barber then fetched Hope from the garage. Both men dragged the dead woman to the lily pond where James arranged the body so that only the head was in the water, making it appear that this wife had gotten dizzy from labor pains and had accidentally collapsed to her watery death. James and Hope left, the barber careful to open his shop at eight that morning to establish his alibi.

With Hope's detailed confession in hand, Southard arrested the errant barber. James' background was then unfolded, a life history replete with more than merely one murder. His real name was Major Raymond Lisemba, born in 1895 in rural Alabama. He had little education and had slaved as a cotton baler until two uncles died within a year of each other and left him a thousand dollars each. These insurance payments gave Lisemba the idea of quick money, one that never failed to obsess him.

Going to Birmingham, Lisemba graduated from a barber's college and changed his name to James. In 1921 he married a Birmingham girl named Maud Duncan. They were divorced when Maud could no longer tolerate James' grotesque love of pain, especially hers. She complained in her suit that her husband's favorite game was to thrust hot curling irons under her fingernails.

Charged with siring several bastards in the Birmingham area, James thought it prudent to move west before several shotgun-toting fathers located him. He opened a small barber shop in Emporia, Kansas, in the 1920s where he met and married Vera

Vermillion, a movie cashier. William Allen White, the notable publisher, often sat in Bob James' chair, getting the usual close shave; Vera opened a beauty parlor next door. This second marriage was short-lived.

A farmer stormed into James' shop one morning, shouting that James had made his buxom daughter pregnant. James fled west that night in a Model-A Ford. He ran out of gas in Fargo, North Dakota, where he opened another barber shop. Within weeks he married Winona Wallace, a tall blonde. They honeymooned near Pike's Peak, Colorado, but their wedded bliss was spoiled when their car, Winona at the wheel, spun out of control and smashed into a boulder. James, who had thrown himself from the auto at the last moment, was uninjured, but Winona had to be taken to the Beth-El Hospital in Colorado Springs for treatment.

Upon her release, James took her to a remote cabin outside of Manitou, Colorado. A few days later the barber stood weeping before J. D. Rogers, Highway Superintendent at Pike's Peak, telling the official: "My poor, dear bride has been killed in an accident."

James had told Rogers that Winona had been suffering dizzy spells since the car accident and she had apparently fainted while getting into the cottage bathtub and drowned. Saddened officials sympathetically helped James remove the body of his beloved to California, where he buried Winona in that gilt-edged Mecca of American dead, Forest Lawn Memorial Park. He then promptly collected fourteen thousand dollars on Winona's life, an insurance policy James had taken out a day before his marriage to the sexy blond.

Returning to Alabama to see relatives early in 1934, James got drunk and woke up in a tourist cabin bed. Next to him was a local girl, one Helen Smith. They were married, Helen informed the traveling barber. James shrugged and took his fourth wife to Los Angeles. By then James could not have sex without being whipped. Helen Smith obliged with a vengeance. "He used to scream and yell somethin' awful," she later told detective Southard. "But he just loved me to whip him."

The whipping stopped cold when Helen learned that James had arranged for a doctor to examine her for an insurance policy. Helen refused, telling James: "I don't believe in insurance. People who have it always die of something strange."

Robert James was having none of that. He told his beloved that "we are not made for each other" and proposed a divorce. Helen agreed.

At the time of his divorce from Helen, James ran a scruffy barber shop in Santa Ana. His living was becoming threadbare and he fielded about for more opportunities, chiefly in the field of insurance. Just such a windfall came his way in the spring of 1934 with the visit of his thickskulled nephew Cornelius Wright, then a sailor stationed in San Diego.

James knew his nephew to be accident-prone—hilariously so, as his history testified. Wright had been hit several times by autos. Scaffolding once collapsed on him. He had been knocked unconscious by a foul ball at a baseball game. Once, when observing builders at a construction site, the crowd around him edged him into the excavation pit, again hospitalizing him. Wright was not even safe in the Navy. While in Honolulu on leave, a fight had erupted in a bar where he was quietly sitting, minding his own business. A flying bottle beaned him on the head and caused him to be hospitalized with a severe fracture. He was the answer to the feverish prayers of dollar-thin Robert James.

"Connie," James had told his disaster-prone cousin, "I want you to have a good time while you're on leave. Take my car, pick up a few girls. Have fun."

Three days later Cornelius Wright, U.S. sailor, drove off a cliff near Santa Rosa and was killed. Robert James collected ten thousand from a new insurance policy he had thoughtfully taken out on his nephew. The car in which Wright had met his end was towed away for junk at James' orders. The mechanic who disassembled the wreck for resale later told detective Southard that "something was wrong with the steering wheel," something, no doubt, Robert James had personally arranged. The barber used the money he collected on his nephew's life to open his posh new barber shop in Los Angeles.

When arrested for the murder of his much-bitten wife, Mary, James was found in a motel court bungalow with a nineteen-year-old floozy whipping him raw. "Don't stop her," begged James of the police. "Can't you see it's love?"

In a quick trial Robert James was sentenced to die on the gallows. Charlie Hope, who turned State's evidence, was given a life sentence. The two snakes, Lethal and Lightnin', were placed on exhibit in the courtroom, which made more than one of the jurors edgy.

But Robert S. James, who was to be known to the inmates of San Quentin as "Rattlesnake" Lisemba, was far from the rope. For four years his lawyers fought for his release, while he remained in the Los Angeles County Jail. He was finally moved to San Quentin in 1940.

James told Warden Clinton P. Duffy repeatedly that he had been framed, that he did not deserve to die. Softly, he purred to Duffy: "Now, warden, you know I'm not guilty. Why don't you help me prove it? I didn't kill my wife and I wasn't after her insurance. I was only trying to help. If it weren't for Conti [Hope], she'd be alive today. He brought the snakes over and started us all drinking until my wife got bitten. I revived her in the tub and then she fell in the pond and drowned. I'm an innocent man."

"That's not the way I heard it," replied Duffy.

"You just don't believe me, warden, do you?" James snapped back. "I can't do anything with you. I'll have to work some other way out." He thought for a moment. Then inmate James shouted: "You're calling me a liar, warden!"

"I'm not calling you a liar. I'm just telling you what the records show."

"Well, the records are wrong."

During James' long court battle to save his life, the method

Robert James on the witness stand, stonily denying the murder of his wife.

of capital punishment in California was legally changed from the gallows to the gas chamber (at the urging of Representative James Holohan, who had once been warden at San Quentin and considered the gallows too cruel a death, the gas chamber much more merciful). The change did not, however, affect Robert James, since he had been sentenced under the old law.

For seven years, James fought the gallows, going all the way to the Supreme Court, which denied his petition for life imprisonment. Before James, the last man to swing off in San Quentin was Harrison Wells, on October 14, 1938, also sentenced under the old execution law. James hoped he would at least get the gas chamber if he had to be killed. After the execution of its first victim, Albert Kessell on December 2, 1935, the gas chamber was thought by those on death row to be much less painful.

When California Governor Culbert L. Olson refused to sign James' commutation order, his execution date was fixed for May 1, 1942. By then "Rattlesnake" James was serene, even

How he did it: While a chagrined Robert James looks on, Charles Hope, James' murder assistant, cooperatively reclines on a courtroom table while a prosecutor plunges his leg into the box that once held the rattlesnakes.

philosophical about his end. He had organized a Bible class on the condemned row. As warden Duffy led him from his cell for the walk to the gallows, James told him, "I've been around here a long time and you have treated me with consideration. But I would rather die than spend the rest of my life in prison. It will soon be all over and I will be with the Lord." As he stepped from his cell, his expression changed, panic raced up his throat. "Those guards are going to force me to go up those thirteen steps and I'm going to have a noose put around my neck. You're going to hang me for something I didn't do!"

"I wish I didn't have to," Duffy mumbled, "but I have no choice. Take it easy."

Robert James, né Major Raymond Lisemba, then went meekly and quietly to his death. Only minutes after his execution—he was the last to be hanged in California—Warden Duffy met with newsmen.

"Can you give us your reaction to his execution, Warden?" quizzed one newsman.

Duffy paused a moment and then blurted angrily: "I wish everyone in California had seen it. I wish they had all seen the flesh torn from Lisemba's face by the rope and his half-severed neck and his popping eyes and his swollen tongue. I wish they had seen his legs swinging and had smelt the odors of his urine and defecation and sweat and caking blood."

"We can't print that, warden," another reporter cried out.

"I know you can't," sighed Duffy, long a foe of capital punishment. "Every legislator who helped pass the law that made it necessary for us all to go through this ordeal should have been with me today."

1936 CHICAGO

Married to Murder

When looking back over the lives of certain murder victims, it seems as if they were inevitably destined for violent ends, inexplicably racing toward death, helpless to turn back the furies that so doggedly pursued them. One stellar soul of such hapless fate was Joseph W. Bolton, Jr., a mild-mannered Chicago businessman who, for all practical purposes, was slated for murder from the moment he stepped to the altar. The odd thing about Mr. Bolton's grim end was that he knew all about it from the beginning.

Bolton married a girl from Kalamazoo in 1922. His wife, Mildred, appeared to be a troubled soul from the start of their anxious union. She was suspicious and possessive of Bolton and imagined him with other women around the clock. Bolton, who stood six feet tall and was myopic, was a docile creature, so shy and retiring that he found it next to impossible to carry on a conversation with a strange female for more than a few minutes. Yet Mildred persisted in her fantasies, thinking her spouse a classic rake, and for his imagined transgressions, she made his life a living hell.

An insurance broker, Bolton, over a period of years, never felt safe from his wife's fury. She would barge into his office and accuse him of having affairs with his secretary, other females in his business, and the wives of his friends. So aggressive were her verbal attacks that Bolton was forced to go into business for himself; his employers could not take the strain.

Hapless Chicago businessman Joseph W. Bolton, who knew for years of his wife's ambition to murder him. (UPI)

Through the years, Mildred's tongue-lashing wrath changed to physical attacks. She beat her husband in public, knocking off his glasses and stepping on them. She attacked him with knife and razor. The police patrol wagon was regularly called to these outrageous scenes to pick up the cantankerous Mildred, a feisty person, short and squat, later described at her trial as a "dusky, dumpy defendant."

Blood flowed, Bolton's blood, on July 22, 1934, as Mildred's passionate paranoia exploded. Officer Joseph Lynch was called to a drugstore in Hyde Park at three o'clock that morning. He found Bolton almost unconscious as a druggist bandaged his right forearm, which had been viciously slashed. He would say nothing as he was removed to the Chicago Hospital. Lynch followed a trail of blood from the pharmacy for two blocks to 5230 University Avenue. At that address, Lynch found Mrs. Mildred Bolton sitting with her feet propped up on the parlor table, casually smoking a cigar. Lynch asked Mildred how her husband came to be slashed.

"He cut himself while shaving" was her cool reply as she blew smoke rings.

"Shaving at three o'clock in the morning?"

"Yes."

Bolton's wife was brought to the hospital where he was being stitched up. He refused to admit that Mildred had attacked him. But by that time, the much-harassed Bolton knew his days were numbered. He was overheard to nervously blurt to her one day: "I wish you would hurry up and get it over with."

Mildred wasted little time after Bolton filed for divorce on January 20, 1936. She purchased a Narizmande, Eibar, Spair .32 revolver on June 11, 1936, along with six bullets, from the Hammond Loan Company, a pawn shop. Four days later, Mildred called on her husband in his tenth-floor office at 166 West Jackson Blvd. Shots soon rang out in the office. Miss Andrea Houyoux, Bolton's secretary, rushed to an elevator and begged the operator to take her down, quick. An elevator starter, Lincoln Knutson, and an electrician from the building's basement, Fred Ferguson, then raced an elevator back up to the tenth floor.

They found Bolton writhing and beating his legs on the hallway floor. He appeared to have been shot in the lungs but he was conscious. Mildred stood casually in Bolton's open office door. "Keep that woman away from me," croaked Bolton to the startled building employees.

Mildred then spoke in a soothing southern drawl: "Why don't you get up and stop faking?" Ferguson raced down the hall for a doctor. Mildred called after him: "Don't you mind! He's putting on an act!"

It was no act. Bolton was removed to a doctor's office, where physicians tried to save his life. Mildred stood around making odd remarks, kissing her dying husband's brow and asking the feverishly working doctors: "Doesn't he have a nice head?" Bolton died within an hour and Mildred was arrested.

From the first moment of her trial, Mildred insisted that Bolton had shot himself, playing the role of the scorned woman. The sob sisters of the press ran errands for her, brought her lipstick and candy. Her fan mail was heavy. One housewife wrote: "You should have killed him whether you did or not." Another penned: "If I had the nerve I would have killed [my husband] ten years ago." A social lioness also wrote: "Mildred, you are a saint and the jury will acquit you with orchids. A group of us is planning to celebrate your first day of liberty with a dinner party and we want you to be our guest of honor."

There were no orchids and no party for Mildred. She finally admitted shooting Joseph W. Bolton, Jr., after deciding not to commit suicide with the revolver she had bought. She was jeal-

Mildred Bolton under arrest; she has just told reporters, "They don't convict women for killing their husbands in Cook County."

247

ous of phantoms, it was clear. Mildred was first sentenced to
death but her sentence was commuted by Governor Henry Hor-
ner to 199 years (and no parole) at the women's penitentiary at
Dwight, Illinois. Mildred Bolton died in her cell on August 29,
1943, committing suicide by slashing her wrists with a pair of
stolen scissors. "I wish to die," her farewell note said, "as I
have lived, completely alone." She had no words for her slain
husband. She had said all that following her confession, to
which she had poignantly added in court: "I loved him, devot-
edly, always." Enough to plan his murder, she might have
added, from the minute the wedding band was slipped onto her
finger.

1937 JAMAICA, NEW YORK
Science Picks the Killer

"There's a dead woman in the lots!" The stranger stood in the
shadow of the doorway through which he had just burst.

Staring bug-eyed at him from his desk was David Nutkis, a
contractor alone in his office warehouse on Beaver Road, Jamaica, Queens County. It was 7:20 A.M., Friday, July 2, 1937.
Nutkis could not discern the features of the excited intruder's
face but did see him point toward the nearby tracks of the Long
Island Railway.

Dashing from the office, Nutkis raced to a pathway on a lot
next to his property, a well-worn shortcut to a railway under-
pass. Close to the abutment of the railway bridge Nutkis spotted
a woman lying on her back. About her head was a pool of coag-
ulated blood.

The roofing contractor turned to stammer his surprise to the
stranger who had brought the news but saw that the man was
sprinting down the road. Nutkis was next startled by a loud cry.
Looking closer, he could see a two-year-old baby girl raise her
head, spattered with blood, next to the woman, crying out.

Without another word, the contractor ran back to his office
and called police. Special investigators were careful to study
the death spot and the body before touching anything. When
the unhurt child was taken away for safekeeping, detectives

noted that a man's black oxford was next to the body. Three feet from the dead woman was a shopping bag, ripped at the edges, containing a woman's blue blouse and some baby clothes.

Medical examiners quickly determined that the dead woman had been killed several hours earlier; her dress was torn, indicating a violent struggle. Squads of detectives combed the area. One investigator was rewarded when he spotted a thirteen-inch piece of concrete caked with blood and human hair, obviously the murder weapon. The woman's skull had been crushed in two places, the result of terrific blows to the head.

Within an hour of the discovery, the dead woman was identified by a neighborhood woman as Mrs. Phennie Perry. Officers were immediately dispatched to her home to locate her husband, Arthur Perry. The child found next to her mother was their daughter, Shirley. When the officers finally removed the body, they were startled to find an assortment of amazing clues as to the killer's identity.

Found was an envelope addressed to one Ulysses Palm at 11008 153rd St., Jamaica; a piece of paper with Palm's name and address on it; a postcard sent to the same man; his electric bill; three photos—two of the same man, one of him in front of a car and one posing in a studio, plus one of a woman; and a receipt book, which contained many names and amounts of money that appeared to be donations. Also discovered beneath the body was an electric iron caked with blood and a three-inch strip of blue broadcloth flecked with blood.

An instant and not unsound theory proposed by the police was that the woman, struggling with her assailant, had torn away a piece of his shirt pocket, which resulted in his personal effects' spilling out. The darkness prevented the slayer from noticing the accident and when his victim fell from his repeated blows, her body covered the clues. With the absence of the woman's handbag, police felt it was also safe to assume that she had been killed while attempting to resist a purse-snatcher.

With tires squealing, detectives raced to the home of Ulysses Palm. They entered his home on 153rd Street. No one was on the premises but the investigators began a thorough search. In a narrow hall between the bathroom and bedroom they found a black oxford shoe that matched the one they had brought from the scene of the killing. In Palm's bedroom, hanging on the back of a chair, was a blue shirt with a strip of broadcloth missing from the pocket. It all seemed so neat to Captain Henry

Flattery, who headed the investigation. Perhaps, he mused, it was too neat.

Back at the Jamaica stationhouse, information on the Perrys and Palms was being assembled. The murdered woman, Phennie Perry, was an attractive twenty-year-old. She and her husband, Arthur, childhood sweethearts, had moved from Jamestown, S.C., to Jamaica, New York, only recently. Perry worked as an iron construction laborer for Joseph W. Falke. He was yet to be found by police.

Ulysses Palm, too, seemed less than suspicious. He and his wife, Hattie, friends and neighbors of the Perrys, were hard-working people with no blemishes on their record. Palm was quickly identified as the man in the photos found at the murder site; his wife was the woman. In addition to being a trusted employee of a chain store in Flushing, police learned, he was a much-admired deacon of the Amity Church in Jamaica, a conscientious and devout leader of the congregation who was entrusted with the care of the church's books and collections. However, all the evidence gathered at the murder scene clearly implicated Deacon Palm.

The key suspect was picked up at work by officers and driven back from Flushing to Jamaica in a squad car. Lieutenant Thomas J. Feeney sat in the back seat with Palm, who persistently got the silent treatment when he asked why he was under escort. Feeney finally said in a calm voice: "You're suspected of murdering Mrs. Phennie Perry."

"What?" Palm almost jumped into the front seat with excitement and shock. "Why should I want to kill her?"

"Maybe you can tell us that."

At the station Feeney held up the torn blue shirt to Palm's startled gaze. "Recognize this?"

"Yes, that's my shirt."

"How about these?" Feeney asked, holding up, one by one, the receipt book, the photos, the postcard and scrap of paper, which Palm identified as his.

When Feeney suddenly whipped out the bloody iron, Palm grimaced. "It looks . . . familiar . . . but . . . my iron . . . that is, my wife's iron . . . doesn't have those stains on it."

Perry, also picked up by police at work, was told that his wife was in the hospital, not dead. "My wife should be in Brooklyn," he said to Detective Michael Kissane. He went on to explain that Mrs. Perry and the baby were to have stayed with her sister in Brooklyn before traveling to South Carolina to visit relatives.

Kissane, according to a plan mapped out for both Palm and Perry, went on the attack, jamming on the brakes and then turning to the man next to him, blurting: "Why did you kill your wife?"

"Kill my wife?" Perry stared back at the officer bug-eyed. His hands clenched the seat white-knuckled. Then he turned away and blankly stared out the window. "That means Phennie is dead," he said slowly.

When Perry was ushered into the Jamaica station, Lieutenant Feeney met him with the question: "Why should anyone want to kill your wife?"

Without hesitation, Arthur Perry replied: "Palm threatened to kill her."

On Monday morning, June 20, Perry patiently told police, Phennie Perry had received a letter. Since his wife was spending the week with her sister in Brooklyn, Perry saw no harm in opening it. "It was signed Ulysses Palm." The missive was short and to the point, according to Perry. Either Mrs. Perry, whom Palm had been secretly interested in for months, became intimate with him or he would kill her. "I thought somebody must be playing a joke," Perry said, shaking his head. "I didn't think Palm would send such a letter. He didn't seem like that kind of person." He had resealed the letter, given it to his wife and waited for a week until Phennie Perry, obviously upset by the note, showed it to her husband, stating that it must be some sort of hoax. The couple watched Ulysses Palm closely for a week, Perry told police, but he never gave Phennie anything other than a neighborly hello.

Phennie's movements with the baby were accounted for by her husband. On the night of her death, she attended the bingo games held at the Plaza Theatre in Jamaica, as was her custom every Thursday night, before going to her sister's home. Perry had stopped by to talk to her at seven o'clock, chatting with her outside the theater, and checking to see if she was still going to South Carolina after seeing her sister.

"That letter from Palm bothered me," Perry admitted to detectives. "I went to Palm's house and showed him the letter. 'You know I can't write as well as that,' he said to me." Perry, not quite sure whether Palm was telling the truth or not, then left, returned home, and then decided to spend the night at his sister's house, which he did.

"What time did you talk to Palm?" quizzed Feeney.

"It was nine fifty-three," said Perry. "I remember because I looked at the clock on the dresser when I got the letter to show to him. I kept the letter hidden behind the dresser." The incriminating letter was at his sister's home, Perry insisted. Police retrieved this missive, which bore out Perry's story. It was turned over to handwriting experts.

The rest of Perry's narrative was backed up by relatives. Phennie's sister knew that Mrs. Perry had received the letter; Phennie had told her how it had upset her. Perry's brother, William Perry, told police that he had been with Arthur the previous night and that his brother had told him that he intended to confront Palm about the letter. Perry's sister and brother-in-law confirmed that Perry had spent the night of the murder with them, arriving at their flat no later than eleven o'clock.

Arthur Perry, however, was held in the lockup. Some cells away, Ulysses Palm, his prospects looking blacker by the moment, paced also behind bars. Everything pointed to Palm as the heartless slayer of pretty Phennie Perry.

"I didn't write that letter," Palm said when police showed him the letter Phennie had received in the mail. The blood-stained shoe, which matched the shoe found in his first-floor apartment was indeed his; but, said Deacon Palm, he had given those shoes to Perry. He was at a loss to explain how the church receipt book, which was normally kept under lock and key in his apartment, had wound up beneath the body of Mrs. Perry. The photos and his other effects also found there similarly left him in a quandary.

What unnerved police, who appeared to have an ironclad case against Palm, was the substantiated fact that he had worked in the Flushing chain store until 10:10 P.M. He hadn't arrived home until 11:15 P.M., taking a trolley and bus en route. This claim was upheld by his employer, who had asked Palm to stay late to take inventory on the night of the murder.

The time involved was narrow for the alibis of both men. Mrs. Perry, it was estimated by medical examiners, had been dead about eight hours before being discovered by the contractor Nutkis; the time of death was fixed at around 11:00 on the dark night of July 1, 1937. It would have been impossible, if Perry had arrived at his sister's home to spend the night at 11:00, and Palm had returned home at 11:15, for either man to have committed the murder.

Detectives went back to grilling Perry. "Palm said he gave you the shoes—the one that was found at the scene of the killing."

"That's right," Perry replied without a flinch, "but I gave them back to him. They were too tight on me."

The suspect was then asked how many times he had seen his wife on the night of the murder. Just the once, he repeated, when he stopped by the theater to talk with her at seven o'clock.

Feeney tossed a signed paper across the desk at Perry. "Here's the statement of an usher at the Plaza Theater. He says you saw your wife and baby twice that night, at seven P.M. and then at nine fifty-one P.M., and that you left with her."

"He's full of beans!"

Both Perry and Palm, under hammering interrogations, failed to budge from their stories. The police kept both in custody but were hesitant to charge either one with homicide. They needed more evidence. Captain Flattery had only one hope. He announced to his investigative team: "It's either Palm or Perry. We can't try both and we can't afford to arrest the wrong one. Let's see what the scientific boys can do with this stuff."

Examiners studied the shoe found at the scene of the crime. There was a small hole in the blood-covered sole of the shoe. They asked detectives to retrieve the socks worn by both Perry and Palm. These were provided. The experts soon discovered a bit of dirt in the center of one of Arthur Perry's socks. When a test of this sock was made, blood of Mrs. Perry's type was identified on it.

Perry was brought back to the examination room and confronted with this new evidence.

"That's plain crazy!" he howled.

"Sit up on that table, Mr. Perry," an examiner told him. The suspect was then thoroughly inspected. (Both men were wearing the same clothes they had worn when arrested.) Perry's feet were examined with special lights. Nothing spectacular was found. When Perry was arrested the sleeves of his work shirt had been rolled up; they still were. An expert carefully rolled

*Arthur Perry of Jamaica,
New York, who planned
the near-perfect murder
of his wife.* (UPI)

down the sleeves. He discovered a suspicious-looking spot on one and applied the benzidine reagent blood test. It confirmed the spot as blood.

Handwriting experts had by then carefully studied the letter ostensibly sent by Palm to Mrs. Perry, comparing it with dozens of handwriting samples by both Perry and Palm. They concluded that it could not have been written by the church deacon but, though it was disguised, the writing was probably that of Arthur Perry.

Using a powerful microscope, it was then determined that the strip of broadcloth from Palm's shirt, which had been found beneath the body, had not been torn as if in a struggle. The strip had been neatly cut for a half inch and then torn away.

There was enough evidence, a grand jury felt, for an indictment to be brought against Arthur Perry on September 23, 1937, on charges of first-degree murder. Perry was brought to trial the following November. The scientific evidence was placed before a jury. Moreover, police proved that Perry, a short time before his wife's murder, had taken out an insurance policy on her life with himself as the sole beneficiary.

The prosecution reconstructed with amazing accuracy the ingenious plot conceived by Perry to establish his neighbor Palm as the murderer of his wife. He had, weeks before, written the threatening letter to his wife, imitating Palm's writing from samples he had collected over several months, thus embedding in the minds of his wife and relatives suspicion of Palm's intentions. He confronted the church deacon on the night of the murder, not as an outraged husband, but as an evidence thief, for at that time, excusing himself to go to Palm's bathroom, he had filched one of Palm's shoes, snipped a piece of his shirt in the bedroom next to the bathroom, swiped three photos, a postcard, a torn piece of paper with Palm's name on it, his church receipts book—all found on Palm's bureau—and departed.

Prosecutors next pointed out how Perry picked up his wife at the Plaza Theatre, escorted her through the empty lot, and killed her, using the stolen iron owned by Mrs. Palm. He carefully left the false clues that would lead to Palm's identification, subsequent arrest, conviction and execution for the murder of a woman he knew only as a friendly neighbor. Perry would then be free to collect the insurance money on his wife's life without one accusing finger pointed in his direction. His amazingly clever plan, thought out months in advance, belied the lower-class mentality Arthur Perry was thought to possess; it was the murder plot of a diabolical genius, one that would certainly have succeeded had it not been for the sublime science of police detection.

Despite his vociferous claims of innocence, Perry was found guilty on November 13, 1937. He was subsequently sentenced to die in Sing Sing's electric chair. Fighting for his life, Perry won a new trial through a technicality. He lost again, this time doubly damned by testimony of an undercover policeman, Sidney Cusbeth, who had shared a cell with Perry and to whom he had admitted the killing.

In a seven-day trial, he was convicted a second time. There would be no more appeals. The killer was stubborn to the last second of life. Arthur Perry insisted to all who would listen to him as he was strapped into the electric chair on August 1939 that he "never harmed a hair on my dear wife's head."

1944 PACIFIC PALISADES, CALIFORNIA
A Most Refined Fiend

Louise Peete has been lost somewhere in the lexicon of murder. Students of this most sinister crime and/or profession have failed to remember this adroit assassin when retelling the fascinating vagaries of such archkillers as Herman Webster Mudgett (known far and wide as the indefatigable killer of more than two hundred under the alias "H. H. Holmes") and the berserk "Son of Sam." Yet lovable Louise has her niche in the dark corner of violent death, one that assures her of hallmark infamy.

To the muddled mind of Louise Peete, however, her image was simply that of a cultured woman, a female of exquisite refinement who had been wronged by the law and misunderstood by society. This sentiment was shared by most who came under Louise's charming sway, particularly a well-meaning social worker, Mrs. Margaret Logan, who, with her equally well-meaning husband Arthur, resided in Pacific Palisades.

Mrs. Logan had often visited the woman's prison in Tehachapi, and there befriended the lady Louise who was serving a life sentence for a killing she insisted she had not committed.

"I covet only two things," Louise once purred, "spiritual understanding and culture." Mrs. Logan could only nod affirmatively to such gracious ambitions. To her, no one who looked as benign as Louise could be guilty of the monstrous acts of which she was convicted, not this matronly, short, slightly plumpish female, with gray eyes, chestnut hair flecked with gray, and a constant, reassuring smile.

Louise, as she constantly reminded her prison keepers, was appalled at the kind of company she was forced to keep behind bars. In one of her many interviews, fashionable Louise pointed out the social discomforts of inconsiderate prison life oppressing her and her sister convicts: "The public must be educated to our needs. We need stepping stones and people send us roller skates. We don't ask for the advantages of a country club or a university, but we seek curative treatment so that when we are liberated we shall be prepared against any recurrence of the so-called mental illness that brought us here.

"There should be some way, too, of segregating the better-educated, more refined women from those who have been brought up in close touch with life's slime and filth. They should be protected against being sullied by it."

Being "liberated," of course, was what Louise needed most. From the day she was imprisoned in 1921 at age thirty-eight, Louise Peete bowed, smiled, and fawned before parole boards in vain efforts to get released. Warden Clinton T. Duffy, who knew Mrs. Peete at San Quentin before she was transferred to Tehachapi in 1933, was one of those who was easily bamboozled by Louise, recalling her as "the clubwoman type. . . . If you met her without knowing who she was, you would have thought her a leader of civic activities in some suburban town." Years later, writing in *88 Men and 2 Women*, Duffy revised his impression, realizing then that she projected "an air of innocent sweetness which masked a heart of ice."

On her tenth try for parole in 1939, aided greatly by Mrs. Logan's expressed belief in her reform, Louise Peete was released, paroled to the care of a Mrs. Latham in Los Angeles. She was permitted to change her name to Anna B. Lee (after Anna Lee, the movie star she so much admired).

All seemed serene in the life of freedom-loving Louise. She earned a little money sewing curtains for a girls' home. During World War II she worked in a servicemen's canteen. Parole officers learned that in 1942, a woman in the canteen building

Crafty Louise Peete shortly after being sent to prison for the murder of J. C. Denton.

had vanished. The woman's home was found in disarray. Since Louise had been her friend, authorities asked her opinion as to the reasons for the disappearance. Simple, explained Mrs. Peete. The elderly woman had fallen on her hip and the injury led to her death. They took her at her word, as scores had been doing for decades, accepting the word of one of America's most lethal liars.

The following year, Mrs. Peete's sponsor, Mrs. Latham, died of natural causes. She was paroled to the custody of her long-standing supporter and friend, Mrs. Margaret Logan, moving into the luxurious Pacific Palisades home of Arthur Logan. The gentle couple greeted the smiling Louise Peete at the door, little realizing exactly whom they were allowing to cross their threshhold.

Born in 1883 as Lofie Louise Preslar in Bienville, Louisiana, the daughter of a socially prominent newspaper publisher, she was kept in the best private schools, including an exclusive New Orleans finishing school for the richest girls in the state. Possessed of a voluptuous body and a vixen-like mind, Louise (she soon dropped the ungainly name Lofie) reportedly became so sexually active in New Orleans that she was expelled and sent home to Bienville where in 1903 she met and married, at age twenty, a traveling salesman named Henry Bosley. With her father's publishing fortune dwindling, Louise bullied Bosley into moving back to New Orleans. Then the couple traveled throughout the South while Bosley sold his wares. In Dallas, during the summer of 1906, Louise was attracted to an oil man staying at her hotel. Bosley found the two together in bed. The salesman, full of misery, committed suicide two days later.

Louise was unmoved. She sold Bosley's belongings and with the proceeds relocated to Shreveport, Louisiana, where she plied the trade of what would be known today as a call girl, expensive and "guaranteed," as she later put it to a confidante. With her prostitutional nest egg, Louise traveled in style to Boston. She set herself up in a comfortable Back Bay home and entertained the fathers and sons of the city's most socially esteemed families, calling herself Louise Gould, and intimating to one and all that she was a member, albeit wayward, of *the* Gould family.

Her business boomed. Yet greed controlled the heart of the beautiful, bountiful Louise, who took to visiting mansions late at night to service her customers. Upon departing, she filched the jewelry from the bedrooms of absent wives. When one of Boston's Four Hundred threatened to expose her, Louise left town in a hurry, taking the next train to Waco, Texas. There she struck up an acquaintance with an oilrigger who had wildcatted a small fortune for himself, a man called Joe Appel who was known to have spent all his gusher money on the diamonds that adorned his fingers, belt buckle and buttons.

It was no more than a week before Appel was found dead, his diamonds missing. Louise, who had been seen about Waco with Appel, was brought in for questioning. She freely admitted to killing the man, shooting him in the head. A special grand jury convened to hear the young lady's story.

Dressed in conservative-looking clothes, Louise played the southern belle horribly wronged by the carpetbagging speculator Appel. "That Northerner tried to rape me," she whimpered. Southern honor had been violated but retribution in the form of a bullet in the head had been exacted by Louise. The jury applauded her as she was released from custody.

It was 1913 when Louise returned to Dallas. Here, down on her luck, she married hotel clerk Harry Faurote, who was smitten by the bosomy Louise. Her unfaithfulness led to Faurote's hanging himself in the hotel basement.

Two years later Louise arrived in Denver and became the idol of a naive door-to-door salesman, Richard C. Peete. They married in 1915. For a while, Louise settled down to a domestic life inside a small house. She gave birth in 1916 to a daughter. The couple talked of going to the Orient to seek their fortune, but Peete's meager income could not even provide the travel fare. Louise Peete grew restless and, following an argument with her husband in the spring of 1920, she decamped for Los Angeles where she would seek her own fortune, alone.

Finding an ad in the *Los Angeles Times* that offered a spacious house for rent on fashionable South Catalina Street, Louise phoned its owner, Jacob Charles Denton, a wealthy mining executive and a devout bachelor. She was soon living in the house, rent free, with Denton as her living companion.

Several weeks of reported lovemaking moved Louise to urge Denton to marry her, particularly when she learned he was a multimillionaire.

"Don't ever mention marriage to me!" he roared back at her over breakfast.

Some days later Louise mysteriously ordered Denton's care-taker to have a ton of dirt dumped into the basement of the sprawling Tudor house. It was done. To quell the caretaker's curiosity, Louise told him that she planned to use the earth to "raise mushrooms," Denton's favorite delicacy.

Then, on May 30, 1920, millionaire Denton utterly vanished. To inquiries by friends as to the whereabouts of the middle-aged man, Louise Peete had a host of stories. As crime historian Miriam Allen deFord was to say of her: "Louise Peete was one of the most superbly imaginative liars on record. She never made up a small story when a big one would do."

One explanation from the inventive Louise was that Denton had had a violent fight with a "Spanish-looking woman," and, in the course of the melee, the hot-blooded Spaniard had pro-duced a small sword and lopped off Denton's arm. He survived, Louise whispered, but he was so embarrassed at losing an arm that he was in hiding.

Amputation must have been much on Louise Peete's mind in those days. When Denton's lawyer, Russ Blodgett, alarmed at the millionaire's failure to meet regular business commitments, called the Denton home, Louise was prepared with another tale. According to writer Alan Hynd, "Denton . . . had to have a leg amputated and he didn't want any of his Los Angeles friends looking at him until the stump had healed sufficiently to wear an artificial limb."

Mollified, friends and business associates accepted these in-credible explanations for some months. In the meantime, Louise took to calling herself Mrs. J. C. Denton. She gave lavish parties at Denton's home, forged his name on checks for consid-erable amounts, which she promptly cashed and spent, and then began systematically to sell off Denton's valuable antique and art collection to avaricious collectors.

She rented rooms in the twenty-room mansion and twice sub-leased the building. Finally she rented the house to a couple named Miller and returned to Denver and her still-adoring hus-band, Richard Peete.

Police, at the urging of lawyer Blodgett, inspected the Den-ton home in September and, shoveling away the dirt in the basement, found the millionaire's body. Authorities immedi-ately wired Louise in Denver, asking her to return to Los An-geles. She did, her husband in tow. None of her wild tales of

259

*Louise tells a
newspaperman that she
hardly knew Jake
Denton, let alone
murdered him, as she is
released from the
women's prison at
Tehachapi, California, in
1939.* (WIDE WORLD)

Denton's disappearance convinced police that she was anything other than the person who had sent a bullet into the back of his skull.

Richard Peete could believe none of the accusations hurled at his wonderful wife when she was tried in January 1921. During the trial Louise nobly asked him to divorce her, "for the child's sake." If true, this consideration was the most magnanimous Louise would make in her scurrilous lifetime. Peete did divorce Louise, who was speedily convicted and sent to prison for life. Up to that time, no woman had ever been executed for murder in California and it was still thought with wrongheaded cavalier logic that such a chivalrous precedent should not be broken.

For thirteen long years, Mrs. Louise Peete (the name she favored among her many names) played the martyred society matron, a lady of culture brutalized. Her husband visited and wrote her regularly, saying he would "wait forever," and that he would "exchange places with her," if the authorities would agree. She finally tired of him and, when she refused to write back in 1924, Richard Peete, on one of his salesman's visits to Tucson, Arizona, blew out his brains.

None of the gory details of Louise's body-strewn past was known by the Logans when they took the sixty-year-old Louise into their home. To the kind-hearted Logans, Mrs. Peete was an affable, amiable lady who provided sterling conversation and warmhearted company. She was then Anna B. Lee, a woman with a new name and a new background.

As such, Louise met a gullible messenger for the Bank of America, one Lee Borden Judson, an elderly widower looking for another good woman. The couple married in May 1944, but Judson continued to live apart from Louise in a small hotel room.

Life with the Logans suddenly became intolerable. Margaret Logan discovered valuables, some jewelry, money disappearing. Before she could confront Louise, Mrs. Peete loudly complained of her husband Arthur. Logan was getting senile, she said, the very reason for all of his recent business setbacks. His mind was failing and he was in need of mental study. Her harangues about Arthur Logan's mental deterioration finally persuaded Margaret Logan to have her husband committed to the psychiatric ward of the Los Angeles Hospital where he was to be observed. Within three weeks, Logan was sent home. There was nothing wrong with him, concluded the doctors.

On May 30, 1944, Mrs. Logan was missing. To Arthur Logan's demands, Louise told him she was critically ill in a hospital and he could not see her. The following month the calculating Louise convinced authorities that Arthur Logan was hopelessly crazy. He was committed to the State Hospital for the Insane, where he died within six months. Louise, who had taken over the Logan house, belongings and savings, adamantly refused to finance Arthur Logan's burial; at her brutal suggestion, his body was turned over to medical students for dissection.

By then Lee Judson was living with Louise in the Logan home. The crotchety bank messenger was perky enough to spot a bullet hole in one of the walls of the Logan home. When he asked his wife about it, she merely shrugged and put a picture over the spot. Louise took to wearing Mrs. Logan's best dresses and Judson once commented: "Won't Mrs. Logan object to you wearing her clothes?" Louise waved off the annoying question.

Judson also uncovered a ten-thousand-dollar insurance policy on Mrs. Logan's life. The beneficiary was Louise. The elderly man thought that, too, peculiar. When raking leaves one day in the back yard, an unnatural mound of earth next to Mrs. Logan's favorite avocado tree caught his attention, but before Judson could inspect the area, Louise accidentally dropped a bucket from a second-floor window that nearly struck the man. "Sorry, sweetheart," Louise cooed down to the startled Judson. "And by the way, stay away from that tree in the future. I always throw water there when I'm cleaning up."

Not until December 1944 did parole authorities grow suspicious of Louise's activities. The reports sent in each month from her parole sponsor, Mrs. Logan, were suspiciously full of too much praise for Louise Peete. The signature at the bottom of each was also a forgery, experts soon determined.

Police officers invaded the Logan home just before Christmas 1944. Old man Judson was so unnerved by their presence that he related every strange thing he had noted in the last six months: the bullet hole in the wall, the insurance policy, the odd mound of earth near the avocado tree. Hurriedly, investigators dug up the area and, not much to their surprise, unearthed the body of Mrs. Logan. She had been shot in the base of the skull (as she was sitting at the hall telephone stand,

Mrs. Peete turns her back to the cameras in 1944 while officials begin to dig up another of her victims, Margaret Logan. (UPI)

it was later learned), and then buried by the energetic Louise.

Mrs. Peete rallied against their accusations. "Oh no, not me. It was that crazy old man Arthur Logan. He went nuts one day and beat his wife to death. What could I do in such an instance with my background? Why, I would be suspected, I knew. Not this time." So she had shipped Logan off to the lunatic asylum and buried his victim, a matter of self defense.

When Mrs. Peete was booked for the murder of Mrs. Logan, Judson was also charged as an accessory. He was acquitted on January 12, 1945, but the shocking realization that his wife was an archmurderess was too much for him. The next day Lee Borden Judson rode an elevator thirteen stories up in a downtown Los Angeles office building, walked dazedly to a window, and leaped to his death.

Instead of fearing for her own life, Louise Peete reveled in the old man's suicide, telling reporters that she still had the animal magnetism that compelled her lovers to end their lives. Her trial was brief; she was convicted of first-degree murder.

This time a jury of eleven women and one man ignored Louise's womanhood and recommended the death penalty. Louise, blithely ignoring her death sentence, read books of philosophy when she was removed to Tehachapi. All her appeals failed.

Louise Peete, who had left San Quentin thirteen years earlier, returned to the prison for execution in the spring of 1947. Warden Duffy greeted her with the words: "Mrs. Peete, I'm sorry to see you here. Is there anything I can do for you?"

Louise Peete's usually beaming face was taut with rage. She spat: "Mr. Duffy, it might interest you to know that those guards kept me *handcuffed* all the way here from Tehachapi. I've never been so humiliated!"

The archkiller was the second woman ever scheduled to die in California's gas chamber, the first being Ethel Leta Juanita Spinelli, executed for the murder of a member of her cheap gang of sneak thieves. Unlike Spinelli, who went to her death with hate in her eyes and a sneer on her lips, Louise Peete was her smiling self, walking ladylike into the gas chamber on the morning of April 11, 1947, sighing and projecting an indignant air; such barbarity was beneath her. Just before the pellets fell, Louise Peete turned to Warden Duffy and, through the glass of the gas chamber, mouthed the words "Thank you" for all the kindnesses he had shown her, a show of the ladylike breeding she so superficially cherished. Within seconds, Louise Peete joined four suicidal husbands, three of her *known* murder victims, and the spirit of another man she had hounded into a mental institution and early death.

"At least she was gracious, even at the end," remarked a witnessing newsman.

"Yeah," retorted another, "that lady had manners that killed."

Playing the eternal victim, Mrs. Peete prays for deliverance from the gas chamber in 1947.

1945 ALEXANDRIA, VIRGINIA

The Accusing Skeleton

Homicide for most police departments is a matter of routine, the system of investigation grinding through the normal channels of checking and rechecking known facts. Seldom do inspecting officers step into the risky area of the unknown, playing the hunch, the notion. Such thought-to-be-cavalier actions rarely pay off in murder suspects, yet for detective Elliott Howe of the Virginia State Police, unorthodox methods solved the riddle of a sixteen-year-old killing, and proved Howe one of America's super sleuths.

On the afternoon of July 2, 1945, Howe answered a call from some workmen who had been clearing out an abandoned well on a farm near Alexandria, Virginia. The dredgers had found a human skeleton deep at the bottom of the well. Howe was not only shown the mortal remains of some unfortunate person but was given other items also found in the well—parts of a wristwatch, a piece of cable, a pair of shoes, bits of cloth, a brass button and a man's signet ring bearing the initials BJE.

Within hours, Howe was in the office of Dr. E. H. Marsteller, the coroner of Prince Williams County. From Marsteller, Howe learned that the remains were fifteen or so years old. Howe next had a dentist, Dr. Earl W. Payne of Arlington, check the teeth in the skull. A day later the detective was in the offices of Dr. T. Dale Stewart, curator of the Division of Physical Anthropology at the Smithsonian Institute in Washington. Following a studied examination, Dr. Stewart provided the officer with these startling facts: "Your bones belonged to a white man of North European stock. He was slim and of medium build—about five-feet-six or five-feet-seven. His hat size was six and seven-eighths or seven. His shoes were probably nine or nine and a half D. Bone lengths indicate he was probably left-handed, and he had an extreme case of pyorrhea. Want any more?"

"Was he murdered?" asked the popeyed Howe.

"He was killed by a heavy blow on the skull. And the bone of his left arm was broken, either just before or just after death. Neither the head nor the arm fracture shows signs of knitting."

Next Howe took the piece of cloth found in the well—a swatch of khaki—and the brass button, and went to Marine Corps Headquarters at Quantico, Virginia. He also took along the dental chart of the skull he had been given by Dr. Payne. The chart matched that of a missing ex-Marine, Brad J. Ellison, the name corresponding to the initials on the signet ring also found in the well. Ellison was twenty-four years old when he was reported missing.

Howe then inspected the records of the Quantico Town Police; Ellison had last been seen in that area. Notes written by a Sergeant Richard Duvall, who had later been killed in the line of duty, revealed that Ellison had dropped from sight on December 29, 1929, and that he suspected two men of killing the ex-Marine but proof was lacking, chiefly the corpse. Duvall's notes maddeningly did not name the two suspects.

Through interviewing neighbors in the area, Howe learned that, following his release from the Marines, Ellison went to live with Frenchy Carney, a small-time bootlegger, and his wife, Effie. Months later Howe learned that Frenchy had been found murdered in a pigsty on March 21, 1931, but that his wife was alive and living with relatives in Quantico. He located and interviewed her. Effie had remarried but was cooperative, telling the detective that she had fallen in love with Ellison and was planning to leave with him when he disappeared. Frenchy went berserk with rage, she stated, when she told him she wanted a divorce to marry Ellison. "Brad went to live on a houseboat down on what was then Squatters Creek with two fellows named Dooley Dent and Scissors Saunders. Frenchy began to offer five hundred dollars to anybody who would kill Brad. I was scared to death."

Howe lost no time in scouring the Squatters Creek area for anyone who would remember the missing Marine. With miraculous luck he found a hunchback named Robert B. Leitch living the tramp life in a piano box; Leitch had been in the area since 1929 and he had plenty to say: "On December 30, the day after Brad disappeared, Saunders had a cut on his head as well as a smashed finger. He showed me a pool of blood behind Dent's car and said he had knocked hell out of Ellison and put him where he wouldn't bother anybody else. . . . So I told one of the Quantico policemen—his name was Duvall—and I tried to help him. Duvall had the creek dragged, but Saunders got the body up and buried it in the woods. When dogs started scratching, Saunders dug up the body again. I don't know what he did with it. Because about that time Dent warned me if I didn't keep my mouth shut, another man would disappear."

Duvall's missing corpse, the only element of his case against Dent and Raymond "Scissors" Saunders unaccounted for, had been identified by the tireless Elliott Howe. The detective tracked down Saunders, who had become a hopeless drunk. He was arrested and tried for Ellison's murder on November 25, 1945. For the first time in the court history of Virginia, the bones of a murder victim were present at the trial of the accused. Saunders was convicted by a jury in 105 minutes and sent to prison.

Howe's investigative work in the Ellison case stands as a hallmark in homicide detection. In less than five months he identified a sixteen-year-old skeleton, pieced together a sixteen-year-old triangle murder, and collected enough witnesses to send the slayer to jail, a feat that brought praise from the reserved FBI chief, J. Edgar Hoover: "Howe's job was one of the most brilliant examples of individual detective work I have ever observed."

1948 BRISTOL, CONNECTICUT

A Christmas Killing

Accident and luck have done much to solve the most baffling of homicides, providing investigators with clues that at first appear to be mystifying but are really beacon lights that flood the face of many a killer. Such was the case that sent the police force of Bristol, Connecticut, into a frenzy on the night of December 25, 1948.

At 2 o'clock that morning, police received a call from a distraught woman who lived in a cottage at the outskirts of Bristol; the caller "found a woman in the snow in my yard. She's either very ill or she's dead."

When detectives arrived, the owner of the cottage, Mrs. Rose Lombardi, led them to an area where a woman in a fur coat was sprawled, explaining that she had stumbled over the body on her way to empty the garbage.

"Who is she?" asked Police Chief Edmund S. Crowley.

Mrs. Lombardi shook her head in wonder. "I never saw her before. I have no idea how she got here—or why."

One thing was certain, according to Medical Examiner Fred T. Tirella. The purple bruises on the dead woman's throat meant that she had been strangled. She had been dead for several hours.

The entire affair had upset Mrs. Lombardi's Christmas dinner. Police were sympathetic, but began a systematic search of the area.

While the nameless corpse was sent to the morgue for further study, detectives scoured the grounds around the cottage. Entering an unlocked barn, they found a car. Inside was a lipstick, a twenty-dollar bill, and several long hairs caught in the screw socket of a rear window frame.

The car was rented to a neighbor who hadn't taken the auto out of the garage for days. He had an alibi. Before leaving the scene, one sharp-eyed detective found a black purse in the snow. It was empty except for a small slip of paper upon which was scrawled the word "rich." These seemingly unimportant items were sent along to the pathologist who was examining the corpse. The woman was in her forties, she wore a dress too tight for her, and she was unknown. She had been strangled to death.

Police were stymied. The clues led nowhere, until a young mortician from nearby Plainville who was helping to prepare the body heard about the slip of paper with the single word "rich" on it. Not until returning home was the mortician's memory jogged. He called the Bristol detectives and said: "Say, we have a family in Plainville named Rich. One of the girls married a Bristol bartender last fall. You might check."

The detectives did check, discovering the identity of the corpse to be that of a Lillian Rich who had wedded one Harold Brackett. Checking with Brackett in Bristol, police learned that he was innocent; he had not seen his estranged wife in months. However, detectives in Plainville discovered that Lillian and two youths, one a burly, tough sort in his early twenties and standing well over six feet tall, had been thrown out of a Plainville cafe for rowdy behavior only hours before the woman was found murdered.

The big youth's description fit that of Joseph W. Therrien, a twenty-three-year-old bad boy with a long record of burglary and car theft. Therrien had spent six months in prison and his probation report had him living with none other than Rose Lombardi. Back to the Lombardi cottage raced police. A detective found a freshly dug hole some distance from the remote cottage, but it was empty. It could well have housed a body.

Chief Crowley confronted Mrs. Lombardi. She hadn't seen her star boarder, Therrien, in several days, she insisted.

"We have a warrant and we're going to search this house,"

*Mrs. Lillian Rich
Brackett, shown with an
unknown escort, met her
murderous end at the
hands of two thrill-
seeking youths in Bristol,
Connecticut. (WIDE
WORLD)*

announced Crowley. With that his men began to check everything in the building. In the basement they found a damp, dirt-
covered woman's dress. Inside the furnace they unearthed from
the ashes a half-burned Social Security card belonging to one
Lillian Rich Brackett. Mrs. Lombardi burst into tears when confronted with these implicating finds. "What a Christmas! Now
you won't believe a word I say."

"Try us," Crowley said.

Mrs. Lombardi told how Therrien and another youth,
eighteen-year-old George L. St. James, had appeared early on
the evening of the twenty-fourth with a strange woman. They
were all drunk and Mrs. Lombardi chased them from the house.
The young men took Mrs. Brackett to the nearby barn-garage
where they raped her in the back seat of the car parked inside
(which explained the hairs caught in the window frame). But
Mrs. Brackett struggled too much and the boys strangled her.
Not knowing what to do next, the boys dug a hole in the ground,
threw the corpse into it, and covered it up. They then told Mrs.
Lombardi what they had done. The landlady feared that they
might have buried the woman alive and ordered them to dig up
Mrs. Brackett. They did, dragging her into Mrs. Lombardi's
kitchen. She was quite dead. While the corpse lay on the
kitchen floor, Mrs. Lombardi served the youths coffee and cake
while they figured out what to do next. Mrs. Lombardi solved
the dilemma. They stripped the corpse of its dirty dress, which
was then hidden in the basement. Mrs. Lombardi put one of
her own dresses on the body, although it was too snug, after she
had scrubbed the corpse in her tub and cleaned off Mrs. Brackett's fur coat and shoes. She was then dumped into a snow bank
and the police called.

"But why on earth did you protect these killers?" asked the
astounded Crowley.

"I had to," Mrs. Lombardi announced matter-of-factly. "Therrien is engaged to my daughter and I didn't want anything to
happen to postpone the marriage."

The wedding was postponed indefinitely. Therrien and St.
James were rounded up and were sent to prison for life. Mrs.
Lombardi, as an accessory, was given a three-year sentence. "I
don't know what the fuss was all about," she reportedly griped.
"I just wanted the young people to be happy."

1949 GRAND RAPIDS, MICHIGAN

Slaying the Lonely Heart

The legions opposed to capital punishment rarely shun any condemned prisoner, yet two murderous creatures utterly failed to rouse one cry of protest over their executions. So vile and cold-blooded were their slayings that no one signed a petition, waved a placard or moaned an epitaph for Raymond Fernandez and Martha Beck before they visited Sing Sing Prison's electric chair during America's struggling post–World War II era.

In less than two years, Fernandez and Beck traveled a path strewn with more than a dozen grisly killings. Oddly enough, though, murder was not this strange couple's aim, but only the side-effect of a cheap con game gone amuck.

It began simply enough with Fernandez operating a Lonely Hearts racket. The Hawaiian-born Spanish American was tall and thin, but heavy of jowl and thick of eyebrow. He covered a nearly bald pate with a trim, black wig. Most of the elderly females who fell for this gigolo's line thought of him as a Latin-lover type, although newsmen later dubbed him "a rather seedy Charles Boyer."

Fernandez concentrated on females in their late fifties and early sixties, answering their lonely hearts ads, sweeping them off their feet with lavish attention. He already had two wives and uncounted children before embarking on his career as a devout bigamist.

One advertisement Fernandez answered was from a lonely woman living in Pensacola, Florida. He was happy to learn the woman was young, but was shocked when meeting her. Mrs. Martha Beck, a registered nurse and a matron of a home for crippled children, was obese, weighing well over two hundred pounds. Oddly, Fernandez fell in love with the roly-poly Martha and admitted his con game. She astounded him by her enthusiastic approval of his livelihood. She, too, wanted to participate.

The couple embarked upon a sinister system of swindling the lovelorn. Fernandez would join a lonely hearts club, enamour a fading female with his dubious charms and then introduce the gullible lady to Martha, who pretended to be Raymond's sister. In many instances, the pair moved into the homes of ladies who married Fernandez.

Such was the case with Mrs. Delphine Dowling, an attractive, twenty-eight-year-old widow living in Grand Rapids, Michigan. After accepting Raymond's marriage proposal, Mrs. Dowling allowed him and Martha to move into her home. The cautious widow, however, delayed the walk to the altar until she was "sure of Raymond's affections."

This blocked the couple's chances of obtaining Mrs. Dowling's money, and Martha could not bear for Raymond to make love to the woman. As had been the case many times before with reluctant ladies, Raymond and Martha brought about their own solution. Mrs. Dowling and her two-year-old daughter, Rainelle, disappeared in January, 1949.

When police, asked to investigate by suspicious neighbors, arrived at the Dowling home, Fernandez and Martha shrugged their shoulders. No, they did not know where Mrs. Dowling had gone, but the officers "could search the house if you like." The police did search, and found, not cleverly concealed at all, a wet patch of cement the size of a grave. Digging down four feet, police found the bodies of Mrs. Dowling and her little girl.

His head adorned with a cheap, ill-fitting toupee, Lonely Hearts killer Raymond Fernandez (left) in custody in Grand Rapids, Michigan.

The "Lonely Hearts Killers" broke down immediately upon questioning. Mrs. Dowling became too suspicious so they gave her an overdose of sleeping pills, they said. The woman, however, struggled against the drug and Fernandez shot her in the head.

They tried to placate Rainelle by buying her a dog, but when the child continued to cry for her mother, Mrs. Beck threw her into a washtub and held her down until she drowned. The killers even boasted there were other victims—seventeen, perhaps more.

Fernandez discussed his murders quite freely with Michigan police, removing his cheap wig and wiping away the beads of sweat that gathered on his glistening pate with a perfume-scented handkerchief thoughtfully provided by Mrs. Beck, who chuckled through the lengthy interrogations. "I'm no average killer," grinned Fernandez. He had been suave and sophisticated in his homicides, he told police. It was business, after all, a way of earning a living.

The lean figure in the lockup complained that Mrs. Dowling's demise netted him only five hundred dollars but he had made as much as six thousand dollars in swindling and killing other lonely heart victims. There was Mrs. Jane Thompson, a widow Fernandez married and took to Spain on a honeymoon. He had returned alone, sadly informing Mrs. Thompson's relatives that she had perished in a horrible train wreck, a railway accident never recorded in any book of disasters. The con man was consoled by Mrs. Thompson's mother, a Mrs. Wilson. He moved into the elderly woman's home and she disappeared a short while later.

Carefree with his conscience, Fernandez recalled a Mrs. Myrtle Young. Oh, yes, he had promised to marry her, taking the woman (and her savings) to Chicago in August 1948. "Poor woman," laughed the con man, "she croaked of over-exertion." He went on to explain in descriptions both vivid and obscene —as was the conduct of both Fernandez and Mrs. Beck throughout their three-week trial—how he drove Mrs. Young to death by compelling her to partake of nonstop sex.

In the tragic instance of Mrs. Janet Fay, a sixty-six-year-old widow living in a Manhattan apartment, murder was nothing more than a jealous whim of Martha Beck. She and Fernandez had *already* obtained every penny of Mrs. Fay's savings. As they were preparing to desert the widow, Mrs. Fay cried out for her beloved Fernandez. Martha grabbed a hammer and crushed the woman's head. With a smile forcing her chubby cheeks wide, Martha Beck told police: "I turned to Raymond and said, 'Look what I've done,' and then he strangled her with a scarf."

Mrs. Fay's remains were packed into a trunk and driven to a small house some miles from New York City where the killers neatly wrapped it in brown butcher paper, then buried it beneath four feet of concrete. Fernandez generously gave the Michigan police the address of the New York cottage, one, he stated, they had cunningly rented just for the purpose of housing the grisly remains of their victims.

Michigan authorities reckoned that since their state had no capital punishment, the murderers might be free on parole in a decade. However, Mrs. Janet Fay was from New York, and that state still punished first-degree murder with execution. Fernandez and Martha were turned over to New York authorities.

Removed to Long Island jail cells, Martha and Raymond shrugged indifference to their fate. So avid was their taste for murder mysteries that warders were kept busy buying pocket-edition thrillers for them. Their trial commenced in July 1949

Fernandez signing his lengthy confession of killings, after which he blurted: "I'm not an average murderer!"

Fernandez shown with one of his victims, Mrs. Myrtle Young, of whom the killer said laughingly: "She croaked of over-exertion!"

Martha Beck, Fernandez' neurotic lover, glumly reading her murder-partner's confession in 1949. (WIDE WORLD)

before Judge Ferdinand Pecora. Both pleaded not guilty by reason of insanity.

On one occasion, as Mrs. Beck was being led to the witness stand, her face coated with rouge, her mouth thick with bright red lipstick, she broke away, waddled quickly to Fernandez, and held him in a bearlike embrace, kissing him passionately on the mouth, then the cheeks, the forehead, the neck. As she was pulled away by several guards, leaving Fernandez proudly bearing a lipstick-covered face, Martha screamed to the court: "I love him! I do love him, and I always will!"

Such theatrics aside, the odd couple was found sane. A jury took little time convicting them of the first-degree murder of the widow Fay. Judge Pecora sentenced them to death on August 22, 1949. Their strange residence in Sing Sing's Death House, prolonged by laborious appeals, remains an unsavory legend in that prison.

Mrs. Beck and Fernandez were placed in cells that allowed them to see each other through an open door that stood between the men's and women's wings of Death Row. They waved at each other and blew kisses. Fernandez regaled his fellow condemned prisoners with his sexual feats, so much that they sarcastically took to calling him the "Mail-Order Romeo." They shouted at him to shut up, but he all the more readily prattled on about his bedroom exploits, his warped logic being that since all thoughts of sex were abandoned by fear in those facing executions, his bragging about sexual conquests therefore proved him unafraid, manly, someone to be respected.

Yet his Death House neighbors found a way to jangle Fernandez' nerves. Any caustic remark about his lover Martha would provoke him to screaming rage. A prisoner once called to him, after returning from the exercise yard: "Hey, Fernandez, that blimp of yours gave me a big greeting today. She wiggled at me!" Raymond Fernandez exploded, shaking the bars in a fury, screaming death threats.

Before they were brought back to court for one of their many appeals, Martha began the love-hate correspondence that marked their Sing Sing imprisonment, writing:

The remains of Janet Fay, one of the many Fernandez-Beck victims, are removed from a New York cottage. (WIDE WORLD)

Martha's not getting on the stand again if we have a new trial. I don't want a new trial if we have to cut each other's throats. Nor do I want one if it means you will refuse to look at me, smile, or speak when possible. I can take everything except a cold shoulder from you . . .

I am glad you waved this a.m. Thanks darling, from the bottom of my heart. Ray—please, Ray—accept these flowers and my love.

Your own Birdbrain

P.S.: If you don't return the flowers, I'll know you added my initials to the bow knot, joining our love together with a tie so tight that nothing can break it.

The next missive promised, as usual, eternal love, one in which Mrs. Beck waxed thickly about the birds she could see flying free beyond her cell window:

If I have to get to the chair to prove my love—I'll go. . . . Maybe I can train them [the birds], darling, to fly to you with a message of love, for I never want you to forget I love you. To me you will always be the man I love.

The Lonely Hearts killers laugh it up with police guards during their New York murder trial.

Thirty *X*'s, standing for kisses, were marked at the bottom of the page, with the flirtatious footnote:

> If only I could deliver them in person!

Weeks later, Martha had learned that Fernandez was talking freely about their evil adventures and her weird fetishes, laughing about such quirks with other prisoners in his wing. She dashed off the following vitriol to him:

> You are a double-crossing, two-timing skunk. I learn now that you have been doing quite a bit of talking to everyone. It's nice to learn what a terrible murderous person I am, while you are such a misunderstood, white-haired boy, caught in the clutches of a female vampire. It was also nice to know that all the love letters you wrote "from your heart" were written with a hand shaking with laughter at me for being such a gullible fool as to believe them.
>
> Don't waste your time or energy trying to hide from view in church from now on, for I won't even look your way—the halo over your righteous head might blind me. May God have mercy on your soul.
>
> M. F. Beck

Keeping pace with Martha's furious correspondence, the couple's lawyers filed appeal after appeal, all being denied, including that of the Supreme Court on January 2, 1951. The date for their execution was set for March 8, 1951. Two others, Richard Powers and John King, both twenty-two, were slated to die at 11:00 P.M. on that date. The young killers, who had murdered a man in an armed robbery, taunted Fernandez to the end, studding their bravado with lines such as "Don't forget, Ray, old boy, we got a date for Thursday, March eighth, at eleven o'clock. And don't forget to bring Martha!"

At this, Fernandez would grit his teeth and yell: "You dirty punks, I'll still be around when you're both dead!" The lonely hearts killer was making reference to a Sing Sing rule that when more than one inmate is executed on the same day, the weaker goes to the chair first; he was, in his own estimation, the only one who "wasn't yellow."

On the appointed day, Powers and King did go first, weeping and shaking, being supported by guards into the "little green room."

275

The thirty-five-year-old Fernandez could not muster any appetite and sent his last meal to other prisoners. He did smoke a Havana cigar and handed over a note, his last official words, to warders for subsequent publication. It read:

> People want to know whether I still love Martha. But of course I do. I want to shout it out. I love Martha. What do the public know about love?

Martha Beck breaks down on learning that she is going to the electric chair.

Martha Beck, age thirty, told her female guards that she was sick and tired of people thinking of her as a fat woman. She would show them. She ordered a simple last meal of fried chicken, fried potatoes and a salad—two helpings each. For the waiting newsmen, Mrs. Beck had written a final message:

> My story is a love story. But only those tortured by love can know what I mean. I am not unfeeling, stupid or moronic. I am a woman who had a great love and always will have it. Imprisonment in the "Death House" has only strengthened my feeling for Raymond.

Fernandez was not, as he had boasted, the last to go to the electric chair that night. He followed Powers and King into the execution room, led wobbly legged and sagging by struggling guards. Mrs. Martha Beck was the last to go, thought by the authorities to be the strongest of all the condemned killers. There was a noticeable smile on her lips as she plopped down into the chair.

1953 KANSAS CITY, MISSOURI
"The Boy Is Driving Us Crazy!"

He was at the end of the line, a derelict of drink and drugs, and Carl Austin Hall, age thirty-four, knew it. Hall's father, a highly esteemed attorney in the Kansas City area, had left him more than two hundred thousand dollars, which he squandered on alcohol and hard-line drugs. When the money ran out, Hall desperately turned to crime to pay his bar tabs and pusher, robbing taxicab drivers in the Kansas City area.

Hall was an inept stick-up man and was quickly apprehended. Sentenced to five years in the Missouri State Prison,
he was paroled within sixteen months, released on April 24,
1953. Waiting for Hall at the time of his release was a forty-
one-year-old heavyset woman with a porcine face and the disposition of an adder, one Bonnie B. Heady, who had been widowed when her bank-robber husband was killed while
attempting to escape prison. Hall had been tipped through the
prison grapevine that Bonnie, one of those misdirected creatures who are enamoured with criminals, was eager to meet
him, having heard of the wastrel's shoddy past through underworld friends.

Bonnie Heady took Hall to her modest one-story home in St.
Joseph, Missouri, where they whiled away the dull hours by
drinking themselves senseless. According to FBI historian Don
Whitehead, "Each of them drank about a fifth of whiskey a
day." During this historic binge, one thought kept recurring in
the booze-soaked brain of Carl Austin Hall, an idea he had
conceived while he had lain awake night after night in the state
prison, a "foolproof" kidnapping.

The minute his thick-tongued thought was broached to Bonnie, she squealed with anticipation. As with all of her ilk, Bonnie Heady thrived on the excitement of the illegal, the thrill of
the illicit. "Why, that's better than sex," she confessed to Hall,
and readily began to organize the kidnap plan with him, detailing exactly how they would abduct the six-year-old son of Robert Greenlease, a wealthy Kansas City resident who owned a
Cadillac dealership.

At 10:55 A.M., September 28, 1953, Bonnie B. Heady, wring-
ing a handkerchief in her pudgy hands to channel her nervous-
ness, stood before the entrance of the French Institute of Notre
Dame de Scion, a private pre–grade school in Kansas City, Missouri. After she had repeatedly rung the doorbell, Sister Morand opened the front door.

Inside the school office, Mrs. Heady appeared in a state of
emotional chaos. "I'm sorry I'm so upset," she told the sister,
telling her that she was the aunt of Bobby Greenlease, Jr., a
student at the school. "Something terrible has happened.
Bobby's mother has had a heart attack. She's in St. Mary's Hospital and calls for the boy all the time. I simply must take him
there at once. It will comfort my sister so much."

"Wait in the chapel, please," Sister Morand told her and then

277

Bonnie Heady's attic bar in her St. Joseph, Missouri, home where, in alcoholic stupors, she and her lover, Carl Austin Hall, planned the kidnapping of Bobby Greenlease, Jr. (UPI)

Bobby Greenlease, Jr., shown only days before his abduction from his Kansas City private school. (UPI)

went to fetch the Greenlease child. When she returned with little blond-haired Bobby, Bonnie Heady was at a pew on her knees. Mrs. Heady stepped from the chapel smiling at Bobby, placing her arm tenderly about his shoulder. "I have been praying for my sister's quick recovery," said Mrs. Heady. "I'm not a Catholic and I don't know whether God heard my prayers." Bobby Greenlease gave no sign that Bonnie Heady was a total stranger to him and went willingly with her outside to a waiting cab.

The cabbie drove Mrs. Heady and the boy to the Katz Parking Lot at Main and Fortieth Streets. He watched as the woman led the boy by the hand to a 1947 Plymouth station wagon. The driver of the car was a balding, sallow-faced man with a receding chin and droopy eyes. The cab driver noted that the man had a scar on his forehead; he looked familiar but the taxi driver could not quite place him.

Swinging out of the parking lot, the man, woman and boy seemed to be chatting amiably, as the car headed south from Kansas City on Highway 169. By this time, Sister Morand, concerned about Mrs. Greenlease, had called St. Mary's Hospital to discover in shock that Bobby's mother was not a patient. The sister then called the Greenlease home. Mrs. Greenlease was well. Bobby's mother, learning from Sister Morand about the unknown woman who had picked up her son, hurriedly called her husband. Robert Greenlease rushed home, called the Kansas City police and they, in turn, phoned the FBI.

The family had not long to wait for word on Bobby. The first ransom letter arrived the morning after the kidnapping, September 24, 1953. It read:

> Your boy been kidnapped get $600,000 in $20s—$10s—Fed. Res. notes from all twelve districts we realize it takes few days to get that amount. Boy will be in good hands—when you have money ready put ad in K.C. Star—will meet you in Chicago next Sunday—Signed Mr. G.
> Do not call police or try to use chemicals on bills or take numbers. Do not try to use any radio to catch us or boy dies. If you try to trap us your wife your other child and yourself will be killed you will be watched all of the time. You will be told how to contact us with money. When you get this note let us know by driving up and down main St. between 39 & 29 for 20 minutes with white rag on car aeriel.
> If do exactly as we say an try no tricks, your boy will be back safe withen 24 hrs—after we check money
> Deliver money in army duefel bag. Be ready to deliver at once on contact.—
> $400,000 in 20s
> $200,000 in 10s

The reaction to this extortion note was staggering since the amount of money demanded was, up to that time, the highest ever in the history of kidnapping in America. Further, the crime itself was anachronistic in that such abductions had not been common since the heyday of gangster-kidnappers in the 1930s; it was thought to be a crime of the past, wholly obliterated by the energetic efforts of the FBI in their gangbuster days. The Bureau, in the Greenlease kidnapping, was hamstrung in that it was still forced to adhere to the seven-day waiting period before intervening as dictated by the 1932 Lindbergh Law. Kansas City police, at the urgent request of the parents, agreed to take no action for five days.

That period of time came and went. Even though the local police and the FBI swarmed throughout the Kansas City area looking for leads, they unearthed nothing. Blithely, the kidnappers continued, over several weeks, to send ransom notes, messages, and conduct phone calls with the nerve-wracked Greenleases and their friends.

One phone call from Hall, calling himself "M," with Mrs. Greenlease at the other end, was reconstructed by federal agents:

Mrs. G.: M, this is Mrs. Greenlease.

M: Speaking.

Mrs. G.: We have the money but we must know our boy is alive and well. Can you give me that? Can you give me anything that will make me know that?

M: . . . A reasonable request, but to be frank with you, the boy is driving us crazy. We couldn't risk taking him to a phone.

Mrs. G.: Well, I can imagine that. Would you do this? Would you ask him two questions? Give me the answer of two questions?

M: Speaking.

Mrs. G.: . . . If I had the answer to these two questions, I would know my boy is alive.

M: All right.

Mrs. G.: Ask him what is the name of our driver in Europe this summer.

M: All right.

Mrs. G.: And the second question, what did you build with your monkey blocks in your playroom the last night you were home. . . . If I can get those answers from you, I'll know you have him and he is alive, which is the thing you know that I want.

M: We have the boy. He is alive. Believe me. He's been driving us nuts.

Mrs. G.: Well, I can imagine that. He's such an active youngster.

M: He's been driving us nuts.

Mrs. G: Could you get those answers?

M: All right.

The anxiety of the Greenleases dragged agonizingly on, Hall and Heady delighting in their cruelty toward the family by making short, incessant phone calls to set up the ransom delivery. Several times the communications, mostly due to the ineptitude of the drunken kidnappers, broke down in folly and failure to

appear. Messages were placed beneath rocks or taped to the
bottoms of mailboxes; notes from the abductors that directed
the go-betweens to notes hidden elsewhere confused those acting on behalf of the frustrated family.

Finally, Hall arranged to pick up the money, eighty-five
pounds of bills amounting to $600,000 jammed into a duffel
bag. It was to be left in high grass near a country lane. The
kidnapper, reeling drunkenly about in the grass, could not locate the money. Hall went back to the phone. On October 4,
1953, his fourteenth phone call to the Greenleases, Hall rang
up his victims at 8:28 P.M. A family friend, Robert Ledterman,
answered:

Ledterman: Greenlease residence. Ledterman speaking.

M: How are you?

Ledterman: Fine. How are you tonight?

M: A little late.

Ledterman: You said eight o'clock. Are we all set?

M: We're all set. We have a perfect plan. It couldn't be
any . . .

Ledterman: How's that now? Give me that again.

M: There could not be any mistake. This is a perfect plan. It
will have to be a little later. I am sorry, too, but we want to
make sure there's no mixup this time.

Ledterman: Yes. Let's get things over—say, by the way, M,
did the boy answer any of those questions?

M: No . . . I couldn't . . . we didn't get anything from him.

Ledterman: Couldn't get anything from him?

M: He wouldn't talk. . . . I'll tell you this much. You will get
him in Pittsburg, Kansas.

Ledterman: You're not bunking me in that, are you?

M: That's the gospel truth.

Two friends of the Greenleases, Ledterman and Norbert S.
O'Neill, according to arrangements made in the phone conversation, placed the duffel bag near a bridge close to the junction
of highways 40 and 10E at midnight. Some hours later, Hall
called the Greenlease home as M to report that the kidnappers
were in possession of the ransom but still hadn't counted it.

Ledterman: I can assure that all the money you demanded is
there.

281

M: Well, I am sure of that. You can tell his mother that she
will see him as we promised within twenty-four hours. . . .
We will certainly be very glad to send him back.

Immediately upon picking up the money, Hall and Bonnie
Heady left for St. Louis. Hall purchased two metal suitcases
and dumped half the ransom money into those, hiding them in
an ash pit in south St. Louis. The rest of the cash Hall took with
him to a hotel room in St. Louis where he and Bonnie proceeded to drink heavily to their success. When Mrs. Heady fell
unconscious from the whiskey, Hall slipped out of the room
with all of the cash he had with him, leaving only $2,000 in
Bonnie's purse.

A day later Hall took several cabs to various spots in St. Louis.
At the end of his travels, pulling on a flask of whiskey all the
way, he began to blabber about his clever exploit to a cab
driver, who tipped the police and the FBI.

St. Louis police arrested both Hall and Heady on the night of
October 6, 1953, only two days after they had obtained the
largest kidnap ransom in U.S. history. Only $295,140 of the
ransom money paid was recovered by federal agents, almost all
of it from the metal suitcases in the ash pit. The rest, more than
$300,000 was never recovered.

For all the promises and assurances Hall had given the

Heavily manacled, Hall and Heady are taken into custody.

FBI officials direct the digging up of Bobby Greenlease's body next to Mrs. Heady's home. (UPI)

Greenlease family, his sadistic cruelty was capped with his bland confession that little Bobby Greenlease was dead; he had murdered the child only a few hours after the abduction, having driven from Kansas City to a deserted farm.

While Mrs. Heady took a stroll in the field, Hall placed his hands about the boy's neck and tried to strangle him. Bobby Greenlease was a feisty youngster. He fought for his life, striking his attacker and squirming repeatedly from his grasp. Hall was prepared for such resistance.

"I had the gun in my coat pocket," he calmly informed FBI agents. "I pulled it out and I shot once, trying to hit him in the heart. I don't know whether I hit him or not for he was still alive. . . . I shot him through the head on the second shot. I took him out of the car, laid him on the ground and put him in a plastic bag. I remember a lot of blood there. This farm where the killing occurred is about two miles south and two miles west of the state line."

After his grim chores were finished, Hall yelled to Mrs.

Heady, who walked back to the car and helped the killer load the body into the rear seat. Once back at Bonnie's St. Joseph home, the two, waiting until nightfall so the neighbors could not see their movements, dragged the plastic-wrapped body to a shallow pit they had prepared some days before the kidnapping, dumped it in, and covered it over with dirt. The next morning, both purchased chrysanthemums, which they planted on top of the grave.

Although she insisted that Hall was the sole killer of the boy, Mrs. Heady was convicted, along with her paramour, on a charge of kidnapping for ransom, after both pleaded guilty in a federal court. The jury recommended the death penalty when they reached their verdict on November 19, 1953.

In reaction to her sentence, Mrs. Heady sneered, "I'd rather be dead than poor." To that end, she and Hall were strapped into separate chairs in the gas chamber of the Jefferson City State Penitentiary of Missouri on December 16, 1953. Carl Austin Hall was pronounced dead at 12:12 A.M. Mrs. Heady outlived him by twenty seconds.

FBI agents to this day still search for the missing $300,000. The kidnappers insisted with their dying gasp that they did not know its whereabouts.

The press of the day wholeheartedly endorsed the execution of Hall and Heady; even the reserved *New York Times* approved of the death penalty in an editorial. When the death penalty was announced in court at the end of the couple's trial, a thunderous applause came from the spectators' gallery.

Bonnie Heady and Carl Austin Hall only minutes after learning of their joint death sentence.

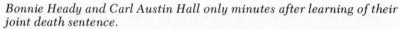

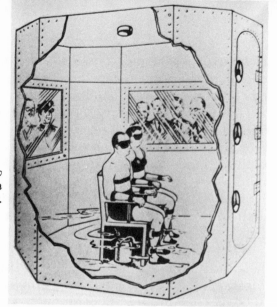

*An artist's rendering of how
Hall and Heady died in
Missouri's gas chamber.*

Because of this case, the federal Lindbergh Law of 1932 was altered so that the FBI could immediately involve itself in any kidnapping case, instead of waiting the mandatory seven days, a legal modification that came, perhaps, too late for Bobby Greenlease, Jr.

1954 TULSA, OKLAHOMA

Murder for Love

Dr. N. Z. Schwelbein, a physician in Tulsa, Oklahoma, was on the phone talking to the wife of his recently deceased patient Samuel Doss. At the other end of the line was Nannie Doss, her voice pleasant, her manner cooperative. Schwelbein told Mrs. Doss that when her husband had been admitted into a hospital in October 1954, the stomach pains he exhibited were highly suspicious, particularly since he had apparently died of them the following day.

"I think an autopsy is necessary to determine the cause of death," Schwelbein patiently explained to Mrs. Doss.

Without a moment's hesitation, the wife replied: "Whatever he had might kill somebody else. It's best to find out."

The results of Dr. Schwelbein's autopsy were more than he

285

had expected. Samuel Doss had been poisoned; his body contained enough arsenic to kill twenty men. Police were dispatched to Mrs. Doss' home.

The woman answering the door was a bespectacled, plump female who had the appearance of a kindly grandmother, although she was only forty-nine years old. When confronted with the evidence found in the autopsy, Nannie clucked in her mild voice: "I don't understand it. How could such a thing happen, poison? All I fed him when he came home . . . was a dish of stewed prunes, and there was certainly no arsenic in that."

When officers asked Nannie Doss to accompany them to headquarters for questioning, she willingly obliged. The interrogations then conducted were grueling, occurring before the 1964 Escobedo and 1966 Miranda Supreme Court decisions that allowed suspects to be represented by lawyers prior to questioning. The police hammered away at Nannie Doss for several days. She smiled and giggled through the ordeal like a teenager, struggling, it seemed, to please the relentless interrogators. But her memory appeared to be incredibly poor.

At one juncture an officer quizzed: "What can you tell us about the death of Richard Morton? He seems to have died long before he should have, about a year and a half ago."

"I never heard of any Richard Morton."

"What? You don't remember your previous husband?"

"Oh, *that* Richard Morton."

"That's the one."

"Yes, I was married to him."

At the end of several punishing days of questioning, Nannie finally remembered everything about Morton. She had poisoned him, yes, she said. She had also given arsenic to Samuel Doss.

Days after Nannie Doss' confession made headlines, police departments all over Oklahoma began calling the Tulsa officers, asking about Mrs. Doss' other husbands—who had also died mysteriously. Of five, four had perished in great pain. The bodies were exhumed. Large amounts of arsenic were found.

Nannie's first husband, it was learned, who had married her when she was but fifteen, had divorced her. He survived, but two of their three children had died early deaths, their symptoms the same—violent stomach pains. (A third child managed to escape Mrs. Doss' prunes and lived to raise a normal family.)

Nannie Doss with husband number three, Arlie Lanning, in 1952.

The hunt through the cemeteries was on. Not only were Nannie's first two children murdered with arsenic poisoning but, after digging up almost every relative the woman was known to have had, medical experts discovered that she had also poisoned her mother, two sisters, the nephew of one husband, and the grandson of another, eleven *known* killings in all.

At her brief trial, Nannie Doss admitted to the wholesale slayings. Yes, she had obtained money from the insurance on her husbands' lives, but these were meager amounts. She took umbrage at the thought of murdering for money. No, the real reason, she said, was that all of her spouses had been dullards, boring her beyond belief. Her marital experiences were not at all like the stories she was addicted to in her favorite magazine, *True Romance.*

"You killed for romance?" the prosecution asked incredulously.

"Yes, that's about it. I was searching for the perfect mate, the real romance of life." Her quest for a meaningful relationship had been blotted with failure, she explained. It was necessary to kill off her husbands to continue the search.

When asked how this schoolgirl motive applied to her mother, sisters and the children, Nannie Doss only shrugged. The jury took only a few hours to convict the woman of mass murder. She was sent to prison for life, where she died of leukemia in 1965. At the time her cell was littered with well-thumbed romance magazines.

Nannie Doss at her trial in Tulsa, Oklahoma, after admitting the murder of four husbands and the poisoning of her mother, two sisters, two children and assorted relatives to bring her total to eleven known killings. She is shown with two of her grandchildren and a shocked Mrs. Melvina Hedrick, one daughter she allowed to live. (WIDE WORLD)

Nannie Doss (left) with unknown mourners at Arlie Lanning's funeral; according to her later confessions, she gave him rat poison for breakfast.

Nannie with husband number four, Richard L. Morton; she poisoned him a month after this snapshot was taken.

1958 WASHINGTON, D.C.

Trapped by a Speck of Dust

Three small boys deciding to get in an hour's fishing before dinner on September 8, 1958, threw their makeshift line—a rope and hanger—into the Anacostia River off the East Capitol Street Bridge in Washington, D.C. Their catch both astounded and frightened them. They had snagged what they first thought to be the largest freshwater fish in history, but when it was tugged to the surface, they were greeted with the body of a woman.

Answering the screams of the boys, police pulled from the watery depths the body of a woman. She was dressed in pajamas and tied with baling wire; around one leg was a concrete block weighing twenty-six pounds. Other than an inexpensive ring on her finger, the identity of the victim remained a mystery; there were no missing-persons reports or available fingerprints to link the young woman with a name.

Then John E. Sulhoff, building engineer of the International Bank for Reconstruction, spotted a news story regarding the unidentified body and wondered if it could have been that of Mrs. Reeves. Mrs. Reeves, a normally punctual woman, had failed to appear on Sunday at the bank building to operate one of the elevators. After calling police, Sulhoff went to the morgue and made a positive identification: Mrs. Ruth Reeves, elevator operator, age thirty-eight. She had held down another job, working in a government building cafeteria in Virginia. Mrs. Reeves lived in a comfortable duplex at 206 Thirty-fourth Street, S.E.

Nothing had been disturbed in the apartment, police noted when they entered. A photograph of the dead woman and a man was found on a desk in Mrs. Reeves' apartment. A neighbor remembered the man in the photo, which led to the identification of one Philmore Clarke, a forty-year-old carpenter who worked on various government construction projects. Clarke was not on the job, having gone on vacation two days before Mrs. Reeves' body was dragged from the river.

Clarke had not been seeing Mrs. Reeves for a number of weeks, police learned. The attractive brunette had a new boyfriend and she had apparently cut off her affair with Philmore

Clarke. When visiting Clarke's residence, officers saw that some of the concrete slabs making up the low wall in front of his house were missing; the remaining slabs were identical to the one that had been tied around Mrs. Reeves' leg. Further, inside Clarke's house was a large spool of baling wire, which matched the wire used to attach the slab to the dead woman. Several detectives surrounded the Clarke home and waited for its occupant to arrive.

Clarke strolled nonchalantly up the walk on Tuesday night, September 9, 1958. He was whistling as if he hadn't a care in the world. Taken to headquarters for interrogation, Clarke had little to say. When informed that his lady friend had been murdered, Clarke only sighed deeply.

"How do you think this murder came about?" grilled one cop.

"God only knows."

"Didn't you threaten Mrs. Reeves when you two broke up?"

"No, never."

"And you deny seeing her in the last week?"

"I didn't say that. Yeah, sure, I saw her. I called her Sunday morning on the phone. She needed some groceries. I got them for her and then dropped them off around noon. That's the last I saw of her."

When police informed Clarke that Mrs. Reeves' upstairs neighbors had heard loud "thumping" noises, the cool-minded suspect only shrugged, saying he had no idea what could have caused such sounds. The neighbors proved most cooperative, interrogators pointed out to Clarke. His car, a 1955 Oldsmobile, had been seen several times in the area of Mrs. Reeves' house, even on the night she was killed.

"A guy in the service owns that car. He shipped out and left it with a girl I know. She loaned it to me."

"Where's the car now? You returned home on foot?"

"I left it in front of a friend's house early yesterday and at night it wasn't there." He shook his head slowly, sadly. "I guess someone stole it."

Boldly, officers revealed the discoveries they had made at Clarke's house, telling him that the concrete slab and wire tied to the dead woman matched the wall of his house and the spool of wire they had found in his hallway.

Philmore Clarke laughed; the officers were inflating both their imaginations and their investigative prowess. "Forget about all that," he told them. "She was probably killed by her new boyfriend or by her ex-husband, and I'll just bet whoever it was took the concrete and the wire from my place to make me suspect in this mess."

The officers sat back in their chairs and stared at Clarke.

"Well, it's possible, right?"

They didn't answer. They knew that the cement blocks and the wire would serve well in court against Clarke but they lacked the evidence that would put him at the scene of the crime. Clarke grinned confidence. He had an alibi. His new girlfriend was with him, in bed, at the very time police claimed Mrs. Reeves had been dumped into the river. When officers confronted the woman, she backed up Clarke's story.

Captain Lawrence Hartnett of Washington's Homicide Squad was not about to give up. The Oldsmobile Clarke had been driving was found only a few blocks away from the suspect's home a few days later. Hartnett ordered that it be picked clean. He specified that the car be painstakingly vacuumed and that everything in the car be minutely examined in the FBI laboratory.

Found were specks of dust, tiny bits of black silica slag. Similar dust specks had been found on Mrs. Reeves' pajamas, and on a pair of shoes worn by Philmore Clarke. At first Hartnett and his officers were in a quandary. Such residue, FBI chemists informed them, was found only in industrial furnaces that maintained incredibly high temperatures.

Visiting the spot where the body was dragged from the Anacostia River, Hartnett and others took many samples of the riverbank earth. Black silica slag was abundantly present in this earth, chemists soon revealed. A canvas of power plants in the area proved successful; the Potomac Electric Power Company's furnaces produced the peculiar residue. The waste material was trucked by an independent firm to the very spot where the body had been found and had been dumped into the river. Though circumstantial, the evidence was strong against Clarke and he was brought to trial.

By the time he appeared in court, police had found a blood spot on the floor of the Oldsmobile that matched Mrs. Reeves' blood type. The prosecution prepared a strong case, its lawyers, with the help of Hartnett's reconstruction of the crime, believing that Clarke had told the truth about visiting Mrs. Reeves on Sunday afternoon—and he had strangled her to death when she refused to see him again. He carefully cleaned up her apartment and left, locking all the doors and windows, taking Mrs. Reeves' key with him. That night, after his lady friend fell asleep, Philmore Clarke rose from his lover's bed, dressed, and drove back to Mrs. Reeves' apartment. He had brought along a concrete slab and wire from his home.

Retrieving the body from the apartment, Clarke drove to the river, edging the Oldsmobile close to the water. He then tied the concrete slab to Mrs. Reeves' leg with the baling wire. The weight of the body and the slab were such that he had to drag the body to the water, thereby coating Mrs. Reeves' pajamas. It was only a quirk of fate that Clarke selected that part of the riverbank where the slag had been dumped, something he would not have noticed in the dark as he went about his grim chores.

When the prosecution entered the courtroom on December 9, 1958, its lawyers were shocked at Clarke's response to Judge John J. Sirica, who had told him to state his plea. "Guilty, Your Honor," stated the defendant in a calm, clear voice. Defense counsel had simply taken advantage of the prosecution's pretrial stipulation that, should the defendant plead guilty to second-degree murder, such a plea would be acceptable, given the lack of eyewitness testimony to prove premeditation of first-degree murder.

The careful disposal of Mrs. Reeves' body, however, was exposed through dogged police and crime laboratory work, when infinitesimal specks of dust proved murder and guilt.

Philmore Clarke received a five-to-twenty-five-years' sentence in the penitentiary.

1962 SAN JOSE, CALIFORNIA

Torture for Love

Unlike the physician killers earlier profiled in this volume, nothing else in the last two centuries compares with the hideous savagery practiced by the medical monster Dr. Geza de Kaplany. An anesthesiologist working in a San Jose, California, hospital, de Kaplany was a Hungarian refugee whose haughty

Dr. de Kaplany and his bride; even then he was thinking of "fixing" her so no other man would possess her. (UPI)

Beautiful Hajna de Kaplany only a few months before her torturous murder in 1962. (WIDE WORLD)

manner and arrogant speech endeared him to no one. Vain and pompous, the thirty-six-year-old doctor pursued and won the heart and hand of a twenty-five-year-old model and one-time beauty queen of the Hungarian community in San Jose.

Hajna de Kaplany had no idea what was in store for her when she moved with her husband into a new apartment in August 1962, a day after their wedding. Some weeks later, de Kaplany was later to state, he was driven to impotency, thinking in his paranoid manner that his beautiful wife was having several affairs with bachelor neighbors. He would fix her, he would "ruin her beauty," as he later sneered.

Early Tuesday morning, August 28, 1962, de Kaplany's neighbors were annoyed to hear blaring music coming from his apartment. A high, thin screech hovered over the music. To those grimacing at the noise, the screech sounded almost human. Despite their vigorous wall-pounding and floor-stomping, neighbors failed to communicate their displeasure. In frustration they called the police.

When officers knocked at the de Kaplanys' door they were greeted by a waxy-skinned, smirking man sweating in his underclothes. He had been hard at work, as officers soon discovered. In the bedroom, officers took one look at Hajna de Kaplany and reeled in horror. She had been tortured, beyond belief.

De Kaplany, it was quickly learned, had decided that no other man would ever possess his wife, no man would ever want to look at her after he "operated" on her. He had prepared well for his task, getting a manicure the day before so that he would not puncture the rubber gloves he donned that terrible morning, a self-protective measure to guard against the sulphuric, hydrochloric and nitric acids he carefully assembled on the bedroom bureau while his beautiful wife slept.

He then jumped upon her, tying her to the bed. De Kaplany went to the new hi-fi equipment he had purchased just for this event and turned up the volume to maximum level. Without a word he walked to the naked woman and held up a note he had written the night before on one of his own prescription forms. It read: "If you want to live—do not shout; do what I tell you; or else you will die."

Although Hajna very much wanted to live, it was impossible not to scream. Systematically, de Kaplany made small cuts all over his wife's body; he then poured acid into these, obliterat-

ing her face and her genitals, as she writhed and screamed in
the worst of physical agonies.

Police interrupted the torture after an hour; Hajna was removed to a hospital with third-degree corrosive burns. When
attendants in the ambulance attempted to apply aid they
burned their hands on her acid-smeared body. A little over a
month later the plucky woman finally died. Geza de Kaplany
was charged with murder and brought to trial on January 7,
1963.

"Not Guilty" and "Not Guilty by Reason of Insanity" were
de Kaplany's joint pleas before the court. On the witness stand
the doctor calmly stated that he had never meant to murder his
beautiful wife, certainly not. The medieval torture he had inflicted was only to disfigure her for life so that men would not
be attracted to her and he would have his peace of mind.

De Kaplany's composure was utterly shattered when the
prosecution exhibited in court photos of the woman as police
had found her. The physician became hysterical viewing his
devilish atrocity, babbling to Judge Raymond G. Callahan: "I
am a doctor! I loved her! If I did this and I must have done this
—then I am guilty!"

Thirty-five days later, on March 1, 1963, Geza de Kaplany
was found guilty. He was given a life sentence but was inexplicably classified by prison authorities as a "special interest prisoner."

The "acid doctor" spent only thirteen years inside prison
before being released in 1975, fully six months before his official parole date in 1976. It was later explained that the doctor's

*Dr. de Kaplany is restrained in court at his
acid-murder trial after seeing a large
autopsy photo of his dead wife. "No!" he
screamed. "What have you done to her?"*

medical expertise was vital to a Taiwan missionary hospital where his knowledge as a "cardiac specialist" was in great need. This alone was astounding in that de Kaplany was far from being a heart specialist.

When probes into the unusual de Kaplany parole unearthed his early and secret release—he was all but smuggled out of the country—Ray Procunier, head of the parole board, resigned "for personal reasons."

From last reports, the "acid doctor" is presently attending to the medical needs of Chinese on Taiwan, patients undoubtedly unaware of de Kaplany's peculiar surgical quirks.

1966 SALT LAKE CITY, UTAH

"We Thought It Was Kind of Funny"

Walter Kelbach, twenty-eight, and his intimate friend, Myron Lance, twenty-five, were ex-convicts whose concepts of morality and sensitivity to human life were (and are) nonexistent by the time they decided, almost casually, to go on a murder spree in the Salt Lake City area just before Christmas 1968. Both homosexuals, the big-boned, blue-jawed Kelbach was obviously the leader, but his pal Lance, sporting a shaved head and the deceptive mannerisms of a studious type, was equally aggressive and lethal.

After popping some pills and drinking great quantities of beer, the pair, on the night of December 17, 1966, drove into a Salt Lake City gas station. Stephen Shea, an eighteen-year-old attendant, filled their tank. Instead of paying him, Kelbach and Lance robbed him of $147. They threw the terrified Shea into the back of their station wagon and drove off into the desert, ordering the youth to undress. In a remote spot Kelbach and Lance sexually assaulted him several times.

While the terrified victim sat huddled in the back of the wagon, the pair then drove on, loudly talking about killing him. "Let's flip a coin to see who wins the job," one of them squealed in demented joy. Kelbach won the toss and jumped into the back of the wagon, stabbing the youth in five places, mortally wounding him. The killers then hurled the naked body alongside the lonely road and drove off at a leisurely pace.

"Did the kid say anything?" quizzed Lance, referring to Shea's last uttered cry for mercy.

"Yeah," snorted Kelbach with a guffaw, "he said 'Oh, my God, I got a wife!' "

"That's kind of funny, really," chuckled Lance.

"Did you see the way he squirmed?" Kelbach added, relishing the brutal slaughter of Stephen Shea. "Wasn't that funny?"

This maniacal sense of humor was exercised again the following night when the pair robbed another gas station worker, a youth named Michael Holtz. He, too, was abducted and taken into the desert where he was sexually attacked by both Kelbach and Lance and then dumped unceremoniously after being stabbed to death by the same stiletto that had been used on Shea. Lance had done the killing this time, one stroke straight into the heart.

When police discovered the second body, a city alarm went out: all gas stations should close at nightfall and older men should be in charge of all stations. The killers, by the night of December 21, 1966, had decided to alter the selection of their victims. Kelbach and Lance hopped into a cab driven by thirty-year-old Grant Creed Strong. They told him to drive them to the Salt Lake City Airport. Strong looked them over and became suspicious. En route to the destination, the driver stopped at his cab headquarters. He informed a dispatcher that he was taking "two fellows out to the airport, but I don't like the looks of them. If I get in trouble, I'll click my microphone twice."

Only a few minutes later, Lance thrust a gun to the head of Grant Strong, demanding all his cash. The driver managed to click his microphone twice before handing over nine dollars. While police cars and some taxis were rushing to Strong's aid, Lance grinned crazily and fired. (He was later to gloat on an NBC network show: "I just pulled the trigger and blood flew everywhere. Oh boy! I never seen so much blood!")

By the time police arrived at the scene, Grant was dead at the wheel of his cab, slumped forward, half his head blown away. His killers were nowhere in sight. Kelbach and Lance had trotted up the road to Lolly's Tavern, which was located near the airport, strolling into the bar at 11:15 P.M., an hour after killing Grant.

Kelbach went to a pinball machine and began to play. Lance, with equal ease, walked up behind a customer sitting at the bar, forty-seven-year-old James Sizemore, and fired a shot into the back of his head, killing him, acting as if the murder was as casual a gesture as slapping a fly. He then told the startled bartender: "This is a stickup." Without a word the bartender handed over every cent in the cash register, a little more than three hundred dollars.

Kelbach and Lance then appeared to move toward the door. They paused, and then, with an air of indifference, they began shooting at the bartender and the four remaining customers sitting petrified at the bar. All five fell to the floor after the pair unleashed a terrific barrage. Two customers were mortally wounded—Mrs. Beverly Mace, thirty-four, and twenty-year-old Fred William Lillie. When the firing ceased, the killers stood their ground for some seconds, staring at the prone bodies, thinking they had wiped out all the witnesses; the bartender and two of the customers were only pretending to be hit.

As the pair walked from the bar, Kelbach remarked: "They owe me a nickel from that pinball machine."

Suddenly the bartender came to life, jumped up, grabbed a pistol from behind the bar and fired through the tavern window at the pair. Kelbach and Lance broke into a wild run. Only a few hours later, both men were captured by police, who stopped their station wagon at a roadblock and put shotguns to their heads. They surrendered meekly.

Quickly brought to trial and convicted, Kelbach and Lance were sentenced to be executed (either by hanging or firing squad, the condemned allowed to select his own end, a Utah distinction). Both men were saved when the Supreme Court abolished capital executions, being, as the five justices put it, "cruel and unusual punishment." (Justice William J. Brennan added that in his opinion such punishment did not "comport with human dignity," an attitude toward human life Kelbach and Lance never exhibited.)

Kelbach and Lance smirked and flaunted their six murders in the 1972 NBC production of "Thou Shalt Not Kill." To them, the killings were incidental antics designed to bring them amusement. Both laughed and joked about the brutal slayings before the cameras. "I haven't any feelings towards the victims," sniggered Lance. "I don't mind people getting hurt because I just like to watch it," grinned Kelbach. Both prisoners then entertained NBC viewers by creating a scenario in which they entered a crowded street armed with a machine gun, preferably a tank, shooting everyone in sight.

"You could see people scattering all over," rejoiced Kelbach. "Windows breaking, people just falling down, blood running all over. It could be exciting."

Kelbach and Lance still reside in the Utah State Penitentiary, where their prison life "comports with human dignity." They receive healthy food, watch their favorite TV fare, and generally enjoy the creature comforts allowed them. And they wait for parole.

The berserk mass killers of Salt Lake City, Walter Kelbach (left) and Myron Lance (center), under police escort.

1968 HOLLYWOOD, FLORIDA
The End of a Super Cop

To his fellow officers in the Hollywood, Florida, police department, husky, always-valiant Robert John Erler was known as "Super Cop." A one-time Green Beret who had served with distinction in Vietnam, Erler, thirty-four years old, possessed almost psychic powers in the capturing of criminals.

On several occasions, Erler, in company with a partner, spotted an auto and, even though the car was not listed on the force's "hot sheet," he *knew* it was stolen. "Pull that car over," Erler would say to his partner.

"How come?"

"That car's been stolen."

After ordering the car to the side of the road, the officers—no surprise to Erler—would learn that indeed the auto had been stolen. There were many instances like that. Erler's instincts caused him to pull over one car that had been used in an armed robbery. Another time a deserted house caught his attention. Single-handed, Erler entered and, after exchanging shots with intruders, captured three thieves. Uncanny, thought his marveling superiors and fellow cops. But such detection came naturally to Robert Erler. What was unnatural about Officer Erler was his uncontrollable compunction to murder.

Erler was one of five boys and two girls in a Phoenix, Arizona, family. His father was a rugged individualist, strict and uncompromising with his children. Erler was raised with the back of a hand. After serving in Vietnam, Erler became a karate and judo expert. He applied for a position on the Hollywood, Florida, police department, and, due to his distinguished service record, was hired.

A short while later, Super Cop married a seventeen-year-old go-go dancer. The couple produced one child, a boy. Mrs. Erler's compulsive buying produced almost insurmountable debts for the cop, causing him to take on extra jobs. They were finally divorced, his wife given custody of the child. Erler lived alone in a trailer home on the beach. When not on patrol instinctively apprehending felons, Erler sat in the beach home alone, brooding, the lapping waves whispering strange words into his ears.

Walking along the beach on August 12, 1968, Erler spied a woman and a young girl sleeping on the sand. He learned that the mother and daughter had traveled from Georgia. They were broke.

"Sleeping on the beach is not permitted," Erler told Mrs. Dorothy Clark and her twelve-year-old daughter, Merilyn. He looked Mrs. Clark over and then offered to let her and the child sleep in his trailer home. "My wife and my two-month-old son are there," he lied.

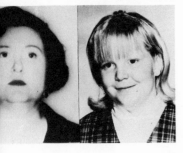

Teenager Marilyn Clark (right), an inexplicable murder victim of a Florida cop, and her mother (left), Dorothy Ammons Clark. (UPI)

Mrs. Clark and her daughter gratefully accepted the offer. Once inside Erler's mobile home they realized the policeman's family was not present. As they turned to go, Erler stood before them naked. "Your mother's going to take care of me," he told Merilyn Clark. Later, outside the trailer, Erler took the girl into a wooded area and shot her five times in the head with a .22-caliber pistol. Near the airport, Erler also shot Mrs. Clark five times in the head. By some sort of miracle the woman survived.

At 6:18 P.M. that night, for reasons that could only be answered by Robert John Erler, the super cop called police headquarters, telling Officer Harold Lenmore that he had killed Mrs. Clark and her daughter. He would not identify himself, only adding in a near-hysterical voice: "If you want to find those bodies, go to the airport—one by the road, one in the water . . . Hurry . . . Catch me, please—please catch me!" He hung up.

The next morning Robert Erler joined the hunt for the bodies as Super Cop, dressed in full uniform. He had no trouble in locating Merilyn Clark's body, calling in the discovery to headquarters. Mrs. Clark was found alive by other officers and taken to a hospital where she slowly recovered from her wounds. During her three-week convalescent period, Erler, ironically assigned to solve the shooting, appeared everywhere in the Hollywood, Florida, community, busily hunting a killer he knew to be himself.

Suddenly, Super Cop quit his post, telling superiors that his elderly mother was dying of cancer in Phoenix and he had to be with her. Erler departed for Phoenix where, some days later, he switched on a TV set to learn that he had been identified as the killer of Merilyn Clark. He turned himself in and, waiving extradition, was taken back to Florida to stand trial.

Mrs. Clark identified the super cop in court as her child's murderer, telling jurors that she "would never forget the mean expression in his eyes." Five officers of the Hollywood Police Department who had listened to the recorded phone call Erler had made to headquarters following the shootings identified the voice as their coworker, the super cop.

Though Erler staunchly maintained his innocence, his defense counsel could only plead with the jury, offering such lines as "This little boy, this boy who has been besieged by troubles is innocent."

Erler was found guilty and sentenced to ninety-nine years with six months at hard labor, meaning that he would not be eligible for parole for thirty-three years. Cops sent to prison are fair game for any inmate and Erler was no exception. He was beaten unmercifully during his four-year stay in the state prison. He was then transferred to a minimum security prison at Belle Glade, Florida, from which he promptly escaped by swimming a moat filled with man-eating alligators.

Erler stayed out of prison by working under assumed names as a laborer in Mississippi, Tennessee and Illinois. He was finally apprehended in the Jackson, Mississippi, post office when he arrived to collect a 3.57 Magnum he had ordered through the mails. He broke loose from the grasp of lawmen as they were escorting him to the street, jumped into his car and led pursuing officers in a wild chase out of town and into a swamp where he tried to escape on foot. He was brought down by shotgun blasts from deputy sheriffs.

The super cop had had enough of running. He was returned to prison where he now resides, embracing a religious life, patiently thumbing through his Bible.

Super cop Robert Erler, who begged fellow officers to arrest him.

1973–74 NEW YORK CITY
The House of Dead Women

In spite of its auspicious name and glorified facade, the Park Plaza Hotel at 50 West Seventy-seventh Street was nothing more than a rattrap with polished door handles. Scores of elderly women, surviving on the most meager of incomes, tolerated the cramped, stuffy rooms of the hotel. Beyond the inconvenience was a growing, gnawing fear in these women that not only were the dark, cavernous halls dangerous, but they were not safe within the walls of their own tiny apartments. Premature death was stalking them, they knew.

Inside the eleven-story gray stone hotel, several women were found dead in the early part of 1973. Police and medical examiners handled the deaths in stereotyped manner. Causes of death varied, according to police, from acute alcoholism to heart attack. On April 10, 1973, Theresa Jordan, thirty-nine, was found suffocated. Apparently, she had also been raped and her apartment looted.

Detectives were not astounded by this discovery, since they were well aware that the hotel was a nesting place for thieves, junkies, and apprentice maniacs. A routine investigation into the Jordan death was conducted. Nothing was uncovered.

With increasing and alarming regularity the police were called to the Park Plaza Hotel. On July 19, 1973, sixty-five-year-old Kate Lewisohn was found trussed up in her bed, strangled, her skull bashed in. She, too, had been raped. Her apartment was ransacked. Again detectives sifted grainy clues and came up empty-handed.

For several months the murders ceased at the Park Plaza. Then, on April 24, 1974, Mabel Hartmeyer, age sixty, was found dead in her room. Her death was at first diagnosed as "occlusive coronary arteriosclerosis." Had the medical examiners bothered to give the body a closer look, they would have learned that Miss Hartmeyer had been strangled and raped.

There was no doubt of murder four days later, when police found Yetta Vishnefsky with a butcher knife plunged to the hilt in her back. The seventy-nine-year-old retired sewing machine operator had been tied up with her own stockings and raped before being killed. Her clothes, scant jewelry, and TV set had been stolen.

The killer or killers were bent on having a hellish summer. Victims littered the Park Plaza rooms through the next three months: Winifred Miller, age forty-seven, pianist and singer, strangled and raped, June 8; Blanche Vincent, age seventy-one, a charwoman, suffocated and raped on June 19 (police examiners originally stated that she had perished of "chronic alcoholism"); Martha Carpenter, age sixty-nine, suffocated and raped on July 1; Eleanor Platt, a sixty-four-year-old sculptor, suffocated and raped on August 30 (her death was originally termed "suspicious" and no cause was listed by examiners).

In all instances, the slayer had taken radios and TVs, possessions amounting to no more than a few hundred dollars. The police had no suspects. They had to wait.

Then, for the first time the killer struck beyond the peeling walls of the Park Plaza. At 9:15 A.M. on September 12, 1974, Dorothy May, a maid, made a frantic call to police, telling officers that her employer, Mrs. Pauline Spanierman, age fifty-nine, was dead, her apartment torn to pieces. Thieves had made off with some valuables, including the widow's TV set.

Detectives entering the Spanierman apartment at 40 West Seventy-seventh Street were all too aware that this building adjoined the Park Plaza, now an infamous murder house. Squads of investigators streamed through the Plaza, grilling residents and visitors. They were told that a man had been seen crawling down the fire escape of Mrs. Spanierman's building at three o'clock that morning. He had been carrying a TV set. Systematically, officers began to knock on every door in the Park Plaza. One man opened his door to inquiring officers. As they entered they saw a TV set near the window. This set was identified as the one belonging to the slain Mrs. Spanierman.

"It's not mine," pleaded the man. "It belongs to Calvin Jackson. He brought it in here early this morning. He's been staying here."

Calvin Jackson was not difficult to locate. He was a twenty-six-year-old porter employed at the Park Plaza Hotel. In custody by that night, Jackson had a long history of drug addiction and assault and robbery, and had once served time in the Elmira Reformatory. He told police that he had been drifting from one cheap hotel to another for five years. Born in Buffalo, New York, Jackson's record revealed that he had last been arrested in November 1973 on charges of felonious robbery and burglary. At that time Jackson had pleaded guilty in plea bargain-

301

ing, his crime then reduced to a misdemeanor; instead of being sent to prison for fifteen years, Calvin Jackson was given a thirty-day jail sentence. He was set free to continue a mass murder-rape spree that would establish an all-time record for the great city of New York. (This arrest and puny punishment undoubtedly caused the hiatus in the series of murders at the Park Plaza.)

Even street-calloused police officers were stunned by the mass slayings. Thomas Makon, the detective-sergeant in charge of the multiple murder investigation, remarked: "I don't know anything that compares with this except for Jack the Ripper." Other officers had more to say. According to the *New York Times*, an unidentified police detective was incensed that even though known murders had taken place at the Park Plaza, "no immediate police action was taken on any of them." The unknown officer, in fuzzy textbook terminology, blamed it all on "depersonalization" of detective squads, plain "lack of interest" on the part of investigating officers, and "objectivization of the areas covered."

Early in the evening of his first night in custody, Calvin Jackson, in a whimpering voice, admitted murdering Mrs. Spanierman. Then he added eight other hapless ladies from the Plaza to his murder list, all of those known to have been killed, plus some, in the Park Plaza. "You had to lean forward to hear him speak," Makon told reporters when he was listening to Jackson's death roll.

The killer went to trial, judged mentally fit, a decision that enraged the defense. Jackson's own testimony struck horror into the jury. In one instance he related the murder of one of the women in a monotone: "I told her I wasn't going to kill her. Then I strangled her with my hands. I made sure she was dead by forcing her face down into a pillow. Then I sat in the room for an hour, watching to make certain she was dead. I sat there and I looked at her all the time."

Asked why, other than to have the TV sets for sale or for his own use, Jackson had robbed, raped and killed his victims, he lamely shrugged and replied in a small voice: "Well, I guess I kind of broke wild there, you know?"

Donald Tucker and Robert Blossner kept hammering away at the insanity question, a last-ditch measure to save their client. Said an impassioned Tucker before the jury: "If Calvin Jackson is not legally insane, who is legally insane? He raped women, some in their seventies and eighties. He raped some of them after death. Is this a legally sane man?

"He went to the refrigerator in nearly every apartment. He prepared a meal and ate it as he watched the body. Sometimes he stayed for an hour. Is this a legally sane man?"

There was no doubt of Jackson's sanity, according to the jury; he was convicted of killing nine women. State Supreme Court Justice Aloysius J. Melia, who had presided over the six-week trial, gave Jackson everything in the book—two life terms for each killing, a total of eighteen life sentences, making Jackson's parole impossible before he had served thirty years in the twenty-first century.

1977 NEW ROCHELLE, NEW YORK

"I'm Sorry for Your Trouble"

At thirty-three years of age Frederick W. Cowan was a man living inside a dangerous past, an unsavory one, thought most who knew the burly weightlifter. Cowan lived with his parents, William and Dorothy Cowan, and two brothers, at 40 Woodbury Avenue in New Rochelle, New York. His normally quiet demeanor was sometimes disrupted by a surly, snapping voice when his passions erupted. Fred Cowan, it would soon be learned, loved but three things: lifting weights above his beefy 250-pound, five-foot-ten-inch frame, lethal guns of all sorts, and Nazi culture—in particular, Adolf Hitler.

Cowan, who worked as a mover at the Neptune Worldwide Moving Company of New Rochelle, was not shy about disclosing his warped love for Nazi ideology. He would swagger down his hometown streets, his great girth occupying most of the sidewalk. A few seconds after passing someone, Cowan would shout "Heil Hitler!" and give the Nazi salute. Most only shook their head at such antics, and snorted under-the-breath murmurs of "Oddball" and "Weirdo."

To those special few whom Cowan befriended he would proudly show his collection of weights, weapons and Nazi memorabilia. His room at home was adorned with large posters of Hitler and Heinrich Himmler, who had once headed the

303

dreaded SS, and with the infamous red flag with a black swastika inside a white circle. His bookshelves sagged beneath the weight of books and periodicals dedicated to Nazi ideals, much of it current propaganda from the National States' Rights Party, an ultra-right-wing group espousing hatred for minorities, especially blacks and Jews.

For close friends, the weightlifter would throw open a large closet, and gloat with the air of a peacock at his weapons display: "What do you think of that, huh?" Before him on racks and wall hooks were scores of handguns, rifles, muskets, bayonets, machetes, and black gloves with loaded knuckles. In the collection the older weaponry dated back to World War II, artifacts—some still coated with ancient caked blood—that made Cowan beam with joy.

One visitor picked up one of Cowan's books on Hitler. The weightlifter had written on the flyleaf: "Nothing is lower than blacks and Jews except the police who protect them."

Such sentiments were not confined to Cowan's dreary room. He made his racial hatred known both on the job and in his neighborhood. Cowan would attack with venom anyone he thought played an "inferior role." Miscegenation rankled him to rage. For pretty Theresa Schmidt, a neighbor who lived only two houses from him and was widely known to be dating a Negro, Cowan showed nothing but bitter contempt.

On the afternoon of August 2, 1975, the twenty-six-year-old blond woman walked around Cowan, who stood flexing his massive muscles on the sidewalk (one forearm bore a large tattoo of the German Iron Cross). The weightlifter sneered at Miss Schmidt and growled to a youngster nearby: "There goes that little nigger lover!"

Theresa Schmidt froze in shock, then turned and asked: "*What* did you say?"

Cowan walked swiftly to his car, unlocking the trunk, yelling at the woman: "Get out of here before I blow your brains out!" With that he produced a rifle from the trunk of his car and aimed it at Miss Schmidt, who took to her high heels, clattering down the street to a delicatessen where she immediately phoned the police for help, telling a dispatcher that her life had been threatened.

Officer Robert Curasi responded to the call. Putting her in the squad car, the officer drove down Woodbury Street. Miss Schmidt, trembling from her traumatic experience, managed to point to a red 1971 Pontiac as that owned by the man who had threatened her. She next picked out three houses, saying he lived in one of them. Curasi did not get out of the squad car to check the Pontiac, according to Miss Schmidt's later story. The woman remarked: "He acted as if this was something very minor. He seemed to have the feeling, since the guy was no longer on the street, that I exaggerated what happened."

She remembered Curasi's turning to her and asking: "Do you go with a black guy?"

"Yes."

"Well, yeah, okay." ("He acted as if everything was now clear, it was understandable.")

That was the end of the one and only police investigation into the turbulent background of Fred Cowan while he was alive. It was not, however, the last of Cowan's threats to Miss Schmidt. Some months later she passed his house. As the weightlifter was talking to a neighbor he held a rifle. When he spotted the handsome blond, he pointed the weapon at her. She was terrified when he pulled back the trigger. Nothing happened. The rifle was not loaded. Because of police indifference to her first complaint against Cowan, Miss Schmidt merely ran from the scene, never bothering to call officers.

The seething cauldrons of racial hatred inside Fred Cowan began to bubble over the brim in late January 1977. He was rude to a customer he thought was Jewish, refusing to move a refrigerator. His superior, Norman Bing, thirty-one, traffic manager for Neptune, suspended Cowan for two weeks. (Cowan had never reacted well to authority; while serving in the Army in Germany he had been convicted of being AWOL in a special court martial. His answer was to promptly go AWOL again, resulting in another conviction.)

Norman Bing knew Cowan hated him. Bing was a Jew. "Cowan didn't like blacks and Jews," Bing nervously remembered weeks later. "It never bothered me. A lot of people are like that. The guys figured he was a lot of talk. He had no history of violence. Everybody said he was a pussycat."

Fred Cowan, to the remorse of sorrowing relatives and the regret of the New Rochelle Police Department, proved anything but a pussycat; rather, he became a berserk rogue lion with teeth and talons ripping at flesh on the morning of February 14, 1977, ironically the anniversary of the St. Valentine's Day Massacre.

His arms adorned with Nazi emblems, wrestler and weight-lifter Fred Cowan is shown outside his New Rochelle, New York, home only weeks before he committed mass murder.

Driving his car into the parking lot of the Neptune Moving Company on Weyman Avenue, Cowan almost casually opened the trunk of his car and in full view of several employees going to work began to gird himself for battle. It was 7:45 A.M., with only a few workers in the area; had he arrived fifteen minutes later, more than three hundred employees would have been present. The burly man said nothing as he slipped bandoliers of ammunition over his military field jacket and around the waist of his battle green pants. He tucked four pistols, one a .45-caliber automatic, into his waistband. (He had no police permits for these pistols.) Snapping two hand grenades to his jacket pockets (these later proved to be only shells), Cowan reached into the trunk of his car and brought forth a German-made, semi-automatic .308-caliber assault rifle with a telescopic sight. He slammed the trunk lid shut and marched stoically into the first-floor offices of the Neptune building, his presumed target being Normal Bing. ("He was going to 'get even' with his Jewish boss," theorized one account later, "the Jew who canned him.")

Approaching the counter at the front entrance, Cowan gazed at the row of glass-partitioned offices fifty feet beyond, obviously searching for Bing. Not seeing his prey, he settled for anyone with a black face, shooting James Green and Joseph Hicks with the assault rifle as they were passing the offices, sending them crashing dead through the shattering glass. Clynt Wynent looked up in wonder from a time clock he was punching. "He got them point blank," he was to recall. "They weren't moving. They looked dead."

Cowan was distracted for a moment—which allowed Bing to dive beneath a desk for safety in one of the offices—when an employee, Ronald Cowell, almost bumped into the killer. "I had one foot out of the door and I was staring at the muzzle of the rifle he was carrying," remembered Cowell. "I started saying 'Please,' and he said, 'Go home and tell my mother not to come down to Neptune.' I didn't look back. I just kept on running."

Swinging into the company cafeteria, Cowan spied Pariyaral Varghese. He opened fire on Varghese, his hailstorm of bullets driving the man into a wall, killing him. By this time Cowan was bleeding from a severe cut on the hand. In his desperate search for Bing he had slashed his hand on the broken glass jaggedly protruding from the glass door of the cafeteria, which he had smashed in a wild burst of frustration. The killer paused a few seconds to wrap a patterned red handkerchief around the hand. With a shrug, Cowan lumbered into the main hallway, heading for the stairs to the second floor. He met Fred Holmes, another black man, on the stairs. Holmes gaped at the gun-festooned Cowan for a few seconds. Without a word Cowan brought his rifle to his shoulder and fired, sending several bullets into Holmes. Leaving his fourth dead man on the stairs, Cowan ponderously climbed the steps.

Bing, realizing Cowan had left the office area, peeped from his shelter beneath the desk. Close to him lay Joseph Russo, shot in the abdomen, moaning in pain. He had been wounded in the barrage that felled Hicks and Green. Bing and others crawled to desk phones and called police. They kept calling every few minutes.

The first to respond was Officer Allen B. McLeod of the New Rochelle Police Department. The thirty-two-year-old cop, one of the most dedicated on the force and a father of two, stepped from his squad car, which pulled up next to Cowan's auto in the parking lot, at 8:15 A.M.

McLeod had barely enough time to peer toward the second floor of the Neptune building and draw his gun. A shot cracked and he fell dead to the pavement. His partner, Raymond Satiro, bravely jumped from the squad car and began to move toward McLeod. Another shot from the second-story window crashed into his leg and sent him sprawling. He tried to crawl to his dead partner but it was impossible.

A police armored personnel carrier turns into the Neptune parking area during the siege.

Bing and others anxiously watched from windows, their heads barely edging over the sills, sickened at the sight of the officers lying in the lot beyond. Suddenly James Parks, a former policeman and company driver, could be seen running across the parking lot. He picked up the service revolver dropped by the slain McLeod, positioning himself at the bottom of a stairway, waiting for the mass killer should he try to flee in that direction.

But Frederick W. Cowan had no thought of escape. This would be his last pathetic stand for his anachronistic beliefs. By ten that morning the Neptune building was in a virtual state of siege. Scores of officers equipped with high-power rifles were perched on rooftops surrounding the building. Four state police helicopters circled above the plant. Since no one could get near the body of the slain McLeod, the New York City Police Department dispatched a tank-like armored personnel carrier to the scene. This crossed the lot without coming under fire from Cowan, officers crouched and moving behind it. McLeod's body was taken away.

In spite of the powerful array of weapons brought to face him, Cowan would not surrender, periodically shouting from his second-story office bastion: "I got plenty of grenades and other guns to last me all day!"

At the mention of grenades, the armored personnel carrier withdrew. Authorities were unsure of Cowan's plan of action or whether he was holding hostages. He did not respond to any messages police barked through bullhorns. Officers in a forward command post finally managed to contact the killer at noon by simply making a phone call to the office where he was huddled.

"What is it you want?" asked one officer.

"I want some food," Cowan said in a dull voice. "Get me some food."

"Anything else?"

The killer paused. "Yes . . . I'm sorry for your trouble. Tell the mayor [New Rochelle Mayor Vincent Rippa] that I'm sorry to be causing the city so much trouble." After equating his carnage with something like a parking violation, Cowan hung up.

The killer's mother was asked to come to the scene to plead with her son to give up. The woman, in tears, her voice breaking as she spoke through a loudspeaker, begged Cowan to surrender. Only silence met her pleas. Dorothy Cowan turned

Building of carnage, the Neptune plant where Cowan made his last gory stand.

away, saying to a friend: "Pray for Freddie. He's gone crazy."

For almost three hours no guns were fired. Cowan and the police played the waiting game. The once-bustling area was silent as a stone. Then, at 2:40 P.M., the quiet was pierced by the sound of a single explosion. Police could not be sure whether the lone shot ringing out was Cowan's killing another employee or his committing suicide.

Three police officers systematically crawled through the offices one by one, clearing out employees and working toward the second floor. Minutes later they found Freddie Cowan, his massive bulk sprawled in the second-floor office, adorned in the battle gear of a long-ago war. The killer of five had sent a .45-caliber bullet into his head.

As stunned officers looked down at him, one leaned close to read the inscription on the belt buckle he was wearing, a relic of Cowan's much-cherished Nazi past. Incredulous, the officer slowly read the inscription aloud: "I will give up my gun when they pry my cold dead fingers from around it."

Cowan's amazing arsenal and Nazi memorabilia found in his home following his slaughter of fellow plant employees.
(UPI)

A Chronology
of Murder in America

The following is a chronology, beginning with the American Revolution, which includes the most infamous and distinctive homicides in the United States. Chapter pages follow those cases treated extensively in the general narrative. (Note: Not included are murders committed for the most part by professional criminals, early-day gangsters, and present-day members of organized crime, whose victims in our country's turbulent history easily surpass ten thousand.)

1773

"Never quite right in his head," according to an early report, Samuel Brand, a farmer, living near Lancaster, Pennsylvania, sets fire to his home with his parents asleep, entering the building to shoot his brother dead. Brand is quickly convicted and hanged on December 18 for the triple murders.

1778

Thomas Goss, who laments to one and all about his unhappy home life in Litchfield County, Connecticut, murders his wife in her sleep; he promptly confesses when neighbors accuse him of the killing (Goss was a strong suspect in a murder twenty years earlier in East Hartford). He is hanged. . . . In Worchester, Massachusetts, Bathsheba Spooner enlists the aid of her lover and three deserting British soldiers to arrange for her elderly husband's murder to gain his considerable riches and to satisfy her Tory sentiments. (page 17)

1783

William Beadle of Weathersfield, Connecticut, who is in the habit of taking a sharp axe and knife to bed with him each night, wakes early on the morning of December 11, 1783, and beheads his wife, Lydia, and his four children before slitting his own throat.

1784

After undergoing a "religious experience," George Williams of Philadelphia suddenly confesses to a murder he had committed seventeen years earlier and for which an innocent man was executed; he is summarily hanged. . . . To gain riches for his new bride, seaman Alexander White kills the captain of his ship but is arrested when the cutter docks in Cow Harbor, Long Island, New York. He is hanged on November 18, 1784.

1785

Impoverished Elizabeth Wilson of East Bradford, Pennsylvania, murders her twin infants, only ten weeks old. Her brother obtains a reprieve from the governor on the date of his sister's execution and rides furiously to Chester, Pennsylvania; slowed by the muddy roads, he arrives twenty-three minutes after Elizabeth Wilson has been hanged on January 3, 1786. (The story, along with the fact that the brother, in his sorrow, became a total recluse, becomes part of Pennsylvania folklore.)

1786

Hannah Ocuish, a Paquot Indian girl who is judged a halfwit, beats to death six-year-old Eunice Bolles in New London, Connecticut, in late 1786 for stealing her strawberries. With no defense counsel, the girl is sentenced to die, and is hanged on December 20, 1786.

To prevent her child from being raised in slavery, Negro Alice Clifton of Philadelphia cuts the throat of her newborn baby. She is reprieved from hanging by authorities and confined in jail for life. . . . John Campbell, John Kease, and Patrick Kinnon burglarize a house in Evesham, New Jersey, stabbing an elderly woman to death. The three are hanged in Burlington, New Jersey, on September 18, 1787.

1789

Five convicts escape from the Walnut Street Jail in Philadelphia in September, killing a man in the process. All five—Burns, Bennett, Logan, Ferguson, and Cronan—are hanged. As a result of this outbreak, Philadelphia authorities abandon the use of convict labor in the streets.

1791

Whiting Sweeting, a hunter in Stephentown, New York, is cornered in a wood by a posse attempting to serve him with a warrant for trespassing. Sweeting, in his attempt to flee, slashes posse member Darius Quimby, who shortly dies of his wounds. After a quick trial, Sweeting, much to the consternation of the local press—who feel his death sentence too severe—is hanged on August 26, 1791.

1792

One-time Tory soldier in the Revolution John Ryer gets drunk in a White Plains, New York, tavern and kills Dr. Isaac Smith, a deputy sheriff attempting to arrest him. Ryer escapes. Governor Clinton posts a reward for him on May 27, 1792. He is apprehended. At his trial, a penitent Ryer proclaims to the court that he is guilty of "excess drinking, card-playing, cock-fighting, cursing, swearing, together with almost every kind of vice, wickedness and debauchery." He is hanged at White Plains on October 2, 1793.

1793

Samuel Frost, who had been acquitted of murdering his father by driving a spike into his head ten years earlier, takes a hoe to Captain Elisha Allen, with whom he has been living in Princeton, Massachusetts. Though authorities admit that Frost's "mind was evidently not formed altogether like those of other persons," he is hanged for the murder on October 31, 1793, at Worcester.

1794

Pirates John Baptist Collins, Augustus Palacha, and Emanuel Furtado rob and murder Enoch Wood, a passenger on board the brigantine *Betsey* while sailing for Boston. The three are quickly caught and hanged on July 30, 1794. . . . Negro Edmund Fortis rapes and kills Pamela Tilton of Vassalborough, Maine. He is executed at Dresden, September 25, 1794. On the gallows Fortis weeps, telling a great throng: "All my life I have been taking things not my own and lying with women."

1795

Pomp, a slave on the farm of Captain Charles Furbush in Andover, Massachusetts, is caught by his master after running away. Furbush strips Pomp naked and flogs him, then ties him to a barn rafter and leaves him to dangle overnight. Waiting until the night of February 11, 1795, Pomp takes revenge by crushing Furbush's head with an axe while the Captain sleeps. Pomp confesses his murder only minutes before being hanged at Ipswich on August 6, 1795.

1796

Abraham Johnstone quarrels with a fellow slave, Thomas Read, and stabs him to death; he is hanged at Woodbury, New Jersey on July 8, 1796. . . . Drunkard Matthias Gotleib, according to one report, enters his home, "intoxicated; his wife being displeased to see him in that situation began to find fault with his conduct." Gotleib's response is to sharpen a butcher knife during his wife's harangue, which he then uses to kill her. He is hanged on October 28, 1796, at Newton, New Jersey.

1797

Benjamin Bailey encounters Jost Follhaber near Machonoy Mountain in Pennsylvania, telling the peddler that he is a hunter. At their camp in the woods on the night of August 11, 1797, Bailey takes Follhaber's wares but is caught in the act; he decides to kill the peddler to prevent identification, shooting him and then splitting his head with a tomahawk. Bailey is apprehended when he attempts to sell off Follhaber's goods. In a nonstop twenty-hour trial, Bailey is convicted; he is hanged in Reading, Pennsylvania, on January 6, 1798. . . . John Hauer of Heidelburg, Pennsylvania, arranges the murder of his entire family to obtain the riches of his dead father-in-law. He is apprehended and convicted. Despite a fervent pretense at being insane, Hauer is hanged on July 14, 1798. (page 27)

1799

In the Ohio wilderness a large posse traps William "Big" Harpe and his brother Wiley "Little" Harpe, who have murdered and robbed dozens of trappers and settlers. Big Harpe is killed, his head sawed off and kept by possemen as a souvenir; Little Harpe escapes the shootout and utterly vanishes.

1800

From early 1800 to 1802, Sam Mason terrorizes travelers along the Natchez Trace, robbing scores and murdering a half dozen men; he is finally tracked down by a professional bounty hunter, Bill Setten, who returns Mason's head in a jar to Natchez. Setten himself is mistakenly identified as Wiley Harpe, the much-wanted killer, and is hanged. . . . A Haitian slave named Gabriel secretly musters a thousand-man army of blacks outside Richmond, intent on capturing the city in a slave revolt and killing most of the white population, but the blacks are halted in their march toward Richmond by a fierce storm; alerted to the plot, white militia disband the invaders two days later. Gabriel, who is found guilty of slitting several throats in his takeover plot, is hanged before the entire Negro population of Richmond some days later.

1801

Another slave, thirty-five-year-old Cyrus Emlay of Chesterfield, New Jersey, axes to death his master, Humphrey Wall, then burns his house to veil the murder. Emlay is quickly caught and hanged on June 12, 1801. According to one account of the day, Emlay "was most agreeable to his execution." . . . Mrs. Josiah Deo, head of a large household in Paltz, New York, decides on the morning of September 6, 1801, that the world is too much for her. After sending several of her offspring on errands, she locks the doors of her home and slits the throats of her three youngest children, following these atrocities with

315

suicide. . . . Jason Fairbanks, disgruntled over his lover's reluctance to marry, slits the throat of Elizabeth Fales, the most beautiful girl in Dedham, Massachusetts. (page 30)

1802

Farmhand Ebenezer Mason, in a raging fit, turns on his employer, William Pitt Allen, crushing his head with a shovel on May 18, 1802. He is hanged on October 7, 1802, explaining his murder to the executioner with "I didn't like him ordering me about."

1803

Cato, a slave on a large farm near Charlestown, New York, rapes and murders May Akins. He is hanged at Johnstown, New York, on April 22, 1803 after confessing on the scaffold and detailing "his corrupt life." . . . Caleb Adams of Windham, Connecticut, slits the throat of five-year-old Oliver Woodworth because the boy "annoyed" him; he is hanged November 29, 1803. . . . Peter Stout feels insulted by fourteen-year-old Thomas Williams on a Dover, New Jersey, street and takes an axe to Williams' head, killing him; he is executed on May 13, 1803.

1804

Richard Dennis, angered over insults hurled at his father in a business meeting by James Shaw, hides on a Charleston, South Carolina, street to appease his honor as a Southern gentleman, shooting Shaw dead when he emerges from a building on August 20, 1804; Dennis is hanged. . . . Mrs. Elizabeth Cannon of Goosecreek, South Carolina, has been having an affair with Joshua Nettles, which is resolved on the night of October 24, 1804, when Nettles murders her husband, John; then, somehow thinking to conceal the crime, he places the body of the slain husband in bed with Mrs. Cannon, who later tells neighbors that her spouse succumbed in illness. The lovers are found out. Nettles is executed; Mrs. Cannon, in a gesture typical of Southern justice, is set free.

1805

Samuel Freeman, a resident of Ashford, Connecticut, suddenly tires of his Indian mistress, Hannah Simons, and beats her to death. Freeman is found guilty and executed on November 6, 1805. . . . Schoolteacher Stephen Arnold of Cooperstown, New York, flies into a rage at his six-year-old niece, Betsy Van Amburgh, over her inability to spell a word and kills her. He is convicted but reprieved at the last moment while standing on the gallows with the rope about his neck; he is later pardoned on grounds of insanity. . . . A sailor, Francisco Dos Santos, on shore leave from a ship docked in New York Harbor, makes lascivious advances to the attractive daughter of wealthy Archibald Graham and is knocked senseless by Graham, who wields a heavy cane on Dos Santos' head; in retaliation, the sailor attacks Graham from an alleyway concealment a few days later with a knife, stabbing him to death. Identified, Dos Santos is quickly convicted and executed.

1806

Josiah Burnham, sharing a debtor's cell in the jail at Haverhill, New Hampshire, is insulted by two fellow prisoners, Joseph Starkweather and Russell Freeman. While the others sleep, Burnham fashions a blade from a scythe accidentally left in his cell and slashes Starkweather and Freeman to death. Despite the eloquent defense mounted for Burnham by a young Daniel Webster, the killer is sent to the gallows. . . . An exasperated farmer, Abel Clemmons of Clarksburg, West Virginia (then Virginia), goes berserk, slaughtering his wife and eight children, for which he is hanged on June 30, 1806. . . . In an attempt to press American sailors into British service aboard English vessels, Captain Henry Whitby orders a cannon shot fired from his ship into the entrance of New York Harbor; the shot kills an American seaman named Pierce. Whitby is seized, convicted and hanged. . . . John Banks of New York City, filled with wrath over his drunken wife's failure to make dinner upon his return from work, hits her with a coal shovel and then slits her throat; he is hanged on July 11, 1806. . . . James Purrington of Maine, brooding over his Bible on the night of July 8, 1806, suddenly slays his wife and seven children, then commits suicide.

1807

New York farmer Alpheus Hitchcock doses his wife's gruel with arsenic at their evening meal, which promptly kills Belinda Hitchcock. He later reveals the murder accidentally and is tried, sobbing before the court that "I thought I could live more agreeably with some other woman than my wife." He is executed in August 1807. . . . David Sanford, a blacksmith in Woodbridge, Connecticut, gets into a violent argument with a customer, Samuel Lee, which results in Sanford's stabbing Lee to death with a pitchfork. The blacksmith is found guilty of manslaughter; he is given thirty lashes and the letter *M* (for *murderer*) is branded on his left hand.

1808

In February Edward Donnelly beats his wife Catherine to death and then attempts to burn her remains in the family fireplace; her teeth are found and Donnelly is subsequently hanged, February 8, 1808. . . . John Joyce, alias Davis, and Peter Matthias, alias Mathews, rob Philadelphia shopkeeper Mrs. Sarah Cross, strangling her to death with her own clothesline. At their trial, the two blacks are defended by Nicholas Biddle and future U.S. Attorney General Richard Rush, but are found guilty and hanged on March 14, 1808. . . . Four convicts —Caleb and Daniel Dougherty, William Morris and William Robinson—escape from the Baltimore jail, killing George Worker in the process. All are apprehended. Morris escapes once more but is recaptured. The four are hanged at Baltimore's new jail on March 14, 1808. . . . Smuggler Cyrus B. Dean, attempting to bring potash into Canada, kills Asa Marsh and Jonathan Ormsby, two revenue agents trying to capture him and others. Dean is later caught and hanged on August 23, 1808, in Burlington, Vermont.

1810

John Frederick Sinclair, a boarder in the New York City home of David Hill, arrives at the house on the night of April 8, 1810, dead drunk. Hill orders him from the house. Sinclair, an unusually spry seventy-seven-year-old, turns on him with a knife and slashes him to pieces. Sinclair is hanged. . . . James Johnson, during a dance given in his New York home, argues loudly with fellow black, Lewis Robinson, before withdrawing a long knife and plunging it into Robinson's chest. He is hanged at the same time Sinclair goes to the gallows. . . . William Clutter, who works as a navigator on board the trading boat of John Farmer, takes an axe to his employer as they glide past Cincinnati in the dark. Clutter is found some days later claiming to be Farmer, and selling Farmer's goods from the boat. He is hanged on June 8, 1810.

1811

Captain Edward Tinker of Newbern, North Carolina, scuttles his ship in an insurance fraud scheme. When a sailor named Edward, one of his crew, refuses to support his story, Tinker takes him hunting and shoots him in the back. The sailor's body is discovered and Tinker is arrested. Other crew members testify against the captain, sealing his fate. Tinker is executed in September 1811. . . . Winslow Russell of Troy, New York, explodes in anger over an order given to him by fellow worker Michael Bockus and, taking an axe, splits Bockus' head. Russell is hanged after delivering to a gallows throng a lengthy speech about distemper. . . . George Hart of New York City returns home drunk and accuses his mistress, Mary Van Housen, of rifling his pockets. When she voices her denial, Hart grabs a club and beats her to death. He is hanged in Manhattan on January 3, 1812.

1812

Nicholas John Crevay, an Indian, moves with his wife to Stoneham, Massachusetts, during the War of 1812 but he is held in low regard by neighbors upset with his constant drinking, cursing and generally repugnant behavior. Four townsmen, having decided to rid themselves of the pesky Crevay, steal up to his rural house at night and shoot both man and wife, Crevay dies of his wounds. Alpheus Livermore and Samuel Angier are sentenced to die but receive commutations of life imprisonment. . . . Mary Cole of Newton, New Jersey, can no longer endure the wrath of Agnes Teaurs, her mother, over her not getting married. She slits her mother's throat and attempts to hide the body beneath the floorboards of her home. The decomposing body arouses visiting neighbors and Mary is arrested. She is hanged on June 28, 1812.

1813

Thomas Burns, angered over not receiving his army pay, gets drunk in an Albany, New York, grogshop and then proceeds to the city armory, where he arms himself. Emerging with shrieking threats against his superior officers, Burns is jumped by other soldiers. Before being subdued, Burns picks a random pedestrian, one John E. Conkling, and shoots him dead. He is hanged June 4, 1813. . . . Alexander M'Gillavrae and Hugh Cameron, two happy travelers passing through the backroads of Connecticut near Delhi, are joined by James Graham; they offer him liquor. The trio begin to argue over the price of horses. The bodies of M'Gillavrae and Cameron are found, their heads crushed, the next day on the road. Witnesses identify Graham as their traveling companion. He is convicted in a two-day trial and condemned.

1814

George Travers, a giddy sort for a Marine, hurls snowballs at guards in the U.S. Navy Yard in Charlestown, Massachusetts, on November 27, 1814. When other Marines accuse him of putting stones in the snowballs, Travers begins hitting them. As he is being dragged to the guardhouse, Travers lunges for a rifle, getting off one shot, which incredibly passes through the bodies of two guards, Thomas Hasey and James McKim, killing both. Travers is found guilty and given a long prison sentence.

1815

Barent Becker of Mayfield, New York, grows tired of his wife, Anne, and poisons her food with arsenic. The farmer is so overcome with guilt that he confesses his deed and is hanged October 6, 1815.

1816

Miner Babcock, a racist living in New London, Connecticut, kills a free Negro named London in full sight of several witnesses; he is hanged on June 6, 1816. . . . John Burwick of Philadelphia often tells friends that he intends to slaughter his family but is thought to be slightly mad, harmless. An outbreak brings neighbors, but before they can interrupt, Burwick manages to stab his wife to death and then slit his own throat, thereby, according to a report of that period, "hurrying his never-dying soul to the bar of God." . . . Lieutenant Richard Smith, stationed with an army detachment in Philadelphia, encounters Mrs. Ann Carson, a ravishing beauty whose husband, Captain John Carson, deserted her several years earlier. They wed but Carson returns, attempts to retrieve his former wife, and in the process is shot dead by Smith; Smith is condemned to death after a brief trial and almost at the insistence of presiding Judge Rush. Desperate, Ann Carson Smith attempts to kidnap Pennsylvania Governor Simon Snyder, thinking to hold him as ransom for the jailed Richard Smith; the plot fails when Smith is hanged. Ann Smith then joins a counterfeit gang and is subsequently arrested; she dies in prison in 1838.

1817

Samuel Green, brigand and one of the United States' first mass-murderers, begins his gruesome career in New England. (page 34) . . . A fight in a Boston groggery results in the death of Gaspard Denegri, whose skull is crushed with a loggerhead. Henry Phillips is accused of delivering the blow; he is convicted of murder, rather than simple manslaughter, and is hanged March 13, 1817. . . . To gain forty dollars belonging to Hugh Fitzpatrick, who has put him up for the night in his Bloomfield, Pennsylvania, log cabin, George Speth Vanhollen splits his host's head with an axe and is later condemned. Vanhollen is brought hard to death, throwing the executioner from the scaffold only seconds before he is hanged on July 26, 1817, at Meadville . . . Another night killer, James Lane takes a club to the sleeping William Dowell in his Gallipolis, Ohio, home while the victim sleeps. He is executed for the murder, but not before Lane devilishly describes how the murder instrument was fitted "with a knot on the end, just fit for my purpose." . . . Abraham Casler, a Schoharie, New York, farmer, feels himself a victim of an unwanted marriage—he had been forced to marry his wife, Catherine, five years earlier—as well as being subjected to his wife's wild fits of frothing rage. Casler slips a mixture of opium and arsenic into his wife's food while the couple stop at an inn in Middleburgh, New York; the innkeeper finds the poisoned food and Casler is exposed. He is hanged at Schoharie on May 29, 1818.

1818

Samuel E. Godfrey, a prisoner at the Vermont State Prison, suddenly goes berserk while walking in the exercise yard and grabs Thomas Hewlet, the warden, who is about to enter a prison building. In full view of the inmate population, Godfrey strangles Hewlet to death before guards can come to the rescue. The killer, who laughs uproariously at the ten thousand–plus spectators who come to see him hang, is executed at Woodstock Green, February 13, 1818. . . . John H. Craig, a scholarly type from an upper-crust family in Chester, Pennsylvania, becomes enraged at Edward Hunter who, he feels, advised his father-in-law to cut him out of his will. Craig settles matters by waiting in ambush with a long rifle and shooting Hunter as he passes a lonely place in a buggy outside of Chester. Following his conviction for murder, Craig begs that he be allowed to walk to the scaffold, which is about a mile from Chester (perhaps originating the term "walking the last mile."). The thirty-one-year-old Craig is hanged on a beautiful Saturday morning, June 6, 1818. . . . In his cups, trooper James Hamilton, stationed at the cantonment near Albany, New York, reels through the camp, cursing one and all in his usual display of ungovernable temper. Spotting a Negro who tells Hamilton he intends to join the army, Hamilton explodes, kicking the black man's backside and driving him from the camp. Major Benjamin Birdsall witnesses this disgraceful conduct and tongue-lashes Hamilton before the entire troop. Minutes later Hamilton, obtaining a rifle from his tent, enters Major Birdsall's quarters and blows away his head. Hamilton drops through the trap on November 6, 1818.

1819

Martin and Michael Toohey, soldiers in an all-Irish regiment, get drunk and then grab the first passerby on a Charleston, South Carolina, street, one James W. Gadsden, using him for bayonet practice and leaving him dead in the gutter. Witnesses quickly identify the killers. Michael is convicted of manslaughter, Martin of murder, the latter escaping jail with a posse hot on his heels; he is shot dead in a hiding place in a tree by a militiaman. . . . James Munks, nurturing a secret hate for Reuben Guild of Bellefonte, Pennsylvania, passes Guild on the Howard Township Road, and then impulsively turns, whips out a pistol and shoots the man dead. Munks is hanged in tears on January 23, 1819. . . . Sheriff William Huddleston visits John Van Alstine at his Sharon, New York, home to collect an overdue debt, calling the farmer to his face "a poor risk." Van Alstine responds by grabbing an oak club and bashing out the sheriff's brains; he buries the body in one of his ploughed fields and flees to Canada, where he is recognized from a wanted circular and seized. The killer is hanged at Schoharie, New York, March 19, 1819. . . . When skinflint Richard Jennings will not agree to sell him some land near Sugar Loaf, New York, James Teed hires Jack Hodges to shoot the crusty old man; the hired assassin only wounds Jennings but Teed's partner, Dunning, finishes off Jennings by beating him to death. Teed and Dunning are informed upon, probably by Hodges, and are hanged after a speedy trial at Goshen, New York. . . . Well beyond sixty, Mathan Foster of Masonville, New York, crankily decides to rid himself of his wife, Eleanor. He purchases arsenic for the job from a local apothecary, remarking to his hometown druggist with a wink that he is "looking about for a new wife." This rank stupidity leads authorities to examine Mrs. Foster's body when she dies a few days later; they easily determine her murder. Attorney General of New York Martin Van Buren is the chief prosecutor against Foster, who is convicted and hanged.

1820

Michael Powers, a resident of Boston, receives a heart-rending appeal from a friend in Ireland, one Timothy Kennedy, begging him to send passage money to America. Powers sends the money and Kennedy arrives on the next boat. Although he is employed within weeks of his arrival, Kennedy refuses to repay his friend. Such ingratitude enrages Powers who, using a broadaxe, kills Kennedy and hides his body by burying it in his cellar. He neglects to discard the axe, which is found blood-smeared, and he is found out. The eloquence of Daniel Webster, Powers' counsel, avails the killer little at his trial. He is convicted and hanged in Boston, April 11, 1820. . . . Hearing that Peter Lagoardette, a member of his band of burglars, is secretly seeing his girl, Manuel Philip Garcia and his henchman Jose Castillano lure Lagoardette to a deserted Norfolk, Virginia, house on March 20, 1820, slaying him with cutlasses and then attempting to burn his body in the fireplace where smoke-smelling constables find the smoldering remains hours later. The murderers are tracked down through laundry marks on clothes left at the murder site, the first instance of such clues employed by police. Both men are hanged at Norfolk, June 1, 1821. . . . Lois Stone of Kinsman, Ohio, living alone with her three small boys, all under the age of five, undergoes a traumatic religious experience not undetected by her neighbors, one of whom later comments that "something unusual was occasionally noticed in the deportment of this woman." On May 15, 1820, Lois Stone drowns her three children and then hides in a closet in her home, where she is found "in a delirious state of mind." Mrs. Stone is sent to prison. . . . John Dahmen, a dedicated murderer, asks Frederick Nolte, a New Albany, Indiana, shopkeeper, if he can spend the night in his store on May 25, 1820. That night Dahmen kills his kind host and steals his money and some goods. He murders another man, John Jenzer, for his purse, depositing his body along with that of Nolte's in a nearby river. Though apprehended, Dahmen escapes to Canada but is traced by the mails and returned to be hanged. His confessions reveal that Dahmen has murdered at least six men in America, three in Europe.

1821

Daniel Davis Farmer is so shocked when Mrs. Anna Ayer, a widow, claims he has fathered her child that he races to her Goffstown, New Hampshire, home and beats her to death with his walking staff. He then tries to burn her house down around the corpse to hide his victim but the smoke from the blaze draws neighbors, who apprehend him. Farmer is executed January 3, 1822 at Amherst.

1822

"It has been working on me for four or five years" is how Wilhemus Vanauken explains the murder of his wife, Leah, whom he has clubbed, knifed and finished off with an andiron. He is hanged at Newton, New Jersey. . . . A domestic dilemma of a different sort confronts John Lechlar of Lancaster, Pennsylvania. He discovers his

323

strumpet wife in bed with a man named Haag, who persuades him not to kill both of them; Haag signs a promissory note to pay a large sum for the indiscretion. When Haag reneges, Lechler dashes home, strangles his wife and hangs her body from an attic beam. He then goes to Haag's home and, when the debtor refuses to open the door, fires two pistol shots through it, instantly killing Haag's wife. The unpaid cuckold is hanged on October 25, 1822.

1823

Jebadiah Kearney, a tinker, is plagued with ghosts, his neighbors in Utica, New York, are later to insist in his defense, but authorities fail to see how such mental aberrations provoke Kearney into strangling to death Joseph Hovious, a bartender, who serves him ale instead of rum, his preferred drink, on July 22, 1823. Before police can catch the madman, Kearney races whooping and hollering into thick woodlands to vanish completely.

1824

Othello Church opens his front door at dawn in answer to loud knocking. He is shot to death. David D. How is arrested for the killing and convicted on strong circumstantial evidence. Though motives are blurry, it is conjectured that How loved Mrs. Church, an attractive brunette, from afar, and could not bear to see her live with someone else. How is hanged on March 19, 1824, at Angelica, New York. . . . About the same time How is planning his murder, an unidentified corpse is found by police wrapped in a blanket on a Manhattan street, the victim's skull split wide. The corpse is displayed at City Hall for three days until someone finally identifies the body as that of James Murray, which leads to the arrest of his roommate, John Johnson. The roommate confesses, saying he used a hatchet on Murray to take his money. Johnson is hanged before fifty thousand people on April 2, 1824, in the heart of New York City. . . . William Bonsall hears intruders in his Upper Darby, Pennsylvania, home on the night of May 22, 1824, and finds four burglars, one of whom stabs him to death. Three of the men are caught but only Michael Monroe, alias James Wellington, is convicted and hanged at Chester, Pennsylvania, on October 20, 1824. . . . Adonijah Bailey is arrested when his friend Jeremiah W. Pollock, with whom he lived, is found dead in a Brooklyn woods, his skull smashed with an axe on October 23, 1824. Convicted, Bailey cheats the gallows by hanging himself in his cell.

Cover of the pamphlet describing the criminal career of Michael Monroe, murderer of William Bonsall in 1824.
(HARVARD LAW LIBRARY)

A. The Store Door the Prisoners first knocked at.——B. The Gate they entered through to the Dwelling.——C. The Door they entered at, and where Lass stood on the Watch——D. A Cave, at the side of the house for storing of provision, milk, &c. for family use.

THE ONLY COPY
OF THE
Life, and the Testimony
That Convicted
Michl. Monroe
alias James Wellington.

AT A COURT OF OYER AND TERMINER,
Held at Chester, Pennsylvania, on the 20th of October 1824.

For the Murder of Wm. Bonsall,
AT HIS DWELLING ON THE DARBY ROAD.

On the Night of the 22d of May, last.
Containing the Testimony of MARY WARNER, PHŒBE BONSALL, DR. MORRIS C. SHALCROSS, &c. before the Court.
Together with a List of the Jury.
This is the Only Original Copy.—All others are Spurious.

Philadelphia: Printed and for Sale at 38 Chesnut St.

1825

Stephen Videto has his eye on the beauteous Mrs. Fanny Mosely of Fort Covington, New York, but the happily married woman shuns him. Videto next gossips loudly about seeing Indians in the district, armed and painted for war. Mrs. Mosely is shot through the window of her home while she is in bed on the night of February 2, 1825. Videto, whose lusts are commonly known, is arrested. He protests, claiming that Indians committed the murder. He is hanged on August 25, 1825 at Malone, New York. . . . Robert Douglass, an infamous counterfeiter, gets into an argument about "honest labor" with Samuel H. Ives in a Troupsburgh, New York, tavern. Douglass ends the debate by stabbing Ives to death. He is hanged at Bath, New York, April 29, 1825. . . . Isaac, Israel and Nelson Thayer rent a room in their Buffalo, New York, farmhouse to John Love. When they see that Love has considerable funds from his loan business, the brothers shoot and then chop up the roomer, mixing his remains with hogs slaughtered on their farm. When none of the brothers can explain how they have come into Love's possessions, they are tried and convicted, all hanged together from a Buffalo scaffold on June 17, 1825. . . . The busybody in Mrs. Maria Schermerhorn is her undoing. When Mrs. Schermerhorn advises a young girl to break off her engagement to one John Van Patten, the rejected suitor asks a friend for the loan of a shotgun. Van Patten knocks on Mrs. Schermerhorn's Rotterdam, New York, home and asks her for some wadding. She turns her back and proceeds up a stairway. Van Patten produces the shotgun from beneath his coat and shoots the woman in the back. The unlucky swain is hanged. . . . James Reynolds, who works on board a small barge in New York Harbor, stops a Negro boy from unloading some stones, telling him to put aside an especially large stone. This very stone is found anchored about the body of Captain W. M. West, Reynolds' employer, some days later. The sailor quickly admits the murder, claiming before his execution on November 18, 1825, that his downfall was due to "bad company who lured me into houses of ill fame." . . . One of the most extravagant murder motives on record is established by John Funston of Philadelphia who shoots and kills William Cartmill, a postboy, from ambush. Minutes before he is hanged on December 30, 1825, Funston shrugs and gives a terse explanation for his deed: "He crumpled up my letters with dirty hands." A popular ballad later honors the hapless postboy.

1826

Down-and-out gambler William F. Hooe convinces plantation owner William Simpson that contraband slaves are to be had. Taking Simpson to the purported secret auction on a dark road outside of Centreville, Virginia, Hooe shoots Simpson in the back for his purse. He is hanged on June 30, 1826, at Fairfax, Virginia. . . . Another Southerner upholding ancient traditions of honor, Jereboam O. Beauchamp, a prominent attorney in Frankfort, Kentucky, avenges his wife's sullied virtue by stabbing Colonel Solomon P. Sharp to death. According to Ann Cooke Beauchamp's repeated accusations to her husband, Sharp, a member of the Kentucky House of Representatives, had been guilty of seducing her two years before her marriage to the youthful attorney. Beauchamp is sentenced to death; his wife, visiting him in jail, convinces him to take his own life and hers. They plunge daggers into each other. Ann Beauchamp dies but Jereboam survives to be hanged, still bleeding from his wound, on July 7, 1826. Man and wife are buried in a common grave.... William Hill, one of a shipload of slaves en route from Baltimore to New Orleans for sale, leads a mutiny on board the schooner *Decatur*, throwing Captain Walter R. Gallaway and a mate overboard; the slaves are captured in Baltimore waters and Hill is hanged at Ellis Island, New York, before large cheering throngs ... Charles Marchant and Sylvester Colson murder Captain Edward Selfridge and his mate, Thomas P. Jenkins, on board the schooner *Fairy*, out of Boston in a brutal act of piracy. (page 38)

1827

Jesse Strang goes to work for John Whipple, owner of a large estate outside of Albany, New York. The hired hand uses the alias "Joseph Orton" since he has recently deserted a wife and child and is in great debt. Elsie Whipple, the owner's wife, takes a liking to Strang and promotes an affair, then suggests her lover kill the husband. After failing to poison Whipple, Strang shoots him through a window as he prepares for bed on May 7, 1827; both Mrs. Whipple and Strang claim it is the work of a passing drunk firing a random shot, but Strang, confronted by a suspicious clergyman, confesses the murder. He is found guilty and hanged in Albany, August 24, 1827. His co-plotter, Mrs. Whipple, is acquitted and she retires to her dead husband's estate.... Levi Kelley, who drives from Cooperstown, New York, to Albany to witness Strang's execution, is profoundly moved by the hanging. Returning to Cooperstown he tells friends that "no one who has ever seen such a horrid spectacle as the hanging of Jesse Strang could ever commit a murder!" Only ten days later, on September 3, 1827, a lame delivery boy is knocked down by Kelley. One of Kelley's boarders, Abraham Spafard, steps forward to prevent Kelley from braining the boy. Kelley whips out a pistol and shoots Spafard dead. Kelley is hanged in Cooperstown on November 21, 1827, after a speedy trial. When a spectator stand erected for the event collapses under the weight of several hundred people, killing two persons, authorities decree that Kelley's hanging be the last public execution in Otsego County, New York.

1828

Robert Bush may be the first murderer to kill in America while under the influence of narcotics. Dosed with opium, he shoots his wife, Sally, in their Westfield, Massachusetts, home. He is sentenced to die on the gallows on November 14, 1828, but eludes the rope by committing suicide in his cell, swallowing a weird poisonous mixture of opium and tobacco.

1829

Catharine Cashiere, a black, gets drunk in a New York City grogshop and, incensed at a remark made to her by another alcoholic, stabs to death Susan Anthony. She is convicted and sentenced to death. Her lawyer writes to the Governor of New York that his client should not hang since "she is completely amoral and unable to distinguish right from wrong," adding that Catharine is "moronic, syphilitic as well as a dypsomaniac." Counters the Governor: "What else makes a criminal but the inability to tell right from wrong?" Catharine Cashiere is hanged at Blackwell's Island, New York, May 7, 1829. . . . Waity Burgess, a self-styled soothsayer, goads her lover Oliver Watkins of Sterling, Connecticut, to murder his wife. (page 44)

1830

Edward Williams' wife complains of body pains. In response, the understanding Williams prepares a special brew for his spouse, camomile tea, magnesia water, and arsenic. (He stupidly purchases three orders of the poison on the day his wife dies.) Williams is executed at Westchester, Pennsylvania. . . . James and Elijah Gray, father and son, get drunk inside the grogshop of Samuel Davis in LeRoy, New York. When the barkeep attempts to throw the rowdy Grays from his place, Davis is stabbed to death. Elijah is freed on his father's insistence that he alone did the murder. James Gray is sent to prison for life.

1831

Amasa Walmsley, a half-breed Indian, gets drunk at a party he gives in his Burrillville, Rhode Island, home. He argues with John Burke over the possession of Burke's mistress, Hannah Prank. When the couple leave, Walmsley follows them into the woods where he beats them to death. Their bodies are found days later and Walmsley is brought to trial. Following his conviction, Walmsley confesses before the court, blaming his murderous act on drink and the fact that he is a member of the Narraganset Indian tribe. In careful and eloquent words he tells the group: "I felt shut out by my complexion and the ignominy which the world has cast upon the tribe to which I belong."

He is hanged June 1, 1832. . . . A swaggering imposter, Lino Amalia Espos y Mina, ingratiates himself with Dr. William Chapman, headmaster of an esteemed Philadelphia school, and his wife, Lucretia, telling the naive couple that he is the son of the Governor of California. They invite him to stay at their luxurious home and, over the course of a few weeks, Mina seduces the willing Lucretia Chapman. To make matters easy for Mina, Dr. Chapman dies following a four-day illness, complaining of stomach cramps. When Mrs. Chapman's jewelry begins to disappear, police investigate, discovering that Mina has been posing as Dr. Chapman and has been selling off his property. The doctor's body is exhumed and arsenic in large doses is found in his body. Mina is found guilty of murder and hanged on June 21, 1832. . . . Nat Turner, a highly educated slave, leads a bloody revolt in Virginia, slaughtering, with sixty other blacks, at least fifty white persons before being subdued on the Parker Plantation. Before he is hanged in November 1831, Turner tells startled jury members convicting him that he has no remorse for his victims, even the hacked-up children: "I viewed the mangled bodies as they lay in silent satisfaction, and immediately started in quest of other victims."

1832

A habitual wife-beater, Guy C. Clark, at the insistence of his wife, Fanny, was arrested for almost knocking an eye from her head. "I'll kill you for this," Clark tells his wife before constables lead him from his Ithaca, New York, home. Upon his release, Clark takes an axe to his wife. He is hanged on February 3, 1832. . . . A cranky peddler, Amos Miner, traveling about Rhode Island in a wagon, the only home his family knows, is stopped by deputies who accuse him of purchasing goods for resale without paying for them. "Call me a cheat, will you?" screams Miner and with that brings down a handaxe from his wagon perch to split the skull of deputy John Smith, killing him instantly. Miner is convicted of murder and executed on December 27, 1833, at Providence.

1833

Joel Clough is smitten by the attractive Mrs. Mary W. Hamilton, a widow. His advances, however, are rebuffed. Visiting the woman, Clough begs for her hand, prostrating himself before her. When she laughs, Clough leaps up and sinks a long knife into her bosom. He is hanged on July 26, 1833. . . . William Teller, while attempting to escape the Connecticut State Prison at Wethersfield, is stopped by Ezra

Hoskins, a guard, whom Teller hits with a wooden beam, killing him. Teller is convicted of murder and hanged at Hartford on September 6, 1833.

1834

Joseph J. Sager, who cannot stand illness, decides to help his rheumatic wife, Phebe, out of her long suffering and doses her food with arsenic. He is convicted of murder (the first on the records as euthanasia) and is hanged on January 2, 1835, at Augusta, Maine.

1835

Mobile, Alabama, businessman Nathaniel Frost is stabbed and robbed while walking home on the night of May 10, 1834. Police arrest Charles R. S. Boyington, who was seen walking with the victim minutes before the attack. Convicted on thin circumstantial evidence, Boyington is condemned to die. . . . When Ephraim Peake, the son of his father's former marriage, comes to live at the ancestral farm in Vermont, his stepmother realizes that she will lose the land to him when her husband dies, the farm being promised to Ephraim. Rebecca Peake fixes Ephraim his favorite meal, hash, liberally peppering it with arsenic. She is turned in by her husband and is sentenced to be hanged; Rebecca Peake dies in prison before she can be led to the gallows, starving herself to death. . . . Manuel Fernandez, a prosperous pirate who has operated at sea under the name of Richard C. Jackson, discovers that John Roberts, one of his band, is trysting with his wife. He approaches Roberts on a Manhattan street, slapping him and challenging him to a duel. "I do not duel," Roberts tells him. "Then you die," shouts Fernandez, and shoots him between the eyes. The pirate is hanged at Bellevue Prison, New York, on November 13, 1835.

1836

When John Earls of Muncy Creek, Pennsylvania, learns that his wife, Catharine, is pregnant, he plans her death, for by that time he is involved in a love affair with another woman. Earls waits until his wife delivers the child. The following day he goes to his local druggist and buys arsenic, stating he intends to rid his place of "mink and muskrats." Only a few hours after he has poisoned his wife, constables burst through the door, tipped by the suspicious druggist, to apprehend the killer. He is condemned to the gallows. . . . The most sensational murder of the 1830s is that of Ellen Jewett, a stunningly beautiful prostitute who is killed by her lover, Richard P. Robinson, who stabs her to death on the night of April 9, 1836, in her bordello bedroom when she threatens to ruin him if he marries the daughter of his employer. Though Robinson's guilt is beyond doubt, he is acquitted, mostly on the belief that "it is no crime to kill a whore," as one of his friends puts it. Robinson is carried from the Manhattan courtroom on the backs of his supporters upon his release amidst wild cheering.

1837

The proof of John Washburn's ineptitude as a thief is obvious to the most simple policeman when he murders William Beaver, a storekeeper, in Cincinnati, Ohio. Not content with merely taking Beaver's savings, Washburn exacts the last penny on his killing by selling Beaver's body to an anatomy professor for study, which leads to his arrest and conviction. Washburn uses the fifty dollars he has received for his victim's corpse to pay for his last sumptuous meal in jail and a new broadcloth suit, which he proudly wears to his own hanging. . . . A little less than four weeks after her marriage, Mariah Francisco of Erie, Pennsylvania, dies, following a short but violent illness. Authorities examining her body find large amounts of laudanum present. Cornelius Henry Francisco is confronted with their suspicions and immediately breaks down, telling police that he and his bride had formed a suicide pact but he had not the courage to complete his end of the bargain. The state proves murder and Francisco is hanged. . . . Octavius Baron steals five hundred dollars from William Lyman in his Rochester, New York, shop on the night of October 23, 1837, killing Lyman in the process. Only hours later, police find the stolen money on Baron, a known thief. He is hanged.

1838

Lewis Willman and Henry Kobler Musselman come across Lazurus Zellerbach, an itinerant peddler, traveling the backroads of Lancaster, Pennsylvania, and, almost on impulse, decide to rob him. As an afterthought, they stab him to death. Authorities find the peddler's goods on them and they are quickly convicted and hanged. . . . William Stewart of Baltimore is impatient to inherit his father's considerable fortune. On June 21, 1838, he accompanies his father, Benjamin Stewart, to some of his property, turning toward him as they are climbing a hill and shooting him several times. To conceal the identity of the

murder victim, Stewart proceeds to obliterate the face by smashing it
with a hatchet. The youth's impatience not only rests with his greed
for his father's money but in his planning of the murder. The clerk
who sold the hatchet to Stewart tells police that "he bought it the
morning his father disappeared. He told me that he didn't care to have
it wrapped, saying 'I'm going to use it soon.'" Further, the pistol
balls used in the shooting of Benjamin Stewart are determined to be
especially made for William Stewart's pistol, the first time ballistics
are employed in pinpointing a killer in the United States. Stewart is
found guilty and given a long prison term. . . . Edward Coleman, an
enormous thug and black gang leader in the notorious Five Points
district of Manhattan, marries one of the beautiful hot-corn girls working the streets (sellers of hot roasted ears of corn); he suspects her of
being unfaithful a few days later and, to the horror of dozens of witnesses, slits her throat in the middle of the street on July 28, 1838. He
is hanged January 12, 1839, the first person to be executed in the New
York Tombs prison.

1839

Eliza Sowers, a girl from a good Philadelphia family, becomes pregnant. Turned out of her house, she goes to Dr. Henry Chauncey, a
known abortionist. Sowers dies during the operation and Chauncey,
in perhaps the first conviction of its kind in the United States, is found
guilty of second-degree murder and given a stiff prison sentence.

1840

On July 10, 1840, John Stone is hanged in Chicago, Illinois, becoming
the first person to be officially executed in the infant city. Stone had
raped and murdered Lucretia Thompson, an attractive housewife who
had spurned his advances. . . . Another rapist-turned-murderer,
Charles Cook, is found guilty of killing Mrs. Catharine Merry on September 22, 1840; he is hanged on December 18 at Schenectady, New
York. . . . A dull brute of a man, Peter Robinson always solves his
problems with the strength of his arm. To dispense with a pesky
banker, Abraham Suydam, of New Brunswick, New Jersey, who
haunts the farmer for his mortgage payment, Robinson lures him to
his home, striking him with a mallet and dragging him to the cellar
where, for three days, he holds him a starving captive. On the night of
December 3, 1840, Robinson descends to the cellar, digs a grave before the horrified banker's eyes, and then throws him into it, bashing

THE
TRIAL, LIFE AND CONFESSIONS
OF
CHARLES COOK,

WHO WAS INDICTED, TRIED AND CONVICTED OF THE MURDER OF MRS. CATHARINE MERRY, (On the 22d day of September last,)

Sentenced to be Executed at Schenectada,

On the 18th December, 1840.

SCHENECTADA:
E. M. PACKARD, PRINTER.
1840.

An 1840 pamphlet describing the crimes and career of rapist-murderer Charles Cook. (HARVARD LAW LIBRARY)

the banker's head with a shovel. When friends learn that the penniless Robinson has retrieved his mortgage, police investigate. Robinson confesses, digs up the body, and is shortly convicted and hanged.

1841

Bradbury Ferguson of Exeter, New Hampshire, quarrels with his wife, who flees to a neighbor's. The irate husband drags her back home and empties a shotgun into her as she is washing the dishes. Ferguson is executed. . . . Moses W. Keen slays his wife in Mason, Kentucky. He is hanged on December 31, 1841, but thinks little of it, cracking jokes and laughing loudly at his own offbeat humor. States one report: "When putting on his shroud, and adjusting the halter about his neck, he made remarks to his attendants indicating a feeling of singular levity, badly suited to his situation." . . . John C. Colt, brother of the famous Samuel Colt, creator of the modern pistol industry, argues with New York City printer Samuel Adams over an additional ten-dollar charge for typesetting in Colt's self-published work on book-

333

keeping. Colt takes a hammer to Adams' head and kills the printer. Colt, following his conviction, is sentenced to hang in the Tombs on November 18, 1842; he begs to marry his common-law wife, Miss Henshaw. She, accompanied by several dignitaries—including John Howard Payne, the composer of "Home Sweet Home"—visits the condemned man in his cell on execution day. Miss Henshaw and Colt are married. An hour later, Colt is dead in his cell, a blade plunged into his heart, a suicide. Reports later state that Colt escaped and another body was substituted for his, but this claim remains unproved.

1842

William F. Comings, at odds with his wife over her spending money, strangles Adeline T. Comings in their Bath, New Hampshire, home, using a handkerchief. Comings then attempts to make the murder appear a suicide by hanging the hapless corpse from a bedpost, but his ruse is too thin and he is convicted and hanged.

1843

Following an argument with his father, Deacon White, Benjamin D. White, age thirty-nine, shoots his father in their Stafford, New York, home. Phrenologists examine White and consider him "mentally defective." He is nevertheless hanged on April 26, 1843. . . . Adam Horn, alias Andrew Hellman, is a wife-murderer known to have killed at least one previous wife before chopping up Malinda Horn in Baltimore, Maryland. A sloppy slayer, Horn buries parts of Malinda's remains in an apple orchard but other parts of her body are discovered in full view lying about his house. He is executed.

1844

Thomas Barrett gets drunk and mistakes a seventy-year-old woman for another, raping a Mrs. Houghton and then killing her to cover up his crime on February 18, 1844, at Luneberg, Massachusetts. Barrett is hanged on January 3, 1845. . . . John and William Gordon arrive in Providence, Rhode Island, from Ireland, and immediately apply for a liquor license. Amasa Sprague, a local pillar of Providence society and a brother to one of the U.S. Senators from the state, squashes the liquor license. The Gordons retaliate by beating Sprague to death on a lonely road. John and William Gordon are indicted for the murder but only John is executed, on February 14, 1845. . . . Burglar Henry Thomas kills Frederick Edwards while robbing the victim's store in Bourneville, Ohio, on November 20, 1844. Held on suspicion,

Thomas admits the murder to a fellow inmate and is later convicted
and hanged on that man's testimony. . . . While her family attends
church, Mrs. Lavinia Bacon is robbed and then stabbed to death in
her Middletown, Connecticut, home. Lucian Hall, who has been seen
to lurk about the Bacon home, and two others are arrested. Hall confesses his guilt at the end of his trial. The other two suspects, completely innocent, are released; Hall is executed. . . . Edward Howard
Rullofson begins his sinister murder career, which is to span almost
thirty years. (page 46)

1845

Orrin DeWolf, a boarder in the Worcester, Massachusetts, home of
William Stiles, is seduced by the voluptuous Mrs. Stiles. At her goad-
ing, DeWolf strangles his landlord with the lady's silk scarf. He blubbers his guilt almost immediately when confronted by authorities.
DeWolf is given a death sentence but this is commuted to life, preach-
ers of the day chalking up the murder not to premeditation but "the
natural results of intemperance and licentiousness." Mrs. Stiles is not
prosecuted. . . . Luscius P. Osborn loans his watch to Andrew P. Potter. When Osborn asks for the return of the watch, Potter, talking to
him at the railroad in Fair Haven, Connecticut, shouts: "I shall keep
it!" Potter, grabbing a pike pole, then crushes Osborn's head. He is
hanged still wearing Osborn's watch in his vest pocket. . . . After one

*Andrew Potter's brutal slaying of
Lucius P. Osborn is depicted in this
1845 broadsheet.* (HARVARD LAW
LIBRARY)

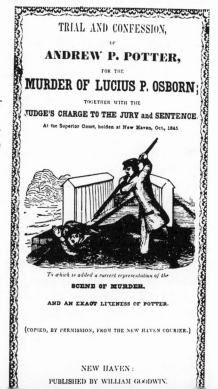

TRIAL AND CONFESSION,
OF
ANDREW P. POTTER,
FOR THE
MURDER OF LUCIUS P. OSBORN;
TOGETHER WITH THE
JUDGE'S CHARGE TO THE JURY and SENTENCE.
At the Superior Court, holden at New Haven, Oct., 1845.

To which is added a correct representation of the
SCENE OF MURDER,

AND AN EXACT LIKENESS OF POTTER.

(COPIED, BY PERMISSION, FROM THE NEW HAVEN COURIER.)

NEW HAVEN:
PUBLISHED BY WILLIAM GOODWIN.

Poisoner Henry G. Green administering the fatal dose to his wife, Mary Ann.

of his mother's many lectures about the unfitness of his wife, Mary Ann, Henry G. Green doses his spouse's food with arsenic. Green is hanged at Troy, New York, September 10, 1845.

1846

When fellow inmate James Gordon refuses to turn over a cigar butt to him, Henry Wyatt strangles Gordon at Auburn Prison, New York, in full view of many guards. Wyatt is hanged. . . . Gambler John Burnett stabs George Sornberger to death on a Schenectady, New York, street. When a deputy sheriff named Steele attempts to interfere, Burnett slashes him to death. Burnett uses one of the first switchblades in murder records in both instances. He confesses to killing Sornberger over a debt, detailing: "I then put my left hand upon the right side of his face, and shutting my eyes hard, cut his throat." He is condemned. . . . Edward A. Pennington beats Simon Davis to death for his farm tools. He throws Davis' body into a cave, but he is found later with the tools and convicted. Pennington is executed in Cincinnati. . . . To cure her husband of drinking, she says, Elizabeth Van Valkenburgh doses his food with arsenic. Arrested, the poisoner admits to killing at least one previous husband in the same fashion. She is hanged in Fulton, New York.

1847

Mary Myers and her lover, John Parker, decide to rid themselves of Mrs. Myers' husband, John. Parker buys a half ounce of arsenic, telling the druggist in Rockland, Pennsylvania, that "the rats are very bad around the house." When John Myers is discovered to have died of arsenic, both Mrs. Myers and Parker are arrested. They are hanged together in Franklin, Pennsylvania. . . . Dr. Valorus P. Coolidge gets rid of a creditor with prussic acid and a club in Waterville, Maine. (page 55) . . . In one of his usual alcoholic stupors, John Haggerty takes an axe to Melchior Fordney and his wife and child, killing all. At his trial, his counsel points out that Haggerty has had a long history of "alcoholic insanity," that he had years earlier murdered another man while drunk, and that while drunk he had shot his horse with a silver bullet, claiming that the animal was an evil spirit. Haggerty is hanged.

1848

Recently released from prison, Charles Langfeldt swears revenge. He slits the throat of a stranger, Mrs. Catherine Rademacher, in Philadelphia, thinking her one of those who had earlier testified against him. He is hanged. . . . Andreas Hall steals twelve hundred dollars from an elderly couple, Noah Smith and his wife, slitting their throats on the night of July 1, 1848. He is captured outside of Troy, New York, which is the site of his execution. . . . Highwayman James Copeland becomes a killer-for-hire, taking a thousand dollars to murder James A. Harvey in Augusta, Mississippi. He shoots Harvey on July 15, 1848, but is not hanged until October 30, 1857, his benefactors and employers, the Wages clan, managing to postpone Copeland's execution for almost a decade. . . . William Terrell gets into a heated argument with James McWilliams on September 14, 1848. Both young men from prominent families, they forget their courtly Southern manners by brawling in the home of a friend. Terrell, knocked down by McWilliams, draws a six-inch blade and stabs McWilliams to death, thus committing the first official homicide in Atlanta, Georgia. Terrell is sentenced to four years in prison on the fuzzy grounds of "voluntary homicide."

1849

William E. Knowlton, a boarder in an Uxbridge, Massachusetts, house, becomes drunk and tries to make love to Prudence Arnold, on the night of January 31, 1849. Rebuffed, he cuts her throat, and then attempts to slit his own—without success. He is hanged. . . . Francis Muir, not receiving his monthly payment on the property near Dinwiddie, Virginia, that he has sold to William Dandridge Epes, attempts to foreclose. Epes shoots Muir and buries his body in his fields. He mails bogus letters from Muir to prove the landlord is still living, but when he pawns Muir's watch, he is arrested. Epes is hanged at Petersburg, Virginia. . . . A classic murder of the nineteenth century is committed by Dr. John White Webster of Harvard, who clubs Dr. George Parkman, his creditor, to death on November 23, 1849, and then tries to burn the body in his laboratory. The remains are discovered by a suspicious janitor. Webster, in a dramatic Massachusetts trial, is convicted; he is hanged August 30, 1850.

Professor Webster of Harvard's medical college, who killed and dissected his chief creditor, Dr. George Parkman.

Dr. Parkman as he appeared only a few months before his murder by Webster.

1850

Henry L. Foote drugs Emily H. Cooper of New Haven, Connecticut, then rapes her. He slits her throat when worrying about the outcome. He is hanged in New Haven on June 19, 1850. . . . John Tilghman is seduced by his beauteous aunt, who encourages him to murder her husband, Joseph T. Tilghman of Kinston, North Carolina. Tilghman first tries to feed arsenic to his uncle, then stabs him to death. He is executed; Mrs. Tilghman is never indicted. . . . Martin Posey, in love with another woman, hires a slave named Appling to kill his wife, Matilda. The murder done, Posey kills Appling, for which he is indicted and hanged in Edgefield, South Carolina. . . . Elvira Streeter is so attractive that her husband, Milton W. Streeter, of Southbridge, Massachusetts, constantly makes jealous threats to her. When Elvira tells Streeter she is leaving him, he goes into a rage and cuts her throat; he then tries to slit his own, but is unsuccessful. Streeter is sent to prison for life.

1851

Edward Moore and Aaron B. Stookey burst into a wild fight on a Manhattan street, April 17, 1851; Stookey stabs Moore to death. He is hanged for murder in the Tombs, September 19, 1851. . . . Because he won't loan him a dollar George T. Gillespie is hit over the head by sailor Joseph Clark, who kills him with a cart-rung. Clark is hanged in the Tombs, February 11, 1853. . . . Victorine Grunsig of New York

City becomes ill and her husband, Otto, nurses her, dosing her with arsenic mixed with sugar. Grunsig is executed February 27, 1852. . . . Seventy-year-old John Windsor of Georgetown, Delaware, slightly daffy, is married to a twenty-four-year-old woman, Nancy Windsor, and is insanely jealous. Thinking her unfaithful, Windsor shoots her. He is sent to prison for life. . . . Resentful of her husband's strictness, Pamela Lee Worms feeds arsenic to her husband, Moses Worms, and, as an afterthought, to her daughter. She is hanged in Pittsburgh, Pennsylvania, January 30, 1852. . . . Portuguese Maurice Antonio fights with Ignacio Pinto over their common-law wife in Gates, New York. Antonio kills Pinto with a club and buries the body under a corncrib, where it is quickly found. Antonio is hanged on June 3, 1852.

1852

When his wife, Fredericka, and his three children join John Erpenstein, coming from Germany to Newark, New Jersey, he realizes his affair with Dora Muller is threatened; Erpenstein gives his wife a bread-and-butter sandwich loaded with arsenic, killing her. He is hanged in Newark on March 30, 1852. . . . Augustus Otis Jennings and three others take a debtor, Edward H. Willard, into the woods near St. Joseph, Missouri, thinking to teach him the error of being a deadbeat. They whip Willard with rawhide, which kills him. Jennings is executed. . . . A sex murderer, Charles Steingraver, is executed in Jackson, Ohio. He was convicted of killing Clarinda Vantilburg, "an idiotic, blind, deaf, dumb and entirely helpless girl of ten years." Several hundred spectators gather at the murderer's public hanging, cheering when he drops through the trap, then tearing his body to pieces. . . . On the morning of July 19, 1852, slave servants in a Richmond, Virginia, household, Jane and John Williams, take a hatchet to Mrs. V. B. Winston and her child. They are hanged separately for the killings on August 22, 1852, first Jane Williams, then John, who is whipped into stepping off a cart with the rope about his neck. . . . The Reverend George Washington Carawan grows suspicious of Clement Lassiter, thinking the schoolteacher of Goose Creek, North Carolina, is secretly wooing his wife, and prepares to murder the young man, only one of a series of killings of which the pastor is later accused. (page 59.)

1853

"I can't stand no more sermons from you," yells Patrick Fitzgerald to his wife, Margaret, who upbraids him for his drinking. He swirls from the table, grabs a pistol and shoots his wife dead on January 17, 1853. He is hanged in New York City's Tombs Prison, November 15, 1853. . . . John Hendrickson of Bethlehem, New York, gets rid of his new but argumentative wife, Maria, by poisoning her food with aconite—the first known use of such poison in an American murder case—but is found out by police. He is executed on March 6, 1853. . . . In Cuyahoga Falls, Ohio, James Parks gets William Beatson drunk after he discovers Beatson is carrying a large sum of money. Parks accompanies the drunken Beatson on his way home and kills him on a dark road, April 13, 1853. To assure that none will identify the corpse, Parks chops off his head and takes it with him, along with Beatson's purse, fleeing to Buffalo, New York, where Parks (along with the victim's head) is captured. Parks is executed. . . . Telling clothier Louis Reese that he will pay for the suit of clothes he has ordered if he will come to a lonely spot outside of Wilkes-Barre, Pennsylvania, Rees W. Evans, eighteen, shoots the storeowner when he arrives on horseback, stealing fifty-five dollars from his pockets and the victim's gold watch, which he is wearing when arrested. Evans' confession is announced before he is hanged, despite his request that it remain unpublished until his death. . . . Thomas Cook and James M. Bickford shoot John B. Secor from ambush outside Franklin, New York, then rob him, on June 6, 1853. Both Cook and Bickford are caught and hanged. . . . When Susan McAnnany refuses sexual favors to James L. Hoare on the night of October 5, 1853, the offended Hoare shoots her in the neck while kissing her. Hoare is hanged in the Tombs, January 27, 1854.

1854

Released from the Marine Hospital in Cincinnati, William Arrison, feeling that he has been mistreated while being doctored, sends a bomb to Hospital Director Isaac Allison, who opens the package in front of his wife on June 26, 1854. Both man and wife are killed. Arrison is first condemned but his sentence is later reduced after a new trial in which he is found guilty of manslaughter. This is the first known homicide in America in which a bomb is employed as the murder weapon. . . . Following his suspicions, Courtland C. Johnson returns unexpectedly to his home in Middletown, Pennsylvania, to find his wife and Nathaniel Colyer brazenly making love in the garden. He fetches a brace of pistols from his study and chases the naked couple throughout the large house, shooting and killing both. He is executed on August 25, 1854 in Harrisburg, despite a strong plea of temporary insanity by his lawyer.

1855

Hugh Corrigan of Blairsville, Pennsylvania, kills his wife and then hides the corpse in a flour barrel. When a neighbor visiting him sits on the barrel, Corrigan grows nervous and tries to burn the body some hours later. The odorous smoke causes the neighbor to return and the deed is discovered. Corrigan is condemned. . . . J. V. Craine, already married, is driven to kill Susan M. Newnham of Ringgold, California, after the lady's parents object to their meetings. Craine is hanged at Colma, California, on October 26, 1855 . . . George W. Green of Chicago poisons his wife but stubbornly denies his guilt. Experts testifying as to their chemical tests to determine the presence of poison—the first such testimony in the history of Illinois homicide—contribute largely to Green's conviction of murder in the first degree. He is sentenced to die but commits suicide in his cell shortly before his scheduled hanging. . . . David F. Mayberry, hearing that Andrew Alger, a prosperous farmer, has just sold his crops and is returning home, hides along a road outside Harmony, Wisconsin, leaping upon Alger as he passes and burying a hatchet in his head. Taking the farmer's money, Mayberry gets roaring drunk and reveals his crime. Convicted, Mayberry laughs at his trial's conclusion, reveling in the fact that the state of Wisconsin has abolished capital punishment. The killer never spends one moment of his life sentence in a cell. Incensed mobs break into the courthouse on July 11, 1855, drag Mayberry to the streets and lynch him on the spot. . . . A vixen at heart, twenty-two-year-old Mrs. Elizabeth Ragan of Piqua, Ohio, not only makes James D. Mowrey her secret lover but compels the gullible youth to poison her husband. Mowrey is reluctant to purchase the necessary poison so Mrs. Ragan dispatches her child to the druggist. The boy has only three cents, seven cents shy of the price of the smallest package of arsenic. Kind neighbors in the store, thinking the poison is to rid the Ragan farm of rats, contribute the necessary money. When Arthur Ragan dies suddenly, authorities investigate. Mrs. Ragan and Mowrey confess and draw long prison terms. . . . Isaac Wood, in order to inherit his brother's vast estate outside Dansville, New York, slips arsenic into the food of David Wood, his wife, Rhoda, and their three children. All die as the result of a strange illness, authorities believe. Wood next poisons his own wife and child in New Jersey and then flees to Illinois where he is later traced and returned to New York for trial. He is convicted and hanged at Geneseo, New York, on July 9, 1858. . . . Conrad Bauer, whose Lager Beer Saloon on Market Street is the most popular groggery in Newark, New Jersey, decides to charge admission. He is collecting fees on the night of August 7, 1855, when John McKinney and several other Irishmen approach, McKinney angrily shouting: "I would rather kill a Dutchman any time than give him a shilling." Some time later, when Bauer is found stabbed to death, McKinney's words are remembered and he is charged and convicted of manslaughter, given a long prison term. . . . Mark Fitzgerald of Sterling, New York, refuses to believe that his son, John, is a "born criminal," mortgaging his farm for bail when his son is charged with robberies. The farmer next finds the family sugar bowl loaded with strychnine and the empty vial in his son's coat pocket. He dismisses the incident. A week later, on August 29, 1855, John Fitzgerald waits until his father, mother and brother go to sleep before killing all three with a hatchet. He is condemned.

1856

Nathan Ellington hates his son-in-law, Adolphus F. Monroe, one day taking a cane to the youth's head to emphasize his disgust. Monroe pulls out a pistol and kills Ellington with a bullet in the head. Sentenced to be hanged on February 15, 1856, Monroe receives a three-month stay of execution from the governor. The people of Charleston, Illinois, respond by breaking into the jail, dragging Monroe to the streets and hanging him from a sturdy oak tree. . . . John Fox expresses his hatred for a neighbor, John Henry, of New Brunswick, New Jersey, by slitting his throat and then taking his body to the river to dispose of it. He chops a hole in the ice and dumps the body through but the corpse bobs up, frozen in ice, some weeks later. Fox is convicted mostly on his own statements showing knowledge of the killing prior to his arrest. He is condemned. . . . James P. Casey, editor of the *Sunday Times* in San Francisco, spots James King, editor of the rival *Evening Bulletin* on the street May 14, 1856, and tells him to draw his weapon. Although King is unarmed, Casey pulls forth a revolver and shoots King dead. Some weeks later, Casey, while awaiting trial, is dragged from his jail cell along with three others and hanged by a lynch mob of more than two hundred thousand San Francisco residents who are in a vigilante mood. . . . George Knight of Poland, Maine, tires of his wife and slits her throat while she sleeps. Evidently, Knight has no thought of escaping punishment for he leaves his razor, the murder weapon, on the pillow next to the dead woman. He is given a life term.

1857

Negro sailor John Dorsey, coming home drunk to his common-law wife, Ann McGirr, alias Ann Hopkins, a black professional prostitute, brawls with her down three flights of stairs at No. 3 Worth Street, Manhattan, on the night of March 10, 1857, slitting her throat in front of scores of witnesses. Dorsey is hanged on July 17, 1857. . . . Mormon Bishop John D. Lee becomes a brigand in Utah, leading dozens of armed renegades dressed as Indians in attacks against immigrant wagon trains for the gold they are carrying. In September 1857, Lee and his cohorts attack a wagon train of 140 immigrants near Mountain Meadows, Utah, killing all except seventeen children. Not until 1875 is Lee accused of the mass murders. After two trials, he is convicted; he is shot by a firing squad on March 23, 1877. . . . New Yorker James Stephens, in love with his niece, begins beating his wife, Sophie. When she is bedridden from her injuries, Stephens doses her lager beer and brandy with laudanum on September 22, 1857. Investigating doctors discover the poison and Stephens is condemned, hanged on February 3, 1860. . . . John Crummins, owner of a liquor store in Manhattan, takes offense at insults hurled at him and his wife by Dennis McHenry on the night of October 10, 1857. Crummins tells McHenry to put down his drink and leave his place. "I'll go, but you dare not follow me," challenges McHenry with a sneer. Crummins then grabs a sword and chases him into the street, passing the blade four times through McHenry's body. The liquor dealer is convicted and hanged on March 30, 1860. . . . James P. Donnelly, an outstandingly good doctor, begins to gamble with Albert S. Moses on August 1, 1857, at the Sea View House in Navisink, New Jersey, losing fifty-five dollars to the sharper. While Donnelly is attempting to steal back his losings that night, Moses awakes; Donnelly stabs him to death with a surgical instrument. He is caught and hanged, January 5, 1858. . . . Unable to face a public scandal, James E. Eldredge of Louisville, New York, poisons his pregnant fiancée, Sarah Jane Gould, giving her arsenic mixed with Dr. Rogers' Syrup of Liverwort & Tar. He dies of consumption in the Canton, New York, jail, March 23, 1859. . . . Charlotte Jones covets the savings of her uncle George Wilson and aunt Elizabeth M'Masters, both in their seventies, residents of Elizabeth, Pennsylvania. She urges her lover, Henry Fife, a penniless shoemaker, and his friend Monroe Stewart to steal the money. They do, but in the process kill the elderly brother and sister. Fife, Stewart and Charlotte Jones are caught some days later carrying the stolen bills. All three are hanged. . . . Edward W. Hawkins, bullyboy and horse thief, is arrested by deputies James M. Land and Jesse Arvine outside Estill, Kentucky. He takes a weapon from Arvine and shoots both men. He is hanged for four murders in all, giving a penitent speech on the gallows.

1858

Thomas Washington Smith's young bride delivers a child five months after their marriage; the wife admits that she has been seduced by her sponsor, Richard Carter, a man of forty-eight. Smith meets Carter in a

Philadelphia hotel and shoots him dead on the spot. He receives a long prison term. . . . On March 6, 1858, Henry Jumpertz, a Chicago barber, learns that his mistress, Sophie Elten Werner, has been unfaithful. He slices her into pieces and packs the remains in a whiskey barrel, which he ships by rail to New York. The grisly barrel is traced, Jumpertz arrested. He is executed. . . . J. Edward Roach, a student at Newark College, learns that upper-classmen intend to distribute pamphlets ridiculing his class. He steals the printed material, shouting, "You'll get these circulars only over my dead body!" Isaac N. Weaver and several other upper-classmen leap upon Roach and he is killed in the scuffle. Weaver is tried for murder and given a short prison term. . . . Oscar F. Jackson murders Henry A. Wallace in Rockford, Minnesota; he is lynched on August 27, 1858 before he can be executed. . . . Thomas M'Keever accuses William H. Buse, a local tough, of stealing his jug of whiskey. Buse's response is to shoot M'Keever through the head with one shot while the victim is sitting in a chair. Buse is hanged at Jacinto, Mississippi, on November 19, 1858. . . . Charles J. Rinehart slays John B. Bodell in an argument in Lexington, Minnesota; Rinehart is lynched by an angry mob thinking he might be released. . . . William A. Choice, the most esteemed actor of Atlanta, Georgia, shoots Calvin Webb, a bailiff, to death on an open street, December 31, 1858. Webb had served the actor a ten-dollar bail process the previous day, injuring his pride. Choice is tried but sent to an insane asylum for a short period of time due to the dramatic efforts of his lawyer.

1859

Daniel E. Sickles, a congressman from New York, later to distinguish himself as a formidable Union general in the Civil War, discovers on February 26, 1859, that his wife, Teresa Bagioli Sickles, has been carrying on a year-long affair with Philip Barton Key, the son of the composer of the national anthem. The next day, the enraged cuckold encounters Key on a Washington street, and draws a pistol, shouting: "You have dishonored my house! You must die!" He shoots Key twice, killing him. Sickles is released on the grounds that he has defended his honor. . . . Ann Bilansky, in league with her young lover, poisons her saloon-and-real-estate-rich husband, Stanislaus Bilansky, on March 12, 1858. (page 62) . . . Lee Ah Bow, a Chinese immigrant, stabs his mistress and two other women in his New York boardinghouse on the night of March 9, 1859; his mistress had served him a cold dinner. He is convicted of murder and sentenced to hang in the Tombs but is reprieved and later released due to the efforts of missionaries thinking he will convert to Christianity. Lee Ah Bow goes on to commit several more homicides before authorities place him permanently in an insane asylum, where he dies on June 23, 1912. . . . Henry Kriegler of Albert Lea, Minnesota, tells a neighbor that he hates one Nelson Boughton and that Boughton has recently jabbed him four times with a pitchfork. "Some day I'll kill him," swears Kriegler aloud. A week later when Kriegler's wife, a subject of his constant beatings, runs to Boughton's home for sanctuary, Kriegler follows and shoots Boughton dead. He is hanged on March 1, 1861.

1860

On the murky night of March 14, 1860, Captain Burr and his two seamen, the brothers Oliver and Smith Watts, are slaughtered in their bunks on board the sloop *E. A. Johnson*, docked in New York Harbor. Their killer, who has looted the ship, is revealed to be the notorious thief Albert E. Hicks, who calls himself "the worst man in the world." Hicks is hanged at Bedloe's Island, Friday, July 13, 1860, before a wildly enthusiastic crowd of more than twelve thousand, most of whom view the execution from cruise boats. . . . Charles Jefferds, in a mistaken belief that his mother will inherit his stepfather's considerable wealth when he dies, shoots John Walton, his stepfather, from ambush, and also John W. Matthews, Walton's friend, who pursues him, killing both men. (page 66) . . . George C. Hersey lives with the Tirrell family in Weymouth, Massachusetts, for four months. Discovering that he has made his fiancée pregnant, he gives Betsy Frances Tirrell a "secret drug," telling her it will create an instant abortion. The drug is strychnine, which kills her. Hersey is hanged. . . . The Reverend Jacob S. Harden of Mount Lebanon, New Jersey, is nagged into marrying a young girl. A fortuneteller informs the mystical Harden that his wife will soon die. The pastor helps the prophecy along by giving his wife arsenic. He is hanged on July 6, 1860.

1861

That John E. Lovering is a total failure at all he attempts is exemplified by his robbery of Henry Auker, an elderly storeowner in McAlisterville, Pennsylvania. The ancient Auker almost kills him before Lovering splits his head with an axe. Lovering is caught almost immediately with loot spilling from his pockets. He is executed January 3, 1862. . . . Private Michael Lanahan is slapped in the face by Sergeant Brennan for being late for guard duty in Washington, D.C., on October 29, 1861. An hour later, Lanahan salutes his sergeant from his post by shooting him in the head. Lanahan is publicly hanged on January 6, 1862, before six regiments of infantry and hundreds of spectators. He shouts his last words: "Goodbye, soldiers, goodbye!"

Andrew J. Pate, an émigré from the Southland to Oregon, argues with George Lamb, who calls Pate a "Southern son of a bitch." With that the two men arm themselves, Lamb with an axe, Pate with a pistol, the latter sending a bullet into his opponent. Pate is executed at Albany, Oregon, on May 27, 1862. . . . Daniel Webster, the warden of the Connecticut State Prison at Wethersfield, is a martinet, treating his prisoners with extreme cruelty. He has inmate Gerald Toole flogged when the prisoner fails to complete work on a dozen boots a day. Fearing that he will be whipped again the next day for not finishing the impossible chore, Toole uses a homemade knife to stab the warden to death. Toole is hanged.

1863

Ephraim Gilman strangles Mrs. Harriet B. Swan to death in Fryeburg, Maine, after she rebuffs his pleas to let him marry her daughter. Gilman is sent to prison for life where he languishes until 1906, when he is pardoned. . . . Dr. David M. Wright of Norfolk, Virginia, a man of sixty, is enraged at the sight of black troops moving through the streets of his town. Wright hisses at the commanding officer, Lieutenant A. L. Sanborn, who orders him arrested. Wright in turn shoots Sanborn dead from his horse. He is condemned. His daughter visits him in jail and he changes into her clothes in an attempt to escape, which fails. Dr. Wright is hanged on July 11, 1863. . . . Charles Lewis kills James Rowand, a jeweler, for his gems in Princeton, New Jersey. He is hanged. . . . Edward W. Green, a normally peace-loving resident of Malden, Massachusetts, impetuously decides to rob the local bank on December 15, 1863—making this the first bank robbery in America —killing the bank's only occupant, Frank E. Converse, and taking away five thousand dollars. Green is questioned by police after it is reported that he is spending a great deal of money. He confesses and is hanged on January 27, 1866.

1864

Encouraged by the wife of Patrick O'Brien, her lover, James Gilbert Jenkins, shoots O'Brien and hides the body in some woods near Napa City, California. The corpse is quickly found by dogs and Jenkins is arrested and tried, confessing with disgust at his sloppy ways to the court: "That whiskey that I drank the morning before I shot O'Brien was what caused me to do it when I did, and in so careless a manner."

He is hanged. . . . John Nance, a Union soldier, also blames his cups
when he is found guilty of murdering William M'Bee, a Confederate,
while drunk. An interesting point is made by his jurors in that had
Nance shot M'Bee while sober he would have been found innocent,
the shooting considered an act of war. Nance is hanged at Rutledge,
Tennessee, on December 27, 1867. . . . One of the most horrendous
mass poisoners ever seen in America, Lydia Sherman, embarks upon
a career of killing. (page 73)

1865

In January, George Baker and George P. Beale, two apprentice
thieves, rob Daniel Delaney of Salem, Oregon, and shoot him in the
process. Found with the money, both men are hanged. . . . Bernard
Friery, who fancies himself a prizefighter, stabs to death Henry Lazurus, a Manhattan barkeep, when Lazurus refuses to fight him on
January 3, 1865. Friery is hanged in the Tombs on August 17, 1866.
. . . John Wilkes Booth, a flamboyant actor with pro-Southern sentiments, and several others form a conspiracy to murder President Abraham Lincoln. Booth shoots Lincoln at Ford's Theatre on April 14,

*Assassin John Wilkes Booth
leaping from the presidential
box after having fatally shot
Abraham Lincoln in Ford's
Theater, on April 14, 1865.*
(NEW YORK HISTORICAL
SOCIETY)

1865, then escapes. Lewis Paine, a mentally defective member of the conspiracy, attempts to kill Secretary of State William Seward but fails. Paine, Mary E. Surratt, and David E. Herold are later hanged. Booth is tracked down to a Virginia farm and killed by Union troops on April 26, 1865. Much remains a mystery in this conspiracy. John H. Surratt, Booth's co-conspirator, escapes to Europe and Africa before being returned for trial. He is released, largely due to Secretary of War Edwin Stanton's influence. There is evidence that points to Stanton's involvement in the killing, along with other important Union leaders opposed to Lincoln's empathetic Reconstruction plans for the South, and members of the British Government in Canada. . . . George Wagner of New York City becomes upset over his wife's inability to please him sexually and crushes her head with a hatchet on July 21, 1865. He is executed March 1, 1867. . . . Dennis Harris and another ex-slave, Henry Brown, break into the Georgia Railroad office in Atlanta, killing stationmaster James R. Crew, but get nothing on November 29, 1865. Harris remains at large for a year, robbing homes in Atlanta, before he is captured and hanged.

1866

Martha Grinder is executed in Pittsburgh after poisoning her neighbor, a Mrs. Carothers. Grinder tells her jurors that she enjoys murder and would have killed more had she had the opportunity. . . . On April 7, 1866, Anton Probst, a handyman on the farm of Christopher Dearing near Philadelphia, systematically begins slaughtering the entire Dearing family. (page 86) . . . Albert L. Starkweather of Manchester, Connecticut, takes an axe to Harriett and Ella Starkweather, his mother and sister, thinking he will inherit the family farm when they die. Starkweather, later judged weakminded by phrenologists measuring his cranium, inherits a hangman's rope. . . . Jeremiah O'Brien stabs his mistress, Lucy A. McLoughlin, alias Kate Smith, a New York harlot, to death during a dance—she reportedly stepped on his toes —on June 20, 1866; he is hanged in the Tombs, August 9, 1867. . . . James T. Wright shoots and kills Johnson W. Bridwell, one-time publisher of Atlanta's *Intelligencer* on July 5, 1866, to stop the newsman from having sex with an aunt. When arrested, Wright blurts to police: "The old drunk had it coming!" He is sent to prison for twenty years. . . . John L. Campbell, a half-breed Sioux, slaughters the family of Andrew J. Jewett near Mankato, Minnesota; Campbell is lynched. . . . Jacob Hodapp murders nineteen-year-old Julius Wochele, a German immigrant, to obtain his forty-dollar gold watch in Norristown, Pennsylvania. Hodapp is hanged.

1867

Bridget Durgan, an Irish immigrant servant, kills Mrs. Ellen Coriell in New Market, New Jersey, with the thought of taking her place in the affections of Dr. Coriell. She is hanged at New Brunswick. . . . G. W. Strong, who moved to California in 1857 where he now lives a life of thievery and murder, pretends to purchase the farm of Francis Holmes outside of Ukiah City, murdering the rancher for his savings. He is caught and hanged. . . . Jane M. Swett, after discovering her husband to be a secret drinker, according to one report "did privately and subtilely, with a gill of whiskey, mingle, put into and mix a large quantity of morphine," which Mr. Swett innocently gulps down, the poison killing him. "I thought to cure him of his evil habit," is Mrs. Swett's only explanation before she is given a six-year prison term. . . . William Parquet is exhumed in Cleveland on a tip in February 1867. Great quantities of arsenic are found in his body and his sister, Sarah M. Victor, is convicted of the murder, sentenced to hang. Mrs. Victor's sentence is commuted to life imprisonment. She is released nineteen years later. . . . James Jeter Phillips of Atlanta murders his wife, Mary, who is ten years his senior, hiding her body on a farm. The victim's corpse is many times dug up and then reburied until she is identified through clothing. Phillips is arrested on suspicion. He is convicted but manages to stave off his execution until July 22, 1870. He confesses his guilt on the gallows. . . . Andreas Roesch of St. Peter, Minnesota, encounters Joseph Saurer, a sixteen-year-old, hunting in the woods. Roesch, a dull-witted brute, takes the youth's rifle from him and kills him with it. Roesch's son, who is present, informs authorities of the murder and Roesch is hanged on March 6, 1868. His wife refuses to bury the corpse.

1868

John Ward murders Mrs. Ephraim Griswold in her Williston, Vermont, home. When apprehended, Ward claims that he was but a hired assassin, paid by Mrs. Griswold's adopted daughter who wanted to inherit her estate. He is not believed and is hanged on March 20, 1868. . . . John Millian is arrested in Virginia, Nevada, for the murder of prostitute Julia Bulette. Some of her furs, jewelry and clothes are found in his possession. Millian is condemned. . . . Hack driver John Real feels that patrolman John Smedick is harrassing him to extort part of the fares he picks up in Manhattan's Tenderloin. On July 1, 1868, Real shouts to officer Smedick from his hack perch: "You'll point that billie at me once too many times!" On July 23, as Real passes Thirty-fifth Street, he spots Smedick, draws a pistol and blows away the top of the policeman's head. He is led laughing to a cell. Real is hanged August 5, 1870. . . . Philadelphia child molester John Hanlon attacks and murders seven-year-old Mary Mohrmann on September 6, 1868. He is caught in the act and swiftly convicted and executed, despite an angry mob trying to break down the prison door to lynch him.

1869

At the urging of Mrs. Nancy E. Clem, her brother, Silas W. Hartman, murders Jacob Young and his wife in their rural home to obtain their hidden savings. Police trace the murder weapon, an axe, and distinctive horseshoe tracks to Hartman's Cold Spring, Indiana, door. Both are condemned but Hartman commits suicide in jail, leaving a wailing Nancy Clem to face the hangman alone. . . . No longer able to stand her tongue-lashings, George S. Twitchell of Philadelphia beats Mary E. Hill, his mother-in-law, to death with a poker. Trying to stage her death as an accident, Twitchell hurls his mother-in-law from a second-floor window but is seen; he is convicted. Just as his death sentence appears about to be commuted to a life term, the despairing Twitchell commits suicide. . . . Successful author and editor of the *New York Tribune* Albert D. Richardson is shot in the editorial rooms of his newspaper by Daniel McFarland. The killer, who has been sitting quietly in the offices, waiting for Richardson to appear, tells arresting officers that the editor has stolen the affections of his divorced wife, Abby Sage, a prominent actress. Abby marries Richardson on his deathbed while McFarland is brought to trial; the case becomes a *cause célèbre*. His lawyer vilifies the victim, labeling him a "scoundrelly lover." McFarland's powerful friends create a whitewash on his behalf as the "betrayed husband." The propaganda moves a jury to release the killer. . . . Chicago trolleycar driver Daniel Walsh disappears only hours after marrying Rose Weldon, a woman he will blatantly murder some months later. (page 89)

1870

An itinerant, Jack Reynolds, calmly walks into the Manhattan home of grocer William Townsend at 192 Hudson Street on a Saturday night, January 29, 1870. He sits down in the living room across from the startled Townsend and says: "I am your brother. I want to stay here all night." Responds the indignant Townsend: "I do not know you. Get out of my house!" With that Reynolds stands up, walks over to Townsend and sinks a shoemaker's knife into Townsend's neck, killing him. Though several doctors insist that Reynolds is hopelessly insane, authorities counter that he was only slightly tipsy at the time of the killing and knew what he was doing, that he is "perfectly fit" to hang. Before Reynolds drops through the Tombs trap on April 8, 1870, he smirks at the executioner and announces to the crowd of witnesses assembled at the foot of the gallows: "This don't impress me much. Hanging is played out in New York." . . . James M. Lowell gloats to himself that his murder of Mary Elizabeth Lowell, his wife, has been a perfect crime. He has bludgeoned her to death on a back road near Lewiston, Maine, in June 1870, burying the corpse in a deserted field. Three years later, the victim's mother has a dream about her vanished daughter, a dream so vivid that she urges sheriff's deputies to accompany her to a field she has seen in her slumber. Amazed police dig up a headless skeleton. Lowell is charged, convicted and sent to prison for life. . . . Stephen M. Ballew, a cowhand on the Golden ranch near Quincy, Illinois, travels with James P. Golden to Texas to purchase horses. He returns alone, telling the Golden family that "poor Jim has been shot by bandits." Ballew weds a Golden daughter, scheming his way into the family inheritance. When Golden's body is found, Ballew is identified as the killer. He is hanged.

1871

Thinking his wife to be cheating on him with one Alfred Rendall, Isaac V. Buckhout invites Rendall to his Tarrytown, New York, home. While the visitor sips some wine in his parlor on New Year's Day, Buckhout shoots him through the head. Buckhout then calmly walks into another room and beats his wife to death. He is convicted after three trials and hanged. . . . Charles Marlow, a brewer in Jamestown, New York, offers to sell his brewery to William Bachmann but when the purchaser arrives with six thousand dollars Marlow changes his mind, settling on murder. He inveigles Bachmann into the brewery's cellar where he axes him to death, then burns the body. Employees find teeth and bones in the ashes some days later. Marlow is tried and given a long prison term. . . . Jacob Rosenzweig of Paterson, New Jersey, performs an abortion on Alice Augusta Bowlsby, who dies during the operation. Rosenzweig panics, packing the body in a trunk and shipping it to Chicago. The trunk is traced back to the abortionist, who is convicted of manslaughter and given a stiff prison sentence. . . . Eugene Shader of Lima, New York, argues with his landlord, Henry Ward, over an increase in his rent; the argument ends when Shader explodes and throws Ward down a flight of stairs. An hour later the two men sit down to dinner. Ward places a pistol on the table next to his soup. "What's that for?" asks Shader. "I bet a dollar I can shoot that fly off the tip of your ear," Ward says. Shader throws down a dollar, sneering: "You don't frighten me." With that Ward fires a shot that hits Shadeı between the eyes. "I lose," remarks Ward as he is led away. He is sent to prison. . . . Another ridiculous argument ends in homicide on April 27, 1871, on board a Broadway trolleycar in New York. William Foster, riding on the front platform of the car, insists upon keeping the front door open. Another passenger, Avery D. Putnam, complains of the cold air and closes the door. Foster opens it. Putnam closes it. The door is opened and closed a half dozen times before Putnam stomps out the platform and says: "What is the matter with you?" He returns to his seat. Before leaving the car at Forty-sixth Street, Foster enters the car, leans down to the seated Putnam and shouts: "What is the matter with you?" He then swings out a car-hook and strikes Putnam in the head with the instrument, killing him. Police arrest the intoxicated killer on the street. Foster is tried before Judge Albert Cardoza and found guilty. He is hanged in the Tombs, March 21, 1873.

1872

Edward S. "Ned" Stokes, a Broadway character, dines at Delmonico's on January 6, 1872, broods over the loss of his flashy showgirl Josie Mansfield to financier Big Jim Fisk, then races to the Broadway Central Hotel to see his estranged paramour. He encounters Fisk who is coming up the grand staircase and, whipping out a Colt revolver, shoots the tycoon, who dies of a stomach wound hours later. Stokes

Edward S. "Ned" Stokes shooting millionaire speculator Big Jim Fisk to death on the grand staircase of the Broadway Central Hotel in 1872.

*Kate Bender with
murder on her mind.*
(NEW YORK PUBLIC
LIBRARY)

*John Bender, who
wielded the
sledgehammer.* (NEW
YORK PUBLIC LIBRARY)

serves a prison sentence, is released, and becomes the toast of New York, operating the elegant Hoffman House, a watering hole for the famous, until his death in 1901.... John Bender, his wife, son, and voluptuous daughter, Kate, who is known as a self-styled healer and spiritualist, settle in a remote spot near Cherryvale, Kansas, establishing an inn. For two years, travelers stopping at the inn, persuaded to stay the night by the sexy Kate, have their evening dinner while sitting on a bench, their backs to a canvas wall. While Mrs. Bender and Kate wait upon the visitors, John Bender and his son wield sledge hammers against the heads of the guests pressed against the canvas, killing them. They steal their guests' money and then crush their bodies beyond recognition before burying them on the prairie. Suspicious lawmen searching for dozens of missing strangers in the area close in a year later but the "Bloody Benders" as they came to be labeled, have disappeared. Eleven bodies are unearthed about the one-story frame inn, which is taken down by angry residents board by board; the Benders are never found.... Near Oak Lake, Minnesota, Bobolink and some other Chippewa renegades invade the log-cabin home of John Cook on April 26, 1871, killing him, his wife, Deantha, and their three children, hacking their bodies to pieces, looting the house and then burning it to the ground. Bobolink is later apprehended, tried and found guilty of murder. He stoically states that he will give his last war whoop from the gallows but never has the chance, conveniently dying in his prison cell of "consumption." Most suspect the Indian has been murdered but proof cannot be obtained since the sheriff buries the killer in an unmarked grave "to prevent the spreading of the disease." ... Enoch F. Spann, a farmer in Preston, Georgia, falls in love with the hired girl, Susan Eberhardt. Both plot the murder of Spann's wife for six weeks. They strangle her while she sleeps on May 5, 1872, Spann tightening a rope around her neck, Susan stuffing a handkerchief into her mouth to prevent her from screaming. Both then flee to Alabama but are returned by a Georgia sheriff. Susan details the crime. A jury of Georgia farmers convicts and condemns both, the foreman rustically recommending to the judge that "Spann die like his wife—with a rope around his neck!" He does.... Franklin B. Evans rapes and kills Georgianna Lovering at Northwood, New Hampshire, on October 25, 1872, hiding the body in some woods. The local sheriff, knowing Evans' history of sexual perversion, suspects he is involved with the missing girl and gets Evans drunk, telling him that if he will show him the spot where the girl's body is buried, he will help him escape to Canada. Evans takes the sheriff to the shallow grave. "Now will you show me the way to get out of this?" asks Evans. "Yes," replies the sheriff, "straight to the hangman, you son-of-a-bitch!" Evans is executed.

The lethal Bender Inn outside Cherryvale, Kansas, where mass murder, as depicted here, was committed by the Bender family in 1872. (TRIPLETT'S "HISTORY, ROMANCE AND PHILOSOPHY OF GREAT AMERICAN CRIMES")

The pulchritudinous Kate Bender giving one of her famous lectures on Spiritualism. (TRIPLETT'S "HISTORY, ROMANCE AND PHILOSOPHY OF GREAT AMERICAN CRIMES")

Frank H. Walworth visits his father in a New York City hotel and shoots him to death, murmuring only to arresting officers: "He mistreated my mother." He is sent to Sing Sing for life. . . . On the night of January 25, 1873, Michael Nixon, in an attempted holdup, sends a bullet into Charles H. Phifer as his victim lounges at the corner of Catherine Street and Bowery. Nixon is hanged May 16, 1873. . . . Ne'er-do-well Charles Mortimer, drinking with his mistress in a Sacramento, California, saloon owned by Mary Gibson, tries to get the proprietress drunk to steal her money. She screams and Mortimer slits her throat. He is hanged May 15, 1873. . . . A disgruntled, unemployed fisherman, Louis Wagner, on March 5, 1873, rows a small boat to the island of Smutty Nose off Portsmouth, New Hampshire, and there chops to pieces Anethe M. Christensen, the wife of his former employer, before ransacking Christensen's home in search of money. The discovery of Mrs. Christensen's body by her husband is thusly described by a contemporary account: "There upon the floor, naked, stiff and stark, is the woman he idolizes . . . stone dead! Dead—horribly butchered! Her bright hair is stiff with blood, the fair head that had so often rested on his breast crushed, cloven, mangled with the brutal axe!" Wagner is found in disguise, and in possession of some of Mrs. Christensen's trinkets. He is found guilty and sentenced to the gallows. A newspaper quotes Wagner bellowing from behind bars: "If de beoples put Louis Wagner on de gallows mit der rope arount his neck, Gott will yet save him. It cannot be oderwise." Wagner is hanged on June 25, 1875, along with John True Gordon, who has murdered three persons, these being the last executions ever held in Maine. . . . William E. Udderzook of Baltimore concocts an insurance swindle wherein his brother-in-law, W. S. Goss, pretends to have perished in his home, which Udderzook torches. When insurance detectives conclude that Goss is still alive, Udderzook murders Goss and buries him in a shallow grave outside Chester, Pennsylvania. The killer is quickly caught and hanged. . . . Emil Lowenstein lures businessman John D. Weston from Brooklyn to West Albany, New York, in a bogus deal, trapping him inside a rooming house where he shoots Weston nine times and then cuts his throat to rob him of more than four hundred dollars. Lowenstein is caught spending the money. He is executed in 1874. . . . Nelson E. Wade grows thirsty in his travels and knocks on the door of John and Isabella McBride near Linden, Pennsylvania. The two elderly misers give Wade a glass of milk and then demand a dollar for the drink. Wade, incensed, charges into their home and beats them to death. He then loots the house, finding their horde of more than sixty thousand dollars in gold. Wade is found exchanging the gold for currency some days later and arrested. He is executed. . . . Alfred Packer, a self-styled frontiersman in Colorado, takes five gold-seekers into mountainous regions near the Gunnison River and, when the food runs out, murders and cannibalizes them, stealing their money. He staggers into an Indian Agency in early 1874 where he confesses his deed, but escapes and is not apprehended until 1883 in Lake City, Colorado, where he is convicted of manslaughter—the state had no provisions for murder at the time—and is given forty years in the Colorado Penitentiary. He is released in 1901 and dies near Denver, Colorado, on April 24, 1907. . . . Sexton Thomas Piper, using his church as a base of operations, begins a murder campaign that terrorizes Boston for two years. (page 92)

1874

John Goodman argues with John Haywood in a business transaction in Sugar Creek, Ohio, on April 8, 1874. Goodman shoots Haywood and then Haywood's wife, Susan, to eliminate any witnesses. When he hides Mrs. Haywood's body in a nearby river, he is seen and later arrested. Goodman is executed December 30, 1874. . . . Daniel O'Mara and his friend Patrick Irving beat Mrs. O'Mara to death. To conceal the murder they drag the corpse to a railroad near Montrose, Pennsylvania, where they place the cadaver on the tracks. A train later severs the body's right arm but investigators follow the trail of blood from the tracks back to O'Mara's front door. He and Irving are arrested and condemned after a speedy trial. . . . A customer of prostitute Ann Freeze in Rutland, Vermont, John P. Phair, noticing her small savings and meager jewelry, jumps from Ann's bed and slits her throat. He is located in Boston some weeks later, selling jewelry known to belong to Ann Freeze. Through legal battles, Phair manages to stay alive for another five years, not executed until 1879. . . . After almost killing another small boy, Jesse H. Pomeroy, a vicious sadist, does kill four-year-old Horace Millen in Boston. He waits for police at the murder scene and proudly tells them that he has also murdered one Katie Curran, a nine-year-old girl, leading them to her buried body. Pomeroy's death sentence is commuted, after two years of waiting for the gallows, to life imprisonment. He serves fifty-two years in prison before dying in 1932, a record of American confinement. . . . William Westervelt, a Broadway tout and one-time cop, engineers the kidnapping of Charles Brewster "Charley" Ross from his Germantown, Pennsylvania, home on July 1, 1874, by two thugs, Joseph Douglass and William Mosher, both later killed in a Brooklyn burglary. Though Westervelt is tracked down and arrested for the first sensational kidnapping in U.S. history, the boy is never found, most believing that Westervelt has drowned him in New York's East River. The kidnapper is given seven years and utterly vanishes upon his release. . . . Joseph LaPage, a French-Canadian lumberjack, kills and mutilates

Marietta Ball, a schoolteacher in St. Albans, Vermont, in late 1874. He is not captured until the following year, when he crushes the skull of a student, seventeen-year-old Josie Langmaid, dragging her body into some woods near Pembroke, New Hampshire, where he mutilates and then sexually attacks the corpse. This necrophiliac killer, the first in the records of American homicide, is hanged in 1875.

1875

In St. Louis, police investigating reports of mass murder enter the home of Julia Fortmeyer, a secret abortionist. They find the corpse of Sarah Beehler's infant daughter and at least two other bodies in the house. A stove yields dozens of human bones. Ms. Fortmeyer is convicted of manslaughter and sent to prison for five years. . . . Blasius Pistorius migrates from Germany to Norristown, Pennsylvania, living in the United States for a little more than a month. He begins shouting at another farmer, Isaac Jaquette, who has driven his cows to drink from the same stream where Pistorius is watering his cattle. Pistorius orders Jaquette to move his cattle to another watering place. Jaquette laughs a refusal. Pistorius draws a pistol and shoots his neighbor dead in sight of a passing farmhand. The killer is hanged. . . . Lusting after his cousin Sara Alexander, a twenty-year-old married woman five months pregnant, Pasach N. Rubenstein inveigles the woman to a secluded rural spot in New Lots (Brooklyn), New York, on the night of December 12, 1875. He attempts to rape her but when she resists, Rubenstein stabs her to death. Detectives discovering the body hours later track the killer through his footprints in the snow. He is convicted and condemned on January 31, 1876, but dies in his cell of illness weeks later. The anti-Semitic propaganda in this case is rampant. One account banners the headline: "The murdered Jewess, being the life, trial and conviction of Rubenstein, the Polish Jew."

1876

On the night of February 15, 1876, John Eli Cannaday, alias John Sneedom, hearing that Marcus Louis of Holly Springs, Mississippi, has secreted a fortune of gold in his home, crushes the old man's head with an axe. Cannaday finds only two dollars and is quickly apprehended. He is hanged on May 24, 1876, in Holly Springs. . . . Intending to rob his parents, Allen C. Laros of North Hampton, Pennsylvania, slips four-and-a-half ounces of arsenic into the family coffeepot. The deadly brew kills his mother and father, and a farm worker; his two brothers and two sisters are also stricken but recover.

Laros, a twenty-two-year-old teacher, filches more than three hundred dollars from his father's coffers and flees. He is apprehended and tried, his lawyer pleading epileptic insanity, which is ignored by the jury. The avaricious schoolteacher is condemned. . . . Panderer William W. Lee, whose bordello in East Burlington, Illinois, is the local scandal, becomes incensed when one of his trollops, Jessie McCarty, takes to drink in lieu of performing her sexual duties. He beats her to death in front of several customers. Lee is hanged.

1877

Frank Yost, a Tamaqua, Pennsylvania, policeman, is shot to death in his bed next to his hysterical wife by a band of home invaders who steal nothing. John Jones, a mine owner, is killed under similar circumstances days later. Working under cover as a Pinkerton detective, James McParlan discovers that these murders and others are the acts of a secret society known as the Molly Maguires, an all-Irish terrorist group based in the fields of Pennsylvania intent on controlling workers and profits from the coal mines (albeit loftily designed to improve the horrendous conditions under which the miners work). Thanks to

A group of Molly Maguires being led to the gallows for execution in 1878.

Nathan W Hart

McParlan's extensive investigations, the Mollies are exposed and dozens are arrested and charged with murder. On June 21, 1877, six Mollies are hanged in Pottsville, Pennsylvania, and four more are executed in Mauch Chunk, Pennsylvania. The ferreting out of Mollies continues for two more years until the last three ringleaders are hanged at Bloomsburg, Pennsylvania, on March 25, 1878, for the killing of Alexander Rea, a mine owner. . . . Freeman Cargin and his wife, along with Norris Alexander and the wife of Charles Smith, form a murder conspiracy to kill Charles Smith to obtain his riches. They hack up Smith on the night of September 13, 1876, in his Saginaw, Michigan, home but their subsequent haggling over the stolen fortune causes leaks to the police. The plot is uncovered. All four murderers are convicted and given life sentences. . . . Perry Bowsher, a resident of Chillicothe, Ohio, has twice been confined to an insane asylum but released. On October 26, 1877, Bowsher passes a tollhouse on the Columbus Pike near Chillicothe and, annoyed by questions put to him by the keepers, Edwin S. and Ann McVay, turns on the elderly couple, slashing them to death. Bowsher then steals their collection money but is quickly captured, his clothes soaked with the blood of his victims. The lunatic is hanged. . . . The residents of Tenants Harbor, Maine, last see Mrs. Sarah Meservey, a recluse, on December 22, 1877, and for five weeks do not check on the elderly woman. She is finally discovered dead in her home, strangled to death. Oddly, Captain Nathan Hart, the town eccentric, tells several persons *before* the discovery of the body about having had a dream in which he saw Mrs. Meservey murdered. Hart is arrested and tried. Deacon Robert Long testifies that "Mr. Hart said that he had dreamed that Wainwright [Seth Wainwright, a Negro handyman in the town] had strangled Mrs. Meservey who fell dead in his arms." Vinal Wall's testimony is even more damaging: "He [Hart] told me of the murder—he told me how the hands were tied, and said the cloud [scarf] was wound three times around the neck and tied in a square knot." Such lucid dreams retold to neighbors on the morning of the discovery seal Hart's fate; he is convicted and sent to prison for life.

1878

Businessman Benjamin F. Hunter loses a seven-thousand-dollar investment in a music publishing firm owned by John M. Armstrong. Hunter's scheme for recouping his loss is to take out a twenty-six-thousand-dollar insurance policy on Armstrong's life. He then lures Armstrong, with the help of his paid accomplice, Tom Graham, to a secret rendezvous in Camden, New Jersey, where he crushes Armstrong's head with an axe on which Hunter has scratched the initials of another man to throw off suspicion. However, Armstrong recovers

*The hanging by hand
of Benjamin F.
Hunter, New Jersey
murderer.*

from the attack, and, hearing this, Hunter visits his home in the guise
of a doctor; he rips away his victim's bandages and causes his death.
Graham is arrested by police as a suspect and immediately confesses.
Hunter is speedily convicted and hanged, spectacularly executed by
hand. . . . Despairing of ever marrying Catherine Dunsbach, rejected
suitor Hilaire Latrimouille sneaks into the woman's Watervliet, New
York, house and cuts her throat while she sleeps. He is found with the
bloody knife a short while later. Latrimouille is hanged. . . . The son
of slaves, John Ten Eyck robs the Sheffield, Massachusetts, home of
David Stillman, killing Stillman and his wife in the process. He is
discovered some days later when trying to buy some hair dye to disguise his appearance. Ten Eyck is condemned. . . . Myron Buel of
Plainfield, New York, lusts after his buxom farm neighbor, Catherine

361

Mary Richards; he rapes her while she is milking cows on June 25, 1878, and then crushes her head with the milking stool, throwing her body into a bull pen to make it appear that the bull has crushed her. Friends to whom Buel has confided his desires inform on him. He is hanged. . . . After Narcissa Canart steals the affections of her husband, Kate Southern of Picken, Georgia, stabs her rival to death. Says one of Kate's defenders: "She was maddened to insanity by the outrageous taunts of a bad woman who had enticed her husband away." Though sentenced to death, it is learned that Mrs. Southern is pregnant; her sentence is commuted by Governor Colquit to life imprisonment. . . . James Madison Stone, on the night of October 5, 1878, breaks into the Washington, D.C., home of his estranged wife, Alberta, and slashes the throat of his sister-in-law, Lavinia Pitcher. He runs raving to the street where neighbors take away the bloody razor from his hand. He later tells police that Lavinia has wrecked his marriage. Stone's execution is the last public hanging in Washington, and a grisly one at that; he is decapitated by the weight of his enormous body as he falls through the trap. . . . Five lumberjacks working in Union Township, Pennsylvania, decide that their incomes must be increased and to that end they insure the life of eighty-year-old Joseph Raber, the local recluse, for thirty thousand dollars, naming themselves—Franklin Stichler, Josiah Hummel, Israel Brandt, Charlie Drews, and Henry F. Wise—as the beneficiaries. They next lure the old man to Indiantown Creek on December 7, 1878, where they drown him. They are all arrested when attempting to collect the insurance money and subsequently hang en masse. . . .

1879

Religious fanatic Charles F. Freeman of Pocasset, Massachusetts, slays his little daughter, Edith, as an offering to God, telling authorities later that "she is a sacrifice like the child of Abraham." The "Second Adventist" is sent to jail for life. . . . Stephen Lee Richards, known as the "Nebraska Fiend," chalks up at least nine murders in the Lincoln, Nebraska, area before reaching age twenty-three. He is condemned for slaughtering the Harlson family of five near Minden, Nebraska. He is hanged on April 26, 1879. . . . Negro Chastine Cox embarks upon a life of crime by breaking into the Manhattan home of Mrs. Jane L. DeForest on the night of June 11, 1879. When Mrs. DeForest enters a room he is ransacking, Cox first gags, then strangles her to death. He is caught fleeing from the house. Cox is hanged on July 16, 1880. . . . Edward Parr is imprisoned in Philadelphia for beating his daughter, Susan Irwin, threatening loudly from his cell that he will kill her upon his release, which he does. Parr is hanged. . . . A self-styled Richmond, Virginia, cavalier, John E. Poindexter, is enraged when an acquaintance, Miss Isabel Cottell, informs him that a shoe clerk, one Charles E. Curtis, has insulted her as she tried on a pair of shoes, telling her that her feet are "too big." To avenge this "insult to Southern womanhood," Poindexter runs to the shoe store and horsewhips Curtis into an apology. Recovering from the shock, Curtis races after Poindexter, attempting to cane him, but Poindexter is too fast for him, pulling forth a pistol and shooting the shoe clerk dead with five shots. Poindexter is convicted of manslaughter.

1880

His relationship with his mistress gone sour, Augustus D. Leighton, a Negro, argues with Mary Dean in front of their Manhattan home on the night of June 13, 1880. She orders him out of the building. "I want my coat," he insists. "You can't have it," she shouts. "By God, I will have it," Leighton screams and slashes her throat in front of dozens of witnesses. He is hanged for murder in the Tombs, May 19, 1882.

1881

William Sindram, a printer, creates several disturbances in the New York City boardinghouse of Catharine Craves and is thrown out by the landlady. He returns on the night of January 25, 1881; Mrs. Craves calls down to Sindram, asking him what he wants. "Come downstairs and I'll show you what I want," Sindram answers. As Mrs. Craves walks down the staircase, Sindram pulls forth a pistol and shoots her. He is convicted and sentenced to die on the gallows, April 21, 1882. Sindram is totally indifferent to his fate, yawning in the hangman's face when asked for his final words. . . . Dr. Thomas Neill Cream, already suspected of several earlier murders, doses one of his Chicago patients, a Miss Stack, with strychnine but outwits police in his budding career as one of this century's strangest mass murderers. (page 94) . . . Dr. P. H. Talbott of Maryville, Missouri, is despised by his family for his rigid ways. As he stands with his son Albert in a bedroom, his other son, Charles, shoots him with a rifle through the window. A detective later earns the confidence of the sons, who tell him how they have murdered their father. Albert and Charles Talbott are hanged. . . . Thinking her lover, wealthy businessman Charles Stiles, is about to leave her, Theressa Sturla orders a candlelight dinner in her luxurious suite in Chicago's Palmer House on the night of July 10, 1882. As Stiles lifts a glass of champagne in toast to her, Theressa shoots the startled paramour through the throat, killing him. She is given a life sentence. . . . Disgruntled office-seeker and religious fanatic Charles Julius Guiteau shoots President James A. Garfield on

Charles Julius Guiteau shooting President Garfield in a Washington, D.C., train station, July 1, 1881. (HARPER'S WEEKLY)

July 1, 1881, as the President enters the Baltimore & Potomac train station in Washington. Garfield dies two months later. Guiteau, in a weird trial in which he acts as his own attorney—cursing both judge and jury—is convicted and sentenced to death. He is hanged on June 30, 1882, after delivering from the gallows a song he has composed while in prison, the first words of which are "I am going to the Lordy." . . . On December 9, 1881, Pasquale Majone, a Manhattan resident, accuses his wife of having affairs with other men. When she denies the accusations, Majone shoots her in the head; her mother, Maria Velindino Selta, rushes into the family kitchen and Majone shoots her, too. Mrs. Majone recovers; the mother-in-law dies of her wounds. Majone is hanged on March 9, 1883. . . . On December 24, 1881, George Ellis, William Neal, and Ellis Craft invade the Ashland,

Kentucky, home of the Gibbons family, raping Fanny and Emma Gibbons, then killing them and their brother, Robbie, with crowbars and axes. They burn the house to hide the crime but are caught with stolen loot some days later and are summarily tried and hanged.

1882

On January 10, 1882, Oscar F. Beckwith has a business disagreement with Simon A. Vandercook in Austerlitz, New York. Beckwith solves the argument by strangling Vandercook and then chopping up his body, burying pieces separately. He is revealed as the murderer when some parts of Vandercook's body, kept by the murderer as "souvenirs," are found in his home. Beckwith is hanged. . . . Two brothers gone wrong, Frank and Henry Rumberger, kill Dan Troutman, an elderly farmer they are attempting to rob near Uniontown, Pennsylvania. They are apprehended selling the farmer's equipment and quickly condemned. . . . Edward Hovey of Manhattan cannot stand the way his sister-in-law criticizes his table manners and shoots her dead over dinner on April 26, 1882. He is executed in the Tombs, October 19, 1883. . . . After poisoning her husband in late 1882, Sarah Jane Robinson poisons her sister, Annie, Annie's husband, Arthur Freeman, and then three of her own children in the Boston area. She is caught when suspicious neighbors demand autopsies and arsenic is discovered. Sarah Robinson is sent to prison for life, dying in her cell in 1905.

1883

William Fox of Nevada, Missouri, has been insulted by J. W. Howard and takes revenge by shooting Howard in the back as he passes in the street on May 20, 1883. Though he tries to commit suicide by chewing matchtops in his cell, Fox survives to hang on December 28, 1883. . . . The town idiot of Laconia, New Hampshire, Thomas Salmon, wanders into the home of James Ruddy, killing Ruddy, his wife and child with an axe, then burning down the house. Police find Salmon dancing about the embers and laughing hysterically. He is sent to prison for life.

1884

Dr. L. U. Beach of Altoona, Pennsylvania, tires of his wife and, after she falls asleep, he drugs her and then dissects her body. Parts of Mrs. Beach's body are later found and the sloppy surgeon is tried and sentenced to death.... Fifteen-year-old Ella Watson of Yorketown, New Jersey, is raped and murdered. Howard Sullivan, a Negro youth, is suspected and held in jail where a black detective, working undercover as a prisoner, obtains a confession from Sullivan, who is later hanged.... Maria Williams, a black prostitute in Manhattan, gives up one lover and becomes mistress to Miguel Chacon, a Cuban Negro. When Maria, on the night of June 20, 1884, decides to return to her original lover, Chacon begs her not to leave him and then shoots her dead in frustration. He attempts to kill the previous lover but is interrupted by police. Chacon goes into hiding but, for the sake of the Cuban community living in New York, "Niazza," leader of the Cuban Revolutionary Society, turns the killer in to police. Chacon is hanged on July 9, 1886.... A Finnish immigrant, John Waisenen, gets drunk; then, with an unknown accomplice, he breaks into the Duluth, Minnesota, home of Joseph Farley, robbing it and killing Farley when he tries to stop them. Waisenen is caught setting fire to Farley's home and with thirty dollars in his pockets, money filched from the victim. The accomplice escapes, but Waisenen is hanged on August 28, 1885, in Duluth, Minnesota, spectators about the gallows sickened when the condemned man's face and hands turn blue as he is slowly strangled by the rope.

1885

Fannie Lilian Madison of Richmond, Virginia, is found floating in a reservoir on March 14, 1885. A check by detectives of her room in a local hotel where she has registered under a different name reveals a slip of paper on which are the initials "TJC." A watch key found at the murder site is traced through local jewelers as belonging to Thomas J. Cluverius, son of a wealthy Virginia family. It is learned that Cluverius has murdered Fannie to keep their marriage a secret. Denying his guilt to the last, Cluverius is condemned and hanged on November 20, 1885.... Charles H. Ruggs, while robbing their Oyster Bay, New York, home, strangles Annie and Lydia Maybee to death. He is later apprehended following another murder and hanged in Queens late in 1885.... Filippo Caruso of Chicago is slaughtered by his closest friends on April 30, 1885 and shipped via trunk to Pittsburgh. (page 118)... W. H. Maxwell, son of an esteemed British family, meets well-to-do C. Arthur Preller in a St. Louis hotel and plots his murder. (page 120)... Maria Barberi slashes her lover to death in a New York bar in early 1885; her ensuing trial is a sensational circus. (page 122)... Henry K. Goodwin, thinking Albert D. Swan is about to steal his telephone patents, shoots Swan in his Lawrence, Massachusetts, office. Goodwin is convicted of second-degree murder and sent to prison.

1886

Betran Bellesford of Creede, Colorado, a prospector, returns to his claim to find George "Crazy" Harris a permanent occupant. Bellesford tells him: "You can go or stay." Harris snorts: "I'll stay," whereupon Bellesford shoots him and returns his body to Creede, telling authorities he was merely protecting his claim. Bellesford is tried for murder but given a light prison sentence.

1887

Killer of dozens of women, mass-murderer Johann Otto Hoch continues his murder-for-profit career in the United States. (page 125) . . . Suspected of several earlier murders, drunken strong-arm tough Tommy Newhouse of New Orleans attacks another roughneck, George Maloney, in a Poydras-Prieur district saloon. The two battle for almost an hour, Maloney using his own wooden leg as a club. Newhouse, with scores watching, finally strangles his opponent to death. Police watching the fight are compelled by citizens to arrest Newhouse, who is convicted of murder and sent to prison for twenty years. . . . John W. Wilson is hanged for murdering Anthony W. Dealy, his employer. Wilson admits to authorities in Chestnut Hill, Pennsylvania that he has murdered Dealy because he would not pay him his wages. Since the ground is frozen at the time of the killing, Wilson explains, he could not bury the corpse, nor could he carry it any great distance as he weighs only a hundred pounds (standing five-feet-two-inches tall), so he was compelled to chop up his victim and distribute the remains piece by piece into a river, where he has been caught in the act. . . . On May 27, 1887, Nels Olson Holong, thinking Lilly Field, the daughter of his employer in Fergus Falls, Minnesota, has slighted him, attacks the fifteen-year-old, committing, according to one account, "one of the most revolting murders in Minnesota history by cutting the girl's throat, slitting her corpse open as a butcher would an animal carcass, and throwing the body to the hogs." Lynch mobs almost snatch Holong from the sheriff before he is hanged on April 13, 1888. . . . Three Minneapolis delinquents, Henry, Peter and Timothy Barrett, hold up a horse-drawn streetcar on July 27, 1887, shooting the conductor and fleeing with twenty dollars. Henry informs on his brothers for amnesty; Peter and Timothy Barrett are hanged together on March 22, 1889. Their parents, owners of a notorious saloon called the "Hub of Hell," do not attend the executions.

1888

John Gibson, a political hack, and special policeman Louis Clare of New Orleans decide to rid themselves of Commissioner Mealey who has been interfering in their rackets. They shoot him to death on January 1, 1888, and are sent to prison for life.... Two days later, Thomas J. Ford, Recorder for New Orleans, eliminates his political rival Cap Murphy by having two assassins shoot Murphy in front of his employees. The killers, John Murphy and Patrick Ford, are hanged.... On July 19, 1888, John Lee and his friend Martin Moe emerge from a saloon in Brandon, Minnesota, spotting Charles Cheline walking in the moonlight. Lee, who has been vying with Cheline for the attentions of one Sophia Mathieson, grabs a pistol at Moe's urgings and shoots Cheline in the head. Both Lee and Moe are condemned but Moe is reprieved as the two men begin walking toward the gallows on February 5, 1889 in Alexandria, Minnesota. Lee is hanged after telling the assembled throng that he is going "to a better place."

1889

Pharmacist Irving Latimer, with a successful practice in Jackson, Michigan, murders his mother on January 24, 1889, to obtain her vast estate but is apprehended days later, his shirt splattered with his mother's blood. He is convicted by a jury twenty minutes after hearing the evidence and is sent to prison for life, paroled in 1935 and dying in 1946.... New Orleans is rocked on January 30, 1889, when Dr. Etienne Deschamps, a self-styled faith healer, espousing the miracles of "magnetic physiology," is found naked in his offices, next to the body of Juliette Deitsch, the teenage daughter of the doctor's most ardent patient, Jules Deitsch, a carpenter. Officials soon realize that the doctor has had sex with the child and has then chloroformed her to death before attempting suicide. He is hanged on May 12, 1892, lavishing curses upon the city coroner, LeMonnier, who has opposed the medical commission's labeling Deschamps insane. The doctor spits from the scaffold: "I am innocent! LeMonnier is the criminal! Adieu!" ... On February 2, 1889, the body of a working girl, Annie Klaus, is found in a snowswept Philadelphia street. She has been shot twice in the head. After interviewing Annie's father, a shoemaker, and several sisters and friends, detective Frank Geyer, who is later to be instrumental in trapping the arch-mass-murderer Herman Webster Mudgett (H. H. Holmes), determines that a streetcar conductor admired by Annie Klaus—she has waited for his car every night on her way home from work—is the likely killer. Within ten hours of the murder, Geyer tracks the man down to his residence; he is Otto Kayser, an albino with white hair and pink eyes. As Heyer enters Kayser's home, the killer's wife emerges, carrying her child, screaming. Her throat has been cut from ear to ear. Detective Geyer dashes up the stairs and breaks into a bedroom just as Kayser leaps upon the bed, slashing his own throat in a bloody suicide. . . . William Brooker grabs a shotgun on the night of November 2, 1889, and marches to the house of Mrs. William P. Coombs in Pine City, Minnesota, where his wife has taken refuge after a violent argument. Mrs. Coombs, who is Mrs. Brooker's sister, hurls insults at Brooker from a second-story window when the enraged husband arrives. Brooker levels his shotgun at her and fires. William Coombs races to the window and he, too, is shot by Brooker, who calmly walks to a neighbor's house and confesses the double shooting, claiming self-defense. He is condemned and is hanged after snorting down a shot of whiskey and taking a long puff on an imported cigar. . . . On September 21, 1889, William Seely Hopkins of Philipsburg, Pennsylvania, can no longer endure the scathing attacks of his mother-in-law or the fact that his wife constantly cuckolds him in the dark parlor of his own home; he shoots both women to death. He turns the gun on himself but only manages to wound himself slightly. Hopkins is hanged at Bellefonte, Pennsylvania, on February 20, 1890. . . . Mrs. George Weidler returns from visiting her physician, Dr. Edward Duggan, angrily telling her spouse that, according to Dr. Duggan, Weidler has given her venereal disease. Weidler explodes, racing to the doctor's office with gun in hand and shooting the physician dead. Weidler is found guilty in Brooklyn, New York, and given a long prison term. . . . Roxana Druse of Little Falls, New York, prepares the laborious murder of her husband. (page 129)

1890

In January 1890, Felix Kampf, nearly *non compos mentis*, suddenly turns on his son, age nineteen, and his daughter, age twenty, and stabs them to death for not bringing his dinner on time. He is hanged in Charlestown, West Virginia, on March 7, 1890. . . . The Washington correspondent for the *Louisville Times*, Charles E. Kinkaid, is fired when ex-congressman from Kentucky William F. Taulbee uses his influence after being attacked in Kinkaid's editorials. The journalist, on February 28, 1890, encounters Taulbee on the Capitol stairs and shoots him in the eye, then dances a wild jig around his prostrate victim. He is convicted of murder and sent to prison for life. . . . Charles P. Buchanan murders a woman named Murphy in New York on April 22, 1890; he remains at large until revealing his crime in correspondence to fellow printers. Buchanan is arrested and convicted, sent to prison for life. . . . The incongruously named Nicely Brothers, Joseph and David, visit Herman Umberger's farm outside Jennertown, Pennsylvania, and, as a ruse to look for the farmer's hoarded money, tell Umberger they are deputy sheriffs with a search warrant looking for stolen property. After uncovering the farmer's twenty thousand dollars, they shoot the old man and flee, but are caught days later with the money. Both are hanged.

1891

Clamdiggers uncover the body of a German immigrant, Carl Emmanuel Ruttinger, off Staten Island on March 13, 1891. The cause of his death is easily determined—he has been choked to death. Officials find a handkerchief stuffed down his throat with the initials "WW" on it, these corresponding to William Wright, the police learn, the victim's brother-in-law. Wright is soon found in the Astor House, a suicide. The motive: Ruttinger had decided to cast off his homosexual relationship with his brother-in-law and was murdered by the frustrated Wright, who then took his own life. . . . One-time widow of an upstanding captain in Salem, Massachusetts, a sixty-year-old prostitute known as "Old Shakespeare" is found brutally slashed to pieces along the New York waterfront. Many feel, with the press providing suggestive details, that Jack the Ripper has taken ship to continue his grisly career in the United States, but authorities soon arrest a flamboyant Algerian named Ameer Ben Ali. The strongest point made by the State at Ali's trial is that the suspect, also called "Frenchy," has been thoroughly examined when arrested and that "human gore" has been scraped from under his fingernails; he is convicted of second-degree murder and is sent to prison, but later pardoned. . . . Dr. John P. Baker of Abingdon, Virginia, has an ailing wife. To cure her illness, Baker gives her arsenic—"as a tonic," he later tries to explain, when charged with murder. Baker is sent to prison. . . . On March 22, 1891, Adelbert Goheen of Fergus Falls, Minnesota, shoots his lover, Rosetta Bray, having fallen in love with another. Condemned, Goheen takes time out briefly from playing his accordion and writing maudlin poetry to curse his jailers; he is hanged on October 23, 1891, shouting with bravado to the executioner: "Let her go, Jack! Goodbye!" . . . In the first case of morphine poisoning before the New York courts, young Dr. Carlyle Harris poisons his secret wife, Mary Helen Neilson Potts, cleverly giving her a box of six pills, only one of which—the last she is to take—he has injected with poison because she was "a rope around" his neck. Harris is convicted and sent to the electric chair, February 9, 1892, protesting his innocence to the last. . . . Dr. Thomas Thatcher Graves of Providence, Rhode Island, seeks to steal the estate of wealthy Mrs. Josephine Barnaby, of which he is the executor, by sending Mrs. Barnaby a bottle of whiskey in Denver where the heiress is visiting. She and a Denver friend, a Mrs. Worrell, drink the whiskey and die. Graves' poisonous gift is traced when he is identified by a man who has mailed the package for him. Graves is condemned but commits suicide by taking poison in his cell in April, 1893. . . . Frank Almy, a burglar attempting to reform, is rejected by Christie Warden of Hanover, New Hampshire, and, in a rage, strangles her on July 17, 1891. He is captured six months later still hiding in the Warden barn. He is condemned.

1892

Dr. Robert Buckanan of New York plots the perfect murder of his wife, a rich one-time bordello madam of whom Buckanan once stated: "Her face is enough to drive a man to drink." (page 133) . . . New Orleans fight promoter Jack Lyons stages a match, which policeman John Hurley breaks up, boxing bouts then being illegal in the city. Lyons loses all control and shoots Hurley in front of hundreds of spectators. He is sent to prison for life.

1893

Capping a long dispute, Robert M. Bean and Samuel Hagar conduct a slugfest down two busy blocks in Nashville, Tennessee. Bean finally pulls a revolver and shoots Hagar five times, his victim staggering another full block before collapsing dead. "I was nothing but a peacemaker," Bean tells his jurors, but he is convicted of second-degree murder and sent to prison for twenty years. . . . Julia Force, a member of one of Atlanta's most prestigious families, is an insane Southern belle who, on February 25, 1893, shoots her sister Minnie for humming too loud and then kills her other sister, Florence, an invalid. She turns herself in and is sent to prison for life. . . . Will Buckley, a Negro farmer living outside Columbia, Mississippi, is shot and killed by nightriders calling themselves the White Caps (a version of the Ku Klux Klan). The victim's brother, hiding in the bushes, identifies the killer as Will Purvis, a local youth, who is convicted and condemned. Purvis' hanging on February 7, 1894 is botched, however, the noose twice breaking, which is interpreted by the assembled crowd as a sign from On High; Purvis is taken back to prison and is pardoned on December 19, 1898. Nineteen years later, a Mississippi planter named Joe Beard, who had been converted to the Holy Rollers before taking to his deathbed, admits with his dying breath that he and a man named Louis Thornhill are the real killers of Buckley. Will Purvis is voted five thousand dollars as compensation for his false

Murder,
America

Diggers in shock as they uncover the skeletal remains of more than two hundred murder victims of the infamous Herman Webster Mudgett in the basement of his "Murder Castle" at 63rd and Wallace streets in Chicago.

imprisonment by the State Legislators. Purvis lives until 1943. . . . Herman Webster Mudgett, alias H. H. Holmes, orders the construction of his "murder castle" in Chicago, to which he lures more than two hundred unsuspecting young females with promises of jobs and marriage, chloroforming them and then dissecting their bodies and burying them in a quicklime pit in the basement of the building at

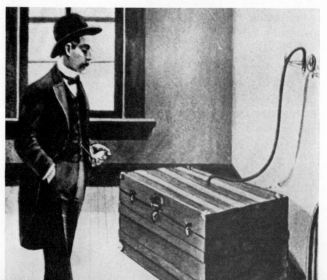

Mudgett, alias "H. H. Holmes," checks his watch to time the asphyxiation of the Pitezel girls.

Sixty-third and Drexel streets in order to obtain their dowries, savings, real estate, stocks. None of these females are missed, all having come to Chicago's World Exposition in 1893 to seek jobs and husbands, most from states bordering Illinois. Holmes becomes America's all-time mass murderer with more than two hundred homicides to his dark credit (these numbers are supported by the human bones later found in his three-story building and assembled by police). After Holmes torches the building and puts in a false insurance claim that causes police to inspect the premises, he flees East, where he murders Benjamin Pitezel and his children in an insurance scheme and is apprehended. He is convicted of the Pitezel murders and admits to killing twenty-seven women in Chicago before his execution stops the litany of death. Holmes is hanged in Philadelphia's Moyamensing Prison on May 7, 1896.

Minneapolis killer Harry T. Hayward, who planned the murder of his fiancée for insurance money in 1894.

1894

Gambler Harry T. Hayward convinces his fiancée, Catherine M. "Kitty" Ging, to insure her life for ten thousand dollars, making him the sole beneficiary. Kitty is then inveigled into taking a moonlit buggy ride with Hayward's partner, Claus Blixt, who puts a bullet into her head at the outskirts of Minneapolis, Minnesota, on December 3, 1894. Before collecting the insurance money, Hayward's scheme is upset by his brother, Adry Hayward, whom he had previously asked to murder Kitty; Adry informs the police of the plan. Blixt, to save his life, also testifies against Hayward, who is convicted and condemned. Hayward asks that the gallows upon which he is to hang be painted a bright fire engine red, his favorite color. His wish is granted. Hayward mounts the scaffold in formal evening dress, his tuxedo impeccable, on December 11, 1895. He casually smokes a cigarette, then adjusts the rope around his neck, suavely telling the executioner: "Pull her tight. I'll stand pat." His neck is not broken as he goes through the trap; Harry Hayward takes several minutes to strangle to death.

Claus Blixt, Hayward's chum, who shot Kitty Ging "as a favor" to Hayward.

Harry Hayward, on the day of his execution, cursing his brother, Adry, who had testified against him.

The trusting and hapless Kitty Ging.

1895

Medical student William Henry Theodore "Theo" Durrant, who is also an assistant Sunday School attendant at San Francisco's Emanuel Baptist Church, attacks attractive Blanche Lamont, a parishioner, inside the church library on April 3, 1895, strangling her to death. He then sexually assaults the body before dragging the corpse to the church belfry. Durrant, on April 13, 1895, next attacks and mutilates Minnie Williams, another churchgoer, strangling her. The victim's screams bring police, who find her body and that of Blanche Lamont.

Sunday school attendant William Henry Theodore "Theo" Durrant dragging the body of his victim, Blanche Lamont, to the belfry of his San Francisco church in 1895.

Parishioners discovering the body of Minnie Williams, another Durrant victim.

Durrant is seized and tried. He is found guilty and sentenced to hang. Appeals delay his execution until January 7, 1898. His oddball parents consume a large roast beef dinner as they sit in the prison death room waiting for the mortician, their son's exposed body, with blackened face and protruding tongue, only feet from their dinner table. . . . Reverend W. E. Hinshaw of Bellville, Indiana, is found wounded by neighbors responding to a disturbance in his house; his wife is found shot through the head. Hinshaw claims robbers have done the deed until one of his flock recalls the Reverend's recent sermon, entitled "A Man's Life Is Not Always in Obeying the Laws that Exist." When accused of killing his wife, Hinshaw mounts the pulpit and defends himself in spirited oratory but he is tried all the same, found guilty, and sent to prison for murder.

Durrant shortly before his execution.

375

William Tayler, a banker, lawyer and one-time state legislator, is charged with receiving stolen cattle outside of Kansas City, Missouri. Gus Meeks is to be a witness against him in court. Tayler and his brother, George, invade the home of the Meeks family, slaughtering Meeks, his wife, and three children. A fourth Meeks child jumps from a window and escapes to tell authorities of the grisly murders. William and George Tayler are quickly convicted and condemned. Bill Tayler hangs but George escapes, only to be recaptured and executed. . . . Pearl Bryan of Greencastle, Indiana, having had an affair with Scott Jackson, a dental student, is enticed to a wooded area near Fort Thomas, Kentucky, being told an abortion has been prepared for her. Jackson, with the help of a friend, Alonzo M. Walling, drugs Pearl, then decapitates her while she lives, hiding her body in the woods, where it is found only hours later by a small boy. Evidence found on the body leads police to Jackson and Walling who are tried, convicted and hanged. . . . Captain Charles I. Nash and his wife are slaughtered in their cabin as the barkentine *Herbert Fuller* sails the Atlantic. (page 137)

Walling and Jackson, escorting Pearl Bryan into a wooded area near Fort Thomas, Kentucky, where they murdered her.

Sausage-maker Adolph Louis Luetgert (standing) instructs one of his workers to crush potash, later used to dissolve the body of Luetgert's wife.

1897

John O'Neil's repeated advances to Hattie Evelyn McCloud of Shelburne Falls, Massachusetts, are rebuffed; the enraged O'Neil assaults Miss McCloud on a country lane, then strangles her. He is quickly caught and executed. . . . Martin George Thorn moves into the Manhattan roominghouse of Mrs. Augusta Nack, which causes bitter arguments between Thorn and Willis Guldensuppe, another roomer, as both men vie for the landlady's affections. The rancor is ended when Mrs. Nack encourages Thorn, in June 1897, to murder Guldensuppe and hack up his body. Pieces of the corpse are found all about Manhattan, police identifying the body by a tattoo on the torso. Inspection of Mrs. Nack's summer cottage in Woodside, New York, reveals bloodstains in the kitchen, the spot where Thorn has dissected his rival. Arrested and brought to trial, Mrs. Nack promptly takes the stand to describe in horrible detail how Thorn has hacked up her ex-boyfriend. Mrs. Nack receives ten years in prison; Martin George Thorn is sent to the electric chair in Sing Sing. . . . Adolph Louis Luetgert of Chicago wearies of his wife, Louise. To be free to carry on his many love affairs, the sausage-maker kills his wife and attempts to boil her body away in a sausage vat inside his plant. Her teeth and some bones are, however, found days later and Luetgert is sent to prison for life. . . . John Moshik encounters businessman John Lemke in Minneapolis' Union Station, October 22, 1897; luring him to a secluded area, he kills him and steals fourteen dollars. Though shot in the back twice and beaten on the head, Lemke lives long enough to identify his assailant. Moshik is hanged on March 18, 1898, telling the hangman on the scaffold: "You haven't got the rope tight enough about my neck!"

1898

On the night of February 7, 1898, New York housewife Martha Place takes an axe to her husband; she will be the first woman to sit in the electric chair. (page 150) . . . Son of an Army general, thirty-year-old Roland Molineux sends a poisoned bottle of liquor to Henry C. Barnet, fellow member of the exclusive Knickerbocker Athletic Club and rival for the affections of one Blanche Cheeseborough. Barnet dies and Molineux marries Blanche. Some weeks later Molineux sends a bottle of poisoned Bromo Seltzer to Harry Cornish, the athletic director of the club, who has bested him in a weight-lifting contest. Cornish's landlady, Mrs. Katherine Adams, takes the Bromo Seltzer to soothe a headache and dies. The bottle is traced to Molineux. He is convicted and sentenced to death but is released from Sing Sing on a technicality eighteen months later; he dies insane in 1917. . . . John Higgins of Adrian, Michigan, murders Lafayette Ladd, a business competitor. Police, knowing of Higgins' quarrel with Ladd, search Higgins' rooms and find a romance story Higgins has written in which the Ladd murder is outlined in detail; the script is used to convict Higgins, who is sent to prison for life. . . . Joseph Ott of Granite Falls, Minnesota, is condemned for beating his wife to death. Before going through the trapdoor on October 20, 1898, Ott tells a crowd of four hundred spectators: "I bid you all good evening!" . . . San Francisco's Cordelia Botkin sends a box of poisoned candies to the home of John Dunning, her estranged lover, in Dover, Delaware. Mrs. Elizabeth Dunning and her friend Mrs. Joshua Deane eat the bonbons and die. The candy is traced to Cordelia Botkin, who is found guilty and given a life sentence, dying in San Quentin in 1910.

1899

Sam Holt, accused of axing to death a farmer, Alfred Cranford, then raping Mrs. Cranford, is dragged from the Newnan, Georgia, jail by a mob on April 23, 1899. The Negro is slashed, burned with kerosene, and disemboweled alive. None of the two thousand participants in this horrendous mob murder is ever charged. . . . Billy Neufeld, a family friend of Mrs. Anna Kronman, visits with the woman in her New

York apartment on August 7, 1899; seeing her chopping ice, he grabs
the axe and delivers several mortal wounds to the woman, stealing
her jewelry. He is caught trying to pawn the gems. Neufeld is convicted in dazzling speed, a jury taking only twelve minutes to con-
demn him. He is electrocuted in Sing Sing.

1900

Itinerant worker Norman Williams murders Oregon pioneer Alma
Nesbitt and her mother for their possessions in their log cabin home
near Hood River. He is tracked down, tried and hanged. . . . Virginia,
Caroline and Mary Wardlaw, daughters of a distinguished South Carolina family, conspire to murder John Snead—Mary Wardlaw's son—
to obtain twelve thousand dollars in insurance money; they will also
murder Colonel C. Martin, Caroline Wardlaw's husband, poisoning
him for insurance money, and, as late as 1909, starve to death Caroline's daughter, Ocey Martin Snead, also for insurance. Virginia Wardlaw commits suicide in prison, Caroline Wardlaw is sent to an insane
asylum for life and Mary Wardlaw is acquitted of Ocey Snead's murder. . . . Belle Gunness of LaPorte, Indiana, begins her gruesome career of murdering a string of wealthy suitors, poisoning more than a
dozen men, then dissecting their bodies and burying the remains in a
pigpen. She disappears after her house burns in 1908. . . . New York–

*Belle Gunness, mass murderer of
suitors in LaPorte, Indiana,
shown with her children.*

Houston lawyer Albert T. Patrick puts in motion an elaborate murder scheme in his planned takeover of the multimillion-dollar estate of tycoon William Marsh Rice. (page 000) . . . Franz Theodore Wallert takes a butcher knife to his wife and four stepchildren on the night of August 20, 1900; the killer of five is hanged at Gaylord, Minnesota, on March 29, 1901.

1901

Anarchist Leon Czolgosz (pronounced *Cholgosh*) approaches President William McKinley at the Pan-American Exposition in Buffalo, New York, on September 6, 1901, standing in the receiving line. When it comes his turn to shake McKinley's hand, Czolgosz points a .32-caliber Ives-Johnson revolver, hidden by a handkerchief (which he has wrapped about his hand; Secret Service agents standing nearby think the man's hand is injured), at the President's stomach. He fires twice; McKinley dies a few hours later. Guards leap upon the assassin, crashing him to the floor. "I done my duty!" screams Czolgosz. "Who are you?" police ask the killer as he is led away. "Fred Nieman," Czolgosz snickers, "Fred Nobody. Nobody killed the President." Be-

Assassin Leon Czolgosz shooting President McKinley in Buffalo, New York, September 6, 1901.

Czolgosz being electrocuted at Auburn Prison two months after his murder of McKinley while doctors and witnesses stand by.

fore he is led to the electric chair in New York's Auburn Prison on October 29, 1901, it is apparent that Czolgosz has acted alone, the mad murder of a malcontent bitter over his parents' poverty, a singular hater of America who can only repeat: "I thought it would be a good thing for this country to kill the President!"

1902

With an iron tie-weight slung about her neck, the corpse of Mrs. Joseph P. Pulitzer (no relation to the newspaper magnate) is found in a New Jersey ditch near Newark. Police trace the tie-weight, a heavy piece of iron to which the reins of a horse are fastened, by checking all the livery stables in New York. One hired rig has been returned without the weight and this leads officers to the home of William Hooper Young, grandson of Mormon leader Brigham Young, a wastrel long since ousted from the Mormon Church. Young has escaped, traveling to upstate New York, where he moves in the guise of a tramp to avoid detection for several months. He is subsequently identified and arrested. Following a speedy trial he is convicted of murder—an act of outright sadism by his own admission—and is electrocuted.

1903

The thirty-year-old Hargis-Cockrill feud in Kentucky boils over when James B. Marcum, a Cockrill ally, is told that he will be murdered. Marcum, town trustee for Jackson, Kentucky, trustee of the Kentucky State College, a leading lawyer and candidate for the court of appeals, carries his youngest child in his arms for nearly a year, "knowing the assassins would not dare risk killing the child," according to one report. "I am doomed," Marcum tells reporters. "Sooner or later they will kill me. But I will not run away." The marked man relaxes his vigilance on May 4, 1903, walking alone from his home to the court-house in Jackson. As he mounts the steps of the courthouse, Curtis Jett and Tom White, two deputy sheriffs on the side of the Hargis clan, step forth and shoot Marcum to death in broad daylight with scores of horrified citizens looking on. In a rare exception to murders in the Kentucky feuds, Jett and White are convicted and sent to prison for life. . . . Lewis W. Lyons, holding a grudge for eight years—he was locked up under suspicion of robbery but exonerated in 1895—walks into the offices of New Orleans District Attorney J. Ward Gurley on the morning of July 20, 1903, demanding for the umpteenth time that Gurley meet him in a duel in satisfaction for the long-ago arrest. When the District Attorney orders him from his office, Lyons takes out a pistol and shoots Gurley three times. "My God, he is murdering me," cries Gurley to his office staff. "Murder! Murder! He murdered me for nothing." With that, Lyons yanks Gurley from the floor to a standing position and shoots him once more, then dashes out as staff personnel rush inside Gurley's office. Lyons tries to plead insanity but is convicted in two trials. He is sentenced to death. As he walks to the gallows on March 24, 1905, Lyons is told to "be brave" by one of the keepers of the Parish Prison. "There's no dunghill in me," retorts the fifty-five-year-old Lyons. "I'll walk to the gallows as easily as I'll walk through that door." His neck and spine are broken instantaneously as he drops through the trap. . . . Two Croations, angered over being fired from the Ferguson Contracting Company in Pittsburgh, Pennsylvania, blow up a buggy on the night of September 25, 1903, killing its two occupants—Samuel T. Ferguson, an owner of the firm, and book-keeper Charles L. Martin; they take the weekly payroll of thirty-six hundred dollars. Police trace Milovar Kovovick and Milovar Patrovick through an old shotgun left at the scene of the murder. Both have fled to Europe, but U.S. police cable Southampton, England, where they are detained. The killers are escorted back to the U.S. and are convicted of the slayings, Kovovick, who threw the dynamite bomb, according to his own confession, being executed, Patrovick being given twenty years in prison.

1904

Wealthy J. Samuel McCue of Charlottesville, Kentucky, staggers from his thirty-room mansion, his shirt covered with blood, arousing neighbors with the cry: "For God's sake, get help! A burglar just shot Fannie and tried to kill me!" Fannie McCue is found dead in an upstairs bathroom, her head bashed in by a blunt instrument, a bullet in her heart, her body dumped into a tub of scalding water. Local police are baffled by the attack until Albert and William Baldwin, owners of the Baldwin Detective Agency, arrive, summoned by relatives. The Baldwins quickly search the mansion and within days name none other than McCue himself as the killer, pointing out that a burglar would not use McCue's own rifle to kill his wife, that such a professional intruder would carry his own weapon; that the gore-coated baseball bat they find in a hallway closet is McCue's and has been used upon the victim; that the broken window through which McCue insists the burglar has entered has a cobweb that is undisturbed (William Baldwin, in a flamboyant display, hurls himself through the window to prove that the cobweb and a plant on the windowsill would have been destroyed); and that McCue's shirt is covered with not his blood but that of his wife, the smear of blood being only waist high, indicating that he has carried his unconscious wife to the tub and there shot her. Further, the Baldwins rip away a bandage on McCue's head, revealing two tiny scratches—superficial wounds, they prove, that could not have caused him to be rendered unconscious at the time of the murder, as McCue had claimed. McCue is hanged in Charlottesville on January 20, 1905. . . . Charles Louis Tucker visits spinster Mabel Page in her Massachusetts home with sex and murder on his mind. (page 178)

1905

When Mrs. John Keller attempts to break up a homosexual liaison between her sixteen-year-old son, Johnny, a St. Paul, Minnesota, bellboy, and William A. Williams, a twenty-seven-year-old itinerant worker, Williams rushes to the Keller home on April 12, 1905, and shoots both Mrs. Keller and her son. He is the last person to be executed in Minnesota, hanged on February 13, 1906. . . . A union agitator in many mining disputes, Harry Orchard, born Albert E. Horsley, after blowing up and killing twenty-six strike-breaking miners in Cripple Creek, Colorado—at the instigation of labor leader Big Bill Haywood—proceeds to Caldwell, Idaho, and, under direct orders from Haywood, plants a bomb on December 30, 1905, in front of the home of Frank Steunenberg, ex-governor of Idaho, who had been marked by union fanatics for murder because he had once called in federal troops to quell violence by miners. Steunenberg is blown to pieces as he enters the front gate outside his home. Orchard is recognized in the street before he can flee town. His room is found to be a regular bomb factory. Orchard confesses, saying: "I always dreaded to do these murders and usually put them off as long as I could." Orchard is condemned to the gallows but through powerful union influence his sentence is commuted to life in prison.

1906

On March 23, 1906, Emma LeDoux, in order to take on a new lover, gives her protector, Albert N. McVicar, a drink of morphine and chloral, which renders him dizzy enough for Emma to shove him into a trunk and lock the lid. McVicar suffocates inside the airless container. Emma then ships the trunk from San Francisco to Jackson, California. She is traced through a furniture dealer who recalls selling her the trunk. After a quick trial, Emma is found guilty and sentenced to hang; her sentence is finally commuted to life imprisonment. The plotting murderess dies in the Tehachapi Women's Prison in July, 1942. . . . George Mitchell, enraged at the psychological hold a self-styled evangelical leader, Joshua II, has over his sister, Esther, and scores of other women in the Corvallis, Washington, area, decides to kill the "mad prophet." Mitchell approaches Joshua II on a Seattle street, puts a pistol to his head and pulls the trigger on May 7, 1906. (page 182) . . . Robert Franklin Stroud, who is to be known as "The Birdman of Alcatraz," slays a bartender in Alaska over a frontier whore; he is sent to prison for manslaughter but murders a guard in Leavenworth's mess hall on March 26, 1916, which guarantees life in prison for "The Birdman." . . . Pittsburgh multimillionaire Harry Kendall Thaw shoots renowned architect Stanford White on June 25, 1906, in front of dozens of theater-goers watching a musical being performed on the roof of Madison Square Garden in New York City. Thaw fires two bullets into White, who dies immediately. Thaw is rushed by police to the Tombs where he explains that he has murdered White because his wife, Evelyn Nesbit, one-time Floradora Girl, had been a sex slave to White before Thaw's marriage to her. Thaw orders catered meals from Delmonico's as he awaits trial in the Tombs. The flamboyant lawyer Delphin Delmas defends Thaw; Wil-

*Millionaire madman Harry K. Thaw sits with his one-time wife and
showgirl Evelyn Nesbit, twenty years after Thaw murdered the brilliant
architect Stanford White.*

liam Travers Jerome, the hard-hitting New York District Attorney,
prosecutes. Delmas advances the theory that Thaw has been stricken
by an attack of "dementia Americana" at the moment he has shot
White, explaining in puzzling methods that such a condition results
from a neurosis peculiar to American males who feel every man's wife
is sacred. The baffled jury accepts the theory and renders a "Not
Guilty" verdict on grounds of insanity. Thaw is sent to the New York
State Asylum for the Criminally Insane at Matteawan, from which he
is released in 1922 to travel around the world as a spectacular playboy,
dying in 1947. . . . Chester Gillette, the nephew of a wealthy factory-
owner in upstate New York, drowns his pregnant girlfriend, Grace
"Billie" Brown, in Big Moose Lake, to cover up his seduction and to
remain free to marry a High Society debutante. The bloody tennis
racket Gillette used to batter Billie Brown unconscious before drown-
ing her is found and is used to trace the youthful killer. Gillette is
found guilty and sentenced to the electric chair, being executed on
December 4, 1906, at Auburn Prison. Author Theodore Dreiser, who
has attended the long Gillette trial, will write his masterpiece, *An
American Tragedy*, from his knowledge of this case.

*Handsome killer of his
sweetheart, Chester
Gillette inspired the
writing of* An American
Tragedy. (UPI)

1907

Walter Lamana, seven-year-old son of wealthy undertaker Peter Lamana of New Orleans, is kidnapped from the entrance of his father's
establishment at 624 St. Philip Street a little after six o'clock in the
evening on June 8, 1907. A ransom note demanding six thousand
dollars in exchange for the boy's life is shortly received by the father.
Peter Lamana rides horseback with the cash in a black satchel to the
outskirts of New Orleans, a secluded area designated for the exchange
by the kidnapper, but no one is there. The kidnapper is frightened off
by the police who follow the unwitting Lamana. Through informers
inside the Italian community, it is learned that a Black Hand ring has
taken the child, whose body is found in a swamp near St. Rose, Louisiana. Ignazio Campisciano, who has led police to the body, informs
authorities that one Angelo Incaratero has strangled the boy, but the
mastermind of the kidnapping is Leonardo Gebbia, who is arrested,
tried and condemned. After long legal maneuvering, Gebbia is led to
the gallows on July 16, 1909. As the noose is placed about Gebbia's
neck, he shouts: "Why ain't they caught the others? How about Tony
Gendusa, Incaratero, Monfre, and Frank Luchesi? [These members
of the kidnap ring are never found.] It's more than two years and they
ain't caught 'em! They never will now, but they're satisfied just so
long as they're hanging me. . . . I told you I was going to be the fall
guy." He hands his half-smoked cigar to the sheriff standing next to
him, who puffs on it as he binds Gebbia's hands. "Do a good job, big
boy," Gebbia tells the hangman. Peter Lamana and a large group of
friends are at the foot of the gallows eating roast beef and drinking
wine as they watch Gebbia go through the trap, his neck breaking
instantly. The rope is removed from the kidnapper and given to Lamana as a souvenir.

1908

Five times married, "Sister" Amy Archer-Gilligan, who has owned
and operated a nursing home in Windsor, Connecticut, draws suspicion from police when neighbors relate how many of her elderly
charges die shortly after entering the home, their life insurance policies paid directly to Sister Amy. Police exhume some of the bodies
and find that her most recent victim, one Charlie Andrews, has been
poisoned. The evangelical nursing home operator is arrested and
tried. The prosecution charges her with the murders of twenty-seven
persons since 1901. Amy Archer-Gilligan is sent to the Wethersfield
Prison for life but is later removed to the insane asylum in Middletown where she dies raving, "yelling for a man in the watches of the

night," according to one report citing her as a declared nymphoman-
iac.

1909

Bible-spouting Carl Loose of New York, a baker, after years of raping
his own daughters, impregnates Maria Loose, then convinces a suitor,
Billy Rooney, that the child is his and that he must marry his daughter.
Rooney weds Maria Loose but deserts her when he discovers that her
delivery of the child does not correspond with the period of time he
has known her. Maria Loose tells authorities of her father's incest, and
while he awaits deportation hearings (to Bremen, Germany, the land
of his birth), he begins to shoot his family over the breakfast table,
yelling: "*Verflucht sei jeder mann hier!* (Everyone here be damned.)"
He wounds one son, Frederick, and kills his daughter Meta, who has
blocked the shot intended for Mrs. Loose. Police arrive minutes later
and Loose meekly surrenders. He is tried and convicted, Judge Foster
sentencing him to death with the words "The gruesome annals of
awful crime contain nothing more shocking than this crime of which
you stand convicted. It is not for me to abate one jot or tittle of the
punishment which the law provides for your offense." Carl Loose
goes to the electric chair in Sing Sing. . . . Dr. John MacGregor of Bad
Axe, Michigan, in lover's league with Mrs. John Sparling, begins the
systematic murder of the Sparling males. (page 184)

1910

Albert Wolter writes to the Bankers' and Merchants' Business College
of New York City, asking to interview an advanced student in stenog-
raphy, specifying a woman. Ruth Wheeler responds to the written
request and disappears. Wolter, a German immigrant living with his
wife, is interrogated by police; he appears nervous, tells officers that,
yes, Miss Wheeler has come to see him but left. The next day neighbors find a bundle on Wolter's fire escape. Inside is a charred-
beyond-recognition torso of a body but a gold chain about the throat
is identified as Ruth Wheeler's. Police soon learn that Wolter as-
saulted and strangled the girl, then tried to burn the body in the
fireplace of his apartment before the return of his common-law wife.
Hearing her knock and thinking it the police, Wolter hurriedly
wrapped the body and shoved it out onto the fire escape where it was
later found. He is sent to Sing Sing's electric chair. . . . Mass-murderer
Albert Fish kills his first victim, a man in Wilmington, Delaware,
according to his confession, twenty-six years later, in which he will

*Cannibal-murderer Albert Fish (second from left) entering Sing Sing in
1936 to be executed.*

also confess to the abduction, murder and sometimes cannibalism of
more than four hundred children, although only six of these homicides are proven before Fish's execution in Sing Sing on January 16,
1936. . . . James P. "Bluebeard" Watson of El Centro, California, is
suspected by his wife of planning her murder. After she informs police, detectives "sweat" the suspect, although they have no evidence
other than possible charges of polygamy. Watson unaccountably tells
them that if he delivers a body to them they must guarantee life imprisonment rather than a death sentence. Surprised, the police readily
agree. Watson leads detectives to a shallow grave in the desert where
they find the body of Nina Deloney. He is convicted of her murder
and sent to San Quentin, where Watson openly brags of murdering at
least fifteen other females, all wives murdered for their money over a
period of ten years. Watson will die in prison. . . . Frank Heideman,
an émigré from Germany, takes a hammer to the head of Marie Smith,
a nine-year-old schoolgirl, in Asbury Park, New Jersey, then chokes
her to death on November 9, 1910. Suspected by investigators, Heideman quits his job in a greenhouse and moves to New York City. There,
a detective operating undercover befriends him, telling him that he
has committed a murder. Heideman, to prove *his* friendship, admits
to the killing of Marie Smith. He is arrested and condemned, sent to
the electric chair in May 1911.

With the paranoid thought that novelist David Graham Phillips has slandered his sister in a fictional profile appearing in *The Fashionable Adventures of Joshua Craig*, Philadelphia socialite and ne'er-do-well son of a wealthy family Fitzhugh Coyle Goldsborough attacks the writer as he is walking through Manhattan's Gramercy Park. Goldsborough approaches Phillips and fires five bullets into him, shouting: "Here you go!" The sixth bullet Goldsborough sends into his own brain after yelling: "Here I go!" Phillips lives for some hours, the writer who had seemed to have a brilliant future dying with the words: "I can fight one bullet, but not five."

1912

Floyd Allen and members of his gang are convicted of bank robbery in a Richmond, Virginia, courtroom on March 14, 1912. "No one will ever take me to the penitentiary!" booms Allen and with that he and his members produce guns that have been smuggled to them, killing Judge Thornton L. Massie, the prosecutor, the sheriff and a woman spectator before an army of deputies subdues them. Allen and the others receive life sentences.

1913

Mary Phagan, a fourteen-year-old factory worker in Atlanta, Georgia, is murdered in the pencil factory of Max Leo Frank. Accused and tried for the murder, Frank is found guilty largely on the dubious testimony of one witness. His death sentence is later commuted but a howling anti-Semitic mob, abetted by the newly reborn KKK, will tear him out of the Milledgeville, Georgia, jail and lynch him on August 16, 1915, in one of the most disgraceful displays of mob violence on record. . . . Shoemaker Gregorio Giordano visits the New York City morgue, identifies a corpse as that of his wife and then faints. Revived, Giordano goes home, leaving officials perplexed. Some hours later, the sliced-up corpse of Giordano's wife, Salvatrice, is found in some woods in Inwood Park. Detectives find near the body a shoemaker's knife and lash. They confront Giordano, asking why he has identified the wrong body. He can't explain. In his dresser bureau they find bloody pants and a shirt covered with gore. Confronted with this, Giordano blurts out a confession, telling police that he has murdered his wife because "she started to pack and leave. I got jealous, thinking maybe she was

389

in love with somebody else. I begged her to stay and asked her to go for a ride in the woods and we could talk things over." When asked why he had hurried to the morgue, Giordano shrugs and states: "For some reason I couldn't keep away from the morgue. I had to get one last look at her." The killer is electrocuted in Sing Sing in April 1914.

1914

Sailors on board the tug *Tillicum* on March 22, 1914, find floating in Puget Sound an empty rowboat with one oar broken and bloody at the end; the bottom of the boat is filled with blood. Seattle detectives surmise that someone has been murdered in the boat. They match hairs found at the end of the broken oar to those found in a hotel room in which a wealthy prospector, Everett C. West, has been living; West has disappeared. Detectives also remember a similar instance, three years earlier, when one Mrs. Saide Buchanan was killed in a boat, the oar used as the murder weapon. They pick up the man suspected of the Buchanan killing, Roy Morhead, who is carrying travelers' checks made out in the name of Everett C. West, the missing prospector. Following an hour of interrogation, Morhead drops his cries of innocence and blubbers to police: "You've got me, but you'll never find the body. I killed West. I got him into the boat and beat him over the head with an oar. One blow laid his skull wide open, and then I robbed him and threw him overboard. But I'm not telling you where. He'll never come up." Morhead is placed in a cell; at dawn jailers find him dead. The murderer has hanged himself by making a rope of his shirt. . . . Henry Spencer woos spinster Allison Hexroat of Wheaton, Illinois. After obtaining her savings, Spencer takes Miss Rexroat on a picnic and, while she munches on a chicken salad sandwich, withdraws a hammer from the picnic basket and bashes out her brains. He steals two of her rings from her fingers, buries her in a shallow grave, and prepares to leave town. Suspicious police pick Spencer up at the train station. He confesses hours later, is tried and condemned, and is hanged in August 1914 before a great crowd of picnickers. . . . In June 1914, Frederick Mors, from Vienna, Austria, takes a position as a nurses' aide in a home for the elderly in the Bronx. From August 9, 1914, to January 4, 1915, Mors murders seventeen elderly patients, mostly with chloroform and arsenic (which he administers to one man in a glass of beer). He is sent to Matteawan State Prison for the Criminally Insane but escapes a decade later, never to be seen again. . . . Tillie Gbrurek, a product of Chicago's Little Poland, begins to poison her husbands for insurance; she will murder at least eight before being caught in 1921. (page 188)

In one of the most baffling murder cases in Philadelphia history, Daniel J. McNichols' decomposed body is found in the cellar of an abandoned building on December 13, 1915, a murder victim whose remains still point to the killer when a dogged and crafty detective takes up the trail of Edward Keller. (page 191)

1916

Dentist Warren Waite embarks on a wholesale murder plan of destroying his in-laws on March 12, 1916, as he first poisons his mother-in-law in New York. (page 194) . . . Frederick Small of Mountainview, New Hampshire, takes out twenty-thousand-dollar life insurance policies on himself and his wife, each the beneficiary of separate policies. On September 28, Small orders a cart driver to take him to the train station where he plans to leave for Boston on business, accompanied, ironically, by Edwin Conner, the man who has sold him the insurance policies. The cart driver hears Small say "Goodbye" at his doorway, but this is a ruse; Small, only hours before, has grabbed a poker and crushed the skull of Florence Arlene Curry Small with eight terrible blows, shot her in the head with a .32 Colt automatic pistol, and strangled her with a cord. He has set a slow fire in the basement of his house. Once in Boston, he mails a postcard to his wife in the presence of his business companion, Edwin Conner, thus, he thinks, establishing the perfect alibi. The fire consumes the house but does not destroy the body; the torso and head are found intact with the tell-tale wounds. Small returns home when hearing of the fire and his conduct and remarks draw suspicion. When asked by the coroner what should be done with the body, Small, startled, responds: "What! Is there anything left to be buried?" He is arrested, charged with murder and tried, many witnesses testifying that Small has often talked of murdering his wife. He is convicted on impressive circumstantial evidence and sent to his death on January 15, 1918, insisting upon his innocence to the end. When entering the room where the gallows has been constructed in the State Prison at Concord, New Hampshire, Small bows to the thirty-five witnesses assembled, and smiles broadly as the hood and rope are put on his head and around his neck.

1917

Unhappy with his long-estranged wife, Alice McQuillan Dunn, Frank Dunn, owner of a postal contract to haul mail from the trains to the post office in St. Paul, Minnesota, hires three killers from Kansas City

—Joseph P. Redenbaugh, only nineteen, Frank McCool, and John Doyle—who are aided by a local bartender and go-between for Dunn, one Mike Moore, to murder his wife on the night of April 26, 1917. They break into the McQuillan house—Alice is living with her parents—and Redenbaugh pushes Katherine McQuillan, who is in bed with her sister, from Alice's side, telling Katherine: "Be calm, be calm, I'm only gonna do a little shooting." Wearing a white mask and a cap low over his eyes, the youthful killer uses a flashlight to distinguish the right victim, aiming a pistol only a few inches from Alice's face. According to Katherine's later testimony: "He fired three shots, one right after another, just as quick as a flash. He pushed me aside before he did any shooting. . . . There was a big hole . . . the whole side of her head was gone." Several men who have been approached in the past by Dunn with his request to kill his wife come forth when hearing of the murder; police soon arrest Dunn and subsequently the other members of the paid-for-murder ring. All are sent to prison for life where they die, except for the boy killer Redenbaugh, who is released on May 9, 1962, at age sixty-four, thought to be "totally rehabilitated." . . . Grace Lusk, a thirty-nine-year-old spinster in Waukesha, Wisconsin, after having a torrid affair with horse doctor David Roberts, shoots her paramour's wife, Mary Roberts, and is sent to prison for nineteen years' hard labor; she is pardoned in 1923.

1918

Gordon Hamby, an honor student in the San Francisco area, robs a bank with an unknown accomplice, gets ten thousand dollars and kills two men in the process. He is later captured in New York and executed for another murder, insisting that he be allowed to wear a white shirt to the electric chair. He sends a message from the death chamber that reads "Tell all the folks out there the little green door is brown."

1919

Charles Chapin, city editor of the *New York Evening World*, shoots his wife, then confesses to police that it was an act of "despondency." He is convicted of second-degree murder and given a life sentence; sent to Sing Sing, he is allowed to cultivate gardens in and outside the prison walls, becoming "The Rose Man of Sing Sing" until his death in 1930 at age seventy-two. Before Chapin's death, his warden, Lewis Lawes, receives a letter from one of Chapin's former employees, which acidly reads: "I knew Mr. Chapin long and from a certain angle intimately in the years he was at the *New York World*. That is, I knew intimately the anguished stories of the hundreds and thousands of young writers whose lives he made a living hell. He was the worst curse our reportorial craft ever enjoyed. I used to think of him a sort of devil sitting on enthroned power in the *World* office and making Park Row gutters flow red with the blood of ambitious young men. If you enjoy him I hope you keep him long and carefully." . . . Julia Wilkins, wife of Dr. Walter Keene Wilkins, age sixty-seven, is attacked and brutally beaten in her Long Beach, New York, home on February 27, 1919. She later dies in the hospital and Wilkins is proved to be the killer, murdering his third wife for her money. Wilkins commits suicide in the local jail before he can be sent to Sing Sing. . . . Thinking his two children are putting hexes on him, superstitious Aurelius Angelino of York, Pennsylvania, strangles them. Angelino is sent to an insane asylum but escapes three times, permanently in 1923. . . . Rosario Borgio of Akron, Ohio, decides to rid himself of police intervention in his rackets and offers a $250 bounty for each policeman murdered by his willing stooges. (page 198) . . . Wealthy Cleveland, Ohio, publisher Daniel D. Kaber, is killed in a bizarre murder plot designed by his loving wife, whose chief adviser is a sinister soothsayer. (page 202)

1920

Lydia Trueblood marries cowboy Ed Meyer in Twin Falls, Idaho, has him take out a ten-thousand-dollar life insurance policy and then poisons him, collecting the money from the insurance company. Insurance detectives looking into Lydia's background discover that she has collected more than twenty-five thousand dollars in life insurance on three previous husbands. Meyer's body is examined and the poison found. Lydia is sent to the state penitentiary in Boise for life. . . . Carl Otto Wanderer of Chicago, a hero of World War I, arranges for a bum to stick up him and his wife so that he can overpower the hobo and appear to be a hero in his wife's eyes, but this is only a ruse to enable him to shoot the bum and his wife, blaming the stick-up man with the murder of his spouse and claiming he has killed the thief in self-defense on the night of June 21, 1920. Wanderer's later confession reveals the motive; learning that his wife is pregnant, he feels "sexually threatened," being a secret homosexual. The clever plan is learned by reporters from the Chicago papers and Wanderer is exposed. He is sent to the gallows on March 19, 1921, going to his death while singing a song entitled "Dear Old Pal of Mine." . . . Carl Panzram, whose background is cluttered with burglary and robbery, buys a small boat and lures sailors with promises of jobs to the harbor in Bridgeport, Connecticut, where he murders them for their money.

By his own later confession before he is executed in Leavenworth's prison yard in 1930 for the murder of a prison employee, Panzram admits to murdering at least twenty-one persons in America and Africa.

1921

Nova Scotia–born Harry Townsend murders his sister, Fay, in a New York tenement building and flees. Police establish his identity by clues left in the apartment and track the bargeman for five years, "laying the wires" by leaving verbal descriptions of the killer with hundreds of bargemen, one of whom informs detectives of Townsend's presence in Philadelphia in 1926 where he is arrested. He is subsequently sent to prison for life after pleading guilty. . . . On the night of August 21, 1921, Father Patrick E. Heslin is called from his rectory of Holy Angels Church in Colma, just outside of San Francisco, answering a plea for help from a mysterious stranger. He is later found murdered, after a kidnapper fails to get the demanded ransom. (page 206)

1922

In Los Angeles on the afternoon of July 6, 1922, former showgirl Clara Phillips decides that murder is the best solution to her husband's philandering. (page 214) . . . Police responding to a disturbance in the Lakehurst, New Jersey, apartment of Ivy and William Giberson on the night of August 13–14, 1922, find Mrs. Giberson in the kitchen, tied and gagged, and her husband, William, a taxi-cab company owner, in the bedroom, sprawled on the bed with a bullet in the base of his skull. Chief of Detectives Ellis Parker, whose brilliant career is to be destroyed in the botched investigation of the Lindbergh case a decade later, interrogates Mrs. Giberson, who claims that two burglars have entered her house, one man remaining to tie her up in the kitchen, the other proceeding into the bedroom, where he shot her husband as he awoke. Mrs. Giberson tells Parker that "the man who was binding me up in the kitchen," after hearing a shot from the bedroom, "shouted to the other man: 'Why the hell did you shoot him?' and the man in the bedroom shouted back: 'I had to—he was waking up.' " Parker has already discovered that Mrs. Giberson is tired of her husband and that she had purchased widow's apparel a week before. Parker tells her: "Why don't you tell the truth, Mrs. Giberson. You know you killed your husband. You admitted it a minute or two back, but you didn't know it." The detective goes on to state that there have been no intruders, that Mrs. Giberson has shot her husband and tied herself up in the kitchen to fake the burglary, pointing out that any burglar would not know that a shot from the bedroom had meant that his partner had shot Giberson, but would have investigated to find out exactly who had been shot. The startled woman blubbers her confession. She is sent to the penitentiary in Trenton, New Jersey, for twenty years. . . . John Magnuson of Marshfield, Wisconsin, feuding with his farmer neighbor James A. Chapman over river rights, sends a bomb, wrapped as a Christmas gift, to the Chapman house on December 27, 1922, which blows up in Chapman's face and also kills Mrs. Chapman, who is standing nearby. Part of the wrapping paper used to package the bomb remains intact and writing thereon is traced to Magnuson, who is sent to prison for life.

1923

Wanted for forging checks in Cleveland, Ohio, John Leonard Whitfield is picked up outside his home on May 11, 1923, a friendly cop, Patrolman Dennis Griffin, allowing Whitfield to say goodbye to his wife in their home before taking Whitfield to the station to book him. On the ride to the station, Whitfield draws a .45 pistol and fires point blank into Griffin's head, killing him. He buries the body in a shallow grave, which is found hours later. A nationwide hunt for Whitfield ensues. Al Felly, owner of a restaurant in Madison, Wisconsin, identifies the killer from a newspaper photo as a man sitting in one of his booths on May 25, 1923. He stalls the man's steak dinner while calling officers. Two detectives respond but Whitfield breaks away from them, dashes in front of a streetcar, which barely misses him, and vanishes up an alley. Some weeks later, the owner of a Detroit, Michigan, lumber company calls police, stating that he believes one of his workers, a man calling himself Sam DeCaro, is none other than the much-wanted Whitfield. Police arrest Whitfield in the lumberyard; he surrenders meekly. The cop killer is given a life term. Whitfield is killed on March 9, 1928, as he attempts to escape the state prison. . . . Pleasant Harris of New Orleans argues with his sweetheart, then beats her unmercifully on the night of May 20, 1923, pistol-whipping Katherine Wilson on the street, only a half block from a police station, before shooting her to death. Police identify the killer within hours but Harris has fled the city. He is found in July 1926, having been arrested in Jersey City. New Orleans police extradite the killer to New Orleans. Harris can do nothing but brag about his exploits in the previous three years, telling officers that he has met dozens of celebrities, including the famous sports writer Ring Lardner and the fighter Harry Greb. "One day my picture was taken at ringside with Firpo [Luis Firpo, the heavyweight contender]," chuckles Harris as he puffs on a cigar. Though convicted and sentenced to death, Harris' sentence is commuted to a life term of hard labor by Governor Huey P. Long.

1924

Wife murderer Gee Jon is the first man to be gassed to death in Nevada, executed in a crudely made gas chamber on February 8, 1924, an act condemned by one newspaper as "one step further from the savage state." . . . Wanda Stopa, brilliant lawyer and hopeful artist, returns from New York to Chicago to kill the wife of the man she loves on April 24, 1924. (page 218) . . . Two brilliant college students, Nathan F. Leopold and Richard A. Loeb, both sons of millionaires, plan the "perfect" (and motiveless) crime by murdering fourteen-year-old Bobbie Franks on May 24, 1924, pretending it to be the work of kidnappers. When the body is found, personal effects of Leopold's are discovered nearby, chiefly a pair of glasses. Loeb, who is undoubtedly the mastermind of the thrill killing, actually joins in the police searches for evidence, throwing suspicion upon himself when he re-

Chicago intellectual murderers, sons of millionaires, Nathan F. Leopold and Richard A. Loeb (front, second and third from left) at their sensational bench trial in 1924.

marks: "If I were going to pick out a boy to kidnap or murder, that's just the kind of cocky little son-of-a-bitch I would pick," meaning Bobbie Franks. The boys are arrested and quickly incriminate each other. They are brought to a bench trial, the quick-thinking move of their lawyer, Clarence Darrow, who makes his appeal for life sentences to the judge, upon whom he cleverly throws the burdensome weight of responsibility for taking their lives. The boys are given life sentences. Loeb is killed by a Stateville inmate, James Day, in January 1936, after sexually attacking Day. Leopold will be paroled on March 13, 1958, largely due to the efforts of the brilliant lawyer Elmer Gertz and the fact that poet Carl Sandburg tells the parole board he would be willing to have the one-time killer in his home. Leopold dies on August 30, 1971, in Puerto Rico, where he has worked as a hospital technician.

1925

Martha Hasel Wise, a forty-year-old widow sweating out a living on a farm outside of Medina, Ohio, falls in love with Walter Johns, a younger man. When her mother laughs at her for such romantic "caprices," Martha poisons her with arsenic on New Year's Day 1925. Her uncle and aunt, Fred and Lily Geinke, also ridicule her affections for Johns, for which Martha puts arsenic in their coffee pot in February 1925. She also attempts to murder the entire Geinke clan, eight in all, by poisoning their water, but these victims recover. Local authorities investigate the deaths, find the arsenic and confront Martha Wise. The local prosecutor, Joseph Seymour, interviews her as a violent rainstorm ensues. Realizing that the deeply religious Martha is unnerved by the rain beating incessantly upon the tin roof of his office building, Seymour plays upon the woman's apprehensions. "Listen, Martha," Seymour tells her, "listen to the raindrops on the roof. They are the voice of God, Martha. Listen—listen to what they are saying —You did, you did, Martha." Mrs. Wise gives a yell and confesses: "Yes, I did it, but it was the devil who told me to do it. He came to me while I was in the kitchen baking bread. He came to me while I was working in the fields. He followed me everywhere. I tried to escape him in my sleep . . . but he came to me everywhere. It was the devil, I tell you, the devil. I poisoned Mom because she made fun of me for falling in love at my age. I poisoned the Geinkes because they made fun of me." Martha Wise's activities, her confession points out, have ranged beyond murder. The area has been plagued by fires and burglaries. Mrs. Wise admits to the break-ins and setting the fires: "I like fires. They were red and bright, and I loved to see the flames shooting up into the sky." In May 1925, Mrs. Martha Hasel Wise is brought to trial, the press dubbing her "The Borgia of America." Her defense, lawyers vainly try to prove, is insanity. Even her lover, Walter Johns, takes the stand to testify that during their lovemaking, Martha "barked like a dog!" The jury nevertheless convicts her of murder in the first degree. The wayward member of the lovelorn is sent to prison for life, where she dies. . . . Katherine Gore, an attractive twenty-two-year-old, is found dead, strangled and raped, in her New York City apartment on East Seventy-seventh Street in September. Her killer is identified as Luke O'Neil, an estranged lover. Police search the city for O'Neil but he has vanished. Not until 1931 do three detectives spot O'Neil walking along East Forty-first Street, heading toward Fifth Avenue. They grab him, but O'Neil breaks away, the detectives in hot pursuit, chasing him onto a moving bus, then down Forty-second Street, finally knocking him out with their gun butts in front of the Public Library. Though several shots have been fired, no one is injured (the police have fired their weapons into the air as warning shots). O'Neil is tried and condemned, but his army buddies from World War I, chiefly Alfred E. Smith, Jr., the son of the former governor of the state of New York, appeal to then-Governor Franklin D. Roosevelt, asking that O'Neil's life be spared in light of his brilliant and heroic war record. In a rare act, Roosevelt commutes O'Neil's sentence to life imprisonment.

1926

Bible student gone wrong Earl Leonard Nelson, who has been raised in an atmosphere of religious fanaticism by an aunt who is also a strict landlady, begins to strangle women, and then rape them—he is a pronounced necrophiliac—murdering Clara Newman, a San Francisco landlady, February 20, 1926. This mad killer will strangle another nineteen women and girls, mostly landladies, coast to coast, until he is apprehended in Canada and is executed on January 12, 1928, for the murder of Mrs. Emily Patterson of Winnipeg.

1927

Corset salesman Henry Judd Gray and his lover, housewife Ruth Snyder, murder Mrs. Snyder's husband, Albert, by bashing in his brains with a paperweight as he sleeps in his Queens, New York, home on the night of March 20, 1927. Detectives quickly trip up Mrs. Snyder who places all blame on Gray; he, in turn, labels Mrs. Snyder as the murderer. Both are found guilty in a sensational trial and condemned. Gray is electrocuted in Sing Sing on January 12, 1928, Mrs. Snyder a few minutes later; a photographer from the *New York Daily News*, using a small camera strapped to his leg, takes a photo of Mrs. Snyder in the chair just as the electric current is sent into her body. The photograph is reproduced in the newspaper the following day, taking up most of the front page, considered to be an all-time low in American journalism. . . . Jesse Watkins, fired from his stable-hand job at the military base of The Presidio, outside of San Francisco, breaks into the home of his former employer, stablemaster Henry Chambers, on the night of August 21, 1927. Chambers awakes as Watkins approaches his bed, pulls forth a pistol and fires three times, slightly wounding Watkins in the cheek. Watkins pounces upon Chambers and takes away the pistol, using it as a club to batter his victim to death. Police, knowing of the feud between Chambers and Watkins, arrest the killer some days later. He is tried and sentenced to life in prison on McNeil Island. . . . Handyman Ludwig Lee chops up his landlady and a neighbor, depositing pieces of the victims all over New York City. (page 224) . . . Earl Leo Battice, the mulatto cook on board the four-master schooner *Kingsway*, cuts the throat of his wife, Lucia, who serves as his galley assistant, when she flirts with other crewmen, as the ship is bound for Africa in August 1927. He is thrown in irons and returned to New York Harbor. Battice is given ten years in the federal penitentiary in Atlanta, convicted of second-degree murder. . . . When Robert Hitchens, an elderly bachelor living in Omar, Delaware, does not answer his doorbell, neighbors crawl through a window on November 5, 1927, to discover Hitchens lying on the floor, his head bashed in, a bullet sent into his body. Mrs. Mary Carey, Hitchens' sister, who lives across the street, arrives to insist that the bachelor has not been murdered: "It looks to me like he's had a hemorrhage and bled to death. Besides, he hasn't an enemy in the world." The case goes unsolved until Lawrence Carey, Mrs. Carey's youngest son, is arrested for housebreaking in Omar on December 5, 1934. Detectives on a hunch grill him about the Hitchens murder. The twenty-year-old breaks down and tells officers that his mother and older brothers, Howard and James, killed the old man for his life insurance, Mrs. Carey promising Howard a new car if he would commit the murder. The mother and brothers are arrested, Howard and James Carey confessing. Mrs. Carey, her hysterical protests in court notwithstanding, is convicted, along with her sons. She and Howard Carey are sentenced to death; James Carey is given life imprisonment. Lawrence is sent to prison for seven years for housebreaking. . . . College student Edward Hickman, to pay for his school tuition, kidnaps, in December 1927, Marian Parker, one of twelve-year-old twin daughters of successful Los Angeles businessman Perry Parker. Hickman forces the girl to write notes to her father asking him to pay the seventy-five-hundred-dollar ransom. He then kills her and inexplicably cuts off the child's legs. Parker meets the kidnapper on a lonely road, giving him the money. Hickman holds up the dead child, who is

Housewife gone wrong, murderess Ruth Snyder went to the electric chair with her lover, Judd Gray.

399

wrapped in a blanket and appears to be sleeping. He drives down the road a block and then places the child next to the highway. Parker rushes to his daughter to find her a mutilated corpse. Hickman flees north but is recognized in Echo, Oregon, arrested and returned to California for trial where he is convicted and condemned. Hickman, a vainglorious type, spends his last hours combing his luxuriant wavy, red hair, polishing his shoes and manicuring his fingernails before mounting the scaffold at San Quentin Prison to be hanged on February 4, 1928. . . . Mrs. Emeline Harrington, a thirty-nine-year-old New York actress, is found beaten to death in her Manhattan apartment on December 29, 1927. Police think it the work of a professional burglar. The murder remains unsolved until January 1928, when a guest at the Hotel Taft in New Haven, Connecticut, skips without paying his bill, leaving his suitcase, the contents of which identify him as Frederick W. Edel. Also found in the case are many papers and jewelry traceable to Mrs. Harrington. Edel, a parole-violator recently released from New York's Dannemora Prison, has been implicated in several earlier murders, two in the Meriden, Connecticut, area in 1925. When Edel attempts to cash a small money order at the post office in Hopkins, Minnesota, a clerk recognizes him from a wanted poster and informs the town marshal, who chases the suspect a mile before Edel falls exhausted and is taken into custody. Edel is returned to New York, tried, and condemned to death.

1928

On February 6, 1928, "Major" Cecil Campbell and his wife, down on their luck, take a room in the Grand Central Hotel and, using ten of the twenty-five cents they have between them, buy a hammer. Mrs. Campbell asks her husband to kill her with the hammer. He crushes her skull and then, as part of their prearranged suicide pact, goes to a window, intending to jump. He loses his nerve, but police pick Campbell up a short while later. "Why didn't you jump?" he is asked. "There was a ledge below the window and so many people down on the street that I couldn't bring myself to do it," he responds. "I was afraid I might hit the ledge and fall on the sidewalk and injure someone." Though he begs for the death penalty at his trial, sympathetic jurors convict him of murder in the second degree. Campbell is sent to prison for twenty years. . . . Gordon Stewart Northcott of Riverside, California, a twenty-year-old who will later be described as a "pathological liar, sadist and degenerate . . . a cold, heartless physical and mental misfit," and whose father has died in an insane asylum, his uncle sent to prison for life after three murder indictments, begins kidnapping young boys, sometimes two and three at a time, holding them captive for weeks while forcing them to submit to his sexual attacks before murdering and dismembering them. His nephew, Stanford Clark, finally informs on Northcott, stating that Northcott and his mother are mass murderers, and that Mrs. Northcott has also participated in the sex orgies with the captive boys and helped to murder and then secretly bury the bodies. Northcott, by then, has fled to Canada. He is extradited, tried and condemned, and sent to the gallows at San Quentin on October 2, 1930. Mrs. Northcott is given a life sentence. Neither will reveal where they have buried the bodies. Northcott goes to his death begging for a blindfold and is led up the thirteen stairs to the rope, asking the prison doctor: "Will it hurt?" Responds the doctor: "No—I've never heard anyone complain."

1929

Black man James E. Bell, yelling to the world that he is being persecuted, runs amok in a residential section of Newark, New Jersey, on March 3, 1929. Using a pistol and shotgun, Bell fires indiscriminately upon five persons, killing Julius Rabinowitz and Charles Ramperger, and wounding three others; he is sent to prison for life.... "I can't stand another day like this," Mrs. Mamie Shey Shoaf tells a neighbor in Lebanon, Kentucky, on May 24, 1929. Hours later, Mrs. Shoaf is found in a cemetery where she has cut the throats of her three children, Catherine, eleven; Ina, seven; and Thomas, two, before slashing her own throat and dying.

1930

Louis Balducci, a Newark, New Jersey, businessman, steps to the street to talk to a friend in a parked car on Seventh Avenue on the night of September 12, 1930. After a brief conversation, he shakes hands with the driver of the car, then turns to go back into his store. He is shot to the pavement and dies minutes later as police rush him to the hospital. Witnesses to the street shooting give police a partial license number and after days of checking, George Segro's plates are identified as belonging to the killer's car. Segro, a friend of Balducci, is convicted of second-degree manslaughter and given fifteen years in prison.... A. D. Payne, a prominent Amarillo, Texas, attorney, plans the unique deaths of his family. (page 227)

1931

Used-furniture salesman Herman Drenth of Clarksburg, West Virginia, though married, has been operating a matrimonial racket for a decade, marrying well-to-do widow women throughout the United

States, taking them back to his "scientific laboratory" in a wooded area beyond Clarksburg, and gassing them to death. Drenth then pockets their bank savings and other properties. Ranging from Spokane, Washington, to Boston, Massachusetts, Drenth explains his absences to his wife as business trips. A farmer living near Drenth's strange concrete blockhouse in the woods complains to police that gaseous odors are constantly belching from the squat building. Police investigate and find a two-room structure, a main "killing room," where Drenth's victims are bound and into which, through an intricate pipe system, he has released poison gas, and the "operations rooms," separated by a large plate glass window through which the killer watches his victims die. When detectives enter this horror house they find the floor coated with human blood, for Drenth has used a hammer on the three children of his latest victim, Mrs. Asta Buick Eicher, before gassing the hysterical Mrs. Eicher to death. He is arrested and charged with these four murders, and with killing another widow, Mrs. Dorothy Lemke, of Worcester, Massachusetts. He is labeled as "America's worst bluebeard," and, under incessant police grilling, finally admits to the five murders after the bodies are discovered in a shallow ditch next to Drenth's "laboratory." Drenth admits to great sexual stimulation when watching his victims die through the plate glass window—"It beat any cat house I was ever in." Police estimate that the mass murderer has killed more than fifty women but he will not help them locate the bodies, sneering at detectives: "You got me on five. What good would fifty more do?" Herman Drenth is hanged on March 18, 1932. . . . Mrs. William Zubitsky and her lover, Joseph Obrieto, murder and then dissect Zubitsky, scattering his body throughout Manhattan, as Mrs. Nack and her lover, Martin George Thorn, did to the hapless Willie Guldensuppe in 1897. The killers, however, neglect to strip the body, leaving an undershirt covering the discovered torso. On the shirt police find a laundry mark that identifies the corpse and leads to the arrest, conviction and condemnation of Mrs. Zubitsky and Obrieto; this case establishes the checking of laundry markings as standard procedure in all homicide cases. . . . Bowery bum Earl Spencer Fox is picked up by Luigi Raffia, who thinks to pass off Fox's body as his own in bilking an insurance firm out of money. Raffia takes Fox to his room where he feeds him a large dinner and provides him with rotgut wine. When Fox is thoroughly drunk, Raffia dumps kerosene over him and sets him afire, believing the flames will obliterate Fox's features and that he will be mistaken for Raffia. Fox unexpectedly leaps up, and, his entire body ablaze, races from the room, shrieking for help and hollering out Raffia's name as his murderer to startled roomers. Raffia is quickly convicted of Fox's death and sent to the electric chair. . . . William Lester Scott of Sasakwa, Oklahoma, gets drunk on the storm-swept night of

November 9, 1931, and beats his wife with a car crank as she runs
crazily about the house. Several blows to the head crush her skull. To
disguise his act, Scott drives his wife to the railroad tracks two miles
south of Sasakwa, parking the car on the tracks at a curve. He watches
until a passenger train thunders into the car, then races home. The
woman's body remains intact and police quickly establish her identity
and the fact that she was murdered. Scott is confronted hours later by
detectives, who find his bloody shirt and pants in a closet in his home.
After two trials, Scott is convicted of murder on April 18, 1935, and is
sent to the state prison at McAlester, Oklahoma for life. . . . Thalia
Massie, the wife of Navy Lieutenant Thomas Massie, stationed in
Hawaii, is raped by five Japanese-Hawaiian beach boys as she takes a
moonlit dip in September 1931. One of the boys, Joseph Kahawawai,
is brought before Massie in Massie's home by two of his sailors, A. O.
Jones and E. J. Lord. When Kahawawai admits the rape, Massie shoots
him in a wild rage. With the help of Jones, Lord and his mother-in-
law, Mrs. Granville Fortesque, Massie attempts to hide the body on a
mountaintop but is discovered. Massie, Lord, Jones and Mrs. Fortesque are tried for murder and masterfully defended by Clarence
Darrow. All are found guilty of murder in the second degree but are
sentenced only to serving one hour in the courtroom dock; they are
then freed. . . . San Francisco tire-store owner Bill Oetting is found in
his small office on December 5, 1931, with a .32-caliber bullet in his
head. His ex-partner, Hermann Nordlund, is soon suspected. When
police arrive at Nordlund's flat to arrest him they find that he has fixed
a shotgun to his chin. The gun is balanced between his knees and a
string is fixed about the triggers, the string tied firmly to a door that
opens to the outer hallway. Anyone entering this way will set off the
gun and blow away Nordlund's head. Through a window, detectives
see a pistol and knife on a small bed, within Nordlund's reach. One
detective leaps through the window, knocks the shotgun away and, as
other police officers rush inside, subdues the maniacal Nordlund, who
is dragged screaming to jail. He admits to murdering Oetting, his slim
excuse being that "the man was too content." Nordlund, despite pleas
of insanity, is sent to prison for life. He is paroled in 1941.

1932

As a way of enriching themselves, five young Bronx, New York, men
decide, in early January 1932, to insure a local drunk, Michael Malloy,
and kill him for the insurance money. Malloy, a man of forty-odd
years, is a regular patron of Tony Marino's speakeasy at 3804 Third
Avenue. Marino, along with Joe Murphy, Dan Kreisberg, Harry Green
and Frank Pasqua, first attempts to poison the heavy-drinking Malloy

with lethal concoctions, including wood alcohol, horse liniment, and turpentine. Malloy, drinking free, consumes great quantities of these deadly brews but fails to fall ill. Harry Green then runs him down several times with his taxi, but Malloy is found and recovers in a hospital. Next, Malloy is fed poisoned sardine sandwiches—mixed with ground-up tacks—but his only response is to ask for more. Next, when in a drunken stupor, Malloy is taken to the Bronx Zoo in the middle of a sub-zero night, stripped by the "Murder Trust," and soaked with water. Instead of freezing to death, Malloy saunters into Marino's speakeasy the following day complaining only of a head cold. He is finally taken to a room on Fulton Avenue where the killers stick a rubber tube connected to a gas tap into Malloy's mouth. He is found dead the next day, Dr. Frank Manzella, reportedly in the gang's employ, signing the death certificate for "Nicholas Mellory"—the name used by the gang to insure Malloy—and stating the cause of death as pneumonia. Murphy collects $800 of the insurance money on Malloy's life. Oddly, it is later estimated that the "murder trust" has spent more than $1,800 to kill Malloy when only a total of $1,788 in insurance money is forthcoming. Suspicious detectives arrest the quintet, and Green turns State's Evidence. The other four are found guilty of murder and sentenced to die; Kriesberg, Marino, and Pasqua

Kidnapper and killer of the Lindbergh child in 1932, Bruno Richard Hauptmann (center) is led into court four years later.

are electrocuted at Sing Sing on June 7, 1934, Murphy on July 5, 1934. Dr. Manzella was convicted as an accessory after the fact, and given a short jail term. . . . Kidnapper Bruno Richard Hauptmann abducts Charles A. Lindbergh, Jr., the only son of America's greatest aviator, from his Sourlands, New Jersey, home on March 1, 1932. He receives fifty thousand dollars in ransom but does not deliver the child, whom he has murdered. Hauptmann is caught in the Bronx, New York, two-and-a-half years later, spending some of the ransom money (twenty thousand dollars of which has been paid to him in traceable old gold certificates.) At his trial, Hauptmann is identified, by Amandus Hochmuth, a Lindbergh neighbor, as the man who drove past the Lindbergh home several times on the day of the kidnapping with a three-section ladder strapped to his auto. The ladder is proved to be made of planks from Hauptmann's attic flooring. Hauptmann is identified as the man collecting the ransom in a Bronx cemetery in the dead of night by go-between Dr. John F. Condon. The murderer is found guilty and sent to the electric chair in the state prison at Trenton, New Jersey, April 2, 1936. Unfounded claims, wholly unsupported by real evidence, later insist that Hauptmann was an innocent man railroaded to his death, a theory utterly dismissed by any and all responsible crime authorities. . . . Mrs. Mamie Schaaf, a wealthy widow of Atlantic City, New Jersey, is found strangled and stuffed into a trunk in a Philadelphia roominghouse. Her body, police learn, was shipped from Atlantic City to a Henry Miller in Philadelphia. Detectives arrive at Mrs. Schaaf's Atlantic City home to discover that her lone boarder, Louis Fine, is also missing. They search Fine's room and find letters addressed to Henry Miller. When Fine returns three days later, police arrest him on suspicion of murder. He is identified as Henry Miller, the man who has rented the Philadelphia room where the body has been found. Though pretending insanity, police overhear Fine remark: "The old fool [meaning Mrs. Schaff]! I wanted her to give me some money. It was the only way I could get it." Fine is convicted and sent to the New Jersey electric chair. . . . When elderly, well-to-do Mrs. Jessie Scott Hughes is found dead in a San Francisco street on the night of August 29, 1932, police first think her the victim of a hit-and-run driver. Suspicions are aroused, however, when Frank J. Egan, San Francisco's Public Defender, comes to the morgue the following day to identify the corpse, weeping as he views Mrs. Hughes' mangled body, and stating: "She was both my friend and my client. I have handled her legal and business affairs for years, ever since I was in private practice. In fact, I'm named beneficiary in her will. As Mrs. Hughes would have wished, I shall take charge of the funeral arrangements." As a careful afterthought, Egan adds without being asked, "I was at the fights in Dreamland Pavilion last night." Curious detectives check on Egan's car and discover that it has the

Winnie Ruth Judd at her
1932 trial, where she was
convicted of killing and
dissecting her two best
friends; the injured arm
is the result of a feeble
suicide attempt.

same tire marks as those left at the scene of the alleged accident and on the concrete floor of Mrs. Hughes' garage. (Mrs. Hughes did not own a car nor drive.) They interview Verne Doran, Egan's chauffeur, and Albert Tinnin, who also works for the Public Defender, both men being ex-convicts released from prison at Egan's insistence. Doran breaks under interrogation and admits that he and Tinnin have murdered the old woman at Egan's directive, so that the Public Defender can collect her money as the heir, Egan being in deep debt. Egan, Doran and Tinnin are sent to prison for life. . . . In a rage over an imagined insult, Winnie Ruth Judd of Phoenix, Arizona, stabs to death her two best friends, Miss Helwig "Sammy" Samuelson and Mrs. Agnes Leroi, chopping up their bodies and shipping them to the Southern Pacific Railroad Station in Los Angeles. When she calls for the shipment, suspicious freight handlers notice blood seeping from the trunk; the killer flees in panic but is soon apprehended, tried and convicted. Miss Judd receives life imprisonment, escapes several times, and is finally paroled in 1971. . . . Rancher Alfred Elliot of Seattle, Washington, is shot through the window of his home on November 11, 1926, by his best friend, John T. Bibeau, who later laughingly explains to police that he murdered Elliot because the rancher taunted him by keeping on the premises a black cat, the symbol of evil. Bibeau is imprisoned for life.

1933

President Franklin D. Roosevelt visits Miami, Florida, on February 15, 1933, with Chicago Mayor Anton Cermak at his side in an open car, which is reduced to a crawl when enthusiastic crowds mob the auto. Political malcontent Joseph Zangara rushes up to the car, screaming: "There are too many people starving to death!" He fires four shots, two wounding spectators, two more striking Cermak, who dies hours later. Zangara is tried for Cermak's murder, found guilty and sent to Florida's electric chair on March 21, 1933. It is later theorized that Zangara has never intended Roosevelt's assassination, but, on orders from the Chicago crime cartel—Cermak had been breaking up Windy City rackets as a reform mayor—Zangara has killed the "right" man, a story not without substantial foundation. . . . Charles Burke, whose wife discovers he is seeing a younger woman, goes berserk when Ella Burke sues him for divorce. He strangles and beats her to death in their lavish New York home, then slices up her body, splashing blood everywhere, to make it appear the work of intruders. Placing the grisly remains in several jars, he packs the dismembered body in the trunk of his car and drives off. He is stopped in Covington, Kentucky, on March 17, 1933, by police checking on his expired license plates. Burke suddenly produces a razor blade and slashes his wrists, dying before he arrives at a hospital. . . . Kenneth Neu, a song-and-dance man at the end of his rope, kills his first victim following a Times Square meeting in New York on September 2, 1933. (page 232) . . . Two home-grown youths, Thomas Harold Thurmond and John Maurice Holmes, kidnap and murder Brooke Hart, twenty-two-year-old heir to a department store fortune in San Jose, California, on November 9, 1933. Thurmond calls Alex Hart to arrange for the ransom payment but he is kept on the phone long enough for his call to be traced, the police picking him up as he haggles with Hart about the payment. He and Holmes are placed in the Santa Clara County Jail in San Jose. A mob of more than fifteen thousand forms in front of the jail on the night of November 26, 1933, only hours after Brooke Hart's body is found in San Francisco Bay. Rioters storm the jail, drag Holmes and Thurmond to the street, and lynch them. This ghastly episode of mob violence, upon which Fritz Lang will later base his movie *Fury,* is lauded by California Governor James "Sunny Jim" Rolfe as "the best lesson ever given the country. . . . I would like to parole all kidnappers in San Quentin and Folsom [prisons] to the fine patriotic citizens of San Jose." . . . Alice Wynekoop, a much-respected

Kidnapper-murderer Thomas Harold Thurmond (center) under arrest only days before a raging mob dragged him and fellow killer John Holmes from their San Jose jail in 1933, lynching both. (WIDE WORLD)

Chicago doctor, takes her daughter-in-law, Rheta Gardner, to her basement surgery to examine her, administering chloroform on the night of November 21, 1933. Hours later she calls in police who find the eighteen-year-old girl dead, a bullet through her breast. When confronted, Dr. Wynekoop confesses, saying that the girl had died under the anesthetic and that she then inexplicably shot her. A jury believes the sixty-two-year-old physician has murdered the girl for her insurance and to accommodate her son, Earle, in ridding him of a pesky wife. Earle Wynekoop confesses to murdering his wife but his claim is discarded as he was miles from the scene of the murder. Dr. Wynekoop is sent to prison for twenty-five years where she dies. . . . Ernest D'Iorio strangles and mutilates pretty Jennie Zablocki in Detroit, Michigan, on December 6, 1933, tying a rope around the girl's neck and then to a doorknob. He disarranges her house to make it appear as though a burglar has entered but he is quickly traced through a car. He explains that Jennie repeatedly criticized him, telling his girlfriend, Sonia Marzek, not to marry him. For this he has taken her life. D'Iorio is sent to prison for forty years, convicted of second-degree murder.

1934

Leo Hall, an apprentice thug in Seattle, Washington, learns from a married woman he is seeing that an elderly couple living in a cottage near Erland Point, Washington, has considerable cash. He drives to the cottage on the night of March 3, 1934, and, after the female accomplice has helped him to bind Mr. and Mrs. Flieder and their guests—Mr. and Mrs. Chenovert, a Mr. Jordan, and Bert Balcom—he robs them, ransacking their place. He then produces a hammer, smashing in the skulls of all six persons. He shoots each one to make sure of death. Not until almost a year later do police pick up the trail leading to Hall's mistress, who hysterically describes the nightmare murders in detail. The thirty-three-year-old Hall is arrested and quickly sentenced to hang in late 1935. . . . To impress their dates, Mickey Fallon and Eddie McDonald attempt to rob a couple parked in their car on New York's Riverside Drive in the early morning hours of March 3, 1934; Fallon shoots Joe Arbona, killing him, and both youths flee. The "show-off killers," as the press dubs them, are quickly apprehended when their girlfriends inform police. Pleading guilty, McDonald is given twenty-five years, Fallon thirty-five years in prison. . . . Middle-aged Eva Coo, bordello madam and owner of a rowdy roadhouse where Prohibition is liberally snubbed by high-positioned patrons living near Cooperstown, New York, decides to enrich herself by murdering a stew-bum named Harry Wright, planning to collect his life insurance. Eva takes the drunken Wright to nearby Crumhorn Mountain, knocks him unconscious in the road with a large mallet and then has her closest friend, Martha Clift, run her car over Wright's body. Police become suspicious when Eva claims the insurance money and grill both Eva and Martha, who confess to the killing. Martha Clift testifies against Eva Coo and receives a prison sentence; Madam Coo goes to Sing Sing's electric chair on June 28, 1935. . . . Robert Allen Edwards, a cultured, highly intelligent young resident of Edwardsville, Pennsylvania, learns that his girl friend, Freda McKechnie, is pregnant. When she insists on marriage, Edwards drives Freda to Harvey's Lake, Pennsylvania, on July 30, 1934, persuading the girl to go swimming. When in the water Edwards slugs Freda with a blackjack, killing her before she sinks in deep water. Hours later, Edwards sits in Freda's house chatting with the McKechnie family when word of her murder is heard. He claims ignorance of her whereabouts. Edwards is arrested when some of his clothes and the blackjack are found near the lake. He is brought to trial, which is attended by Theodore Dreiser (the case is identical to the Chester Gillette case profiled in his *American Tragedy*). After a grueling examination, Edwards confesses on the witness stand, explaining that he wanted to marry another girl and that killing Freda appeared to be the only solution to his problems. Following Edward's execution, Freda's father, George McKechnie, meets reporters, recounting how the boy-next-door, Edwards, grew up with his daughter. "I'm sorry for Dan Edwards, and his wife," states McKechnie, "and that other boy of theirs, too. But Robert Edwards took my little girl's life, and justice has been done—as far as it can be done." . . . Several hundred persons gather in a torchlight political parade in Kelayres, Pennsylvania, on the night of November 5, 1934. They march past the home of John J. "Big Joe" Bruno, a town politician they hope to unseat. Suddenly rifle volleys open up on the crowd, killers from ambush behind trees and bushes shooting down nearly fifty persons, five of whom are killed. Bruno; his brother, Philip; his sons, Alfred and James; and another relative, Tony Orlando, are charged and found guilty of what becomes known as the "Keystone Massacre." They are given long prison terms.

1935

Youthful William Schweitzer, sisters Loretta and Florence Jackson, and Jean Miller befriend Howard Carter Dickinson, a New York lawyer on business in Detroit. (Dickinson is a nephew of Charles Evans Hughes.) After a drinking party on the night of June 7, 1935, Schweitzer and the girls take Dickinson for a ride. The girls ask to get out on Joy Road in the city's Rouge Park. Schweitzer stops the car, the girls get out and then hear a shot. They turn to see Schweitzer dragging Dickinson from the car. He shoots the lawyer again, in the head, as his body topples to the road. He takes $134 from the dead man's pockets, counting it and then complaining: "That's a helluva little bit of money to kill a man for. I thought he'd have plenty of fifties—well, at least he can't talk." After a shopping spree in Chicago, the youths are picked up and quickly convicted of the murder, all of them given life terms. . . . Gerald Thompson, a factory worker in Peoria, Illinois, has been abducting women in the area, driving them along lonely country roads where he has stripped and tied them in front of his car's glaring headlights before raping them, sixteen in all by June 15, 1935, when he murders his last rape victim, Mildred Hallmark. His car, especially equipped with straps and locks to hold victims, is discovered. Thompson confesses and is sent to the electric chair in the Illinois State Penitentiary at Joliet on October 15, 1935. . . . When Mary Francis Creighton and her husband, John, move into a small cottage in Baldwin, Long Island, New York, few think of them as anything other than a quiet, happily married couple. The pair, in the early 1920s, have already been tried and acquitted on a murder charge of poisoning with arsenic Mary's younger brother, Raymond Charles Avery. Mary is later charged with the poisoning by arsenic of her mother-in-law, Mrs. John Creighton, Sr., for which she is narrowly acquitted. The couple befriend Everett and Ada Applegate. When the Applegates fall upon hard Depression times, the Creightons invite them to live in their tiny cottage. Because of cramped quarters, the Creightons' teenage daughter, Ruth, sleeps with the Applegates, mainly with Everett Applegate, who has sexual intercourse with the child repeatedly. Because his overweight Ada complains of this pedophiliac relationship, Applegate and Mary Creighton, who has perversely encouraged the relationship, poison Mrs. Applegate's food. Authorities, thinking a dangerous disease has killed the woman, perform an autopsy, discover the poison, and charge Mary Creighton and Applegate with murder. They are convicted and sent to Sing Sing's electric chair on July 16, 1936. . . . Los Angeles barber Robert James, who has, for a decade, been a murdering Bluebeard for insurance money, accomplishes the bizarre murder of his last wife on August 15, 1935, for which he will be known as "Rattlesnake James." (page 234) . . . Ada Franch Rice, the fifty-eight-year-old estranged wife of the mayor of Nome, Alaska, takes a young lover, Ralph Jerome Von Braun Selz. When Mrs. Rice is reported missing from her home by neighbors, police arrest Selz, who has been cashing her checks. He is grilled for two weeks and then admits to murdering the woman for her money; then he changes his story, saying that he crushed her head by accident with a poker while battling "a wild Hungarian" who broke into their house in Palo Alto, California. He leads police to a remote site in the Santa Cruz Mountains where they dig up Mrs.

Rice's body. Reporters at the scene spark Selz to strange comments and actions. "If you guys want a sensation," he tells them, "try hauling a corpse around in a car with the hoot owls hooting at night." Selz does wild clog dances around the shallow grave and then bows, stating: "I'm going to Hollywood when I get through here." A wide, maniacal smile plays constantly on the killer's face, which causes the press to dub him "the laughing killer." Selz is convicted and sent to prison for life, where he resides at the time of this writing.

1936

Floyd Horton and Mrs. Anna Johnson of Bedford, Iowa, conspire to murder Horton's wife, Elta, giving her capsules of strychnine—enough to kill thirty men, according to a later coroner's report—to "cure her nervous stomach." The woman dies on February 15, 1936. She is found by police clutching her abdomen, which leads to an autopsy and the discovery of the poison. Horton and Mrs. Johnson are interrogated separately, each told by police that the other is informing. Both admit to the murder. Both are given life sentences. . . . On the night of June 17, 1936, Albert Walter, Jr., saunters into police headquarters, informing a startled desk sergeant that he has killed a business college student, Blanche Cousins, whom he met on a transcontinental bus ride from Salt Lake City to San Francisco only days earlier. He takes police to her apartment and shows them her body. Lighting a cigarette, Walter lackadaisically explains: "I always knew I'd kill a woman. When I was fourteen years old I had an unfortunate experience with a woman older than I. She wrecked my life and embittered me against all women. I've tried to lead a normal life, but this hatred and bitterness keeps cropping up in spite of me. I left my wife in New York because I was afraid I'd kill her. When I was with Blanche Cousins this hatred surged up in me again. I want to be hanged and forgotten." Despite pleas by the Public Defender, who claims Walter is insane, court-appointed psychiatrists pronounce Walter sane enough to hang. He is sent to the gallows. . . . On June 11, 1936, Chicago businessman Joseph W. Bolton, Jr., is shot in his office and crawls for help to the outer hallway. As he bleeds to death his wife, Mildred, stands nearby and chattily tells a shocked elevator operator that "he's putting on an act." (page 245) . . . Winfred Howe dies in the U.S. Veterans' Hospital in Bath, New York, on November 13, 1936. An autopsy reveals massive arsenic poisoning. Police question Howe's visitors, learning from Howe's ailing wife that the dead man has in the past sprayed his potatoes in the basement with an arsenate of lead spray. At first officers conclude he has died of inhaling the arsenic fumes. Neighbors, however, insist that the deceased has never sprayed his potatoes, and add that Howe, forty-five, constantly quarreled with his sixty-five-year-old wife. Mrs. Winfred Howe denies killing her husband, challenging police to "prove it." Placed on trial, she admits to feeding her husband arsenic, "but only once, and only to make him sick. I didn't intend to kill him." She is sentenced to twenty years to life in the State Prison for Women at Bedford Hills. The murderess laughs when hearing the sentence, telling the court: "Twenty years to life. How silly. With tuberculosis and diabetes I can't live half that long." She doesn't.

1937

Grover Whalen, New York City's ambassador of good will, who has led the tumultuous parades for world celebrities through the tickertape-strewn streets of Manhattan, walks onto the stage of the Manhattan Opera House on the night of January 17, 1937, to address 671 guests gathered to honor Barney Shapiro, president of the Garment Truckmen's Benevolent Association of New Jersey. Just as Whalen begins his speech, the loud voice of a tipsy man is heard singing "Pennies from Heaven." The man is thirty-three-year-old truck driver Frank Cicero. Two men, Joseph Berger and Gabriel Klar, angered over this outburst, get up from another table, rush Cicero and stab him to death. They have fled by the time police arrive but their identities are soon forthcoming when police compel the entire audience to resume their table seats, count heads and check the guest list. Berger and Klar, who have murdered a man over a song, are sent to prison for a maximum of ten years, found guilty of second-degree manslaughter. . . . Sixty-year-old Cora Webner and her husband, Will, run a crazy mail-order matrimonial scam from their farmhouse outside Pocahontas, Arkansas. Each of them marries at least a hundred times, robbing and leaving their various spouses throughout the Southland before returning to the farm. When Will Webner begins to argue with Cora, the energetic bigamist poisons him and tosses his body into the storm cellar where, days later, its decaying flesh draws buzzards, which Cora attempts to shoot with a shotgun. When passersby smell the overpowering odor they complain to local authorities, who merely question Cora. She blows up, screaming at one visiting officer: "That smell comes from dead chickens. Them birds comin' round here are chicken hawks. If you think I kilt my man and buried him in the storm cellar, then why don't you go down there and take a look-see?" The officer declines and departs. Cora then moves to St. Louis. When the new owners of the farm move in, they find Webner's body. Cora is arrested, but before she is tried, she takes strychnine in her jail cell. . . . Robert Irwin, a twenty-nine-year-old New York sculptor, depressed over being rejected for a job as a taxidermist at the Museum of Natural History, first decides to commit suicide, but opts for murder, going to the home of one-time sweetheart Ethel Gedeon on the night of March 27, 1937. After chatting with Ethel's mother in the kitchen over coffee, Irwin suddenly attacks her, choking her for twenty minutes until she is dead. He places the corpse under a bed, then attacks Ethel's younger sister, Ronnie, a beautiful model, strapping her to a bed. Ronnie Gedeon recognizes him in the darkened room and blurts: "Bob, I know you are going to get in trouble for this." The recognition brings her death. Irwin later states: "The minute she said that I clamped down on her and choked her until she was lifeless. I turned on the lights and ripped off her chemise, leaving her on top of the bed, her mother's body lying beneath. At that moment she was the most repulsive thing I ever knew." Knowing that Frank Byrnes, a roomer in the apartment, has seen him talking to Mrs. Gedeon, Irwin, carrying an ice pick, slips into Byrnes' room and stabs him to death. "Byrnes was asleep. I struck him the first time in the temple, as far as I could go. The pick was about six inches long. After sticking him once, the poor fellow lay there twitching but did not bleed. He did not make any outcry. I wanted to put him out of his misery, so I stabbed him a number of other blows about his head [seven in all]." Before leaving the premises, Irwin absentmindedly takes an alarm clock and two photos of Ronnie Gedeon, after not finding any of Ethel. He later laments: "Do you know, that's the one thing I'm ashamed of —stealing that clock. To kill is one thing, but to be a sneak thief!" Irwin is quickly apprehended. To many he is obviously demented. At one time in the past, Irwin begged a physician to castrate him, and being refused, performed the bloody, half-finished operation on himself. This he did, according to later explanations, to channel all his energies into his art and homespun philosophy, which he terms "visualizing." He later rants that "every organism, upon reaching maturity, sacrifices itself to the task of reproduction. In other words, the driving force in back of our lives, which can be used for other purposes, we sacrifice to the task of reproduction. I realized that if I could once bottle that up with her [Ethel], I didn't need her. It's a great deal of fun to monkey around with a woman. It's a great deal of fun to have five dollars and spend it. But if by foregoing the five dollars you later get a million dollars . . ." Irwin is defended by Samuel Leibowitz. Though obviously unbalanced, his plea of insanity is ignored and he is sent to prison for life. . . . Arthur Perry of Jamaica, New York, cleverly plans the murder of his wife, establishing what will appear to be an ironclad case against his neighbor. (page 248) . . . Near Franklin Park, Illinois, petty thief John Henry Seadlund and James Atwood Gray kidnap seventy-two-year-old Charles S. Ross, a greeting-card manufacturer, on September 25, 1937. Hiding in Spooner, Wisconsin,

*Mocking the guilty
verdict that would send
him to the Illinois
electric chair, kidnapper-
murderer John Henry
Seadlund made
headlines in 1937. (UPI)*

Seadlund murders Ross; then, when he receives the fifty-thousand-dollar ransom, he and Gray flee to California. FBI agents track Seadlund down at the Santa Anita Racetrack on January 14, 1938, J. Edgar Hoover flying to Los Angeles to take personal charge of the kidnapper's capture. (Hoover is later to state of Seadlund: "He was the most vicious killer I ever knew.") Seadlund is returned to Illinois and convicted of the kidnapping-murder. The murderer jokes in court, asking officials with a laugh: "Will I get hanged or fried?" He is electrocuted two months later. . . . Paul Dwyer of South Paris, Maine, thinks his seventeen-year-old girlfriend, Barbara Carroll, is pregnant. Her father, Francis Carroll, who is the local sheriff, insists that the youth come to the home of Dr. James Littlefield, where Barbara will be examined to determine her condition. Dwyer agrees and then attempts to extort money from Sheriff Carroll by telling him that he possesses letters from Barbara in which the daughter claims to have been repeatedly raped by her father. Dwyer is later found asleep in his car by New Jersey police. In the auto's trunk are found the battered bodies of Dr. Littlefield and his wife. Dwyer stands trial and is sent to prison for life. In prison he insists that Carroll murdered the Littlefields for unknown reasons and ordered him to dispose of the bodies. So strong is the evidence against Sheriff Carroll that he is put on trial. His daughter, Barbara, sets up a booth outside the courtroom and sells autographed photos of herself to interested spectators. Carroll is convicted of murder and he, too, is sent to prison for life but is released in 1950. Dwyer remains in prison.

1938

On the night of April 29, 1938, Harvey L. Roush arrives at the Delaware, Ohio, home of Homer T. Myers, his partner in business, asking that Myers receipt his personal note for fifteen hundred dollars. Roush reaches into his pocket as if to withdraw the cash; Myers marks the note "paid in full." Roush withdraws a .38-caliber revolver and shoots Myers. Mrs. Myers races into the room to scuffle with the killer, who empties his gun into her. He then sets the house ablaze but firefighters, on the scene some minutes later, find the bodies with the tell-tale bullet holes. When Roush is interviewed routinely by police he quickly breaks down, admitting he killed the Myers couple over financial setbacks. He is tried and condemned. . . . Albert Dyer lures three Los Angeles children into a ravine where he sexually attacks them before killing them. Like the Michigan child killer three decades later, Dyer cleans their bodies and arranges their clothing, before praying over their bodies: "God, please save the soul of this child and save my soul and forgive me for what I have done." Dyer is apprehended while attempting to molest another child. He confesses and is hanged. . . . Joe Ball, forty-four-year-old owner of a sprawling and successful tavern outside San Antonio, Texas, employs three dozen waitresses at a time to serve his wealthy customers in seductive outfits. Many of these young women disappear; Ball explains that they are itinerants, that he has a large turnover in help. When Hazel Brown, one of the waitresses, disappears, Texas Rangers learn that she has told her banker that she is Ball's intended. Ball denies he planned to marry Hazel. A Ranger probe reveals that Ball has been banking enormous amounts of money beyond his business revenues. Witnesses come forward to shudderingly describe how Ball has been murdering his waitresses to obtain their savings and salary and tips, at least twenty women in all over a two-year period, strangling them, chopping up the bodies and feeding the remains to five pet alligators he keeps in a pool behind his tavern. States one terrified witness to Rangers: "I just happened to stumble into Joe cutting up a couple of bodies one night. He was feeding the pieces to the alligators, heads and all. Well, he saw me and threatened me. He said he'd kill me and feed me to the alligators, too, if I didn't leave town. So I left town." When Rangers enter Ball's tavern on September 24, 1938, to arrest him, the mass-killer leaps for the cash register, pulls out a revolver and blows out his brains. . . . Railroad clerk Rodney Greig meets Leona Vlught on his twenty-first birthday in Oakland, California. A few days later, on December 6, 1938, he takes the girl on a drive. He later tells the story that the girl is despondent, that she has had a miserable life and no hope, that she has tried to take poison but didn't have the nerve, begging Greig to kill her as they sit in the car. Greig shows her a sharp hunting knife. She allegedly pleads: "Rodney, you'd be doing me a great favor if you stabbed me with that." He does, plunging the knife into her right breast. After sitting in the car smoking cigarettes for twenty minutes, Greig then slits the girl's throat several times. Reporters later claim that Greig drinks the blood from her neck wounds, labeling him "The Vampire Killer," a charge Greig denies. Arrested the following night, Greig willingly confesses the murder. He is sent to San Quentin's gas chamber.

1939

Alice Austin and her lover, Ted Simmons, of Hardin County, Illinois, give mechanic Ira Scott fifty dollars to plant a bomb in the car of Earl Austin, Alice's estranged husband. On March 20, 1939, Austin and his sweetheart, Lacene McDowell, take the car for a ride; it blows up after a few miles, killing Austin and mortally injuring Miss McDowell. Detectives find the remains of the dynamite bomb, which leads them to Scott. He exposes his employers, stating that he did not know that the bomb had been intended to kill anyone, a fabrication proved by the fact that he had run the fuse back to the exhaust manifold, where it could not be ignited unless the car was in operation. Alice Austin, Simmons and Scott are given fourteen years in prison.

1940

Les Wilson, frontrunning candidate in the sheriff's race in Okaloosa County, Florida, is shot to death on March 15, 1940, as he sits with his family in his Crestview, Florida, home. The unknown killer has fired a shotgun through a glass window only a few feet from Wilson's head. Police work on the case for ten years but are unable to unearth any clues. The victim's son, Ray Wilson, despite threats and bribes to quit the race, runs for the same sheriff's post in 1956 and wins in a landslide. He immediately begins investigating his father's murder, and, after travelling almost twenty thousand miles, interviewing two hundred persons, and spending eighteen months of time, Wilson finds three witnesses who pinpoint the killers of his father. They testify against Doyle and Jessie Cayson, who murdered Les Wilson to keep lucrative businesses through their political connections. The brothers, boyhood friends of Ray Wilson, are sent to prison for life.

1941

Mrs. Ethel Leta Juanita Spinelli, a homely fifty-two-year-old harridan, gathers a youthful San Francisco gang about her and her common-law husband, Mike Simeons, to commit petty thefts. They rob and kill Leland Cash, an owner of a San Francisco barbecue stand, then flee to the Arlton Hotel in Sacramento. When it appears that nineteen-year-old Robert Sherrard may talk about the killing, the Duchess, as Mrs. Spinelli is called by gang members, slips chloral hydrate "knock-out" drops into the youth's whiskey. He is then bashed on the head for good measure and dragged to a car and taken to the Freeport–Clarksburg Bridge, his body being dumped into the Sacramento River. Gang member Albert Ives informs on the Duchess and her minions. She is arrested, tried and sentenced to death, going into San Quentin's gas chamber on November 22, 1941, the first woman to be executed in California. (The only other woman previously put to death in the state is recorded only with the first name "Juanita," a Mexican woman who killed a man attempting to rape her in 1851 and who was lynched by an anti-Mexican mob in Downieville, California.) ... Well-to-do Walter Lewis Samples of South Memphis, Tennessee, is admitted to the Veteran's Administration Hospital on February 27, 1941. The Spanish-American War veteran complains of intense abdominal pains; he dies in paroxysm hours later. Doctors quickly learn Samples has been poisoned. Before dying, Samples told physicians that his only meal before entering the hospital was bacon and eggs, toast and two glasses of milk, pointing out that the milk left that morning has been unusual in that *two* bottles instead of the usual one had been left. Police retrieve the bottle and discover the remaining milk poisoned. A further investigation of Samples' house reveals an enormous collection of photos of females, many in lascivious poses, scantily attired, and autographed to "Daddy Samples." The deceased's personal phone directory reveals hundreds of phone numbers of married, single and spinster women in the Memphis area, all of whom, at one time or another, carried on torrid affairs with super womanizer Samples, many of them unable to ignore his calls and refrain from visiting him long after they became married. In the course of interviewing these females intoxicated with Samples' lovemaking, police encounter Mrs. Harvey Collins, the wife of a successful contractor. She denies having anything to do with Samples' death but police find the murdered man's will, which makes her the beneficiary, hidden in one of the shoes she is wearing. She is arrested. Her husband then comes forward, claiming that his wife is innocent, that he alone poisoned Samples for his money. Both are tried and found guilty, each given twenty years and a day to make parole difficult. At a retrial, Mrs. Collins jumps up and screams to the court: "I can't stand it any longer. My husband is innocent. I did it alone and he's been trying to protect me." Mrs. Collins goes on to explain that the only way she could escape the almost hypnotic sexual hold Samples held on her was to murder him. Mrs. Collins is sent to prison for twenty years.

1942

Religious fanatic Donald Fern, married and the father of five, lures a young woman, Alice Porter, to an abandoned church on an Indian Reservation near Pueblo, Colorado, on April 22, 1942, and, to satisfy his sadistic drives, crucifies the woman. He is apprehended and sent to prison. . . . Farrington Graham Hill slays a hotel clerk in Hollywood over his bill. Before he is executed in San Quentin's gas chamber, Hill requests music be played, specifically "Tales from the Vienna Woods." Kindhearted Warden Clinton Duffy, who cannot find a record of the work anywhere only hours before the execution, asks musicians among the prison population to record the work, which they do. Hill goes to his death "a happy man, humming along with the music." . . . Giovanni Leonidas, a hermit living in a shack in Sismundo Valley, California, is attacked in his hut by two young men demanding his hoarded gold on the night of September 6, 1942. When Leonidas refuses, he is tied to a chair, his shoes removed and his feet burned with matches by both men. He still refuses to tell the men where his treasure is. He is beaten and his place ransacked. Police, answering the screams of a child who peeks into the shack to see the carnage, find the hermit dying. No clues to the murderers' identities are unearthed until a milkman reports a blue Ford with a woman and two men in it stopping in front of the hermit's shack on the day of the murder. The car, a rental, is found days later; it leads police to arrest twenty-two-year-old John Elbert, his friend Phil Ferdinand, a young boxer, and Ferdinand's girlfriend, eighteen-year-old Josephine Humphrey, who has just recently left her husband. Mrs. Humphrey breaks down and admits that she went with the two men to the hermit's shack to find his rumored gold, witnessing the beating and torture. Ferdinand also admits the killing. Both Elbert and Ferdinand are given life sentences; Mrs. Humphrey receives a suspended sentence. No gold, then or now, is ever found on the premises. . . . Jake Bird kills two women in Evanston, Illinois, when they interrupt him as he burglarizes their house. He uses an axe to chop them to death. Bird's career as a killer-burglar will not be stopped until police apprehend him in Tacoma, Washington, on October 30, 1947, after he has axed to death Mrs. Bertha Kludt and her attractive seventeen-year-old daughter, Beverly June Kludt. Bird, who admits to more than ten such axe killings, is hanged.

1943

Successful corporation lawyer John Franklin Noxon, Jr., of Pittsfield, Massachusetts, calls police to his home. They find his mongoloid infant son dead, apparently electrocuted—the child has wrapped its arm around an extension cord with exposed wires. Noxon states that he left the infant alone in his workshop only for a few minutes and returned to find the boy dead. Noxon, immensely disliked in the community, is arrested and charged with murdering his son, a mental defective he cannot tolerate. The lawyer is condemned on slim evidence; his sentence is commuted to life imprisonment. He is paroled in 1945. . . . Lewis Wolfe checks into the St. George Hotel in downtown Brooklyn with his wife, Paula, on December 30, 1943. Paula Wolfe, who has been in Europe and separated from her husband for several years, tells him of her nymphomania and recounts in long, detailed stories her escapades with dozens of lovers, ending her tales with a sneering: "You're not a man, or you'd kill me for all this." When Paula Wolfe falls asleep, her husband takes his heavy shoe and strikes her repeatedly on the head, crushing her skull. He informs police of the murder and is given a life sentence in Dannemora State Prison.

Louise Peete, who has already served a long sentence for murder, grows tired of her "sponsors" in Pacific Palisades, California, and carefully plots the extermination of Mrs. Margaret Logan and her husband. (page 255)

1945

William Heirens, a seventeen-year-old Chicago burglar, enters the home of Mrs. Josephine Alice Ross, experiencing sexual climax merely by secretly being on the premises, according to his later testimony. When the twice-divorced Mrs. Ross wakes at his noise, Heirens runs to her bed and slashes her throat from ear to ear and then proceeds to mutilate the corpse. He later robs several more apartments in Chicago, including that of thirty-three-year-old Frances Brown on December 10, 1945, shooting the ex-WAVE when she emerges from a bathroom. He stabs her twice and then inexplicably puts the corpse in a bathtub and washes it. On the bathroom mirror, Heirens writes in lipstick: "For Heavens' sake, catch me before I kill more. I cannot control myself." Heirens goes on to kidnap and dissect six-year-old Suzanne Degnan on January 7, 1946, and is not apprehended until breaking into another apartment. Heirens denies all charges of murder, stating that his best friend, "George Murman," (George *Murder-man*) is the guilty party; "Murman" is, in reality, Heirens' alter ego, to whom he writes letters. Heirens is found guilty and given three consecutive life terms; he is, at this writing, still attempting to be paroled. . . . Deputy sheriff Arthur R. Eggers arrives at his San Bernardino, California, home to see a man leaving the house. Finding his wife naked in bed, he shoots her and then cuts off her head and hands. ("I loved her," he will later state, "that's why I cut off her head and hands—I had gone so nuts I thought I could keep them and look at them whenever I wanted.") He is quickly apprehended, tried and sentenced to death in San Quentin. "They'll never execute me," he tells guards. "They wouldn't send a deputy sheriff to the gas chamber." Eggers is sent to the gas chamber in 1948. . . . Leo Pacarella murders his girl friend, Ethel Marie Beaver, in her Detroit apartment when she tells him she is going to marry another man. He strangles her to death, stuffs a handkerchief down her throat, slips the body beneath the bed and flees to Saginaw, Michigan. Police track him down months later. Pacarella, a homicidal maniac according to Detroit psychiatrists, receives a seven-to-fifteen-year sentence. . . . A skeleton is found at the bottom of a well on an Alexandria, Virginia, farm; it sparks a one-man detective hunt to solve a sixteen-year-old murder mystery. (page 263)

Chicago archkiller William Heirens in 1945; he stubbornly applies for parole to this day.

1946

Erwin Walker, having established a noteworthy war record, returns to Los Angeles and goes on a robbery spree of small stores, wielding a submachinegun, which he uses on two officers in April 1946, wounding both. Some weeks later he kills Highway Patrolman Loren C. Roosevelt when the officer asks why he is loitering near a grocery store. The cop killer is caught on a tip from the girl he is dating and, following a speedy trial, sent to San Quentin to be gassed. Walker appears to crack up mentally weeks before his execution and only hours before he is to die, seven prison psychiatrists observe his animal-like behavior in his cell and declare him insane. He is sent to the state mental hospital at Mendocino, where it takes twelve years for him to recover his sanity. Governor Edmund G. Brown commutes Walker's death sentence to life imprisonment in 1961. The story of Irwin Walker is made into the film, *He Walks by Night*.

1947

LaVerene Borelli, thirty-eight years old, finds her younger husband, Gene, making love to another woman, and, after guzzling many drinks in a San Francisco bar, returns home on May 9, 1946, takes her husband's automatic from a bureau drawer, and empties four bullets into him while he sleeps. She then swallows strychnine and fires two bullets into her own breast but survives. Jake Erlich takes her defense and manages, through surprising legal maneuvers, to reduce Mrs. Borelli's conviction to manslaughter, for which she receives a minimal sentence in the woman's prison at Tehachapi, being paroled on March 10, 1953.

1948

Houston, Texas, police receive a phone call from Steve Mitchell on the afternoon of December 16, 1948, informing them that he has just shot his wife. He is arrested and says that his wife has been sleeping away from home, that he told her they are through and she began hitting him, then ran into the bathroom. He fired his pistol at her through the door, killing her as she sat on the commode. To reporters, Mitchell declares: "My wife left me. She sued me for divorce. She wanted half my property. I had a right to shoot her. Don't you think I had a right to shoot her for that?" The flamboyant lawyer Percy Foreman takes Mitchell's case but it proves fruitless. Foreman cannot alter jury opinion after hearing evidence of Mitchell's guilt; he is found guilty. Mitchell is condemned and electrocuted in Huntsville Prison, September 25, 1951, the only client of Percy Foreman's to be executed. . . . Lillian Rich Brackett is slain by two joy-seeking youths in Bristol, Connecticut, on December 25, 1951. (page 266)

1949

Mrs. Delphine Dowling and her infant daughter of Grand Rapids, Michigan, are slain in January 1949 by Raymond Fernandez and Martha Beck, who will be known to the world as the "Lonely Hearts Killers." (pages 269) . . . World War II hero Howard Unruh goes berserk on the streets of Camden, New Jersey, and kills thirteen persons inside of twelve minutes. He barricades his house against a police siege. A clever reporter from the *Camden Courier Post* calls Unruh and asks him how many persons he has killed. "I don't know," Unruh answers. "I haven't counted them but it looks like a pretty good score." Unruh surrenders minutes later. When a cop holding him asks if he is crazy, Unruh calmly replies: "I'm no psycho. I have a good mind." He is sent to the New Jersey State Mental Hospital for life.

1950

Always an incorrigible, Ernest Ingenito of Minotola, New Jersey, argues with his young wife, Theresa, on November 17, 1950; when she flees to her father's house, Ingenito follows, shooting her and eight others of the Mike Mazzoli family, killing seven. He is apprehended and sent to the New Jersey State Hospital for life, adjudged a hopeless maniac. . . . Itinerant bad boy William Cook, after robbing motorists in Texas, stops Carl Mosser on Highway 66 between Claremore and

Killer of thirteen in a berserk mass-murder spree, Howard Unruh sits stonily in custody in a Camden, New Jersey, lockup. (UPI)

Mass murderer William Cook (center, handcuffed) is led from a California courtroom after hearing his death sentence in 1951.

Tulsa, Oklahoma. Cook jumps into the car and abducts Mosser, his wife, Thelma, and their three small children. Cook shoots all five, including the family dog, and drops them down a well. He stops a police car, ties up the deputy, and roars off in the deputy's auto. Next he pulls over the car of salesman Robert H. Dewey, robbing and killing him. Cook drives to Mexico where he is arrested and returned to the United States; tried and convicted, he is executed at San Quentin on December 12, 1952.

1951

Gertrude Morris, thinking her husband, Milton, a successful San Francisco insurance executive, is having an affair with his attractive secretary, goes to her husband's office and makes a scene. Milton returns home that night and packs his bags. Gertrude points a pistol at him as he holds an armful of shirts and shoots him in the back. "Go for the doctor," he pleads, but Gertrude Morris can only vomit and collapse. She revives hours later, changes her clothes, and then asks neighbors to fetch the police. She never denies her guilt, and she insists that the state execute her. Jake Erlich, in a brilliant defense, emotionally appeals to the jury, detailing the lonely, miserable life of Gertrude Morris, a woman without friends who has slaved to send her husband through school and who, at forty-four, has been ignored and deceived. The jury is convinced, convicting the killer of only manslaughter. She receives a term of one to ten years in the state prison. Before she is led away, Gertrude Morris screeches at the reporters' gallery: "I am a criminal! I murdered someone! I owe the state a life!" She then turns to her lawyer, Erlich, who has lost eight pounds during the ten-month trial and looks an emaciated wreck, spitting at him: "You missed your vocation. You should have been on the stage. . . . Well, Master, I suppose this is one more feather in your cap? . . . I am not satisfied. I still believe in a life for a life. I am not paying my debt to society. I have no hopes, no longings—nothing!" . . . Sex pervert August Jagusch, whose wife has left him because of his abnormal lovemaking, takes up with a New York whore, Mildred Fogarty, strangling her to death in June 1951 when, after long sexual bouts, she laughingly tells him she has gonorrhea. Jagusch is later captured by police with his wife's help. He is to say of the murder: "Her body collapsed, but I kept squeezing until her neck felt like mashed potatoes in my hands. It wasn't much harder than strangling a cat, and it made me feel good—real good." Jagusch is found guilty of second-degree murder and given twenty years in prison. He was released from Auburn State Prison in New York on August 23, 1967.

Hilda Rose Pagan, a pretty sixteen-year-old high school girl in San Francisco, is found horribly beaten to death in Mission Park on March 24, 1952. Her eighteen-year-old boyfriend, Roman Ivan Rodriguez, is brought in for questioning and admits to the killing, saying that when he could not bring himself to have intercourse with Hilda—who, he insists, urged him on—she called him "a queer," hitting him. He struck her back, using his fists, shoes, belt buckle, leaving her dead on the grass at Mission Park. Rodriguez is given a long prison term. . . . Baltimore salesman G. Edward Grammer, in love with another woman, chooses to murder his wife instead of divorcing her, bashing in her head and then faking a car accident, which fails to convince police (officers find a rock placed on top of the accelerator, a device commonly employed to cause a driverless car to keep moving). When brought in for questioning, Grammer admits to second-degree murder. He recants his confession during his trial, pleading "Not Guilty." Evidence for premeditated murder is overwhelming and Grammer, convicted and condemned, is hanged in the Maryland Penitentiary on June 11, 1954.

1953

A case of "bad company" is how Barbara Graham will later explain her bludgeoning to death an elderly woman named Monohan in Burbank, California, on March 9, 1953. Graham and four other thugs enter the woman's home in search of the elderly spinster's hoarded gems. When she puts up a struggle, Graham hits her with the butt of a gun, crushing her skull. No jewels are uncovered by the thieves, who quickly turn on one another when they are tracked down by police. Barbara Graham and two others are condemned; she is sent to the gas chamber on June 3, 1953. . . . Carl Austin Hall and Bonnie Heady kidnap and murder Bobby Greenlease, Jr., in Kansas City, Missouri, on September 23, 1953. (page 276) . . . Carl J. Folk, after being confined in a mental institution for three years following his rape and torture of a seventeen-year-old girl in Albuquerque, New Mexico, enters a camper owned by Raymond Allen, parked at an Arizona rest area on December 1, 1953. Folk ties up Allen and, for seven hours, in another room of the camper, rapes and tortures his twenty-two-year-old wife, Betty. Allen manages to break his bonds, escape and retrieve a revolver hidden beneath his driver's seat. He finds Folk pouring gasoline on his dead wife and ten-month-old baby, preparing to burn them. Allen shoots Folk in the stomach, wounding him. The child survives. Folk is quickly adjudged sane and is condemned, sent to the gas chamber in March 1955. . . . Eight-year-old Stella Darlene Nolan disappears in Los Angeles. Not until 1970 will Mack Ray Edwards, haunted by the murder of six children, come forward, showing Stella's grave to police and asking to be put to death. Edwards, impatient at waiting to be executed, will hang himself in his prison cell. . . . Chicago grocery store owner Vincent Ciucci, in order to live with another woman, chloroforms his wife, Anne, and three children on December 4, 1953, and attempts to hide the murders by torching his apartment. Firemen appear too soon for Ciucci's purposes, put out the blaze and find the bodies. After all appeals fail, Ciucci is sent to the electric chair in 1962.

1954

Farmer Edward Gein, a long-time ghoul who has been cannibalizing the bodies from graves he has robbed in the Plainfield, Wisconsin, area, shoots and cannibalizes Mary Hogan. This extraordinary cannibal, necrophile and murderer will not be apprehended until 1957, after he kills Mrs. Bernice Worden; he is sent to a mental institution for life. . . . Famed 1920s poet Maxwell Bodenheim, over whose lost love several women committed suicide in the Jazz Age, is shot to death on February 7, 1954, in a Bowery slum by Harold Weinberg, who is having an affair with Bodenheim's wife. He also knifes Ruth Bodenheim to death. Weinberg is apprehended and sent to New York's Matteawan State Hospital for the Criminally Insane for life. . . . On March 4, 1954, William Snyder Byers, at the urgings of sixteen-year-old Theresa Gresch, murders Theresa's mother, Anna, in her Manhattan apartment because of Mrs. Gresch's attempts to stop her daughter from seeing Byers. The killer is sent to the electric chair; he dies with an indifferent shrug, chewing bubblegum. Theresa Gresch is sent to prison for twenty years. . . . Robert William Jordan of Elizabeth City, North Carolina, upon hearing that he is about to be inducted into the Army, goes berserk on September 9, 1954. The twenty-two-year-old shoots four fellow workers with a rifle in a locker freezer plant, killing three men and wounding a woman. Jordan, given a life sentence, explains that his fellow workers "laughed at me." . . . Filipino houseboy Bart Caritativo murders his employers, wealthy Camille and Joseph Banks of Stinson Beach, California, on September 10, 1954, and then attempts to fake an awkward will in which he is to inherit their property. Caritativo is sent to San Quentin's gas chamber on October 24, 1958. . . . Dovie Dean, an Ohio grandmother of eight, feeds rat poison to her husband. She is sent to the electric chair showing no remorse, labeled by the press as the "Murderess Without

Tears." . . . Nannie Doss of Tulsa, Oklahoma, is questioned about the mysterious death of her husband, at which time she admits not only to poisoning him but also a half dozen other husbands and relatives. (page 285)

1955

University of California accounting student Burton W. Abbott of San Francisco abducts and strangles to death fourteen-year-old Stephanie Bryan on April 28, 1955. In a long, sensational trial, Abbott is found guilty, the jury convinced of his guilt when Stephanie's bra and schoolbooks are found in the killer's basement. Abbott is sent to the gas chamber, March 14, 1957. . . . Judge Charles E. Chillingworth and his wife, Marjorie, disappear from their West Palm Beach, Florida, estate on June 14, 1955. Not until 1960 does a thug-for-hire, Floyd Albert Holzapfel, admit that he and others murdered the judge and his wife, taking them out in a boat, binding them with chains, and bashing in their heads until they sank, all at the orders of Joseph Alexander Peel, Jr., a one-time judge himself, and racketeer. Chillingworth had been interfering in Peel's rackets, states Holzapfel, and was therefore eliminated. Holzapfel is sent to the electric chair, Peel to two life terms. . . . Mrs. Wilma Frances Allen, an attractive thirty-four-year-old housewife, steps from a Kansas City, Missouri, beauty parlor on August 4, 1955, and goes to her car in a parking lot. A man jumps in next to her, telling her to drive into the country—across the state line into Kansas. About twenty miles from Kansas City, the man

One-time Florida judge Joseph A. Peel, Jr., was given a life sentence after arranging for the murder of his nemesis, Judge Charles E. Chillingworth, in 1955. (WIDE WORLD)

forces her to stop in a farmer's field and strips the woman, stealing her jewelry. As she begs for her life in the back seat of the car, telling the thief of her children, he mercilessly shoots her twice in the head and dumps her body in the field. A massive hunt involving six hundred local and state police ensues. The body is found but not until November do authorities get a clue to the killer's identity. A San Francisco woman calls the FBI, telling agents that she believes her son, Arthur Ross Brown, who has a long record of sex offenses, is crazy and dangerous and is, perhaps, the murderer of Mrs. Allen. Brown answers the description of a man who has recently shot a sheriff in Wyoming following a burglary. Agents stake out the address of Brown's favorite aunt in San Francisco, where he is later found sleeping in a parked car. Brown quickly admits killing Mrs. Allen, telling agents that "I was looking for someone to rob. She looked wealthy." He insists that he did not rape the woman, but stripped her only to prevent identification (examination of the body upholds his claim). Brown also insists that he is sane. He is sent to the gas chamber in the Missouri State Prison on February 24, 1956. . . . United Airlines Flight 629 blows up eleven minutes after leaving Denver's Stapleton Airport on November 1, 1955. Officials checking the passenger list find that heiress Mrs. Daisie Walker King has taken out three policies before takeoff, making her son, Jack Gilbert Graham, the beneficiary. It is also quickly learned that the plane has been bombed. Graham is interviewed by police who find bomb-making apparatus in his home. After severe grilling, Graham cracks, admitting that he planted the bomb in his mother's luggage to obtain her life insurance money. He is convicted and sent to the gas chamber in the Colorado State Penitentiary on January 11, 1957.

1956

Patrolman Gerald H. Mitchell stops a motorist for going through a stop sign in Paoli, Pennsylvania, on the night of February 29, 1956. The driver is youthful Danny Metcalf, a five-foot-three-inch stickup artist from Massachusetts who shoots Mitchell dead from the car and flees. Roadblocks are set up to apprehend the killer, but he crashes through a bridge barricade near Gladwyne, Pennsylvania, running through a wooded area to evade pursuing police. Metcalf bursts into the home of Mrs. Margaret Loweth on the morning of March 1, 1955, clubbing her unconscious in her kitchen with a monkey wrench. Her eleven-year-old son, Billy, runs downstairs with a .22 rifle, shooting Metcalf in the finger before he can land a killing blow on Mrs. Loweth. Metcalf disarms the boy. Bandaging the woman's head and using her and the boy as hostages, Metcalf orders them to drive through the roadblocks around Gladwyne. When police stop the car they notice blood trickling down Mrs. Loweth's cheek. Before they can jump Metcalf, the youthful killer puts a gun to Billy's head, shouting to Mrs. Loweth: "Drive on fast, or I'll shoot!" Mrs. Loweth drives the car around police vans, officers holding their fire after seeing the automatic at Billy Loweth's head. A few miles from the roadblock, Mrs. Loweth purposely jams on the brakes, which sends her car into a ditch. She jumps from one side of the car. Metcalf grabs the boy and, still holding the weapon to his temple, begins backing into the woods. Police arrive and train their weapons on Metcalf and his hostage. Metcalf stumbles in the brush; Billy Loweth dashes away to freedom. Before Metcalf can shoot the boy, the police open up and the killer flops backward, dead, riddled by more than a dozen bullets.

1957

When fifteen-year-old Victoria Zielinski of Mahwah, New Jersey, is reported missing on March 4, 1957, police interview Edgar Herbert Smith, one of the girl's boyfriends. He states ignorance. Victoria's body is then found in a sandpit. Smith is confronted with a pair of his own jeans, covered with blood and found at the scene of the murder. He claims he loaned the jeans to a friend, but his weak explanation is discarded by a jury that condemns him. Smith spends a record fourteen years on Death Row in the Trenton Prison. He files fourteen appeals and is granted thirteen stays of execution. During his confinement, Smith writes to columnist William F. Buckley who, after receiving almost three thousand pages of handwritten appeals from the prisoner, is convinced of his innocence and begins a massive campaign to free the prisoner. With Buckley's help, Smith writes two best-sellers, including *Brief Against Death*. Thought to be rehabilitated, Smith is released in 1971. Five years later in San Diego, he attacks Lefteriya Ozbun in his car, attempting to steal her weekly paycheck, stabbing her. The woman manages to escape and Smith, wanted by police, calls his mentor, Buckley, leaving his phone number when finding the columnist not available. Buckley turns the number over to FBI agents, who arrest Smith at his Las Vegas, Nevada, hotel. At trial on the attempted robbery charge, Smith admits that he murdered the Zielinski girl, crushing her head with a baseball bat when she refused to have sex with him. Before being sent back to prison, Smith states: "For the first time in my life, I recognized that the devil I had been looking at the last forty-three years was me." . . . On June 26, 1957, a psychopathic musician, Melvin David Rees, stops a car near Annapolis, Maryland, shooting Margaret Harold after she rebuffs his advances. In 1959, Rees will stop a car driven by Carroll Jackson outside of Fredericksburg, Virginia, shooting Jackson, suffocating his eighteen-month old child, and raping and killing Mildred

Jackson and her four-year-old daughter. Four more teenage girls are found raped and strangled in Maryland, all Rees' work. FBI agents finally track the killer of nine to a West Memphis, Arkansas, store where Rees is a piano salesman. He surrenders without a struggle. At his trial, Rees' diary, replete with detailed descriptions of the murders, is used to convict the "sex beast," as the press dubs the killer. Rees is put to death in Virginia for the Jackson murders in 1961. . . . Amateur photographer Harvey Murray Glatman of Los Angeles lures model Judy Ann Dull to his apartment on August 1, 1957; has her pose for "bondage photos," telling her they will appear in some men's magazines; and then, when she is bound, rapes and strangles her, burying her in a shallow desert grave 125 miles east of Los Angeles. Glatman will use essentially the same procedure to murder Mrs. Shirley Bridgeford and Ruth Mercado in 1958. He is apprehended while trying to murder another woman, Lorraine Vigil, and promptly confesses to his brutal slayings. Glatman is sent to the gas chamber on August 18, 1959. . . . Lincoln, Nebraska, garbageman Charles Starkweather goes on a murder spree with his teenage girlfriend Caril Ann Fugate on December 1, 1957, murdering gas station attendant Robert Colvert. In the following month he will murder nine more persons, shooting and stabbing at will, including Caril's own mother, baby sister and stepfather. He is finally captured with his sweetheart outside Douglas, Wyoming, following a nationwide manhunt involving more than twelve hundred police officers. Starkweather, who admits to the mass killings with a sneering laugh, is sent to Nebraska's gas chamber on June 25, 1959. Caril Fugate receives a life term but is paroled in 1977.

Charles Starkweather, the Nebraska Terror of 1957, killer of ten.

Mrs. Ruth Reeves' strangled body is found by boys fishing in the Anacostia River in Washington, D.C., on September 8. The baffling murder is finally placed at the door of Philmore Clarke, a hard-working carpenter. (page 288) . . . Lowell Lee Andrews, an overweight (310 pounds) eighteen-year-old honor student in Wolcott, Kansas, walks into the family living room on November 28, 1958, and shoots his sister, mother, and father dead as they watch television. Hours later he claims that burglars are responsible for the triple killing but breaks down and admits the slayings, telling police that he wants to inherit the family money in order to travel to Chicago to become "a hired gun." After devouring two fried chickens, with extra helpings of mashed potatoes, green beans, ice cream and pie, Andrews is hanged in the prison yard of Leavenworth Prison. . . . Hitchhiker James Donald French, who has recently been released from a California reformatory, is picked up near Amarillo, Texas, on December 10, 1958 by Franklin Boone. At French's gunpoint, Boone drives back and forth between Texas and Oklahoma until the hitchhiker tires of the game and shoots Boone through the head outside Stroud, Oklahoma. Following his apprehension, French strangles his cellmate, Eddie Shelton. He is convicted of both murders and is electrocuted in the Oklahoma State Prison.

1959

Penny Bjorkland, an attractive but mentally disturbed eighteen-year-old blond living in Daly City, California, impulsively takes her .38-caliber target pistol with her on a drive in the hills about San Francisco. She encounters gardener August Norry and empties the pistol into him. She is caught by police who trace her target practice ammunition to a sporting goods store listing her as a purchaser. Penny is sent to prison for life, stating that she killed the hapless Norry "to see if I could and not worry about it afterwards." . . . Dr. Bernard Finch of Los Angeles and his attractive lover, Carole Tregoff, plan and execute the murder of Finch's wife, Barbara, pistol-whipping her to death in the family driveway on July 18, 1959, pretending it to be the work of intruders. When Dr. Finch's attaché case—containing rubber gloves, hypodermic needles, a butcher knife, clothesline and .38-caliber ammunition—a "murder kit," as it were—is found, the doctor and his sweetheart are put on trial, both convicted of second-degree murder and given life terms. Tregoff will be paroled in 1969, Finch in 1971. Each refused to contact the other when released. . . . James Gordon Palmer, a twenty-one-year-old, kills three persons—a bait-shop owner, a waitress in a roadside cafe and a gas station attendant—in

Missouri, Illinois and Tennessee, before returning home to Jersey-ville, Illinois where he attempts to rob the Gorman Brothers' Construction Company. He takes seven men hostage in the plant offices on October 9, 1959, training a repeating rifle on them, ordering Louis Gorman to tie the men up, stating that when they are all bound he is "going to shoot them in the head." Gorman, seeing the killer off-balance for a moment as he shifts his weight while kneeling, jumps Palmer, knocking the rifle from his hands, and sending him to the floor with a powerhouse right. The workmen tie up the killer and deliver him to the sheriff. Palmer receives a 180-year prison term. Gorman receives a citizen's medal. . . . Richard E. Hickock and Perry E. Smith, both neurotic thieves, break into the rural home of Herbert W. Clutter, thinking to steal reportedly hoarded money. When they find no appreciable sums, Hickock and Smith murder Clutter, his wife and their daughter and son. Hickock and Perry are tracked down by intrepid detective Al Dewey of Kansas, and arrested in Las Vegas. Both men are executed in Kansas, hanged on April 14, 1965. Author Truman Capote attempts to provide a rationale for the senseless Clutter killings in his book *In Cold Blood.*

1960

Chester Weger, a twenty-one-year-old employee at the posh Starved Rock Lodge in Illinois, follows three Chicago socialites who are strolling through the woods on March 14, 1960. He attempts to steal a camera from one of the women, then decides to rob all three, ordering Mrs. Linquist, Mrs. Frances Murphy, and Mrs. Lillian Oetting deep into the woods. When the women resist, Weger grabs a tree limb and bashes in their heads. He next drags the bodies into a cave where he partially disrobes the victims to make his robbery-murders appear to be sex killings. Boys hiking find the bodies and police respond. The only clues available are the rope binding the women and the professional sailors' knots used by the killer. Detectives meticulously work on the meager clues for several months, finally determining that the rope came from the lodge. Weger, who has already passed two lie detector tests, fails when two more tests are administered by John Reid of Chicago. Blood is then found on Weger's jacket. Weger has been a Marine and is known to be able to tie the most intricate knots, his friends tell police. Confronted with this evidence, Weger breaks down and confesses. He later recants his story but is convicted and sent to prison for life. . . . Berkeley, California, student Joseph Howk, Jr., who changed his name to Mohammed Abdullah when embracing the Islamic religion, is rebuffed by fellow student Sonja Lilliam Hoff, whom he shoots on July 13, 1960, on the steps of the University of

California library in Berkeley. He sends a bullet into his own head but survives to be condemned. His death sentence is commuted to life imprisonment by Governor Edmund G. Brown for reasons of insanity. . . . Ann Gibson Tracy, a cocktail waitress in posh Laguna Beach, California, feels that her sometimes boyfriend Amos Stricker, a wealthy contractor, is two-timing her. She shoots her lover over dinner in his home on November 14, 1960. The killer admits the murder and is given a life term, her only comment being: "I loved him. I wouldn't have hurt him for anything in the world."

1961

Oregon plumber Richard Marquette lures Joan Caudle of Portland to a lonely place where he rapes and strangles her, then dismembers her corpse, scattering the remains in the woods where they are shortly found. Marquette is tracked down and sent to prison, but is paroled within twelve years. Almost upon release, Marquette slays another woman and, in April 1975, he attacks Betty Wilson of Salem, Oregon, savagely dissecting her body. Again the plumber is traced and is sent back to prison for life.

1962

Boston area women are attacked and strangled to death in almost wholesale murders, beginning on June 14, 1962, when fifty-five-year-old Anna Slesers is found murdered in her Back Bay apartment. Thirteen victims in all from 1962 to 1964 will make up the list of females killed at the hands of what the press will call "The Boston Strangler," a man later identified as Albert DeSalvo, thought to be insane, and who, in 1966, pleads "Not Guilty" to the mass murders and is sent to the Bridgewater State Hospital. On November 26, 1973, he is stabbed through the heart and killed in Walpole State Prison in Massachusetts. . . . Dr. Geza de Kaplany plans the murder of his beautiful wife in San Jose, California, in one of the most brutal killings recorded in the annals of homicide. (page 291)

1963

Douglas Godfrey, fifteen years old, armed with a .22-caliber pistol, shoots at various persons in Bloomfield Township, Michigan, a posh bedroom suburb of Detroit, on the night of January 26, 1963, making police think a random sniper is loose, before carefully shooting his mother, Mary Godfrey, through the kitchen window of his home.

*President Kennedy's
assassin, Lee Harvey
Oswald, shown only
minutes before he was
killed by Jack Ruby in
1963.* (UPI)

When police inspect the body of the attractive thirty-eight-year-old blond, they notice Douglas' indifference and, later, his lack of sorrow at her funeral. Upon questioning, Godfrey breaks down and admits the murder, telling authorities he killed his mother because she would not allow him to attend dances or go to movies. . . . In Manhattan, on August 28, 1963, Janice Wylie, twenty-one-year-old daughter of author Max Wylie and niece of writer Philip Wylie, is found murdered with her roommate, Emily Hoffert, both young women stabbed to death and mutilated, then tied together with bedsheets. Not until 1965 do New York police receive a tip that a heroin addict, Richard Robles, was in the area of the Wylie apartment on the day of the murder. Robles is arrested. After confessing, he is found guilty and sent to prison for life. . . . Lee Harvey Oswald shoots and kills President John F. Kennedy in Dallas on November 22, 1963. Two days later, while in the custody of seventy police officers, Oswald is shot to death in the city-jail garage by Dallas nightclub owner Jack Ruby, who is later convicted and sentenced to death, but who dies of cancer in jail before execution. Massive investigations into charges of a conspiracy in the assassination fail to prove such charges as anything other than theory.

1964

Catherine Genovese, known as "Kitty" to her Long Island neighbors, returns to her Kew Gardens, New York, home from work at three o'clock in the morning, March 13, 1964. As the attractive twenty-eight-year-old approaches her apartment, only a hundred feet distant, a man who has been loitering on the block stabs her. Kitty Genovese screams: "Oh, my God, he stabbed me! Please help me! Please help me!" A window on the upper floor of the apartment house is thrown open and a man's voice yells: "Let that girl alone!" The assailant shrugs and moves off. When the window closes and lights are turned off, the man returns and stabs her again. "I'm dying, I'm dying," cries Kitty Genovese. Though there are thirty-eight witnesses watching the woman being attacked, no one peering from the windows immediately calls police, let alone races to her defense. The attacker returns to a white sedan parked down the street. Kitty Genovese crawls bleeding to the rear of the apartment building, enters a rear door and collapses at the base of the stairs. The attacker gets out of his car, goes to the rear of the building and, finding Miss Genovese, stabs her again until she dies, his assaults taking thirty-five minutes. He casually drives from the area. Then someone calls police, who appear inside of two minutes. Six days after the killing, a twenty-nine-year-old factory worker, Winston Moseley, is arrested for the murder. In addition to the Genovese slaying, Moseley confesses to two other murders of women in the New York area. When asked why they did nothing to prevent the murder, or, at least, call police to the rescue, the thirty-eight witnesses respond with the almost universal statement: "I didn't want to get involved." . . . Charles Howard Schmid, Jr., who is later to be known as "The Pied Piper of Tucson," begins luring young girls into the Arizona desert, where he rapes and kills them, beginning with fifteen-year-old Alleen Rowe on May 31, 1964. (On the night of the murder, the twenty-two-year-old Schmid has been guzzling beer in a friend's house when he suddenly jumps up yelling: "I want to kill a girl! I want to do it tonight! I think I can get away with it!") Schmid will go on to murder in Tucson seventeen-year-old Gretchen Fritz and her thirteen-year-old sister, Wendy, on August 16, 1965, before his friends inform on him. He is given the death penalty but is saved by the Supreme Court decision on capital punishment. He is presently serving two life terms.

1965

On February 21, 1965, Malcolm Little, Black Muslim leader who has renamed himself Malcolm X, steps before his followers in Manhattan's Audubon Ballroom to deliver an address. After his opening remarks, three men rush him on stage, one man, Thomas Hagan, shooting and killing the black leader with a shotgun at close range. Hagan is immediately taken into custody . . . Anesthiologist Dr. Carl Coppolino, a womanizer previously suspected of murdering the husband of one of his paramours, is accused by Mrs. Majorie Farber, a jealous lover, of murdering her husband—she tells police she has injected her husband with succinylcholine chloride under his supervision—and that he also murdered his wife, Carmela, in order to marry another woman, Mary Gibson. In a highly technical trial, Coppolino is convicted of murdering his wife and is sent to prison for life. . . . Michael Andrew Clark, sixteen-year-old son of a Long Beach, California, couple, takes fifteen dollars from his mother's purse on March 25, 1965; he grabs his father's big-game Swedish-made military rifle and a bagful of armor-piercing shells, gets into his mother's car and drives north on Route 101, arriving at Santa Maria and climbing Solomon Hill (ironically named after Solomon Pico, a bloodthirsty highwayman of a century before who waylaid Wells-Fargo stages from this very site, a fact unknown to the Clark boy). Clark begins to shoot at motorists, striking the driver of the first car in his sights, William Reida, and killing his five-year-old son, Kevin, then mortally shooting Joel W. Kocab in the next car, and, some cars behind that, killing Charles Christopher Hogan. Before police arrive, Clark murders three persons in passing autos and wounds eleven others. When officers charge up the hill firing at the sniper, Clark turns the weapon on himself. He is found dead. . . . Indianapolis, Indiana, housewife Gertrude Wright Baniszewski supervises the torture-murder of her foster child, sixteen-year-old Sylvia Likens, in her home, her own children carrying out the incredibly brutal slaying in her basement on October 26, 1965, branding the girl with white-hot needles with the words "I am a prostitute," before crushing her skull on the concrete floor. Sylvia's crippled fifteen-year-old sister, also left with Mrs. Baniszewski, informs police, who arrest the woman. Mrs. Baniszewski is sent to prison for life, the children to foster homes.

1966

Richard Franklin Speck, an itinerant garbageman and sometime seaman, breaks into the Chicago living quarters of nine nurses working at Chicago Community Hospital on the night of July 13–14, 1966, binding the girls in a bedroom, then taking them one by one into other rooms of the apartment where he stabs and strangles them to death, with Corazon Amurao hiding beneath a bed, the only survivor. Speck's mass slaughter is described in detail by Miss Amurao who also identifies the killer when he is found, his wrists slashed, in a Chicago flophouse. Speck is given the Jovian sentence of more than four hundred years in jail, but he is nevertheless eligible for parole, his last appeal in 1976 being rejected. . . . Mentally disturbed Charles Whitman, a twenty-five-year-old ex-Marine and student at the University of Texas in Austin, sits down at a typewriter in his home on July 31, 1966, writing: "I don't quite understand what is compelling me to type this note. I have been to a psychiatrist. [Dr. Maurice Heatly, on March 29, 1966] I have been having fears and violent impulses. I've had some tremendous headaches in the past. I am prepared to die. After my death, I wish an autopsy on me be performed to see if there's any mental disorder." Whitman next writes that he will kill his wife, Kathy. He picks her up from work and leaves her at their apartment. He drives to his mother's home, where he plunges a knife into her chest and shoots her in the back of the head. He returns to his typewriter: "I have just killed my mother. If there's a heaven, she's going there. If there's not a heaven, she's out of her pain and misery." Whitman next walks into his bedroom and stabs his wife to death while she sleeps. That morning, August 1, 1966, Whitman arms himself with several pistols and a powerful 33-mm. Remington rifle, stuffing his pockets with ammunition. He also takes a large supply of food and water. Enroute to the tower on the university campus, which will give him a commanding view, twenty-seven floors high, of the entire campus, Whitman purchases a .30-caliber carbine and several boxes of ammunition from a gunshop. He lugs the entire arsenal by dolly to the top floor of the tower, killing receptionist Edna Townsley by bash-

Richard Speck, killer of eight nurses in Chicago.
(UPI)

ing in her skull with a gun butt when she asks what he wants. Barricading himself on the tower walkway, Whitman begins to shoot any human coming into his gunsight, killing sixteen persons and wounding another thirty people, picking his targets at random. During the course of his sniping, in which Whitman proves himself a deadly marksman, more than a hundred Austin policemen return his fire. Officers, headed by patrolman Ramiro Martinez, then charge the observation deck from the floor below and Whitman dies in a withering fusillade. Martinez is wounded. Later found in psychiatrist Heatly's notes are the following words: "At one point he said he was thinking about going up on the tower with a deer rifle and start shooting people." . . . Arland Withrow, a good-looking seventeen-year-old of Ypsilanti, Michigan, receives a phone call on the night of October 16, 1966, and leaves his house. His naked and sexually abused body is found in a Port Huron creek four days later. Upon questioning Withrow's friends, police learn that an older man named "Ralph" has had homosexual associations with several of them, including Arland Withrow. The man's description tallies with that of Ralph Nuss, a social worker in the Federal Correctional Institution south of Ypsilanti. Nuss is taken into custody and admits the homosexual killing, as well as that of another. Nuss is sent to prison for life. . . . Two black men, Rubin "Hurricane" Carter, a prominent middleweight boxer, and John Artis, enter a Patterson, New Jersey, bar and shoot down three white persons—James Oliver, part-owner and bartender of the Lafayette Grill, Fred Nauykas and Hazel Tanis. After two sensational trials, both men are found guilty and sent to prison for life. . . . Mark Alan Smith of McHenry, Illinois, begins attacking young women, killing and raping them in northern Illinois. He will be apprehended years later and confess to the rape-murders of seven females, the latest being twenty-two-year-old Janice Bolyard, with whom Smith worked in a chemical plant in Evanston, Illinois. Smith receives five hundred years in prison. . . . Robert Benjamin Smith, an eighteen-year-old high school senior of Mesa, Arizona, enters the Rose-Mar College of Beauty in Mesa, armed with a pistol and knife. He orders five women, a three-year-old girl, and a baby, to lie on the floor in a wheel, their heads at the center. One of the terrified women tells him: "There'll be forty people in here in a few minutes." Smith replies in a dull tone: "I'm sorry, but I didn't bring enough ammunition for them." Woman-hater Smith then proceeds to execute all lying on the floor. Mrs. Joyce Sellers shields her baby with her own body, absorbing the bullets meant for the child; she then rises with a bullet in her head and attempts to attack Smith, who stabs her to death. Smith calmly strolls outside and into the arms of policemen rushing forward. "What's going on in there?" one cop asks. Smith laughs hysterically, saying: "I've just killed all the women in there." Before being sent to prison for life, Smith tells reporters: "I wanted to get known, just wanted to get myself a name." . . . On December 17, 1966, two blood-thirsty homosexuals, Walter Kelbach and Myron Lance, abduct, rape and stab to death gas station attendant Stephen Shea outside of Salt Lake City, Utah. They will kill four more persons in cold blood before their murder spree is ended. (page 294)

1967

Motorcyclist John Norman Collins begins brutally murdering female students in the Ypsilanti, Michigan, area, stabbing and raping women until 1969 when bloodstains and his own hair are traced to the murders. He has long been a suspect of the "co-ed murders," and has intimated to many that he is the killer of seven females. He is tried for the murder of eighteen-year-old Karen Sue Beckemann and found guilty, sent to prison for life. . . . Thomas Eugene Braun and Leonard Maine signal to Mrs. Deanna Buse from their car that something is wrong with her tire as they pass her near Redmond, Washington, on August 19, 1967. When the attractive Mrs. Buse stops and gets out to check the car, big teenager Braun orders her at gunpoint into a nearby woods, where he orders her to strip. He sends five bullets into her head (an autopsy later states that the woman has not been raped). The youths, driving Mrs. Buse's car, next kill a fisherman, Samuel Leger-wood, on an Oregon lumber trail, stealing his car and setting fire to Mrs. Buse's auto, on August 27. As they drive into northern California the two killers pick up two hitchhikers on Route 120. They rape Susan Bartolomei several times, shooting her and also killing her friend Timothy Luce. The girl survives to describe her assailants. The car Braun is driving is identified by Constable Ed Chafin of Jamestown, California, parked in front of a local hotel. Several more officers are called; they charge into the room occupied by Braun and Maine. Both men are arrested after a brief scuffle. Braun is sentenced to death but the execution is postponed following the Supreme Court's decision on capital punishment; Maine is given a life term. . . . Fat, short Stephen Weinstein, who owns a Philadelphia shop, Ye Olde Tobacconist Ltd., makes it his hobby to invite college youths to his establishment, give them ham sandwiches with thick mustard that is drugged, and, when they pass out, rape and beat them. When finished, Weinstein orders his helper, Clark Vestry, an oversized fourteen-year-old, to drive the boys to remote areas, kill them, and hide the bodies. Vestry merely takes the youths home, telling them to "stay away from Weinstein." John Green, eighteen-year-old university freshman, is drugged and raped in October 1967, but Weinstein has trouble reviving him. Weinstein pours ammonia down Green's throat, killing him. Vestry and some friends dump the body in a trunk into the Delaware River. It is found four days later and friends pinpoint Weinstein by remembering that Green, only hours before he disappeared, was searching for a store selling antique pipes, which leads police to Weinstein's shop. The homosexual killer confesses after being apprehended in New York City. He is given a life term.... Janie Gibbs, having married when only fifteen, is a grandmother at age thirty-eight, appearing to be a happily married woman and religious pillar of Cordelle, Georgia; she takes out thirty-one thousand dollars in life insurance on the lives of her husband, three sons, and infant grandson, then poisons them all. Receiving the insurance money, Grannie Gibbs gives 10 percent of the insurance funds to her church, where she continues to teach Sunday School. When suspicious authorities suggest autopsies be performed on the Gibbs' bodies, Grannie fumes, stating that such medical practices are against her religion. Her daughter-in-law, however, insists that the body of her husband be examined. Poison is found and Grannie Gibbs admits killing her five family members. Not until 1976 will the mass killer be judged sane enough to stand trial. She is convicted and given five life terms.

1968

James Earl Ray, an escaped felon, rents rooms in Memphis, Tennessee, under the aliases of Eric Starvo Galt and John Willard; then, on the evening of April 4, 1968, he shoots, with a 30-06 Remington pump rifle, civil rights leader Martin Luther King as King steps out onto the second-floor balcony of his motel room to greet friends. King, shot in the throat, dies wordlessly an hour later as Ray flees first to Canada, then to Europe, where he is apprehended; he is extradited for trial. He pleads guilty and is given a ninety-nine-year prison term. Much of Ray's background in the assassination—the large amounts of money at his disposal, his well-organized escape route, mysterious calls he received while hiding in Canada—suggests that there has been a conspiracy to murder King, but all subsequent investigations fail to prove this fact.... Palestinian fanatic Sirhan Bishara Sirhan waits for Senator Robert Kennedy to finish addressing a crowd jubilant at his California primary sweep in the Embassy Ballroom of the Los Angeles Ambassador Hotel on June 5, 1968. When Kennedy walks offstage, Sirhan moves forward with a small group of wellwishers, extending a campaign poster rolled around a .22-caliber revolver he holds in his hand. Quickly he fires several shots, one bullet striking Kennedy in the head. The assassin is subdued by bodyguards but Kennedy is dying. The youth quickly admits the murder, confessing later in court. He is condemned but his appeals have kept him alive to this writing. ... Much-honored policeman Robert John Erler of Hollywood, Florida, spots a woman and her daughter on a beach on August 12, 1968, and inexplicably plans a double murder. (page 297)

Robert Kennedy's assassin, Sirhan Bishara Sirhan; this photo was taken only minutes after Sirhan was taken into custody in 1968. (WIDE WORLD)

1969

Camellia Jo Hand, an eight-year-old living in Ocoee, Florida, disappears with her dog on April 10, 1969. Four days later the dog is found dead and, near the carcass, a shallow grave yields the child's mutilated body. Two bloody razor blades are found nearby. Informants tell police that a car was seen near the child's home on the day of her disappearance and later at the murder site, one with "19" on the license plate. Officers spot a car with these numbers on April 16 parked in an Ocoee shopping center. They arrest the owner, Kenneth Ray Wright, a twenty-nine-year-old painter. His fingerprints match those on the razor blades used to kill the Hand girl. He is sent to prison for life. . . . Vagrant Charles Manson gathers a weird hippie cult about him at Spahn Ranch near Los Angeles and, acting on his orders, several of his cultists brutally slay actress Sharon Tate and four others, following this mass murder with the double killings of Leno and Rosemary LaBianca. Following a prolonged and nationally sensational trial, Manson and three of his moronic followers, Susan Atkins, Leslie Van Houten, and Patricia Krenwinkel, are condemned, but all survive when the death penalty is abolished. . . . On October 27, 1969, an Indian student, Prosenjit Poddar, kills Tatiana Tarasoff, a fellow University of California student, after the girl rebuffs him. Poddar catches her on the front porch of her home and stabs her two dozen times. When Poddar is arrested, it is learned that his psychologist has been told in advance by the killer of his intentions and that the psychologist has sent a warning letter to the police, a letter that the medico's superior demanded be returned and destroyed, which it was, only days before the slaying. Following Poddar's conviction of manslaughter, the killer spends four years in prison before being deported to India. In July 1976 the California Supreme Court will rule that any psychotherapist with prior knowledge of an intended murder must, under law, warn the victim, as well as authorities, a ruling that comes sadly too late for Miss Tarasoff.

1970

Edmund Emil Kemper III, 280 pounds, a massive six feet nine inches tall, who is "a born killer" to many authorities who examine his horrendous murder record, begins picking up hitchhiking college girls in the Santa Cruz, California, area. (His mother works in the administration office of the University of California in Santa Cruz. The UCSC sticker on his car, obtained by her to enable him to park his auto in the university parking lot, makes co-eds think him safe—a university official.) Kemper shoots the victims, then practices necrophilia by having sex with their dead bodies or pieces of the bodies after he has dissected them. He often sleeps with the corpses for several days before disposing of them, and, like the chilling protagonist of Emlyn Williams' play *Night Must Fall*, he wraps parts of the bodies in plastic and carries them with him, usually in the trunk of his auto. Kemper's murderous inclinations are, ironically, known to authorities; at age fifteen, he shot his grandmother and grandfather to death on August 27, 1964, while staying on their farm, telling startled psychiatrists: "I just wondered how it would feel to shoot Grandma." Kemper was sent to the Atascadero State Mental Hospital but was released in 1969 by the California Youth Authority, against the advice of hospital psychiatrists, and sent to live with his mother in Santa Cruz. Kemper spends most of his time in a bar called the Jury Room near the Santa Cruz courthouse, swapping stories with local policemen. The mass murderer, with an estimated IQ of 136, will, on the night of April 20, 1973, creep into his mother's bedroom and bash out her brains, then dissect her body, similarly murdering his mother's best friend, a Mrs. Hallet, some hours later; he will then flee to Pueblo, Colorado, where, after calling Santa Cruz police to confess this horrid murder in detail, he will be apprehended and sent to prison for life.

1971

Juan Vallejo Corona, a thirty-eight-year-old Mexican immigrant who has made good as a labor contractor near Yuba City, California, is accused of being responsible for the disappearance of twenty-five migrant workers in his employ. Police arrive at Corona's home, conducting a thorough investigation of his house and a nearby bunkhouse on the Sullivan ranch, which Corona uses as a barracks for his workers. From twenty-five shallow graves his victims are removed, all of them stabbed, axed, clubbed and shot to death. Denying his guilt, Corona is placed on trial. His blood-coated machete and boots are introduced as evidence against him, along with his own damning personal ledger in which many of his victims and their belongings, which he has stolen, are listed. Following forty-five hours of deliberation, the jury finds Corona guilty and he is sent to Soledad Prison for twenty-five consecutive life terms. Corona is attacked, much like Albert DeSalvo, the reputed Boston Strangler, stabbed by fellow prisoners thirty-two times, which causes him the loss of an eye in 1973. . . . John Gilbert Freeman, of Phoenix, Arizona, thinking that the husband of Norvella Bentley has run away with his wife, enters Mrs. Bentley's home on the night of September 3, 1971, with two .38-caliber revolvers and begins shooting all present, killing Mrs. Bentley; her sixteen-year-old daughter, Pam; Pam's husband, Frank Martin, age eighteen; and four of Mrs. Bentley's other children: Tina, ten; Adam, three; Tracy, two; and nine-month-old Charlotte, whom he finds sleeping in a rear bedroom. Freeman, a psychotic upholsterer, after being confined in a mental institution for four years, is almost released on the grounds that he is found mentally competent and the fact that he has not been indicted for the seven murders, a count that makes Freeman the worst mass-killer in Arizona history. Freeman is subsequently ordered by the Supreme Court to stand trial and, found guilty, is given seven consecutive life terms. He claims innocence to the end, shouting to the court: "It wasn't me! I didn't kill them! They were murdered by Communists!"

1972

Between October 1972 and February 1973, Herbert William Mullin, of Santa Cruz, California, murders thirteen persons, almost indiscriminately, although he is later to state that most of his victims are "human sacrifices" to ward off earthquakes. The victims include a priest hearing his confession, whom he stabs to death; four youths camping, whom he shoots as they emerge from their tent; two families slaughtered in their houses; and an old man he shoots in a backyard before delivering wood to his parents' home, a killing so blatant that police squads pick up the clean-cut young man before he can travel more than a few blocks. Though Mullin has been long known to be mentally disturbed, he is not confined until his thirteenth murder, then receiving life imprisonment. The well-mannered Mullin states at his trial that significant punishments for previous offenses would have served as a deterrent to his multiple slayings: "If I had gotten one year for resisting arrest [on a minor charge occurring in 1968], I would never have killed anyone because jail is a deterrent. What were they waiting for? Until I broke a big law so I would spend the rest of my life in jail? . . . If I had spent five years in jail I never would have killed anyone because jail is a horrible experience."

1973

On June 3, 1973, Henry Brisbon and three others drive up behind the moving car of Dorothy Cerny and her fiancé, James Schmidt, and as they proceed down Highway I-57 near Flossmoor, Illinois, bump their car repeatedly until the couple pull to the side of the road to inspect the damage. Brisbon then shoots the couple. He is apprehended a short time later, tried and given one thousand to three thousand years in prison. . . . Mark James Robert Essex, a twenty-three-year-old black from Emporia, Kansas, who has been thrown out of the U.S. Navy as a "troublemaker," decides on wholesale murder on January 7, 1973, to express his smoldering passions, writing with spray

paint on the walls of his shabby apartment: "Hate White People Beast
of the Earth," and "Kill White Devil and Kill White Pig." Armed with
a .44 Magnum rifle and carrying great amounts of ammunition, Essex
goes to New Orleans' downtown Howard Johnson's Motel, driving to
a fourth-floor parking area and then running down hallways and into
rooms, setting fires and shooting only white guests. He encounters a
black maid, taking her keys, and screaming: "The revolution is on!
Don't worry, sister, we're only shooting whites today." (Oddly, Essex
has already murdered one black man, ballistics tests later prove; he
shot police cadet Alfred Harrell III the day before.) When firemen
arrive to pump water on the six floors burning in the hotel, Essex fires
on them, as well as police returning his fire, as he takes refuge on the
hotel roof eighteen floors above. After he kills six persons—including
honeymooners Dr. Robert Stegall and his wife, two hotel officials, and
three policemen—and wounds sixteen others, a marine helicopter,
jammed with expert machinegunners, makes fifteen sweeps of the
roof, spraying the area. Essex emerges from a stone blockhouse on the
roof to fire at the copter and is cut in half by police marksmen. . . . On
August 8, 1973, Houston, Texas, police receive a call from eighteen-
year-old Elmer Wayne Henley, Jr., who drawls: "Listen, you better
come on over. I killed a guy." The victim, police soon learn, is thirty-
three-year-old electrician Dean Corll, who has murdered at least
twenty-seven youths, ages thirteen to eighteen, after administering
unimaginable tortures upon them, strangling and shooting them,
along with castrating them before wrapping them in plastic bags and
burying them in a boathouse pit near his Pasadena, Texas, home. The
homosexual killer, Henley tells police, was about to torture him after
he had passed out following a drug party (sniffing acrylic paint), but
he persuaded the mass killer to free him so that he could help him
murder other youths, which has been his capacity all along. Once
free, as Corll goes to work on another boy, Henley shoots Corll with
the electrician's own gun, killing him. Henley is found guilty of murdering—along with his mentor, Corll—six Houston youths, and receives six ninety-nine-year terms in prison. Another youth, David
Owen Brooks, who has also procured homosexual youths for Corll's
insane perversities in return for drugs, liquor and money, receives a
life term. . . . William Steelman and Douglas Gretzler, vagrants and
holdup men, run into a storm outside Victor, California, on November
6, 1973, breaking into the home of Walter and Joanne Parkin and
killing the couple, their four children, and three others, after compelling Parkin to give them four thousand dollars from his store safe.
Less than three days later, the murderous pair are tracked down and
captured. At least eleven other deaths in California and Arizona are
attributed to the killers, who receive death sentences but who remain
alive today on Death Row. . . . On December 31, 1973, John Wayne
Wilson, a homosexual prostitute in New York City, is taken home by

Roseann Quinn, where, unable to perform sexually, he slashes the girl to pieces, then mutilates her. Wilson, a mental case from Indiana, who later becomes Judith Rossner's unsavory killer in *Looking for Mr. Goodbar,* is found six weeks later in Indianapolis, admitting the murder; he hangs himself in jail. . . . Calvin Jackson, a Manhattan porter, commits mass murder for the sake of secondhand TV sets. (page 300)

1974

In July 1974, twenty-five-year-old actress Karin Schlegel answers a *Show Business* ad asking for young women to try out for a film, going to a studio on Waverly Place in Greenwich Village. Her body is found by police; she has been strangled, knifed and sexually abused. The man who placed the ad, using the alias "Williamson," is the building's superintendent, Charles Yukl, who is quickly tried and given a life sentence. . . . Allen King, a twenty-five-year-old Manhattan resident, murders a Roman Catholic priest whom he attempts to hold up. King, apprehended almost at the scene of the killing, appears before New York Supreme Court Justice Bernard Dubin, who sentences him to twenty-five-years-to-life. "I'll do you, too!" yells King to the judge. Dubin points out that the priest made no resistance, yet "his life was destroyed." King only smirks before being led away, sneering: "Want a handkerchief. It's so bad." . . . During a series of petty robberies in the greater Chicago area, thirty-three-year-old Gary Duane Rardon murders three men in November 1974. He is found guilty three years later and sentenced to forty to one hundred years in prison. Turning to the relatives of the victims in court, Rardon apologizes, adding: "I know it doesn't do any good, but you deserve that. In fact, you deserve my life." . . . On December 30, 1974, honor student Anthony F. Barbaro of Olean, New York, uses a rifle to kill the school custodian of his high school, and, while firing from the windows of this school, also kills a woman in a parked auto and a utility company worker passing the school. Firemen responding to the blazes he has set in the school are greeted by his sniper fire; eleven of them are wounded before police capture the mentally disturbed youth. Barbaro hangs himself in his jail cell.

1975

Gun enthusiast James Ruppert appears to go berserk in Hamilton, Ohio, on Easter Sunday 1975, firing thirty-five bullets into eleven members of his family. The forty-one-year-old Ruppert meekly surrenders to arriving police, stating that he went crazy because his mother incessantly combed his hair, talked babytalk to him, and tried to make him into a homosexual. At his trial, the prosecution carefully details another motive: that the mass killing was perpetrated in order to gain the family inheritance of three hundred thousand dollars; that Ruppert intended to be caught by police, be termed insane, spend a few years in an asylum, and emerge a rich man after being "rehabilitated." He is found guilty and given eleven consecutive life terms. ... On probation for murder, Russell Lee Smith terrorizes Dayton, Ohio, on a one-man murder rampage, May 24, 1975, shooting his girlfriend and killing two others, wounding eleven persons at random, including a family exiting a movie theater, firing through the doors of residents who will not answer his calls from outside their homes. After kidnapping and raping two girls, killing one, Smith turns his pistol on himself, committing suicide. ... Town drunk and day laborer Erwin Simants of Sutherland, Nebraska, enters the home of his best friend, James Kellie (who has recently bailed him out of jail for public drunkenness), carrying a rifle. He methodically shoots Kellie, his wife, children and grandchild, ten-year-old Florence Kellie, sexually attacking both the child and grandmother before his own family turns him in to the police. Simants is given the death penalty but presently waits on Death Row for execution. ... Freddie Martin of Chicago exemplifies his hatred for the aged by murdering four persons, a woman and three men, all in their seventies. He receives a life sentence.

1976

Allen Leroy Anderson, a thirty-four-year-old vagrant with a long backlist of felonies, steals the car and credit cards of the director of a halfway house where he lives in Seattle, Washington, and drives through twenty states, robbing scores of persons and killing at least eight. He pleads guilty to murder in Minnesota and is given a life sentence. ... High on cocaine, Moses Pearson explodes in lethal wrath, driving through central Georgia shooting persons at random, killing three and wounding thirteen on April 25, 1976. Taking several persons hostage in commandeered cars, the mass killer is finally surrounded by deputies from whom he has stolen a car, wrecking it in a high-speed pursuit. Pearson, realizing he is trapped, puts a pistol to his head, killing himself. ... Former police cadet David McRae, Jr., age twenty-two, is, according to Norfolk, Virginia, authorities eager to "eliminate crime," and, to that end, he enters a shabby bar, shoots four persons he suspects of being pimps and prostitutes, then blows out his own brains in May 1976. ... On August 19, 1976, outside of Lincoln, Nebraska, a self-styled revolutionary, Michael Edward Drabing, stabs to death wealthy hog farmer Lloyd Schneider, his wife, Phyllis, and their seventeen-year-old daughter, Teri, to satisfy his "kill-the-rich" philosophy. He is apprehended before he can carry out his plans to murder the Governor of Illinois and other politicians. Drabing falls asleep at his own trial, calling it "a farce." He is given a life sentence. . . . Mrs. Patty Bolin, a forty-year-old Columbus, Ohio, housewife, purchases a .22-caliber pistol on Thanksgiving Day. On December 8, without warning, Mrs. Bolin turns on her husband, Ronald, shooting him dead in their upper-middle-class home. She next shoots her daughter Pamela Jean, age twelve. Her 9-year-old son, Todd, races from the house yelling: "She's shooting everyone! She's shooting up the place!" He reenters the home after asking neighbors to call the police, thinking to help his sisters. His mother shoots him dead as he enters the kitchen. Another daughter, fifteen-year-old Alicia Ann, walks into the house. Her mother aims the pistol at her and squeezes the trigger three times but the weapon misfires. "Alicia, go to your room," her mother tells her in a low voice while she attempts to fix the pistol. The girl runs from the house, tripping over the body of her brother but escaping. A policeman arrives, peeks in the window and ducks when Mrs. Bolin aims the weapon at him. He hears a dull popping sound. Mrs. Bolin has committed suicide.

1977

On February 14, 1977, American Nazi Fred Cowan goes on a murder rampage in New Rochelle, New York. (page 303) . . . On November 19, 1977, Leonard Warchol of Chicago is watching TV when he tells his stepdaughter, twenty-five-year-old Mrs. Pam Pastorino, that he does not want her sister, fifteen-year-old Debbie Saylor, to make pizza in his kitchen (the sisters live in another apartment). Mrs. Pastorino promptly hits Warchol over the head with a lead pipe while her sister repeatedly stabs the man with a seven-inch butcher knife. The sisters are convicted; Mrs. Pastorino is sent to prison for sixty years, Debbie Saylor sent to the custody of a youth center.

1978

Theodore R. Bundy, former law student, beats five women on January 15, 1978, clubbing to death students Lisa Levy and Margaret Bowman in the Chi Omega sorority house at Florida State University. When arrested, Bundy tells police that he has fantasies about young women and that he "feels like a vampire." Bundy, who has been convicted of a 1974 kidnapping in Utah, and who faces two other murder charges in Colorado and Florida, is convicted and given the death penalty on July 25, 1979. . . . Richard Trenton Chase, a twenty-eight-year-old killer, slashes and shoots six persons in California between January

23 and January 27, 1978. He has earlier been known to eat live birds
and more than once has been found in Nevada naked in a field, covered with the blood of a cow he has slaughtered. Chase admits not
only to the killings, but, in one instance, to drinking his victim's
blood. He is found guilty and given a life sentence. . . . Mrs. Marilyn
Dietl drives her eighteen-year-old daughter, Judy, down a rural road
outside Burlington, Vermont, on May 5, 1978, pulls to the side of the
road, and calmly withdraws from her purse a .38-caliber Smith and
Wesson revolver. She shoots her daughter, later explaining to police
that she killed her child rather than allow her to become a prostitute
in Boston. Mrs. Dietl is found guilty of second-degree murder and
sent to the Chittenden County Correction Center for from five to fifteen years. . . . Young Am Pin, a forty-five-year-old Chinese-American
living in Essex, Maryland, has endured his wife's abuse for twenty-
five years—Im Sook Pin, a year older than he, has repeatedly over the
years beaten him with a wooden mallet when angry, taunted him with
her extramarital affairs, and limited his spending to a fifty-cent weekly
allowance. In July 1978, Pin argues with his wife over her purchase
of a new casette tape recorder, then strangles her and chops up her
body into thirty-five pieces, storing the remains in jars and paint cans.
When these grisly contents are found, Pin is arrested, tried and convicted of second-degree manslaughter. He is given twenty-five years
in prison. . . . Dan White, a former city supervisor in San Francisco,
former honored policeman and firefighter, walks into City Hall on
November 27, 1978 and, following brief discussions with Mayor
George Moscone and city supervisor Harvey Milk, an avowed homosexual, shoots and kills both men. Moscone tells White he will not be
reappointed as supervisor, White relates; "It was like roaring in my
ears. And that was it. I just shot him. It was over." Immediately following this killing, White walks into Milk's office. "I thought, 'Well, I'm
going to talk to Harvey.' It was like my head was going to burst. I just
wanted to talk. Then he [Milk] started kind of smirking. He smirked
at me and said, 'Too bad.' I got all flushed up and hot and shot him."
White is convicted of voluntary manslaughter and given eight years in
prison. Following the conviction, five thousand homosexuals (of the
city's estimated two hundred thousand homosexuals, roughly one-
third of the city population) stage city-wide riots, attacking police cars
and smashing the glass on the front doors of the City Hall. San Francisco's chief of police—who has in the past removed the American
flag from his office, recruited homosexuals into the police department,
and openly posed with a prostitute and a transvestite at San Francisco's "Hooker's Ball"—resigns on July 15, 1979, as a direct result of
the homosexual riot of May 21, 1979. . . . John Wayne Gacy, a thirty-
six-year-old contractor living in a modest home in Norwood Park
Township, Illinois, is questioned by police regarding the disappearance of youths in his area. The twice-divorced, admitted homosexual

445

*Chicago contractor and Democratic party worker shakes hands with
Rosalynn Carter when the first lady visited the Windy City for a party rally;
Gacy, in late 1977, confessed to police that he had killed thirty-two youths
in homosexual murders, burying most of the bodies in the crawlspace
beneath his suburban Norwood Park home.* (CHICAGO SUN-TIMES)

quickly confesses to having abducted, sexually abused and murdered
thirty-two youths; twenty-seven of the bodies are later dug up from
shallow graves in the crawlspace beneath his home (the other five
bodies Gacy claims to have thrown in the river). Gacy, who is known
to his neighbors as "a nice fellow," has been in the habit of throwing
parties for children, at which times he dressed up like a clown. When
recruiting workers for his contracting business, Gacy made sexual
advances to many, telling some: "I have already killed some people."
Gacy, who at this writing still awaits trial, becomes the third-worst
mass-murderer in this country, with a count of thirty-two, after H. H.
Holmes, killer of more than two hundred in the nineteenth century,
and Johann Otto Hoch, slayer of more than fifty.

First degree murder

Bibliography

The research for this book was done in libraries and archives throughout the United States, in addition to many interviews and lengthy correspondence. The author's own files, exceeding more than a quarter of a million separate entries and a personal crime library of more than 25,000 volumes, were heavily employed. The most helpful published sources follow.

Books

Abrahamsen, D. *Crime and the Human Mind*. New York: Columbia University Press, 1949.

Adleman, Robert H. *The Bloody Benders*. New York: Stein and Day, 1970.

Alexander, F. *Fundamentals of Psychoanalysis*. New York: W. W. Norton, 1951.

——, and Staub, M. *The Criminal, the Judge and the Public*. Glencoe, Ill.: The Free Press, 1956.

Alix, Ernest Kahlar. *Ransom Kidnapping in America, 1874–1974*. Carbondale, Ill.: Southern Illinois University Press, 1978.

Altman, Jack, and Ziporyn, Marvin. *Born to Raise Hell*. New York: Grove Press, 1967.

Anonymous. *Streetwalker*. London: The Bodley Head, 1959.

Anslinger, Harry J., and Ousler, Will. *The Murderers*. New York: Farrar, Straus and Cudahy, 1961.

Aptheker, Herbert. *Nat Turner's Slave Rebellion*. New York: Grove Press, 1966.

Arieti, S., and Meth, J. A. *American Handbook of Psychiatry*. New York: Basic Books, 1959.

Asbury, Herbert. *The Gangs of New York*. New York: Knopf, 1927.

——. *Gem of the Prairie*. New York: Knopf, 1940.

——. *The French Quarter*. New York: Knopf, 1940.

Atwell, Benjamin H. *The Great Harry Thaw Case*. Chicago: Laird & Lee, 1907.

——. *Memoirs of an Assassin*. New York: Yoseloff, 1959.

Bayer, Mary Fannell. *Early Days on Boston Common*. Boston: Privately printed, 1910.

Barkas, J. L. *Victims*. New York: Scribner's, 1978.

Barnes, David. *The Metropolitan Police*. New York: Baker & Godwin, 1863.

Barnes, H. E., and Teeters, N. K. *New Horizons in Criminology*. New York: Prentice-Hall, 1953.

Bayer, Oliver Weld (ed.) *Cleveland Murders*. New York: Duell, Sloan and Pearce, 1947.

Bell, Arthur. *Kings Don't Mean a Thing*. New York: Morrow, 1978.

Bemis, George. *Report of the Case of John W. Webster*. Boston: Little, Brown, 1850.

Bentley, W. G. *My Son's Execution*. London: W. H. Allen, 1957.

Berger, Meyer. *The Eighty Million*. New York: Simon & Schuster, 1942.

Berns, Walter. *For Capital Punishment*. New York: Basic Books, 1974.

Bierstadt, Edward Hale. *Curious Trials & Criminal Cases*. Garden City, N.Y.: Garden City Publishing Co., 1928.

Biggs, J., Jr. *The Guilty Mind*. New York: Harcourt, 1955.

Birmingham, George A. *Murder Most Foul!* London: Chatto and Windus, 1929.

Block, Eugene B. *The Wizard of Berkeley*. New York: Coward-McCann, 1958.

——. *Fifteen Clues*. Garden City, N.Y.: Doubleday, 1965.

——. *The Fabric of Guilt*. Garden City, N.Y.: Doubleday, 1968.

Bolitho, William. *Murder for Profit*. London: Jonathan Cape, 1926.

Bontham, Alan. *Sex Crimes and Sex Criminals*. New York: Wisdom House, 1961.

Borchard, E. M. *Convicting the Innocent*. New Haven, Conn.: Yale University Press, 1932.

Borowitz, Albert. *Innocence and Arsenic Studies in Crime and Literature*. New York: Harper & Row, 1977.

Boswell, Charles, and Thompson, Lewis. *The Girls in Nightmare House*. New York: Gold Medal, 1955.

Boucher, Anthony (ed.). *The Quality of Murder*. New York: E. P. Dutton, 1962.

Brace, Charles Loving. *The Dangerous Classes of New York*. New York: Wynkoop & Hallenbeck, 1880.

Bradford, Judge Kermit. *Miracle on Death Row*. Waco, Texas: Chosen Books, 1977.

Brearley, H. C. *Homicide in the United States*. Chapel Hill, N.C.: University of North Carolina Press, 1932.

Bromberg, W. *Crime and the Mind*. Philadelphia: J. B. Lippincott, 1948.

Browne, Douglas, and Brock, Alan. *Fingerprints, Fifty Years of Scientific Crime Detection*. New York: E. P. Dutton, 1954.

Bullough, Vern L. *The History of Prostitution*. New Hyde Park, N.Y.: University Books, 1964.

Burt, Olive Woolley. *American Murder Ballads*. New York: Oxford University Press 1958.

Busch, Francis X. *Prisoners at the Bar*. Indianapolis: Bobbs-Merrill, 1952.

Butterfield, Roger. *The American Past*. New York: Simon & Schuster, 1947.

Byrnes, Thomas. *Professional Criminals of America*. New York: Cassell & Co., 1886.

Caesar, Gene. *Incredible Detective: The Biography of William J. Burns*. Englewood Cliffs, N.J.: Prentice-Hall, 1968.

Canning, John. *50 True Tales of Terror*. New York: Bell Publishing Co., 1972.

Carey, Arthur A. *Memoirs of a Murder Man*. Garden City, N.Y.: Doubleday, Doran and Company, 1930.

Carrington, Frank G. *The Victims*. New Rochelle, N.Y.: Arlington House, 1977.

———. *Neither Cruel Nor Unusual*. New Rochelle, N.Y.: Arlington House, 1978.

Casey, Lee. *Denver Murders*. New York: Duell, Sloan and Pearce, 1946.

Cassity, J. H. *The Quality of Murder*. New York: The Julian Press, 1958.

Chaplain Ray. *God's Prison Gang*. Old Tappan, N.J.: Fleming H. Revell Co., 1977.

Churchill, Allen. *A Pictorial History of American Crime*. New York: Holt, Rinehart & Winston, 1964.

Clinton, Henry Lauren. *Celebrated Trials*. New York: Harper & Bros., 1896.

Coates, Robert M. *The Outlaw Years*. New York: Macaulay, 1930.

Cohen, Louis H. *Murder, Madness and the Law*. New York: World Publishing Co., 1952.

Cohen, Sam D. *100 True Crime Stories*. New York: World, 1946.

Collins, Ted (ed.). *New York Murders*. New York: Duell, Sloan and Pearce, 1944.

Cooper, Courtney Riley. *Designs in Scarlet*. Boston: Little, Brown, 1939.

Corder, Eric. *Murder, My Love*. New York: Playboy Press, 1973.

Cox, Robert V. *Deadly Pursuit*. New York: Cameron House, 1977.

Crane, Milton. *Sins of New York*. Boni & Gaer, 1947.

Crapsey, Edward. *The Nether Side of New York*. New York: Sheldon, 1872.

Crouse, Russell. *Murder Won't Out*. Garden City, N.Y.: Doubleday, Doran & Co., 1932.

Darrow, Clarence. *The Story of My Life*. New York: Scribner's, 1932.

Day, Oscar F. G. *The Ging Murder and the Great Hayward Trial*. Minneapolis: Minnesota Tribune Co., 1895.

Dean, John. *The Indiana Torture Slaying*. Chicago: Bee-Line Books, 1967.

de Ford, Miriam Allen. *Murderers Sane & Mad*. New York: Abelard-Schuman, 1965.

de la Torre, Lillian. *The Truth about Belle Gunness*. New York: Gold Medal, 1955.

Demaris, Ovid. *America the Violent*. New York: Cowles Book Co., 1970.

Dempewolff, Richard. *Famous Old New England Murders.* Brattleboro, Vt.: Stephen Daye Press, 1942.

de Rham, Edith. *How Could She Do That?* New York: Clarkson N. Potter, 1969.

Derleth, August. *Wisconsin Murders.* Sauk City, Wis.: Mycroft and Moran, 1968.

Dickson, G. *Murder by Numbers.* London: Robert Hale, Ltd., 1958.

Dorman, Michael. *King of the Courtroom: Percy Foreman for the Defense.* New York: Delacorte Press, 1969.

Douthwaite, L.C. *Mass Murder.* New York: Holt, 1929.

Drago, Henry Sinclair. *Wild, Woolly & Wicked.* New York: Pocket Books, Inc., 1962.

Duffy, Warden Clinton T., as told to Dean Jennings. *The San Quentin Story.* Garden City, N.Y.: Doubleday, 1950.

Duffy, Warden Clinton T., with Hirshberg, Al. *88 Men and 2 Women.* Garden City, N.Y.: Doubleday, 1962.

Duke, Thomas S. *Celebrated Cases of America.* San Francisco: James H. Barry Co., 1910.

Elman, Robert. *Fired in Anger.* Garden City, N.Y.: Doubleday, 1968.

Emery, J. Gladstone. *Court of the Damned.* New York: Comet Press, 1959.

Erbstein, Charles E. *The Show-Up: Stories Before the Bar.* Chicago: Covici, 1926.

Erickson, Gladys A. *Warden Ragen of Joliet.* New York: E. P. Dutton, 1957.

Evans, Clyde (ed.). *Adventures of Great Crime Busters.* New York: New Power Publications, 1943.

Farley, Philip. *Criminals of America.* New York: Farley, 1876.

Fawkes, Sandy. *Killing Time.* New York: Taplinger, 1979.

Fenichel, O. *The Psychoanalytic Theory of Neurosis.* New York: W. W. Norton, 1945.

Fenwick, Robert. *Alfred Packer.* Denver: Denver Post, 1963.

Fergusson, Erna. *Murder & Mystery in New Mexico.* Albuquerque, N.M.: Armitage Editions, 1948.

Fiaschetti, Michael. *You Gotta Be Rough.* Garden City, N.Y.: Doubleday, Doran, 1930.

Finn, John T. *History of the Chicago Police.* Chicago: Police Book Fund, 1887.

Forbes, Abner, and Green, J. W. *The Rich Men of Massachusetts.* Boston: W. V. Spencer, 1851.

Fosdick, Raymond B. *American Police Systems.* New York: Century, 1920.

Fowler, Gene. *The Great Mouthpiece.* New York: Covici-Friede, 1931.

Frank, Gerald. *The Boston Strangler.* New York: New American Library, 1966.

Furlong, Thomas. *Fifty Years a Detective.* St. Louis: C. E. Barnett, 1912.

Furneaux, Rupert. *The Medical Murderer.* London: Elek Books, 1957.

Gantt, Paul H. *The Case of Alfred Packer, The Man Eater.* Denver: University of Denver, 1952.

Gelb, Barbara. *On the Track of Murder.* New York: William Morrow, 1975.

Gertz, Elmer. *A Handful of Clients.* Chicago: Follett, 1965.

Geyer, Frank. *The Holmes-Pitezel Case.* Philadelphia: Geyer, 1896.

Godwin, John. *Alcatraz: 1868–1963.* Garden City, N.Y.: Doubleday, 1963.

Gollomb, Joseph. *Crimes of the Year.* New York: Liveright, 1931.

Graham, Stephen. *New York Nights.* New York: Doran, 1927.

Great True Stories of Crime, Mystery and Detection. Pleasantville, N.Y.: Reader's Digest Assoc., 1965.

Gribble, Leonard R. *Famous Feats of Detection and Crime.* Garden City, N.Y.: Doubleday, Doran, 1934.

———. *Murders Most Strange.* London: John Long, 1959.

———. *Compelled to Kill.* London: John Long, 1977.

Griffiths, Major Arthur. *Mysteries of Police and Crime.* London: Cassell & Co., 1901.

Gross, Hans. *Criminology Psychology.* Boston: Little, Brown, 1915.

Gurwell, John K. *Mass Murder in Houston.* Houston, Tex.: Cordovan Press, 1974.

Guttmacher, M. S. *The Mind of the Murderer.* New York: Farrar, Straus, and Cudahy, 1960.

Hahn, Jon K., with McKenney, Harold C. *Legally Sane.* Chicago: Regnery, 1972.

Hamer, Alvin C. (ed.) *Detroit Murders.* New York: Duell, Sloan and Pearce, 1948.

Hardy, Allison. *Kate Bender, The Kansas Murderess.* Girard, Kan.: Haldeman-Julius, 1944.

Hecht, Ben. *A Child of the Century.* New York: Simon & Schuster, 1954.

Heimer, Mel. *The Cannibal, The Case of Albert Fish.* New York: Lyle Stuart, 1971.

Helpern, Milton, M.D. *Autopsy.* New York: St. Martin's Press, 1977.

Henry, A. F., and Short, J. F. *Suicide and Homicide.* Glencoe, Ill.: The Free Press, 1954.

Hentig, Hans von. *The Criminal and His Victim.* New York: Yale University Press, 1948.

Higdon, Hal. *The Crime of the Century.* New York: Putnam's, 1975.

Hirsch, Phil (ed.). *The Killers.* New York: Pyramid Publications, 1971.

Hoffman, F.L. *The Homicide Problem.* Newark, N.J.: Prudential Press, 1925.

Holbrook, Stewart. *Murder Out Yonder.* New York: Macmillan, 1941.

Holtzoff, H. (ed.). *Encyclopedia of Criminology.* New York: Philosophical Library, 1949.

Hooton, E. A. *The American Criminal.* Volume I. Cambridge, Mass.: Harvard University Press, 1939.

Hoover, J. Edgar. *Persons in Hiding.* Boston: Little, Brown, 1938.

Horan, James D. *The Pinkertons, The Detective Dynasty That Made History.* New York: Crown, 1967.

House, Brant (ed.). *Crimes That Shocked America.* New York: Ace Books, 1961.

Houts, Marshall. *They Asked for Death.* New York: Cowles, 1970.

Hynd, Alan. *Sleuths, Slayers, and Swindlers.* New York: Barnes, 1959.

———. *Brutes, Beasts and Human Fiends.* New York: Paperback Library, 1964.

Inbau, F. E., and Reid, J. E. *Lie Detection and Criminal Interrogation.* Baltimore: Williams and Wilkins, 1953.

Irving, H. B. *A Book of Remarkable Criminals.* New York: George H. Doran, 1918.

Jackson, Joseph Henry (ed.). *The Portable Murder Book.* New York: Viking Press, 1945.

———. *San Francisco Murders.* New York: Duell, Sloan and Pearce, 1947.

James, John T. *The Benders in Kansas.* Wichita, Kan.: Kan-Okla Publishing Co., 1913.

Jenness, John Scribner. *The Isles of Shoals.* New York: Hurd & Houghton, 1873.

Jesse, F. Tennyson. *Murder and Its Motives.* New York: Alfred A. Knopf, 1924.

———. *Comments on Caine.* London: Heinemann, 1948.

Johnston, James A. *Alcatraz Island Prison.* New York: Scribner's, 1949.

Kavanagh, Marcus. *The Criminal and His Allies.* Indianapolis: Bobbs-Merrill, 1928.

Kenny, C. S. *Outlines of Criminal Law.* London: Cambridge University Press, 1947.

Kilgallen, Dorothy. *Murder One.* New York: Random House, 1967.

Kingston, Charles. *Remarkable Rogues; Some Notable Criminals of Europe and America* London: John Lane, 1921.

Kirkpatrick, Ernest E. *Voices from Alcatraz.* San Antonio, Tex.: Naylor, 1947.

Kling, Samuel G. *Sexual Behavior & the Law.* New York: Bernard Geis, 1965.

Knox, Thomas W. *Underground.* Hartford, Conn.: Burr, Hyde, 1873.

Kobler, John. *Some Like It Gory.* New York: Dodd, Mead, 1940.

Kwartler, Richard (ed.). *Behind Bars.* New York: Random House, 1974.

Lane, Roger. *Policing the City: Boston, 1822–1885.* Cambridge, Mass.: Harvard University Press, 1967.

Langford, Gerald. *The Murder of Stanford White.* Indianapolis: Bobbs-Merrill, 1962.

Laurence, John A. *Extraordinary Crimes.* London: Sampson Low, 1931.

Lavigne, Frank C. *Crimes, Criminals and Detectives.* Helena, Mont.: State Publishing Co., 1921.

Lavine, Sigmund. *Allan Pinkerton, America's First Private Eye.* New York: Dodd, Mead, 1963.

Lawes, Warden Lewis Edward. *Twenty Thousand Years in Sing Sing.* New York: R. Long & R. R. Smith, Inc., 1932.

———. *Meet the Murderer.* New York: Harper Bros., 1940.

Lawson, John D. *American State Trials.* St. Louis: F. H. Thomas Law Book Co., 1914.

LeBlanc, Jervy, and Davis, Ivor. *5 to Die.* Los Angeles: Holloway House, 1970.

Leopold, Nathan F., Jr. *Life Plus 99 Years.* Garden City, N. Y.: Doubleday, 1958.

Lewis, Alfred Henry. *Nation-Famous New York Murders.* Chicago: M. A. Donohue, 1912.

Lewis, John B., and Bombaugh, Charles C. *The Goss-Undderzook Tragedy.* Baltimore: James H. McClellan, 1896.

Logan, Guy B. H. *Masters of Crime.* London: Stanley Paul, 1928.

———. *Rope, Knife and Chair.* London: Stanley Paul, 1930.

Lunde, Donald T. *Murder and Madness.* New York: The Portable Standard, 1975.

Lustgarten, Edgar. *The Murder and the Trial.* New York: Scribner's, 1958.

———. *The Illustrated Story of Crime.* Chicago: Follett, 1976.

MacDonald, John M. *The Murderer and His Victim.* Springfield, Ill.: Charles C. Thomas, 1961.

Mackaye, Milton. *Dramatic Crimes of 1927.* Garden City, N.Y.: Doubleday, Doran, 1928.

Mackenzie, Frederic A. *Twentieth Century Crimes.* Boston: Little, Brown, 1927.

———. *The Trial of Harry Thaw.* London: Geoffrey Bles, 1928.

Makins, John R. (ed.). *Boston Murders.* New York: Duell, Sloan and Pearce, 1947.

Marten, Manuel Edward. *The Doctor Looks at Murder.* Garden City, N.Y.: Doubleday, Doran, 1937.

McCallum, John D. *Crime Doctor.* Mercer Island, Wash.: The Writing Works, Inc., 1978.

McComas, Francis. *The Graveside Companion.* New York: Obolensky, 1962.

McCord, W., and McCord, J. *Origins of Crime.* New York: Columbia University Press, 1959.

McKernan, Maureen. *The Amazing Crime and Trial of Leopold and Loeb.* New York: New American Library, 1957.

Mills, James. *The Prosecutor.* New York: Pocket Books, 1970.

Minot, G. E. *Murder Will Out.* Boston: Marshall Jones, 1928.

Morley, Christopher. *Fifth Avenue Bus.* Philadelphia: J. B. Lippincott, 1931.

Morris, A. *Homicide: An Approach to the Problem of Crime.* Boston: Boston University Press, 1955.

Moser, Don, and Cohen, Jerry. *The Pied Piper of Tucson.* New York: Signet Books, 1967.

Murray, George. *The Madhouse on Madison Street.* Chicago: Follett, 1965.

Nash, Jay Robert. *Dillinger: Dead or Alive?* Chicago: Henry Regnery Co., 1970.

———. *Citizen Hoover.* Chicago: Nelson-Hall, 1972.

———. *Bloodletters and Badmen: A Narrative Encyclopedia of American Criminals from the Pilgrims to the Present.* New York: M. Evans, 1973.

———. *Hustlers and Con Men.* New York: M. Evans, 1976.

———. *Among the Missing: An Anecdotal History of Missing Persons from Ancient Times to the Present.* New York: Simon and Schuster, 1978.

Neustatter, W. L. *The Mind of the Murderer.* London: Johnson, 1957.

Noble, John Wesley, and Averbuch, Bernard. *Never Plead Guilty.* New York: Farrar, Strauss and Cudahy, 1955.

O'Brien, Frank M. *Murder Mysteries of New York*. New York: W. F. Payson, 1932.
O'Connor, Richard. *Courtroom Warrior*. Boston: Little, Brown, 1963.
O'Donnell, B. *Should Women Hang?* London: W. H. Allen, 1956.
Olsen, Jack. *The Man with the Candy*. New York: Simon and Schuster, 1974.
Orchard, Harry. *The Confessions and Autobiography of Harry Orchard*. New York: Doubleday, Page, 1907.
O'Sullivan, F. Dalton. *Crime Detection*. Chicago: O'Sullivan Publishing, 1928.

Pearson, Edmund Lester. *Studies in Murder*. New York: Macmillan, 1924.
———. *Murder at Smutty Nose*. Garden City, N.Y.: Doubleday, 1927.
———. *Five Murders*. Garden City, N.Y.: Doubleday, 1928.
———. *Instigation of the Devil*. New York: Scribner's, 1930.
———. *More Studies in Murder*. New York: H. Smith and R. Haas, 1936.
Penfield, Thomas. *Dig Here!* San Antonio, Tex.: Naylor, 1962.
Pinkerton, Alan. *Criminal Reminiscences and Detective Sketches*. New York: G. W. Dillingham, 1878.
Pinkerton, Matthew W. *Murder in All Ages*. Chicago: Pinkerton & Co., 1898.
Pollack, O. *The Criminality of Women*. Philadelphia: The University of Pennsylvania Press, 1950.
Porges, Irwin. *The Violent Americans*. Derby, Conn.: Monarch Books, 1963.
Porter, Garnett Clay. *Strange and Mysterious Crimes*. New York: McFadden, 1929.

Quimby, Ione. *Murder for Love*. New York: Covici, 1931.

Radin, Edward D. *12 Against Crime*. New York: G. P. Putnam's, 1953.
The Record of Crimes in the U.S. Buffalo: Faxon & Co., 1834.
Reik, T. *Myth and Guilt*. New York: Braziller, 1957.
Reinhardt, J. M. *The Murderous Trail of Charles Starkweather*. Springfield, Ill.: Thomas, 1960.
Reiwald, P. *Society and Its Criminals*. New York: International University Press, 1950.
Remarkable Trials of All Countries. New York: S. S. Peloubet & Co., 1882.
Reynolds, Quentin. *Headquarters*. New York: Harper & Bros., 1955.
Reynolds, Ruth. *Murder 'Round the World*. New York: Justice Books, 1953.
Rice, Robert. *The Business of Crime*. New York: Farrar, Straus & Cudahy, 1956.
Rodell, Marie F. (ed.). *New York Murders*. New York: Duell, Sloan and Pearce, 1944.
Rogers, Kenneth Paul. *For One Sweet Grape*. New York: Playboy Press, 1974.
Rosenthal, A. M. *Thirty-Eight Witnesses*. New York: McGraw-Hill, 1964.
Roughhead, William. *Malice Domestic*. New York: Doubleday, Doran, 1929.
Rowan, David. *Famous American Crimes*. London: Frederick Muller, Ltd., 1957.
Rowan, Richard Wilmer. *The Pinkertons, A Detective Dynasty*. Boston: Little, Brown, 1931.
Rumbelow, Donald. *The Complete Jack the Ripper*. Boston: New York Graphic Society, 1975.

Samuels, Charles. *The Girl in the Red Velvet Swing*. New York: Fawcett, 1953.
———. *Death was the Bridegroom*. New York: Fawcett, 1955.
Sandoe, James (ed.). *Murder, Plain and Fanciful*. New York: Sheridan, 1948.
Schultz, Gladys Denny. *How Many More Victims: Society and the Sex Criminal*. Philadelphia: J. B. Lippincott, 1966.
Shore, W. Teignmouth (ed.). *Trial of Thomas Neill Cream*. (Notable British Trials) London: William Hodge & Co., 1923.
Simpson, Helen (ed.). *The Anatomy of Murder*. New York: Macmillan, 1937.
Singer, Kurt (ed.). *My Strangest Cases*. Garden City, N.Y.: Doubleday, 1958.
Smith, Edward Henry. *Famous American Poison Mysteries*. New York: Dial Press, 1927.

Smith, Sir Sydney. *Mostly Murder*. London: Harrap, 1959.

Soderman, H. *Policeman's Lot*. New York: Funk and Wagnalls, 1956.

Sparrow, Gerald. *Women Who Murder*. New York: Abelard-Schuman, 1970.

Steiger, Brad. *The Mass Murderer*. New York: Award Books, 1967.

Stekel, W. *Compulsion and Doubt*. New York: Liveright, 1950.

Stern, Philip Van Dorn. *The Man Who Killed Lincoln*. New York: Random House, 1935.

Stone, Dr. James W. *Report of the Trial of Professor John W. Webster*. Boston: Phillips, Sampson & Co., 1850.

Stone, Irving. *Clarence Darrow for the Defense*. Garden City, N.Y.: Doubleday, 1941.

Strange and Mysterious Crimes. New York: Macfadden, 1929.

Sullivan, Robert. *The Disappearance of Dr. Parkman*. Boston: Little, Brown, 1971.

Sutherland, E. H., and Cressey, D. R. *Principles of Criminology*. Philadelphia: Lippincott, 1959.

Sutton, Charles. *The New York Tombs and Its Secrets and Mysteries*. New York: U.S. Publishing Co., 1874.

Tallant, Robert. *Ready to Hang*. New York: Harper & Bros., 1952.

Tannenbaum, Frank. *Crime and the Community*. New York: Columbia University Press, 1938.

Thaw, Harry K. *The Traitor*. New York: Dorrance, 1926.

Thaxter, Celia. *Among the Isles of Shoals*. Boston: Houghton Mifflin, 1873.

Thompson. C. J. S. *Poison Mysteries in History*. Philadelphia: J. B. Lippincott, 1932.

Train, Arthur. *True Stories of Crime from the District Attorney's Office*. New York: McKinley, Stone & MacKenzie, 1908.

Traini, Robert. *Murder for Sex*. London: William Kimber, 1960.

Trenerry, Walter N. *Murder in Minnesota*. St. Paul: The Minnesota Historical Society, 1962.

Triplett, Col. Frank. *History, Romance and Philosophy of Great American Crimes and Criminals*. Hartford, Conn.: Park Publishing Co., 1885.

Van Every, Edward. *Sins of New York*. New York: Frederick A. Stokes Co., 1930.

Vitray, Laura. *The Great Lindbergh Hullabaloo*. New York: Fargo, 1932.

Walling, George. *Recollections of a New York Chief of Police*. New York: Caxton, 1887.

Warren, John H. *Thirty Years Battle with Crime*. Poughkeepsie, N.Y.: A. J. White, 1874.

Washburn, Emory. *Sketches of the Judicial History 'of Massachusetts*. Boston: Little, Brown, 1840.

Webster, Daniel. *Argument on the Trial of John Francis Knapp, The Works of Daniel Webster*, Volume 6. Boston: Little, Brown, 1851.

Weihofen, H. *The Urge to Punish*. New York: Farrar, 1956.

Weinberg, Arthur (ed.). *Attorney for the Damned*. New York: Simon & Schuster, 1957.

Wellman, Francis L. *The Art of Cross-Examination*. New York: Macmillan, 1903.

———. *Gentlemen of the Jury: Reminiscences of Thirty Years at the Bar*. New York: Macmillan, 1924.

Wellman, Manly Wade. *Dead and Gone*. Chapel Hill, N.C.: North Carolina Press, 1955.

Wertham, Frederic. *Dark Legend*. London: Gollancz, 1947.

———. *The Show of Violence*. New York: Doubleday, 1949.

———. *The Circle of Guilt*. New York: Rinehart, 1956.

West, Don. *Sacrifice Unto Me*. New York: Pyramid, 1974.

Whipple, Sidney. *The Lindbergh Crime*. New York: Blue Ribbon Books, 1935.

Whitehead, Don. *The F.B.I. Story*. New York: Random House, 1956.

Whitelaw, D. *Corpus Delicti*. London: Geoffrey Bles, 1936.

Williams, Jack Kenny. *Vogues in Villainy*. Columbia, S.C.: University of South Carolina Press, 1959.

453

Wilson, Colin. *A Casebook of Murder*. New York: Cowles, 1969.
Wilson, Samuel Payntor. *Chicago and Its Cesspools of Vice and Infamy*. Chicago: n.p., 1910.
Wolfgang, M. E. *Patterns in Criminal Homicide*. Philadelphia: University of Pennsylvania Press, 1958.
————. *Studies in Homicide*. New York: Harper and Row, 1967.
Woollcott, Alexander. *While Rome Burns*. New York: Viking Press, 1934.
————. *Long, Long Ago*. New York: Viking Press, 1943.
Wren, Lassiter. *Masterstrokes of Crime Detection*. Garden City, N.Y.: Doubleday, Doran, 1929.
Wright, Sewell Peaslee (ed.). *Chicago Murders*. New York: Duell, Sloan & Pearce, 1945.

Periodicals

"Accessory After the Fact." *Southern Ruralist*, June 15, 1913.
"America and the Sixth Commandment." *The Outlook*, February 16, 1907.
"Analytical Chemistry of Murder." *Current Literature*, March 1906.
Ansbacher, H. L., Ansbacher, R., Shiverick, D., and Shiverick, K. "Lee Harvey Oswald." *Psychoanalytic Review*, January 5, 1966.
"Anti-Semitism and the Frank Case." *Literary Digest*, January 16, 1915.
Asbury, Herbert. "Days of Wickedness." *American Mercury*, November 1927.
"The Atlanta Massacre." *The Independent*, October 4, 1906.

Banay, R. S. "A Study of 22 Men Convicted of Murder in the First Degree." *Journal of Criminal Law*, 34:106, 1934.
————. "Study in Murder." *Annals of the American Academy of Political Science*, 284, 1952.
Barnhart, K. E. "A Study of Homicide in the United States." *Birmingham-Southern College Bulletin*, 5:25, 1932.
Barton, E. "Murder in the Mountains and the Metropolis." *The Independent*, July 26, 1906.
Batt, J. C. "Homicidal Incidence in the Depressive Psychoses." *Journal of Mental Science*, 94, 1948.
Bell, A. "Fate of the Boys Next Door." *Esquire*, March 1974.
Bell, Daniel. "Crime as an American Way of Life." *Antioch Review*, June 1953.
Bender, C. "Children and Adolescents Who Have Killed." *American Journal of Psychiatry*, 116, 1960.
"The Benders of Kansas." *Kansas Magazine*, September 1886.
Bendiner, R. "The Man Who Reads Corpses." *Harper's Magazine*, February 1955.
Berg, I. A., and Fox, V. "Factors in Homicide Committed by 200 Males." *Journal of Social Psychology*, 26, 1947.
Berger, Meyer. "Lady in Crepe." *The New Yorker*, October 5 and 12, 1935.
"Big Martha." *Time*, March 14, 1949.
Blackman, N., Weiss, J. M. A., and Lamberti, J. W. "The Sudden Murderer." *Archives of General Psychiatry*, 8, 1963.
"Blanket over Homicide." *The Nation*, April 25, 1966.
"Bluebeard on the Beach." *Time*, May 28, 1973.
Bolhower, M. B. "Murder for Thirty Cents." *Scribner's Magazine*, April 1941.
Brearley, H. C., and Seagle, W. "How Often We Murder and Why: Review of Homicide in the U.S." *The Nation*, May 25, 1932.
Buckley, J. M. "Assassinations of Kings and Presidents." *Century Magazine*, November 1901.
Bullock, H. A. "Urban Homicide in Theory and Fact." *Journal of Criminal Law*, 45:565, 1955.

Bunker, H. A. "Mother Murder in Myth and Legend." *Psychoanalytical Quarterly*, 13:19, 1944.

Burkholder, Edwin V. "Those Murdering Benders." *True Western Adventures*, February 1960.

Campbell, C. "Portrait of a Mass Killer." *Psychology Today*, May 1976.

Cannon, W. B. "Voodoo Death." *American Anthropology*, 44:169, 1942.

Carlson, Eric T. "The Unfortunate Dr. Parkman." *American Journal of Psychiatry*, December 1966.

Carpenter, A. "Pattern for Murder." *Science Digest*, June 1947.

"The Case of Leo M. Frank." *The Outlook*, May 26, 1915.

"Catch Me If You Can." *Newsweek*, February 26, 1968.

Champion, H. "Nice Murderer—The Search for a Motive." *The Nation*, March 22, 1958.

Childers, J. E., and Snyder, J. "Death Was a Phantom Lodger." *Denver Post*, February 7, 1960.

Coffee, M. "Badlands Revisited." *Atlantic Monthly*, December 1974.

Cole, K. E., Fisher, G., and Cole, S. S. "Women Who Kill." *Archives of General Psychiatry*, 19, 1968.

Collins, F. L. "Mistakes That Trap Murderers." *Science Digest*, June 1947.

Conrad, William, and Greenwood, Robert. "The Bender Legend." *Kansas Magazine*, 1950 (pages 27–32).

"Cop-Killer at Nineteen—Why?" *Literary Digest*, May 30, 1931.

Creel, George. "Unholy City." *Collier's*, September 2, 1939.

Cruvant, B. A., and Waldrop, F. N. "The Murderer in the Mental Institution." *Annals of the American Academy of Political Science*, 284, 1952.

Davidson, G. M. "Psychiatric Aspects of the Law and of Homicide." *Psychiatric Quarterly Supplement*, 20, 1946.

Davis, Hartley, and Smyth, Clifford. "The Land of Feuds." *Munsey's Magazine*, November 1903.

"Death Follows Art." *Time*, March 22, 1976.

deFord, Miriam Allen. "The Case of Leopold and Loeb." *True Crime Detective Magazine*, October 1952.

Dershovitz, Alan P., and Goldsberg, Arthur J. "Declaring the Death Penalty Unconstitutional." *Harvard Law Review*, June 1970.

"Doomed Sixty in New York." *Harper's Weekly*, October 24, 1908.

Dorpat, T. L. "Suicide in Murderers." *Psychiatric Digest*, 27, 1966.

"Due Process of Law in the Frank Case." *Harvard Law Review*, XXVII, 1915.

Duncan, G. M., Frazier, S. H., Litin, E. M., Johnson, A. M., and Barron, A. J. "Etiological Factors in First Degree Murder." *J.A.M.A.*, 168:1755, 1958.

"Easier to Get Away with Murder?" *U.S. News and World Report*, February 11, 1955.

"Easing Up on Murderers—Why?" *U.S. News and World Report*, November 29, 1957.

"Easy Times for Murderers." *Literary Digest*, October 4, 1924.

"Education and Murder." *Literary Digest*, October 18, 1924.

"Electrodes for Two: Raymond Martinez Fernandez and Mrs. Martha Beck." *Newsweek*, August 29, 1949.

"Emotional Insanity." *Independent*, August 27, 1908.

"End of the Frank Case." *The Outlook*, September 15, 1915.

Ennis, Phillip. "Crimes, Victims and the Police." *Transaction*, June 1962.

"Expanding the Unwritten Law." *The Nation*, July 25, 1907.

Fabing, H. D. "On Going Berserk: A Neurochemical Inquiry." *American Journal of Psychiatry*, 113:409, 1956.

Ferrero, G. "Ideas of Murder Among Men and Animals." *Popular Science*, October 1897.

"Four Murders." *Time*, July 14, 1961.

Freedman, L. Z. "Assassination." *Postgraduate Medicine*, 37, 1965.

Freeman, J. "Murder Monopoly: The Inside Story of a Crime Trust." *The Nation*, 150:645, 1940.

Friendly, Fred. "A Crime and Its Aftershock." *New York Times Magazine*, March 21, 1976.

Galvin, J. A. V., and Macdonald, J. M. "Psychiatric Study of a Mass Murderer." *American Journal of Psychiatry*, 115, 1959.

Garfinkel, H. "Notes on Inter- and Intra-Racial Homicides." *Social Forces*, 27, 1949.

"Ghostly Images of a Ghastly Murder." *Life*, March 28, 1960.

Gibbens, T. C. N. "Sane and Insane Homicide." *Journal of Criminal Law*, 49, 1958.

Giese, D. J. "Why Was Carol Killed?" *Saturday Evening Post*, September 14, 1963.

Goins, G. "Hooch and Homicide in Mississippi." *American Mercury*, October 1939.

———. "Dice and Death in Dixie." *American Mercury*, July 1941.

Gold, M. "Suicide, Homicide, and the Socialization of Aggression." *American Journal of Sociology*, 63, 1958.

Goldberg, H. "Crimes of Darkness." *Cosmopolitan*, April 1959.

Greenacre, P. "Conscience in the Psychopath." *American Journal of Orthopsychiatry*, 15:495, 1945.

Grinnell, C. E. "Modern Murder Trials and Newspapers." *Atlantic Monthly*, November 1901.

Gross, Karl. "The Paranoic Murderers." *Journal of Criminal Psychopathology*, 1:166, 1939.

Harlan, H. "Five Hundred Homicides." *Journal of Criminal Law*, 40:736, 1950.

Harris, John P. "Beautiful Katie." *Kansas Magazine*, 1936 (pages 43–49).

Hastings, D. W. "The Psychiatry of Presidential Assassinations." *Journal-Lancet*, 85, 1965.

Hastings, G. B. "How the Police Make Criminals." *The Survey*, May 15, 1909.

"He Killed Three Times." *Newsweek*, August 24, 1959.

Henderson, Mark. "Murder Tavern." *The Great West*, May 1968.

"Highest Law." *The Outlook*, January 30, 1909.

"High Murder Rate in the South." *Literary Digest*, September 16, 1933.

Hill, D., and Pond, D. A. "Reflections on 100 Capital Cases." *Journal of Mental Science*, 98:23, 1952.

Hoffman, F. L. "Murder and the Death Penalty." *Current History*, June 1928.

———. "The Homicide Record for 1931." *Spectator*, March 31, 1932.

Holbrook, S. H. "Murder at Harvard." *American Mercury*, February 1948.

"Homicide as an Amusement." *The Independent*, October 11, 1906.

"House of Horror Stuns the Nation." *Life*, December 2, 1957.

"Houston Horrors." *Time*, August 20, 1973.

Howe, William F. "Some Notable Murder Cases." *Cosmopolitan*, August 1900.

Huie, William Bradford. "Case of the Murdered Tourist." *Coronet*, March 1950.

Iams, J. "Search for the Strangler." *Saturday Evening Post*. May 18, 1963.

"I'll Kill You If You Scream." *Time*, July 9, 1951.

"In Cold Blood—The Herbert Clutter Family." *Time*, November 30, 1959.

"Increase of Lawlessness in the United States." *McClure's*, December 1904.

"Increase of Lawlessness in the U.S." *Living Age*, January 7, 1905.

"Ingrate Murder Case." *Newsweek*, September 16, 1946.

"Insanity of Assassins." *The Independent*, November 7, 1901.

Jackson, D. "The Evolution of an Assassin." *Life*, February 21, 1964.

James, M. "Annals of Crime." *New Yorker*, December 6, 1941.

Jarman, Rufus. "The Pinkerton Story." *The Saturday Evening Post* (series), May 15, 22, 29, and June 5, 1948.

Johnson, P. H. "Who's to Blame When a Murderer Strikes?" *Life*, August 12, 1966.

Kahn, M. W. A. "Superior Performance IQ of Murderers as a Function of Overt Act." *Journal of Social Psychology*, 76, 1968.

"Killers of the Clutter Family." *Time*, January 18, 1960.

"Killer on a Rampage; W. E. Cook." *Newsweek*, January 22, 1951.

Kilpatrick, J. J. "Murder in the Deep South." *The Survey*, October 1943.

Konigsberg, M. "Personal Touch Traps a Murderer." *Reader's Digest*, November 1942.

Kuehn, J. L., and Burton, J. "Management of the College Student with Homicidal Impulses." *American Journal of Psychiatry*, 125, 1969.

Kurland, A., Morgenstern, J., and Sheets, C. A. "Comparative Study of Wife Murderers Admitted to a State Psychiatric Hospital." *Journal of Social Therapy*, 1, 1955.

Langberg, R. "Homicide in the United States." *Vital Health Statistics*, 20, 1967.

Leacock, S. "Such Fine Murders We're Having!" *Collier's*, November 1, 1924.

Lee, Henry. "The Ten Most Wanted Criminals in the Past 50 Years." *Liberty Magazine*, Fall 1972.

"Leopold-Loeb Decision." *New Republic*, September 24, 1924.

Lester, D. "Suicide, Homicide, and the Effects of Socialization." *Journal of Personality and Social Psychology*, 70, 1968.

Levin, Meyer. "Leopold Should be Freed!" *Coronet*, May 1957.

Lewellen, J. "How to Make a Killer Confess." *Saturday Evening Post*, March 31, 1956.

Lindner, R. M. "The Equivalent of Matricide." *Psychoanalytical Quarterly*, 17, 1948.

Lombroso, C. "Why Homicide Has Increased in the United States." *North American Review*, December 1897 and January 1898.

Lovett, R. M. "Crime and Publicity: Leopold, Loeb, and Chicago." *New Republic*, June 25, 1924.

Lunde, D. T. "Our Murder Boom." *Psychology Today*, November 1975.

"Lust for Blood as an Incentive to Murder." *Current Literature*, August 1909.

Macdonald, J. M. "The Threat to Kill." *American Journal of Psychiatry*, 19, 1970.

Mackaye, M. "Youthful Killers." *The Outlook*, January 2, 1929.

Magee, H. W. "Dust Traps the Criminal." *Popular Mechanics*, July 1935.

Malmquist, C. "Premonitory Signs of Homicidal Aggression in Juveniles." *American Journal of Psychiatry*, 128, 1971.

Manchester, William. "Murder Tour of New England." *Holiday*, May 1961.

"Manhunt." *Newsweek*, April 1950.

Martin, John Bartlow. "The Master of Murder Castle." *Harper's Magazine*, November 1943.

———. "Nathan Leopold's Thirty Desperate Years: Murder on His Conscience." *Saturday Evening Post* (series), April 2, 9, 16, 23, and May 28, 1955.

Matthews, Franklin. "Murder as a Labor Weapon." *Harper's Weekly*, June 2, 1906.

Maynard, L. M. "Murder in the Making." *American Mercury*, June 1929.

McDade, Thomas M. "The Parkman Case." *American Book Collector*, May 1959.

McGarry, William A. "Government by Murder." *The Independent*, October 27, 1917.

M'Clure, R. L. "The Mazes of a Kentucky Feud." *Independent*, September 17, 1903.

Megargee, E. I. "Assault with Intent to Kill." *Transaction*, 2 and 6, 1965.

Michelson, C. "Man Killers at Close Range." *Munsey's Magazine*, November 1901.

"Millions and Murder." *Literary Digest*, July 31, 1915.

Miner, J. R. "Church Membership and the Homicide Rate." *Human Biology*, 1:1247, 1928.
"Mother Knew Best." *Time*, March 17, 1947.
"Murder and the Law." *The Nation*, April 13, 1913.
"Murder at Starved Rock." *Time*, March 28, 1960.
"Murder by Wholesale." *Literary Digest*, July 22, 1922.
"Murder in California." *Time*, November 19, 1973.
"Murder in Missouri." *The Outlook*, January 13, 1932.
"Murder in New York." *The Nation*, August 12, 1931.
"Murder Mysteries, U.S. Homicide Statistics." *The Survey*, May 15, 1932.
"Murder, New Jersey Style." *Look*, March 10, 1970.
"Murder on the Delta." *Newsweek*, September 20, 1948.
"Murder Will Out." *Newsweek*, January 28, 1952.
"Murderous Country." *World's Work*, April 1907.
"Murderous Maniacs at Large." *Literary Digest*, September 19, 1925.
"Murders and Robberies Are Down." *U.S. News and World Report*, September 30, 1955.
"Murders by Poison." *Harper's Weekly*, November 8, 1902.
Murray-Aaron, E. "Poisons and Poisoners." *Scientific American*, August 1, 1891.
"Must a Free People Be Homicidal?" *World's Work*, January 1905.
"Mystery of Cruelty." *The Nation*, May 28, 1908.

"Nebraska Gothic." *Newsweek*, November 26, 1973.
"New York's War on Child-Killing Gangs." *Literary Digest*, August 15, 1931.
"Nicest Person." *Newsweek*, August 20, 1973.

Oswald, F. L. "Assassination Mania." *North American Review*, September 1900.

Palmer, G. "Crimes Against Children." *Literary Digest*, October 2, 1937.
Palmer, John Williamson. "The Pinkertons." *Century Magazine*, February 1892.
Park, R. E. "Murder and the Case Study Method." *American Journal of Sociology*, November 1930.
Parker, I. C. "How to Arrest the Increase of Homicides in America." *North American Review*, January 1896.
"Parole and Murder." *The Nation*, May 6, 1936.
Pearson, Edmund. "Perfect Murder." *Scribner's Magazine*, July 1937.
Peters, W. "Why Did They Do It?" *Good Housekeeping*, June 1962.
"Philadelphia's Deplorable Murder." *Literary Digest*, October 13, 1917.
Phillips, Stephen H. "The Webster Case." *Monthly Law Reporter*, May 1850.
Piliavin, Irving, and Briar, Scott. "Police Encounters with Juveniles." *American Journal of Sociology*. September 1964.
Pokorny, A. D. "Moon Phases, Suicide, and Homicide." *American Journal of Psychiatry*, 121, 1964.
———. "Human Violence." *Journal of Criminal Law, Criminology, and Police Science*, 56, 1965.
Poole, L. "Murder Clues in a Test Tube." *Science Digest*, January 1955.
"Portrait of a Killer: Ed Gein." *Time*, December 2, 1957.
Progoff, I. "The Psychology of Lee Harvey Oswald." *Journal of Individual Psychology*, 23, 1967.

"Quiet One." *Time*, March 7, 1960.
Quinney, R. "Suicide, Homicide, and Economic Development." *Social Forces*, 43, 1965.

Radin, E. D. "Invisible Clues That Trap Killers." *Science Digest*, September 1950.
Ramage, B. J. "Homicide in the Southern States." *Sewanee Review*, February 1896.

Ranck, S. H. "Punishment to Fit the Crime." *American Journal of Sociology*, March 1901.

Randolph, John. "Alfred Packer, Cannibal." *Harper's Weekly*, October 17, 1874.

Reichard, S., and Tillman, C. "Murder and Suicide as Defenses Against Schizophrenic Psychosis." *Journal of Clinical Psychopathology*, 11:149, 1934.

Riis, Jacob A. "How the Other Half Lives." *Scribner's Magazine*, January 1937.

"Robbery and Murder." *The Outlook*, November 28, 1923.

Robinson, Archie. "Murder Most Foul." *American Heritage*, August 1964.

Rolph, C. H. "Those Who Murder." *The Nation*, May 14, 1960.

Rothstein, D. A. "Presidential Assassination Syndrome." *Archives of General Psychiatry*, 11, 1964.

Rousseau, V. "Lawless New York." *Harper's Weekly*, December 26, 1908.

Rowe, Fayette. "Kate Bender's Fate Still Mystery of Pioneer Kansas." *Wichita Eagle Magazine*, September 26, 1954.

Ruotolo, A. "Dynamics of Sudden Murder." *American Journal of Psychoanalysis*, 28, 1968.

"Safest of All Crimes." *The Independent*, January 29, 1903.

Saltus, E. "Champion Poisoners." *Cosmopolitan*, February 1902.

Sargent, D. "Children Who Kill." *Social Work*, 7, 1962.

Scherl, S. J., and Mack, J. E. "A Study of Adolescent Matricide." *Journal of American Child Psychiatry*, 5, 1966.

Schilder, P. "The Attitudes of Murderers Toward Death." *Journal of Abnormal and Social Psychology*, 31, 1936.

Schmid, C. F. "Study of Homicides in Seattle." *Social Forces*, 4:745, 1926.

Schwarzkopf, H. N. "Handsome Killer." *Scribner's Magazine*, February 1941.

Scott, J. P. "Anatomy of Violence." *The Nation*, June 21, 1965.

"Secrets of the Farm." *Newsweek*, December 2, 1957.

"Sentimentality in Murder Trials." *Review of Reviews*, November 1908.

"Sex Killer at Eighteen." *The Nation*, June 8, 1957.

Shipley, M. "Crimes of Violence in Chicago and in Greater New York." *Review of Reviews*, September 1908.

Shupe, L. M. "Alcohol and Crime." *Journal of Criminal Law*, 44:661, 954.

"The Sickles Case." *Harper's Weekly*, March 26, 1859.

"The Sickles Case." *Harper's Weekly*, April 2, 1859.

"The Sickles Tragedy at Washington." *Harper's Weekly*, March 12, 1859.

"The Sickles Verdict." *Harper's Weekly*, May 7, 1859.

Smith, S. "The Adolescent Murderer." *Archives of General Psychiatry*, 13, 1965.

"The Sniper." *Newsweek*, February 18, 1963.

"Speck Handled with Care." *Life*, July 29, 1966.

Stack, Andy. "The Killers' Week-Long Blood Orgy." *Official Detective Magazine*, May 1971.

Stearns, A. W. "Homicide in Massachusetts." *American Journal of Psychiatry*, 4:725, 1924.

Swallow, Richard. "Where Is the Infamous Katie Bender?" *Real Detectives*, September 1932.

Taves, L. "Day of Terror." *Good Housekeeping*, April 1959.

Teale, E. "Is It Murder?" *Popular Science*, September 1940.

"The Tenderloin." *American Notes and Quotes*, August 1945.

Tharter, Celia. "A Memorable Murder." *Atlantic Monthly*, May 1875.

"Thaw, Becker, *et al.*" *The Independent*, August 9, 1915.

"Tragedy in the Canyon." *Newsweek*, March 28, 1960.

Train, Arthur. "The Patrick Case, Complete." *The American Magazine*, May 1907.

Turner, George Kibbee. "The Man-Hunter." *McClure's*, June 1913.
"Twenty-four Years to Page One." *Time*, July 29, 1966.

Wakefield, E. "Brand of Cain in the Great Republic." *Living Age*, January 2, 1892.
Waldron, E. "Murder Tour of the Midwest." *Holiday*, August 1961.
Waldrop, F. C. "Murder as a Sex Practice." *American Mercury*, February 1948.
Wallace, J., Jr. "Inspiration for Murder." *Coronet*, August 1949.
Wallace, L. "Prevention of Presidential Assassinations." *North American Review*, December 1901.
Weinstein, E. A., and Lyerby, O. "Symbolic Aspects of Presidential Assassination." *Psychiatry*, 32, 1969.
Weisz, A. E., and Taylor, R. "American Presidential Assassinations." *Diseases and the Nervous System*, 30, 1969.
Wertham, Fredric. "It's Murder." *Saturday Review of Literature*, February 5, 1949.
Westley, William A. "Violence and the Police." *American Journal of Sociology*, July 1953.
Wheeler, C. A. "Broadcasting Photo Circular Finds Murderer." *American City*, May 1940.
White, A. D. "Assassins and Their Apologists." *The Independent*, August 21, 1902.
"Who Is the Real Murderer?" *Literary Digest*, December 15, 1931.
"Why Murder Will Out." *Newsweek*, April 2, 1945.
"Why So Much Blood Is Spilled in Dixie." *Literary Digest*, June 18, 1932.
Wilkinson, S., and Toland, J. "Why They Killed the People They Loved." *Cosmopolitan*, March 1960.
Wilmer, H. A. "Murder, You Know." *Psychiatric Quarterly*, 43, 1969.
Wittman, O., and Astrachan, M. "Psychological Investigation of a Homicidal Youth." *Journal of Clinical Psychology*, 5, 1949.
Wolf, W. "Poison Murders Solved by Test-Tube Sleuths." *Popular Science*, August 1935.
Wolfgang, Marvin E. "A Sociological Analysis of Criminal Homicide." *Federal Probation*, 25, 1961.
Woodbury, C. "America's Greatest Manhunt." *American Magazine*, December 1952.
Woods, S. M. "Adolescent Violence and Homicide." *Archives of General Psychiatry*, 5, 1961.

Yoder, M. "Murder by Mail." *Saturday Evening Post*, July 12, 1952.
"Young Man with a Gun: W. E. Cook." *Time*, January 22, 1951.

Zimmern, H. "Enrico Ferri on Homicide." *Popular Science*, October 1896.

Bulletins, Documents, Pamphlets, Reports

Abott A. Abott. *The Assassination and Death of Abraham Lincoln*. New York: American News Co., 1865.
Abrahamsen, D. "A Study of Lee Harvey Oswald." *Bulletin of the New York Academy of Medicine* 43 (1967).
The Address of Abraham Johnstone. Philadelphia: N.p., 1797.
The American Bloody Register. Boston: E. Russell, 1784.
An Account of the Curtis Homicide. Richmond, Va.: Dispatch Steam Presses, 1879.
An Account of the Execution of Samuel Green. Boston: N. Coverly, 1822.
An Account of the Murder of Richard Jennings. Newburgh, N.Y.: Benjamin F. Lewis, 1819.
An Account of the Murder of Thomas Williams. Trenton, N.J.: Sherman & Mershon, 1803.

An Analysis or Outline of the Life and Character of Josiah Burnham. Hanover, N.H.: Moses Davis, 1806.

An Awful Warning to the Intemperate: Trial, Conviction, Sentence, and only True Copy of the Confession of Catherine Cashiere to the Murder of Susan Anthony. New York: C. Brown, 1829.

An Awful Warning to the Youth of America. Report of the Trial of Octavius Baron. Rochester, N.Y.: Shepard, Strong & Dawson, 1838.

Argument of Hon. Edward Pierrepont to the Jury on the Trial of John H. Surratt for the Murder of President Lincoln. Washington, D.C.: Government Printing Office, 1867.

The Ashland Tragedy . . . A History of the Killing of Fanny Gibbons. Ashland, Ky.: J.M. Huff, 1883.

The Assassin's Doom, Full Account of the Jail Life, Trial and Sentence of Charles J. Guiteau. New York: Richard K. Fox, 1882.

The Authentic Confession of Jesse Strang. New York: E. M. Murden & A. Ming, Jr., 1827.

The Authentic Life of John C. Colt. Boston: S.N. Dickinson, 1842.

Authentic Narrative of the Murder of Mrs. Rademacher. Philadelphia: G.B. Zieber, 1848.

Baldwin, Rev. George C. *Awful Disclosures: The Life and Confessions of Andreas Hall.* Troy, N.Y.: J.C. Kneeland & Co., 1849.

Barnes, David M. *Trial of John Hendrickson, Jr.* Albany, N.Y.: Barnes & Hevenor, 1853.

The Barrel Mystery, or the Career, Tragedy and Trial of Henry Jumpertz. Chicago: Norris & Hyde, 1859.

Basutoland Medicine Murder. London: Her Majesty's Stationary Office, 1958.

Beach, David. *A Statement of the Facts Concerning the Death of Samuel Lee and the Prosecution of David Sanford for Murder.* New Haven, Conn.: Beach, 1807.

The Beach Tragedy, The Trial of Dr. L.U. Beach. Altoona, Pa.: Call Steam Printing House, 1884.

Belfry Murder in Boston. Philadelphia: Old Franklin Publishing House, 1875.

The Bellville Tragedy, Story of the Trial and Conviction of Rev. W.E. Hinshaw for the Murder of His Wife. Indianapolis, Ind.: Sentinel Printing Co., 1895.

Boyington, Charles R.S. "A Statement of the Trial of Charles R. S. Boyington." Mobile, Ala.: *Mercantile Advertiser,* 1835.

A Brief Account of the Life, Christian Experience and Execution of Courtland C. Johnson. Harrisburg, Pa.: Hamilton Printers, 1854.

Brown, Christian. *Trial and Confession of William Hill.* New York: Brown, 1826.

Buse, William H. *The Life, Confessions and Adventures of William H. Buse.* Memphis, Tenn.: Hutton & Clark, 1859.

Butler, Franklin. "John Ward, or the Victimized Assassin." Windsor, Vt.: *Vermont Journal,* 1869.

Butler, J.E. "Trial of Jane M. Swett." Biddeford, Me.: *Union & Journal,* 1867.

Carpenter, S.C. *Report of the Trial of Richard Dennis.* Charleston, S.C.: G.M. Bounetheau, 1805.

———. "Report of the Trial of Joshua Nettles." Charleston, S.C.: *Charleston Courier,* 1805.

Carrigan, E.C. *John P. Phair, A Complete History of Vermont's Celebrated Murder Case.* Boston: Carrigan, 1879.

Channing, Henry. *The Execution of Hannah Ocuish.* New London, Conn.: T. Green, 1786.

"The Chesaning Murder!" East Saginaw, Mich.: *Saginaw Daily Courier,* 1877.

The Church Belfry Murder in Boston. Philadelphia: Old Franklin Publishing House, 1875.

Clark, Aaron. *Trial of James Graham.* Albany, N.Y.: J. Bull, 1814.

Cluverius, Thomas J. *My Life, Trial and Conviction.* Richmond, Va.: Andrews, Baptist & Clemmitt, 1887.

The Cold Springs Tragedy. Indianapolis, Ind.: A.C. Roach, 1869.

Commonwealth v. George Baker. Boston: Frank P. Hill, 1887.

Confession of Adam Horn. Baltimore: James Young, 1843.

Confession of Augustus Otis Jennings. St. Joseph, Mo.: K.J. Bastin & Co., 1853.

The Confession of Benjamin Bailey. Reading, Pa.: J. Schneider, 1798.

Confession of Edward Donnelly. Carlisle, Pa.: A. Louden, 1808.

Confession of Elizabeth Van Valkenburgh. Johnstown, N.Y.: G. Henry and W.N. Clark, 1847.

Confession of John Battus. Philadelphia: Richard Folwell, 1800.

Confession of John H. Craig. New York: N.p., 1818.

Confession of John Joyce. Philadelphia: Bethel Church, 1808.

Confession of John Burnett. Schenectady, N.Y.: N.p., 1846.

Confession of Joseph Baker. Philadelphia: Richard Folwell, 1800.

Confessions of Two Malefactors, Teller & Reynolds. Hartford, Conn.: Hamer & Comstock, 1833.

Craine, J. V. *The Conspirators' Victims.* Sacramento, Calif.: Gardiner & Kirk, 1855.

Dana, J.G., and Thomas, R.S. *A Report of the Trial of Jereboam O. Beauchamp.* Frankfort, Ky.: Albert G. Hodges, 1826.

The Dansville Poisoning Case. Dansville, N.Y.: George A. Sanders, 1858.

Day, Martin C. "Death in the Mail." Providence, R.I.: *Providence Journal,* 1892.

Day, Oscar F.G. *The Ging Murder and the Great Hayward Trial.* Minneapolis, Minn.: Tribune Co., 1895.

The Dearing Tragedy. Philadelphia: C.W. Alexander, 1866.

A Deed of Horror! Trial of Jason Fairbanks. Salem, Mass.: W. Carlton, 1801.

Dodge, Daniel. *Trial of Peter Robinson.* Newark, N.J.: Aaron Guest, 1841.

The Drinker's Farm Tragedy. Richmond, Va.: V.L. Fore, 1868.

Dudley, J.H. *The Climax in Crime of the Nineteenth Century, Being an Authentic History of the Trial, Conviction and Execution of Stephen Merris Ballew.* Quincy, Ill.: N.p., 1872.

Dunton, Alvin R. *The True Story of the Hart-Meservey Murder Trial.* Boston: Dunton, 1882.

Echeverria, M. Gonzalez. *The Trial of "John Reynolds" Medico-Legally Considered.*

Edgar, W.F. *Trial of Allen C. Lavos.* Easton, Pa.: Cole & Morwitz, 1877.

Emory, B.B. "Life, Trial and Confession of Rees W. Evans." Wilkes-Barre, Pa.: *The Times,* 1863.

Farmer, Daniel Davis. *The Life and Confessions of Daniel Davis Farmer.* Amherst, N.H.: Elijah Mansur, 1822.

Fithian, J.B. *The Assassination of J. Clarke Swayze.* Topeka, Kan.: Blade Printing, 1877.

The Five Fiends, or The Bender Hotel Horror in Kansas. Philadelphia: Old Franklin Publishing, 1874.

Fontaine, Felix G. *Trial of the Honorable Daniel E. Sickles.* New York: R. M. DeWitt, 1859.

Foote, Henry Leander. *A Sketch of the Life and Adventures of Henry Leander Foote.* New Haven, Conn.: T.J. Stafford, 1850.

Forsee, Peter A. *Five Years of Crime in California or the Life and Confession of G.W. Strong.* Ukiah City, Forsee, 1867.

Freeman, E.H. *The Veil of Secrecy Removed, The Only True and Authentic History of Edward H. Ruloff.* Binghamton, N.Y.: Carl and Freeman, 1871.

French, John A. *Trial of Professor John W. Webster for the Murder of Dr. George Park-man in the Medical College*. Boston: Herald Steam Press, 1850.

A Full Account of the Awful Murder of the Winston Family. Richmond, Va.: John D. Hammersley, 1852.

A Full Account, The Lives and Crimes of the "Molly Maguires." Philadelphia: Barclay & Co., 1877.

A Full and Particular Narrative of the Life, Character and Conduct of John Banks. New York: N.p., 1806.

Fuller, Daniel. *Trial of John Lechler*. Lancaster, Pa.: Hugh Maxwell, 1822.

The Genuine Declaration and Confession of William Morris. Philadelphia: N.p., 1808.

Glaser, D., Kenefick, D., and O'Leary, V. *The Violent Offender*. Washington, D.C.: U.S. Printing Office, 1968.

Godfrey, Samuel E. *A Sketch of the Life of Samuel E. Godfrey*. Hanover, Vt.: David Watson, 1818.

"The Goss-Udderzook Tragedy." Baltimore: *Baltimore Gazette*, 1873.

The Great Trunk Mystery of New York. Philadelphia: Barclay & Co., 1871.

The Grinder Poisoning Case. Pittsburgh, Pa.: John P. Hunt & Co., 1866.

Hatie, Joseph C. *Commonwealth of Pennsylvania vs. Blasius Pistorius*. Norristown, Pa.: Stephen S. Remak, 1876.

A History of the O'Mara Murder Trial. Montrose, Pa.: E.B. Hawley & Co., 1874.

Holmes' Own Story. Philadelphia: Burke & McFetridge Co., 1895.

Holmes' The Arch Fiend, or A Carnival of Crime. The Life, Trial, Confession and Execution of H.H. Holmes. Cincinnati, O.: Barclay & Co., 1895.

Horrid Massacre! Sketches of the Life of Captain James Purrington. Augusta, Me.: Peter Edes, 1806.

Hotchkiss, A.S. *The Manchester Homicide*. Hartford, Conn.: *Hartford Daily Courant*, 1866.

Hubbell, William Wheeler. *The Commonweal of Pennsylvania vs. George S. Twitchell, Jr.* Philadelphia: E.C. Markley & Son, 1869.

Hummel, A.H. *Trial and Conviction of Jack Reynolds*. New York: American News Co., 1870.

Hunt, Holloway Whitfield. *A Sermon Preached at the Execution of Matthias Gotlieb*. Newton, N.J.: N.p., 1796.

The Hunter-Armstrong Tragedy. Philadelphia: Barclay & Co., 1878.

Impartial Account of the Trial of Ebenezer Mason. Dedham, Mass.: H. Mann, 1802.

Incidents in the Life of Milton W. Streeter. Pawtucket, R.I.: H.F. Tingley, 1850.

In Prison and On the Scaffold. (Achey, Guetig and Merrick). Indianapolis: Ned Reed & Co., 1879.

The Interesting Trial of William F. Hooe. New York: Joseph M'Cleland, 1826.

Jenks, Ira C. *Trial of David F. Mayberry*. Janesville, Wis.: Baker, Burnett & Hall, 1855.

Jennings, J.S. *Trial of James Parks*. Akron, O.: Laurie & Barnard, 1855.

Kidder, Reuben. *The Life and Adventures of John Dahmen*. Jeffersonville, Ind.: Smith & Bolton, 1821.

Larned, Edward C., and Knowles, William. "A Full Report of the Trial of John Gordon and William Gordon." Providence, R.I.: *Daily Transcript*, 1844.

Life and Adventures of Henry Thomas. Philadelphia: T.B. Peterson, 1848.

"Life and Adventures of Manuel Fernandez." New York: *New York Sun*, 1835.

Life and Career of the Most Skillful and Noted Criminal of His Day, Charles Motimer.
Sacramento, Calif.: Record Steambook, 1873.

Life and Confession of Cato. Johnstown, N.Y.: Abraham Romyen, 1803.

"Life and Confession of Charles Steingraver." Ashland, O.: *Ohio Union*, 1852.

Life and Confession of George Acker, the Murderer of Isaac Gordon. New York: Baker & Godwin, 1860.

Life and Confession of Henry Wyatt. Auburn, N.Y.: J.C. Merrell & Co., 1846.

Life and Confession of John Johnson, the Murderer of James Murray. New York: Brown & Tyrell, 1824.

Life and Confession of Miner Babcock. New London, Conn.: Samuel Green, 1816.

Life and Confession of Moses W. Keen. Maysville, Ky.: N.p., 1842.

Life and Confession of Stephen Lee Richards. Lincoln, Neb.: State Journal Co., 1879.

Life and Dying Confession of James Hamilton. Albany, N.Y.: Printing Office, 1818.

Life and Dying Confession of John Van Alstine. Cooperstown, N.Y.: H. & E. Phinney, 1819.

Life and Execution of Jack Kehoe, King of the "Mollie Maguires." Philadelphia: Barclay & Co., 1881.

Life and History Together with the Details of the Trial of Bill Fox. Sedalia, Mo.: J. West Goodwin, 1884.

Life and Trial of Perry Bowsher. Chillicothe, O.: Edward Kauffman, 1878.

Life and Writings of Adolphus F. Monroe. Cincinnati, O.: N.B. Aulick, 1857.

Life, Crimes and Confession of Mrs. Julia Fortmeyer. Philadelphia: Barclay & Co, 1875.

Life, Flight, Capture, Trial and Execution of Edward Alonzo Pennington. Cincinnati: E. Shepard, 1846.

Life of Elizabeth Sowers. Philadelphia: P. Augustus Sage, 1839.

Life of Henry Phillips. Boston: Russell, Cutler & Co., 1817.

Life of the Chicago Banker, George W. Green. Chicago: Mellen & Co., 1855.

Life, Secret Confession and Execution of Rugg, The Fiend. Philadelphia: Barclay & Co., 1885.

Life, Trial, and Confession of Frank C. Almy. Laconia, N.H.: John J. Lane, 1892.

Life, Trial, Confession and Conviction of John Hanlon. Philadelphia: Barclay & Co., 1870.

Life, Trial, Confession and Execution of Albert W. Hicks. New York: Robert M. DeWitt, 1860.

Life, Trial and Conviction of Edward Stokes. Philadelphia: Barclay & Co., 1873.

Life, Trial and Execution of Edward H. Ruloff. Philadelphia: Barclay & Co., 1871.

"Life, Trial, Execution and Dying Confession of John Erpenstein." Newark, N.J.: *Daily Advertiser*, 1852.

The Linder Tragedy, History of Nelson E. Wade, the McBride Murderer. Williamsport, Pa.: Gazette & Bulletin Printing House, 1873.

Maccarty, Thaddeus. *The Guilt of Innocent Blood Put Away.* Norwich, Conn.: John Trumbull, 1778.

The Manheim Tragedy, A Complete History of the Double Murder of Mrs. Garber and Mrs. Ream, With the Only Authentic Life and Confession of Alexander Anderson. Lancaster, Pa.: H.A. Rockafield, 1858.

The Man of Two Lives, Being an Authentic History of Edward Howard Ruloff, Philologist and Murderer. New York: American News Co., 1871.

"The Marlow Murder!" Jamestown, N.Y.: *Daily & Weekly Journal*, 1871.

Marsh, Rev. John. *A Narrative of the Life of William Beadle.* Hartford, Conn.: Bavil Webster, 1783.

McBath, Will R., and Adkins, E.W. *Life, Trial and Confession of John Nance.* Knoxville Tenn.: Brownlow & Haws, 1867.

A Melancholy Narrative of the Late, Unhappy Samuel Brand. Lancaster, Pa.: Francis Bailey, 1774.

A Minute and Correct Account of the Trial of Lucian Hall. Middletown, Conn.: Charles H. Pelton, 1844.

The Mollie Maguires, A Thrilling Narrative of the Rise, Progress and Fall of the Most Noted Band of Cut-Throats of Modern Times. Tamaqua, Pa.: Eveland & Harris, 1876.

Morgan, C.R. *The Commonwealth of Pennsylvania versus Edward Parr.* Philadelphia: Gillen & Nagle, 1879.

Mrs. Hull's Murder. Philadelphia: Old Franklin Publishing House, 1880.

Murder of the Meek Family. Kansas City, Mo.: Ryan Walker, 1896.

The Murder on Dr. Tiedeman's Farm. Philadelphia: John Campbell, 1867.

Narrative of the Life and Dying Speech of John Ryer. Danbury, Conn.: Nathan Douglas, 1793.

Narrative of the Life of James Lane. Chillicothe, O.: John Bailhache, 1817.

Noonan, E. A. *The Trunk Tragedy, A Complete History of the Murder of Preller and the Trial of Maxwell.* St. Louis, Mo.: St. Louis News Co., 1886.

The Northwood Murder. Manchester, N.H.: N.p., 1873.

Neale, John C. "A Terrible Tragedy, The Execution, Life and Crime of Felix Kampf." Charleston, W. Va.: *Charleston Daily & Weekly Star,* 1890.

The Official Report of the Trial of John O'Neil. Boston: Wright & Potter, 1901.

Packer, William F. *Report of the Trial and Conviction of John Earls.* Williamsport, Pa.: N.p., 1836.

Peixotto, Edgar D. *Report of the Trial of William Henry Theodore Durrant.* Detroit: The Collector Publishing Co., 1899.

The People Against Edward H. Ruloff. New York: Drossy & Co., 1872.

Pittman, Benn. *The Assassination of President Lincoln and the Trial of Conspirators.* New York: Moore, Wilstach & Baldwin, 1865.

Pitts, Dr. J.R. S. *Life and Bloody Career of the Executed Criminal James Copeland.* Jackson, Miss.: Pilot Publishing Co., 1874.

Plummer, Jonathan. *Dying Confession of Pomp.* Newburyport, Mass.: Blunt & March, 1795.

The Poison Fiend! Life, Crimes and Conviction of Lydia Sherman, the Modern Lucretia Borgia. Philadelphia: Barclay and Co., 1872.

Pomeroy, Jesse H. *Autobiography of Jesse H. Pomeroy.* Boston: J.A. Cummings, 1875.

Potter, C.E, *Report on the Trial of Bradbury Ferguson.* Concord, N.H.: Morrill, Silsby & Co., 1841.

Potter, Rev. William J. *A History of the Pocasset Tragedy.* New Bedford, Mass.: Charles W. Knight, 1879.

Powers, Michael. *Life of Michael Powers.* Boston: Russell & Gardner, 1820.

Remault, J. Edwards. *The "Car-Hook" Tragedy.* Philadelphia: Barclay and Co., 1873.

Report of the Case of Ephraim Gilman. Portland, Me.: Stephen Berry, 1863.

Report of the Evidence and Points of Law arising in the Trial of John Francis Knapp for the Murder of Joseph White. Salem, Mass.: W. & S.B. Ives, 1830.

Report of the Trial and Conviction of John Haggerty. Lancaster, Pa.: J.H. Pearsol, 1847.

Report of the Trial and Conviction of Louis H. F. Wagner. Saco, Me.: William S. Noyes & Co., 1874.

Report of the Trial of Martin Posey. Edgefield, S.C.: Advertiser Print, 1850.

Report of the Trial of Edward Williams. Westchester, Pa.: Harnum & Hemphill, 1830.

Report on the Trial of Adonijah Bailey. Windham, Conn.: N.p., 1825.

Report on the Trial of William F. Comings. Boston: S.N. Dickinson, 1844.

Richards, George. *The Trial of Alpheus Hitchcock.* Utica, N.Y.: Seward & Williams, 1807.

Romeyn, Herman M. *Report of the Trial of Nathan Foster.* Kingston, N.Y.: Joseph S. Smith, 1819.

Rubenstein, or The Murdered Jewess, Being A Full and Reliable History of This Terrible Mystery of Blood. Philadelphia: Old Franklin Publishing House, 1876.

The Sad Case of Mrs. Kate Southern. Philadelphia: Old Franklin House Publishers, 1878.

A Short Account of the Trial of Cyrus Emlay. Burlington, N.J.: S.C. Ustick, 1801.

Sickels, H.E. *Reports of Cases decided in the Court of Appeals of the State of New York,* Vol. 136. Albany, N.Y.: James B. Lyons, 1893.

Sketch of the Life and Adventures of Guy C. Clark. Ithaca, N.Y.: N.p., 1832

Sketch of the Trial of Mary Cole. New Brunswick, N.J.: J.W. Kirn, 1812.

Speech of David Paul Brown in the Case of the State of Delaware Against Isaac N. Weaver. Philadelphia: Robb, Pile & M'Elroy, 1858.

Speech of Henry L. Clinton to the Jury on the Part of the Prosecution on the Trial of Isaac V. W. Buckout. Westchester, N.Y.: N.p., 1871.

Stanford, Rev. John. *Trial, Conviction, Sentence, and Only True Copy of the Confession of Catherine Cashiere.* New York: C. Brown, 1829.

Stern, Samuel. *Thrilling Mysteries of the Rubenstein Murder.* New York: S. Stern & Cohn, 1876.

Strobel, Martin. *A Report of the Trial of Michael & Martin Toohey.* Charleston, S.C.: A.E. Miller, 1819.

A Succinct Narrative of the Life and Character of Abel Clemmons. Morgantown, Va.: J. Campbell, 1806.

The Sugar Creek Tragedy, Life and Confession of John Goodman. Ottawa, O.: Sentinel, 1875.

Ten Eyck, John. *The Life of John Ten Eyck.* Pittsfield, Mass.: David O'Connell, 1878.

Toole, Gerald. *An Autobiography of Gerald Toole.* Hartford, Conn.: Lockwood & Co., 1862.

Treadwell, Gordon W. *Myron Buel, The Murderer of Catherine Mary Richards.* Binghamton, N.Y.: Republican Print, 1879.

Trial and a Sketch of the Life of Amos Miner. Providence, R.I.: H.H. Brown, 1833.

Trial and Confession of Andrew P. Potter. New Haven, Conn.: William Goodwin, 1845.

Trial and Confession of John Funston. New Philadelphia, Ohio: S. Patric, 1825.

Trial and Conviction of Abraham Casler. Schoharie, N.Y.: N.p., 1817.

Trial and Conviction of Jack Reynolds. New York: American News Co., 1870.

Trial and Execution of Thomas Barrett. Boston: Skinner & Blanchard, 1845.

Trial, Life and Confessions of Charles Cook. Schenectady, N.Y.: E.M. Packard, 1840.

"Trial, Life and Confessions of John Van Patten." Schenectady, N.Y.: *Mohawk Sentinel,* 1825.

Trial of Alpheus Livermore. Boston: Watson & Bangs, 1813.

Trial of Capt. Henry Whitby. New York: Gould, Banks, and Gould, 1812.

Trial of Capt. John Windsor. Milford, Del.: J.H. Emerson, 1851.

Trial of Charles Lewis. Princeton, N.J.: Standard Office, Printers, 1863.

Trial of Edward Tinker. Newbern, N.C.: Hall, Bryan & Watson, 1811.

Trial of Emil Lowenstein. Albany, N.Y.: William Gould & Son, 1874.

Trial of George Travers. Boston: T.G. Bangs, 1815.

Trial of Henry Ward. Tunkhannock, Pa.: Tunkhannock Republican, 1871.

Trial of Herman Webster Mudgett, alias H.H. Holmes. Philadelphia: George T. Bisel, 1897.

"Trial of James P. Donnelly." Freehold, N.J.: *Monmouth Inquirer,* 1857.

"Trial of John Fox." New Brunswick, Conn.: *The Freedonian,* 1856.

Trial of Joseph Lapage, The French Monster. Philadelphia: Old Franklin Publishing House, 1876.

Trial of Levi Kelley. Cooperstown, N.Y.: The Watch Tower, 1827.

Trial of Mrs. Rebecca Peake. Montpelier, Vt.: E.P. Walton & Sons, 1836.

Trial of Orrin De Wolf. Worcester, Mass.: Thomas Drew, Jr., 1845.

Trial of Pasach N. Rubenstein. New York: Baker, Voorhis & Co., 1876.

Trial of the Rev. George W. Carawan. New York: N.p., 1854.

Trial of Robert Douglass. Bath, N.Y.: B.F. Smead, 1825.

Trial of Sager for the Murder of His Wife. Augusta, Me.: Luther Severance, 1834.

Trial of Stephen Arnold. Cooperstown, N.Y.: E. Phinney, 1805.

Trial of Stephen Videto. Malone, N.Y.: Telegraph Office, 1825.

Trial of William Dandridge Epes. Petersburg, Va.: J.M. H. Brunet, 1849.

Trial of William Stewart. Baltimore: Bull & Tuttle, 1838.

True and Authentic Life and Confession of Joel Clough. Philadelphia: Robert Desilver, 1833.

Truth Stranger Than Fiction. Lydia Sherman, Confession of the Arch-Murderess of Connecticut. Philadelphia: T.R. Callender & Co., 1873.

Vanauken, Wilhemus. *The Trial of Wilhemus Vanauken.* Kingston, N.J.: Plebian Office, 1822.

Van Kleek, Rev. Robert B. *Confession of Henry G. Green.* Troy, N.Y.: R. Rose, 1845.

Victor, Sarah M. *The Life Story of Sarah M. Victor.* Cleveland, O.: Williams Publishing Co., 1887.

Wade, Stuart C. *Harry T. Hayward's Life, Trial, Confession and Execution.* Chicago: E.A. Weeks & Co., 1896.

The Walworth Parricide! New York: Thomas O'Kane, 1873.

Waterman, Elijah. *A Sermon Preached at Windham, November 29, 1803, Being the Day of Execution of Caleb Adams for the Murder of Oliver Woodworth.* Windham, Conn.: John Byrne, 1803.

Welch, Moses C. *The Gospel to be Preached to All Men, Illustrated, in a Sermon Delivered in Windham at the Execution of Samuel Freeman.* Windham, Mass.: John Byrne, 1805.

West, R.A. "The Great Mollie Maguire Trials." Pottsville, Pa.: *Chronicle*, 1876.

Whiting, Sweeting. *The Narrative of Whiting Sweeting.* Lansingburg, N.Y.: Sylvester Tiffany, 1791.

Wilbour, Charles E. *Trial of Charles M. Jefferds for Murder.* New York: Ross & Tousey, 1862.

Wood, R.E. *Life and Confessions of James Gilbert Jenkins.* Napa City, Calif.: C.H. Allen, 1864.

Woodruff, Ephraim T. *The Sovereignty of God.* Warren, O.: Hapgood & Sprague, 1820.

Woodruff, Leonard. *The Infernal Machine. Trial of William Arrison.* Cincinnati, O.: H.H. Robinson & Co., 1854.

Yerrinton, James M.W. *Report of the Case of George C. Hersey.* Boston: A. Williams & Co., 1862.

———. *The Official Report of the Trial of Henry K. Goodwin.* Boston: Wright & Potter, 1887.

———. *The Official Report of the Trial of Thomas W. Piper.* Boston: Wright & Potter, 1887.

———. *The Official Report of the Trial of Sarah Jane Robinson.* Boston: Wright & Potter, 1888.

York, Mary E. *The Bender Tragedy.* Mankato, Kan.: G.W. Neff, 1875.

Index